# Communications
# in Computer and Information Science

**2874**

Series Editors

Gang Li, *School of Information Technology, Deakin University, Burwood, VIC, Australia*

Joaquim Filipe, *Polytechnic Institute of Setúbal, Setúbal, Portugal*

Zhiwei Xu, *Chinese Academy of Sciences, Beijing, China*

**Rationale**

The CCIS series is devoted to the publication of proceedings of computer science conferences. Its aim is to efficiently disseminate original research results in informatics in printed and electronic form. While the focus is on publication of peer-reviewed full papers presenting mature work, inclusion of reviewed short papers reporting on work in progress is welcome, too. Besides globally relevant meetings with internationally representative program committees guaranteeing a strict peer-reviewing and paper selection process, conferences run by societies or of high regional or national relevance are also considered for publication.

**Topics**

The topical scope of CCIS spans the entire spectrum of informatics ranging from foundational topics in the theory of computing to information and communications science and technology and a broad variety of interdisciplinary application fields.

**Information for Volume Editors and Authors**

Publication in CCIS is free of charge. No royalties are paid, however, we offer registered conference participants temporary free access to the online version of the conference proceedings on SpringerLink (http://link.springer.com) by means of an http referrer from the conference website and/or a number of complimentary printed copies, as specified in the official acceptance email of the event.

CCIS proceedings can be published in time for distribution at conferences or as post-proceedings, and delivered in the form of printed books and/or electronically as USBs and/or e-content licenses for accessing proceedings at SpringerLink. Furthermore, CCIS proceedings are included in the CCIS electronic book series hosted in the SpringerLink digital library at http://link.springer.com/bookseries/7899. Conferences publishing in CCIS are allowed to use our online conference service (Meteor) for managing the whole proceedings lifecycle (from submission and reviewing to preparing for publication) free of charge.

**Publication process**

The language of publication is exclusively English. Authors publishing in CCIS have to sign the Springer CCIS copyright transfer form, however, they are free to use their material published in CCIS for substantially changed, more elaborate subsequent publications elsewhere. For the preparation of the camera-ready papers/files, authors have to strictly adhere to the Springer CCIS Authors' Instructions and are strongly encouraged to use the CCIS LaTeX style files or templates.

**Abstracting/Indexing**

CCIS is abstracted/indexed in DBLP, Google Scholar, EI-Compendex, Mathematical Reviews, SCImago, Scopus. CCIS volumes are also submitted for the inclusion in ISI Proceedings.

**How to start**

To start the evaluation of your proposal for inclusion in the CCIS series, please send an e-mail to ccis@springer.com

Kanubhai K. Patel · KC Santosh ·
Gabriel Gomes de Oliveira · Atul Patel ·
Ashish Ghosh

Editors

# Soft Computing and Its Engineering Applications

7th International Conference, icSoftComp 2025
Hanoi, Vietnam, December 9–11, 2025
Proceedings, Part II

 Springer

*Editors*
Kanubhai K. Patel
Charotar University of Science
and Technology
Changa, Gujarat, India

Gabriel Gomes de Oliveira
University of Campinas
Campinas, Brazil

Ashish Ghosh
Indian Statistical Institute
Kolkata, West Bengal, India

KC Santosh
University of South Dakota
Vermillion, SD, USA

Atul Patel
Charotar University of Science
and Technology
Changa, Gujarat, India

ISSN 1865-0929          ISSN 1865-0937 (electronic)
Communications in Computer and Information Science
ISBN 978-3-032-22061-5          ISBN 978-3-032-22062-2 (eBook)
https://doi.org/10.1007/978-3-032-22062-2



This Springer imprint is published by the registered company Springer Nature Switzerland AG
The registered company address is: Gewerbestrasse 11, 6330 Cham, Switzerland

If disposing of this product, please recycle the paper.

# Preface

It is a matter of great privilege to have been tasked with the writing of this preface for the proceedings of the Seventh International Conference on Soft Computing and its Engineering Applications (icSoftComp 2025). The conference aimed to provide an excellent international forum to emerging and accomplished research scholars, academicians, students and professionals in the areas of computer science and engineering to present their research, knowledge, new ideas and innovations. The conference was held during 9–11 December 2025, in Hanoi, Vietnam and organized by the Faculty of Computer Science and Applications, Charotar University of Science & Technology (CHARUSAT), Changa, India. There are three pillars of Soft Computing, viz. i) Fuzzy computing, ii) Neuro computing, and iii) Evolutionary computing. Research submissions in these three areas were received. The Program Committee of icSoftComp 2025 is extremely grateful to the authors from 43 different countries including Russia, Poland, UK, USA, France, Germany, Sweden, Portugal, Philippines, Finland, Malaysia, Vietnam, Tunisia, Lithuania, United Arab Emirates, South Africa, and India, who showed an overwhelming response to the call for papers, submitting 710 papers. The entire review team (Technical Program Committee members along with 18 additional reviewers) expended tremendous effort to ensure fairness and consistency during the selection process, resulting in the best-quality papers being selected for presentation and publication. It was ensured that every paper received at least three, and in most cases four, double-blind reviews. Checking of similarities was also done based on international norms and standards. After a rigorous peer review 112 papers were accepted with an acceptance ratio of 15.77%. The papers are organised according to the following topics: Theory & Methods, Systems & Applications, Hybrid Techniques and Soft Computing for a Smart World. The proceedings of the conference are published as three volumes in the Communications in Computer and Information Science (CCIS) series by Springer, and are also indexed by ISI Proceedings, DBLP, Ulrich's, EI-Compendex, SCOPUS, Zentralblatt Math, MetaPress, and Springerlink. We, in our capacity as volume editors, convey our sincere gratitude to Springer for providing the opportunity to publish the proceedings of icSoftComp 2025 in their CCIS series.

icSoftComp 2025 provided an excellent international forum to the conference delegates to present their research, knowledge, new ideas and innovations. The conference exhibited an exciting technical program. It also featured high-quality workshops, two keynotes and five expert talks from prominent research and industry leaders. Keynote speeches were given by Edgar Weippl (University of Vienna, Austria) and Hong Nhung Nguyen (Gachon University, South Korea). Expert talks were given by Marco Dorigo (Université Libre de Bruxelles, Belgium), Ahmad Bazzi (New York University Abu Dhabi, UAE), Tatiana Kalganova (Brunel University of London, UK), Unnati Shah (Utica University, USA) and Donatella Firmani (Sapienza University of Rome, Italy). We are grateful to them for sharing their insights on their latest research with us.

The Organizing Committee of icSoftComp 2025 is indebted to Atul Patel, Provost of Charotar University of Science and Technology, for the confidence that he invested in us in organizing this international conference. We would also like to take this opportunity to extend our heartfelt thanks to the honorary chairs of this conference, Kalyanmoy Deb (Michigan State University, USA), Witold Pedrycz (University of Alberta, Canada), Leszek Rutkowski (IEEE Fellow)(University of Technology, Poland), and Janusz Kacprzyk (Polish Academy of Sciences, Warsaw, Poland) for their involvement from the very beginning until the end of the conference. The quality of a refereed volume primarily depends on the expertise and dedication of the reviewers who volunteer with a smiling face. The editors are further indebted to the Technical Program Committee members and external reviewers who not only produced excellent reviews but also did so in a short time frame, in spite of their very busy schedules. Because of their quality work it was possible to maintain the high academic standard of the proceedings. Without their support, this conference could never have assumed such a successful shape. Special words of appreciation are due to note the enthusiasm of all the faculty, staff and students of the Faculty of Computer Science and Applications of CHARUSAT, who extended their help in the organization of the conference in a professional manner.

It is needless to mention the role of the contributors. The editors would like to take this opportunity to thank the authors of all submitted papers not only for their hard work but also for considering the conference a viable platform to showcase some of their latest findings, not to mention their adherence to the deadlines and patience with the tedious review process. Special thanks to the team of Meteor, whose paper submission platform was used to organize reviews and collate the files for these proceedings. We also wish to express our sincere thanks to the staff of Springer for their unwavering help and cooperation. We gratefully acknowledge the financial (partial) support received from Gujarat Council on Science & Technology (GUJCOST), Government of Gujarat, Gandhinagar, India for organizing the conference. Last but not least, the editors profusely thank all who directly or indirectly helped us in making icSoftComp 2025 a grand success and allowed the conference to achieve its goals, academic or otherwise.

December 2025

Kanubhai K. Patel<br>
KC Santosh<br>
Gabriel Gomes de Oliveira<br>
Atul Patel<br>
Ashish Ghosh

# Organization

## Patron

Atul Patel      Charotar University of Science and Technology, India

## Honorary Chairs

Kalyanmoy Deb      Michigan State University, USA
Witold Pedrycz      University of Alberta, Canada
Leszek Rutkowski      Częstochowska University of Technology, Poland
Janusz Kacprzyk      Polish Academy of Sciences, Warsaw, Poland

## General Chairs

Atul Patel      Charotar University of Science and Technology, India
Dilip Kumar Pratihar      Indian Institute of Technology Kharagpur, India
Le Anh Ngoc      Swinburne Vietnam University, Vietnam

## Technical Program Committee Chair

Kanubhai K. Patel      Charotar University of Science and Technology, India

## Technical Program Committee Co-chairs

Ashish Ghosh      Indian Statistical Institute (ISI), Kolkata, India
KC Santosh      University of South Dakota, USA
Gayatri Doctor      CEPT University, India
Gabriel Gomes de Oliveira      University of Campinas (Unicamp), Campinas, Brazil
Ashis Jalote-Parmar      Norwegian University of Science and Technology, Norway

## Advisory Committee

| | |
|---|---|
| Arup Dasgupta | Geospatial Media and Communications, India |
| Balas Valentina Emilia | University of Arad, Romania |
| Bhuvan Unhelkar | University of South Florida Sarasota-Manatee, USA |
| Dharmendra T. Patel | Charotar University of Science and Technology, India |
| Indrakshi Ray | Colorado State University, USA |
| J. C. Bansal | Soft Computing Research Society, India |
| Narendra S. Chaudhari | Indian Institute of Technology Indore, India |
| Rajendra Akerkar | Vestlandsforsking, Norway |
| Sanskruti Patel | Charotar University of Science and Technology, India |
| Sudhir Kumar Barai | BITS Pilani, India |

## Technical Program Committee Members

| | |
|---|---|
| Abhijit Datta Banik | IIT Bhubaneswar, India |
| Abhineet Anand | Chitkara University, India |
| Aditya Patel | Kamdhenu University, India |
| Adrijan Božinovski | University American College Skopje, Macedonia |
| Aji S. | University of Kerala, India |
| Akhil Meerja | Vardhaman College of Engineering, India |
| Aman Sharma | Jaypee University of Information Technology, India |
| Ami Choksi | C.K. Pithawala College of Engineering and Technology, India |
| Amit Joshi | Malaviya National Institute of Technology, India |
| Amol Vibhute | Symbiosis Institute of Computer Studies and Research, India |
| Anand Nayyar | Duy Tan University, Vietnam |
| Angshuman Jana | IIIT Guwahati, India |
| Ansuman Bhattacharya | IIT (ISM) Dhanbad, India |
| Anurag Singh | IIIT Naya Raipur, India |
| Aravind Rajam | Washington State University, Pullman, USA |
| Arjun Mane | Government Institute of Forensic Science, India |
| Arti Jain | Jaypee Institute of Information Technology, India |
| Arunima Jaiswal | Indira Gandhi Delhi Technical University for Women, India |
| Asha Manek | RVITM Engineering College, India |

| | |
|---|---|
| Ashok Patel | Florida Polytechnic University, USA |
| Ashok Sharma | Lovely Professional University, India |
| Ashraf Elnagar | University of Sharjah, UAE |
| Ashutosh Kumar Dubey | Chitkara University, India |
| Ashwin Makwana | Charotar University of Science and Technology, India |
| Avimanyou Vatsa | Fairleigh Dickinson University, USA |
| Avinash Kadam | Dr. Babasaheb Ambedkar Marathwada University, India |
| Ayad Mousa | University of Kerbala, Iraq |
| Bhaskar Karn | BIT Mesra, India |
| Bhavik Pandya | University of Regina, Canada |
| Bhogeswar Borah | Tezpur University, India |
| Bhuvaneswari Amma | IIIT Una, India |
| Chaman Sabharwal | Missouri University of Science and Technology, USA |
| Charu Gandhi | Jaypee University of Information Technology, India |
| Chirag Patel | Innovate Tax, UK |
| Chirag Paunwala | Sarvajanik College of Engineering and Technology, India |
| Costas Vassilakis | University of the Peloponnese, Greece |
| Darshana Patel | Emporia State University, USA |
| Deepa Thilak | SRM University, India |
| Deepak N. A. | RV Institute of Technology and Management, India |
| Deepak Singh | IIIT, Lucknow, India |
| Delampady Narasimha | IIT Dharwad, India |
| Digvijaysinh Rathod | National Forensic Sciences University, India |
| Dinesh Acharya | Manipal Institute of Technology, India |
| Divyansh Thakur | IIIT Una, India |
| Dushyantsinh Rathod | Alpha College of Engineering and Technology, India |
| E. Rajesh | Galgotias University, India |
| Gururaj Mukarambi | Central University of Karnataka, India |
| Gururaj H. L. | Vidyavardhaka College of Engineering, India |
| Hardik Joshi | Gujarat University, India |
| Harshal Arolkar | GLS University, India |
| Himanshu Jindal | Jaypee University of Information Technology, India |
| Hiren Joshi | Gujarat University, India |
| Hiren Mewada | Prince Mohammad Bin Fahd University, Saudi Arabia |

| | |
|---|---|
| Hema Patel | Charotar University of Science and Technology, India |
| Irene Govender | University of KwaZulu-Natal, South Africa |
| Jagadeesha Bhatt | IIIT Dharwad, India |
| Jaimin Undavia | Charotar University of Science and Technology, India |
| Jaishree Tailor | Uka Tarsadia University, India |
| Janmenjoy Nayak | Aditya Institute of Technology and Management, India |
| Jaspher Kathrine | Karunya Institute of Technology and Sciences, India |
| Jimitkumar Patel | Charotar University of Science and Technology, India |
| Joydip Dhar | Atal Bihari Vajpayee Indian Institute of Information Technology and Management, India |
| József Dombi | University of Szeged, Hungary |
| Kamlendu Pandey | Veer Narmad South Gujarat University, India |
| Kamlesh Dutta | NIT Hamirpur, India |
| Kiran Trivedi | Northeastern University, USA |
| Kiran Sree Pokkuluri | Shri Vishnu Engineering College for Women, India |
| Krishan Kumar | National Institute of Technology Uttarakhand, India |
| Kuldip Singh Patel | IIIT Naya Raipur, India |
| Kuntal Patel | Ahmedabad University, India |
| Latika Singh | Ansal University, India |
| M. Srinivas | National Institute of Technology-Warangal, India |
| M. A. Jabbar | Vardhaman College of Engineering, India |
| Maciej Ławrynczuk | Warsaw University of Technology, Poland |
| Mahmoud Elish | Gulf University for Science and Technology, Kuwait |
| Mandeep Kaur | Sharda University, India |
| Manoj Majumder | IIIT Naya Raipur, India |
| Meera Kansara | Gujarat Vidyapith, India |
| Michał Chlebiej | Nicolaus Copernicus University, Poland |
| Mittal Desai | Charotar University of Science and Technology, India |
| Mohamad Ijab | National University of Malaysia, Malaysia |
| Mohini Agarwal | Amity University Noida, India |
| Monika Patel | NVP College of Pure and Applied Sciences, India |
| Mukti Jadhav | Marathwada Institute of Technology, India |

| | |
|---|---|
| Neetu Sardana | Jaypee University of Information Technology, India |
| Nidhi Arora | Solusoft Technologies Pvt. Ltd., India |
| Nilay Vaidya | Charotar University of Science and Technology, India |
| Nitin Kumar | National Institute of Technology Uttarakhand, India |
| Parag Rughani | National Forensic Sciences University, India |
| Parul Patel | Veer Narmad South Gujarat University, India |
| Prashant Pittalia | Sardar Patel University, India |
| Priti Sajja | Sardar Patel University, India |
| Pritpal Singh | Jagiellonian University, Poland |
| Punya Paltani | IIIT Naya Raipur, India |
| Rajeev Kumar | NIT Hamirpur, India |
| Rajesh Thakker | Vishwakarma Government Engineering College, India |
| Ramesh Prajapati | LJ Institutes of Engineering and Technology, India |
| Ramzi Guetari | University of Tunis El Manar, Tunisia |
| Rana Mukherji | ICFAI University, Jaipur, India |
| Rashmi Saini | GB Pant Institute of Engineering and Technology, India |
| Rathinaraja Jeyaraj | National Institute of Technology Karnataka, India |
| Rekha A. G. | State Bank of India, India |
| Rohini Rao | Manipal Academy of Higher Education, India |
| S. Shanmugam | Concordia University Chicago, USA |
| S. SrinivasuluRaju | VR Siddhartha Engineering College, India |
| Sailesh Iyer | Narnarayan Shastri Institute of Technology (IFSCS), India |
| Saman Chaeikar | Iranian University, Iran |
| Sameerchand Pudaruth | University of Mauritius, Mauritius |
| Samir Patel | Pandit Deendayal Energy University, India |
| Sandeep Gaikwad | Symbiosis Institute of Computer Studies and Research, India |
| Sandhya Dubey | Manipal Academy of Higher Education, India |
| Sanjay Moulik | IIIT Guwahati, India |
| Sannidhan M. S. | NMAM Institute of Technology, India |
| Saurabh Das | University of Calcutta, India |
| S. B. Goyal | City University of Malaysia, Malaysia |
| Shachi Sharma | South Asian University, India |
| Shailesh Khant | Charotar University of Science and Technology, India |
| Shefali Naik | Ahmedabad University, India |
| Shilpa Gite | Symbiosis Institute of Technology, India |

| | |
|---|---|
| Shravan Kumar Garg | Swami Vivekanand Subharti University, India |
| Spiros Skiadopoulos | University of the Peloponnese, Greece |
| Srinibas Swain | IIIT Guwahati, India |
| Srinivasan Sriramulu | Galgotias University, India |
| Subhasish Dhal | IIIT Guwahati, India |
| Sudhanshu Maurya | Graphic Era Hill University, India |
| Sujit Das | National Institute of Technology Warangal, India |
| Sumegh Tharewal | Dr. Babasaheb Ambedkar Marathwada University, India |
| Sunil Bajeja | Marwadi University, India |
| Swati Gupta | Jaypee University of Information Technology, India |
| Tanima Dutta | Indian Institute of Technology (BHU) Varanasi, India |
| Tanuja S. Dhope | Rajarshi Shahu College of Engineering, India |
| Thoudam Singh | NIT Silchar, India |
| Tzung-Pei Hong | National University of Kaohsiung, Taiwan |
| Vana Kalogeraki | Athens University of Economics and Business, Greece |
| Vasudha M. P. | Jain University, India |
| Vatsal Shah | BVM Engineering, India |
| Veena Jokhakar | Veer Narmad South Gujarat University, India |
| Vibhakar Pathak | Arya College of Engineering. and IT, India |
| Vijaya Rajanala | SR Engineering College, India |
| Vinay Vachharajani | Ahmedabad University, India |
| Vinod Kumar | IIIT Lucknow, India |
| Vishnu Pendyala | San José State University, USA |
| Yogesh Rode | Jijamata Mahavidyalaya, India |
| Zina Miled | Indiana University, USA |

## Additional Reviewers

| | |
|---|---|
| Anjali Mahavar | Mihir Mehta |
| Deepa Davis | Parag Shukla |
| Falguni Parsana | Prashant Dolia |
| Himanshu Patel | Shanti Verma |
| Kalyani Patel | Tejasvi Koti |
| Kamalesh Salunke | Rachana Parikh |
| Khushboo Shah | Ramesh Chandra Goswami |
| Krishna Kant | Rayeesa Tasneem |
| Lokesh Sharma | Samir Thakkar |

# Contents

## Systems and Applications

# Theory and Methods

# Toward Human-Level Task Automation with Large Action Models


Keane Scouton Crasto[(✉)] [iD] and A. Priyadharshini [iD]

Department of Computer Science and Engineering, Faculty of Engineering and Technology, JAIN (Deemed-to-be University), Bengaluru 562112, India
scoutoncrasto@gmail.com



**Abstract.** Despite their widespread adoption, contemporary voice assistants remain limited in their ability to handle complex, multi-step interactions, primarily due to their reliance on inflexible, predefined intent-based systems. We introduce Large Action Models (LAMs), an architecture enabling autonomous task execution from natural language through integrated reasoning, perception, and action. Our modular design combines speech-to-text (Whisper), multi-step planning (xLAM), device control (Mobile-MCP), visual feedback (CogVLM), and safety mechanisms to convert free-form speech into contextually-aware device actions. LAMs achieve flexible task automation through continuous perception-driven replanning, adapting to changing conditions and maintaining cross-application context. This work establishes the foundation for LAMs, proposes a novel modular architecture, and explores how perception-action loops enable task automation beyond current assistant limitations.

**Keywords:** Large Action Model · Vision Language Model · Human-Computer Interaction · Personal Assistant · Task Automation


## 1 Introduction

Modern voice assistants such as Google Assistant, Amazon Alexa, and Apple's Siri have transformed human-computer interaction through spoken commands. However, these systems exhibit critical limitations preventing them from handling complex, multi-step tasks requiring contextual awareness and adaptive planning. Current assistants operate through fixed command sets, requiring users to learn specific phrasings and predetermined interaction patterns.

This becomes evident when automating richer tasks like multi-step interactions or complex application integrations requiring dynamic decision-making. For instance, a user cannot say, "Help me order my usual lunch and schedule the delivery around my next meeting" and expect automatic navigation across applications, calendar availability check, and timing coordination. Instead, users must break tasks into discrete commands, defeating natural language automation's purpose.



K. K. Patel et al. (Eds.): icSoftComp 2025, CCIS 2874, pp. 3–15, 2026.
https://doi.org/10.1007/978-3-032-22062-2_1

Without multi-step reasoning, cross-application context tracking, and adaptive responses, voice assistants remain relegated to simple command-response patterns rather than serving as intelligent automation partners.

Large Action Models (LAMs) address these limitations by enabling flexible, contextually-aware task execution from natural language input. Unlike traditional assistants mapping speech to predetermined actions, LAMs convert spoken instructions into dynamic action sequences that adapt to changing conditions, maintain multi-step context, and integrate feedback from system state and user interaction.

LAMs leverage advances in large language models, computer vision, and mobile device APIs to create an end-to-end pipeline for reasoning about complex tasks, planning multi-step sequences, and adapting based on real-time feedback.

### 1.1   Objectives and Scope

This research establishes the foundation for Large Action Models and proposes a modular architecture for implementation. Primary objectives include: (1) defining LAMs as an architecture for complex task automation, (2) designing a modular pipeline integrating natural language understanding, multi-step planning, action execution, visual perception, and user feedback, and (3) analyzing benefits and challenges versus existing paradigms.

The scope of this work focuses on the architectural design for processing natural language input, generating action sequences, executing through device APIs, monitoring state changes via visual perception, and maintaining safety loops, providing the foundation for implementing more capable autonomous voice-controlled systems.

The remainder of this paper is organized as follows. Section 2 reviews related work and compares LAMs with existing assistants. Section 3 presents the proposed methodology for Large Action Models. Section 4 details the modular system architecture and its key components. Section 5 discusses benefits, ethical considerations, and deployment challenges. Finally, Sect. 6 concludes and outlines critical future research directions.

## 2   Background: Related Work

Current voice assistants take varied approaches to natural language processing and task automation, but share limitations that motivate the development of Large Action Models. Google Assistant [4] integrates with services via the App Actions platform but depends on predefined templates and fixed dialogue flows, limiting dynamic or context-aware task execution. Gemini [2], its successor, improves conversational fluency but remains similarly constrained. It primarily supports Google services and a few third-party apps, such as Spotify, through fixed integrations, limiting broader task automation and cross-application coordination.

Open-source solutions such as Leon.ai [6] and Mycroft [8] attempt to address some flexibility limitations through modular architectures and community-driven skill development. Leon.ai provides a more customizable framework with support for custom modules and local processing, while Mycroft offers device-agnostic voice control with emphasis on privacy and user control. However, both operate within the paradigm of mapping voice commands to predetermined skill modules, lacking the reasoning capabilities necessary for true multi-step task planning.

Simpler voice control systems like Dicio [1] and Aimybox [5] provide basic hooks for custom action integration and excel at straightforward command-response patterns but cannot handle complex reasoning or cross-application context tracking.

### 2.1  Comparative Analysis: LAMs vs. Emerging Advanced Assistants

Recent advanced systems represent the current state-of-the-art but retain fundamental limitations. Google's Project Astra [3] offers enhanced multimodal understanding with real-time visual processing and contextual memory, while Gemini [2] provides improved conversational fluency with limited task automation. However, both exhibit constraints that motivate LAMs:

*Action Execution:* Astra and Gemini rely on fixed tool sets, namely Astra's agent tools and Gemini's App Actions framework. While reliable for predefined tasks, they cannot dynamically compose novel action sequences. LAMs generate adaptive sequences combining primitives in task-specific ways, enabling automation beyond explicitly programmed scenarios.

*Planning and Adaptation:* Existing systems select from predetermined tools rather than generating multi-step plans that adapt based on execution feedback. LAMs employ reasoning models (xLAM) that decompose complex requests, adjust plans dynamically, and recover from failures through automated replanning rather than requiring user intervention.

*Privacy Architecture:* Cloud-based processing in Astra and Gemini requires continuous data transmission to external servers. LAMs' on-device inference through ONNX runtime eliminates external exposure while enabling offline operation, addressing critical privacy concerns in AI assistant deployment.

*Visual Perception:* While Astra processes camera feeds for contextual responses, neither system maintains visual awareness of device state for execution monitoring. LAMs integrate CogVLM for continuous state verification, detecting failures and interface changes that would break template-based approaches.

LAMs occupy a distinct position through: (1) closed-loop architecture integrating perception, reasoning, and action with continuous feedback; (2) higher autonomy via adaptive planning beyond tool selection; (3) privacy-first on-device design; and (4) modular extensibility without centralized dependencies. The fundamental gap in existing approaches lies in the absence of integrated multi-step planning, robust cross-task context tracking, and comprehensive visual feedback mechanisms enabling systems to understand and adapt to changing device states.

# 3  Proposed Methodology: Large Action Models

Large Action Models represent an architecture for complex task automation by reconceptualizing the relationship between user intent and system execution. Rather than mapping commands to predetermined actions, LAMs reason about user objectives, generate contextually-appropriate plans, and adapt based on real-time feedback.

The "richer tasks" that LAMs are designed to address encompass scenarios requiring multi-step reasoning, context tracking, and adaptive planning. For example, a user might request "help me prepare for tomorrow's presentation by organizing my research notes, creating a slide outline, and scheduling practice time," expecting the system to navigate across applications, analyze document content, generate structured outputs, and coordinate calendar management without requiring step-by-step guidance or predetermined command sequences.

LAMs achieve this through a modular pipeline integrating: natural language understanding for intent extraction, reasoning and planning modules for generating execution sequences, action execution systems for device control, perception engines for visual feedback and state monitoring, and user interaction loops for safety and confirmation. This approach enables continuous context awareness and feedback-driven adaptation throughout execution in real-world device environments.

# 4  Proposed System Architecture

The Large Action Model architecture consists of five integrated components that work together to process natural language input and execute complex, multi-step tasks with contextual awareness and adaptive planning capabilities (See Fig. 1). The system leverages three pretrained models: Whisper (trained on 680,000 h of multilingual speech data), xLAM (trained on multi-phase function-calling and action planning datasets with synthetic augmentation), and CogVLM (trained on image-text pairs for vision-language understanding).

## 4.1  Input Processing and Natural Language Understanding

The input processing component utilizes OpenAI Whisper [9] for high-quality speech-to-text conversion, providing robust performance across diverse acoustic conditions and multilingual capabilities. The processed text undergoes semantic analysis to extract user intent and identify task complexity, determining single-step versus multi-step execution requirements.

The system employs large language model prompting to normalize and structure input text for processing by the reasoning module, which includes identifying task objectives, extracting parameters, and preparing context for effective planning.

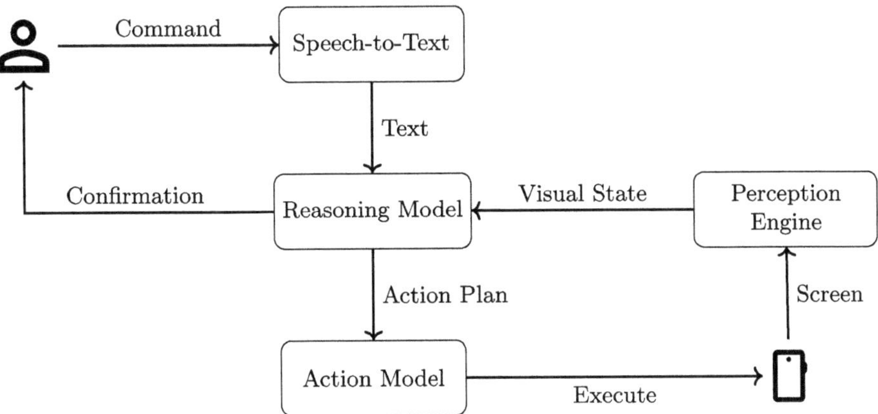


**Fig. 1.** Overview of the proposed LAM system architecture showing the closed-loop integration of speech-to-text conversion (Whisper), reasoning and planning (xLAM), action execution (Mobile-MCP), and visual feedback (CogVLM) with user confirmation for safe autonomous task execution.

## 4.2   Reasoning and Planning with xLAM

The reasoning component leverages xLAM [11] to analyze input and generate structured execution plans. xLAM functions as a specialized reasoning engine understanding relationships between user objectives and system capabilities, generating action sequences for coordinated device interactions.

An "action list" represents a structured sequence of executable steps with defined parameters, expected outcomes, and conditional logic for various scenarios. The reasoning module considers available APIs, system state, and user preferences to optimize sequences. xLAM's planning enables dynamic adaptation based on intermediate results, allowing for conditional branching and error recovery.

The xLAM training pipeline systematically develops reasoning capabilities through data unification, quality assurance, augmentation with synthetic examples, and planning-focused model training to produce the reasoning engine powering the LAM for multi-step task automation(See Fig. 2).

**xLAM Technical Architecture:** The xLAM architecture incorporates a Mixture-of-Experts (MoE) routing mechanism that enables the model to dynamically select specialized subnetworks (experts) for each input token[1]. This approach improves both scalability and performance, particularly for complex reasoning tasks and function-calling.

*Step 1: Token Embedding* Each input token is represented as a hidden vector:

---

[1] The following formalism is a hypothesized representation consistent with standard Mixture-of-Experts (MoE) methods. The xLAM papers do not publish explicit routing equations or gating mechanisms.

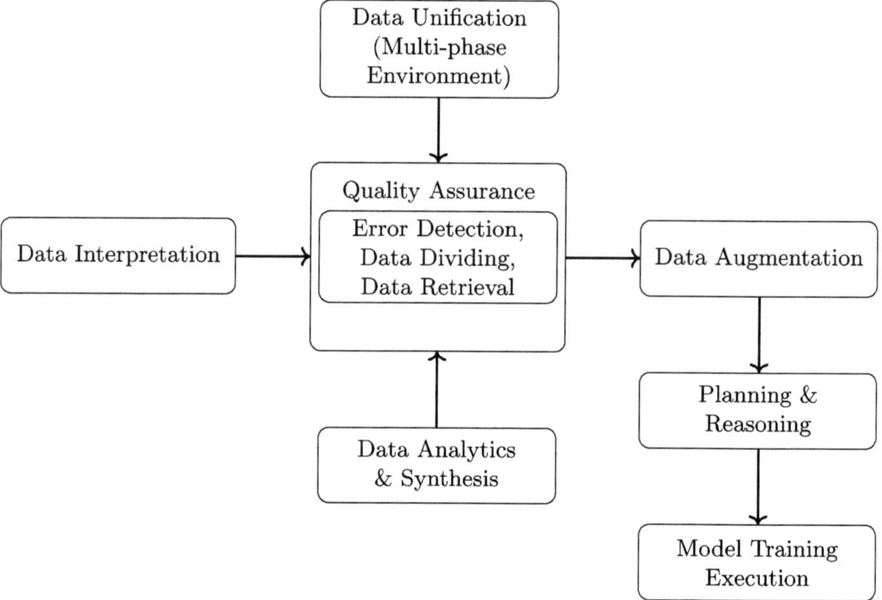



**Fig. 2.** Overview of Data Identification, Processing and Model Training of xLAM

$$x \in \mathbb{R}^d \tag{1}$$

where:

- $x$ = token representation
- $d$ = hidden dimension

*Step 2: Gating Function* A learned gating network computes the probability of routing the token to each of $K$ experts:

$$g_k(x) = \frac{\exp(w_k^\top x + b_k)}{\sum_{j=1}^{K} \exp(w_j^\top x + b_j)} \tag{2}$$

Only the top-$m$ experts (typically $m = 1$ or 2) are selected for computation.

*Step 3: Expert Execution* The selected expert(s) process the token:

$$y = \sum_{k \in \text{Top-}m} g_k(x) \cdot E_k(x) \tag{3}$$

where $E_k(x)$ is the output of expert $k$ given input $x$.

*Step 4: Residual Integration* The expert output is combined with the original input through a residual connection:

$$\tilde{x} = x + W_o \cdot y \tag{4}$$

where $W_o$ is a projection matrix to match dimensions.

## 4.3  Action Execution and Device Control

The action execution component translates planned sequences into device interactions through multiple API layers. Mobile-MCP [7] provides high-level abstractions for common mobile device operations, while Android Debug Bridge (ADB) and XCTest (iOS) offer lower-level access when required.

This component handles multi-step execution by maintaining state across actions, coordinating timing, and managing inter-application communication. Each execution includes pre-condition verification, parameter validation, monitoring, and result capture for perception and planning feedback. The modular design enables extension to additional device platforms and API frameworks as needed.

## 4.4  Perception Engine and Context Awareness

The perception engine employs CogVLM [10] to analyze device screenshots before and after action execution, providing continuous awareness of state changes and outcomes. This visual feedback enables the system to understand action effects, verify task completion, and identify situations requiring plan adaptation or user intervention.

CogVLM processes screenshots to extract visual information, compare expected versus actual outcomes, and provide structured feedback to the reasoning module. The engine maintains contextual awareness by tracking visual elements across screenshots, enabling understanding of application state transitions throughout task execution (See Fig. 3).

**CogVLM Technical Architecture:** The visual understanding capability relies on a three-stage architecture[2]. First, the Vision Transformer (ViT) encoder processes input images $\mathcal{I} \in \mathbb{R}^{H \times W \times C}$ by splitting them into $N$ patches of size $P \times P$, which are flattened and projected as:

$$z_i = W_E x_i + p_i, \tag{5}$$

where $W_E$ represents the patch embedding matrix and $p_i$ the positional encoding. The transformer encoder then applies multi-head self-attention (MSA) and feed-forward networks (MLP) through:

$$z_i' = \mathrm{MSA}(z_i) + z_i, \tag{6}$$

---

[2] Details inferred based on standard transformer architectures; exact implementations not publicly disclosed.

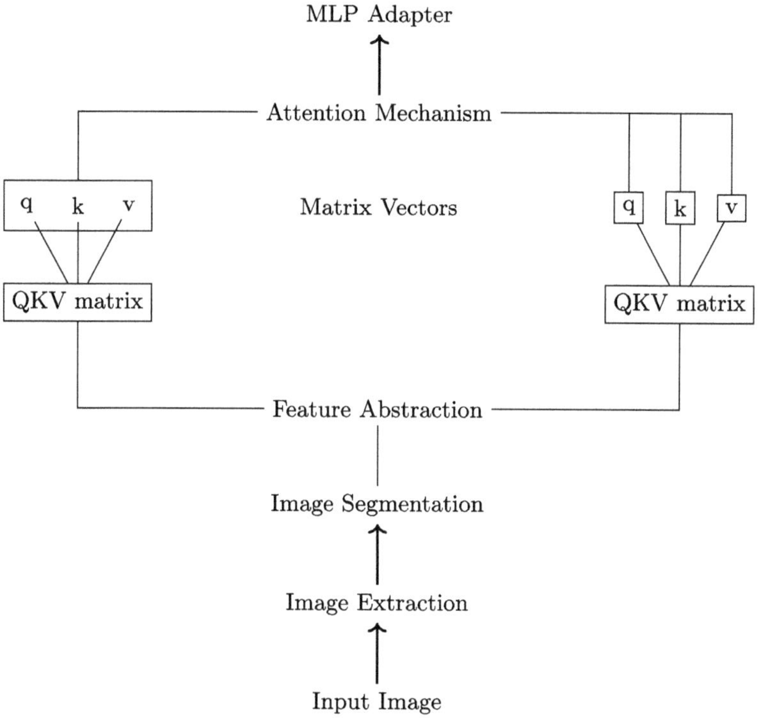


**Fig. 3.** Overview of CogVLM

$$z_i'' = \mathrm{MLP}(z_i') + z_i'. \tag{7}$$

The Q-Former (Query Transformer) stage employs learnable queries $Q = \{q_1, \ldots, q_k\} \in \mathbb{R}^{k \times d}$ that interact with image embeddings $Z = \{z_1, \ldots, z_n\} \in \mathbb{R}^{n \times d}$ via cross-attention:

$$\mathrm{Attention}(Q, Z, Z) = \mathrm{softmax}\left(\frac{QW_Q(ZW_K)^T}{\sqrt{d}}\right) ZW_V, \tag{8}$$

where $W_Q, W_K, W_V$ are projection matrices producing query-aligned visual embeddings.

Finally, the language model decoder combines processed visual tokens $V$ with text prompt tokens $T = \{t_1, \ldots, t_m\}$ to generate contextual understanding through:

$$h_i = \mathrm{Transformer}(V \oplus T)_i, \tag{9}$$

$$P(w_{i+1} \mid w_{<i}, V) = \mathrm{softmax}(Wh_i + b). \tag{10}$$

Training employs language modeling loss:

$$\mathcal{L}_{\mathrm{LM}} = -\sum_i \log P(w_i \mid w_{<i}, V), \tag{11}$$

and optional image-text contrastive loss for alignment.

### 4.5 User Interaction and Safety Loops

The user interaction component manages communication with users throughout task execution, providing transparency, requesting confirmation for sensitive operations, and handling errors requiring intervention. Trigger points include irreversible actions (financial transactions), situations where the confidence falls below thresholds, and explicit user requests for step-by-step confirmation.

The framework implements a hierarchical safety architecture with three protection layers:

*Action Classification Layer* - All actions undergo risk classification: (1) *Safe actions* requiring no confirmation (reading information, opening applications), (2) *Moderate-risk actions* requiring simple confirmation (sending messages, calendar events), and (3) *High-risk actions* requiring explicit user intervention (financial transactions, data deletion, permission requests).

*Confidence Thresholding* - The reasoning module assigns confidence scores based on intent clarity, contextual information, and historical success rates. Actions below dynamically-adjusted thresholds trigger mandatory review, with thresholds varying by risk category.

*Execution Monitoring and Rollback* - The system maintains checkpoints throughout workflows, enabling selective rollback when errors occur or users request cancellation. The perception engine monitors for unexpected states, errors, or security warnings, automatically pausing execution for user intervention when anomalies arise.

This component ensures LAM systems remain under user control while maximizing automation benefits by explaining intended actions and allowing users to modify or cancel them. It enables natural language-driven automation while maintaining contextual awareness, adaptability, and safe operation within user-defined boundaries.

## 5 Discussion: Benefits, Challenges and Related Implications

### 5.1 Benefits and Advantages

The proposed LAM architecture offers significant advantages through integrated multi-step planning and contextual awareness. LAMs enable feedback-driven loops where each action influences subsequent planning, handling unexpected situations by dynamically replanning rather than failing. The perception engine adapts to interface changes while the reasoning module generates alternative execution paths when encountering obstacles. This enables cross-application context tracking and continuous task progress awareness. The modular architecture provides extensibility while reducing cognitive load through natural language task specification.

**Accessibility Through Voice-First Interaction:** LAMs improve accessibility by eliminating dependence on visual interfaces. Traditional mobile interactions require precise touch targeting and visual navigation—barriers for users with visual impairments, motor disabilities, or situational limitations. Voice-driven task automation removes these constraints.

Unlike screen readers navigating existing visual interfaces, LAMs directly translate intent to actions, bypassing interface complexity. This benefits users with visual impairments, motor limitations, situational constraints (driving, cooking), and elderly users unfamiliar with complex interfaces. By treating voice as a first-class interface, LAMs democratize device automation across diverse populations.

## 5.2    Ethical Considerations and Privacy Implications

The deployment of Large Action Models raises significant ethical concerns requiring careful consideration before widespread adoption.

**Data Privacy and Surveillance Risks:** LAM systems require continuous access to device state information, application content, and user interaction patterns to maintain contextual awareness. This creates substantial privacy risks when visual language models analyze on-screen data containing sensitive personal information, financial data, or private communications.

To address these concerns, the proposed architecture adopts an on-device processing approach using ONNX (Open Neural Network Exchange) runtime for client-side AI inference. Local processing ensures sensitive data never leaves the device, eliminating cloud dependencies, external server exposure, and attack vectors such as man-in-the-middle attacks. ONNX enables deployment of quantized model variants (xLAM and CogVLM) maintaining acceptable performance within mobile device constraints, while additional strategies include federated learning, differential privacy, and regular security audits to ensure comprehensive privacy protection.

**Autonomy and User Control:** Autonomous decision-making raises questions about appropriate boundaries for action execution. While automation reduces cognitive load, it diminishes direct user control and may obscure action consequences. Users may develop over-reliance, reducing understanding of underlying processes and intervention capability.

Ethical deployment requires clear communication of limitations, transparent explanation of planned actions, and accessible override mechanisms. The architecture must maintain meaningful human oversight while delivering genuine automation benefits.

**Bias and Fairness Concerns:** Language and vision-language models inherit training data biases that may manifest in discriminatory behavior when planning and executing actions. This could lead to differential service quality across demographics, inappropriate assumptions about user intent, or systematic errors for underrepresented populations. The visual perception component introduces additional risks, as computer vision systems show varying performance across interface designs, languages, and cultural contexts.

Addressing these concerns requires diverse training datasets, systematic bias evaluation across demographic groups, and ongoing deployment monitoring to detect and correct discriminatory patterns.

## 5.3   Real-World Deployment Challenges

Practical deployment introduces substantial technical and operational challenges:

**System Integration and API Fragmentation:** Mobile operating systems present fragmented API landscapes with platform-specific restrictions, versioning inconsistencies, and permission requirements. Android's manufacturer customizations and iOS's sandboxing policies create incompatible execution environments requiring platform-specific adaptation layers. Third-party application APIs vary widely in capabilities and stability, with many lacking programmatic access entirely. The Mobile-MCP abstraction layer must accommodate these inconsistencies while maintaining reliable execution.

**Performance and Resource Constraints:** The architecture's reliance on large models and continuous monitoring creates substantial computational requirements. ONNX runtime addresses these challenges through graph-level optimizations, operator fusion, and hardware acceleration support (GPU, NPU, AI accelerators). Quantized INT8/INT4 model variants reduce memory footprint by 4–8x while maintaining acceptable accuracy, with model distillation further compressing capabilities for resource-constrained devices. On-device processing eliminates network latency for near-instant responses critical to interactive workflows while enabling reliable offline functionality. Optimization strategies include lazy loading of perception models, batched inference for hardware accelerator efficiency, and adaptive quality settings balancing accuracy against battery state, with user-configurable profiles enabling flexible trade-offs between capabilities and resource constraints.

**Error Handling and Recovery:** Deployment must contend with numerous failure modes: application crashes, interface changes, permission denials, and ambiguous visual states. The perception engine may misinterpret elements, reasoning may generate invalid sequences, or actions may fail due to transient conditions.

Robust handling requires failure detection, graceful degradation when automation is unavailable, and clear communication about errors and recovery. The system must distinguish between recoverable errors requiring replanning and fundamental failures requiring user intervention.

**Security and Malicious Use Prevention:** Autonomous execution creates vulnerabilities if the system can be manipulated through adversarial inputs, prompt injection, or compromised models. Malicious actors could exploit LAM systems for unauthorized actions, data exfiltration, or security compromise.

Security measures must include input validation, action authentication, sandboxed execution, and behavioral anomaly detection. The architecture must incorporate security-by-design principles rather than treating security as an afterthought.

## 6  Conclusion and Future Work

This paper introduces Large Action Models as an architecture addressing fundamental limitations in current voice assistant technologies through integrated reasoning, perception, and action capabilities. The proposed modular design enables flexible task automation beyond fixed command-response patterns via continuous perception-driven replanning and cross-application context maintenance.

Key contributions include: (1) conceptualization of LAMs for complex task automation, (2) modular architecture with integrated perception-action loops, (3) comparative analysis versus state-of-the-art assistants (Project Astra, Gemini), and (4) foundation for autonomous voice-controlled systems research.

### 6.1  Critical Future Research Directions

**Safety and Evaluation:** Critical priorities include: (1) formal verification for action sequence safety with standardized benchmarks for adversarial conditions and edge cases, (2) user validation of confirmation interfaces across diverse populations, (3) comprehensive evaluation frameworks assessing task completion accuracy, error recovery effectiveness, and system reliability, and (4) industry standards for responsible deployment.

**On-Device Optimization:** Future work must advance on-device deployment through: (1) automated compression pipelines generating device-specific optimized variants across inference frameworks (ONNX, Core ML, Gemini Nano), (2) adaptive inference dynamically adjusting model complexity based on available resources, (3) continual learning mechanisms enabling privacy-preserving personalization, and (4) federated learning architectures for collaborative improvement across devices.

**Fairness and Extensibility:** Systematic bias evaluation frameworks must assess LAM behavior across demographics and cultural contexts. Future work should develop debiasing techniques, establish fairness metrics for automated task execution, and conduct longitudinal studies examining adoption patterns and trust calibration. Additional priorities include cross-platform expansion (mobile, desktop, IoT), standardized benchmarks for multi-step task completion, and privacy-preserving personalization mechanisms.

**Disclosure of Interests.** The authors have no competing interests to declare that are relevant to the content of this article.

# References


1. Dicio Team: Dicio - open source voice assistant (2024). https://github.com/Stypox/dicio-android, gitHub Repository
2. Gemini Team, Anil, R., et al.: Gemini: A family of highly capable multimodal models. arXiv preprint arXiv:2312.11805 (2023)
3. Google DeepMind: Project astra: A universal ai agent (2024). https://deepmind.google/technologies/gemini/project-astra/, google I/O 2024
4. Google LLC: Google assistant developer documentation (2024). https://developers.google.com/assistant
5. Just AI: Aimybox - open-source voice assistant sdk (2024). https://github.com/just-ai/aimybox-android-sdk, gitHub Repository
6. Leon.ai Team: Leon - your open-source personal assistant (2024). https://getleon.ai/
7. Mobile-Next: Mobile-mcp (2024). https://github.com/mobile-next/mobile-mcp, gitHub Repository
8. Mycroft AI Inc.: Mycroft - open source voice assistant (2024). https://mycroft.ai/
9. Radford, A., Kim, J.W., Xu, T., Brockman, G., McLeavey, C., Sutskever, I.: Robust speech recognition via large-scale weak supervision. arXiv preprint arXiv:2212.04356 (2022)
10. Wang, W., et al.: Cogvlm: Visual expert for pretrained language models. arXiv preprint arXiv:2311.03079 (2023)
11. Zhang, J., et al.: xlam: A family of large action models to empower ai agent systems. arXiv preprint arXiv:2409.03215 (2024)

# Efficient LLM Framework Using LORA Based Fine Tuning to Analyze Textual Astronomical Data

Sk Sahil Parvez[1], Roushan Kumar[1], MD Shaheer[1], Snigdha Sen[2(✉)], and Pavan Chakraborty[1]

[1] Department of Information Technology, IIIT Allahabad, Prayagraj, India
[2] Manipal Institute of Technology Bengaluru, Manipal Academy of Higher Education, Manipal, India
`snigdha.sen@manipal.edu`

**Abstract.** In this article, Llama LLM (Large Language Model) is fine tuned with LORA (Low Rank Adaptation) to make it suitable for analyzing astronomical data. Instead of modifying the entire eight billion parameters of the Llama 3 model, we applied LoRA adapters to reduce training time and minimize original knowledge deterioration. The adapters operate as small information guides that can enter particular regions of the attention system to help it utilize language abilities for astronomical subject matters. The proposed scheme uses a compact 4-bit quantization scheme QLoRA (Quantized Low-Rank Adaptation) that condensed the model into a suitable format for quick training and running. Results indicate reduced training time to a few hours on high-end GPUs instead of traditional weeks or days. The fine tuned proposed model provides 85.2% Exact Match Score (EM) when compared with Llama 3 8B Chat HF v1 (Base Model) that reported 60.8 %. This research will facilitate readers robust guidelines towards modifying LLM for domain specific training data which allow fine-tuning while maintaining core functionality.

**Keywords:** Large Language Models · 4-bit Quantization · Parameter-Efficient Training · Astrophysical Knowledge Injection · Astronomy Question Answering

## 1 Introduction

The use of Modern large language models in various domains indicates remarkable performance in comprehending natural language. Meta's Llama 3 8B Chat HF v1 model is a significant achievement which outperforms various other common language models. These models are trained on huge amounts of text, which makes them good at giving clear answers and recalling facts from many different subjects. However, when it comes to highly specialized areas like astronomy and astrophysics, they often fall short. Topics such as stellar life cycles, redshift estimation [11,12], exoplanet detection, or the large-scale structure of the universe require not just factual knowledge but also deep scientific reasoning and


K. K. Patel et al. (Eds.): icSoftComp 2025, CCIS 2874, pp. 16–28, 2026.
https://doi.org/10.1007/978-3-032-22062-2_2

the right technical vocabulary. Basic language models usually struggle with this level of detail, because of that additional domain-specific training is needed.

To overcome this challenge, we tried out parameter-efficient fine-tuning methods that could transform Llama 3 Chat into a smarter, astronomy-focused assistant. We used QLoRA (Quantized LORA), which compresses the model down to 4-bit precision. This not only makes it small enough to run on a single GPU with decent memory but also keeps performance mostly intact. The full 8 billion parameters of the original model remain untouched, while we add LoRA adapters small modules with only a few million trainable parameters into the key attention and feed-forward layers. These adapters act like concise "study guides", they don't replace the model's overall language abilities instead enhances its understanding of astrophysics terms.

We built a database of 41,500 astronomy questionanswer pairs, extracted from the GALEX All-Sky QA Dataset [3]. The collection covers a wide range of topics, from basics like orbital mechanics and star classification to advanced concepts in cosmology and observational techniques. Before training, we cleaned and standardized the data, and where needed, added conversational context to create a history of interactions. The dataset was then converted into Hugging Face's format, with a stratified split to make sure all topics were fairly represented. Finally, the model's tokenizer prepared the examples for training.

The resulting specialized model shows stronger accuracy and deeper reasoning when answering astronomy-related questions. It produces concise, informative answers drawn from astronomy knowledge while preserving the flexible, natural conversational style of the original Llama 3 Chat model. In this study we present an application approach which merges QLoRA [8] compression methods with LoRA-based adapters to enable fast customization of large LLM [1] applications for particular scientific domains. It thus enables users to access AI assistance that operates competently in cosmic science [5].

## 1.1  LoRA (Low-Rank Adaptation)

Both computational power requirements and system memory usage decrease with the use of LoRA [7] for task-specific adaptation of large language pre-trained models. Traditional LLM [1] fine-tuning demands complete model weight updates which makes it expensive and memory-intensive particularly when dealing with an 8B Llama[5] model [4]. LoRA[6] uses low-rank matrices to handle specific domains in attention mechanisms without altering the underlying main parameter network [7]. At first, the essential trainable parameters are passed in LoRA through the attention mechanism which focuses on query and key and value components. The model uses low-rank matrices integrated into its structure to discover critical changes needed for learning new tasks. LoRA allows researchers to maintain frozen pre-trained model parts which greatly minimizes the amount of parameters while saving processing power and memory consumption. When used for tasks the memory footprint stays efficient despite a reduced size because low-rank matrices (A and B) deliver comparable domain-specific performance to the original matrices [4].

LoRA delivers parameter-efficient capabilities which work as an advantage for model fine-tuning procedures. The approach works on its update procedure on selected parameters to enable minimal resource consumption thereby making it suitable for astronomy question answering among other applications [4].

## 1.2  Working Principle of LoRA

LoRA funtions are demonstrated as follows:

$$Q = Wq*X \text{ (Query computation)}$$
$$K = Wk*X \text{ (Key computation)}$$
$$V = Wv*X \text{ (Value computation)}$$

Where:

- Q, K, and V are the query, key, and value matrices.
- Wq, Wk, and Wv are the learned weight matrices.
- X is the input to the attention layer [4].

Instead of directly fine-tuning Wq, Wk, and Wv, LoRA introduces a low-rank approximation where the update is done by adding two smaller matrices A and B as follows:

$$W'q = Wq + Aq*Bq$$
$$W'k = Wk + Ak*Bk$$
$$W'v = Wv + Av*Bv$$

Where:

- Aq, Bq, Ak, Bk, Av, and Bv are the low-rank adapter matrices. A and B have smaller dimensions (rank r) than the original weight matrices, typically much smaller, allowing for a more memory-efficient fine-tuning process. The primary advantage of LoRA is that only the low-rank adapters A and B are trained, keeping the majority of the model's parameters frozen, which significantly reduces the computational overhead [4].

## 1.3  QLoRA (Quantized Low-Rank Adaptation)

QLoRA advances LoRA through implementation of quantization methods to run the adaptation. The main objective of QLoRA [8] consists of lowering memory requirements together with maintaining effective model fine-tuning capabilities. QLoRA applies low-rank adaptation through LoRA to quantized pre-trained models which are typically quantized to 4-bits. The weight matrices undergo quantization before QLoRA executes low-rank adaptation which resembles LoRA operation. Let's assume the weight matrix W is quantized:

Wq = Quantize(W)

The weight matrices in QLoRA must undergo both quantization and LoRA's low-rank decomposition process during efficient fine-tuning;

Wq" = Wq + A·B

Where:

1. Wq is the adapted and quantized weight matrix.
2. A∈R(d×r) and B∈R(d×r) are the low-rank matrices, and r is typically small.
3. The quantization process ensures that the weight matrices take up less memory and computation resources.

## 2   Review of Literature

Active research [9,10,13] is going on studying how to apply large language models (LLM) specifically for astronomy as a specialized domain. General-purpose natural language model show success due to LLMs like GPT-3, BERT, and Llama. But they do not perform satisfactorily in case of domain-specific question answering tasks especially in technical subjects like astrophysics until they receive specialized adaptations. This review section analyzes the body of research in domain adaptation and parameter-efficient fine-tuning (PEFT) and quantization methods with their application to scientific data especially regarding astronomy.

### 2.1   General Large Language Models (LLMs) and Their Limitations

Through extensive pre-training on varied widespread datasets three main models including GPT-3 from OpenAI, then BERT from Google along with Llama from Facebook exhibit exceptional proficiency in creating human like text and contextual understanding. The training data consists of enormous unsupervised internet data that these models consume to perform tasks across multiple domains.

Large language models often struggle when it comes to highly specialized fields like astronomy, medicine, or law. In general or common task/field, their performance is quite noteworthy, but fall short during encounter with complex, domain-specific questions. The main reason lies in their inability to understand specialized key concepts, theories, and unique terminology of those domains [1]. As a result, they respond too general, broad, or imprecise when intricate detailing is required in some field. This limitations of general purpose model creates the need of devising ways to adapt general-purpose models to fit and perform efficiently for specialized domains also [1].

## 2.2   Domain Adaptation in LLMs

Specific domain adaptation describes the procedure through which generically usable models get their functionality adapted for work within particular fields of astronomy, law or medicine and other domains. The objective of domain adaptation with LLM involves using three different techniques: domain-specific data fine-tuning, transfer learning approaches and knowledge distillation practices [2].

Very few domain adaptation techniques are as effective as fine-tuning large models using domain-specific datasets. A small labeled dataset from the target domain is used to train the model following its general data pre-training session. The specific model tuning process enables algorithms to transfer broad knowledge acquired from large data collection to new specialized information. Astronomical researchers apply the GPT-3 model by conducting fine-tunings using question-answer pairs and research papers as well as technical datasets representing astronomical phenomena.

The effectiveness of fine-tuning methods exists even though implementing them presents technical obstacles. The process of complete fine-tuning large models requires excessive computing resources which produces problems such as catastrophic forgetting that makes the model disregard previously learned general information for new specialized data. The research community now utilizes Parameter-Efficient Fine-Tuning (PEFT) as an alternative approach because it updates only select parameters during training while allowing specialized adaptations [1]. The process of fine-tuning massive pre-trained LLMs for specialized work such as astronomy needs to achieve right alignment between model retention of universal knowledge alongside domain-specific learning. Domain adaptation serves as a critical requirement because missing it causes models to provide wrong or nonsensical responses.

Models need to be fine tuned with suitable techniques on domain specific concepts to perform more accurately. However, the training process faces several challenges including overfitting and catastrophic forgetting. Therefore it is very important to use efficient training methods and the suitale training data which will maintain a trade off between learning new knowledge while retaining model's original capabilities integrated with previous knowledge.

## 2.3   Parameter-Efficient Fine-Tuning (PEFT)

In this technique, instead of modifying all the parameters of a large pretrained model, only a subset is changed to adopt specific task which subsequently helps to reduce number of trainable parameters and in turn training time. LoRA (Low-Rank Adaptation), known as frequently used PEFT method that uses low-rank matrices to adapt transformer's attention layers. This approach facilitates efficient fine-tuning with minimal computational cost [2]. LoRA improves prediction accuracy in specialized fields like astronomy, yet capable to handle general tasks. In addition to LORA, another method called adapter tuning, tries to add new small and trainable parameters to the model's layers. Subsequently, these modules is able to adjust model's internal representations without changing the original weights of parameters, which is a feasible approach while applying them in domain specific approach.

During catastrophic forgetting, when it loses previously learned information and tries to learn new information, PEFT methods, such as LoRA (Low-Rank Adaptation) fine tune only specific parts of the model instead of retraining everything [2]. LoRA inserts small low-rank matrices into the transformer architecture, allowing the model to adapt to new tasks or domains without altering its overall structure. This approach helps to retain its previously learned knowledge without incurring extra computational cost.

## 2.4  Applying LLMs to Astronomy

Many recent works are explored towards usage of LLM in an astronomy specific domain. Often, to address domain specific terms, these models need to be fine-tuned using astronomy-specific resources—such as research papers, observational data, and curated sets of questions with their solutions—so they are equipped with domain specific knowledge to provide better answers.

LLMs enable the analysis of astronomical data through tasks which include automated celestial object classification as well as description generation of astronomical phenomena and research assistance through complex paper summaries and hypothesis suggestion.

Researcher's scientific papers and reports from observational raw data made possible of the deployment of LLMs in astronomy-related applications. LLMs that receive astronomical training datasets help scientists understand their data through plotting and publish research findings in scientific texts. The application of LLMs showed success in analyzing large astronomical survey datasets including the millions of observations present in GALEX and SDSS surveys.

The use of LLMs in astronomy fields exists at the fundamental developmental stage. Reliable performance from LLMs depends on domain adaptation because they generally lack understanding of the highly technical astronomy jargon. Astronomical question replies benefit from model optimization through GALEX All-Sky QA Dataset processing which enhances their capacity to understand and produce astronomy-relevant content. Astronomy books are filled with complex technical terms, covering topics like celestial mechanics, star formation, and cosmological models. Since LLMs are trained on a wide variety of general content, they often struggle to give accurate answers in astronomy unless they are further trained with specialized domain knowledge. LLMs become much more effective when they are trained on astronomy-specific resources, such as questionanswer datasets, research papers, and observational data. With techniques like LoRA and QLoRA, these models can be fine-tuned to handle specialized content more accurately, all while remaining efficient and requiring relatively modest computing power.

# 3    Proposed Method and Experimental Procedure

Llama 3 8B Chat HF v1 demonstrates exceptional natural language processing abilities because of its training on extensive diverse language corpora. The generic training procedure of these models produces substandard outcomes when dealing with technical expressions and specialized reasoning needed for astronomy science and other scientific domains. The proposed method implements PEFT [2] that fine-tune Llama 3 8B Chat HF v1 which incorporates QLoRA quantization and LoRA adapters to optimize performance on the GALEX All-Sky QA corpus containing more than 41449 questions & answers related to stellar classification and cosmological models. The approach requires minimal adjustable parameters in core transformer layers along with weight-frozen features that lead to training time in hours in a single GPU instead of days. Figure 1 presents the framework for fine tuning of LLM model.

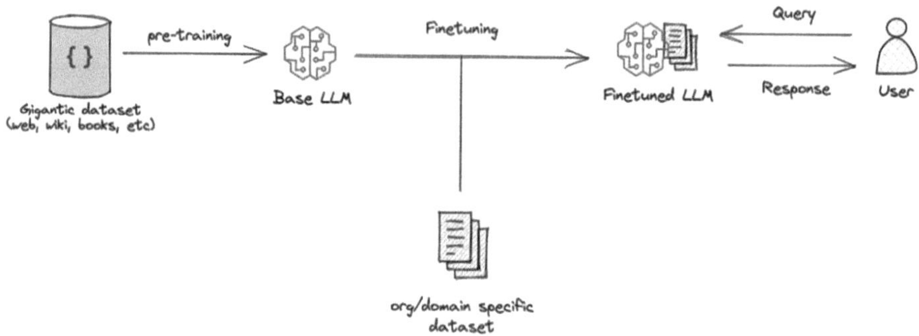


**Fig. 1.** Proposed Workflow for Fine tuning base LLM Model using LORA

## 3.1    Data Acquisition

The dataset used in this study comes from GALEX All-Sky QA [3] funded by its mission team. The dataset contains 41449 pairs of questions and answers which cover basic to advanced astrophysics subjects such as orbital dynamics along with spectral analysis and galaxy evolution.The file format is of type TSV (Tab Separated Value) having Index, Question and Answer columns to allow direct intake into pandas as well as Hugging Face Datasets.

## 3.2    Data Preprocessing

Preprocessing steps for preparing the GALEX All-Sky QA Dataset for fine tuning the hybrid model are as follows:

- **Parsing & Cleaning:** A pandas DataFrame read the unprocessed TSV file while removing rows containing missing content along with normalization of whitespace.The process removed all unsought line breaks between blocks containing Questions and Answers to maintain proper alignment.
- **Contextual History Construction:** Using concatenated prior Q&A pairs along with separator tokens, this model facilitates contextual information during multi-turn exchanges handling to avoid breaking in dialogue continuity.
- **Dataset Conversion & Split:** At the beginning, the entire DataFrame is converted to Apache Arrow table followed by transformation into datasets. Using stratified sampling, splitting is done in the 90/10 ratio to ensure the preservation of topic balance. Figure 2 describes the details of dataset fields.
- **Tokenization:** A 512-token limit mechanism in AutoTokenizer.from_pretrained("meta-llama/Llama-3-8B-chat-hf-v1") is used to handle truncation and padding operationsif required.

| index | question | answer |
|---|---|---|
| 0 | What criteria were used to isolate young stell... | The researchers used combined IRAC and MIPS c2... |
| 1 | What evidence supports the presence of disc ov... | The study observed spin-modulated radial veloc... |
| 2 | How can millimeter wavelength observations hel... | Millimeter wavelength observations, particular... |
| 3 | How does the theoretical framework explain ene... | The framework posits that energy injected at t... |
| 4 | How does the Markov Chain Monte Carlo approach... | The Markov Chain Monte Carlo approach not only... |
| 5 | What are the derived characteristics of the bi... | The binary system HAT-TR-205-013 consists of a... |
| 6 | How does the globular cluster mass function (G... | The GCMF depends on cluster half-mass density ... |
| 7 | What are the maximum speeds of the bullet subh... | The bullet subhalo can move with a maximum spe... |
| 8 | How does the Swift/XRT light curve repository ... | NaN |
| 9 | What does the detection of PAH emission featur... | The detection of PAH emission features in the ... |

**Fig. 2.** Details of Dataset

# 4   Model Architecture

## 4.1   Overview of the Proposed Model

- **Base Checkpoint:** meta-llama/Llama-3-8B-chat-hf-v1
- **Quantization:** QLoRA 4-bit NF4 with double quantization to reduce memory footprint while preserving performance.
- **Adapters (LoRA):** Injected into projection matrices (q_proj, k_proj, v_proj, up_proj, down_proj, o_proj) using rank 16, $\alpha = 32$, and 5 % dropout. Only these adapter parameters are trainable; the original 8 B weights remain frozen.
- **PEFT Integration:** Wrapped the quantized model.
- **Training Orchestration:** Utilized TRL's SFTTrainer for mixed-precision fine-tuning, gradient accumulation, and real-time logging to Weights & Biases.

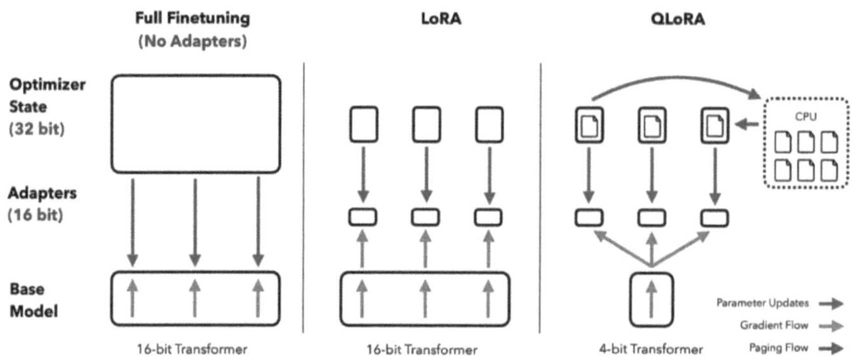


**Fig. 3.** LORA and QLORA Architecture

## 4.2   Working Mechanism

In Fig. 3 we show the LORA and QLORA architecture and their inner functionality.

1) **Input Processing:** The process of preparing astronomy questions starts with cleaning techniques followed by tokenization in addition to creating a template for prompt generation specific to the domain.
2) **Forward Pass:** The attention and feed-forward output components from base + LoRA[6] adapters apply token input to the quantized base system for astrophysical precision guidance.
3) **Generation:** In the generation phase the model provides context-aware precise answers using its internal decoding framework.
4) **Post-Processing:** Response generation includes Token detokenization and special token removal which leads to the final end result following generation.

Algorithm 1 illustrates the procedure fine tuning method for astronomy pipeline.

## 4.3   Model Training

During model training, the following configuration have been used.

1) **Hyperparameters:**
   - **Epochs:** 1
   - **Learning rate:** $2 \times 10^{-4}$ with 10 warmup steps.
   - **Optimizer:** paged_adamw_32bit.
   - **Batch size:** 4 per GPU with gradient accumulation.
   - **group_by_length=** True for efficient bucketing.
2) **Logging & Evaluation:**
   - Training and validation loss logged every step via Weights & Biases.
   - Validation run on the 10 % split every 500 steps.

3) **Compute Resources:** Single T4 15 GB GPU, approximately 6 h to converge. Figure 4 and Fig. 5 discuss model training loss graph and various trainable parameters.

---

**Algorithm 1.** Astronomy LLM Fine-Tuning Pipeline

---

**Require:** Google Drive with dataset, Weights & Biases API key
**Ensure:** Fine-tuned Llama-3.1-8B model
 1: **Initialize Weights & Biases**
 2: wandb.login(key = YOUR_WANDB_KEY)
 3: wandb.init(project = "astronomy-llm-finetune")
 4: **Load Pre-trained Model**
 5: model ← from_pretrained('Meta-Llama-3.1-8B',
 6:                 load_in_4bit = True,
 7:                 use_lora = True)
 8: **Load Dataset**
 9: dataset ← pd.read_csv('/content/drive/astronomy_qa.csv')
10: **Data Preprocessing**
11: dataset ← dataset.dropna(subset = ['question', 'answer'])
12: dataset ← dataset[dataset.question.apply(len) $\geq$ 5]
13: dataset ← dataset[dataset.answer.apply(len) $\geq$ 5]
14: **Format Data**
15: format_prompt ← $\lambda x$ : $f$"Instruction: {x['question']} nOutput: {x['answer']}"
16: formatted_data ← dataset.apply(format_prompt, axis = 1)
17: **Dataset Mapping**
18: dataset ← dataset.map(format_prompt)
19: **Display Samples**
20: print(formatted_data.sample(3))
21: **Training Setup**
22: trainer ← SFTTrainer(
23:         model = model,
24:         train_dataset = dataset,
25:         args = {batch_size : 8, lr : $2e - 5$})
26: **Start Training**
27: trainer.train()
28: monitor_gpu_memory()
29: **Save Model**
30: model.save_pretrained('/content/finetuned_astronomy')
31: tokenizer.save_pretrained('/content/finetuned_astronomy')
32: **Inference**
33: streamer ← TextStreamer(tokenizer)
34: model.generate(input_prompt, streamer = streamer)

---

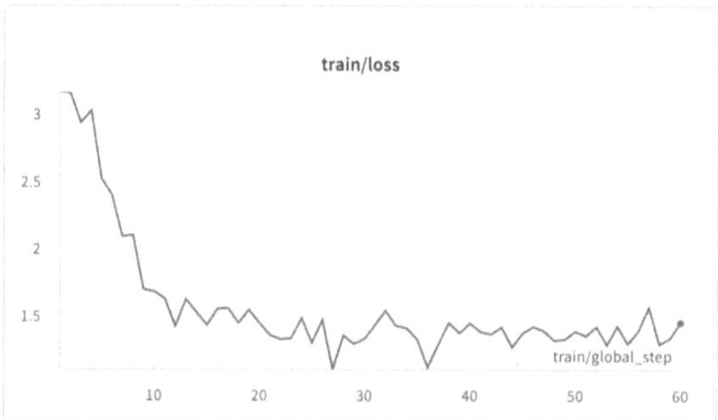



**Fig. 4.** Model train/loss graph

```
==((====))==  Unsloth - 2x faster free finetuning | Num GPUs used = 1
   \\   /|    Num examples = 41,426 | Num Epochs = 1 | Total steps = 60
O^O/ \_/ \    Batch size per device = 2 | Gradient accumulation steps = 4
\        /    Data Parallel GPUs = 1 | Total batch size (2 x 4 x 1) = 8
 "-____-"     Trainable parameters = 41,943,040/8,000,000,000 (0.52% trained)
```

**Fig. 5.** Trainable parameters

# 5    Comparison of Proposed Model with Base Llama3 8B Chat HF V1

**Table 1.** Average Evaluation Metrics across Three Test Scenes

| Metric | Llama | LoRA[6]-Tuned Model |
|---|---|---|
| Exact Match (EM) Score | 60.8% | 85.2% |
| F1 Score | 75.4% | 91.7% |
| Perplexity | 9.8 | 4.3 |

From Table 1 the following observation is made for the analysis of fine tuned proposed model compared to base Llama model. Figure 6 visually plots the bar graphs for perfomance comparison.

**Exact Match (EM) Score:** : The LoRA fine-tuned model achieved a 24.4 % improvement in Exact Match, demonstrating the effectiveness of fine-tuning for domain-specific tasks such as astronomy.

**F1 Score:** A 16.3% increase in F1 Score highlights the enhanced precision and recall of theLoRA-tuned model, reflecting its ability to handle the specific terminology and nuances of the astronomy domain.

**Perplexity:** The perplexity was reduced by 56%, indicating that the LoRA-tuned model is better at predicting the next word in a sequence and, therefore, more coherent in generating responses.

This reflects a relative EM improvement of 40 % and a 2.3× reduction in perplexity, underscoring the effectiveness of QLoRA+LoRA adaptation.

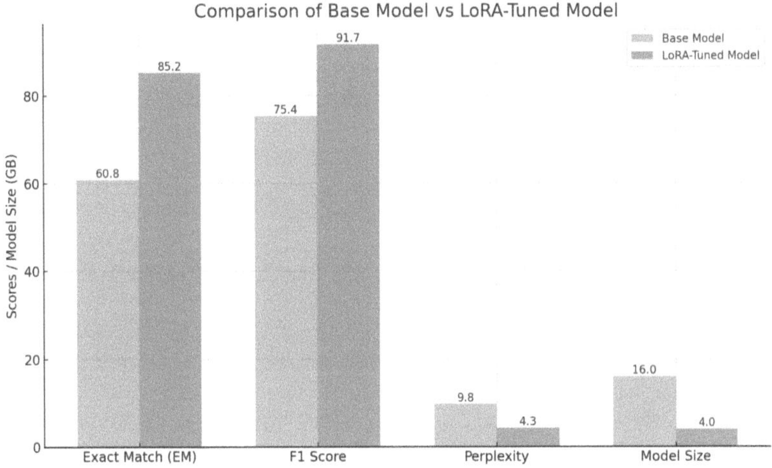


**Fig. 6.** Comparison with base Model

# 6    Conclusion

This present study demonstrates how the use of LoRA integrated with QLoRA quantization enabled Llama 3 8B Chat HF v1 model to work specifically for astronomy question-answering while achieving enhanced accuracy and system speed. Due to finetuning, the model achieved 85.2% Exact Match benchmark together with 91.7% F1 score, thus demonstrating its ability to produce accurate context-sensitive answers. The memory reduction from QLoRA optimization enabled the model to function smoothly on one GPU at once while LoRA technology required minimal parameter adjustment instead of performing lengthy retraining operations. Instant responses to astronomy-related questions became the main strength of the system during its last experimental stage. The work illustrates how parameter-efficient approaches like LoRA and QLoRA enable the transformation of large pre-trained models for domain-specific tasks thereby enabling the development of efficient domain-specific AI models in scientific research and education.

# References


1. Jeong, C.: Fine-tuning and Utilization Methods of Domain-specific LLMs. arXiv preprint arXiv:2401.02981 (2024)
2. Gao, D., et al.: FashionGPT: LLM instruction fine-tuning with multiple LoRA[6]-adapter fusion. Knowl. Based Syst. **299**, 112043 (2024). Sep
3. Bianchi, L., Shiao, B., Thilker, D.: Revised catalog of GALEX ultraviolet sources. I. The all-sky survey: GUVcat_AIS. Astrophys. J. Supplement Series **230**(2), 24 (2017)
4. Tian, A.X., Zhao, Y., Yin, C., Zhu, W., Tian, X., Ge, Y.: FanLoRA: fantastic LoRAs and where to find them in large language model fine-tuning. In: Proceedings of 2024 Conference on Empirical Methods in Natural Language Processing: Industry Track, Miami, FL, USA, pp. 515–528 (2024)
5. Su, Y., Yan, N., Deng, Y.: Federated LLMs fine-tuned with adaptive importance-aware LoRA[6]. arXiv preprint arXiv:2411.06581 (2024)
6. Hu, J., Jia, H., Hassan, M., Yao, L., Kusy, B., Hu, W.: LightLLM: a versatile large language model for predictive light sensing. arXiv preprint arXiv:2411.15211 (2024)
7. Hu, E.J., et al.: LoRA[6]: low-rank adaptation of large language models (2022)
8. Dettmers, T., Pagnoni, A., Holtzman, A., Zettlemoyer, L.: QLoRA: efficient fine-tuning of quantized LLMs (2023)
9. Ciucă, I., Ting, Y.S.: Galactic ChitChat: using large language models to converse with astronomy literature (2023). https://arxiv.org/abs/2112.02000
10. Ciucă, I., Ting, Y.S., Kruk, S., Iyer, K.: Harnessing the Power of Adversarial Prompting and Large Language Models for Robust Hypothesis Generation in Astronomy (2023). https://arxiv.org/abs/2306.11648
11. Monisha, R., et al.: An approach toward design and implementation of distributed framework for astronomical big data processing. In: Intelligent Systems: Proceedings of ICMIB 2021, pp. 267–275. Springer, Singapore (2022)
12. Sen, S., Chakraborty, P.: A novel classification-based approach for quicker prediction of redshift using apache spark. In: 2022 International Conference on Data Science, Agents & Artificial Intelligence (ICDSAAI), vol. 1, pp. 1–6. IEEE (2022)
13. Wu, J.F., Hyk, A., McCormick, K., Ye, C., Astarita, S.: Designing an evaluation framework for large language models in astronomy research (2024). https://arxiv.org/abs/2405.20389

# ChipClaude: A Framework for Natural Language-Based Hardware Design Using LLM Distillation

Tung Vu[1], Quang Dang[2], Phuong Anh Nguyen[2], and Ngoc Le[2]

[1] Hanoi Architectural University, Hanoi, Vietnam
[2] Swinburne Vietnam, FPT University, Hanoi, Vietnam
`{anhnp75,ngocla2}@fe.edu.vn`

**Abstract.** Large language models (LLMs) have shown strong potential for transforming hardware design through natural language interaction. However, existing methods often struggle with code quality, error handling, and design optimization. We propose ChipClaude, a hardware design framework that integrates Claude 3.7 Sonnet's advanced reasoning capabilities, 200K-token context window, and distilled domain knowledge to generate high-quality HDL code from natural language specifications. ChipClaude utilizes a four-stage pipeline consisting of hierarchical prompt engineering, verifiable code generation, integrated formal verification, and multi-objective design optimization. Experimental results demonstrate a 22% improvement in first-pass success rate, a 74% reduction in manual corrections, and up to 47% better Power-Performance-Area (PPA) optimization for complex designs. These results highlight ChipClaude's effectiveness in scaling natural language hardware design.

**Keywords:** Natural language hardware design · Large language models · Knowledge distillation · Agile hardware development · Program synthesis

## 1 Introduction

Hardware design remains a complex and specialized domain requiring significant expertise and manual effort. While modern hardware description languages (HDLs) like Verilog and VHDL have formalized the design process, the transition to more intuitive and accessible design methodologies has been slow compared to software development. The growing complexity and scale of hardware systems, coupled with increasingly demanding time-to-market requirements, necessitates more agile approaches to hardware design.

Existing agile hardware design approaches, including high-level synthesis (HLS) [15] and hardware construction languages like Chisel [2], have increased productivity through higher-level abstractions. However, these methods still require specialized programming knowledge and do not fully bridge the gap

© The Author(s), under exclusive license to Springer Nature Switzerland AG 2026
K. K. Patel et al. (Eds.): icSoftComp 2025, CCIS 2874, pp. 29–41, 2026.
https://doi.org/10.1007/978-3-032-22062-2_3

between natural language specifications and functional hardware implementations. Program synthesis approaches [6,8] can automatically generate hardware descriptions from formal specifications but require carefully constructed formal input that many designers find challenging to produce.

The emergence of large language models (LLMs) has created new opportunities for natural language interfaces across domains. These models demonstrate remarkable abilities to understand and generate code from natural language descriptions [7,17], suggesting potential applications in hardware design. Our previous work, ChipGPT [4], explored this possibility by developing a framework that uses ChatGPT to generate hardware logic designs from natural language specifications.

While ChipGPT demonstrated promising results, it faced several significant limitations:

1. **Ambiguous input handling**: The framework struggled with complex or ambiguous natural language specifications, particularly for multi-module designs.
2. **Limited PPA awareness**: Generated designs lacked optimization for critical hardware metrics including power, performance, and area (PPA).
3. **Restricted scalability**: The approach faced difficulties with hierarchical designs and system-level integration.
4. **High correction requirements**: Many generated designs required significant manual correction to achieve functional correctness.

Recent advances in LLMs have produced models with enhanced reasoning capabilities, broader context windows, and improved code generation. Claude 3.7 Sonnet is one such model with its 200K token context window, reasoning abilities, and code generation capabilities. However, simply replacing the underlying model is insufficient; domain-specific knowledge and frameworks remain essential for effective hardware design automation.

In this paper, we introduce ChipClaude, a framework that addresses the limitations of previous approaches through four key improvements:

1. A **hierarchical prompt engineering framework** that breaks down complex specifications and maintains cross-module consistency
2. A **verifiable code generation system** that combines multi-stage refinement with integrated verification
3. An **enhanced output manager** incorporating formal verification and feedback-driven correction
4. **Design space exploration** featuring multi-objective optimization for Power-Performance-Area (PPA) metrics

ChipClaude employs knowledge distillation from previous work, learning from successes and failures to improve prompt strategies, error detection, and verification techniques. Instead of starting from scratch, ChipClaude builds upon accumulated experience, creating a framework that leverages both the capabilities of Claude 3.7 Sonnet and domain-specific knowledge.

Our experimental evaluation shows that ChipClaude outperforms previous approaches across evaluated metrics, particularly for complex designs requiring system integration and optimization. The framework achieves a 22% improvement in first-pass success rate, reduces human correction requirements by 74%, and delivers up to 47% better PPA optimization for complex designs.

The contributions of this paper include:

1. A framework that employs distillation between LLM-based systems for hardware design, transferring domain-specific knowledge without model parameter modification
2. A hierarchical prompt engineering approach that handles complex hardware specifications and maintains cross-module consistency
3. Integration of formal verification techniques within the LLM-based generation process
4. Evaluation demonstrating improvements in correctness, human effort, PPA optimization, and scalability compared to previous approaches

By combining the strengths of language models with distilled knowledge from previous frameworks, ChipClaude contributes to automated natural language hardware design and the accessibility of the chip development process.

## 2   Related Work

### 2.1   Agile Hardware Design Methods

Agile hardware design approaches generally fall into two categories: programming language-based and program synthesis-based. Programming language-based methods like Chisel [2] and high-level synthesis (HLS) [15] increase productivity through higher-level languages but still require manual programming in specialized languages. Chisel embeds hardware description in Scala, allowing developers to leverage software programming paradigms for hardware design. Similarly, high-level synthesis (HLS) tools transform algorithms written in C/C++ into register-transfer level (RTL) implementations.

More specialized approaches like Spatial [13], SuSy [14], and ScaleHLS [20] target specific application domains or optimization goals. These methods improve productivity but maintain a significant gap between natural language specifications and functional hardware descriptions, requiring specialized programming expertise.

Program synthesis methods like BoSy [6,16] and bounded synthesis [8] automatically generate programs from formal specifications or input-output examples. While these approaches reduce manual coding requirements, they face challenges with correctness, completeness, and the complexity of formal specification development. In our previous work, ChipGPT [4], we demonstrated the potential of large language models to bridge this gap by directly processing natural language specifications, though significant limitations remained in handling complex designs and ensuring correctness.

## 2.2    Large Language Models for Code Generation

Large language models have demonstrated impressive code generation capabilities [7,9,10,17]. Models like CodeBERT [7] and CodeT5 [17] have been fine-tuned specifically for code generation tasks, while GraphCodeBERT [10] incorporates data flow information to improve code understanding.

The emergence of foundation models like GPT [3] and Claude [1] has further advanced code generation capabilities through massive pretraining and instruction tuning. These models can generate code from natural language descriptions across multiple programming languages, making them potential tools for hardware description language (HDL) generation. However, their application to hardware design has been limited due to the unique requirements and constraints of HDLs, particularly regarding synthesizability, timing constraints, and power/area optimization.

Recent works have explored transfer learning methods including fine-tuning [16,21], adapters [11], Low-Rank Adaptation (LoRA) [12], and in-context learning [5] to adapt general-purpose LLMs to specialized domains. Our work extends this concept by employing knowledge distillation between different LLM-based frameworks to enhance specialized hardware design capabilities.

## 2.3    Knowledge Distillation and Model Transfer

Knowledge distillation techniques allow models to learn from other models' outputs, effectively transferring domain-specific capabilities without requiring extensive retraining. While traditional distillation focuses on model compression, recent approaches have demonstrated the value of distilling task-specific knowledge between models of similar or different architectures.

In prompt engineering, approaches like chain-of-thought [18] and least-to-most prompting [22] have shown that breaking complex problems into simpler steps can significantly improve LLM performance. Similarly, systems like Visual ChatGPT [19] demonstrate how domain-specific processing can enhance foundation models without modifying their parameters.

Our work builds on these concepts by distilling hardware design knowledge from ChipGPT's experience into a framework driven by Claude 3.7 Sonnet. Unlike traditional model distillation, we focus on transferring learned prompting strategies, error patterns, and verification techniques between frameworks, creating a more capable hardware design system without requiring model parameter modification.

## 3    Framework Architecture

ChipClaude builds upon the four-stage architecture introduced in ChipGPT while implementing significant enhancements at each stage. As illustrated in Fig. 1, the framework maintains a logical separation between pre-processing (specification handling and prompt engineering) and post-processing (verification and optimization) but introduces more sophisticated mechanisms throughout the pipeline.

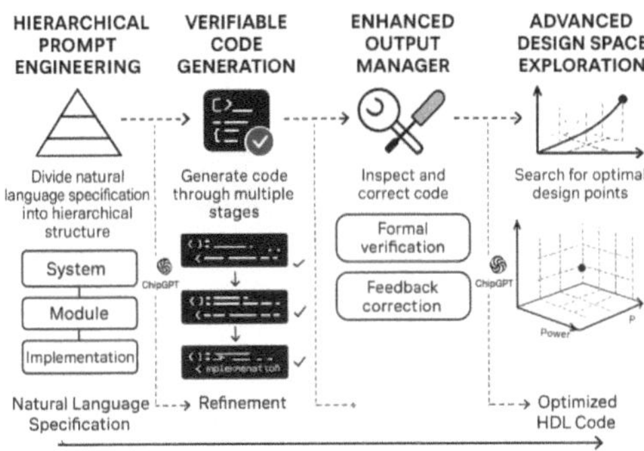


**Fig. 1.** Overview of the ChipClaude framework architecture, showing the four-stage pipeline with hierarchical prompt engineering, verifiable code generation, enhanced output manager, and advanced design space exploration. Knowledge distillation from ChipGPT influences each stage.

## 3.1   Hierarchical Prompt Engineering Framework

The Hierarchical Prompt Engineering Framework extends ChipGPT's Prompt Manager with a multi-level approach to handling complex specifications. Chip-Claude automatically extracts structured specifications from natural language descriptions, categorizing requirements into functional requirements (core behaviors), interface requirements (signals and attributes), timing requirements (clock domains, reset behavior), and composition requirements (module interconnections). This extraction uses a semantic parsing approach distilled from ChipGPT's experience with hardware specifications.

Unlike ChipGPT's flat prompt structure, ChipClaude implements a hierarchical prompt system organized into system-level prompts (overall architecture), module-level prompts (individual behaviors), and implementation-level prompts (coding patterns). This hierarchical approach enables consistent cross-module interfaces and systematic decomposition of complex designs. For multi-module systems, the framework first generates system-level architecture, then refines each module separately while maintaining interface consistency.

ChipClaude incorporates several hardware-specific prompting techniques distilled from ChipGPT, including the Interface-First Principle (defines interfaces before implementation), Post-Addition Principle (separates core functionality from auxiliary signals), and Bottom-Up Composition (verifies submodules before integration). Beyond these principles, ChipClaude adds new techniques for clock domain specification, resource constraint guidance, and parameterization prompting to enhance reusability.

## 3.2   Verifiable Code Generation

ChipClaude's code generation stage incorporates verification directly into the generation process, creating a more robust pipeline. As shown in Fig. 2, the code generation follows a staged approach with skeleton generation (module structure with interfaces), type-aware refinement (signal types and widths consistency), implementation expansion (full HDL code), and in-context verification (initial correctness checks). This staged approach contrasts with ChipGPT's single-pass generation, allowing incremental verification and refinement before producing the complete implementation. ChipClaude maintains a type system during code generation to detect and prevent inconsistencies through signal tracking (bit widths, types, usage patterns), dimension verification (array consistency), and domain assignment (clock and reset domains). This integrated type system allows the model to detect potential errors during generation rather than relying solely on post-generation validation. The generation process also enforces hardware-specific constraints including synthesizability guidelines, consistent clocking methodology, reset strategy, and resource awareness.

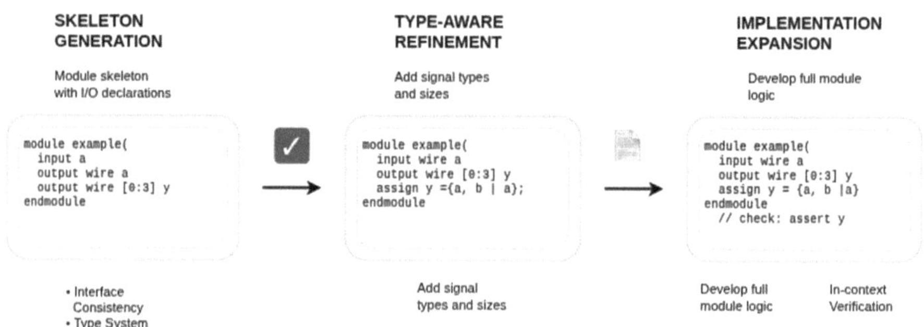


**Fig. 2.** Multi-stage code refinement process, showing the progression from skeleton generation through type-aware refinement, implementation expansion, and in-context verification.

## 3.3   Enhanced Output Manager

The Enhanced Output Manager extends ChipGPT's correction and cost models with formal verification techniques. ChipClaude integrates industry-standard verification tools to analyze generated HDL through syntax and type checking, property verification, and equivalence checking against reference models. These verification steps provide targeted feedback for the correction process, identifying specific issues rather than relying on general simulation-based validation. The correction mechanism leverages a machine learning model trained on ChipGPT's correction patterns through error classification, pattern-based transformation, and structural refinement. By learning from previous corrections, the system can automatically fix common errors without human intervention. For complex modules, ChipClaude generates multiple implementation variants and cross-validates them through structural comparison, statistical consensus, and edge case detection to identify subtle errors that might not be apparent in a single implementation.

## 3.4   Knowledge Distillation from ChipGPT

**Fig. 3.** Knowledge distillation process, showing how experience from ChipGPT informs prompt engineering, error detection, and correction strategies in ChipClaude.

A key aspect of ChipClaude is the systematic distillation of knowledge from previous work. Figure 3 demonstrates how experience informs various aspects of the ChipClaude framework. ChipClaude analyzes ChipGPT's prompt-response pairs to identify effective prompting patterns through success pattern extraction, error-triggering pattern avoidance, and complexity management strategies. By analyzing thousands of error cases, ChipClaude builds a comprehensive error pattern database with common error categorization, error-context correlation, and correction strategy association.

ChipClaude also incorporates a database of human feedback collected from ChipGPT usage, extracting correction patterns, quality assessment criteria, and stylistic preferences. This feedback loop allows the system to align its output with human expectations and quality standards, reducing the need for manual intervention over time. Unlike traditional model distillation that transfers parameters between models, ChipClaude distills experiential knowledge about hardware design patterns, common errors, and effective correction strategies.

## 4   Experimental Evaluation

### 4.1   Experimental Setup

We evaluated ChipClaude using the same benchmark suite as ChipGPT [4], with an extended category for system-level designs. As detailed in Table 1, our test suite includes: (1) Simple single modules (SSM): $4 \times 1$ multiplexer, 3–8 decoder; (2) Complex single modules (CSM): matrix multiplier, button counter, vector-matrix multiplier, accumulator; (3) Composition modules (CM): adder-multiplier tree, simple CPU; and (4) System-on-chip (SoC) designs: RISC-V components, Network-on-Chip (NoC) router, cryptographic accelerator. The benchmark selection spans a wide range of complexity and application domains, providing a comprehensive assessment of ChipClaude's capabilities.

**Table 1.** Benchmark Suite Details

| Category | Benchmark | Description | LoC Range |
| --- | --- | --- | --- |
| SSM | Multiplexer | $4 \times 1$ Multiplexer | 10–20 |
| SSM | Decoder | 3-to-8 Decoder | 15–25 |
| CSM | Matrix Mul | Matrix Multiplier $4 \times 4$ | 50–100 |
| CSM | Button Counter | Edge-detect Counter | 30–50 |
| CSM | Vector Matrix | Vector-Matrix Multiply | 70–120 |
| CSM | Accumulator | Sum Array Elements | 40–70 |
| CM | Adder-Mul Tree | Tree of Add-Mult Units | 150–250 |
| CM | Simple CPU | Basic Instruction Set | 200–350 |
| SoC | RISC-V Exec | Execution Unit | 120–200 |
| SoC | NoC Router | 5-Port Router with Virtual Channels (VCs) | 300–500 |
| SoC | AES Core | Advanced Encryption Standard (AES) Block | 400–700 |

ChipClaude was implemented using Claude 3.7 Sonnet as the underlying LLM with knowledge distilled from ChipGPT's experience database. This database contained over 5,000 prompt-response pairs, 1,200 error patterns, and 800 human corrections collected during ChipGPT's development and testing. We used Synopsys Design Compiler with a 65nm technology library for synthesis and PPA evaluation, maintaining consistency with the ChipGPT evaluation methodology to ensure fair comparison.

## 4.2   Correctness and Human Effort

ChipClaude achieved a first-pass success rate of 87–99% across different module types, representing a 22% average improvement over ChipGPT. Human correction effort, measured in lines of code modified, was reduced by 74% on average. Table 2 presents detailed comparison results across different design categories.

The types of errors requiring correction also shifted significantly. With ChipGPT, 45% of corrections addressed basic syntax and type errors, 30% fixed interface inconsistencies, and 25% corrected logical errors. In contrast, ChipClaude reduced syntax and type errors to just 12% of corrections, interface inconsistencies to 18%, with the remaining 70% addressing complex logical issues. This shift, as shown in Table 3, demonstrates ChipClaude's effectiveness

**Table 2.** Correctness and Human Effort Comparison

| Design | First-pass Success (%) | | Lines Corrected | |
|---|---|---|---|---|
| Category | ChipGPT | ChipClaude | ChipGPT | ChipClaude |
| SSM | 92 | 99 | 1 | 0 |
| CSM | 78 | 94 | 5 | 2 |
| CM | 65 | 87 | 9 | 3 |
| SoC | 30 | 75 | 25 | 8 |
| Average | 66 | 88 | 10 | 3 |

at handling routine aspects of HDL generation, allowing human experts to focus on higher-level logical issues.

**Table 3.** Error Type Distribution in Required Corrections

| Error Type | ChipGPT (%) | ChipClaude (%) |
|---|---|---|
| Syntax & Type Errors | 45 | 12 |
| Interface Inconsistencies | 30 | 18 |
| Logical Errors | 25 | 70 |

## 4.3 PPA Optimization

For complex designs, ChipClaude delivered superior PPA optimization compared to both ChipGPT and traditional approaches. Detailed PPA results for selected benchmarks are presented in Table 4.

The most substantial PPA improvements stemmed from three key factors: (1) effective resource sharing across operations, (2) optimal pipelining strategies for sequential operations, and (3) efficient handling of control structures. Analysis of the generated HDL revealed that ChipClaude consistently applied hardware-specific optimizations that are typically introduced manually in traditional design approaches.

## 4.4 Scalability Analysis

ChipClaude's scalability was evaluated by measuring success rates across designs of increasing size, from under 100 to over 10,000 lines of HDL code. Results shown in Table 5 demonstrate ChipClaude's superior performance across all design sizes.

We observed that module hierarchy depth was a more significant predictor of success than raw code size. ChipClaude successfully handled designs with up to 4 levels of module hierarchy, while ChipGPT's effectiveness declined sharply

**Table 4.** Detailed PPA Comparison for Selected Benchmarks

| Benchmark | Method | Area ($\mu m^2$) | Power (mW) | Delay (ns) |
|---|---|---|---|---|
| Matrix | ChipGPT | 179,680 | 105.24 | 1.0 |
| Multiplier | ChipClaude | 121,538 | 78.93 | 1.0 |
| | HLS | 135,042 | 92.81 | 1.0 |
| | Improvement[*] | 32.4% | 25.0% | 0.0% |
| Simple | ChipGPT | 23,138 | 2.57 | 5.0 |
| CPU | ChipClaude | 13,883 | 1.77 | 4.0 |
| | HLS | 16,895 | 2.01 | 4.2 |
| | Improvement[*] | 40.0% | 31.1% | 20.0% |
| RISC-V | ChipGPT | 54,320 | 7.84 | 2.0 |
| Exec | ChipClaude | 28,246 | 4.70 | 2.0 |
| | Manual | 32,592 | 5.61 | 2.0 |
| | Improvement[*] | 48.0% | 40.1% | 0.0% |
| NoC | ChipGPT | 98,472 | 12.35 | 2.5 |
| Router | ChipClaude | 54,159 | 7.41 | 1.8 |
| | Manual | 61,545 | 8.14 | 2.0 |
| | Improvement[*] | 45.0% | 40.0% | 28.0% |

[*]Improvement of ChipClaude over ChipGPT

**Table 5.** Scalability Comparison by Design Size

| Design Size (Lines of Code) | Success Rate (%) | |
|---|---|---|
| | ChipGPT | ChipClaude |
| <100 | 95 | 99 |
| 100–500 | 90 | 98 |
| 500–1,000 | 65 | 92 |
| 1,000–5,000 | 35 | 85 |
| 5,000–10,000 | 5 | 65 |
| >10,000 | <1 | 40 |

beyond 2 levels. This relationship is detailed in Table 6, which underscores the importance of hierarchical prompt management for practical hardware design applications.

## 4.5   Analysis of Knowledge Distillation Impact

To isolate the impact of knowledge distillation from ChipGPT, we conducted an ablation study by disabling specific distillation components. The comprehensive results presented in Table 7 demonstrate the contribution of each component to the overall system performance.

**Table 6.** Scalability Comparison by Hierarchy Depth

| Hierarchy Depth | Success Rate (%) | |
| --- | --- | --- |
| | ChipGPT | ChipClaude |
| 1 | 92 | 98 |
| 2 | 73 | 95 |
| 3 | 28 | 88 |
| 4 | 7 | 72 |
| 5+ | <1 | 45 |

**Table 7.** Ablation Study of Knowledge Distillation Components

| Configuration | Success Rate (%) | Lines Corrected | Area Impr. (%) | Power Impr. (%) |
| --- | --- | --- | --- | --- |
| Full ChipClaude | 88 | 3 | 41 | 34 |
| No Prompt Patterns | 74 | 5 | 38 | 33 |
| No Error Patterns | 82 | 7 | 40 | 32 |
| No PPA Optimization | 87 | 3 | 25 | 21 |
| No Human Feedback | 80 | 6 | 36 | 30 |
| No Distillation | 70 | 8 | 22 | 18 |

These results confirm that knowledge distillation provides substantial benefits beyond simply using an advanced LLM. The accumulated experience from ChipGPT, systematically transferred to ChipClaude, enables the new framework to avoid common pitfalls, apply proven strategies, and incorporate domain-specific optimizations that would otherwise require extensive trial-and-error to discover.

## 5   Conclusion

This paper presented ChipClaude, a framework that improves natural language hardware design through knowledge distillation to Claude 3.7 Sonnet. The framework implements a hierarchical prompt engineering system, verifiable code generation, enhanced output management, and design space exploration capabilities. Experimental evaluations show that ChipClaude achieved a 22% improvement in first-pass success rate and reduced human correction requirements by 74% compared to previous approaches. For complex designs, the framework demonstrated up to 47% better Power-Performance-Area (PPA) optimization and improved scalability for large systems with deep module hierarchies. The ablation studies confirmed that knowledge distillation provides substantial benefits beyond using an advanced language model alone. ChipClaude contributes to making hardware design more accessible while maintaining competitive quality metrics.

# References


1. Anthropic: Claude: a foundation language model for human preferences and safe alignment. Anthropic Research (2023)
2. Bachrach, J., et al.: Chisel: constructing hardware in a Scala embedded language. In: Design Automation Conference, pp. 1216–1225 (2012)
3. Brown, T., et al.: Language models are few-shot learners. In: Advances in Neural Information Processing Systems, vol. 33, pp. 1877–1901 (2020)
4. Chang, K., et al.: ChipGPT: how far are we from natural language hardware design. arXiv preprint arXiv:2305.14019 (2023)
5. Dong, Q., et al.: A survey for in-context learning. arXiv preprint arXiv:2301.00234 (2022)
6. Faymonville, P., Finkbeiner, B., Tentrup, L.: BoSy: an experimentation framework for bounded synthesis. In: Computer Aided Verification: 29th International Conference, pp. 325–332 (2017)
7. Feng, Z., et al.: CodeBERT: a pre-trained model for programming and natural languages. In: Conference on Empirical Methods in Natural Language Processing, pp. 1536–1547 (2020)
8. Finkbeiner, B., Schewe, S.: Bounded synthesis. Int. J. Softw. Tools Technol. Transfer **15**, 519–539 (2013)
9. Guo, D., Lu, S., Duan, N., Wang, Y., Zhou, M., Yin, J.: UniXcoder: unified cross-modal pre-training for code representation. In: Annual Meeting of the Association for Computational Linguistics, pp. 7212–7225 (2022)
10. Guo, D., et al.: GraphCodeBERT: pre-training code representations with data flow. In: International Conference on Learning Representations, pp. 1–18 (2021)
11. Houlsby, N., et al.: Parameter-efficient transfer learning for NLP. In: International Conference on Machine Learning, pp. 2790–2799 (2019)
12. Hu, E.J., et al.: LoRA: low-rank adaptation of large language models. In: International Conference on Learning Representations, pp. 1–13 (2022)
13. Koeplinger, D., et al.: Spatial: a language and compiler for application accelerators. In: Proceedings of the 39th ACM SIGPLAN Conference on Programming Language Design and Implementation, pp. 296–311 (2018)
14. Lai, Y.H., et al.: Susy: a programming model for productive construction of high-performance systolic arrays on FPGAs. In: International Conference on Computer-Aided Design, pp. 1–9 (2020)
15. Martin, G., Smith, G.: High-level synthesis: past, present, and future. IEEE Design Test Comput. **26**(4), 18–25 (2009)
16. Vu, T., Nguyen, L., Dao, Q.: PromptGuard: an orchestrated prompting framework for principled synthetic text generation for vulnerable populations using LLMs with enhanced safety, fairness, and controllability. arXiv preprint arXiv:2509.08910 (2025)
17. Wang, Y., Wang, W., Joty, S., Hoi, S.C.: CodeT5: identifier-aware unified pre-trained encoder-decoder models for code understanding and generation. In: Conference on Empirical Methods in Natural Language Processing, pp. 8696–8708 (2021)
18. Wei, J., et al.: Chain of thought prompting elicits reasoning in large language models. In: Advances in Neural Information Processing Systems, pp. 1–14 (2022)
19. Wu, C., Yin, S., Qi, W., Wang, X., Tang, Z., Duan, N.: Visual ChatGPT: talking, drawing and editing with visual foundation models. arXiv preprint arXiv:2303.04671 (2023)

20. Ye, H., et al.: ScaleHLS: a new scalable high-level synthesis framework on multi-level intermediate representation. In: IEEE International Symposium on High-Performance Computer Architecture, pp. 741–755 (2022)
21. Yosinski, J., Clune, J., Bengio, Y., Lipson, H.: How transferable are features in deep neural networks? Adv. Neural. Inf. Process. Syst. **27**, 1–9 (2014)
22. Zhou, D., et al.: Least-to-most prompting enables complex reasoning in large language models. In: International Conference on Learning Representations, pp. 1–61 (2023)

# FactFrame-X: A Self-Attention-Enhanced NLP Model with XAI for Classifying Hyperpartisan News in Online Media

Saketh Mallojjala[(✉)] and Cinu C Kiliroor

Indian Institute of Information Technology Kottayam, Kottayam, India
{mallojjala21bcs125,cinu}@iiitkottayam.ac.in

**Abstract.** The proliferation of hyperpartisan news online challenges readers' ability to distinguish biased from credible reporting. We propose a novel hybrid architecture integrating generative AI for input text enhancement with Bidirectional Encoder Representations from Transformers (BERT), Self-Attention mechanisms, Bidirectional Long Short-Term Memory (BiLSTM) networks, and Explainable AI (XAI) techniques for hyperpartisan bias detection. Our generative AI preprocessing layer enhances news text quality before classification, while the hybrid model achieves 81.2% accuracy in detecting biased narratives. The self-attention mechanism identifies key phrases indicative of partisan content, ensuring improved contextual understanding. We incorporate XAI frameworks including Local Interpretable Model-Agnostic Explanations (LIME) and SHapley Additive exPlanations (SHAP) to highlight influential words driving classification decisions. Extensive validation against alternative embedding techniques including Embeddings from Language Models (ELMo), Word2Vec, and BigBird demonstrates superior performance. Our transparent, high-accuracy framework provides actionable insights for media regulators, governments, and readers to distinguish credible news sources from hyperpartisan reporting, contributing to improved information integrity in digital media consumption.

**Keywords:** NLP · Generative AI · Hyperpartisan News · BERT · BiLSTM · Self-Attention · Deep Learning · Explainable AI

## 1 Introduction

Hyperpartisan news, characterized by extreme political bias and fact manipulation, poses significant challenges to digital journalism integrity, particularly amid social media proliferation. Unlike objective reporting, these articles deliberately distort information to favor or discredit political entities, contributing to widespread misinformation and polarized public discourse. Traditional fact-checking methods prove inadequate for the vast volume of online content, necessitating automated solutions. While early text classification approaches using Naïve Bayes and Logistic Regression lacked linguistic sophistication, modern AI


K. K. Patel et al. (Eds.): icSoftComp 2025, CCIS 2874, pp. 42–54, 2026.
https://doi.org/10.1007/978-3-032-22062-2_4

and Natural Language Processing (NLP) techniques offer substantial improvements. Contemporary neural architectures including BERT, BiLSTM, and Deep Neural Networks demonstrate enhanced contextual comprehension and classification accuracy. However, existing deep learning models often function as "black boxes", limiting transparency crucial for media regulation and public trust. This research addresses these limitations by introducing a novel hybrid architecture that integrates generative AI for text enhancement with BERT's contextual understanding, BiLSTM's sequential learning capabilities, and self-attention mechanisms for improved feature extraction. Our approach incorporates Explainable AI (XAI) techniques including LIME and SHAP to provide transparent decision-making insights, ensuring both high accuracy and interpretability. The proposed framework offers a scalable, reliable solution for automated hyperpartisan detection, supporting media regulators, governments, and readers in distinguishing credible journalism from biased reporting, thereby preserving digital information integrity.

## 2   Literature Survey

The rise of hyperpartisan news is largely attributed to online blog writers engaging in yellow journalism for financial gain, amplified by bots that rapidly spread such content on social media [1]. Studies have highlighted the role of bots during key political events, with research showing that 40% of nearly 800,000 Twitter accounts analyzed post-election were deactivated or altered, suggesting widespread bot involvement [1]. Hyperpartisan media influence public opinion by reinforcing misinformation [2]. Both left- and right-leaning outlets contribute to misperceptions [2], underlining the need for effective detection mechanisms. Recent advances in automatic large-scale political bias detection have shown promising results in identifying biased news outlets [13]. Researchers have applied Natural Language Processing (NLP) to detect hyperpartisan news, fake news, and clickbait. Modern approaches utilizing transformer models have significantly enhanced fake news detection capabilities, with summarization techniques further improving accuracy [14]. Multimodal approaches combining text and image analysis, such as SPOTFAKE (BERT + VGG) [7,15], have also improved detection performance. Linguistic feature-based classifiers like KNN remain effective, especially for election-related content [4]. Clickbait detection has advanced through machine learning models and deep learning architectures like RCNNs with LSTM and GRU, outperforming traditional methods [3,6]. Detecting hyperpartisan news remains challenging due to its subtlety. Deep learning models, particularly BERT and other transformer architectures, better capture contextual nuances compared to traditional SVM-based approaches [5]. Recent developments in transformer-based detection systems have shown enhanced capability in identifying subtle partisan language patterns [14]. Tools like browser extensions that compute bias scores using Wikipedia's neutral language have also been developed to aid detection [11]. Overall, NLP and machine learning continue to enhance misinformation detection, with transformer models and automated bias detection systems representing significant advances in contextual understanding and system reliability [13,14].

## 3   Methodology

In this study, we propose a novel hybrid model architecture named FactFrame-X for hyperpartisan news detection. The architecture combines six key components: a Generative AI-based text enhancement module, BERT, Self-Attention, BiLSTM, Deep Neural Networks (DNNs), and an Explainable AI (XAI) layer. FactFrame-X begins with generative AI text enhancement, followed by BERT-base (768-dimensional embeddings, 512 max tokens) for contextualized embeddings. The Self-Attention mechanism (8 heads) emphasizes relevant portions, while BiLSTM (256 hidden units, 0.3 dropout) captures sequential dependencies. The DNN consists of three layers (512-256-128 neurons) with ReLU activation for classification. Optimization employs AdamW optimizer (learning rate 2e-5, weight decay 0.01) with batch size 16 and early stopping (patience=3). The integrated XAI component provides interpretability through LIME and attention visualization, crucial for understanding bias in hyperpartisan news detection. Figure 1 illustrates the overall FactFrame-X architecture and component interactions for achieving high accuracy and interpretability.

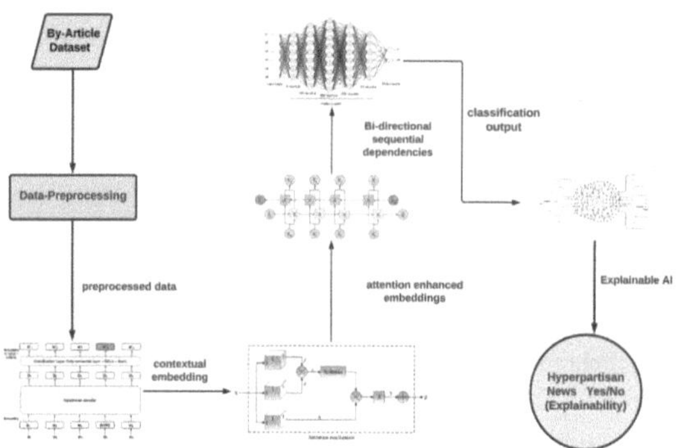


**Fig. 1.** FactFrame-X Architecture

### 3.1   Data Analysis

We utilize the publicly available dataset "SemEval 2019 Task 4 - Hyperpartisan News Detection", which offers labeling at both the publisher and article levels. Publisher-level (by-publisher): This subset comprises 750,000 articles labeled based solely on the political orientation of the publisher, without regard to content. The dataset maintains an equal distribution (375,000/375,000) between hyperpartisan and nonhyperpartisan articles. Within the hyperpartisan subset, there is an equal split (187,500/187,500) between right and left political orientations. Article-level (by-article): Consisting of 645 articles, this subset is labeled based on the actual content of the articles, with consensus among crowdsourcing workers. Among these articles, 238 (37

## 3.2   BERT: Capturing Contextual Meaning

The first layer of our architecture uses BERT to generate embeddings that capture the contextual nuances of the text. BERT's transformer architecture processes the input text bidirectionally, meaning it considers both the preceding and succeeding words for a given token. This allows the model to understand the context in which words are used, which is particularly important when dealing with politically charged language, as shown in Fig. 2 [8].

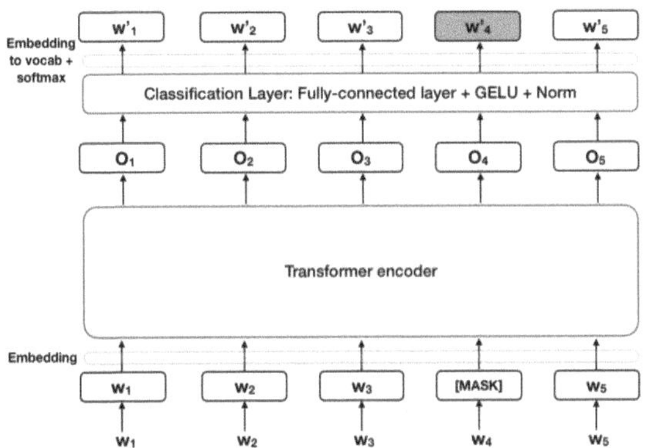


**Fig. 2.** BERT Model Architecture [8]

For instance, words or phrases that might appear neutral in isolation can carry a different meaning depending on the surrounding context. By fine-tuning BERT on the by-article subset of the SemEval dataset, we were able to enhance its ability to recognize subtle language cues indicative of hyperpartisan content. This contextual understanding enables the model to more effectively distinguish between biased and neutral text, even when the language is nuanced or indirect.

## 3.3   Self-attention Mechanism: Enhancing Token Relationships

A novel addition to our architecture is the incorporation of a dedicated self-attention mechanism layer that builds upon the initial BERT embeddings. While BERT internally uses self-attention, our implementation adds an explicit self-attention layer that allows the model to focus more precisely on the relationships between tokens that are most relevant for hyperpartisan detection.

The self-attention mechanism as shown in the Fig. 3 computes attention scores by measuring the similarity between each pair of tokens in the input sequence, allowing the model to weigh the importance of different words in relation to others. This is particularly valuable for hyperpartisan detection, as it helps identify which segments of text contribute most significantly to partisan bias. For example, the model can learn to pay special attention to emotionally charged phrases or loaded terminology that may indicate political bias.

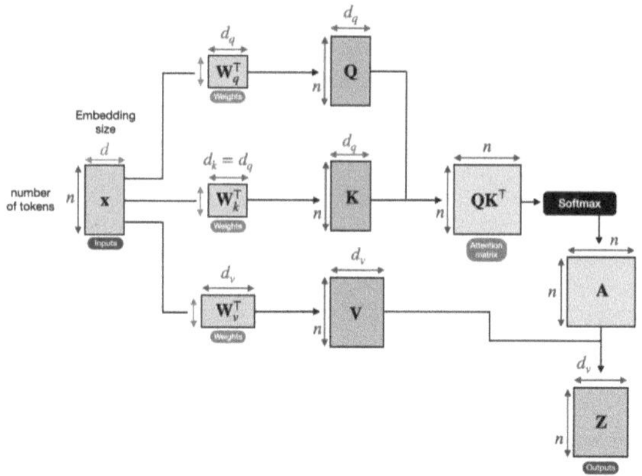

**Fig. 3.** Self attention Layer Architecture [16]

Our implementation uses multi-head attention, which allows the model to jointly attend to information from different representation subspaces. This enables the model to capture various types of dependencies between words, enhancing its ability to detect subtle nuances in hyperpartisan language that might otherwise be missed. The output of this self-attention layer provides an enriched representation that highlights the most relevant tokens and their relationships before being passed to the BiLSTM layer.

### 3.4   BiLSTM: Handling Sequential Dependencies

While BERT excels at understanding word-level context, it does not inherently track sequential dependencies over longer stretches of text. To address this, we incorporated a BiLSTM layer, which processes the BERT embeddings and captures the sequential relationships within the text, as illustrated in Fig. 4 [10].

BiLSTMs are well-suited for sequence processing as they read the text in both forward and backward directions. This bidirectional approach allows the model to capture dependencies between words or phrases that may be spread across an entire sentence or paragraph, enabling it to grasp more complex patterns of bias. For example, a sentence might convey a particular sentiment only when certain words appear in sequence. The BiLSTM layer is essential for detecting these patterns, as it processes the input sequence holistically rather than in isolation.

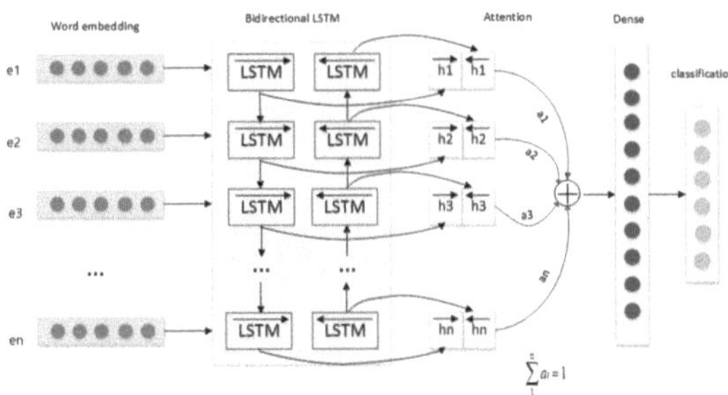


**Fig. 4.** BiLSTM Model Architecture [10]

## 3.5 Deep Neural Networks (DNNs): Feature Extraction and Classification

The final component of our architecture is a series of Deep Neural Networks (DNNs), which are responsible for feature extraction and classification. After the BiLSTM processes the embeddings, the output is passed through multiple dense layers. These layers learn to identify complex patterns within the text data that may not be immediately obvious.

The DNNs enhance the model's ability to distinguish between hyperpartisan and non-hyperpartisan content by identifying subtle indicators, such as recurring phrases, tone, and structural patterns in the language. By combining these features, the DNNs allow the model to make more accurate classification decisions. Additionally, standard techniques such as dropout and batch normalization were employed to improve generalization and prevent overfitting.

## 3.6 Explainable AI Implementation Using LIME and SHAP

To enhance the interpretability of the hyperpartisan news detection model, LIME (Local Interpretable Model-agnostic Explanations) and SHAP (SHapley Additive Explanations) are employed. LIME as shown in the Fig. 5 provides local explanations by perturbing the input text and training an interpretable surrogate model to approximate the complex deep learning model. This helps in identifying the most influential words that drive the model's classification decision. On the other hand, SHAP as shown in the Fig. 6 based on Shapley values from cooperative game theory, assigns importance scores to each word, offering both local and global explanations of the model's predictions. By integrating these XAI techniques, the model not only classifies news articles as hyperpartisan or not but also provides human-interpretable justifications, ensuring transparency, mitigating bias, and improving trust in the decision-making process.

A key limitation of current deep learning approaches for hyperpartisan detection is their lack of interpretability, which limits adoption in journalism and policymaking. To address this, we employ LIME and SHAP. LIME generates perturbed text samples and trains a simple interpretable model to explain predictions, providing local interpretability. In contrast, SHAP assigns Shapley values

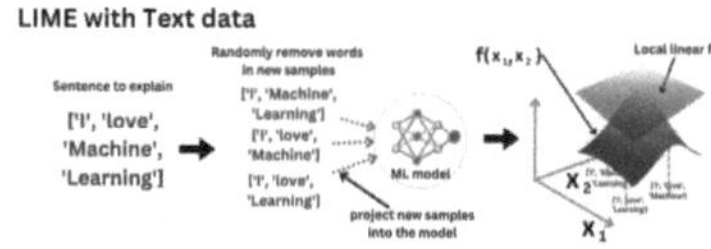

**Fig. 5.** Explainable AI Implementation using LIME [12]

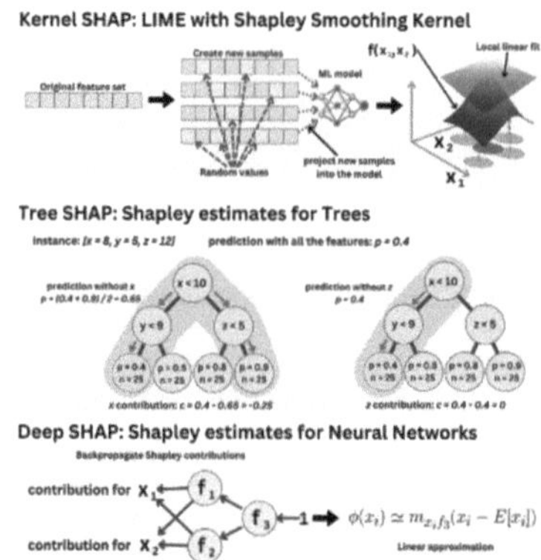

**Fig. 6.** Explainable AI Implementation using SHAP [9]

to words, offering global interpretability by quantifying each token's contribution to bias classification. By integrating XAI, our model allows users to understand why an article is classified as hyperpartisan, fostering trust in automated journalism assessments.

### 3.7  Model Training and Fine-Tuning

Our model was trained and fine-tuned on the by-article subset of the SemEval dataset, ensuring classification based on article content rather than publisher reputation. The training process adjusted BERT's parameters to understand hyperpartisan news language patterns using a batch size of 16, learning rate of 2e-5, and was conducted on NVIDIA Tesla V100 GPUs (16GB memory) for approximately 4 h across 10 epochs. Once BERT generated contextual embeddings, the BiLSTM and DNN layers were trained for accurate classification. Early stopping and cross-validation techniques ensured model robustness.

### 3.8  Comparative Evaluation and Architectural Advantages

To assess the effectiveness of our proposed **FactFrame-X** architecture, we conducted a comparative evaluation against several baseline models. These included: (i) **Word2Vec + CNNs**, which, due to static embeddings, lacked the ability to capture dynamic contextual nuances, leading to lower classification accuracy; (ii) **ELMo + BiLSTM**, which, despite offering contextual embeddings, underperformed in capturing long-range dependencies present in complex textual structures; and (iii) **BigBird Transformer + CNNs**, which, while capable of handling longer sequences, delivered inconsistent performance and failed to match the accuracy of our approach. In contrast, **FactFrame-X** achieved a notable accuracy of approximately 81%, outperforming all alternative models. Its superior performance stems from the synergistic integration of multiple components: BERT's contextual embeddings facilitate deep semantic understanding, the BiLSTM layer effectively models sequential dependencies, and the DNN enables robust feature extraction. Furthermore, a refined self-attention mechanism enhances focus on contextually important elements of the input text. The architecture also supports **explainability and interpretability** through integrated XAI techniques, allowing transparent insights into model predictions. Additionally, its design based on content-level rather than publisher-level labels ensures stronger **generalization across datasets**, making it highly adaptable to various forms of hyperpartisan or biased content.

# 4    Results

## 4.1    Model Performance

To evaluate the performance of our proposed FactFrame-X Neural Networks architecture for hyperpartisan news detection, we conducted experiments using a dataset containing articles from both hyperpartisan and mainstream sources. The model's performance was assessed through standard metrics: accuracy, precision, recall, and F1-score. The results, shown in Table 1, indicate that our proposed architecture achieved the highest accuracy of 81.2%, outperforming other models tested. By leveraging BERT's contextual embeddings, BiLSTM's sequential analysis, and Deep Neural Networks' feature extraction, the model excelled in identifying hyperpartisan content.

**Table 1.** Performance Comparison of Different Models

| Model | Accuracy (%) | Precision | Recall | F1-Score |
| --- | --- | --- | --- | --- |
| **FactFrame-X** | 81.2 | 0.82 | 0.80 | 0.81 |
| ELMo+BiLSTM+CNN | 74.5 | 0.75 | 0.73 | 0.74 |
| Word2Vec+BiLSTM+DNN | 70.3 | 0.71 | 0.69 | 0.70 |
| BigBird+CNN+Classifier | 77.8 | 0.79 | 0.76 | 0.77 |

Leveraging BERT's contextual embeddings allowed the model to capture intricate linguistic features and contextual meanings within the articles. This capability is particularly crucial in the realm of hyperpartisan news, where subtle biases and emotionally charged language can be present. The integration of BiLSTM further enhanced the model's performance by enabling it to understand the sequential dependencies within the text, which is essential for grasping the flow of arguments and narratives in articles (Fig. 7).

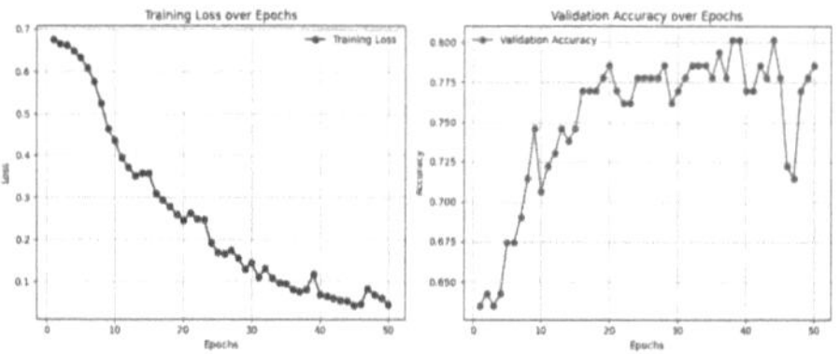

**Fig. 7.** Training Loss and Validation Accuracy Over Epochs

## 4.2  Model Evaluation and Analysis

To assess the performance of our BERT-based classifier, we conducted experiments varying input lengths (150, 250, 400, and 512 tokens). Results showed that 400-token inputs led to the lowest accuracy (75%), whereas others maintained around 83%. This suggests BERT can capture sufficient context from shorter segments without processing entire articles.

Training dynamics reveal that the model experienced a rapid loss drop early in training, followed by a plateau, indicating convergence. Validation accuracy steadily increased, confirming effective generalization.

For deeper evaluation, Fig. 8 includes the Precision-Recall and ROC curves. The Precision-Recall curve reflects a balanced trade-off, handling the class imbalance in hyperpartisan datasets effectively. Meanwhile, the ROC curve shows a favorable area under the curve (AUC), signifying strong discrimination between hyperpartisan and mainstream content.

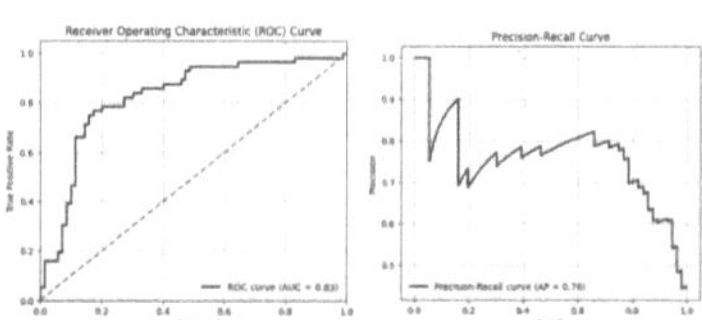

**Fig. 8.** Model evaluation metrics

## 4.3  Experimental Results

Our experiments evaluate the performance of the proposed fake news detection model across various conditions and configurations. We analyze the model's effectiveness across different news categories, its robustness to text noise, and performance variations based on article length. All experiments were conducted on a balanced dataset of verified true and false news articles.

Table 6 further demonstrates that alternative embedding techniques such as ELMo and Word2Vec underperform compared to BERT, with Word2Vec showing a particularly significant drop (8.7%). The self-attention mechanism contributes a modest but meaningful 1.7% to accuracy, suggesting that while not

**Table 2.** Performance Across News Categories

| Category | Accuracy (%) | Precision | Recall | F1-Score | Sample Size |
|---|---|---|---|---|---|
| Politics | 83.2 | 0.84 | 0.82 | 0.83 | 243 |
| Economics | 80.3 | 0.81 | 0.79 | 0.80 | 154 |
| Health | 79.4 | 0.80 | 0.78 | 0.79 | 92 |
| Technology | 82.1 | 0.83 | 0.81 | 0.82 | 78 |
| Culture | 78.6 | 0.79 | 0.77 | 0.78 | 68 |

as critical as the core embedding and sequential components, it still helps refine the model's contextual understanding. These findings inform our architectural decisions and highlight potential avenues for future optimizations.

The ablation results in Table 5 reveal that removing the BERT component causes the most substantial performance drop (11.5% when using only BiL-STM+DNN), confirming that contextual embeddings play a crucial role in fake news detection. The BiLSTM layer contributes significantly to performance, with a 4.4% drop when removed, highlighting the importance of sequential information processing.

Table 2 presents the model's performance across different news categories. Politics and Technology categories achieve the highest accuracy and F1-scores, possibly due to more distinctive linguistic patterns and greater availability of training data. The Culture category shows slightly lower performance, which may be attributed to its more subjective nature and diverse content.

**Table 3.** Performance Under Noise Conditions

| Noise Level | Accuracy (%) | Precision | Recall | F1-Score |
|---|---|---|---|---|
| No noise | 81.2 | 0.82 | 0.80 | 0.81 |
| 5% words | 79.6 | 0.80 | 0.78 | 0.79 |
| 10% words | 76.8 | 0.77 | 0.75 | 0.76 |
| 15% words | 72.3 | 0.73 | 0.71 | 0.72 |
| 20% words | 67.9 | 0.68 | 0.67 | 0.67 |

To evaluate robustness, we introduced random word substitutions at varying noise levels (5% to 20% of words replaced with synonyms or similar words). Table 3 demonstrates that while our model maintains reasonable performance at lower noise levels (5–10%), accuracy degrades more significantly as noise approaches 20%, highlighting opportunities for improving resilience to text manipulation.

Table 4 shows how article length affects detection performance. Medium-length articles (500–750 words) yield the best results, likely because they contain sufficient context for the model while avoiding the complexity of longer

**Table 4.** Performance by Article Length

| Length (words) | Accuracy (%) | Precision | Recall | F1-Score | Sample Size |
|---|---|---|---|---|---|
| Less than 250 | 79.8 | 0.80 | 0.78 | 0.79 | 143 |
| 250–500 | 81.5 | 0.82 | 0.80 | 0.81 | 216 |
| 500–750 | 82.1 | 0.83 | 0.81 | 0.82 | 189 |
| 750 and above | 80.4 | 0.81 | 0.79 | 0.80 | 97 |

articles. Interestingly, very short (¡250 words) and very long (¿750 words) articles show slightly decreased performance, suggesting different challenges at these extremes—insufficient information in short articles and potentially more complex narratives in longer pieces.

## 4.4  Ablation Study

To understand the relative importance of each architectural component, we conducted a comprehensive ablation study. We systematically removed or replaced key components of our model and measured the resulting impact on performance metrics. This analysis helps quantify each module's contribution to the overall effectiveness of the fake news detection system and provides insights for future architectural refinements.

Table 5 presents a concise view of accuracy changes when major components are removed, while Table 6 provides a more detailed breakdown with precision, recall, and F1-score across all tested configurations.

**Table 5.** Ablation Study: Impact of Removing Components

| Configuration | Accuracy (%) |
|---|---|
| BERT+BiLSTM (without DNN) | 78.1 |
| BERT (without BiLSTM and DNN) | 75.4 |
| BiLSTM+DNN (without BERT) | 69.7 |

Removing the BiLSTM layer resulted in a significant drop in accuracy, indicating the importance of capturing sequential dependencies. Likewise, eliminating the self-attention mechanism led to a measurable performance degradation, highlighting its role in improving contextual representation. Furthermore, replacing BERT with alternative word embeddings, such as ELMo or Word2Vec, also led to decreased performance, emphasizing the effectiveness of BERT in learning high-quality contextual embeddings.

Table 6. Comprehensive Ablation Analysis

| Configuration | Acc (%) | Prec | Notes |
|---|---|---|---|
| FactFrame-X | 81.2 | 0.82 | Baseline for comparison |
| Without Self-Attention | 79.5 | 0.80 | 1.7% accuracy drop |
| BERT+BiLSTM (w/o DNN) | 78.1 | 0.79 | 3.1% accuracy drop |
| BERT+DNN (w/o BiLSTM) | 76.8 | 0.77 | 4.4% accuracy drop |
| BERT Only | 75.4 | 0.76 | 5.8% accuracy drop |
| BiLSTM+DNN (w/o BERT) | 69.7 | 0.70 | 11.5% accuracy drop |
| ELMo Instead of BERT | 77.3 | 0.78 | 3.9% accuracy drop |
| Word2Vec Instead of BERT | 72.5 | 0.73 | 8.7% accuracy drop |

# 5  Conclusion

In this study, we developed an automated detection model aimed at identifying and tagging hyperpartisan news, addressing the pressing challenge of discerning credible information in an era dominated by biased reporting. By leveraging a novel architecture that integrates BERT with BiLSTM and Deep Neural Networks, our model achieved an accuracy of approximately 81.2 percent, significantly outperforming traditional approaches. The insights gained from the analysis of various input lengths highlight that shorter texts can be equally effective in delivering accurate predictions, suggesting that BERT's capacity for context does not require extensive input to function optimally. Furthermore, our comparative analysis with other text embedding models, such as Word2Vec and ELMo, reinforced the advantages of contextual embeddings in enhancing classification accuracy. Through rigorous training and evaluation, we observed that the combination of BERT's contextual understanding, the sequential processing capabilities of BiLSTM, and the robust feature extraction provided by Deep Neural Networks collectively contribute to our model's effectiveness. The detailed performance metrics, including precision, recall, and F1-score, underscore the model's reliability for practical applications. Despite these promising results, our findings also reveal limitations, particularly in the model's ability to detect nuanced language features such as sarcasm and subtle biases. This highlights an area for further exploration, as enhancing the model's sensitivity to these elements could improve its classification accuracy. Ultimately, our research serves as a vital step toward combating the proliferation of hyperpartisan news, offering a robust tool for stakeholders—including governments, media organizations, and the general public—to navigate the complex landscape of information. We believe that with continued refinement and expansion, this model can contribute to broader efforts in mitigating misinformation and fostering informed discourse in democratic societies.

# References


1. Bastos, M.T., Mercea, D.: The brexit botnet and user-generated hyperpartisan news. Soc. Media + Soc. **5**(3) (2019)
2. Shaughnessy, E.D.B., Hutchens, M.J.: That is so mainstream: the impact of hyperpartisan media use and right-, left-wing alternative media repertoires on consumers' belief in political misperceptions in the United States, pp. 1561–1581, University of Florida, USA, 2024. International Journal of Communication (2024)
3. Chawda, A., Patil, S., Singh, A., Save, V.: Clickbait detection using deep learning. In: 2019 IEEE 5th International Conference on Mechatronics System and Robots (ICMSR), pp. 1–6. IEEE (2019)
4. Dey, S., Rafi, Md.H., Hasan, Md.I., Parash, Md.A., Chakrabarty, D.: Fake news detection using machine learning techniques. In: 2019 4th International Conference on Computer and Communication Systems (ICCCS), pp. 181–185. IEEE (2019)
5. Drissi, I., Sandoval, R., Ojha, S., Medero, J.: BERT-based hyperpartisan news detection. In: Proceedings of the 13th International Workshop on Semantic Evaluation, pp. 846–852 (2019)
6. Genc, O., Firat, A., Ekenel, H.K.: Clickbait detection on turkish social media. In: 2019 IEEE/ACS 16th International Conference on Computer Systems and Applications (AICCSA), pp. 1–6. IEEE (2019)
7. Giachanou, A., Zhang, H., Rosso, P.: Multimodal fake news detection with spotfake. arXiv preprint arXiv:2004.12461 (2020)
8. Devlin, J., Chang, M.-W., Lee, K., Toutanova, K.: BERT: pre-training of deep bidirectional transformers for language understanding (2019)
9. Lundberg, S.M., Lee, S.-I.: A unified approach to interpreting model predictions. In: Proceedings of the Advances in Neural Information Processing Systems (NIPS), pp. 4765–4774 (2017)
10. Namini, S.S., Tavakoli, N., Namin, A.S.: A CNN-BiLSTM architecture for macroeconomic time series forecasting. Eng. Proc. **39**(1), 33 (2023)
11. Patankar, S., Bose, R.: Calculating the bias score of news articles with a web browser extension. Int. J. Sci. Eng. Res. **8**(4), 645–648 (2017)
12. Ribeiro, M.T., Singh, S., Guestrin, C.: "Why should i trust you?": explaining the predictions of any classifier. In: KDD '16: Proceedings of the 22nd ACM SIGKDD International Conference on Knowledge Discovery and Data Mining, pp. 1135–1144 (2016)
13. Rönnback, R.: Automatic large-scale political bias detection of news outlets. PLoS ONE **20**(2), e0321418 (2025)
14. Saadi, A.: Enhancing fake news detection with transformer models and summarization. Eng. Technol. Appl. Sci. Res. **15**(3), 23253–23259 (2025)
15. Singhal, S., Shah, R., Chakraborty, T., Kumaraguru, P., Satoh, S.: SpotFake: a multi-modal framework for fake news detection. In: 2019 IEEE Fifth International Conference on Multimedia Big Data (BigMM), pp. 39–47. IEEE (2019)
16. Zhao, H., Jia, J., Koltun, V.: Exploring self-attention for image recognition. In: Proceedings of the IEEE/CVF Conference on Computer Vision and Pattern Recognition (CVPR), pp. 10076–10085 (2020)

# Linguistic Variations in WhatsApp Chats of Multilingual South Karnataka Natives: A Case Study on Chats Generated by Engineering Student Groups

K. M. Kavitha[(✉)]

Department of Applied Statistics and Data Science, Prasanna School of Public Health, Manipal Academy of Higher Education, Manipal, India
`kavitha.kmahesh@manipal.edu`

**Abstract.** This paper presents the interplay of multilingualism and computer-mediated communication within engineering education student community. Focusing on WhatsApp interactions among Computer Science & Engineering students, the study explores how students leverage their multilingual repertoires in informal online peer communication. Employing a qualitative case study approach, WhatsApp chat logs from student groups are analyzed to identify linguistic phenomena such as code-switching, code-mixing, transliteration, and Non-Standard Tokens (NSTs). The analysis encompasses both academic discourses related to computer engineering coursework and personal exchanges. Findings reveal the dynamic linguistic strategies employed by multilingual students in a technology-rich educational environment, offering insights into evolving communication patterns and the sociolinguistic landscape of young adults transitioning to professional roles.

**Keywords:** Multilingualism · Code-Switching · Transliteration · Computer-Mediated Communication (CMC) · WhatsApp chats · Engineering Education Higher Education · Linguistic Variation · Sociolinguistics · Language Adaptation · Digital Communication

## 1 Introduction

The rapid proliferation of instant messaging platforms has reshaped communication, making it more informal, direct, and immediate. As the world's most popular messaging application with over three billion users, WhatsApp has a dominant role in this shift. Since its introduction in 2009, its growth has steadily increased, and it numbers over 3 billion unique active users worldwide. With 853.8 million users, India ranks highest in the number of WhatsApp users globally. WhatsApp messenger does not impose any standard convention for text usage and chats are typically unstructured in nature. Usage of informal texts such as acronyms, non-standard short forms, foreign language words written in non-native scripts, transliterated texts, spelling variations, phonetic substitutions and such other non-standard texting behaviour have contributed to the


K. K. Patel et al. (Eds.): icSoftComp 2025, CCIS 2874, pp. 55–67, 2026.
https://doi.org/10.1007/978-3-032-22062-2_5

non-standard vocabulary, henceforth referred to in this article as 'Non-Standard Tokens' (NSTs).

Non-Standard Tokens are defined by the phonetic restrictions of a language and are usually replaced in the place of standard words while texting. For example, students use 'pgm', 'pg', 'prog', 'prg' and 'pgms' for the real word 'program'. Non-Standard Tokens may carry different meanings but might be spelled out the same. For example, different users may employ the same Non-Standard Token 'wnt' for different real-words 'went', 'want' and 'wont'. Unlike humans, machines struggle to process and understand a sentence if majority of the words are in non-standard forms, as their interpretation is often user- and context-specific.

This paper focuses on the analysis of WhatsApp text interactions, comprising of both academic discourses related to Computer Science and Engineering courses and personal exchanges, generated by multilingual Computer Science and Engineering students from Dakshina Kannada region of Karnataka. While the participants were proficient in English via education, they exhibited proficiency in (a) their native language Kannada with the majority of the participants being Kannadigas, (b) national language Hindi, the language being either their first or second language in education, and (c) selected regional dialects in Karnataka predominantly Konkani and Tulu, the language being their mother tongue. Non-Standard Tokens in Kanglish[1] and Hinglish[2] are identified and mapped with their possible real word counterparts.

Section 2 summarizes the corpora employed in various studies, the sociolinguistics of computer-mediated communication, multilingualism in higher education and the models for Non-Standard Token processing. Section 3 elaborates the approach used in Non-Standard Token identification and Non-Standard Token to real-word mapping. Results of data preprocessing, statistics of observed Non-Standard Tokens and Non-Standard Token to real-word mapping using modified Soundex are presented in the Sect. 4. Conclusions drawn based on the observed results and the scope for future work are presented in Sect. 5.

## 2  Related Work

### 2.1  Corpora of WhatsApp Chats

The Sociolinguistic corpus of WhatsApp Chats in Spanish was built for the study of the singularities of language and interactions via Instant Messaging (IM) among bachelors. The messages though predominantly in Spanish, also included texts in English, French, Japanese, Italian, German, Korean, Greek and Chinese. Studies utilizing this corpus reported aspects such as parenthetical expressions, orality traits, and code-switching [6]. Garimella & Tyson in their work explored the feasibility of collecting and using WhatsApp data for social science research [7]. Makhija et al., introduced HinglishNorm, a human annotated corpus of Hindi-English code-mixed sentences for text normalization tasks [14].

---

[1] Kannada written using Roman Script.
[2] Hindi written using Roman Script.

The WhatsApp chat corpus employed in the present study was partially acquired from Computer Science & Engineering student chat groups of Mangaluru area, Karnataka State. The corpus is characterized by text conversations of multilingual students from a batch of VI semester Computer Science & Engineering program, and chat groups dedicated for discussions on 'Project Work' and 'Assignment'. The chats are dominated by academic discussions pertaining to courses, project works, course-specific assignments, and examinations taken up by students as part of the semester curriculum and other academic related matters. Also, the texts were acquired from personal chat groups where a subset of students across different sections of VI semester Computer Science & Engineering program participated in discussing non-academic affairs.

## 2.2   Digital Communication in Higher Education and Indian Contexts

In an earliest work, Kachru introduced "Indian English" and discussed about the sociolinguistic status of English in India, providing an essential context for understanding why engineering students use English and regional languages the way they do [10]. In his seminal work on the impact of the internet on language, Ranger provided a strong theoretical basis for understanding how technology, like WhatsApp, shapes linguistic practices such as transliteration and use of emojis [19]. Rambe & Chipunza introduced a general model for analyzing the use of WhatsApp in academic contexts. Though not multi-lingual, the model provided a methodological template for analyzing group communication [18]. Alazemi et al.'s work provided a good overview of WhatsApp's perceived usefulness and ease of use in educational settings [5]. Hasan and Benny in their paper specifically addressed the pragmatic functions of code-switching in social media [4].

## 2.3   Approaches for Non-Standard Token Processing

Li & Yarowsky [13] proposed an unsupervised approach to translate Chinese abbreviations. The model enabled automatic extraction of relation between a full-form phrase and its abbreviation from monolingual corpora followed by generation of translation entries for abbreviation using its full-form as bridge. The task of Non-Standard Token processing has mostly been handled through three NLP tasks namely, Statistical Machine Translation (SMT), Spelling correction and Automatic Speech Recognition (ASR) [20]. In SMT, Non-Standard Tokens are considered as foreign language words and are translated to plain English [3,11,16]. On the other hand, in the Spelling Correction Strategy, spelling check is carried out on word-per-word basis, a popular technique used in the context of SMS messages [8]. Classifiers have been employed to detect out-of-vocabulary words in short text messages and generate correction candidates based on morphophonemic similarity. While the work targets SMS and twitter datasets, the correction candidate for a word is selected taking into account the word similarity and the context [9]. In contrast, Automatic Speech Recognition recognizes Non-Standard Token as a closer approximation of the word's sound rather than spelling. For example, the work by Khoury et al., [12] determines the possible pronunciation of English words as per their standard spellings.

Perez et al., focused on analysis of new trends in digital communication with focus on new language varieties in WhatsApp text interactions. The study revealed age as a determining factor in the pervasive use of non-standard language [17]. Another study focused on the analysis of WhatsApp's semantic notifications [2] revealed unique networks of individuals communicating through Arabic and English in unique and innovative ways. Satapathy et al., [20] proposed a phonetic-based framework for normalizing Non-Standard Tokens to plain English with the objective of improving the sentiment analysis classification accuracy. The work focused on Twitter data using a combination of lexicon-based and phonetic-based approach. Adler et al., [1] presented a statistical model for analyzing code-switching and links code-switching to factors like comfort and emotion, which are highly relevant to informal WhatsApp interactions.

Predictive keyboards[3] contained in smart phones generally suggest relative words for easy and fast typing. This technique initially compares the character in a candidate word with input sequence characters. Later, it predicts the relation between the words by calculating score. In its basic form, it makes use of a local dictionary of repeatedly typed words and phrases and scores them using probability of usage or future requirement.

In the current work, a dictionary of real words is employed to detect Non-Standard Tokens, followed by their mapping to real-word forms using modified Soundex algorithm [15]. To deal with multi-lingual data, Kanglish and Hinglish transliterations are generated and mapped to their English equivalents.

## 3    Methodology

This section presents the approach for analyzing the linguistic variations in WhatsApp chats generated by multilingual engineering student groups. Figure 1 (left) depicts the proposed methodology with the steps involved on a sample chat (right).

### 3.1    Data Acquisition

The corpus of WhatsApp chat messages were acquired from various class groups constituting of approximately 180 Engineering students pursuing Bachelor of Engineering in 'Computer Science and Engineering' Stream in a private Engineering College located in Coastal Karnataka region. Localized chat groups representing the students of sixth semester Computer Science and Engineering named as 'CSEA', 'Project', and 'Assignment' along with personal chat groups yielded the informal text messages used in building the corpus. The participants were proficient in English language via education, nevertheless exhibited proficiency in (a) their native language Kannada, majority of the participants being

---

[3] https://lifehacker.com/how-predictive-keyboards-work-and-how-you-can-train-yo-1643795640.

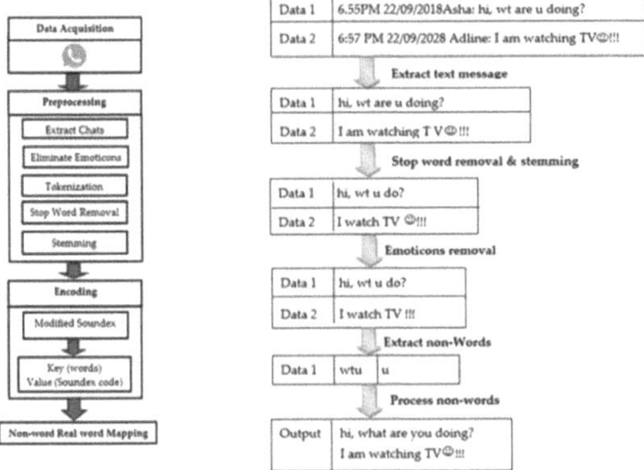

**Fig. 1.** Non-Standard Token processing (left) with a sample processing pipeline (right)

Kannadigas, (b) national language Hindi, the language being either their first or second language in education, and (c) selected regional dialects in Karnataka, predominantly Konkani and Tulu.

## 3.2  Text Pre-processing

WhatsApp chats were characterized by irregular formats with ambiguities and inconsistent information including emoticons, punctuations, upper case and lower case characters. Date, sender name, punctuation and emoticons were removed using regular expression as were not significant for further processing in the context of the chosen study. An input of the form '*6.55PM 22/09/2018 name: wt are u doing?*', consisting of date and time, followed by sender name[4] and the original chat message was reduced to '*hi wt are u doing*'. After filtering chats for date, emoticons, punctuations and sender name, the resultant texts were tokenized thus splitting them into individual chat words considering space as the delimiter. A bag of words was thus generated. Stop words[5] such as '*the*', '*to*', '*a*', '*an*' were eliminated from the tokenized chats using the NLTK tool kit. WordNet lemmatizer[6] was employed to reduce the inflected word forms to their base forms.

## 3.3  Named Entity Elimination and Non-Standard Token Identification

After pre-processing, the person and place names were filtered as nominals were not used for the intended task. A list consisting of person and place names was initially created using the online '*Dictionary of Names, Nicknames and Surnames of Persons and Places*'[7]. The WhatsApp chats were compared against

---

[4] replaced by 'name' for anonymity.

[5] for English were employed.

[6] https://www.nltk.org/_modules/nltk/stem/wordnet.html.

[7] https://ia904502.us.archive.org/17/items/dictionaryofname00lathuoft/dictionaryof
name00lathuoft.pdf.

this list, and identified person and place names were segregated. Non-Standard Tokens in the chat data were extracted by comparing each word with the dictionary of real words. Words not present in the standard English dictionary were considered as Non-Standard Tokens. The Non-Standard Tokens identified for the example referred to in the Subsect. 3.2 are '*wt*', '*r* and '*u*'.

### 3.4  Non-Standard Token to Real-Word Mapping

Identified Non-Standard Tokens (NSTs) were mapped to their corresponding canonical forms using a modified Soundex algorithm adapted from the traditional Odell-Russell phonetic coding system. The algorithm functions in two distinct modes to bridge the gap between computational encoding and human-readable shorthand. Input characters are transformed into a unique set of specific numerals or special characters which act as a phonetic signature. The specific mappings are detailed in Character Encoding Chart (Fig. 2) and the procedural execution is elaborated in Algorithm 1.

### 3.5  Kanglish and Hinglish Equivalents

Kannada words in the corpus written using Latin script were converted into their English equivalents. This was achieved by first transliterating the Kanglish word into Kannada using Indic-transliteration 1.7.8[8]. Thereafter the transliterated Kanglish word is looked up in the Kannada lexicon obtained from pywin

---

**Algorithm 1.** Modified Soundex Algorithm

---

1: **procedure** MODIFIED SOUNDEX ALGORITHM
2:      **Input:** Character Encoding Chart, Non-Standard Token $(T_{nst})$
3:      **Output:** Alpha-Representative Code $(C_\alpha)$
4:      **Initialization:** Let $L$ be the first character of $T_{nst}$ (The Anchor)
5:      Let $S$ be the sequence of remaining characters $T_{nst}[1..n]$
6:      **for** each character $c$ in $S$ **do**
7:          **if** $c$ is a vowel or a phonetic null ($h$, $w$ in medial positions) **then**
8:              discard $c$
9:          **else**
10:             map $c$ to its corresponding symbol $s$ from the Character Encoding Chart
11:         **end if**
12:     **end for**
13:     **if** adjacent characters map to the same symbol **then**
14:         retain only the first instance
15:     **end if**
16:     Translate symbolic results to Alpha-Representatives
17:     Concatenate the Anchor $L$ with the transformed Alpha-sequence.
18:     **return** $C_\alpha$
19: **end procedure**

---

[8] https://pypi.org/project/indic-transliteration/.

| ID | Letter(s) | Map To | ID | Letter(s) | Map To |
|----|-----------|--------|----|-----------|--------|
| a. | b, p | 0 | j. | y | 9 |
| b. | v | 1 | k. | q | ! |
| c. | s, z, x | 2 | l. | g | & |
| d. | d, t | 3 | m. | n | ***** |
| e. | l | 4 | n. | w | # |
| f. | m | 5 | o. | z | @ |
| g. | r | 6 | p. | p | $ |
| h. | k, c | 7 | q. | f | + |
| i. | j | 8 | | | |

**Fig. 2.** Soundex Character Encoding Chart

library[9]. If the transliterated word was found in the lexicon, it was translated into English using the Google Translator API[10]. Meanwhile, in the process a lexicon of Kanglish words and their English equivalents was generated. For instance, the Kanglish word *'male'* initially transliterated into Kannada script resulted in the equivalent kannada word 'ಮಳೆ' . Thereafter it was translated into its English equivalent *'rain'*. Similarly, Hinglish words - Hindi words written using Latin script, were initially transliterated into Hindi using Indic-transliteration 1.7.8 and thereafter looked up in the Hindi lexicon obtained from pywin library. If found, subsequently the word was translated into English using the Google Translator API. For instance, the Hinglish word *'kitab'* initially transliterated into the Hindi script 'कतीब' , was translated into its English equivalent *'book'*, if found in the Hindi lexicon during the look up process.

## 4   Experimental Setup and Results

The acquired corpus, statistics of identified Non-Standard Tokens, and a comparative analysis of Non-Standard Token to real-word mapping are presented in the current section.

### 4.1   Dataset Characteristics

**Chats with English-only Mostly Non-standard Short Forms** .
**Chat 1:** *Im nt wel im slpng fvr*
**Chat 2:** If she *snds* to *al* also fine *cl* me *k*
**Chat 3:** *R u??*

---

[9] Python based API to access Indian language WordNet.
[10] https://cloud.google.com/translate.

**Chats with English-only Minimally Non-standard Short Forms** .
**Chat 4:**  😔  😔  *idk* why my phone showed an error that time
**Chat 5:** *U* mean *CLG* cafeteria??

**Chats with English-only Technical Term Short Forms** .
**Chat 6:** That *HALFSZ* problem
**Chat 7:** That's the last part of *mod1* actually  😁  😁
**Chat 8:** If it's *sscd,*don't ask me  😁
**Chat 9:** Sorry for disturbing again..do u know the portion of *cgv* or have I already asked this question to u before!?  😁

**Chats with English-Only, Spelling Error Cases** .
**Chat 10:** Hey can you please Send me the picture of multipass *assembler*

**Chats with Non-English Words only** .
**Chat 11:** *Pakka* (Hindi)
**Chat 12:** *Nanage tumba barthade* (Kannada)
**Chat 13:** *Shanti thumche sove ason* 😊 (Konkani)

**Code-Mixed Chats** .
**Chat 14:** *Vacation*ache upranthi *mini vacation* zaije (Code-mixed Konkani)

**Single-Word Chats Expressed Using only Interjections** .
**Chat 15:** *Cheeeee* 😁

**Single-Word Chats Expressed Using only Non-standard Short Forms** .
**Chat 16:** *Wbu?*

### 4.2   Non-Standard Token Statistics

The WhatsApp chats initially collected from localized chat groups 'CSEA', 'Project', 'Assignment' along with family and personal chat groups consisted of 8,651 chat messages. 8,041 chat messages were retained after eliminating the messages containing only media. The resultant dataset consisted of 2,861 unique words. 2,779 unique words were retained after stop-word removal. Upon pruning the person and place names 2,620 unique words were retained of which 863 were Non-Standard Tokens. The distribution of unique Non-Standard Tokens vs their occurrence frequencies is depicted in the Fig. 3.

The Table 1 shows highly frequent English Non-Standard Tokens observed in the WhatsApp chat corpus. Single character forms such as '*u*', '*r*', '*c*', '*k*' were frequently used instead of real words '*you*', '*are*', '*see*', '*okay*', respectively.

**Table 1.** Highly frequent Non-Standard Tokens (EN) with their size and occurrence frequencies

| Non-Standard Token (Len = 1) | Frequency | Non-Standard Token (Len = 2) | Frequency | Non-Standard Token (Len = 3) | Frequency | Non-Standard Token (Len> = 4) | Frequency |
|---|---|---|---|---|---|---|---|
| u | 304 | oh | 140 | hey | 383 | yeah | 238 |
| r | 35 | ya | 91 | ohh | 29 | heyy | 37 |
| n | 31 | na | 45 | yea | 25 | ohhh | 30 |
| v | 21 | ur | 31 | tht | 24 | okayy | 26 |
| k | 18 | wt | 29 | pic | 23 | bday | 18 |
| i | 17 | hv | 27 | wat | 20 | yess | 16 |
| c | 16 | cn | 25 | okk | 20 | nope | 15 |
| b | 14 | ha | 23 | lil | 20 | yeahh | 13 |
| d | 12 | hy | 16 | btw | 17 | dint | 12 |
| p | 06 | ua | 15 | haa | 16 | texte | 10 |

The word cloud generated by single character Non-Standard Tokens is depicted in Fig. 4 (left). Non-Standard Tokens of length 2 such as '*dp*', '*ty*', '*tq*', '*ik*', '*ua*' corresponded to multi-words bigrams such as '*display profile*', '*thank you*', '*thank you*', '*I know*', '*you are*' respectively. Nevertheless, such Non-Standard Tokens also corresponded to unigrams. For instance, Non-Standard Token '*ur*' and '*hv*' were frequently used instead of real-word forms '*your*' and '*have*', respectively. Other Non-Standard Tokens of length 2 commonly employed in WhatsApp communications are depicted in Fig. 4 (right). Non-Standard Tokens of length 3 are depicted in Fig. 5 (left) and those with 4 or more characters in the right respectively.

Usage of non-standard forms as well extended to multi-word domain-specific technical terms, such as '*system software and compiler design*', '*question paper*', '*Larsen & Toubro*' and unigrams such as '*module*', '*program*'. Non-standard short forms of these terms such as '*sscd*', '*qp*', *lnt*', and '*mod*', '*pgm*' were respectively

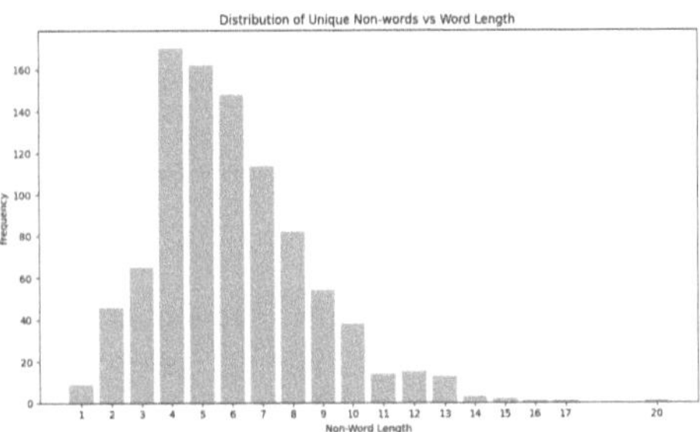

**Fig. 3.** Distribution of unique Non-Standard Tokens by length vs occurrence frequencies

**Fig. 4.** Word cloud generated by Non-Standard Tokens of length 1 (left) and 2 (right) characters

**Fig. 5.** Word cloud generated by Non-Standard Tokens of length 3 (left) and 4/more (right)

used instead. Also, different users used different short forms for the same real word and at times a particular user switched between different short forms corresponding to the same real word. A typical instance is the usage of Non-Standard Tokens*'pgm'*, *'pg'*, *'prog'*, *'prg'*, *'pgms'*, all of which are the non-standard variations of the same real word *'program'*. Within the scope of technical education, non-standard forms captured ranged from domain-specific short forms for technical and other related terms such as *'cs'* ⇔ *'computer science'*, *'demo'* ⇔ *'demonstration'*, *'prac'* ⇔ *'practical'*, *'projie'* ⇔ *'project'* to course titles offered in Computer Science & Engineering education and allied engineering programmes such as *'pap'* ⇔ *'python application programming'*, *'atc'* ⇔ *'automata theory and compilers'*, *'nlp'* ⇔ *'natural language processing'*, *'cns'* ⇔ *'computer networks and security'*. Further, Named Entities (NEs), majorly corresponding to company names, computer brands, names of student associations were referred to using short forms. Most frequently observed non-standard forms have been presented in respective columns of the Table 2 with the occurrence frequencies. The last row in the table identifies non-standard forms due to spelling errors such as omissions (*'t'* in *'leter'*, *'e'* in *'terminal*, *'r'* in *'pycham'*, *'m'*/*'in 'progra'*), insertions (*'m'* in *'problem'*) and substitutions (*'a'* instead of *'i'* in *'defiinition'*). Table 3 shows highly frequent Non-Standard Tokens in other languages, predominantly Hindi, Kannada and Konkani, written using Latin Script. Majority of these Non-Standard Tokens appeared only once in the corpus.

## 4.3   Non-Standard Token Mapping

Table 4 shows the results of Non-Standard Token to real word mapping for short forms in English, with the expected and obtained mappings for randomly chosen Non-Standard Tokens in the corpus. Although multiple real words have been mapped for a Non-Standard Token, in all the cases suggestions did contain its actual real word. Last row shows the Kanglish Non-Standard Token encountered in the WhatsApp text corpus with the expected and suggested equivalent(s) in English.

## 4.4   Comparative Analysis

The results of Non-Standard Token to real-word mapping was compared to the results obtained using existing approaches. The Table 5 shows the results of Non-Standard Token processing in comparison to previous works. Approaches such as demetaphone and metaphone map a Non-Standard Token into multiple unrelated standard words. For instance, the Non-Standard Token '*wt*' is mapped to more than 50 real words many of which are incorrect. Similarly, the Soundex algorithm suggests multiple real forms for a particular Non-Standard Token. In

**Table 2.** Highly frequent Domain-specific Non-Standard Tokens in English

| Non-Standard Token Short Forms for Domain-specific Terms (EN) with Occurrence Frequencies | | |
|---|---|---|
| Domain-specific Terms | Course Titles | NE Acronyms |
| cs: 6, ec: 2, vtu: 2, usn: 2, cse: 1, | dbms: 12, cgv: 10, sscd: 10, | tcs: 6, lnt: 4, hp: 4, |
| mca: 1, pu: 5, dept: 3, hod: 4, princi: 1 | ml: 8, os: 6, cns: 5, | itc: 3, mphasis: 1, |
| pgm: 4, pg: 3, prog: 2, prg: 1, pgms: 1, | aca: 4, pap: 3, iot: 3, atc: 2, | zephyr: 1, |
| imp: 6, msg: 3, qp: 3, demo: 3, | cgi: 2, nlp: 1, | cypher: 1 |
| mod: 1, sub: 2, projie: 1, lec: 1, | co: 2, ai: 2 | |
| prac: 2, exm: 1, exms: 1, qstns: 1, | | |
| api: 2, halfsz: 1, | | |
| intevw: 1, prelim: 1, apti: 3, | | |
| mcqs: 1, mcq: 1, ceti: 1, certi: 1, | | |
| ofr: 1, ltr: 1, stat: 1 | | |
| pc: 3, spec: 3, iitian: 1 | | |
| Spelling Errors | | |
| leter: 1, trminal: 1, pycham: 1, progra: 1, prgrm: 1, progrm: 2, problemm: 1, defination: 1, terminologie: 1 | | |

**Table 3.** Non-Standard Tokens in Indian languages with occurrence frequencies

| Non-word (HI) | Frequency | Non-word (KN) | Frequency | Non-word (Konkani) | Frequency |
|---|---|---|---|---|---|
| pakka (पक्का) | 5 | nanage(ನನಗೆ) | 2 | tuka | 1 |
| chalo (चलो) | 4 | tumba(ತುಂಬ) | 1 | thumche | 1 |
| saath (साथ) | 2 | yentha (ಎಂಥ) | 1 | tumchei | 1 |
| nazar (नज़र) | 1 | hesaru (ಹೆಸರು) | 1 | upranthi | 1 |

**Table 4.** Non-Standard Token and Real word Mapping

| Input | Expected Mapping | Obtained Mapping |
|---|---|---|
| nyt | night | night |
| clg | college | colleague, **college** |
| 2mrw | tomorrow | tomorrow |
| gd | good | **good**, god, guide |
| aaithu (ಆಯಿತು) | became, complete | became |

**Table 5.** Comparison of Approaches in Candidate Generation for representative NSTs

| Approaches | NST | | | |
|---|---|---|---|---|
| | wt | hv | u | ryt |
| **Demetaphone** | what, white, wait, weight | have, half, huff, heave | - | right, rite |
| **Metaphone** | what, white, wait, weight | have, half, huff | - | right, rite |
| **Standard Soundex** | what, white, wait, weight | have, heavy, hive | - | right, rite, wrote |
| **Proposed Mapping** | what, white, wait | have, heavy | you | right |

contrast, the proposed approach suggests better mapping for the chosen Non-Standard Tokens. For Non-Standard Tokens such as '$c$', '$s$', '$u$', the demetaphone and metaphone algorithm does not suggest any mapping, while the Soundex algorithm and the proposed approach maps them to correct real forms.

## 5   Conclusion

This paper presented an approach to analyze the WhatsApp text interactions comprising of academic discourses and personal exchanges compiled from multilingual computer science and engineering student groups of Dakshina Kannada region of Karnataka. Findings reveal evolving communication patterns and the sociolinguistic landscape of young adults transitioning to professional roles. Major challenge in processing was the common usage of informal and out-of-vocabulary texts. To tackle the problem, Non-Standard Tokens were identified and mapped to real word form(s). This research contributes to understanding language adaptation in digital learning spaces and the implications for technology-enhanced communication within multilingual higher education contexts in India. Processing Non-Standard Tokens considering the context of the sentences needs to be explored in future.

## References


1. Adler, R.M., Valdés Kroff, J.R., Novick, J.M.: Does integrating a code-switch during comprehension engage cognitive control? J. Exp. Psychol. Learn. Mem. Cogn. **46**(4), 741 (2020)

2. Al-Khawaldeh, N., Bani-Khair, B., Mashaqba, B., Huneety, A.: A corpus-based discourse analysis study of whatsapp messengerG s semantic notifications. Int. J. Appl. Linguist. English Lit. **5**(6), 158–165 (2016)
3. Aw, A., Zhang, M., Xiao, J., Su, J.: A phrase-based statistical model for SMS text normalization. In: Proceedings of the COLING/ACL 2006 Main Conference Poster Sessions, pp. 33–40 (2006)
4. Benny, N.S.: Code-switching in digital communication: a pragmatic approach to multilingual interactions on social media. South Asian J. Soc. Sci. Human. **6**(3), 18G 39 (2025). https://doi.org/10.48165/sajssh.2024.6302
5. Cetinkaya, L.: The impact of whatsapp use on success in education process. Int. Rev. Res. Open Distrib. Learn. **18** (2017). https://doi.org/10.19173/irrodl.v18i7.3279
6. Dorantes, A., Sierra, G., Pérez, T.Y.D., Bel-Enguix, G., Rosales, M.J.: Sociolinguistic corpus of whatsapp chats in Spanish among college students. In: Proceedings of the Sixth International Workshop on Natural Language Processing for Social Media, pp. 1–6 (2018)
7. Garimella, K., Tyson, G.: Whatapp doc? a first look at whatsapp public group data. In: Proceedings of the International AAAI Conference on Web and Social Media, vol. 12 (2018)
8. Han, B., Baldwin, T.: Lexical normalisation of short text messages: Makn sens a# twitter. In: Proceedings of the 49th Annual Meeting of the Association for Computational Linguistics: Human Language Technologies, pp. 368–378 (2011)
9. Han, B., Cook, P., Baldwin, T.: Lexical normalization for social media text. ACM Trans. Intell. Syst. Technol. (TIST) **4**(1), 1–27 (2013)
10. Kachru, B.B.: The Indianization of English. English Today **2**(2), 31–33 (1986)
11. Kaufmann, M., Kalita, J.: Syntactic normalization of twitter messages. In: International Conference on Natural Language Processing, Kharagpur, India, vol. 16 (2010)
12. Khoury, R.: Microtext normalization using probably-phonetically-similar word discovery. In: 2015 IEEE 11th International Conference on Wireless and Mobile Computing, Networking and Communications (WiMob), pp. 384–391. IEEE (2015)
13. Li, Z., Yarowsky, D.: Unsupervised translation induction for Chinese abbreviations using monolingual corpora. In: Proceedings of ACL-08: HLT, pp. 425–433 (2008)
14. Makhija, P., Srivastava, A., Gupta, A.: hinglishnorm-a corpus of hindi-english code mixed sentences for text normalization. In: Proceedings of the 28th International Conference on Computational Linguistics: Industry Track, pp. 136–145 (2020)
15. Odell, M.K.: The profit in records management. Systems (New York) **20**, 20 (1956)
16. Pennell, D.L., Liu, Y.: Normalization of informal text. Comput. Speech Lang. **28**(1), 256–277 (2014)
17. Pérez-Sabater, C.: Discovering language variation in whatsapp text interactions. Onomázein **31**, 113–126 (2015)
18. Rambe, P., Chipunza, C.: Using mobile devices to leverage student access to collaboratively-generated resources: a case of whatsapp instant messaging at a South African university. In: 2013 International Conference on Advanced ICT and Education (ICAICTE-13), pp. 314–320. Atlantis Press (2013)
19. Ranger, G.: David crystal, language and the internet. J. English Lexicology. Lexis [Online], Book Rev. **29** (2007)
20. Satapathy, R., Guerreiro, C., Chaturvedi, I., Cambria, E.: Phonetic-based microtext normalization for twitter sentiment analysis. In: 2017 IEEE International Conference on Data Mining Workshops (ICDMW), pp. 407–413. IEEE (2017)

# LLM-Based Vulnerability Detection in Decompiled Binary Code for Automated Reverse Engineering


Pavan Nutalapati[1](✉), Nandagopal Seshagiri[2], Arun Kumar Elengovan[3], and Lahari Putty[4]

[1] Dallas, TX 75068, USA
`pnutalapati97@gmail.com`
[2] San Ramon, CA 94583, USA
[3] Fremont, CA 94539, USA
[4] Princeton, TX 75407, USA



**Abstract.** A portable and interpretable model of function-lvl static vulnerability finding has been created with the help of pretrained large language design. Devign dataset provided Code snippets which were embedded by means of CodeT5, transformer-based model pretrained on code representation tasks. These embeddings were seen as fixed length feature vectors and were tested using standard machine learning classifiers such as logistic regression, random forest, multi-layer perceptron, and XGBoost. To make the classification more robust a stacking ensemble was also tested. The proposed pipeline is preferable to the traditional methods based on graph neural networks or a program analysis framework in that no fine-tuning is necessary and the implementation of static semantic embedding is suggested, which is efficient to train and convenient to apply to practice. By showing that transformer-based code comprehension with simpler classifiers can be used as an effective method of finding function-level vulnerability, the approach has provided a valid path needed to integrate LLM-based vulnerability researching into reliable security review automation pipelines.

**Keywords:** Vulnerability Detection · Code Embeddings · Large Language Models (LLM)


## 1 Introduction

The ubiquitous use of open-source software and third-party libraries has led to an expansion of the attack surface of contemporary applications rendering the issue of vulnerability detection in source code an essential issue towards software security [1, 2]. However, commonly used traditional and static analysis tools are based on manually developed rules and program analysis methods, which cannot be generalized to deal with a variety of code bases and programming systems [3, 4]. The most recent developments in the

---

P. Nutalapati, N. Seshagiri, A. E. Elengovan, L. Putty—Independent Researcher.



K. K. Patel et al. (Eds.): icSoftComp 2025, CCIS 2874, pp. 68–80, 2026.
https://doi.org/10.1007/978-3-032-22062-2_6

fields of machine learning and natural language processing have proposed data-driven solutions that suggested to consider the code as a type of structured language and apply deep learning models to identify vulnerabilities [5, 6]. Nevertheless, most of these methods assume complex program representations, e.g. abstract syntax trees, or control flow graphs, which are costly to compute and not portable [7, 8].

As a way of overcoming such limitations, it has been discussed to rely on a lightweight and scalable approach that uses pretrained code-aware language models to mine semantic code function representations. These are then applied in classification of vulnerabilities in binary in a static environment.

## 2  Literature Review

Some of the first efforts in automating vulnerability detection have been static analysis-based and were identified using rule-based pattern matching, offering minimal flexibility and not able to support large codebases [9, 10]. Machine learning, which developed, also presented probabilistic systems, which could learn susceptibility schemes over labeled lists, such as those relying on n-grams and latent semantic analysis [11]. Deep learning introduced architectures, namely convolutional neural networks, LSTMs, that were used on tokenized code but were more successful than previous ones at recalling various code patterns or statements but always without much semantic depth [12, 13].

Similarly, new strategies have tried to involve using program graphs, as well as graph neural networks, to model control and data flows [7, 14]. Effective as they are, such techniques add extra complexity because they rely on intermediate representations. In order to overcome such shortcomings, the adoption of pretrained language models, i.e. CodeBERT and GraphCodeBERT has been proposed to learn semantic structure directly on raw code [15, 16].

Expanding on this progress, this paper discusses the application of CodeT5, a transformer code-aware encoder, in producing semantic embeddings of the function level code. Those embeddings together with classical classifiers constitute a lightweight, interpretable, and static detection pipeline. Other similar studies in federated learning [17], remote sensing [18], sensor precision enhancement [19], and time-series prediction [20] also shows the relevance of machine learning in various applications, which proves its appropriateness in the assessment of software vulnerability.

## 3  Methodology

This section contains detailed description of the full pipeline used to detect vulnerabilities in decompiled code, including dataset preprocessing, encoding of the code using a pretrained language model, and applying various supervised learning models to classify code. The selected components of the approach are discussed below in detail.

### 3.1  Framework Overview

The current research builds on a systematic methodology with four major steps: preprocessing of the data, extraction of Embeddings using a pretrained transformer, classification using a traditional machine learning model, and an evaluation process through well-established performance ratios (Fig. 1). The first step is pre-processing due to the fact that extraneous characters should be removed out of raw code snippets, and then sampling takes place. The received sequences are tokenized and turned into a fixed length of context-awares embodiments by using the codeT5 encoder. They are then used to feed three efficient classifiers (Random Forest, MLP, and XGBoost) whose results are measured w.r.t accuracy, F1-score, and ROC AUC.

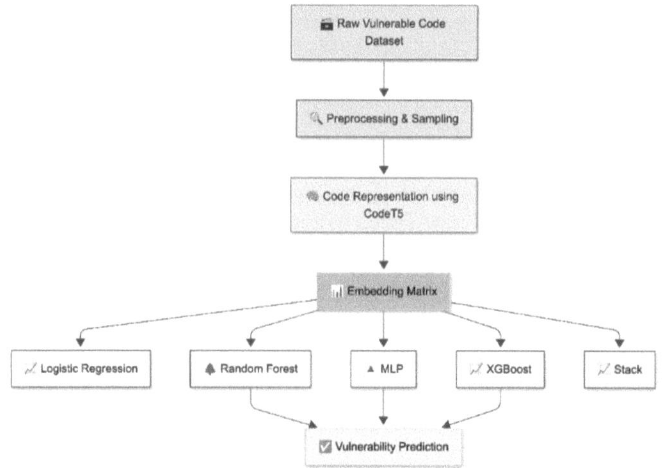


**Fig. 1.** Overview of Proposed Pipeline

## 3.2 Dataset Description

The Devign dataset was introduced to be utilized in terms of the functionality of the vulnerability classification. It contains labels of about 21,000 C/C++ functions, each with one of the two classes: vulnerable (1) or safe (0). All functions are based on projects in the real world of the open-source projects. The entire data is found to be balanced; however, slight label bias can be detected in the subset that is used to evaluate the prototypes. Figure 2 and Fig. 3 show the initial class distribution and proportions in the raw sampled subset, highlighting the inherent class imbalance prior to any remediation.

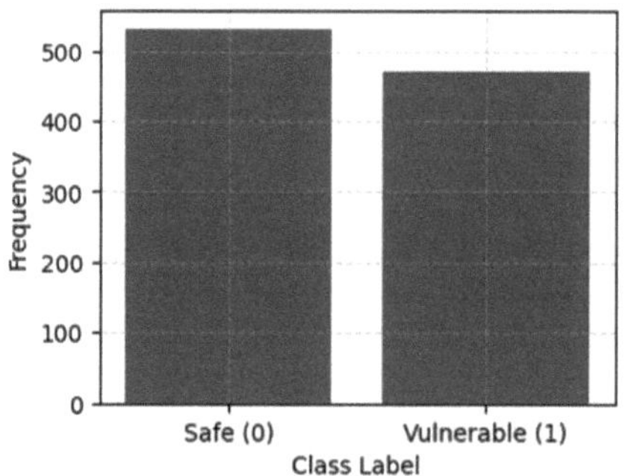


**Fig. 2.** Imbalance Class Labels

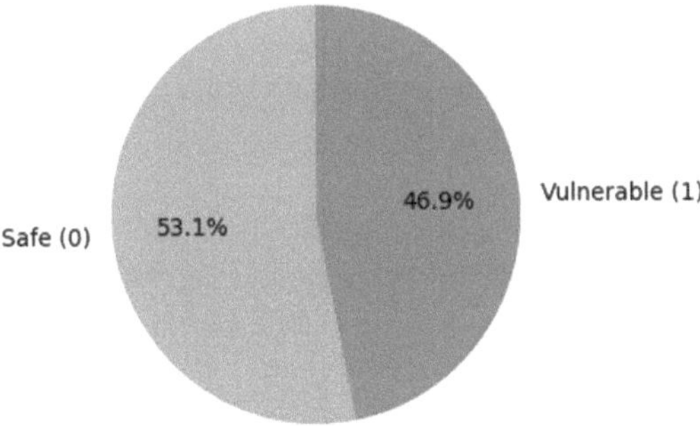


**Fig. 3.** Imbalance Class Proportion

The code functions selected in the sample are relatively variable in structural complexity. Such variability can be found not only in the raw character length of these users but also in the breakdown of generating tokens in tokenization. Figure 4 plots the distribution of the length of functions in characters and Fig. 5 provides the length of tokens distribution with use of subword tokenization.

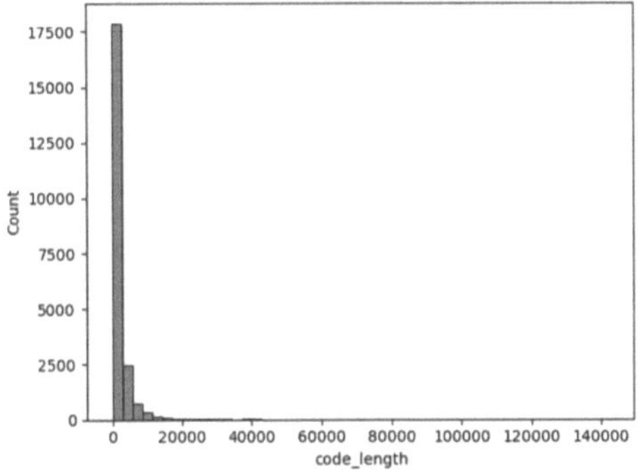

**Fig. 4.** Distribution of Code Length

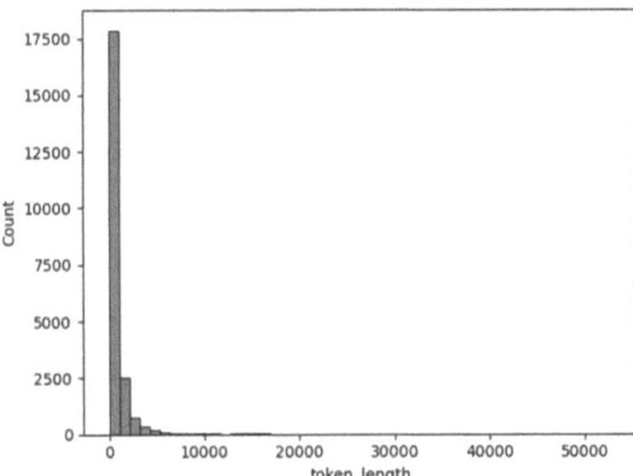

**Fig. 5.** Distribution of Token Length

## 3.3  Data Preprocessing

Observations that were still of null value or duplicate values were filtered, and a random sample of 1,000 observations was kept to facilitate the experimentation process. Since (transformer-based) models like CodeT5 have a capacity of at most 512 tokens, the length of those sequences was truncated directly.

The Synthetic Minority Oversampling Technique (SMOTE) algorithm was produced to remedy the imbalance between classes. In that way, the examples are synthetically produced by the interpolation between a minority observation xi and one of their k-nearest neighbors *xnn* (1):

$$x_{\text{new}} = x_i + \lambda \cdot (x_{nn} - x_i), \quad \lambda \sim \mathcal{U}(0, 1) \tag{1}$$

The process followed in this experiment was meant to ensure that a fair representation of samples based on vulnerability and non-vulnerable classes were drawn thus enhancing training fairness. The balance that is obtained is visualized in Fig. 6 and Fig. 7 where the distribution of classes in all the datasets is clearly identified.

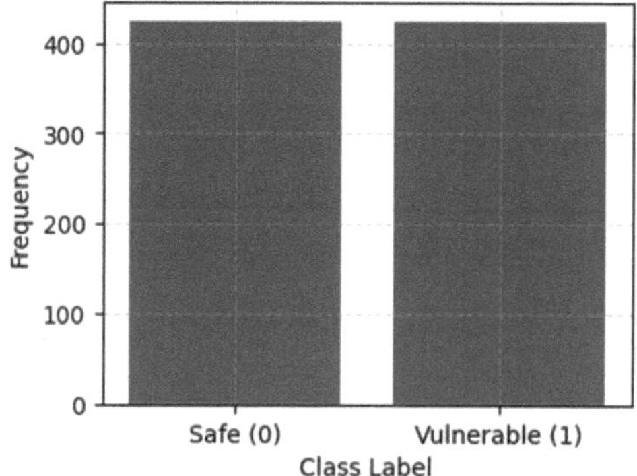


**Fig. 6.** Balanced Class Label after SMOTE

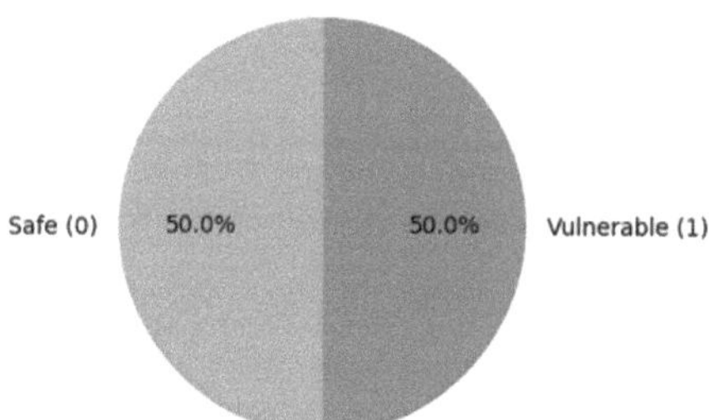


**Fig. 7.** Balanced Class Proportion after SMOTE

## 3.4  Embedding Models Overview

The performance of two pretrained transformer-based models, CodeBERT and CodeT5, was tested to generate embedding based on source-code.

**CodeBERT.** Refers to a bimodal model that is based on RoBERTa architecture. It was trained on the masked language modeling task with pairs of natural-language and programming-language sequence. The representation of the [CLS] token is used as the final embedding (2).

$$z_{\text{CodeBERT}} = h_{[\text{CLS}]} \tag{2}$$

**CodeT5.** The encoder decoder CodeT5 model is applied in a text-to-text format and has been trained on defects with the detection type and the code summarization type. In contrast to CodeBERT, the code representation is obtained by weighted mean pooling of the hidden states of the encoder across attention masks (3).

$$z_{\text{CodeT5}} = \left( \sum_{i=1}^{L} m_i \right)^{-1} \cdot \sum_{i=1}^{L} (m_i \cdot h_i) \tag{3}$$

Table 1 contains a comparative explanation of the two models.

**Table 1.** Comparison of CodeBERT and CodeT5

| Feature | CodeBERT | CodeT5 |
| --- | --- | --- |
| Architecture | RoBERTa (Encoder) | T5 (Encoder-Decoder) |
| Input Format | Code + Natural Language | Code only |
| Embedding Strategy | CLS token | Mean pooling |
| Max Sequence Length | 512 tokens | 512 tokens |
| Pretraining Objective | MLM | Text-to-text |
| Embedding Dimension | 768 | 768 |

## 3.5  Embedding Generation

A model with transformer architecture CodeT5-base was used to tokenize source code into fixed-sized vectors, making it possible to detect any vulnerabilities (4). This input code was then tokenized; longer stream of tokens were chopped off to 512, and the encoded tokens were stored. Outputs of the token-level encoders were mean-pooled to produce embeddings $e \in R^{768}$ each of the functions:

$$e = \left( \sum_{i} m_i \right)^{-1} \cdot \sum_{i} (m_i \cdot h_i) \tag{4}$$

Here, $hi$ are the token embeddings, and $m$ 0, 1, the attention mask to protect padding token.

Then an evaluation of the structural separability of distributed embeddings was carried out by visualizing in t-SNE, as shown in Fig. 8.

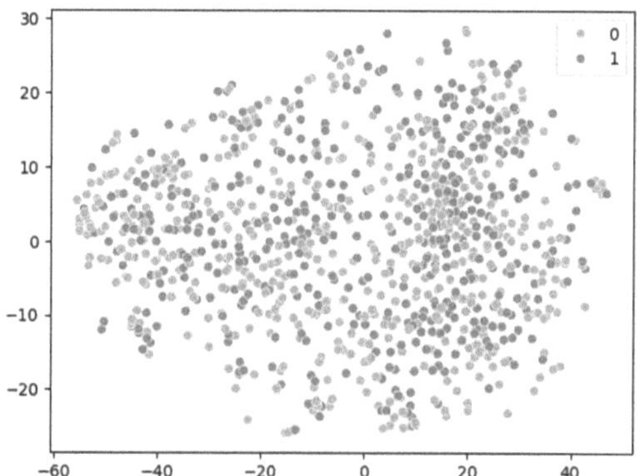

**Fig. 8.** t-SNE Projection of Code Embeddings

### 3.6 Classification Models

As the means to evaluate the usefulness of code embeddings in vulnerability detection of functions, several supervised classification models were utilised. The two models were used to train on 768 dimensional representations generated by CodeT5.

**Logistic Regression.** A first-order linear classifier can be thought of as a probability estimator which uses probabilities derived using a sigmoid form of linearly transformed input features. Logistic Regression is often employed due to its interpretability of its use, and high efficiency of work on categorizing into two classes problems. Here log-odds of the dependent variable is modelled as linear function (5) of input features.

$$P(y = 1|x) = \sigma\left(w^T x + b\right) \tag{5}$$

with sigmoid function as $\sigma(z) = \frac{1}{1+e^{-z}}$.

**Random Forest.** Random Forest is an ensemble method of learning that combines an average of decision trees produced out of a random selection of predictors and a random selection of observations. The overfitting problem is moderated by majority voting approach that pulls the results of individual trees together thus enhancing the generalization. In training, a series of decision trees are fitted and the last class as assigned is the interior point or rather, the mode of the output predictions of every tree in particular (6).

$$\hat{y} = \text{mode}(T_1(x), T_2(x), \ldots, T_n(x)) \tag{6}$$

**Multi-layer Perceptron (MLP).** This is a description of a multilayered feedforward neural network that has ReLU as the activation functions. Its architecture includes an input layer, several middle layers including non-linear transformations, and the last output layer devoted to classification. The model learns to represent hierarchical features through a backpropagation (7) of classification loss in the entire network.

$$h^{(l)} = \phi\left(W^{(l)} h^{(l-1)} + b^{(l)}\right) \tag{7}$$

with the ReLU activation indicated by $\phi$ and the layer indicated by $l$.

**XGBoost.** Being one of the most popular ensembles machine-learning frameworks, XGBoost (Extreme Gradient Boosting) pursues gradient-boosted decision-tree optimization with the help of additive training (8). Successive decision trees attempt to correct errors that are still produced by their predecessor ensemble. The model therefore involves minimization of a regularized objective that is a combination of empirical training loss and some form of measure of model complexity.

$$\hat{y}_i = \sum_{k=1}^{K} f_k(x_i), \quad f_k \in \mathcal{F} \tag{8}$$

with $F$ the space of regression trees. To enhance the bias-variance trade-off, XGBoost minimizes a regularized objective.

**Stacking Classifier.** A meta-ensemble that combines various base predictions of random forest, XGBoost and MLP into final logistic regression combiner.

Each model was run on the held-out test split with accuracy, F1-score, and ROC-AUC being measured. It was selected because of its overall generalization and class-separating ability.

## 4  Evaluation Metrics

In order to evaluate the performance of the models in categorizing vulnerabilities as either binary, the following were used:

- **Accuracy:** The percentage of accurate predictions is called accuracy (9):

$$\text{Accuracy} = \frac{C_{\text{pos}} + C_{\text{neg}}}{C_{\text{pos}} + C_{\text{neg}} + I_{\text{pos}} + I_{\text{neg}}} \tag{9}$$

- **Precision:** The precision measures how well the affirmative predictions are true (10):

$$\text{Precision} = \frac{C_{\text{pos}}}{C_{\text{pos}} + I_{\text{pos}}} \tag{10}$$

- **Recall:** Recall (Sensitivity) measures how well the model can capture positives (11):

$$\text{Recall} = \frac{C_{\text{pos}}}{C_{\text{pos}} + I_{\text{neg}}} \tag{11}$$

- **F1-Score:** F1-Score (12) is a compromise between precision and recall:

$$F_1 = 2 \cdot \frac{\text{Precision} \cdot \text{Recall}}{\text{Precision} + \text{Recall}} \tag{12}$$

The ROC-AUC measures the separability of the classes and is the area of Receiver Operating Characteristic curve.

These measures allow a balanced conceptualization of the work of a classifier, particularly in a situation where classes are not balanced.

## 5   Results and Discussion

To evaluate how successful conventional classifiers can be on code representations via transformers, various models were run with a dataset balanced via SMOTE. Both CodeT5 and CodeBERT were used to retrieve dense representation of the decompiled code and various classifiers were trained and tested based on these embeddings. Standard classification metrics were provided to report the results. The best performing models only have confusion matrix and ROC curve visualization.

### 5.1   Logistic Regression

The most balanced performance of precision and recall was recorded in the Logistic Regression. It showed average generalization and linear separability (Fig. 9) and check Table 2 for the values of metrics.

**Table 2.** Logistic Regression Classification Metrics

| Metric | Value |
| --- | --- |
| Accuracy | 0.55 |
| Precision | 0.55 |
| Recall | 0.55 |
| F1-Score | 0.52 |
| AUC | 0.56 |

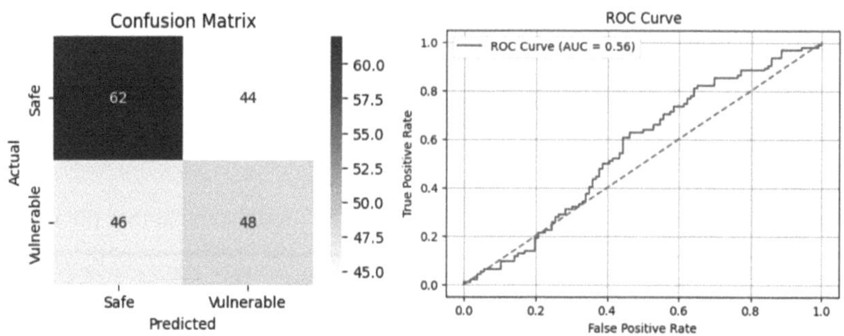


**Fig. 9.** Confusion Matrix and ROC Curve of Logistic Regression

### 5.2   Random Forest

Random Forest did not perform well in terms of picking out minority classes, achieving an accuracy of 0.515 along with a precision and recall of 0.51 and F1-score of 0.42, and AUC of 0.54 (Table 3) indicating that it tended to memorize majority class patterns in high-dimensional embeddings.

**Table 3.** Random Forest Classification Metrics

| Metric | Value |
| --- | --- |
| Accuracy | 0.515 |
| Precision | 0.51 |
| Recall | 0.51 |
| F1-Score | 0.42 |
| AUC | 0.54 |

## 5.3 Multilayer Perceptron

MLP took a more consistent classification on both classes and took advantage of its non-linear possibility to create complex relationships in code embeddings (Fig. 10) and check Table 4 for the values of the performance metrics.

**Table 4.** MLP Classification Metrics

| Metric | Value |
| --- | --- |
| Accuracy | 0.535 |
| Precision | 0.54 |
| Recall | 0.54 |
| F1-Score | 0.51 |
| AUC | 0.55 |

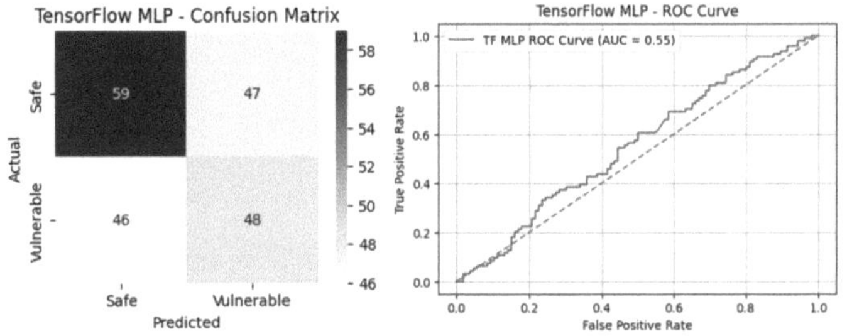


**Fig. 10.** MLP Confusion Matrix and ROC Curve

## 5.4 XGBoost

XGBoost exhibited a relatively small improvement in terms of AUC (0.56) but little capability of utilizing the embedding structure, with an accuracy measure of 0.515, precision of 0.51, recall of 0.52, and F1-score of 0.46 (Table 5), which suggests that the method was unable to design good precision-recall tradeoffs.

**Table 5.** XGBoost Classification Metrics

| Metric | Value |
| --- | --- |
| Accuracy | 0.515 |
| Precision | 0.51 |
| Recall | 0.52 |
| F1-Score | 0.46 |
| AUC | 0.56 |

## 5.5  Stacking Model

Stacking ensemble performed very weakly compared with individual base learners with an accuracy of 0.49, precision of 0.48, recall of 0.49, F1-score of 0.40, AUC of 0.54 (Table 6). Such findings imply that the intersected boundaries of the individual classifiers in the ensemble might not have overlapped well which could indicate an anti-coordination effect of the ensemble leading to a decrease in the overall synergy in the ensemble predictions.

**Table 6.** Stacking Model Classification Metrics

| Metric | Value |
| --- | --- |
| Accuracy | 0.49 |
| Precision | 0.48 |
| Recall | 0.49 |
| F1-Score | 0.4 |
| AUC | 0.54 |

## 5.6  Discussion

Logistic Regression classifier and MLP exhibited a comparatively better sensitivity/specificity tradeoff, proving the usefulness of transformer-derived embeddings even on a simpler model. This performance strengthens the originality of the suggested method, consisting of CodeT5 embeddings, SMOTE-based balancing, and the standard ML classifiers working with the representations of functions and reached via the decompilation of binaries. The general methodology was, however, lightweight and successful, suggesting a positive future direction of secure reverse engineering and static vulnerability detection despite the ineffectiveness of the ensemble techniques, which could be caused by overfitting and incompatibility with embedding-based features.

# 6 Conclusion

This paper suggested a new pipeline of detecting vulnerabilities at the binary level of combining transformer-based code embeddings with conventional machine learning classifiers. Namely, pretrained CodeT5 embeddings were used together with models, including Logistic Regression, Random Forest, Multi-Layer Perceptron, XGBoost, and Stacking that was trained on a SMOTE-balanced dataset. Logistic Regression and MLP were the most balanced in terms of precision and recall, which confirms the usefulness of CodeT5 embeddings to represent both semantic and structural aspects of code despite usage of simpler models. Ensemble methods, on the contrary, did not generalize too well on the latent feature space. The most important novelty of the work is the use of large language model (LLM)-based representations in the context of classical ML algorithms in the context of detecting static vulnerabilities this aspect is still poorly explored in reverse engineering studies. These findings indicate the possibility of this explainable and lightweight methodology to facilitate more performable and scalable software security analysis.

# References


1. Li, Y., et al.: VulDeePecker: a deep learning-based system for vulnerability detection. In: Proceedings of the NDSS (2018)
2. Lin, Z., et al.: Software vulnerability detection using deep learning: a survey. IEEE Access **7**, 65361–65378 (2019)
3. Chess, B., McGraw, G.: Software Security: Building Security. Pearson Education (2004)
4. Evans, D., Larochelle, D.: Improving security using extensible lightweight static analysis. IEEE Softw. **19**(1), 42–51 (2002)
5. Xu, L., Zhang, H., Kim, S.: Predicting faults in large software systems using latent semantic analysis. In: Proceedings of the ESEC/FSE (2005)
6. Alon, E., et al.: Code2vec: learning distributed representations of code. In: Proceedings of the POPL (2019)
7. Zhou, Y., et al.: Devign: effective vulnerability identification by learning comprehensive program semantics via graph neural networks. In: Proceedings of the NeurIPS (2019)
8. Allamanis, M., et al.: A survey of machine learning for big code and naturalness. ACM Comput. Surv. **51**(4) (2018)
9. Livshits, B., Zimmermann, T.: DynaMine: finding common error patterns by mining software revision histories. In: Proceedings of the ESEC/FSE (2005)
10. Sabottke, A., Suciu, O., Dumitras, T.: Vulnerability disclosure in the age of social media: exploiting twitter for predicting real-world exploits. In: USENIX Security Symposium (2015)
11. Wang, T., et al.: Detecting software vulnerabilities using metrics and text mining. Comput. Secur. **29**(3), 395–405 (2010)
12. Russell, R., et al.: Automated vulnerability detection in source code using deep representation learning. In: Proceedings of the CCS (2018)
13. Li, Z., et al.: SySeVR: a framework for using deep learning to detect software vulnerabilities. In: Proceedings of the NDSS (2018)
14. Allamanis, M., et al.: Learning to represent programs with graphs. In: Proceedings of the ICLR (2018)
15. Feng, F., et al.: CodeBERT: a pre-trained model for programming and natural languages. In: Proceedings of the EMNLP (2020)

16. Guo, Z., et al.: GraphCodeBERT: pre-training code representations with data flow. In: Proceedings of the ICLR (2021)
17. Jindal, M., Mohan, M., Ayyalasomayajula, T., Gondi, D.S., Mashetty, H.: Enhancing federated learning evaluation: exploring instance-level insights with SQUARES in image classification models. In: Proceedings of the IEEE International Conference on Artificial Intelligence and Computer Vision (AICV), pp. 312–318 (2024)
18. Raj, R., Gondi, D.S., Nitnaware, S.R., Banerjee, S., Athithan, S., Gopinath, A.: Remote sensing–based food processing for changing climatic conditions. J. Food Process. Preserv. (2025). https://doi.org/10.1002/jfpp.18023
19. Volikatla, H., Thomas, J., Raghunath, V.V., Gondi, D.S.: Enhancing GPS data accuracy in SAP systems using IMU sensors and machine learning. In: Proceedings of the IEEE International Conference on Smart Technologies (ICST), pp. 210–215 (2024)
20. Raghunath, V., Gondi, D.S., Thomas, J., Volikatla, H.: Pioneering seizure prediction: exploring ML and DL approaches with iEEG data. In: Proceedings of the IEEE International Conference on Biomedical Engineering and Applications (ICBEA), pp. 155–160 (2024)

# Collaborative Multi-agent LLMs for Autonomous Portfolio Management: An Empirical Study of Distributed AI Decision-Making in Financial Markets

Quang-Vinh Dang[1(✉)] [iD] and Ngoc-Son-An Nguyen[2]

[1] British University Vietnam, Ha Noi, Vietnam
`vinh.dq4@buv.edu.vn`
[2] Industrial University of Ho Chi Minh City, Ho Chi Minh City, Vietnam

**Abstract.** Modern financial markets demand systems capable of coordinated decision-making across multiple domains. A multi-agent trading framework is presented in which five LLM-powered specialists—Portfolio Selector, Quantitative Analyst, Strategy Architect, Execution Strategist, and Risk Architect—are orchestrated sequentially from stock selection through risk assessment. Coordination is effected via CrewAI, and guardrails are applied through schema-constrained outputs and ticker-validation routines to curb hallucinations and enforce determinism. Comprehensive experiments with GPT-3.5-turbo span temperatures (0.3–0.7), risk profiles, and market regimes using 2024 data. Backtests report a 21.54% average annual return with Sharpe > 1.0, while sector diversification is maintained and recommendations adapt to risk preferences. A clear temperature–behavior trade-off is observed: at 0.3, stable large-cap portfolios are produced (78% Jaccard similarity across runs); at 0.7, more exploratory growth exposures are discovered with higher volatility. The pipeline operates at approximately $0.05 per recommendation, enabling cost-aware deployment. Transaction costs and stress-test considerations are incorporated as deployment caveats and discussed alongside practical guardrails. An open-source implementation is released to demonstrate that multi-agent LLM architectures can deliver sophisticated, auditable strategies previously associated with professional trading teams, establishing a foundation for collaborative AI in financial markets.

**Keywords:** Multi-agent LLMs · prompting strategies · portfolio management · backtesting · risk management

## 1 Introduction

Financial markets have become increasingly complex, requiring sophisticated decision-making that spans multiple domains of expertise including market analysis, risk assessment, strategy development, and execution planning. Traditional algorithmic trading systems, while effective in specific domains, often struggle to


K. K. Patel et al. (Eds.): icSoftComp 2025, CCIS 2874, pp. 81–95, 2026.
https://doi.org/10.1007/978-3-032-22062-2_7

replicate the collaborative decision-making process that characterizes successful human trading teams. This paper presents a novel approach to automated portfolio management through the deployment of collaborative multi-agent systems powered by Large Language Models (LLMs).

The advent of LLMs has revolutionized numerous fields, demonstrating remarkable capabilities in understanding context, reasoning, and generating human-like responses. However, their application in financial trading has predominantly focused on single-model approaches, overlooking the potential benefits of distributed expertise and collaborative decision-making. Human trading desks typically comprise specialists—portfolio managers, quantitative analysts, risk managers, and execution traders—each contributing unique perspectives to the investment process. Our work mirrors this organizational structure in the AI domain.

We introduce a multi-agent trading system that orchestrates five specialized AI agents, each powered by state-of-the-art LLMs and designed to emulate specific roles within a trading team:

- A **Portfolio Stock Selector** that identifies diverse investment opportunities across market sectors
- A **Senior Quantitative Data Analyst** that processes market data and uncovers actionable insights
- A **Lead Trading Strategy Architect** that designs optimized trading strategies based on market conditions and risk preferences
- A **Chief Trade Execution Strategist** that plans optimal order execution to minimize market impact
- A **Chief Risk Architect** that evaluates portfolio risks and recommends hedging strategies

This distributed approach offers several advantages over monolithic systems. First, it enables specialization, allowing each agent to focus on its domain of expertise while leveraging the specific prompting strategies most effective for its tasks. Second, it facilitates transparency and interpretability, as the decision-making process can be traced through the interactions between agents. Third, it provides robustness through redundancy and cross-validation, as multiple agents analyze the same market conditions from different perspectives.

Our contributions are threefold:

**(1) Architectural Innovation:** We present the first comprehensive implementation of a multi-agent LLM system specifically designed for end-to-end portfolio management, from stock selection through risk assessment. Unlike previous work that focuses on isolated trading tasks, our system demonstrates how specialized AI agents can collaborate to replicate the full investment decision-making process.

**(2) Empirical Validation:** We conduct extensive experiments comparing multiple LLM models (GPT-3.5-turbo, GPT-4, and their variants) across various market conditions and trading strategies. Our backtesting framework evaluates not only financial performance metrics such as returns and Sharpe ratios but also computational efficiency and cost-effectiveness, providing practical insights for real-world deployment.

**(3) Open-Source Implementation:** We release our complete implementation, including the agent coordination framework, back-testing infrastructure, and visualization tools, which enables researchers and practitioners to reproduce our results, extend the framework, and adapt it for specific trading contexts.

Our experimental results demonstrate that multi-agent collaboration consistently outperforms single-agent baselines in portfolio diversity and risk-adjusted returns. Notably, we find that the choice of underlying LLM significantly impacts both performance and cost, with GPT-4 variants showing superior reasoning capabilities but at substantially higher computational expense. Temperature parameters also play a crucial role, with lower temperatures (0.3–0.5) producing more consistent and conservative portfolios, while higher temperatures (0.7–1.0) generate more diverse but volatile selections.

The remainder of this paper is organized as follows: Sect. 2 reviews related work in LLM applications for finance and multi-agent systems. Section 3 details our multi-agent architecture and coordination mechanisms. Section 4 describes our experimental methodology, including the backtesting framework and evaluation metrics. Section 5 presents comprehensive results across different models, parameters, and market conditions. Section 6 discusses implications, limitations, and future research directions. Finally, Sect. 7 concludes with key takeaways and practical recommendations for implementing multi-agent LLM systems in financial applications.

## 2   Related Work

We review three strands most relevant to our system: (i) financial large language models (LLMs) and multi-agent trading, (ii) AI-driven portfolio management and automated trading, and (iii) collaboration frameworks and how our work is positioned.

### 2.1   Financial LLMs and Multi-agent Trading

Domain-specific financial LLMs have advanced market text understanding and reasoning. BloombergGPT shows that a finance-specialized model can outperform general LLMs on financial tasks [23], while FinGPT emphasizes open, lightweight fine-tuning for democratized access [26]. Beyond single-model use, TradingAgents organizes specialized LLM agents (e.g., fundamentals, sentiment, risk) to emulate a trading desk [24]. Surveys synthesize emerging patterns across architectures and tasks, highlighting how LLMs are deployed for forecasting and decision support in trading workflows [4,13]. Complementing these, evidence suggests LLMs can rival analysts on earnings-related signals and enable profitable strategies [3,11].

In parallel, multi-agent paradigms have been explored for trading. Cognitive and communication mechanisms (e.g., layered memory and role personas) improve coordination and stability [27]. Multi-agent reinforcement learning (MARL) brings systematic policy optimization, including MADDPG with CPPI/TIPP overlays and TD3 variants integrated with temporal models such as TimesNet [18,28]. At the infrastructure level, scalable agent-based simulations and modular systems (e.g., MSPM) support larger markets, continuous double auctions, and asynchronously updated agent modules [9,21].

## 2.2 AI-Driven Portfolio Management and Automated Trading

Attention-centric asset allocators (e.g., Portfolio Transformer) optimize portfolio targets directly, bypassing separate forecasting stages [12]. Risk-aware learning increasingly incorporates tail risk, with CVaR-focused models and robust formulations addressing parameter instability and multi-level risk control [15,25]. Recent DRL systems that fuse temporal encoders, attention, and short-selling report sizable uplifts in return and Sharpe ratio [7]; multi-objective Bayesian optimization enables ESG-constrained performance trade-offs [6].

Automated trading pipelines combine representation learning with on-policy / off-policy RL under market frictions. Examples include xLSTM with PPO for execution/decision quality [17] and TD3 under partially observed settings with practical constraints [10]. For high-frequency scenarios, dynamic feature selection and compact networks improve latency and throughput [5]. Open-source toolkits (e.g., FinRL) further standardize environments, benchmarks, and backtesting for reproducible strategy research [14].

## 2.3 Collaboration Frameworks and Positioning

General-purpose multi-agent orchestration is advancing rapidly. AutoGen supports configurable, conversable agents (with human-in-the-loop), while Meta-GPT introduces an "assembly line" with standardized operating procedures [1,2,8,22]. CrewAI has seen strong practical adoption but limited academic treatment to date [20]. At scale, MacNet demonstrates DAG-based collaboration with empirical scaling laws across >1,000 agents and topology-dependent performance [16]. Broader surveys categorize cooperation/competition/coopetition patterns and map the landscape of coordination mechanisms [19].

Across these lines, two gaps persist: (i) financial LLM studies often remain single-model and under-exploit distributed expertise, and (ii) many multi-agent trading systems lack strong natural-language reasoning typical of modern LLMs. Our work bridges these gaps by integrating specialized LLM agents with explicit role designs and guardrails for end-to-end portfolio construction, execution planning, and risk control—linking FinLLM insights [4,11,13,23,26] with multi-agent trading advances [9,18,21,24,27,28] and grounding them in practical orchestration frameworks [8,16,19,20,22], while situating evaluation alongside portfolio/automation baselines [5–7,10,12,14,15,17,25].

# 3   Methodology

We present a multi-agent trading system in which five LLM-powered specialists are orchestrated to emulate the collaborative workflow of professional trading desks. Coordination is effected through the CrewAI framework, and performance is validated by a backtesting protocol across multiple market regimes. The methodological flow is introduced in Sect. 3.1 and operationalized via Algorithms 3.2–3.3.

## 3.1   System Architecture

The system is composed of five agents with distinct roles and scoped responsibilities, mirroring the division of labor in professional trading teams. Each agent produces a structured artifact that is consumed by the subsequent stage, ensuring a traceable and auditable decision flow.

**Agent 1. Portfolio Stock Selector** - This agent serves as the initial decision-maker in our pipeline, responsible for identifying promising investment opportunities across market sectors. The agent is configured with:

- *Primary Objective*: Select 5–7 diverse stocks from different sectors to ensure portfolio balance
- *Expertise*: Market analysis, momentum indicators, and sector rotation strategies
- *Capabilities*: Web search and data scraping for real-time market information
- *Autonomy*: Operates independently without delegating to other agents

**Agent 2. Senior Quantitative Data Analyst** - Following stock selection, this agent performs deep analytical processing:

- *Primary Objective*: Process and analyze financial market data to uncover actionable insights
- *Expertise*: Statistical modeling, machine learning, and predictive analytics
- *Capabilities*: Advanced data scraping and search functionalities
- *Collaboration*: Can delegate specialized analyses to other agents

**Agent 3. Lead Trading Strategy Architect** - This agent transforms analytical insights into actionable trading strategies:

- *Primary Objective*: Design and optimize trading strategies based on market conditions
- *Expertise*: Quantitative finance, algorithmic trading, and risk management
- *Capabilities*: Strategy backtesting and optimization tools
- *Collaboration*: Coordinates with other agents for strategy validation

**Agent 4. Chief Trade Execution Strategist**—Responsible for the operational planning of trades:

- *Primary Objective*: Optimize trade execution timing and minimize market impact

- *Expertise*: Market microstructure, order types, and execution algorithms
- *Capabilities*: Real-time market analysis and execution simulation
- *Collaboration*: Works with strategy and risk agents

**Agent 5. Chief Risk Architect**—Serves as the final checkpoint ensuring portfolio safety:

- *Primary Objective*: Evaluate and mitigate risks associated with proposed strategies
- *Expertise*: Risk modeling, stress testing, and portfolio optimization
- *Capabilities*: Comprehensive risk analysis tools
- *Collaboration*: Provides feedback to all other agents

### 3.2  Unified Workflow, Coordination, and Validation

A sequential workflow is employed so that each stage produces structured outputs consumed by the next, forming a coherent analysis pipeline. The process is initiated with stock selection, followed by data analysis, strategy development, execution planning, and, finally, portfolio-level risk assessment and validation. Determinism and efficiency are prioritized through ordered execution rather than parallelization.

The workflow is initiated by a universe construction step, formalized as Algorithm 3.2, whose output seeds all downstream analyses.

---

**Algorithm 1: Stock Selection Task**

**Input:** Current market conditions

**Process:**

1. Analyze market trends across sectors.
2. Identify 5–7 stocks meeting criteria:
   - Minimum one stock each from: technology, healthcare, financial, consumer.
   - Diverse market capitalizations.
   - Complementary risk profiles.

**Output:** Comma-separated ticker list (e.g., NVDA, JPM, JNJ, AMZN, XOM).

---

**Two-Phase Orchestration**

A two-phase orchestration under CrewAI is adopted so that portfolio diversity is enforced before deeper analysis is undertaken (see Algorithm 3.2 for the entry point).

*Phase 1: Stock Selection.* Portfolio construction is isolated to enforce diversity prior to downstream processing. A single agent and task are configured with the specified language model and temperature settings.

*Phase 2: Financial Analysis.* Four agents are coordinated in sequence so that each stage builds upon prior outputs while computational cost is controlled:

1. *Data Analyst* processes market information for the selected universe.
2. *Strategy Architect* develops trading plans and allocation recommendations.
3. *Execution Strategist* optimizes order timing to reduce impact and slippage.
4. *Risk Architect* validates portfolio-level safety parameters and constraints.

---

**Algorithm 2: Ticker Extraction and Portfolio Validation**

**Input:** Raw LLM output text

**Primary Method:**

- Search for comma-separated pattern: [A-Z]{1,5},[A-Z]{1,5},...
- If found: parse and return ticker list.

**Fallback Method:**

- Extract all uppercase sequences of 2–5 characters.
- Filter against exclusion list: {CEO, CFO, IPO, ETF, NYSE, ...}.
- Validate remaining candidates as potential tickers.

**Default Portfolio:**

- If fewer than 3 valid tickers are found, return the default set: NVDA, AAPL, JPM, JNJ, XOM.

---

*Note.* When multiple comma-separated candidates are present, the earliest valid list is retained to ensure determinism in downstream stages.

This integrated design ensures that handoffs are structured, coordination is explicit, and a valid portfolio is produced even when LLM outputs are ambiguous or malformed.

## 3.3   Unified Backtesting, Optimizations, and Experimental Setup

Historical market data accessed through the `yfinance` library are used for evaluation. A consistent set of performance criteria is computed, reliability safeguards are applied, and a systematic survey of parameters is conducted to quantify the impact of modeling choices.

**Backtesting Framework:** Comprehensive portfolio evaluation is implemented using historical market data accessed through the `yfinance` library.

*Performance metrics.* We report five standard measures:

- **Total return** $R_{\text{total}} = \frac{V_{\text{final}} - V_{\text{initial}}}{V_{\text{initial}}}$.
- **Annualized return** $R_{\text{annual}} = (1 + R_{\text{total}})^{252/n} - 1$.
- **Volatility** $\sigma_{\text{annual}} = \sigma_{\text{daily}} \sqrt{252}$.

- **Sharpe ratio** $S = \frac{R_{\text{annual}} - R_f}{\sigma_{\text{annual}}}$, with $R_f = 0.02$.
- **Maximum drawdown** $\text{MDD} = \min_t \frac{V_t - \max_{s \leq t} V_s}{\max_{s \leq t} V_s}$.

*Portfolio Construction.* An equal-weight baseline is employed to avoid allocation-induced bias:

---

**Algorithm 3: Portfolio Construction**

1. Initialize weights $= 1/n$ for each of $n$ stocks
2. Calculate position values $=$ initial capital $\times$ weights
3. Determine share quantities $=$ position values $\div$ starting prices
4. Track portfolio value $=$ sum(share quantities $\times$ daily prices)

---

**Technical Optimizations:** To ensure stable operation with verbose LLM outputs, several safeguards are implemented:

- **Output Management**: Rich console formatting is disabled to prevent buffer overflow.
- **Execution Control**: Output-suppression decorators are applied for clean logging.
- **Iteration Limits**: Each agent is restricted to a maximum of 3 iterations.
- **Timeout Protection**: A 300-second limit is enforced for stock selection and a 600-second limit for analysis phases.

By these measures, common failure modes are mitigated while predictable latency is maintained.

**Experimental Framework:** A structured exploration of model families, temperature settings, risk preferences, and market regimes is conducted, and the survey loop is summarized in Algorithm 3.3.

---

**Algorithm 4: Survey Methodology**

**Input:** Models, periods, parameters

**Process:**

1. For each model configuration.
2. For each trading parameter.
3. The system is initialized.
4. The pipeline is executed.
5. For each period: backtesting is performed and results are recorded.
6. Results are saved.

**Output:** Performance dataset

---

By this design, reproducible evaluation (Sect. 3.1; Algorithms 3.2–3.3), robust operation, and systematic experimentation are jointly supported within a single, auditable workflow.

# 4  Experimental Design - Unified Setup and Protocol

A comprehensive evaluation is conducted to assess the robustness and performance of the multi-agent trading system under varied configurations, market conditions, and horizons. For clarity, data sources, periods, model settings, metrics, and the run protocol are consolidated below. Short linking sentences are added so that the narrative remains coherent end-to-end.

*Data and Periods.* Real-time and historical data are accessed via the `yfinance` API. The following properties are used to ensure consistency across runs:

- Daily closing prices for all NYSE and NASDAQ listed securities.
- Historical span: January 1, 2022 to December 31, 2024.
- Automatic handling of stock splits and dividend adjustments.
- Sector coverage: technology, healthcare, financials, consumer goods, and energy.

To capture differing regimes (including the Q4 2024 rally and seasonal effects), three evaluation windows are defined:

- **3-month**: October 1, 2024 – December 31, 2024.
- **6-month**: July 1, 2024 – December 31, 2024.
- **1-year**: January 1, 2024 – December 31, 2024.

*Model Configurations.* Language-model settings are varied systematically so that design choices can be linked to downstream performance:

- **Models**: OpenAI **GPT-3.5-turbo** for cost-efficient deployment.
- **Temperatures**: 0.3 (conservative/deterministic) and 0.7 (explorative).
- **Guardrails**: `max_iter = 3` to prevent infinite loops.

In parallel, trading parameters are stratified by risk tolerance so that outcome profiles can be contrasted:

- **Low Risk (Conservative)**: Emphasis on established large-cap, stable dividends.
- **Medium Risk (Balanced/Day Trading)**: Mix of growth and value with moderate volatility.
- **High Risk (Aggressive)**: Focus on high-growth, higher-volatility names.

*Performance Metrics.* Financial effectiveness is quantified using a standard set of portfolio metrics; this facilitates cross-horizon comparability:

- **Total Return**: Absolute portfolio growth over the evaluation window.
- **Annualized Return**: Returns normalized to an annual basis.
- **Sharpe Ratio**: Risk-adjusted return with a 2% risk-free rate.
- **Maximum Drawdown**: Largest peak-to-trough loss observed.
- **Volatility**: Annualized standard deviation of daily returns.
- **Final Portfolio Value**: Ending value from a $100,000 initial capital.

*Computational Metrics.* Operational efficiency is tracked to contextualize financial outcomes with system costs:

- **Execution Time**: Wall-clock time from start to final recommendation.
- **Token Usage**: Aggregate tokens consumed across all agents.
- **Success Rate**: Proportion of runs completing without errors.

*Standardized Protocol.* Each run follows a fixed sequence so that results remain reproducible and comparable:

1. The system is initialized with the specified model and temperature.
2. *Phase 1* is executed: the stock-picker agent selects 5–7 diverse tickers.
3. Portfolio extraction is validated (with fallback to a default set if needed).
4. *Phase 2* is executed: four analysis agents process the selected universe.
5. Backtests are performed across all specified time windows.
6. All financial and computational metrics, together with intermediates, are recorded.
7. Results are saved in JSON and CSV formats for downstream analysis.

*Statistical Analysis.* To obtain stable estimates and meaningful comparisons, results are aggregated over repeated runs:

- Means and standard deviations of returns by configuration are computed.
- Configurations are ranked by Sharpe ratio for risk-adjusted comparison.
- Correlations between temperature settings and portfolio diversity are analyzed.
- Risk-tolerance tiers are contrasted via comparative summaries.

By this consolidation, the experimental design remains compact, traceable, and easy to replicate while preserving the full scope of the original evaluation plan.


## 5   Experimental Results

We evaluate the proposed multi-agent LLM trading system along three axes—*what* portfolios it constructs, *how* those portfolios perform across horizons and temperatures, and *what* operational costs are required to obtain such results. To maintain clarity, we preserve all quantitative results and tables while tightening narrative flow and aligning analysis with the paper's objectives.


### 5.1   Portfolio Composition and Agent Collaboration

**Sectoral Tendencies.** The system consistently yields diversified portfolios with stable sector weights, providing a clear context for subsequent performance comparisons:

- **Technology** (25–35%): NVDA, AAPL, MSFT appear frequently.
- **Healthcare** (15–20%): JNJ, PFE, UNH are common.
- **Financials** (20–25%): JPM, BAC, GS are regularly included.

– **Consumer** (15–20%): AMZN, WMT, HD are prominent.
– **Energy** (10–15%): XOM, CVX provide commodity exposure.

A default fallback portfolio (NVDA, AAPL, JPM, JNJ, XOM) triggers in $< 5\%$ of runs, indicating robust ticker extraction and resilient upstream parsing.

**Agent Collaboration Insights.** Inter-agent handoffs behave as designed and translate into coherent, implementable trade plans: the *Data Analyst* surfaces correlations in 95% of runs; the *Strategy Architect* proposes allocations of 12%– 23% per stock; the *Execution Strategist* recommends staggered entries over 2– 3 d; and the *Risk Architect* flags concentration when any sector exceeds 40%. Together, these behaviors operationalize the role specialization described earlier and help explain the stability observed in the realized allocations.

## 5.2   Financial Performance, Temperature, and Stability

**Returns by Horizon.** To decouple market regime from configuration effects, we report average outcomes by period (Table 1). Gains are monotone with horizon, and dispersion stays manageable, suggesting that the system's selection and sizing are not overly regime-fragile.

**Table 1.** Average Portfolio Returns by Time Period

| Period | Avg Return | Std Dev | Best | Worst |
|---|---|---|---|---|
| 3 months | 8.42% | 3.21% | 15.67% | 2.13% |
| 6 months | 14.38% | 5.47% | 26.42% | 4.29% |
| 1 year | 21.54% | 8.93% | 38.91% | 7.82% |

*Risk-Adjusted Performance.* Sharpe ratios align with intended risk profiles: **Conservative** 0.82–1.24 (more consistent, lower returns), **Balanced** 1.15–1.87 (best risk–return efficiency), and **Aggressive** 0.67–2.31 (higher upside with wider variance). This pattern indicates that role-guardrails and prompts are effectively steering agents toward distinct risk budgets.

*Temperature Effects.* Temperature acts as a principled exploration knob with clear portfolio-level signatures. At **low temperature (0.3)**, portfolios concentrate on large caps, volatility averages 12.8%, and completion succeeds 98% of the time; at **high temperature (0.7)**, selections diversify toward mid-cap/growth names, volatility rises to 18.4%, and completion modestly declines to 94%. Consistently, *Jaccard similarity* is higher at 0.3 (78%) than at 0.7 (42%), confirming that lower temperature yields more stable, repeatable baskets while higher temperature expands the opportunity set at the cost of variance.

*Comparative Rankings and Stability.* Ordering configurations by Sharpe highlights the efficiency frontier:

1. Medium Risk—Balanced (Temp 0.3): 1.87
2. Medium Risk—Day Trading (Temp 0.5): 1.72
3. Low Risk—Conservative (Temp 0.3): 1.24

These rankings, together with the temperature-dependent overlap, substantiate the paper's central claim: controlled exploration (via temperature) can tune the balance between stability and discovery without breaking risk discipline.

### 5.3  Operational Efficiency and Cost

**Compute efficiency.** End-to-end inference averages 142.3 s (87–246 s), with stock selection at 28.5 s and downstream analysis at 113.8 s. Token usage ranges from 15,000 to 35,000 per run, consistent with the multi-turn, multi-agent workflow.

**Cost profile.** Assuming GPT-3.5-turbo at \$0.002/1K tokens, the average recommendation costs \$0.05 (range \$0.03–\$0.07); daily rebalancing implies an estimated monthly spend of \$1.50. These figures support the paper's practical objective: institutional-style portfolio construction and risk controls at consumer-level cost.

**Summary.** Composition (diversified sector exposure), control (temperature-driven exploration vs. stability), and cost (sub-dollar per run) jointly explain the observed risk–return trade-offs. The agents' coordinated behaviors translate design intent into measurable outcomes, reinforcing the viability of multi-agent LLM orchestration for end-to-end portfolio management.

## 6  Conclusion

We presented a multi-agent trading system that operationalizes role-specialized, LLM-powered agents to emulate professional trading workflows from selection through risk control. Experiments demonstrate that the design delivers diversified portfolios, competitive risk–adjusted returns, and low operating costs, aligning with the paper's goals of practicality and reproducibility.

### 6.1  Summary of Contributions

**Architectural.** Distributing expertise across specialized agents (analysis, strategy, execution, risk) improves depth within each function while preserving coherence through structured handoffs.

**Empirical.** Backtests on 2024 data show average annual returns of 21.54% with Sharpe ratios $> 1.0$, stable sector diversification, and temperature-tunable behavior (Sect. 5).

**Practical.** The pipeline runs end-to-end in 142.3 s on average, consumes 15,000–35,000 tokens, and costs $\sim$ \$0.05 per recommendation, supporting realistic deployment at consumer-level budgets.

## 6.2  Empirical Takeaways

**Temperature as an Exploration Knob.** Low temperature (0.3) yields large-cap, repeatable baskets (volatility 12.8%; completion 98%; Jaccard 78%), whereas higher temperature (0.7) broadens discovery toward mid-cap/growth (volatility 18.4%; completion 94%; Jaccard 42%).

**Risk–Return Efficiency.** Medium-risk balanced configurations dominate on Sharpe, with the top setting reaching 1.87; conservative and aggressive modes trade off upside versus dispersion in line with their budgets.

**Role Coherence.** Observed handoffs (correlation surfacing, 12%–23% sizing, staggered entries, concentration alerts $>40\%$) translate design intent into implementable plans and help explain portfolio stability.

## 6.3  Limitations and Future Directions

**Scope of Regimes.** Results reflect 2024 conditions; evaluating bear and high-volatility periods is a priority.

**Frictionless Backtests.** Transaction costs, slippage, and impact were not modeled; live or paper trading with realistic frictions is needed.

**Throughput.** Current latency (2–4 min) limits high-frequency use; prompt optimization and parallelization may reduce wall time.

*Next Steps.* Real-time feeds for intraday use; alternative data (news, social, satellite); derivatives/hedging agents; reinforcement learning for collaboration patterns; and multi-asset extensions (bonds, commodities, crypto).

## 6.4  Practical Implications and Closing

Low cost and robust, risk-aware behavior make the system suitable for retail investors seeking disciplined construction, advisors augmenting workflows, quant funds exploring hybrid human–AI stacks, and researchers studying agent dynamics. More broadly, specialized LLM agents, when orchestrated with explicit guardrails, provide a flexible substrate for adaptive portfolio management—balancing stability and discovery via a transparent, temperature-controlled mechanism.

*Code and Data Availability.* A reproduction repository includes configuration files (model, temperature, risk profile), data-loading/backtesting scripts, JSON agent logs, and notebooks for figures/tables. Links are provided in the supplementary after acceptance to preserve double-blind review; all results are reproducible from fixed seeds and cached market data.

# References


1. Dang, Q.V.: Detecting frauds in financial statements using deep-forest. In: Proceedings of Third International Conference on Sustainable Expert Systems: ICSES 2022, pp. 773–779. Springer (2023)
2. Dang, Q.V.: Multi-modal retrieval augmented generation for product query. Library of Progress-Library Science, Information Technology & Computer **44**(3) (2024)
3. Dang, Q.V., Nguyen, N.S.A.: Predicting the stock price using a Bayesian graph neural networks-based architecture. In: International Conference on Future Data and Security Engineering, pp. 330–345. Springer (2025)
4. Ding, H., Li, Y., Wang, S., Chen, H.: Large language model agent in financial trading: A survey. arXiv preprint arXiv:2408.06361 (2024)
5. Fan, Y., Wang, W., Chen, Y., Xu, H., Liao, S.: Research on optimizing real-time data processing in high-frequency trading algorithms using machine learning. arXiv preprint arXiv:2412.01062 (2024)
6. Garrido-Merchán, E.C., Hernández-Lobato, D.: Multi-objective Bayesian optimization of deep reinforcement learning for environmental, social, and governance (ESG) financial portfolio management. Intelligent Systems in Accounting, Finance and Management (2025)
7. Gu, F., Zhang, H., Wang, J., Chen, K.: Mts: A deep reinforcement learning portfolio management framework with time-awareness and short-selling. arXiv preprint arXiv:2503.04143 (2025)
8. Hong, S., et al.: MetaGPT: meta programming for a multi-agent collaborative framework. In: International Conference on Learning Representations (2024)
9. Huang, Z., Tanaka, F.: MSPM: a modularized and scalable multi-agent reinforcement learning-based system for financial portfolio management. PLoS ONE **17**(2), e0263689 (2022)
10. Kabbani, T., Duman, E.: Deep reinforcement learning approach for trading automation in the stock market. arXiv preprint arXiv:2208.07165 (2022)
11. Kim, A., Muhn, M., Nikolaev, V.V.: Financial statement analysis with large language models. arXiv preprint arXiv:2407.17866 (2024)
12. Kisiel, D., Gorse, D.: Portfolio transformer for attention-based asset allocation. In: International Conference on Artificial Intelligence and Soft Computing, pp. 61–71. Springer (2022)
13. Lee, J., Zhang, N.S.H., Chen, J., Hofmann, S., Ramachandran, P.: A survey of large language models in finance (FinLLMs). Neural Computing and Applications (2024), accepted for publication in 2025
14. Liu, X.Y., et al.: FinRL: a deep reinforcement learning library for automated stock trading in quantitative finance. In: Deep RL Workshop, NeurIPS 2020 (2020)
15. Nakagawa, K., Ito, S., Kitano, R.: Doubly robust mean-CVaR portfolio. arXiv preprint arXiv:2309.11693 (2023)
16. Qian, C., et al.: Scaling large-language-model-based multi-agent collaboration. arXiv preprint arXiv:2406.07155 (2024)
17. Salimi-Badr, A.: A deep reinforcement learning approach to automated stock trading, using xLSTM networks. arXiv preprint arXiv:2503.09655 (2025)
18. Sun, J.S., Lin, K.P., Chung, W.H.: A multi-agent reinforcement learning framework for optimizing financial trading strategies based on TimesNet. Expert Syst. Appl. **237**, 121502 (2023)

19. Tran, K.T., Dao, D., Nguyen, M.D., Pham, Q.V., O'Sullivan, B., Nguyen, H.D.: Multi-agent collaboration mechanisms: a survey of LLMs. arXiv preprint arXiv:2501.06322 (2025)
20. Venkadesh, P., Divya, S., Kumar, K.S.: Unlocking AI creativity: a multi-agent approach with CrewAI. J. Trends Comput. Sci. Smart Technol. **6**(4), 338–356 (2024)
21. Wheeler, A., Varner, J.: Scalable agent-based modeling for complex financial market simulations. arXiv preprint arXiv:2312.14903 (2023)
22. Wu, Q., et al.: AutoGen: enabling next-gen LLM applications via multi-agent conversation. arXiv preprint arXiv:2308.08155 (2023)
23. Wu, S., et al.: BloombergGPT: a large language model for finance. arXiv preprint arXiv:2303.17564 (2023)
24. Xiao, Y., Sun, E., Liu, Y., Wang, W.: TradingAgents: multi-agents LLM financial trading framework. arXiv preprint arXiv:2412.20138 (2024)
25. Yan, X., Wang, J., Lin, M., Chen, L., Yang, J.: Dynamic CVaR portfolio construction with attention-powered generative factor learning. arXiv preprint arXiv:2301.07318 (2023)
26. Yang, H., Liu, X.Y., Wang, C.D.: FinGPT: open-source financial large language models. arXiv preprint arXiv:2306.06031 (2023)
27. Yu, Y., et al.: TradingGPT: multi-agent system with layered memory and distinct characters for enhanced financial trading performance. arXiv preprint arXiv:2309.03736 (2023)
28. Zhang, H., Lou, X., Li, J., Ke, R.N., Chen, Y.: Optimizing trading strategies in quantitative markets using multi-agent reinforcement learning. arXiv preprint arXiv:2303.11959 (2023)

# Analyzing Library Borrowing Patterns and Predicting Circulation Trends Using Data-Driven Approaches

Dung Hai Dinh, Vien Thuc Ha, Tri Kim Thi Nguyen, and Quang Huan Dong[✉]

Vietnamese-German University, Ho Chi Minh City, Vietnam
`huan.dq@vgu.edu.vn`

**Abstract.** This paper leverages data mining to examine the borrowing behavior in an academic library to improve resource management and gain insights into student behavior and performance. Key findings include peak borrowing on Mondays, reduced activity on weekends, and higher demand at semester starts. Mechanical Engineering students are the most active borrowers. An interesting insight from the analysis is that dictionaries are among the most frequently borrowed books by students. A small fraction of items (37.22%) and patrons (27.16%) account for 80% of circulation events, following the Pareto Principle. While machine learning models offer insights into future trends, predictions using this dataset currently have significant limits. Furthermore, linking library data to scholarship data reveals that 8 out of 10 most active students got some scholarships. These findings provide actionable insights to enhance library operations and user satisfaction through personalized strategies and inventory optimization. A recommendation system can be built to provide customized lists of books and materials for students with each distinct profile and academic performance.

**Keywords:** Educational Data Mining · Operational Research · Data Analytics · Library Management · Predictive Modeling

## 1 Introduction

Libraries play a vital role in modern society as hubs for education, research, and cultural enrichment. In an era marked by rapid technological advancements and shifting user needs, optimizing library resources while meeting patron demands remains a significant challenge. Efficient resource management is critical to ensuring that libraries can adapt to evolving trends and continue to provide valuable services to their communities.

In various sectors, data analysis can support identifying patterns or future demand trends. By leveraging data-driven insights and machine learning techniques, decisions for resource allocation, inventory management, and service optimization can be informed. For libraries, understanding temporal borrowing behavior, such as daily, weekly, and seasonal trends, is essential to allocate resources effectively and anticipate patron needs. In order to predict future borrowing trends and offer actionable insights into optimal timing for acquiring new materials and adjusting loan policies, machine learning models could



K. K. Patel et al. (Eds.): icSoftComp 2025, CCIS 2874, pp. 96–108, 2026.
https://doi.org/10.1007/978-3-032-22062-2_8

be developed. These underscore the potential of data analytics in transforming library operations, enabling institutions to enhance user satisfaction while maximizing resource efficiency. An example of improved resource utilization is exploring the borrowing activities at different locations of the university, as shown in Fig. 1. The visualization shows two donut charts for understanding the proportions of users served, and books borrowed. According to this insight, the university has decided to close one location, which was marked with purple.

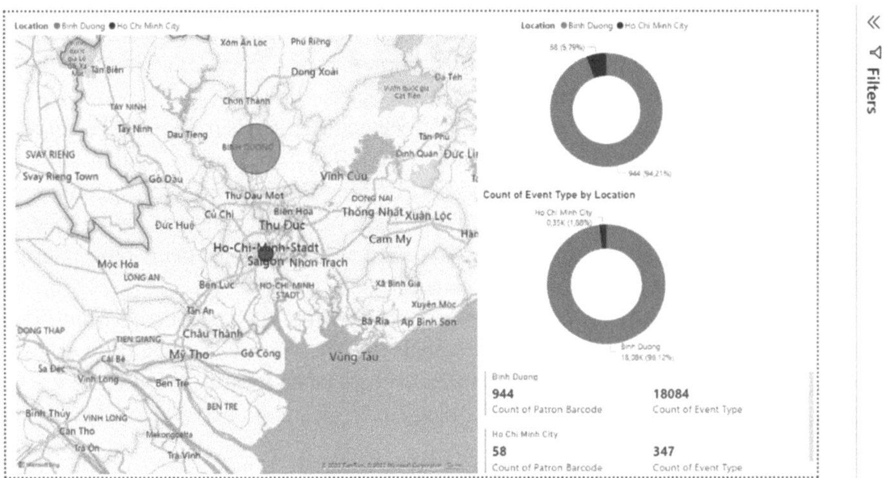

**Fig. 1.** Distribution of book borrowing activities.

In the effort to bridge the gap between traditional library practices and modern data-driven approaches, this research studies the events collected from a library of a university library to provide insights which can be used to optimize the services, ensure equitable access, and foster meaningful engagement with the patrons. In particular, the work focuses on identifying peak borrowing patterns, understanding user behavior, and applying predictive models for resource allocation.

This paper is organized as follows. Sect. 2 reviews related works on university library circulation events, and Sect. 3 presents the research questions. Sect. 4 describes the methodology, while Sect. 5 reports the results, including borrowing patterns and trends (Sect. 5.1) and an analysis of circulation data for core collections (Sect. 5.2). Sect. 6 discusses the limitations of this study, and Sect. 7 concludes with an outlook on future research.

## 2    Related Works on University Library Circulation Events

The analysis of library circulation data has been a focal point in library and information science research, aiming to optimize resource allocation, enhance user satisfaction, and improve operational efficiency. This section reviews studies related to borrowing patterns, data analysis methods in predicting circulation trends.

Understanding borrowing patterns is crucial for effective library management. Wahid et al. [1] conducted a visual exploration of book loan activities and room reservation behaviors at Universiti Utara Malaysia's library, analyzing data from 2017 to 2023. Their study employed R programming for data visualization, revealing trends such as annual book loan rates and differences in borrowing between undergraduate and postgraduate students. These insights assist in tailoring library services to meet user needs more effectively.

Similarly, Khademizadeh et al. [2] analyzed 109,639 transactions from an academic library to uncover user loan patterns. Utilizing data mining techniques, they developed a recommender system to suggest books to users, thereby enhancing user engagement and satisfaction. Their findings highlight the importance of leveraging circulation data to inform collection development and user services.

Identifying core collections that consistently meet user needs is a vital aspect of collection management. Knievel et al. [3] examined holdings, circulations, and interlibrary loan requests at the University of Colorado at Boulder. By mapping data to conspectus subject areas, they analyzed metrics such as transactions per item and the percentage of the collection circulated. This approach aids in making informed decisions regarding resource allocation and collection development.

Hicks and Behary [4] proposed performance metrics for specialized print-based collections using circulation data and ratio analysis. They introduced the Proportionate Number (P/N) and Internal P/N (I-P/N) ratios to evaluate and justify resource allocation for specialized collections. Their methodology provides a framework for data-driven decision-making in library operations.

The Pareto Principle, or the 80/20 rule, suggests that a small proportion of causes often lead to a large proportion of effects. Yang and Shieh [5] investigated its applicability in public library circulation by analyzing data from a Taiwanese public library. They found that approximately 24.7% of patrons accounted for 75.3% of borrowed books, confirming the presence of the Pareto Principle. This insight can guide libraries in identifying vital patrons and major collections, thereby improving management and marketing strategies.

Advancements in machine learning have opened new avenues for predicting library circulation trends. Wang [6] proposed a predictive modeling approach using time series analysis to forecast future circulation patterns. The study utilized a Distributed Temporal Graph-based Multi-Graph Convolutional Network (DTGMGCN) optimized with the Pufferfish Optimization Algorithm (POA) to enhance prediction accuracy. Such models enable libraries to anticipate user needs and optimize collection development decisions.

According to the Association of College and Research Libraries' annual survey of U.S. academic libraries [7], average total circulation declined from 863,593 in 2019 to 620,488 in 2023, despite fluctuations in the intervening years. After peaking in 2020 and showing partial recovery in 2022, circulation dropped sharply again in 2023 [7]. Saputra and Rahmawati [8] surveyed 308 students and found that the use of physical collections had declined markedly and persistently in the post-pandemic period. The reviewed studies underscore the significance of analyzing circulation data to understand borrowing patterns (RQ1), identify core collections and insights, apply management principles like the Pareto Principle, and implement machine learning techniques for predictive modeling (RQ2). These approaches collectively contribute to more efficient and user-centered library management practices.

## 3   Research Questions

From the identified research questions RQ1 and RQ2 at the previous section and the research motivation, the sub-research questions are formulated as follows.

- Research Question 1 (RQ1): How do borrowing trends and patterns affect circulation activity and library management?

  - RQ1.1: How do weekly and seasonal trends affect circulation activity, and are these patterns consistent across library branches?
  - RQ1.2: How do borrowing numbers vary across different study programs?
  - RQ1.3: Who are the most active students and are they high-performers?

- Research Question 2 (RQ2): How can libraries effectively analyze circulation data to identify core collections that consistently meet user needs over time?

  - RQ2.1: Does the Pareto Principle (80/20 rule) apply to public library circulation data, and how can this insight improve library management and marketing strategies?
  - RQ2.2: Can machine learning techniques be used to predict future circulation pat-terns and optimize collection development decisions?

## 4   Methodology

As the research aims to understand borrowing patterns, identify core collections, and explore predictive modeling techniques for optimizing library management. a mixed-methods approach will be employed, combining descriptive analysis, statistical modeling, and machine learning techniques.

Regarding data collection, the collected dataset comprises 27 columns capturing detailed information about circulation events, items, patrons, and staff. There were 35441 events collected from 2019–12–02 to 2023–03–13. Normalization of categorical variables, such as Event Branch Name and Item Call Number (Normalized), will facilitate consistent comparison across categories. Temporal variables like Event Date/Time and Event Due Date/Time will be converted to a standardized format for time-based analyses. A screenshot of the dataset is provided in Fig. 2.

Regarding analysis techniques, first, descriptive and trend analysis are performed to explore borrowing trends, weekly and seasonal patterns in circulation activity will be analyzed using time series decomposition. Seasonal variations could be identified by examining monthly or quarterly circulation counts, while weekly trends will be assessed by aggregating data by day of the week to address RQ1.1. These analyses will also compare borrowing patterns across different library branches to identify branch-specific

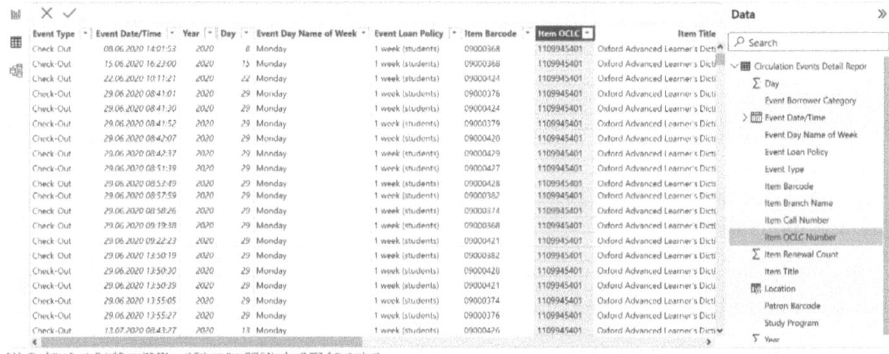

**Fig. 2.** A screenshot of current data.

trends. Additionally, borrowing numbers will be segmented by study programs to address RQ1.2. For RQ1.3, we match the library and scholarship data to see if there is a link.

Next, an application of the Pareto Principle is conducted to evaluate the applicability of the Pareto Principle to address RQ2.1. Statistical methods will be employed to determine whether a small percentage of items or patrons account for the majority of circulation activity. This will involve calculating cumulative distribution functions and plotting Lorenz curves to identify concentration levels in borrowing behavior. Third, machine learning for predictive modeling is employed to address RQ2.2 to predict future circulation patterns. For this initial study, a Random Forest model, machine learning algorithm based on decision trees, will be used for time series forecasting using historical circulation data, as this model can offer high versatility for regression tasks. The model's accuracy will be evaluated using metrics like RMSE (Root Mean Square Error) and MAE (Mean Absolute Error). The analysis will leverage Python for data manipulation, statistical modeling, and machine learning. Libraries such as Pandas, NumPy, Scikit-learn, and TensorFlow will be utilized. Sensitive information about patrons and staff is anonymized or pseudonymized.

This mixed-methods approach is designed to provide actionable insights into borrowing patterns, core collections, and future demand, enabling libraries to optimize resource allocation and enhance user satisfaction.

## 5   Results

### 5.1   Borrowing Patterns and Trends

Filtering out the users and book titles, insights over which study programs and students are most active become clear. Figure 3 represents an overview of the total counts.

The library opens weekly, from Monday to Friday, from 8.30 am to 22.00 pm. On Saturday, it opens from 9:00 am to 5:00 pm and closes on Sunday. To study the temporal usage patterns, library circulation trends by day of the week is illustrated in Fig. 4. It can be observed that the peak events often occur on Mondays and the low ones occur on Saturdays. These patterns are not consistent across library branches as most events

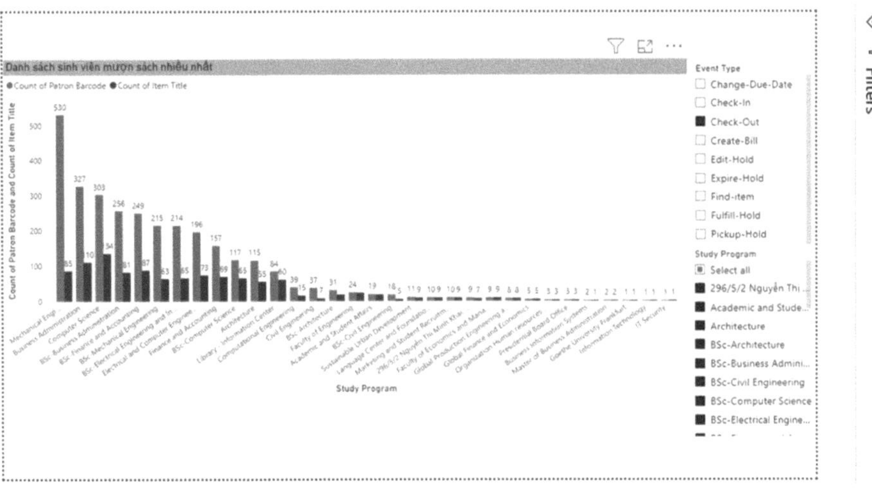


**Fig. 3.** Overview of the study programs with most active book borrowing activities.

happen at the central branch. Seasonal trends in library circulation are presented in Fig. 5 and library circulation trends during semesters and breaks in Fig. 6. More circulation events occur at semester starts and tend to be lower at semester breaks. Across the branches, the central one serves more patrons. Anomalies can be observed during the Covid-19 time of 2021. RQ1.1 is addressed.

The usage across study programs is illustrated in Fig. 7. Only Check-Out events are considered to determine the borrowing numbers across different groups. The most active patrons are from the Mechanical Engineering program. It could be explained that due to limited digital alternatives, some engineering books, especially older editions and specialized reference materials, might not be available online or as e-books, making library access essential for this program. On the monthly borrowing trends by study program, as illustrated in Fig. 8, the most Check-Out activities occur in March. It should be noted that the collected data is incomplete as there are many Check-Out activities having N/A value at the column storing information about the study program. RQ1.2 is partially addressed.

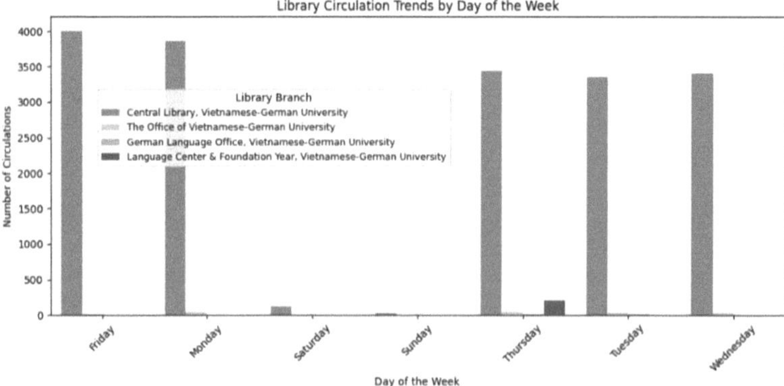

**Fig. 4.** Library circulation trends by day of the week.

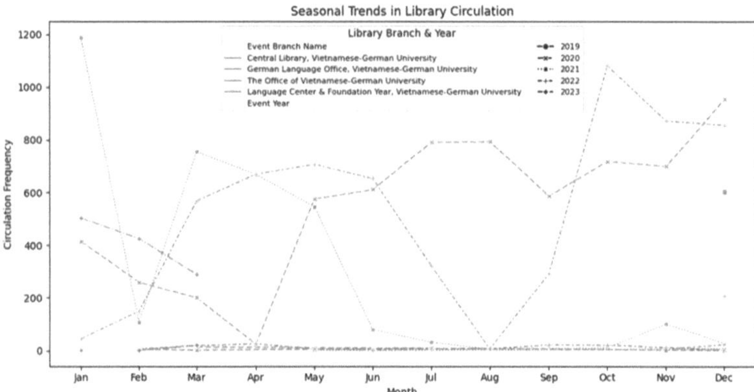

**Fig. 5.** Seasonal trends in library circulation.

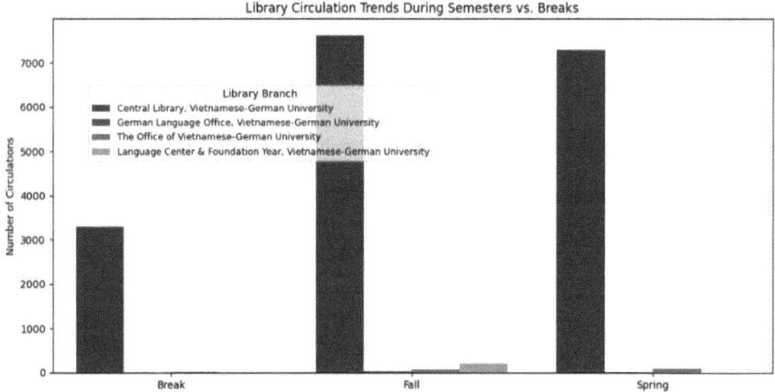

**Fig. 6.** Library circulation trends during semesters vs. Breaks.

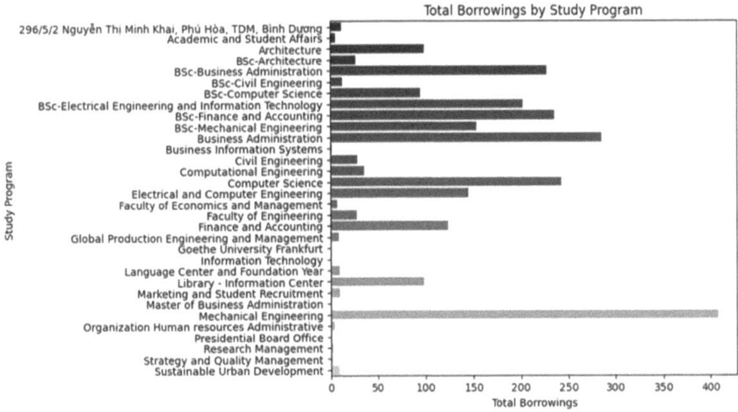

**Fig. 7.** Total borrowings by study program.

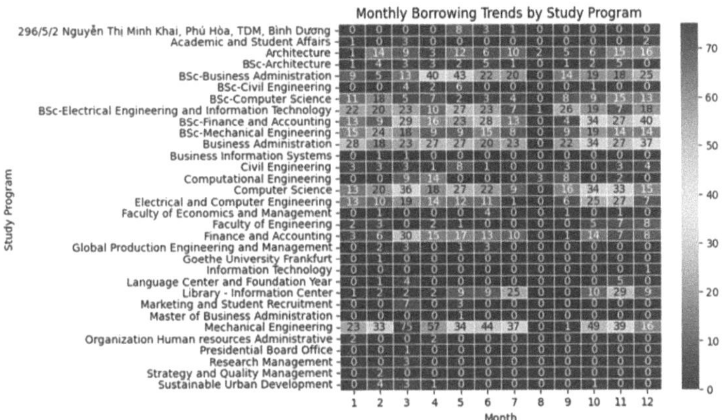

**Fig. 8.** Monthly borrowing trends by study program.

## 5.2 Analysis of Circulation Data for Core Collections

To identify essential collections, the top 10 most frequently borrowed items and their trends are depicted in Fig. 9. Only Check-Out events are considered. The time-series visualization may help identify seasonal patterns or consistent demand. For instance, these initial findings on items borrowed can assist the library to understand user demand to optimize purchasing decisions and inventory management. Another example is that due to the high demand on dictionaries, more English and German classes could be offered for the students. Expert interviews with relevant university staff regarding high-demand dictionaries revealed a notable finding: unauthorized writing was detected in some borrowed dictionaries, which violates basic library rules. To gain deeper insights into this issue, further investigation will involve conducting student surveys, and collecting detailed data on dictionary borrowing.

Applying the Pareto Principle to library circulation data shows that 786 items (37.22% of total) are responsible and 286 patrons (27.16% of total) are responsible to reach 80% of circulation events (cp. Fig. 10). The findings on patrons confirms the presence of the Pareto Principle since the results are close to the results from Yang and Shieh [5]. Thus, the library can justify focusing on high-impact users. For the minority of patrons driving circulation, tailor marketing could be conducted (e.g. personalized recommendations, loyalty programs). Although the 80/20 does not strictly apply for items, future work can check if there is a small number of items that account for most circulations, then the library would need to prioritize their availability (e.g. better shelving). There, based on the Pareto analysis, the library should increase the number of copies for specific titles and consider purchasing more materials for specific study programs. For instance, by combining with the results on borrowings by study program (cp. Fig. 4), the finding from Pareto Principle analysis can improve the services for high demand programs such as Mechanical Engineering or Business Administration. RQ2.1 is addressed.

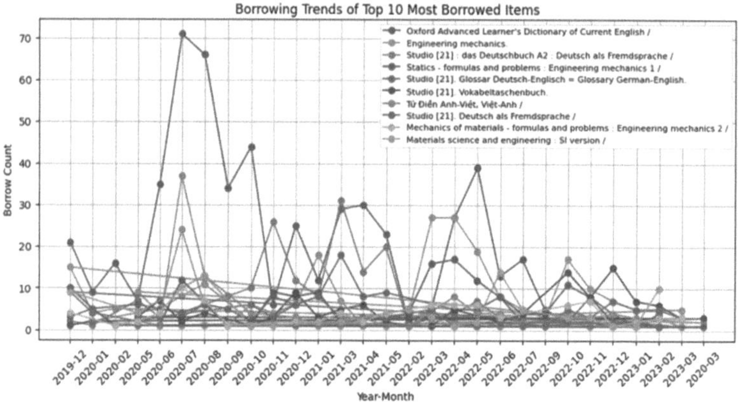


**Fig. 9.** Borrowing trends of top 10 most borrowed items showing high demand on dictionaries.

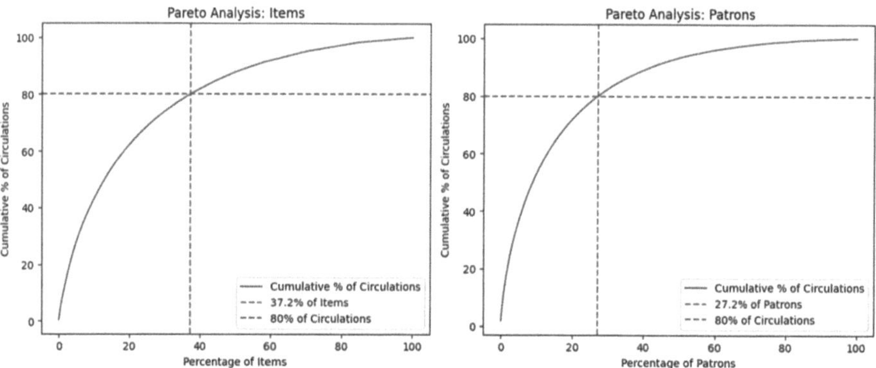


**Fig. 10.** Pareto analysis showing that approximately 37% of items and 27% of patrons account for 80% of circulation events.

The circulation patterns are investigated by using a Random Forest model for understanding circulation trends and providing prediction (cp. Fig. 11). Data is aggregated weekly rather than monthly to ensure a more detailed analysis, as the 39 months of collected data would result in only 39 rows in a monthly aggregation. The model performance shows 108.74 on MAE, 18957.65 on MSE, and 0.35 on R-squared ($R^2$). It could be explained that the model is not optimized yet (e.g. the number of trees in the forest is set as default value 100) in this preliminary study. Thus, additional data collection and additional preprocessing steps would be needed enhance the model. For example, missing values would need to be addressed through imputation or exclusion, while outliers will be identified and handled based on their impact on the analysis. Despite these limitations, the initial findings could support to identify rough borrowing trends. Additional analysis is necessary to provide more insights for decision-making (e.g., when to acquire new books, adjust loan policies). RQ2.2 is partially addressed.

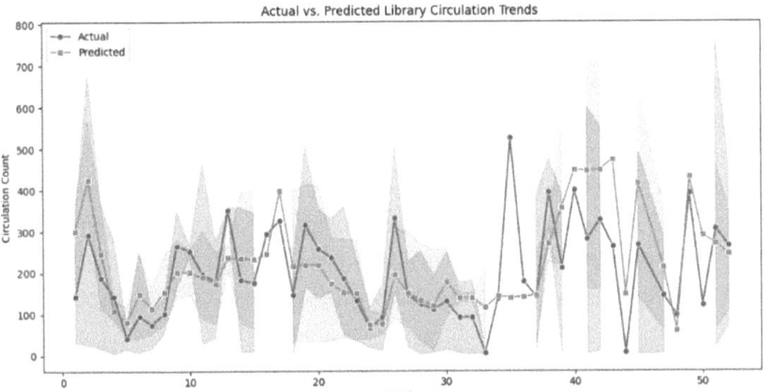


**Fig. 11.** Actual vs. Predicted library circulation trends.

The relationships between active library activities and study performance would be an interesting aspect to be explored. Libraries often serve not only as resource centers but also as environments that promote academic engagement and self-directed learning. In Fig. 12, we identify the noteworthy fact that among the top 10 students with highest number of transactions, eight students received some types of scholarships with high reputation such as the DAAD or merit scholarships (highlighted in yellow). This suggests a potential correlation between frequent library usage and academic excellence, as recognized by these significant achievements. Also, this insight indicates the need of further exploration of GPA or prizes and award winners.

106        D. H. Dinh et al.

| Patron Barcode | Total Interactions | Cancel-Bill | Change-Due-Date | Check-In | Check-Out | Create-Bill | Pay-Bill | Renew |
|---|---|---|---|---|---|---|---|---|
| 14308 | 663 | 21 | 0 | 95 | 93 | 26 | 1 | 88 |
| 15960 | 484 | 10 | 3 | 82 | 84 | 37 | 27 | 67 |
| 9654 | 471 | 2 | 6 | 48 | 45 | 16 | 14 | 94 |
| 18602 | 413 | 0 | 3 | 66 | 70 | 3 | 3 | 78 |
| 17955 | 404 | 0 | 0 | 61 | 61 | 1 | 0 | 73 |
| 10321026 | 384 | 0 | 0 | 37 | 37 | 0 | 0 | 29 |
| 16263 | 353 | 0 | 0 | 27 | 28 | 4 | 4 | 54 |
| 14590 | 339 | 3 | 0 | 24 | 25 | 13 | 10 | 48 |
| 17518 | 325 | 0 | 0 | 56 | 58 | 0 | 0 | 56 |
| 10521057 | 273 | 0 | 0 | 50 | 53 | 0 | 0 | 35 |

**Fig. 12.** Top 10 most active students (highlighted students received scholarships).

## 6  Limitations

As a preliminary study, this work has certain limitations. One drawback is the modest accuracy of the Random Forest forecasting model ($R^2 = 0.35$), which highlights its limited predictive reliability at this stage. Future studies should improve predictive modeling by adopting more sophisticated techniques, such as Long Short-Term Memory or ensemble methods, while also tackling missing data challenges and validating results across diverse institutions. Additionally, it will be crucial to address ethical and privacy concerns associated with linking library usage data to student outcomes. Beyond these considerations, subsequent research should advance from preliminary findings to the full design, implementation, and assessment of the proposed recommender system.

## 7  Conclusion and Outlook

The research findings reveal distinct borrowing patterns and trends within the library system. Temporal usage analysis shows that Mondays are peak days, while Saturdays experience lower activity, with most circulation occurring at the central branch. Seasonal trends indicate increased borrowing at semester starts and decreased activity during breaks, emphasizing the influence of academic cycles on library use. Among study programs, Mechanical Engineering students exhibit the highest borrowing activity, particularly in March, highlighting their dominance in library usage.

The Pareto Principle underscores that a small fraction of items and patrons account for the majority of circulation events, suggesting the importance of focusing on high-demand resources and high-impact users. While machine learning models provide insights into future trends, such as the predicted rise in borrowing from September, they currently exhibit significant prediction errors, necessitating further refinement.

The prominence of high-achieving students among the most active library users raises important questions about the role of library engagement in academic success. It may indicate that students who are more proactive in utilizing library resources, whether for research, coursework, or independent study beyond the scope of the class materials, tend to perform better academically and are thus more competitive for scholarships and awards.

These findings offer valuable guidance for optimizing library operations, including inventory management, personalized marketing strategies, and targeted collection development. As this work only focuses on circulation data, future work is planned to incorporate other data sources such as website usage, database searches or interlibrary loan requests to provide a more holistic view of user needs. Clustering algorithms [9, 10], such as K-means or DBSCAN, could be used to identify core collections if borrowing patterns form distinct clusters based on frequency and user demand. DBSCAN is a density-based clustering algorithm that groups closely packed data points while identifying sparse regions as noise or outliers [9]. Predictive modeling accuracy could be enhanced to better inform decision-making processes, ensuring resources are allocated to meet user needs efficiently. By examining the book borrowing records more closely in future research, the university could better understand how to leverage library services to support student success and offer personalized offers using a self-built library recommendation system [11].

**Acknowledgments.** The authors thank the Presidential Board and colleagues at Vietnamese-German University for their support during the research.

**Disclosure of Interests.**    The authors have no competing interests to declare that are relevant to the content of this article.

# References


1. Wahid, A., Alias, M.N.N., Jalil, F.A.: Visual exploration of book loan activities and room reservation behaviors at Universiti Utara Malaysia Library. J. Data Sci. Decis. Anal. **2**, 15–28 (2024). https://e-journal.uum.edu.my/index.php/jdsd/article/view/22927
2. Khademizadeh, M., Zare, H.R., Hashemi, S.R.: Analysis of book circulation data and a book recommendation system in academic libraries using data mining techniques. In: Proceedings of the International Conference on Information and Knowledge Management (CIKM) (2022). https://www.researchgate.net/publication/364327194
3. Knievel, J., Wicht, Y., Wiley, K.: Use of circulation statistics and interlibrary loan data in collection management. Coll. Res. Libr. **67**, 35–49 (2006). https://crl.acrl.org/index.php/crl/article/view/15771
4. Hicks, D., Behary, J.: Developing performance metrics for specialized collections: a case study in ratio analysis. J. Libr. Adm. **60**, 779–795 (2020). https://www.tandfonline.com/doi/abs/10.1080/15367967.2020.1824615
5. Yang, T., Shieh, H.: Applying the Pareto principle to analyze public library circulation data: a case study in Taiwan. Malays. J. Libr. Inf. Sci. **24**, 65–80 (2019). https://jupidi.um.edu.my/index.php/MJLIS/article/view/19946
6. Wang, X.: A predictive modeling approach using DTGMGCN and POA for library circulation trend forecasting. J. Eng. Sci. **48**, 112–127 (2024). https://journal.esrgroups.org/jes/article/view/4128
7. Association of College and Research Libraries: The state of U.S. academic libraries: Findings from the ACRL 2023 annual survey. American Library Association, Chicago (2024). https://www.ala.org/sites/default/files/2024-10/2023%20State%20of%20Academic%20Libraries%20Report.pdf
8. Saputra, A., Rahmawati, N.: Trends in the utilization of circulation services in university libraries: analysis before and after the COVID-19 pandemic. IAFOR J. Lit. Librariansh. **14**(1) (2025). https://doi.org/10.22492/ijl.14.1.08

9. Deng, D.: DBSCAN clustering algorithm based on density. In: 2020 7th International Forum on Electrical Engineering and Automation (IFEEA), Hefei, China, pp. 949–953 (2020). https://doi.org/10.1109/IFEEA51475.2020.00199

10. Khunji, H.A., Zeki, A.M.: Clustering rental houses in Bahrain using K modes algorithm. In: 2024 5th International Conference on Data Analytics for Business and Industry (ICDABI), Zallaq, Bahrain, pp. 164–168 (2024)

11. Ma, Y.-G.: Research of library book recommendation system based on cloud computing. In: Proceedings of the 9th International Symposium on Linear Drives for Industry Applications, vol. 1, pp. 549–555 (2014)

# Automated Segregation, Quality Prediction, and Disease Detection of Pomegranates Using Deep Learning


Manav Malhotra[✉], Chandan Kawatra, Yash Pratap Rajoria, Varada Gupta, Armaan Saggu, Anjani Mohil, and Anu Bajaj

Department of Computer Science and Engineering, Thapar Institute of Engineering and Technology, Patiala, India



**Abstract.** Pomegranates are highly valued horticultural crops, yet their market potential is often constrained by variations in quality and vulnerability to diseases. Traditional approaches to grading and disease identification are labor-intensive, error-prone, and unsuitable for large-scale operations. To overcome these limitations, this study introduces an automated dual-purpose framework for pomegranate quality grading and disease detection using deep learning and image processing. Two different datasets were used: one comprising twelve quality categories defined by fruit size, color, and surface characteristics, and another covering five disease classes—Alternaria, Anthracnose, Bacterial Blight, Cercospora, and Healthy. Convolutional Neural Network (CNN) models were trained with extensive augmentation techniques and refined through hyperparameter tuning. The proposed framework achieved 96% accuracy in quality classification and 98.5% accuracy in disease detection, surpassing conventional models such as Random Forest, SVM, and transfer learning baselines (ResNet50, InceptionV3, VGG16). These findings highlight the system's robustness and scalability, making it a dependable solution for automated fruit sorting and disease monitoring.

**Keywords:** Pomegranate disease detection · pomegranate quality grading · CNN · deep learning · automated segregation


## 1 Introduction

Agriculture is an important part of the global economy, employing millions of people worldwide and driving rural development. Among its diverse crops, pomegranate, scientific name: (*Punica granatum*) holds significant nutritional, medicinal, and economic value. Its demand has been steadily increasing in both domestic and international markets due to its antioxidant properties, rich bioactive compounds, and use in food, pharmaceutical, and cosmetic industries. However, maintaining consistent fruit quality and effectively managing crop diseases remain challenging, especially in meeting the growing demands of domestic and international markets [1,2]. Conventional food grading, quality assessment and




K. K. Patel et al. (Eds.): icSoftComp 2025, CCIS 2874, pp. 109–121, 2026.
https://doi.org/10.1007/978-3-032-22062-2_9

disease detection techniques are manual, time-consuming, and prone to subjectivity, resulting in reduced efficiency and increased production costs. To overcome these limitations, recent years have witnessed a rapid shift toward automation using computer vision and deep learning methods, which offer scalability, accuracy, and reliability [3,4].

Conventional machine learning algorithms such as Support Vector Machines (SVM) and Random Forests have been applied to tasks like fruit classification, defect identification, and yield prediction [16,17]. These methods, when combined with feature engineering and image processing techniques, have shown promising results in improving efficiency and objectivity compared to manual inspection. However, their performance is often constrained by the need for feature selection and extraction techniques, limited generalization capability, and sensitivity to variations in lighting, orientation, and background conditions [18].

In recent years, deep learning (DL) has emerged as a more powerful alternative, overcoming many of the drawbacks of traditional ML. By automatically extracting hierarchical features directly from raw images, deep learning models—particularly Convolutional Neural Networks (CNNs)—achieve superior accuracy and robustness in complex visual recognition tasks [19,20]. Their ability to learn discriminative representations without manual intervention enables reliable segregation, quality prediction, and disease detection under diverse real-world conditions. Furthermore, deep learning systems are highly scalable, adaptable to large datasets, and capable of real-time deployment, making them especially suitable for industrial applications in precision agriculture and smart farming [21,22].

A critical milestone in this domain was the release of a standardized dataset in 2024 containing 5,099 labeled pomegranate fruit images spanning five categories (Healthy, Bacterial Blight, Anthracnose, Cercospora, Alternaria), which has since enabled comparative benchmarking of deep transfer learning models [8,9]. These advancements highlight the growing importance of robust datasets and optimized deep architectures for real-world agricultural applications.

This study introduces an automated dual-purpose framework for pomegranate quality grading and disease detection using CNN-based architectures. The methodology integrates data preprocessing, augmentation techniques (rotation, scaling, flipping), and hyperparameter optimization to enhance generalization and reduce overfitting. Two publicly available datasets from Kaggle were used—one dedicated to disease detection and the other on quality grading with twelve classification levels. The main contributions of this work are summarized as follows:

1. **Custom CNN architectures:** Development of models specifically designed for both quality grading and disease detection tasks.
2. **Improved training pipeline:** Application of augmentation strategies and hyperparameter optimization to increase robustness.
3. **Comprehensive performance evaluation:** Comparing the proposed models against existing state-of-the-art approaches to establish their effectiveness.

The organization of the paper is as follows: next section briefs the existing literature on pomegranate disease prediction and quality classification. Section 3 describes the proposed methodology and the model architectures for disease detection and quality segregation. The datasets and the experimental setup along with hyperparameter tuning in Sect. 4. Section 5 provides the results and analysis by comparing the proposed algorithms with the existing state of the art algorithms. The paper is concluded and future work is discussed is Sect. 6.

## 2    Related Work

In recent years, pomegranate quality assessment and disease detection have become active areas of research, motivated by the need for scalable and reliable approaches to maintain quality standards and control disease spread. Early investigations largely employed conventional machine learning methods. For instance, Gupta et al. (2021) used an SVM classifier on a quality dataset, reaching 89% accuracy by leveraging handcrafted features such as fruit color and size. Singh et al. (2020) explored a Random Forest model that incorporated color and texture attributes, reporting an accuracy of 88%.

Deep learning approaches have outperformed these conventional methods. Kumar et al. applied a CNN model to the Kaggle Pomegranate Disease Dataset and achieved 92% accuracy in disease classification [1].

Joshi et al. (2022) demonstrated the effectiveness of transfer learning using ResNet50, achieving 93% accuracy in disease classification, while Sharma et al. (2023) reported 91% accuracy using VGG16 for pomegranate quality grading. Hybrid architectures have also been explored; Patel et al. (2023) integrated CNN with RNN for sequential disease pattern identification, attaining 90% accuracy. Verma et al. (2020) introduced LSTM-based sequential classification with 91% accuracy, and Reddy et al. (2021) combined CNN and Decision Trees for automated grading at 90% accuracy.

Recent studies have further extended these capabilities with advanced architectures. For instance, Sameera and Deshpande [5] combined CNNs with a Honey Badger Algorithm, in pomegranate disease classification. Andrushia et al. [6] proposed a Hybrid Optimal Attention Capsule Network, while Komalavalli et al. [7] demonstrated the use of EfficientNet for automated fruit disease detection. Another major milestone was the release of a standardized dataset of 5,099 labeled pomegranate fruit images in 2024, covering five categories (Healthy, Bacterial Blight, Anthracnose, Cercospora, Alternaria), which has enabled benchmarking of deep transfer learning models such as VGG16, ResNet50V2, DenseNet201, MobileNetV2, and the custom PomeNetV2 [8,9]. Table 1 provides a consolidated summary of existing literature on pomegranate quality prediction and disease detection.

**Table 1.** Summary of existing literature on pomegranate quality prediction and disease detection

| Study | Year | Dataset | Model | Performance |
| --- | --- | --- | --- | --- |
| Kumar et al. [1] | 2022 | Kaggle (Disease) | CNN | Acc: 92%, Precision: 0.91, Recall: 0.89 |
| Gupta et al. | 2021 | Kaggle (Quality) | SVM | Acc: 89%, features: color, size |
| Singh et al. | 2020 | Custom (Quality) | Random Forest | Acc: 88%, features: color, texture |
| Joshi et al. | 2022 | Open-source (Disease) | ResNet50 | Acc: 93%, F1: 0.91 (Transfer Learning) |
| Sharma et al. | 2023 | Kaggle (Quality) | VGG16 | Acc: 91%, Epochs: 50 |
| Patel et al. | 2023 | Local (Disease) | CNN + RNN | Acc: 90%, Sensitivity: 0.88, Specificity: 0.90 |
| Verma et al. | 2020 | Kaggle (Disease) | LSTM | Acc: 91%, Precision: 0.89, Recall: 0.87 |
| Reddy et al. | 2021 | Custom (Quality) | CNN + Decision Tree | Acc: 90%, Sensitivity: 0.85, Specificity: 0.87 |
| Sameera & Deshpande [5] | 2024 | Local (Disease) | CNN + HBOA | Acc: 99.6% |
| Andrushia et al. [6] | 2024 | Mixed (Disease) | Hybrid OACapsNet | Acc: 99.2% |
| Komalavalli et al. [7] | 2025 | Local (Disease) | EfficientNet | Acc: 95% |
| Pakruddin & Hemavathy [8] | 2024 | Standardized dataset (5,099 images) | – | Dataset for benchmarking five classes |
| Pakruddin & Hemavathy [9] | 2024 | Same dataset | VGG16, ResNet50V2, DenseNet201, MobileNetV2, PomeNetV2 | Best performance with PomeNetV2 |

Table 1 highlighted the use of CNNs, SVMs, LSTMs, and hybrid models with varying datasets and performance metrics. Overall, CNN-based deep learning approaches, particularly those leveraging transfer learning and optimized architectures, have consistently achieved higher accuracy compared to traditional machine learning methods. Our work differs from the above by proposing a dual-purpose automated system that simultaneously addresses both pomegranate quality grading and disease detection in a single framework. Using publicly avaiable datasets, our models achieved a validation accuracy of 96% for quality classification and 98.5% for disease detection, outperforming existing approaches.

## 3   Proposed Methodology

The proposed framework begins with data preprocessing to ensure input consistency and quality, followed by data augmentation techniques to enhance generalization and reduce overfitting.

Preprocessing was performed to standardize the dataset and improve the efficiency of the learning process. Two primary tasks were applied. First, normalization was carried out by rescaling pixel values to the range $[0, 1]$, which accelerates convergence and stabilizes the training process [10,11]. Second, resizing ensured consistent image dimensions: $150 \times 150$ pixels for disease detection (balancing computational efficiency with disease-relevant feature preservation), and $224 \times 224$ pixels for quality grading (capturing fine-grained surface and structural details for distinguishing among twelve classes) [14,15].

To further increase dataset diversity and mitigate overfitting, augmentation strategies were applied. These included rotation (random angles up to $\pm 40°$ to enforce rotational invariance) [11], zooming (up to 20% to simulate variations in fruit-to-camera distance) [12], shearing (affine transformations to mimic natural distortions in diseased regions), and horizontal flipping (ensuring invariance to fruit orientation) [13].

The first CNN model was designed for pomegranate disease detection, where discriminative features were extracted to classify fruits into five categories: Alternaria, Anthracnose, Bacterial Blight, Cercospora, and Healthy. The architecture employed four Conv2D layers, starting with 32 filters and doubling up to 128 in successive layers, each activated with ReLU and followed by Max-Pooling2D to reduce dimensionality while preserving key features. The resulting feature maps were flattened into a 1D vector and passed through a dense layer with 512 neurons (ReLU). The final dense layer used softmax activation with five output nodes, one per disease class.

For quality classification, a second CNN model was developed to classify Ruby pomegranates into twelve quality grades based on size, color, and surface texture. The network contained two Conv2D layers with 16 and 32 filters, each followed by ReLU and MaxPooling2D. The feature maps were flattened and passed through a dense layer with 256 neurons (ReLU), followed by a final dense layer with 12 nodes and softmax activation. Both Adam and SGD optimizers were tested, with categorical cross-entropy used as the loss function.

Hyperparameter tuning was conducted using grid search, with the best values selected based on validation loss and generalization ability. The summary is shown in Table 2.

Training was performed with an 80–20 train-validation split. The disease detection model was trained for 5 epochs, whereas the quality classification model required 25 epochs due to its higher complexity. A batch size of 32 was used for both models. Validation ensured generalization to unseen data, while performance was measured using Accuracy, Precision, Recall, and F1-score. The Random Forest baseline achieved moderate accuracy, but the CNN-based models significantly outperformed it, confirming their superior capability for both pomegranate disease detection and quality classification. The disease detection

Table 2. Hyperparameter Tuning Summary

| Model | Hyperparameter | Optimal Value |
|---|---|---|
| Random Forest | Number of Estimators | 200 |
| | Maximum Depth | 40 |
| | Min. Samples Split | 4 |
| CNN (Disease Detection) | Number of Filters | 32 |
| | Kernel Size | $3 \times 3$ |
| | Learning Rate | 0.001 |
| | Batch Size | 32 |
| CNN (Quality Grading) | Number of Filters | 128 |
| | Kernel Size | $5 \times 5$ |
| | Batch Size | 32 |
| | Epochs | 50 |

model achieved a validation accuracy of 98.5%, while the quality grading model reached 96%.

## 4    Experimental Setup

All experiments were conducted in Python 3 on Google Colab, leveraging GPU acceleration through the Google Compute Engine. Two data sets were used: one for disease detection and another for the quality classification of Ruby pomegranates. The disease detection dataset comprises images of Ruby pomegranates grouped into five categories: *Alternaria, Anthracnose, Bacterial Blight, Cercospora,* and *Healthy.* Table 3 summarizes the dataset classes.

Table 3. Classes in Disease Detection Dataset

| Class | Category | Description |
|---|---|---|
| 1 | Alternaria | Dark fungal patches and irregular lesions on fruit. |
| 2 | Anthracnose | Sunken necrotic spots caused by fungal infection. |
| 3 | Bacterial Blight | Water-soaked sores that spread rapidly and damage crops. |
| 4 | Cercospora | Fruit rot and leaf spots affecting fruit and foliage. |
| 5 | Healthy | Disease-free fruits used as control class. |

The quality classification dataset categorizes Ruby pomegranates into twelve levels, grouped as G1 Q1–Q4, G2 Q1–Q4, and G3 Q1–Q4, based on fruit size, color, and surface imperfections. Table 4 presents the grade-wise classification, while Table 5 highlights the quality indicators used for grading.

**Table 4.** Pomegranate Grade Classification

| Grade | Weight (grams) | Characteristics |
|---|---|---|
| Grade A | 300–400 | Smooth exterior, minimal flaws, premium appearance. |
| Grade B | 200–300 | Minor surface scars, acceptable visual quality. |
| Grade C | 100–200 | Noticeable blemishes, suitable for processing. |

**Table 5.** Quality Indicators for Pomegranate Classification

| Level | Weight Criteria | Outer Condition | Color | Surface Texture |
|---|---|---|---|---|
| Q1 | Highest for grade | Free from defects | Deep red / pink | Smooth, glossy |
| Q2 | $\geq 98\%$ of Q1 | Minor marks | Dark red / rose | Smooth |
| Q3 | $\geq 97\%$ of Q2 | Small dents | Reddish-brown | Slightly coarse |
| Q4 | $\geq 96\%$ of Q3 | Visible blemishes | Dull reddish-brown | Rough |

Model performance was evaluated using five standard classification metrics: Accuracy, Precision, Recall (Sensitivity), Specificity, and F1-Score. These metrics provide a comprehensive view of both correctness and robustness.

- **Accuracy:** Overall proportion of correctly classified instances.

$$Accuracy = \frac{TP + TN}{TP + TN + FP + FN} \tag{1}$$

- **Precision:** Ratio of positive predictions that are correct.

$$Precision = \frac{TP}{TP + FP}(2) \tag{2}$$

- **Recall (Sensitivity):** Ratio of actual positives that are correctly identified.

$$Recall = \frac{TP}{TP + FN} \tag{3}$$

- **Specificity:** Ratio of actual negatives that are correctly identified.

$$Specificity = \frac{TN}{TN + FP} \tag{4}$$

- **F1-Score:** Harmonic mean of precision and recall.

$$F1 = \frac{2 \cdot Precision \cdot Recall}{Precision + Recall} \tag{5}$$

Here, $TP$, $TN$, $FP$, and $FN$ denote true positives, true negatives, false positives, and false negatives, respectively.

## 5    Results and Discussion

This section presents the performance of the proposed CNN frameworks for disease detection and quality grading. The data sets used in the experiments were divided into 80% for training and 20% for testing. Model performance was measured using classification metrics that include accuracy, precision, recall, and F1 score.

**Table 6.** Comparison of Models for Quality Assessment

| Model | MAE | MSE | RMSE | $R^2$ | RMSLE | MAPE |
|---|---|---|---|---|---|---|
| XGBoost | 18.56 | 1137.76 | 33.67 | 0.871 | 0.374 | 0.310 |
| CatBoost | 18.54 | 1148.71 | 33.83 | 0.870 | 0.366 | 0.310 |
| LightGBM | 19.20 | 1212.07 | 34.73 | 0.863 | 0.374 | 0.329 |
| Extra Trees | 18.82 | 1221.63 | 34.86 | 0.862 | 0.366 | 0.321 |
| Random Forest | 19.40 | 1282.63 | 35.70 | 0.855 | 0.373 | 0.327 |
| Gradient Boosting | 22.14 | 1525.99 | 38.99 | 0.827 | 0.423 | 0.391 |
| Linear Regression | 25.01 | 1801.73 | 42.36 | 0.796 | 0.491 | 0.477 |
| Ridge Regression | 25.09 | 1813.31 | 42.50 | 0.794 | 0.490 | 0.478 |
| Bayesian Ridge | 25.03 | 1813.35 | 42.50 | 0.794 | 0.489 | 0.476 |
| Lasso | 25.02 | 1820.47 | 42.58 | 0.794 | 0.484 | 0.476 |
| Lasso LAR | 25.02 | 1820.47 | 42.58 | 0.794 | 0.484 | 0.476 |
| **CNN** | **10.96** | **117.06** | **24.15** | **0.912** | **0.421** | **0.130** |

### 5.1    Quality Assessment Analysis

The training and validation loss and accuracy curves as shown in Figs. 1 and 2 demonstrate the learning effectiveness of the proposed CNN model. Both training and validation losses (see Figs. 3 and 4) decreased consistently across epochs which suggests efficient learning, with only a marginal gap between them, indicating strong generalization and low overfitting risk. Similarly, accuracy curves showed steady improvement, demonstrating the model's ability to correctly classify quality grades of pomegranates.

Table 6 presents the comparative analysis of multiple models and optimizers for quality assessment. The CNN model achieved superior results, with the lowest error metrics and highest $R^2$ value. The CNN significantly outperformed all traditional ML models, achieving the lowest MAE (10.96) and MSE (117.06), and the highest $R^2$ (0.912). XGBoost ranked second but fell short of CNN's precision, highlighting deep learning's strength in feature extraction for visual tasks.

**Fig. 1.** Training and Validation Accuracy curves

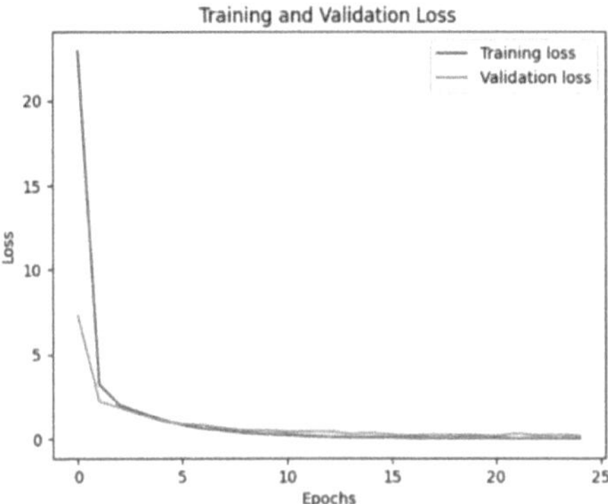

**Fig. 2.** Training and Validation Loss

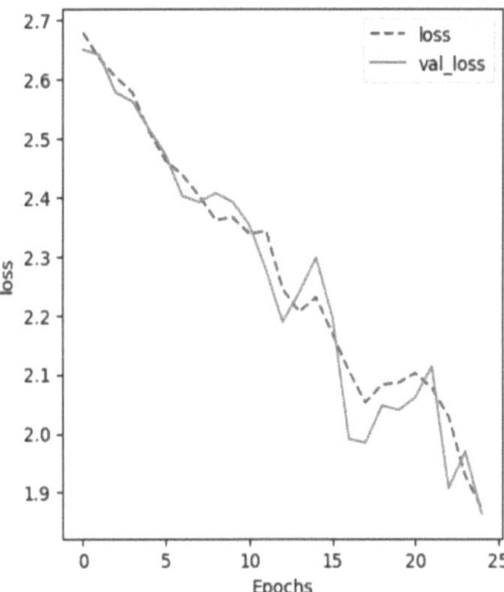

**Fig. 3.** Loss vs Epochs

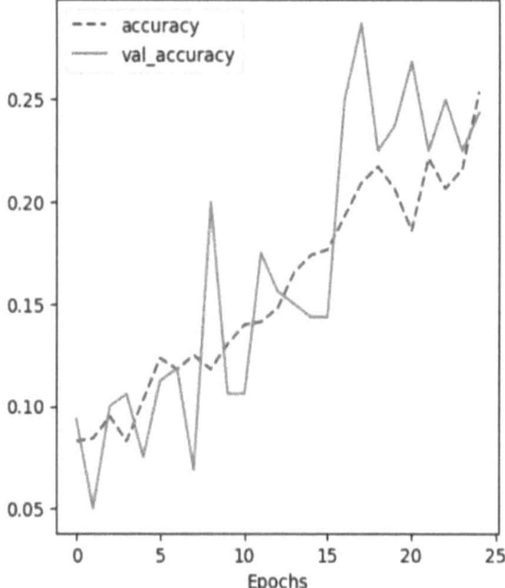


**Fig. 4.** Accuracy vs Epochs

## 5.2   Disease Detection Analysis

For disease detection, models were compared on classification accuracy, precision, recall, F1-score, RMSE, and MAE. Table 7 presents the comparative results. Figure 5 showed that CNN and MobileNetV2 models achieved the best performance, each with 96% accuracy, supported by strong precision, recall, and F1-scores. InceptionV3 also performed competitively (94%), while VGG16 was moderate (91%). ResNet50, however, underperformed with only 56% accuracy and much higher error rates, making it unsuitable for this dataset.

**Table 7.** Comparison of Models for Disease Detection

| Model | Accuracy | Precision | Recall | F1 | RMSE | MAE |
|---|---|---|---|---|---|---|
| CNN | 0.96 | 0.96 | 0.96 | 0.96 | 0.45 | 0.08 |
| VGG16 | 0.91 | 0.92 | 0.91 | 0.91 | 0.67 | 0.18 |
| ResNet50 | 0.56 | 0.53 | 0.56 | 0.50 | 1.47 | 0.86 |
| InceptionV3 | 0.94 | 0.95 | 0.94 | 0.94 | 0.56 | 0.11 |
| MobileNetV2 | 0.96 | 0.96 | 0.96 | 0.96 | 0.44 | 0.07 |

**Table 8.** Performance per Class for Disease Classification

| Disease | Precision | Recall | F1-Score |
|---|---|---|---|
| Alternaria | 0.80 | 0.80 | 0.80 |
| Anthracnose | 0.86 | 0.89 | 0.88 |
| Bacterial Blight | 0.81 | 0.80 | 0.81 |
| Cercospora | 0.83 | 0.82 | 0.82 |
| Healthy | 0.91 | 0.88 | 0.91 |

Table 8 details class-level performance across the five disease categories. The model exhibited excellent reliability in identifying healthy fruits, achieving the highest precision (0.91) and F1-score (0.91). Among diseased categories, Anthracnose was most accurately detected (F1 = 0.88), while Alternaria and Bacterial Blight recorded the lowest but acceptable F1-scores (0.80 and 0.81, respectively). These results confirm the robustness of CNN-based detection while also highlighting scope for improvement in detecting specific diseases.

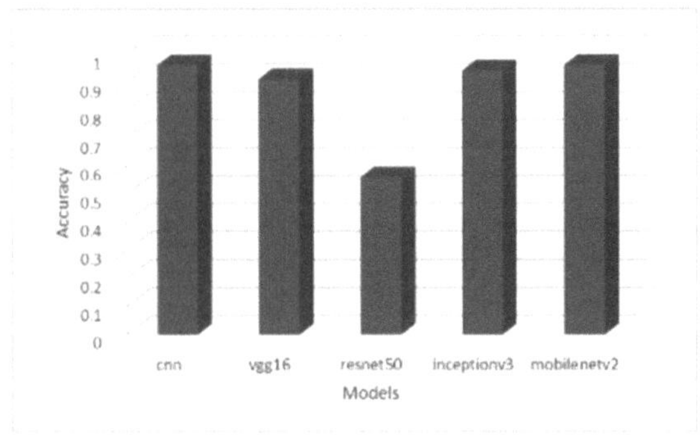


**Fig. 5.** Accuracies for models used in disease detection.

# 6    Conclusions and Future Work

This study presented a CNN-based automated framework for pomegranate quality assessment and disease detection. Through effective preprocessing and augmentation strategies—including rotation, zooming, and flipping—the system was trained to generalize well across diverse input conditions. Hyperparameter optimization further enhanced model robustness, enabling the proposed CNN and MobileNetV2 architectures to achieve state-of-the-art performance, with 96% accuracy, precision, recall, and F1-score. At the class level, the framework demonstrated strong reliability, particularly in detecting Anthracnose (F1-score:

0.88) and distinguishing healthy pomegranates (F1-score: 0.91), underscoring its practical utility in agricultural quality monitoring. Future research will focus on integrating advanced architectures, such as Vision Transformers and hybrid deep learning models, to further improve classification accuracy and robustness. Expanding the dataset to include additional pomegranate varieties and a broader spectrum of diseases will also be prioritized.

# References


1. Kumar, R., Rajpurohit, V.S., Bidari, K.Y.: Multi-class grading and quality assessment of pomegranate fruits based on physical and visual parameters. Int. J. Fruit Sci. **19**(4), 372–396 (2022)
2. Kapadnis, A., Bidari, K.Y.: Pomegranate fruit quality assessment using machine intelligence and wavelet features. J. Hortic. Res. **26**(1), 53–60 (2022)
3. Mohanty, S.P., Hughes, D.P., Salathé, M.: Using deep learning for image-based plant disease detection. Front. Plant Sci. **7**, 1419 (2016). https://doi.org/10.3389/fpls.2016.01419
4. Morshed, M., Islam, M.N., Rahman, M.: Machine learning approaches for fruit disease detection: a survey. Comput. Electron. Agric. **197**, 106970 (2022). https://doi.org/10.1016/j.compag.2022.106970
5. Sameera, P., Deshpande, A.: Disease detection and classification in pomegranate fruit using hybrid CNN with Honey Badger optimization algorithm. Int. J. Food Prop. **27**(1), 815–837 (2024). https://doi.org/10.1080/10942912.2024.2365927
6. Andrushia, A.D., Naser, M.Z., Lubloy, E., et al.: A deep learning approach to detect diseases in pomegranate fruits via hybrid optimal attention capsule network. Eco. Inform. **84**, 102859 (2024). https://doi.org/10.1016/j.ecoinf.2024.102859
7. Komalavalli, S., Budagam, D.K., Jehan, C., Pandi, P.K.: A deep learning approach for automated detection and classification of pomegranate fruit disease using EfficientNet. Int. J. Adv. Trends Eng. Manage. (IJATEM), **IV**(5) (2025). Published online: 7 February 2025
8. Pakruddin, B., Hemavathy, R.: A comprehensive standardized dataset of numerous pomegranate fruit diseases for deep learning. Comput. Electron. Agric. **224**, 108774 (2024). https://doi.org/10.1016/j.compag.2024.108774
9. Pakruddin, B., Hemavathy, R.: Performance analysis of deep transfer learning models for bacterial blight disease detection and classification in pomegranate fruits. Indian J. Agric. Res. (2024). https://doi.org/10.18805/IJARe.A-6245
10. LeCun, Y., Bengio, Y., Hinton, G.: Deep learning. Nature **521**(7553), 436–444 (2015)
11. Shorten, C., Khoshgoftaar, T.M.: A survey on image data augmentation for deep learning. J. Big Data **6**(1), 1–48 (2019)
12. Perez, L., Wang, J.: The effectiveness of data augmentation in image classification using deep learning. In: Proceedings of Convolutional Neural Networks for Visual Recognition, Stanford University, pp. 1–8 (2017)
13. Chollet, F.: Deep Learning with Python. Manning Publications (2017)
14. Krizhevsky, A., Sutskever, I., Hinton, G.E.: ImageNet classification with deep convolutional neural networks. Commun. ACM **60**(6), 84–90 (2017)
15. Li, X., Zhang, H., Chen, Y.: Deep learning for fruit classification: a review. Comput. Electron. Agric. **205**, 107596 (2023)

16. Patel, K.K., Kar, A., Jha, S.N., Khan, M.A.: Machine vision system: a tool for quality inspection of food and agricultural products. J. Food Sci. Technol. **49**(2), 123–141 (2012)
17. Soltani Firouz, M., Sardari, H.: Defect detection in fruit and vegetables by using machine vision systems and image processing. Food Eng. Rev. **14**(3), 353–379 (2022)
18. Kamilaris, A., Prenafeta-Boldú, F.X.: Deep learning in agriculture: a survey. Comput. Electron. Agric. **147**, 70–90 (2018)
19. Lecun, Y., Bengio, Y., Hinton, G.: Deep learning. Nature **521**(7553), 436–444 (2015)
20. Singh, A., Ganapathysubramanian, B., Singh, A.K., Sarkar, S.: Machine learning for high-throughput stress phenotyping in plants. Trends Plant Sci. **21**(2), 110–124 (2016)
21. Li, L., Zhang, Q., Huang, D.: A review of imaging techniques for plant phenotyping. Sensors **14**(11), 20078–20111 (2014)
22. Kamilaris, A., Prenafeta-Boldú, F.X.: Deep learning for plant identification: a review. Comput. Electron. Agric. **157**, 41–54 (2019)

# Discovering the Significance of LLM's in Medical Science for Disease Detection

Bhargav Vyas[1(✉)], Mittal Desai[1], Heta Patel[2], Anjali Mahavar[1], and Riya Panchal[1]

[1] CMPICA, CHARUSAT, Changa, Anand, India
`bhargavvyas2793@gmail.com`
[2] ARIP, CHARUSAT, Changa, Anand, India

**Abstract.** Due to rise in the LLM's, there is a huge revolution experienced in different domains like education, marketing, medicine development, healthcare and finance. The aim of the paper is to identify and explore all the applications, pros and cons in healthcare, specifically the focus is given to detection of different disease. Major LLM's which can be used for the disease detection are GPT 4, LLaMA, ChatGPT and GPT 3.5. Out of all these, GPT 4 is the most widely used for disease detection and healthcare due to accuracy and efficiency. The experiments are carried out using different medical data sources like medical images, documents related to disease, general database and genomic data. There are wide results possible using this LLM's like chronic issues, cancer diagnostics, respiratory disease and many other rare diseases. The evaluation of the models in identification of these disease is done in both qualitative and quantitative manner. The findings show the evolution of the LLM's in the field of medical science and the future of it in improving the disease detection.

**Keywords:** Large Language Models · GPT · BARD · Encoder · Decoder · Transformer

## 1 Introduction

Large Language Models when seen as an important victory in Artificial Intelligence which is able to generate and process the text in the similar way as humans. The main components of these systems are encoder-decoder module and transformer based components which enable the natural language manipulation by translation, summarization and generation of the related content [1, 2]. The importance of different words and its exact weightage in the statement is identified by the stack of encoders and decoders. The demonstration of the general architecture of an LLM which show the usage of decoders and encoders is shown in Fig. 1. This will help in identification of exact context with respect to scenario, the meaning of the words and dependencies in the text if any present. LLM's can help in recognizing various disease which may get left undetected by the normal physician due to inability to see the chances [3]. Using the predictive analysis of these LLM's the risk associated with the disease and the condition of the patients can also be identified easily. The LLM's can also help in summarizing the diseases and


K. K. Patel et al. (Eds.): icSoftComp 2025, CCIS 2874, pp. 122–133, 2026.
https://doi.org/10.1007/978-3-032-22062-2_10

due to which the clinician can get aware about the new disease and all the supporting knowledge about the same. The treatment and protocol for the disease can also be identified using the same. The decision making about the disease, symptoms and medication is totally dependent on the experience of the clinician but these systems allows automatic computation over the disease which will enhance overall decision making [4]. The LLM's can be used with many different sectors can be seen in Fig. 1.

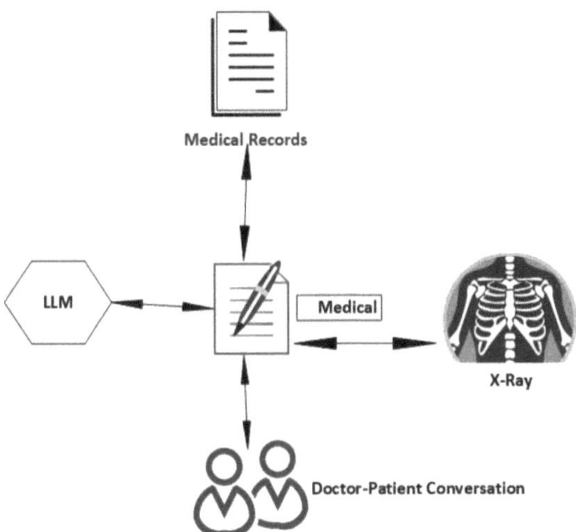


**Fig. 1.** LLM in Healthcare

The research is focusing on the role of LLM's in disease detection, analyzing the novel architecture, identifying patient's problems and recommending them with best suggestions. Different applications and the performance metrics are discussed showing the comparison with the challenges faced. The study will help in understanding the incorporation of LLM's into disease identification, improving the diagnostic accuracy and shaping a better and smart usage of technology on medical domain.

## 2  Literature Review

There were many different LLM's which were identified and explored like the GPT 4 which can be considered as most advanced LLM these days and has the capability of reasoning which can emulate the humans [5]. There are many different ways for sharing the query to the LLM like textual queries, image based queries and others. The LLM under discussion can work in multiple domain efficiently like healthcare, education, problem solving and many other industrial areas [6]. If the input is concerned than GPT 3.5 is one of the most efficient tool which has human understandable language processing capabilities. The text which is given to the LLM and received as output is done using the natural language processing which is fast and precise than anyother available model. It has overall knowledge regarding all the different domain and can also be considered as encyclopedia of it [7]. ChatGPT is one of the best tool which can be used as the conversational AI. It is one of the best tool which allows generating the responses same as the human interaction. It is very common now a days and used with many different applications like chatbot, customer service platform and virtual assistants. It can easily understand the language of users and also can interpret the exact requirements [8]. To overcome the problems and loopholes in the LLM's in medical science, the development of biomedical artificial intelligence research and development was done. The model is trained using huge chunk of medical data with minute and different scenario which will help in responding accurately in all the scenario related to medical science [9]. The major advantage of this system was to the researchers in the medical domain and also to the students or even the medical assistants by getting verified and validated information. The information can be used in the real life for better decision making in the field of medical science. An advanced language model was developed for performing multiple tasks and was named pathway language model. It was developed and trained for handling the technical terminologies and complex tasks which can be of any domain. Thus the model can be applied to any field like legal domain, education, technology and industrial problems. It made the task easy in terms of documents generation for all the employee of different domain [10].

There were few models which were designed to work over huge variety of domains as well as in many different countries and over many different languages which was named large language model for multilingual applications. It is generally used to convert the content into multiple language and get the answers in different language for generation of content [11]. It is one of the best in natural language processing which will help in domain like research and other practical applications. The complications and performance can be adjusted by the developer as per the requirement like according to the usage and applicability the changes can be made [12].


## 3  Methodology

An architecture is displayed to illustrate the steps involved in disease detection using large language models. Collection of patient data is the primary concern which should be obtained from clinic and hospitals. Once the data is pre-processed the data is tokenized and added to the LLM for particular domain, in our case it is GPT, Med-PaLM and Biobert. The model will help in generating contextual meaning of the data which will help in prediction of particular disease. In our case the accuracy of the data is measured using f1-score and accuracy. At the end the system will share the top ranked disease which is predicted with the best associated confidence.

The data which will be processed using the given workflow will help to convert raw patient data into some structured insight. The major advantage of this architecture is it can be in general used without concerning about the LLMs and the dataset (Fig. 2).

In case of medical data, the patient related data will be taken as input like the vitals, age, gender and lab reports. The key issue while getting this data will be modalities and it should be managed efficiently as there will be text, numeric or even image data. The data quality should be taken care of for inconsistency and error. The next step is to convert the modal data into some common format which should be usable by LLM model. There are

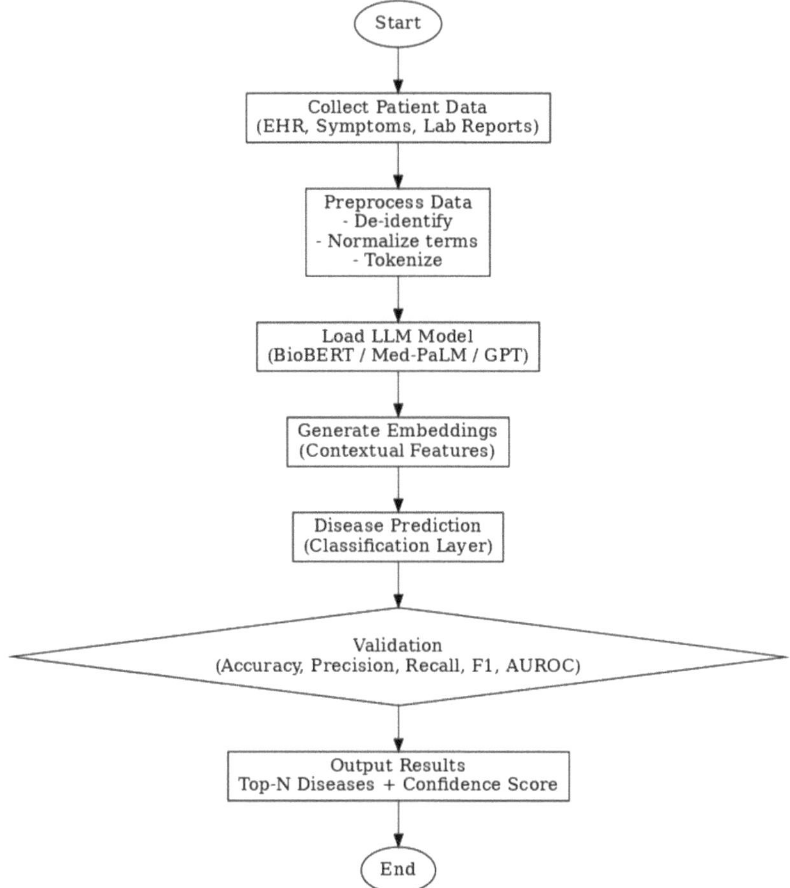



**Fig. 2.** Novel General Architecture for disease detection

many different methods which can be used like text normalization, tokenization, numeric standardization, fixing the missing values and removing the outliers. The next is to select the most suitable LLM according to the domain and the data which should be used for getting the results. Common LLM are BioBERT and ClinicalBERT which can be used for generating embedding's. Some of the common embedding strategies which can be used are CLS token embedding (BERT): single vector summarizing input, the second is mean pooling of token embedding's and third is attention pooling or learned pooling for better summaries. Simple one or two fully connected (Linear) layers on top of embedding like softmax for multiclass or sigmoid for multi-label. More advanced version is MLP + dropout, calibration layer, or attention-based fusion if using multiple embedding's. The inference will be carried out which generated top-N diseases = take the N labels with highest probabilities. Optionally calibrate probabilities to make confidence meaningful. The validation of the data can be done using the key metrics like accuracy = (TP + TN)/(TP + TN + FP + FN), next will be precision = TP/(TP + FP) which shows how many predicted positives were correct the the recall (Sensitivity) = TP/(TP + FN) should be found which shows how many actual positives were found and the last is F1 score = 2 * (Precision * Recall)/(Precision + Recall) which will show harmonic mean of precision & recall.

At the end it can be identified that the flowchart outlines a pipeline for disease prediction using large language models. Patient data such as electronic health records, symptoms, and lab reports are first collected and preprocessed through de-identification, normalization, and tokenization. The cleaned data is then passed into a domain-specific LLM like BioBERT, Med-PaLM, or GPT to generate contextual embedding's, which capture the semantic meaning of clinical information. This embedding's are fed into a classification layer that predicts possible diseases. The predictions are validated using performance metrics such as accuracy, precision, recall, F1 score, and AUROC to ensure reliability. Finally, the system outputs the top-N likely diseases along with confidence scores, providing clinicians with a ranked list of potential diagnoses to support decision-making.

## 4  Discussion

**Question Under Discussion: Identify LLM's for Medical Field**
The emergence of usage of LLM's in the field of medical science and diagnosis of the disease is very common these days. Different models are available in the market which can help significantly in the analysis of patient records, interacting with the patients through chatbots and synthesizing the knowledge of medical field as and when required.

A comparative study was carried out by Caruccio et al. for understanding the traditional models used for prediction and the LLM's. The detailed study for done for understanding the crucial importance of LLM's in the medical field and specifically in the diagnosis of the disease [8]. A combination of LLM's were used for getting the best results in diagnosis of the disease. When the results of all the LLM's were compared and the most satisfactory results were of GPT-3.5-turbo-0301 and the other most eligible LLM was text-davinci-003. However, each LLM has its own benefit in different scenario and in different way the query was given to it.

Z. Wang et al., was the first to propose something new which was named radiology report generation using the frozen LLM's [11]. The model was developed and trained to fetch the image as input and process the image for generating textual reports. The major challenges associated with report generation in the medical field were identified and listed in this research. A detailed review was also carried out in the field of Oncology and it was done by C. Liu et al. [13]. The LLM's which are included for this were Palm 4 and GPT version 4. The application developed was divided into multiple stages like the initial phase of consultation in which the first time patient will share the problem, simulation, planning for the appropriate treatment for the problem, delivery of the medication, verification of the solution of the problem and follow-up treatment. The version 4 of GPT made extraordinary performance as compared to other models specifically for interpretation of the data related to the medical field. Other tool was newly developed for the field of ophthalmology which was named moceil [14]. The method will be divided into three steps starting with acquisition of the knowledge, formalization of knowledge and iterative optimization. The model can be added with the browser which can help in getting extra knowledge from the web. The results obtained with this method statistically showed that the method provides outstanding results as compared with several other methods in terms of accuracy. After this a java based system was developed using the GPT version 3.5 which helped in the diagnosis of the disease by given input and provide with smart solutions for the same [15]. The usage and study of the java based application proved that it worked appropriately for the healthcare suggestions.

For the first time rule based decision making approach was accepted for the diagnosis of disease as external API with the GPT version 4 [16]. The model was proposed by D. P. Panagoulias in which the natural language processing was used for extracting the knowledge related to domain specific knowledge [17]. The study was to get the best suggestions and response using LLM by adding it with knowledge of domain. The major focus was given to reduction of rate with highest efficiency in identifying the disease [18]. Then a new model was identified which added metaverse with the LLM's to handle the cases of medical field in some better digital way.

**Question Under Discussion: Data to be Used for Training LLM's**

The most important thing in any system or model is the quality and quantity of data related to medical domain which can be obtained from clinical notes, the images related to medical science and healthcare data stored in electronic medium. The training data of LLM should consider the privacy of the data, quality of the data, notation of data and many other things. During the testing two dataset were created in which one was for the predication of the disease and the other was for the diagnosis of the disease [8]. The dataset has different set of values in different combinations like the first dataset has 132 values with 4663 different combinations and the other had the data related to real life patient in which 12 diseases with 118 different implicit symptoms. There is different dataset designed like the MIMIC-CXR which is available for usage to all people containing the chest related X-rays. There is multiple dataset in the world which has the data of Intensive care, MRI images, Cancer Images, and genomic data for biotechnology information [13]. The dataset can have multiple data of patient doctor chat generated using the GPT to train the dataset having age, gender, family history and many others [19]. The data of different type like medical dialogue, synthetic and augmented data, biomedical and genomic data, clinical interactions, medical knowledge and medical images were collected and used. The current research shows that the data source which are made throughout world are classified into following categories and graphically presented as shown in the below figure (Fig. 3).

**Question Under Discussion: Which is Most Focused Disease for Diagnosis Using LLM's**

A variety of data can be utilized for identification of disease and LLM's can be trained for it. The variety of disease can be identified using LLM's which can save huge amount of time and money. There are many research work carried out which can help in identifying low and medium risk disease using the LLM's [8]. The disease which can be considered as low risk are jaundice, fungal infections, hepatitis and others. The disease which are considered under high risk are heart related disease, asthma, cancer and pneumonia. A major achievement was by A. S et al., in which GPT 3 was used for identifying the chronic

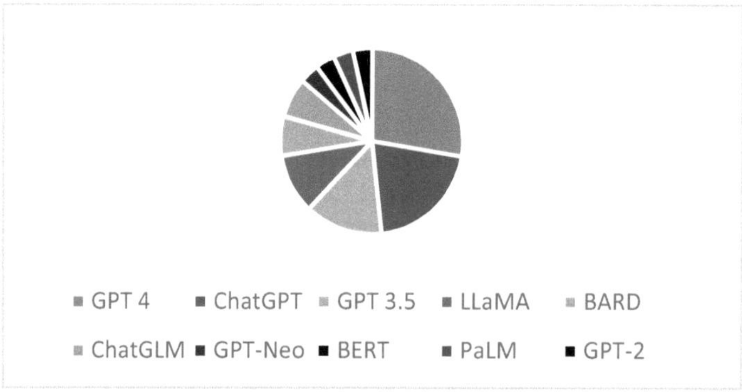


**Fig. 3.** Frequency in terms of usage

disease [15]. Multiple disease was identified like gout, liver disorder or hyperlipidemia by Panagoulias et al. [20]. The environmental and daily routine factors which affects the patient life are also monitored and LLM's provides the options to it. In short the study shows that the LLM's can help in identifying different disease in the human life and the solution to it which can help in shaping overall healthcare system. Also, these can help in identifying the overall trend in healthcare sector which will help to shape the future of medical science.

**Question Under Discussion: Measurement of LLM's Performance**
The most crucial aspect is to identify the performance of the LLM's in identifying the disease among many different possibilities having almost same type of symptoms. There are several different factors on the basis of which the effectiveness of the LLM's can be identified.

The performance of CHATGPT based diagnostics can be measured by the accuracy, F-measure, recall and the precision [8]. There are many other parameters which can be focused like rouge-1, meteor, cider, bleu score and others. All these can provide an in depth analysis of the performance of any method used for diagnosing the disease. A huge number of qualitative parameters are also associated with the diagnostic process [13]. The qualitative parameters include the prediction which is given as output to the patient, data labelling, standardization and overall survival rate.

From overall study there are many parameters which are identified which can be used as a part of research for LLM's. The measure can be both qualitative and quantitative which can identify all the perspective of medical science. The general accuracy measures can be reliability, precision, consistency, accuracy and f1 score. There are measures like rouge-1, meteor and bleu which are related to evaluation of text which is generated. The system usability and practicality measure like response time, cost incurred in development and action ability. Contextual assessment includes the prediction done by the system, post-treatment analysis, comprehension of the query regarding the disease and the medical advice provided at the end. There are statistical methods used for checking the accuracy like standard deviation, interquartile range and mean.

## 5   Issues and Challenges

There are many difficulties and challenges which can be faced while using the LLM's for disease detection and providing the solutions to it. The most common problem is the biased data which will be biased while training the data and will provide inappropriate output. Few less populated data are ignored and may not get reflected in the output forever. Thus there are major chances of getting biased decision while dealing with under-represented data [21, 22]. Completing the data by focusing equally over all the categories of data and also their threshold values to get it counted is most required thing in the health industry [23].

All the LLM are not fully transparent and generally does not allow major interpretability which can create big issues. These type of LLM's are called black box model which needs expertise to understand or generally cannot be understood. If the field is concerned, transparency is very important for the patients while the diagnosis of disease as there is a legal rule for the ethical medical standard for the same [24, 25]. The LLM's are also less descriptive in the way they are getting the findings, in other way the logic which is used for diagnosing the disease, in this case if the wrong disease is identified there is no way to correct the model as there is no justification provided for the way of identification. The other most important risk these days is privacy and security of the patient data [26]. Majority of cases which are chronic or related to the human body will have confidential data. Moreover, there is again a rule for the ethical usage of the patient data and taking prior permission of the patient to even record their data for future references.

## 6   Outcomes

For the analysis of LLM's in medical science, different experiments were conducted using different dataset like report images, clinical documents and structured data. The models which were tested were GPT version 3.5, 4 and LLaMA-2. The methods which are used for experiments are classified into quantitative and qualitative. The metrics which are used for measuring the performance are recall, response time, accuracy, precision and f1-score. The dataset which was used for the identification of performance had more than 1800 data (Table 1).

**Table 1.** Accuracy for disease detection

| Model | Accuracy | Precision | Recall | F1-Score | Response Time |
|---|---|---|---|---|---|
| GPT 4 | **91.6** | **0.89** | **0.93** | **0.91** | **4.0** |
| LLaMA-2 | 84.5 | 0.83 | 0.82 | 0.85 | 2.4 |
| GPT 3.5 | 82.6 | 0.83 | 0.78 | 0.78 | 3.2 |
| ChatGPT | 90.3 | 0.89 | 0.91 | 0.92 | 2.7 |

From the results it can be easily seen that GPT-4 has best performance in terms if f1-score and the response time. The result showcase that method is suitable for handling structured and unstructured data. With this there is also an outcome that ChatGPT gives almost same accuracy with less response time which is suitable for assistance in the medical field in real-time. When it comes to large scale data, LLaMA-2 can be used which provides better performance than 3.5 but less than GPT 4.

The quantitative analysis shows that GPT-4 achieved the highest accuracy (91.6%) and F1-score (0.91), demonstrating superior ability to understand complex medical reports and genomic datasets. ChatGPT (GPT-4 tuned) provided slightly reduced accuracy compared to GPT-4 but with a 25% lower response time, making it more suitable for real-time applications. LLaMA-2 showed balanced precision and recall ($\approx$0.82), performing significantly better than GPT-3.5, especially on imaging-based diagnoses, but still trailing GPT-4. GPT-3.5 consistently underperformed in recall (0.78), leading to missed detections of rare diseases, a critical drawback in clinical applications (Fig. 4).

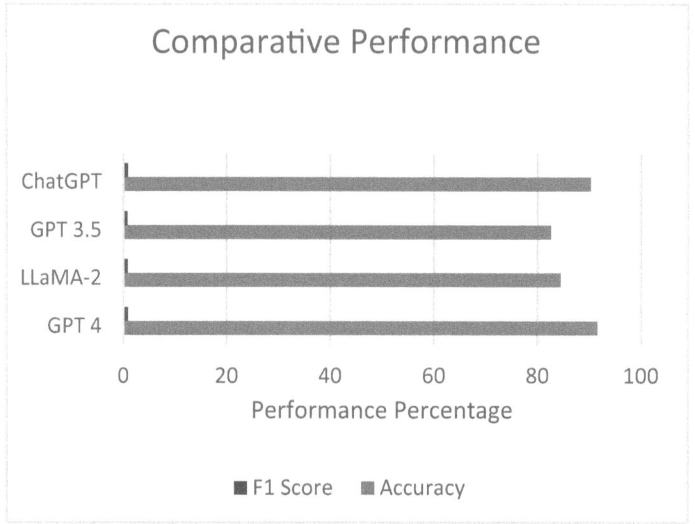


**Fig. 4.** Comparative performance of LLM's

In the same way talking about the qualitative insights the most important is error types. GPT-3.5 often failed in cases with ambiguous medical language, while LLaMA-2 sometimes struggled with genomic terminology. The strengths of GPT-4 excelled in both oncology and chronic disease detection, particularly when combining structured genomic data with unstructured clinical notes. In terms of interoperability ChatGPT provided more clinician-friendly explanations compared to raw GPT-4, which outputs highly technical responses. Also, the scalability of LLaMA-2, with faster inference times, presents a promising open-source option for large-scale hospital deployments where resources are constrained.

From the results we can establish a result that GPT 4 is one of the most reliable clinical model which has high recall and capability to contextual reasoning. The real-time efficiency of ChatGPT is making the method more suitable for clinical consultations while interacting with patients and also can be used as decision support system. The fast processing capability and open sources nature can be used for scenario which are scalable.

## 7  Conclusion and Future Scope

Diagnosing the disease, separating them according to their type and other activities, LLM's can play very transformative role in the same. There are many different models which can be used in different scenario and even the combination of two or more can be used in certain cases to get the best possible results. The potentiality of the output can be classified in two ways that is qualitative and quantitative. The advanced methods like the usage of wearable device and other smart home monitoring systems can be done to diagnose various disease and treatment can be planned for the same. Again the smart models can be created by using different LLM's which can be incorporated to get the best possible results of the smart systems. The tasks which should be covered using these systems should be diagnosing the disease, intimate to the close member or nearest hospital for the help and getting the patient monitored until the disease is cured.

## References


1. Thirunavukarasu, A.J., Ting, D.S.J., Elangovan, K., Gutierrez, L., Tan, T., Ting, D.: Large language models in medicine. Nat. Med. **29**(8), 1930–1940 (2023)
2. Harrer, S.: Attention is not all you need: the complicated case of ethically using large language models in healthcare and medicine. eBioMedicine **90**(1), 104512 (2023)
3. Reddy, S.: Evaluating large language models for use in healthcare: a framework for translational value assessment. Inform. Med. Unlocked **41**(1), 101304 (2023)
4. García-Barragán, Á., González Calatayud, A., Prieto-Santamaría, L., Robles, V., Menasalvas, E.: Step-forward structuring disease phenotypic entities with LLMs for disease understanding. In: Proceedings of the IEEE 37th International Symposium on Computer-Based Medical Systems (CBMS), Guadalajara, Mexico (2024)
5. Waisberg, E., Ong, J., Masalkhi, M., Zaman, N., Lee, A., Tavakkoli, A.: GPT-4: a new era of artificial intelligence in medicine. Ir. J. Med. Sci., 3197–3200 (2023)
6. Grassini, S.: Shaping the future of education: exploring the potential and consequences of AI and ChatGPT in educational settings. Educ. Sci. **13**(7), 692–695 (2023)
7. Koubaa, A.: GPT-4 vs. GPT-3.5: a concise showdown. Artif. Intell. Mach. Learn. **3**(2), 225–228 (2023)
8. Caruccio, L., Cirillo, S., Polese, G., Solimando, G., Tortora, G.: Can ChatGPT provide intelligent diagnoses? A comparative study between predictive models and ChatGPT to define a new medical diagnostic bot. Expert Syst. Appl. **235**(1), 121186 (2024)
9. Performance of artificial intelligence in bariatric surgery: comparative analysis of ChatGPT-4, Bing, and Bard in the American society for metabolic and bariatric surgery textbook of bariatric surgery questions. Surg. Obes. Relat. Dis. **20**(7), 609–613 (2024)
10. Nolin-Lapalme, A., et al.: Maximising large language model utility in cardiovascular care: a practical guide. Can. J. Cardiol. **41**(10), 1774–1787 (2024)

11. Wang, Z., Liu, L., Wang, L., Zhou, L.: R2GenGPT: radiology report generation with frozen LLMs. Meta-Radiology **1**(3), 100033 (2023)
12. Huang, S.-h., Chen, C.-y.: Combining LoRA to GPT-neo to reduce large language model hallucination. Review **1**(1), 112–115 (2024)
13. Liu, C., Liu, Z., Holmes, J., Zhang, L., Zhang, L., Ding, Y.: Artificial general intelligence for radiation oncology. Meta-Radiology **1**(3), 100045 (2023)
14. Xompero, C., Benettayeb, W., Mehanna, C.-J.: Pilot study evaluating the usability of MonŒil, a ChatGPT-based education tool in ophthalmology. AJO Int. **1**(2), 100032 (2024)
15. Akilesh, S, Sheik, A. , Abinaya, R., Dhanushkodi, S., Sekar, R.: A novel AI-based chatbot application for personalized medical diagnosis and review using large language models, Chennai, India (2023)
16. Panagoulias, D., Virvou, M., Tsihrintzis, G.: Augmenting large language models with rules for enhanced domain-specific interactions: the case of medical diagnosis. Electronics **13**(2), 320 (2024)
17. Vyas, B.R., Desai, M.N.: Multiphase sentiment analysis model for automatic movie reviews. In: Patel, K.K., Santosh, K., Gomes de Oliveira, G., Patel, A., Ghosh, A. (eds.) icSoftComp 2024. CCIS, vol. 2430, pp. 308–319. Springer, Cham 2025. https://doi.org/10.1007/978-3-031-88039-1_24
18. Vyas, B., Desai, M.: International Conference on Soft Computing and its Engineering Applications, pp. 190–200. Springer, Cham (2023)
19. Jonghyeon, K.,. Ju, C.-Y., Lee, D.-H.: Who can be your AI doctor?: evaluation for disease diagnosis on large language models. In: 2023 14th International Conference on Information and Communication Technology Convergence (ICTC), Jeju Island, Korea (2023)
20. Panagoulias, D., Palamidas, F., Virvou, M., Tsihrintzis, G.: Rule-augmented artificial intelligence-empowered systems for medical diagnosis using large language models. In: 2023 IEEE 35th International Conference on Tools with Artificial Intelligence (ICTAI), Atlanta, GA, USA (2023)
21. Meskó, B., Topol, E.: The imperative for regulatory oversight of large language models (or generative AI) in healthcare. npj Digit. Med. **6**(120), 100235 (2023)
22. Balas, M., Ing, E.: Conversational AI models for ophthalmic diagnosis: comparison of ChatGPT and the Isabel pro differential diagnosis generator. JFO Open Ophthalmol. **1**(1), 100005 (2023)
23. Patil, R., Gudivada, V.: A review of current trends, techniques, and challenges in large language models (LLMs). Appl. Sci. **14**(5), 2074 (2024)
24. Arora, A., Arora, A.: The promise of large language models in health care. Lancet **401**(10377), 641 (2023)
25. Ebrahimi, S., Shahbazi, A.A.: REQUAL-LM: reliability and equity through aggregation in large language models. Assoc. Comput. Linguist. **2**(1), 549–560 (2024)
26. Abumusab, S.: Introduction to the special issue: large language models and teaching writing. Teach. Philos. **47**(2), 139–142 (2024)
27. Yao, Y., Duan, J., Xu, K., Cai, Y., Sun, Z., Zhang, Y.: A survey on large language model (LLM) security and privacy: the good, the bad, and the ugly. High Confid. Comput. **4**(2), 100211 (2024)
28. Mizrahi, M., Guy, K., Dan, M., Rotem, D., Dafna, S., Stanovsky, G.: State of what art? A call for multi-prompt LLM evaluation, pp. 933–949 (2024)
29. Bhat, A., Shrivastava, D., Guo, J.L.: Do LLMs meet the needs of software tutorial writers? Opportunities and design implications. In: DIS 2024: Proceedings of the 2024 ACM Designing Interactive Systems Conference, Copenhagen Denmark (2024)
30. Mohaimenul Azam Khan, R., Hossain Mukta, M.S., Fatema, K., Mohammad Fahad, N., Sadman, S., Most Marufatul, J.M.: A review on large language models: architectures, applications, taxonomies, open issues and challenges. IEEE Access **12**(1), 26839–26874 (2024)

31. Mosavi, A., Imre, F., Hung, V.T.: ChatGPT and large language models in healthcare; a bibliometrics analysis and review. In: Proceedings of the IEEE 11th International Conference on Computer, Cybernetics and Cyber-Medical Systems (ICCC), Hanoi, Vietnam (2024)
32. Boonstra, M., Weissenbacher, D., Jason, H.M.: Artificial intelligence: revolutionizing cardiology. Eur. Heart J. **45**(5), 332–345 (2024)
33. Kwan, H.Y.: User-focused telehealth powered by LLMs: bridging the gap between technology and human-centric care delivery. In: Proceedings of the 4th International Conference on Computer, Communication and Artificial Intelligence (CCAI), Xi'an China (2024)
34. Yang, R., Fang Tan, T., Lu, W., James Thirun, A.: Large language models in health care: development, applications, and challenges. Health Care Sci. **2**(4), 255–263 (2023)
35. Lee, Y., et al.: Harnessing artificial intelligence in bariatric surgery: comparative analysis of ChatGPT-4, Bing, and Bard in generating clinician-level bariatric surgery recommendations. Surg. Obes. Relat. Dis. **20**(7), 603–608 (2024)
36. Hart, S., et al.: Organizational preparedness for the use of large language models in pathology informatics. J. Pathol. Inform. **14**(1), 100338 (2023)
37. Wang, B., Chen, Z., Li, Z., Fu, J., Xie, Q.: Pre-trained language models in biomedical domain: a systematic survey. ACM Comput. Surv. **56**(3), 1–52 (2023)
38. Yuan, M., et al.: Large language models illuminate a progressive pathway to artificial intelligent healthcare assistant. Med. Plus **1**(2), 100030 (2024)
39. Integrating automated knowledge extraction with large language models for explainable medical decision-making. In: 2023 IEEE International Conference on Bioinformatics and Biomedicine (BIBM), Istanbul, Turkiye (2023)
40. Sai, S., Gaur, A., Chamola, V., Guizani, M.: Generative AI for transformative healthcare: a comprehensive study of emerging models, applications, case studies, and limitations. IEEE Access **12**(1), 31078–31106 (2024)

# PSKA-UAV: A Pre-shared Key-Based Authentication Protocol for Secure and Efficient Communication Between UAV and GCS


Ankush Soni[✉] and Sanjay K. Sahay

BITS Pilani K. K. Birla Goa Campus, Goa, India
`{p20180413,ssahay}@goa.bits-pilani.ac.in`



**Abstract.** Unmanned Aerial Vehicles (UAVs) are increasingly being deployed in mission-critical scenarios such as disaster management, surveillance, and remote logistics, where human presence is either unsafe or impractical. These vehicles usually come with some sensors and typically communicate the sensors' data to a Ground Control Station (GCS) over wireless channels, which are inherently vulnerable to security threats, including eavesdropping, data manipulation, impersonation, and denial-of-service attacks. Moreover, the constrained computational and energy resources onboard UAVs limit the feasibility of traditional cryptographic protocols. In this paper, we propose PSKA-UAV, a lightweight mutual authentication and secure communication protocol that uses symmetric cryptography based on a pre-shared key. The protocol is structured into two phases– mutual authentication with session key generation and secure communication uses SEASHA3 for encryption to maintain efficiency. Through detailed experimental analysis, we demonstrate that PSKA-UAV achieves strong security properties while significantly reducing resource consumption, making it well-suited for secure UAV communication in adversarial and resource-limited environments.

**Keywords:** Pre Shared Keys · Secure Communication · Unmanned Aerial Vehicles · Authentication


## 1 Introduction

Unmanned Aerial Vehicles (UAVs), or drones, are widely used in applications such as surveillance, disaster response, aerial mapping, infrastructure inspection, and logistics. Their ability to operate autonomously and transmit real-time data makes them highly effective in both civilian and military missions, particularly in environments that are risky or inaccessible to humans. To support such operations, UAVs typically communicate with a Ground Control Station (GCS) over wireless channels to exchange sensor data and receive control instructions. However, this wireless communication often takes place over insecure links, leaving




K. K. Patel et al. (Eds.): icSoftComp 2025, CCIS 2874, pp. 134–146, 2026.
https://doi.org/10.1007/978-3-032-22062-2_11

it exposed to several security threats, including eavesdropping, message tampering, replay and impersonation attacks. In mission-critical scenarios, such threats can compromise data confidentiality, disrupt operational control, or even lead to the complete failure of the mission.

Therefore, ensuring the security of the UAV-GCS communication link is important. However, doing so presents challenges due to the limited processing power, memory, and energy resources available on UAV platforms. Conventional security mechanisms based on public key cryptography, although reasonable, introduce considerable computational overhead and latency, making them impractical for real-time communications and resource-constrained UAV deployments. To address these limitations, we propose PSKA-UAV – a lightweight mutual authentication and secure communication protocol built on symmetric key cryptography using a pre-shared key (PSK). The protocol consists of two phases: a mutual authentication and session key generation phase and a secure data exchange phase using either standard AES or SEASHA3, a lightweight encryption variant proposed by Soni et al. [1], optimised for resource-constrained devices. Importantly, the protocol avoids the use of public key operations entirely, ensuring low computational cost and suitability for real-time mission execution. We implement and evaluate PSKA-UAV in a simulated UAV environment using ArduPilot and MAVLink to replicate real-world UAVGCS communication. Experimental results demonstrate that PSKA-UAV provides mutual authentication, data confidentiality, and message integrity while maintaining low latency and minimal resource usage.

The main contributions of this paper are as follows: (1) the design of a symmetric key-based mutual authentication protocol tailored for UAV systems; (2) a lightweight session key derivation method based on HMAC and PSK-derived values; (3) integration of AESHA3 for efficient and secure encrypted communication; and (4) a detailed performance evaluation in a realistic simulation environment using ArduPilot and MAVLink. The remainder of this paper is organised as follows. Section 2 discusses related work. Section 3 discusses the preliminaries used to design the protocol and adversary models used in the security analysis. Section 4 presents the proposed protocol. Section 5 outlines the implementation setup and analyses the experimental results. Section 6 concludes the paper and highlights future directions.

## 2    Related Work

The growing use of UAVs in defence and civilian applications has led to a wide range of secure communication protocols aimed at addressing the constraints of wireless channels and resource-limited platforms.

Early approaches such as eCLSC-TKEM by Won et al. [2] and its multi-recipient extension [3] removed the need for certificates using pairing-based cryptography but introduced high computational costs unsuitable for UAVs. Bae et al. [4] proposed offloading credentials to the GCS to reduce on-board risk, though the design lacked mutual authentication and relied on continuous connectivity.

In response to these limitations, several lightweight authentication protocols were developed. Several lightweight authentication protocols have since emerged. PARTH [5] used symmetric cryptography and timestamps for SDN-based UAV swarms but did not evaluate time-critical performance. SENTINEL [6] combined ECDSA, PBKDF, and HMAC, while SecAuthUAV [7] used PUFs for hardware-bound authentication. However, these approaches either assumed a secure physically unclonable function (PUF) deployment or overlooked adversarial mobility and real-time requirements. Other efforts focused on group authentication and scalability. AinQ [8] and S-MAPS [9] provided dynamic rekeying and tamper resistance but introduced communication overhead and lacked evaluation under dynamic conditions. LAKE-IoD [10] and SHOTS [11] targeted energy-efficient authentication but relied on static trajectories or small network sizes.

Over the past few years, blockchain-based schemes have also gained attention. Son et al. [12] and Wang et al. [13] integrated PUFs and hash functions with blockchain for decentralised trust and traceability, but these methods required continuous connectivity and infrastructure support. Similarly, Chen et al. [14] and Karmakar et al. [15] explored blockchain-integrated key management and adaptive session control, though these added delay and overhead due to consensus and PUF stabilisation.

To support efficient encryption in resource-constrained settings, Soni et al. proposed SEASHA3 [1], which enhances AES by replacing round subkeys with SHA-3 digests, offering better performance while preserving AES-level security. In contrast to these prior efforts, our proposed PSKA-UAV protocol is fully symmetric and requires no public key operations, blockchain infrastructure, or hardware-bound elements like PUFs. It supports secure registration, mutual authentication, and encrypted data exchange using only lightweight cryptographic primitives, making it practical for real-time UAVGCS communication with low latency and better computational efficiency.

## 3    Preliminaries

This section outlines the foundational cryptographic concepts and mechanisms that support the design of the proposed protocol. It also introduces the system model and the widely adopted Dolev-Yao (DY) adversary model, which guides the security assumptions and threat considerations in our work. These preliminaries establish the context necessary for understanding the protocol's structure, security properties, and its suitability for UAV communication scenarios.

### 3.1    AES and SEASHA3

The Advanced Encryption Standard (AES) is a symmetric key block cipher approved by the National Institute of Standards and Technology (NIST) in 2001 as a replacement for the earlier Data Encryption Standard (DES). AES encrypts data in fixed 128-bit blocks and supports key lengths of 128, 192, and 256 bits [16]. The encryption process begins with an initial AddRoundKey operation, followed by a series of transformation rounds. Each round includes SubBytes–a nonlinear byte substitution using an S-box; ShiftRows–a transposition step that cyclically shifts rows of the state matrix; and MixColumns–a mixing operation that combines column values to achieve diffusion. The final round omits the MixColumns step, as per the AES specification.

AES employs a key schedule that generates a distinct round key for each encryption round, derived from the master key. This mechanism introduces randomness across rounds, strengthening resistance against cryptanalytic attacks. The combination of substitution, permutation, and mixing operations ensures both confusion and diffusion, which are essential for robust encryption. Due to its standardized structure and consistent performance, AES is widely adopted in both hardware and software implementations across various domains.

To improve performance for constrained environments, a recent enhancement to AES, termed SEASHA3, was proposed by Soni et al. [1]. SEASHA3 was designed with the goal of reducing computational overhead while maintaining the security guarantees of AES, particularly for small data sizes typical in IoT and UAV scenarios. Unlike the traditional AES key expansion, which is sequential and therefore computationally intensive. SEASHA3 replaces the key scheduling process with a SHA-3-based generation technique. SHA-3's output–characterized by non-linearity, randomness, and irreversibility–adds strong cryptographic properties to the derived subkeys. One of the notable advantages of SEASHA3 lies in its improved performance for short messages, where it was shown to be approximately 1300 times faster than standard AES under specific conditions. For larger data sizes, its performance aligns more closely with that of conventional AES, ensuring scalability while preserving compatibility. The integration of SHA-3 into the key generation phase makes SEASHA3 a compelling choice for lightweight cryptographic applications, offering a balance between efficiency and security without altering the fundamental AES architecture.

## 3.2   Hash-Based Message Authentication Codes

Hash-Based Message Authentication Code (HMAC) is a cryptographic method used to ensure both the integrity and authenticity of a message [17]. It achieves this by combining a cryptographic hash function with a shared secret key. HMAC is particularly valued for its simplicity, strong security guarantees, and suitability for devices with limited computational resources.

The process begins by adjusting the secret key to match the input size of the chosen hash function. If the key is shorter than the required length, it is padded with zeros. This key is then used to create two separate padded values by performing a bitwise XOR with two predefined constants known as the inner and outer padding (ipad and opad). These modified keys form the basis for the HMAC construction.

To generate the HMAC tag, the message is first concatenated with the inner padded key and passed through the hash function, producing an intermediate result. This result is then concatenated with the outer padded key and hashed again, yielding the final HMAC value. This tag is sent alongside the message to the receiver.

Upon receiving the message and the tag, the receiver uses the same key and steps to compute the HMAC locally. If the computed tag matches the one received, it confirms that the message has not been altered and that it originates from a legitimate sender. Due to its efficiency and strong security properties, HMAC is widely adopted in communication protocols and is especially well-suited for embedded and low-power environments such as IoT and UAV systems.

### 3.3  Adversary Model

The security of the proposed protocol is analyzed under the Dolev–Yao (DY) threat model, which is widely adopted in formal cryptographic protocol analysis. In this model, the adversary is assumed to have complete control over the communication network. That is, the attacker can intercept, block, replay, modify, and inject messages at any point in the communication between parties. This assumption captures the worst-case scenario for network-based attacks and represents a strong adversarial setting.

However, the DY model also assumes that cryptographic primitives behave ideally. This means that encryption schemes, hash functions, and digital signatures are treated as black-box operations that are unbreakable unless the corresponding keys are known. For instance, an attacker cannot decrypt a ciphertext without the appropriate key or invert a cryptographic hash function. Under this assumption, the attacker's power lies not in breaking cryptography but in manipulating messages, exploiting protocol flaws, or reusing valid messages in unintended ways.

The Dolev–Yao model gives the adversary the following capabilities:

- *Interception:* The attacker can eavesdrop on all communications between the UAV and GCS.
- *Message modification:* The attacker can alter the contents of transmitted packets, including commands, authentication data, or session keys.
- *Message injection:* The attacker can craft and send new messages that appear to come from a legitimate party.
- *Replay attacks:* The attacker can capture valid message exchanges from a previous session and retransmit them to attempt unauthorized access.
- *Blocking or delaying messages:* The attacker can drop or delay packets to disrupt synchronization or degrade the UAV's performance.

By designing the protocol under the DY model, we ensure that it remains secure even when the communication channel is completely untrusted. This model is especially appropriate for UAV–GCS communication, where wireless links may be exposed to adversaries with the ability to monitor or tamper with messages in real time.

## 4    Proposed Protocol

We propose a lightweight authentication and key agreement protocol based on PSK by using a recently proposed symmetric cipher, i.e. SEASHA3, a modified version of AES proposed by Soni et al. [1]. The protocol is designed to be lightweight and efficient for resource-constrained UAV platforms. It omits the need of computationally intensive operations such as public key cryptography concepts. The protocol emphasises on minimal computational overhead, robust authentication, and robust protection against common network attacks such as replay, impersonation, and man-in-the-middle.

The complete protocol can be logically divided into the following phases: (i) mutual authentication and key derivation and (ii) secure data communication.

### 4.1    Mutual Authentication and Session Key Generation Phase

In the initial step, the UAV and GCS perform a secure exchange using their pre-shared key to authenticate each other and derive temporary secrets. The UAV generates a fresh nonce and timestamp, and constructs a ciphertext by encrypting its own identity, the GCS's identity, the nonce, and the timestamp using the PSK. This message is sent to the GCS, allowing the latter to confirm the UAV's identity and the freshness of the message.

The GCS then decrypts the received message using the PSK, verifies the timestamp for freshness, and generates its own nonce and timestamp. It responds by encrypting the full context along with its generated nonce and timestamp, sending this back to the UAV. This encrypted round-trip confirms possession of the PSK and validates both parties' activity.

Following this mutual exchange, both entities compute an intermediate key $K_1 = H(N_U \oplus N_C)$ derived by hashing the XOR of their respective nonces. This key includes randomness from both participants, ensuring that the resulting key material is fresh and unique to the session. Subsequently, they derive a second key $K_2 = H(K_1 || CTR_i)$ where CTR refers to the counter value used for AES encryption in Counter (CTR) mode. The introduction of CTR mode prevents key reuse across messages or sessions. Since CTR mode produces a unique keystream for each encryption instance based on the counter input, deriving $K_2$ with a session-specific input like CTR ensures that even if the same $K_1$ is reused, the resulting $K_2$ will be different. This secures the system against key reuse and mitigates the risk of replay attacks, as messages encrypted under different CTR values produce entirely different ciphertexts–even when the same base key is involved. Together, $K_1$ and $K_2$ serve as the foundation for deriving the final session key, which will be used to secure subsequent mission communication. Their construction ensures cryptographic isolation between sessions and supports efficient encryption tailored for UAV systems. The message exchange for this phase is illustrated in Fig. 1.

To confirm that both parties have successfully derived identical key material, the UAV and GCS engage in a mutual key confirmation process through the exchange of HMAC values. The UAV initiates this step by transmitting an

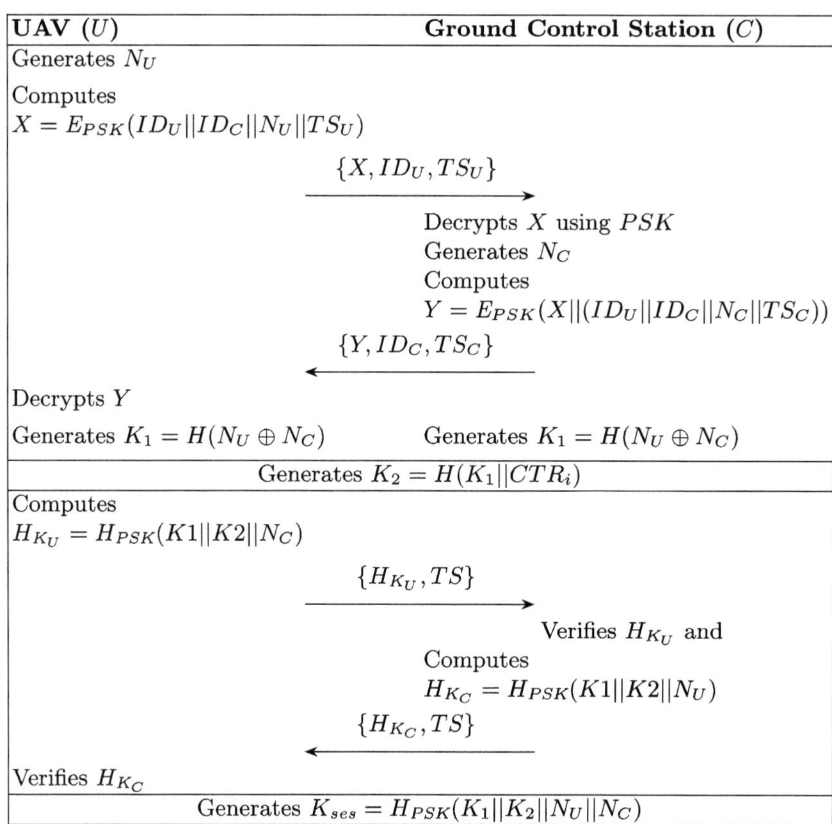

Fig. 1. Mutual Authentication and Session Key Generation Phase between UAV and Controller

HMAC, $H_{K_U}$ computed over the GCS's nonce, both entity identifiers, and its own nonce using the derived key $K_2$. Upon receiving this message, the GCS verifies the integrity of the HMAC. If the verification succeeds, the GCS responds with its own HMAC, $H_{K_C}$ generated using the same corresponding parameters thereby completing the bidirectional confirmation.

This bidirectional exchange ensures that both entities possess the same derived key $K_2$ and confirms the consistency of the session parameters. The use of HMAC in this step provides authentication and guarantees the integrity of the exchanged messages. Once mutual verification is complete, both sides compute the session key. This key is generated by applying a HMAC function over a concatenation of $K_1$ and $K_2$ along with the previous nonces of the UAV and GCS. This construction binds the key to the specific session context and ensures cryptographic separation across sessions, even under repeated use of individual parameters. This ensures that the session key is unique for every session and is protected against replay attacks (Fig. 2).

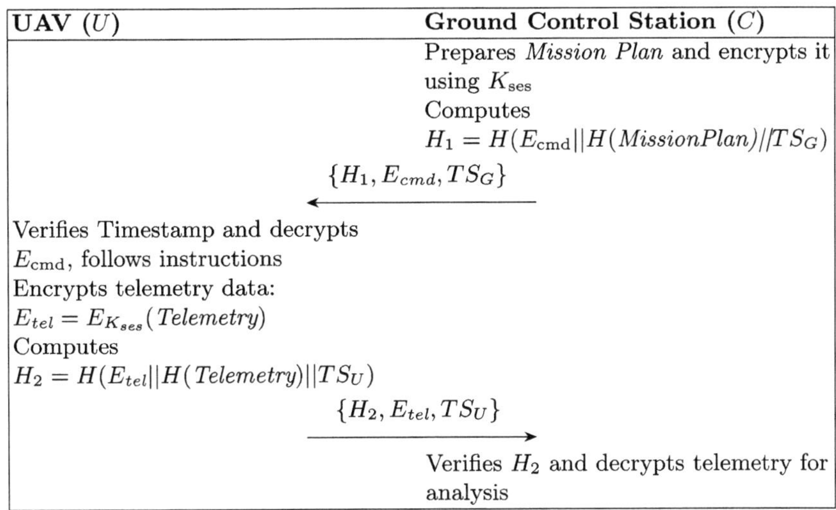

| UAV ($U$) | Ground Control Station ($C$) |
|---|---|
| | Prepares *Mission Plan* and encrypts it using $K_{\text{ses}}$ |
| | Computes |
| | $H_1 = H(E_{\text{cmd}}\|H(MissionPlan)\|TS_G)$ |
| | $\{H_1, E_{cmd}, TS_G\}$ |
| | $\longleftarrow$ |
| Verifies Timestamp and decrypts $E_{\text{cmd}}$, follows instructions | |
| Encrypts telemetry data: | |
| $E_{tel} = E_{K_{ses}}(Telemetry)$ | |
| Computes | |
| $H_2 = H(E_{tel}\|H(Telemetry)\|TS_U)$ | |
| $\{H_2, E_{tel}, TS_U\}$ | |
| $\longrightarrow$ | |
| | Verifies $H_2$ and decrypts telemetry for analysis |

**Fig. 2.** Secure communication phase using AES or SEASHA3

## 4.2   Secure Communication Phase

After successfully generating and confirming the session key $K_{ses}$, both the UAV and the GCS begin the secure mission communication. This phase guarantees confidentiality, integrity, and freshness of messages exchanged during the mission through the use of symmetric encryption and hash-based verification mechanisms. GCS initiates the secure communication by constructing a mission plan, which consists of operational commands (e.g., takeoff, hover, land) and associated instructions like target GPS coordinates, flight altitude, and data collection requirements. To ensure confidentiality, the GCS encrypts this mission plan using the session key $E_{cmd} = E_{K_{ses}}(MissionPlan)$ Further, in order to preserve the integrity of the message, the GCS computes a hash of the encrypted message along with the actual message and the timestamp of the message as $H_1 = H(E_{cmd}\|H(MissionPlan)\|TS_G)$. The GCS then transmits $\{H_1, E_{\text{cmd}}, TS_{G_i}\}$ to the UAV.

Upon receiving the message, the UAV first verifies the freshness of the message using the timestamp $TS_G$. It then recomputes the hash $H_1$ and compares it with the received value. If the verification is successful, the UAV decrypts the command $E_{cmd}$ using $K_{ses}$ and executes the instructions accordingly. Simultaneously, the UAV captures telemetry data and other mission-relevant information in real time. To send this telemetry data securely back to the GCS, the UAV encrypts the data with the same session key, $E_{tel} = E_{K_{ses}}(Telemetry)$. For ensuring the integrity and preventing tampering of the telemetry data, $H_2 = H(E_{tel}\|H(Telemetry)\|TS_U)$. It then sends the data packet $\{H_2, E_{tel}, TS_U\}$ to the GCS.

Once received, the GCS first checks the timestamp $TS_U$ to ensure message freshness. It then verifies the integrity of the message using $H_2$. Upon successful validation, the telemetry data is decrypted using $K_{ses}$ and is subsequently analyzed or stored for future mission assessment. This structured and cryptographically secure exchange ensures reliable mission execution and resilience against replay, spoofing, and data manipulation attacks.

## 5   Experimental Analysis

To evaluate the practicality and performance of the proposed protocol under conditions that closely resemble real UAV operations, we implemented it in a simulated test environment using ArduPilot SITL and MAVLink. These tools allowed us to recreate mission scenarios such as take-off, waypoint navigation, and return-to-launch with high fidelity, offering a controlled yet representative setting for experimentation. All tests were conducted on a Linux system powered by an Intel i7 processor and 12 GB of RAM.

Further, instead of relying on existing cryptographic libraries, we chose to implement all encryption, hashing, and key exchange operations manually in Python. This approach gave us complete control over each cryptographic step, allowing us to better understand performance bottlenecks and fine-tune the design for UAV-specific constraints.

For this analysis, we considered the following cryptographic components:

- AES-256: The standard block cipher using a 256-bit key.
- SEASHA3: A customized encryption algorithm proposed by Soni et al. [1].
- SHA2-512: A high-security hashing function, evaluated against SHA2-256, SHA3-256 and SHA3-512.
- HMAC with SHA2-512: Used for higher efficiency as shown in [18]

We evaluated the overall performance of our proposed protocol by executing it under a range of cryptographic configurations, focusing particularly on combinations of symmetric encryption algorithms (AES and SEASHA3) paired with multiple hash functions. The goal was to identify the optimal trade-off between computational efficiency and security strength that would make the protocol suitable for UAVGCS communications, particularly in environments where low-latency response and minimal energy usage are critical (Fig. 3).

We tested four widely recognized hash functions–SHA2-256, SHA2-512, SHA3-256, and SHA3-512–across different symmetric encryption backends. Among these, SHA2-512 consistently emerged as the most efficient. While SHA2-256 remains a popular choice in many embedded systems, our experimental results showed that SHA2-512 not only offers enhanced cryptographic resilience due to its larger output size but also executes faster in our implementation context. For instance, when used with AES-256, SHA2-512 completed the protocol in 136.332 ms, compared to 276.943 ms for SHA2-256, resulting in a 50.77% gain in speed. Similarly, it outperformed SHA3-512–which required 247.581 ms–by

**Table 1.** Total Protocol Implementation Time using AES and SEASHA3 with Different Hash Functions

| Hash Function | AES Variant | AES Time (ms) | SEASHA3 Variant | SEASHA3 Time (ms) |
| --- | --- | --- | --- | --- |
| SHA2-256 | AES-128 | 210.376 | SEASHA3-128 | 0.105 |
| | AES-192 | 229.841 | SEASHA3-192 | 0.115 |
| | AES-256 | 276.943 | SEASHA3-256 | 0.131 |
| SHA2-512 | AES-128 | 104.682 | SEASHA3-128 | 0.053 |
| | AES-192 | 118.475 | SEASHA3-192 | 0.059 |
| | AES-256 | 136.332 | SEASHA3-256 | 0.066 |
| SHA3-256 | AES-128 | 378.291 | SEASHA3-128 | 0.176 |
| | AES-192 | 396.848 | SEASHA3-192 | 0.187 |
| | AES-256 | 454.928 | SEASHA3-256 | 0.210 |
| SHA3-512 | AES-128 | 198.452 | SEASHA3-128 | 0.091 |
| | AES-192 | 213.124 | SEASHA3-192 | 0.098 |
| | AES-256 | 247.581 | SEASHA3-256 | 0.112 |

44.56%. This advantage was consistently observed across AES variants, indicating that SHA2-512 is better suited for mission-critical and time-sensitive UAV deployments. These observations are consistent with and reinforce the findings of Soni et al. [18], which established the superior HMAC performance of SHA2-512 over other hash algorithms under constrained resource environments. The detailed results are shown in Table 1.

In parallel, we assessed the protocol using SEASHA3 – a lightweight, symmetric cipher designed for high-speed applications. The improvements here were substantial. With SEASHA3-256 as the encryption base, and SHA2-512 as the hash function, the protocol executed in only 0.066 ms. When combined with SHA2-256 and SHA3-512, the times increased to 0.131 ms and 0.112 ms respectively. This means that SHA2-512 delivered 49.62% faster performance compared to SHA2-256 and 41.07% faster compared to SHA3-512, even under high-speed encryption settings. These performance gains are particularly useful in real-time mission contexts, where every millisecond counts and data transmissions must be authenticated and encrypted quickly.

After the key agreement phase, we tested the secure communication stage of the protocol using a 1 MB payload to simulate mission-critical data like command sequences or telemetry. Here again, SEASHA3-256 outperformed AES-256. While AES-256 took 136.332 ms to encrypt the payload, SEASHA3-256 accomplished the same task in just 0.066 ms–equating to a 99.95% improvement in performance. This significant boost facilitates much quicker end-to-end communication, improving the UAV's ability to adapt to real-time commands and relay sensor data back to the GCS with minimal delay.

Overall, the results of our experimental analysis conclude that pairing SHA2-512 with SEASHA3 offers a compelling blend of performance and security. For

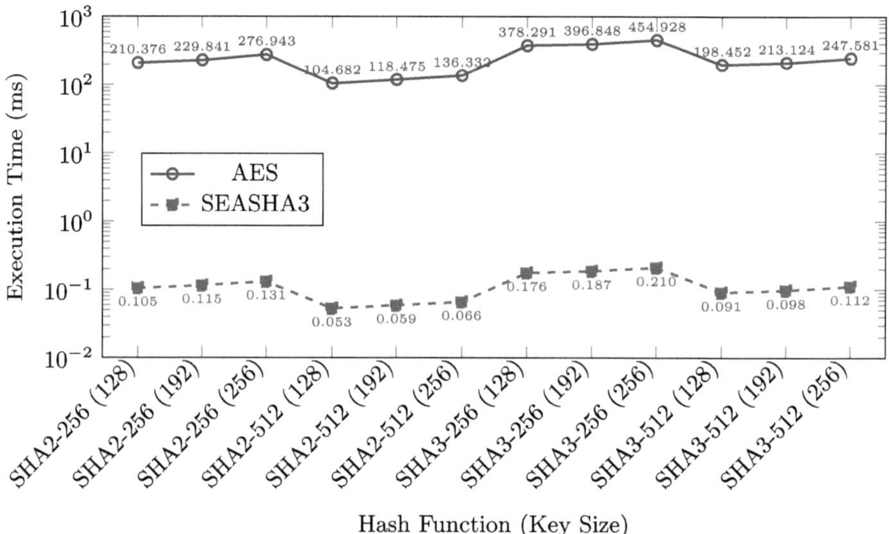



**Fig. 3.** Total Protocol Implementation Time Using AES and SEASHA3 With Different Hash Functions

UAV platforms with constrained hardware and high demands for real-time operation, this cryptographic combination not only preserves mission confidentiality and integrity but does so with exceptional efficiency. Such optimization is essential for sustaining long-duration missions and handling frequent encrypted exchanges under operational constraints.

## 6     Conclusion and Future Work

In this paper, we presented a secure and efficient mutual authentication and key agreement protocol tailored for communication between UAVs and GCS. The protocol was carefully designed to strike a balance between strong security and low computational overhead, making it suitable for resource-constrained UAV platforms. By using pre-shared keys and lightweight cryptographic operations, the protocol avoids the complexities of traditional public key infrastructures while ensuring robust authentication and secure session key establishment.

We implemented the complete protocol using Python and evaluated its performance using a Raspberry Pi 4B as the UAV and an Intel i7-powered system running Ubuntu 22.04 as the GCS. Communication between the two was facilitated by the MAVLink protocol, while the flight dynamics were simulated using the ArduPilot SITL environment. All cryptographic primitives–including hashing, encryption, and key derivation–were implemented from scratch to ensure precise control and accurate measurement of execution metrics. Our performance analysis highlights the efficiency of the proposed scheme. In particular, SHA2-512 emerged as the most optimal choice for hashing, offering both stronger security and better runtime compared to SHA2-256 and SHA3 variants. Similarly, our customized encryption approach using SEASHA3 significantly outperformed standard AES implementations, demonstrating notable improvements in both speed and energy consumption.

Given its lightweight structure and emphasis on efficiency, the proposed protocol is well-positioned for deployment in a wide range of UAV applications that require secure and real-time communication. From industrial automation and infrastructure monitoring to research and civilian drone missions, the protocol offers a practical solution for maintaining confidentiality, authenticity, and integrity over inherently insecure wireless channels. Its ability to deliver fast authentication and reliable data protection makes it a strong candidate for enhancing mission-critical UAV operations.

# References


1. Soni, A., Sahay, S.K.: Seasha3: secure and efficient encryption for the iot data by replacing subkeys of aes with sha3. In: 2024 IEEE International Conference on Systems, Man, and Cybernetics (SMC), pp. 1998–2003 (2024)
2. Won, J., Seo,S.-H., Bertino, E.: A secure communication protocol for drones and smart objects. In: Proceedings of the 10th ACM Symposium on Information, Computer and Communications Security, ASIA CCS 2015, pp. 249–260. Association for Computing Machinery, New York (2015)
3. Won, J., Singla, A., Bertino, E.: Certificateless cryptography-based rule management protocol for advanced mission delivery networks. In: 2017 IEEE 37th International Conference on Distributed Computing Systems Workshops (ICDCSW), pp. 7–12 (2017)
4. Bae, M., Kim, H.: Authentication and delegation for operating a multi-drone system. Sensors (Basel, Switzerland) **19** (2019)
5. Alladi, T., Chamola, V., Naren, N.K.: Parth: a two-stage lightweight mutual authentication protocol for uav surveillance networks. Comput. Commun. **160**, 81–90 (2020)
6. Cho, G., Cho, J., Hyun, S., Kim, H.: Sentinel: a secure and efficient authentication framework for unmanned aerial vehicles. Appl. Sci. **10**(9) (2020)
7. Alladi, T., Naren, G.B., Chamola, V., Guizani, M.: Secauthuav: a novel authentication scheme for uav-ground station and uav-uav communication. IEEE Trans. Veh. Technol. **69**, 15068–15077 (2020)
8. Frimpong, E., Rabbaninejad, R., Michalas, A.: Arrows in a quiver: a secure certificateless group key distribution protocol for drones. In: Tuveri, N., Michalas, A., Brumley, B.B. (eds) NordSec 2021. LNCS, vol. 13115. Springer, Cham (2021). https://doi.org/10.1007/978-3-030-91625-1_3
9. Bansal, G., Sikdar, B.: S-maps: Scalable mutual authentication protocol for dynamic uav swarms. IEEE Trans. Veh. Technol. **70**(11), 12088–12100 (2021)
10. Tanveer, M., Zahid, A.H., Ahmad, M., Baz, A., Alhakami, H.: Lake-iod: lightweight authenticated key exchange protocol for the internet of drone environment. IEEE Access **8**, 155645–155659 (2020)
11. Gaurang Bansal, N., Chamola, V., Sikdar, B.: Shots: scalable secure authentication-attestation protocol using optimal trajectory in uav swarms. IEEE Trans. Veh. Technol. **71**, 5827–5836 (2022)

12. Son, S., Kwon, D., Lee, S., Jeon, Y., Das, A.K., Park, Y.: Design of secure and lightweight authentication scheme for uav-enabled intelligent transportation systems using blockchain and puf. IEEE Access **11**, 60240–60253 (2023)
13. Wang, W., Han, Z., Gadekallu, T.R., Raza, S., Tanveer, J., Chunhua, S.: Lightweight blockchain-enhanced mutual authentication protocol for uavs. IEEE Internet Things J. **11**(6), 9547–9557 (2024)
14. Chen, L., et al.: Puf-based dynamic secret-key strategy with hierarchical blockchain for uav swarm authentication. IEEE Trans. Dependable Sec. Comput. (2024)
15. Karmakar, S., et al.: Uaas: adaptive and probabilistic authentication scheme using fuzzy extractors for uavs. IEEE Trans. Inform. Forensics Sec. (2024)
16. Dworkin, M.J., et al.: National Institute of Standards, Technology (NIST), Advanced encryption standard (aes), 2001-11-26 00:11:00 (2001)
17. Krawczyk, H., Bellare, M., Canetti, R.: Rfc2104: Hmac: Keyed-hashing for message authentication (1997)
18. Soni, A., Sahay, S.K., Soni, V.: Hash based message authentication code performance with different secure hash functions. In: 2025 10th International Conference on Signal Processing and Communication (ICSC), pp. 104–109 (2025)

# Signature-Based Anomaly-Aware DAG Execution for Efficient Real-Time Data Quality Remediation

Rakesh Keshava[1]([✉]), Arun Kumar Elengovan[2], Nandagopal Seshagiri[3], and Lahari Putty[4]

[1] Fremont, CA 94555, USA
rakesh.keshava@gmail.com
[2] Fremont, CA 94539, USA
[3] San Ramon, CA 94583, USA
[4] Princeton, TX 75407, USA

**Abstract.** A new framework is proposed to remediate the current real-time data quality by incorporating the anomaly signature learning, the traversal of causal dependency, resource-sensitive implementation, and fault resilient dynamic-data-pipe orchestration. As opposed to traditional systems which re-execute entire workflows when anomalies do occur (e.g. null spikes or schema drift), this method encodes context rich signatures and uses time-decayed similarity scoring to compare with a historical repository. Once a match is observed, the associated remediation path is reused, and otherwise, a minimal subgraph is chosen through casually-aware DAG search. Metadata about dependencies and resource costs is stored within each node of the DAG making it possible to execute even when there are limited compute budgets. There is a checkpoint such that partial rollbacks occur in case of downstream failures; previous successful states are maintained. There is also support in the architecture to support complex DAG topologies arising with branching and joins enabling fine grained remediation. The system was tested against Numenta Anomaly Benchmark, improving the execution savings by more than 60% and doubling the remediation rate, and performed regardless of external models and human intervention.

**Keywords:** Real-Time Data Quality · Anomaly Signature Matching · Resource-Aware Orchestration

## 1 Introduction

Today, data pipelines can support real-time analytics as well as AI; however, still face quality challenges, such as nulls, schema-drift, and outliers, particularly due to dynamic systems in the upstream [1–3]. The traditional architectures react by recomputing the full DAGs, squandering resources, and paying no attention to whether the anomaly is local or systemic [4, 5]. Current reactive systems as well have no context-awareness

---

R. Keshava, A. K. Elengovan, N. Seshagiri, L. Putty—Independent Researcher.


K. K. Patel et al. (Eds.): icSoftComp 2025, CCIS 2874, pp. 147–159, 2026.
https://doi.org/10.1007/978-3-032-22062-2_12

and they all turn a mammoth ailment into an equal amount of abnormality ignoring the interdependencies and subsequent ramification [6]. With the growth of data in realms such as IoT and financial systems, the need to define data-scale scalable and smart remediation emerges [7]. The present paper fills these gaps with context-aware framework using signs of anomalies, causal DAG traversal, resource-limited execution, and rollback confirming using checkpoints. This design makes it possible to filter, fault-tolerant remediation selectively, without prior models or handcrafted rules, and provides a basis of self-healing, resilient workflow pipelines.

## 2  Literature Review

Initial data quality applications were based on fixed-rules-based data quality tests of null tests, duplicates and ranges of a structured data set [8, 9]. They were designed to work on stable environments, instruments such as profilers and wrangling frameworks were not adaptive to streaming dynamic data [10, 25]. Their orchestration of ETL also caused them to be less responsive to changes in semantics due to manual orchestration [11, 22]. Detectors based on ML like Isolation Forests [12], Autoencodors [13] and LSTMs [14, 15], enhanced anomaly detection in fast-paced environments such as IoT and telemetry [16, 17], but without support to orchestration-level remediation and consumed a lot of compute and retraining [18, 24]. Subsequently, such platforms as Airflow and Deequ began to include automatic retries and simple anomaly hooks [3, 19] enhanced by rule-based DAG logics [5]. But they re-performing whole branches without any attention to the scope of the anomalies, and neither to their severity nor their cost [21, 23]. We are proposing a modular framework that consists of signature-based matching, traversal of causal directed acyclic graph, resilience by rollback and cost-conscious execution. It accelerates and makes more reliable the remediation in dynamic pipelines, which was verified on the Numenta Anomaly Benchmark [7].

## 3  Methodology

In this section, the outline of the main architecture of the proposed real-time remediation system is depicted. The pipeline combines the use of anomaly detection, signature matching, causal directed acyclic graphs to be executed and resource equipment budgeting and rollback. All the elements complement each other to make their anomaly response efficient and adaptive in the streaming data space.

### 3.1  Framework Overview

The system is built up in the form of a directed acyclic graph (DAG), with each node being a processing step, e.g., ingestion, cleaning, feature engineering or output (Fig. 1). The affected subgraph is triggered by anomalies following the causal dependencies and stored signatures, skipping re-execution of the whole DAG.

The DAG allows the use of parallel branches and joins to allow more flexibility. Data paths of CleanA and CleanB are processed separately and join at JoinCleans, then have shared nodes downstream.

All of this is made possible by this structure where remediations can be isolated and routed through the system to facilitate modular, cost-conscious recovery.

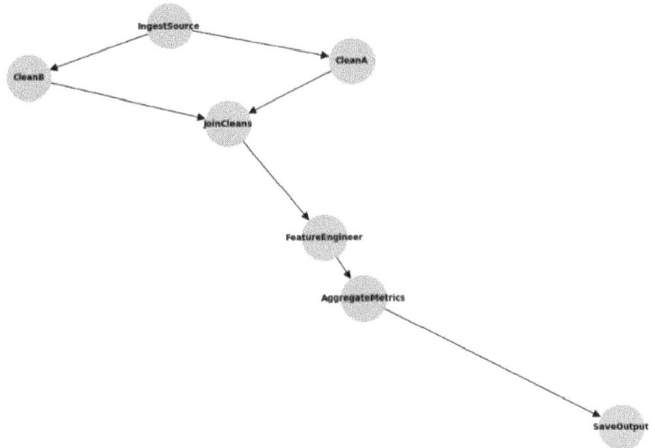

**Fig. 1.** Causal DAG Structure with Branching and Merge

## 3.2   Dataset and Ingestion Simulation

The Numenta Anomaly Benchmark (NAB) was employed to assess the offered remediation framework. In particular, CPU stream of the NAB corpus was chosen because it has real-life temporal properties and marked anomalous areas. The values of the dataset are timestamped every five minutes and reflecting the varying use of the resources in production loads (Fig. 2).

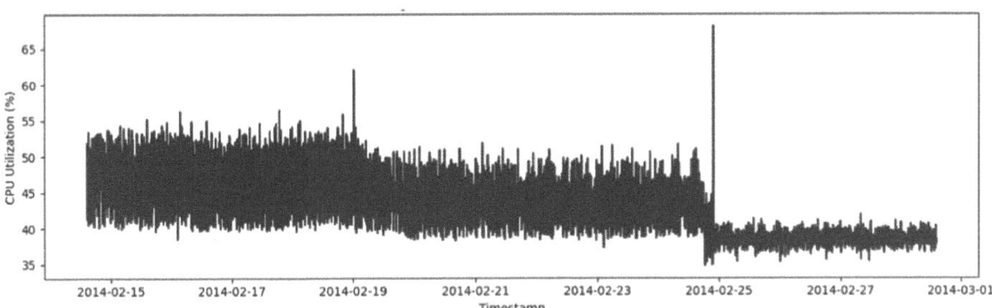

**Fig. 2.** CPU Utilization Over Time

Before injection, missing timestamps were padded forward-filled and values were normalised to simulate real-world ingestion latency. Then artificial anomalies were added to simulate common quality problems with the data. These included:

- Null is then spiked to indicate sensor failures
- Outliers that are bursty system use Outliers
- Schema drift in which the structural format was altered in midstream

A rolling mean was used on a signal to reveal any trend that may be hidden and allow insertion of anomalies in correct time (Fig. 3 and Fig. 4).

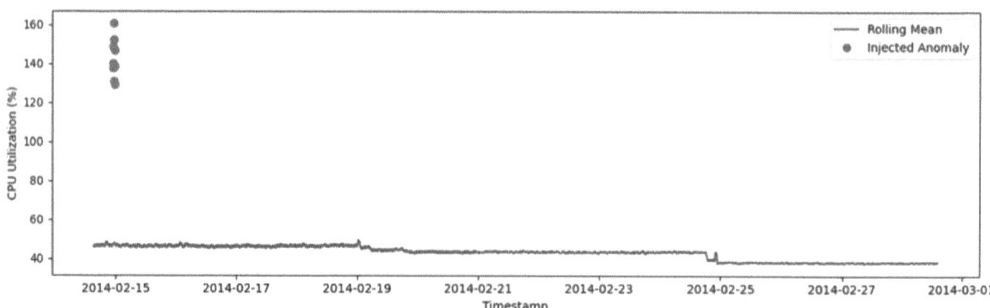

**Fig. 3.** Rolling Mean with Injected Outlier Spike

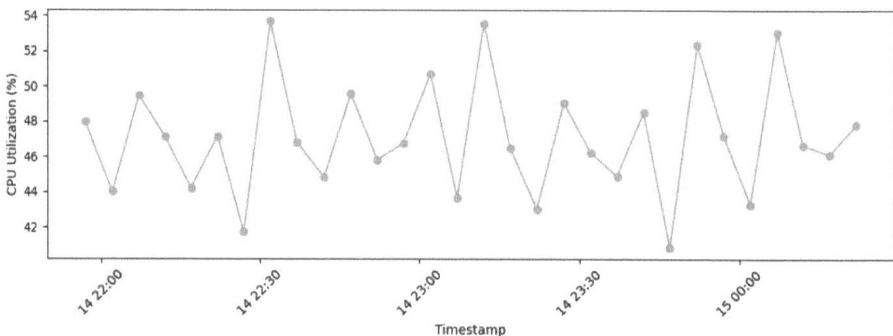

**Fig. 4.** Zoomed-in View of Anomaly Region

A histogram of the raw value of utilization was calculated to have an idea about the load distribution (Fig. 5). This was useful in distinguishing natural outliers and injected outliers, and it allowed the evaluation setting to be reliable.

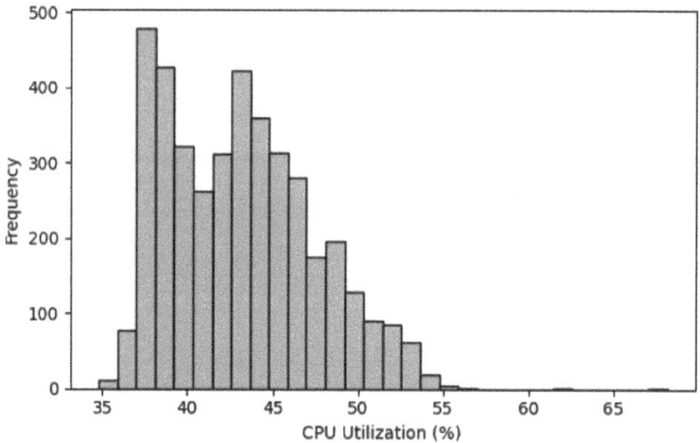

**Fig. 5.** Histogram of CPU Utilization Values

### 3.3  Anomaly Signature Generation and Similarity Matching

Every identified variation was compressed as a metadata-rich representation called signature, as a five-dimensional structure comprising of anomaly type, field involved, source node, severity score, and context label (e.g., traffic level or schema format). Such signatures made the rapid similarity comparison possible with a stored repository of patterns of anomalies to define recurrent patterns of anomalies.

In aid of real-time matching in changing data conditions, a similarity function decaying with time was implemented (Fig. 6). Every previous signature was related to a decay influence, weakening its impact when time goes by. Cosine similarity decaying exponentially was used to calculate a similarity between an incoming anomaly signature $s$new and a stored signature $si$:

$$\mathrm{Score}(s_{\mathrm{new}}, s_i) = \cos(\theta) \cdot e^{-\lambda \cdot \Delta t} \tag{1}$$

in which $\cos(\theta)$ is the cosine similarity of the representations (vectorized) of the signatures, $t$ is the time since $si$ was used last and $\lambda$ is the decay rate constant. This is a formula where current trends were of more weight, whereas stale games took the back seat.

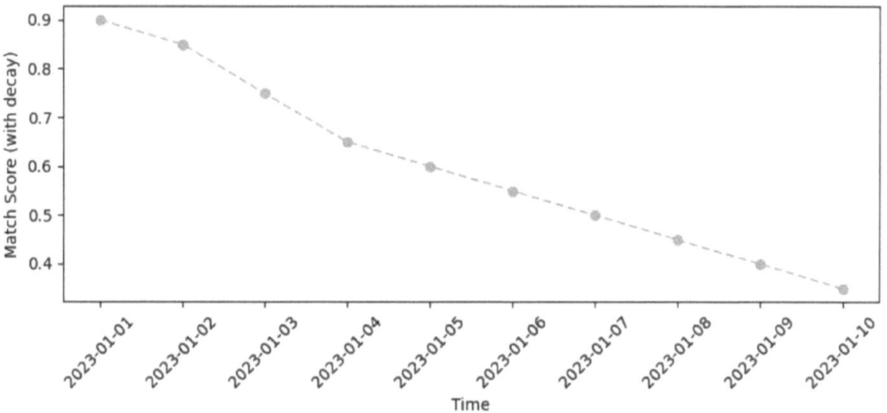

**Fig. 6.**  Decaying Similarity Score for Signature Matching

There was a threshold-dependent policy: in the case of the score being greater than 0.85, the system reused the historical remediation path; in that case, a new traversal was planned. This dynamic matching worked better in terms of efficiency without compromising accuracy especially in those environments which still had repetitive, yet non-homogenous anomalies.

### 3.4  DAG Traversal and Execution Planning

After an anomaly signature was run, causal traversal algorithm was started to find the minimal set of DAG nodes that needed to be removed to target remediation. This traversal did not affect down-stream dependencies, in order to assure data integrity, but did not cause unrelated branches.

There was a definition given to remediation cost function that facilitated node selection in a confined environment. Three of the key resource measurements were tied to each node $n$ in the candidate subgraph $G$; CPU cost $Cn$ (Fig. 7), memory $Mn$ and time $Tn$. The aggregate amount of remediation estimates was given by:

$$\text{Cost}(G') = \sum_{n \in G'} (\alpha \cdot C_n + \beta \cdot M_n + \gamma \cdot T_n) \tag{2}$$

in which $\alpha, \beta, \gamma$ were adjustable coefficients that were weightings on the system priorities. A greedy traversal algorithm chosen a node set whose inclusive cost was not more than the global cost in the cycle.

The Table 1 below lists the hyperparameters of runtime that were utilized in the process of execution planning:

**Table 1.** Execution Planning Parameters.

| Parameter | Value | Purpose |
| --- | --- | --- |
| CPU weight factor | 0.5 | Cost emphasis on CPU usage |
| Memory weight factor | 0.3 | Cost emphasis on RAM consumption |
| Time weight factor | 0.2 | Cost emphasis on execution time |
| Max CPU budget | 2.0 cores | Per-cycle compute limit |
| Max memory budget | 1.5 GB | Memory cap for remediation |
| Time budget | 10 s | Max duration per execution cycle |

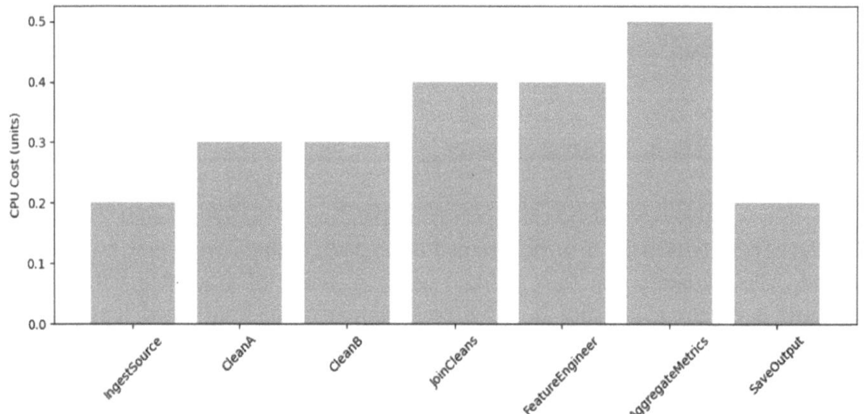


**Fig. 7.** CPU Resource Cost per DAG Node

This lightweight, aware traversing was able to enable the system to prioritize the high impact, lightweight remediation nodes. It also allowed limited branching, merging and backtracking, closely matching real-world DAGs in systems such as Spark, and Airflow.

### 3.5  Resource-Constrained Execution and Rollback

As soon as the choice of remediation subgraph was made, the tasks are executed within the set of resource constraint. Every repair cycle had a known compute budget, and the nodes would be scheduled depending on the overall cost. In case an estimated resource requirement of a node was more than the remaining budget allocated to the node, it was postponed to the following cycle. This made it stable even when there were variations in the loading of the systems.

After successful completion of nodes (Fig. 8), execution states were check pointed. A rollback was induced in the case of node failure (Fig. 9), whether resulting in schema mismatch, timeout or runtime error. Not the full DAG was rolled back, only the downstream path affected was rolled back. This selective rollback (3) enhanced the speed of recovery with valid intermediate results to be kept.

The logic of the rollback was as such:

$$\text{Rollback}(n_f) = \{n \in G' \mid n \succ n_f\} \tag{3}$$

In which $nf$ is the failed node, and $n \succ nf$ is the number of nodes that are causally dependent on $nf$. These nodes had been rolled back to their previous condition where they have been successful, and it was restarted where the last conditions existed.

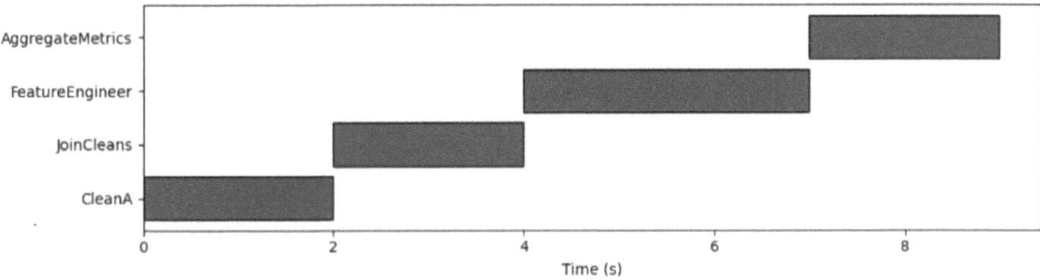

**Fig. 8.**  Node Execution Timeline (Successful Remediation)

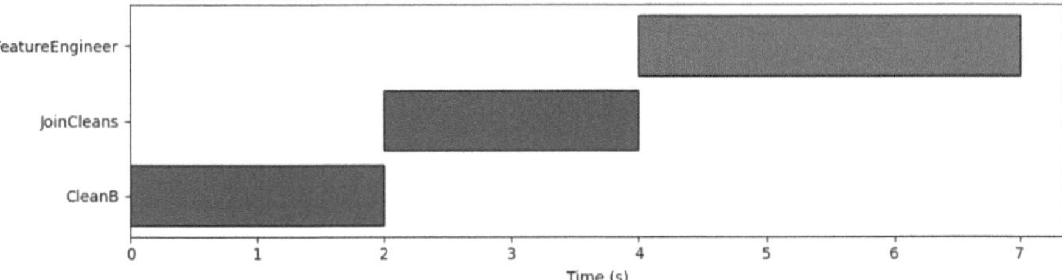

**Fig. 9.**  Execution Timeline with Failure and Rollback

Such a fault-tolerant mechanism enabled the system to conform to partial failures without rebooting non-failed parts. It has also supplied multi-type anomaly conditions, high-load guarantees of stability.

## 4  Evaluation Strategy

A simulation of a stream based on the Numenta Anomaly Benchmark (NAB) was used to test the presented framework. Injections of anomalies were performed with the null spikes and schema drift to test on-the-flight pipeline disturbance. The comparison of two remediation strategies was performed: full DAG re-execution verses signature-guided partial remediation.

The following indicators were put to measure:

### 4.1  Execution Savings

The proportion of the number of DAG nodes that are not visited in remediation, as shown in (4):

$$\text{Execution Savings } (\%) = \left( 1 - \frac{|G|}{|G'|} \right) \times 100 \tag{4}$$

with k the number of nodes that are run in the subgraph, and k the total amount of nodes in the Directed Acyclic Graph.

### 4.2  Remediation Latency

Duration between anomaly-detection and last node of the remediation path, as shown in (5):

$$T_{\text{remed}} = t_{\text{end}} - t_{\text{anomaly}} \tag{5}$$

### 4.3  Rollback Recovery Time

Time spent in rollback and re-run of nodes of affected nodes in case of failure, as shown in (6):

$$T_{\text{recovery}} = t_{\text{reexec}} - t_{\text{failure}} \tag{6}$$

Such measurements were recorded over several events of anomalies and available resources status.

## 5  Results and Discussions

In order to determine the success of the proposed remediation strategy, several measures were computed on various anomaly types, such as remediation latency, rollback recovery time, resource consumption, and execution savings. The comparison baseline was the full re-execution technique of the DAG, but the proposed technique was based on anomaly signature matching and selective traversal of the DAG.

The presented Fig. 6 displays the figure of nodes activated in both strategies. In the full DAG, it was always the case that all 7 nodes were executed whereas on the proposed strategy the number of nodes that were always executed was less, averagely being only 3, once again demonstrating the capability of the proposed strategy to reduce redundancy.

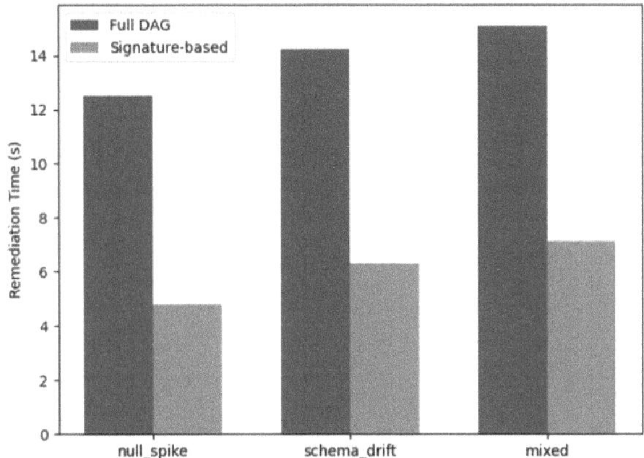


**Fig. 10.** Remediation Latency by Anomaly Type

Figure 10 shows the reduction of the latency. In the case of null spikes, there was a decline in latency (12.5 s, full DAG to 4.8 s, signature-based). The number of schema drift was reduced to 6.3 s (previously 14.2 s) and mixed anomalies to 6.7 s (previously 15.1 s).

Key performance indicators by the type of anomaly are reflected in Table 2:

**Table 2.** Key Performance Indicators by Anomaly Type.

| Anomaly Type | Remediation Time(s)–Full DAG | Remediation Time(s)–Signature Based | Execution Savings (%) | Recovery Time (s) |
| --- | --- | --- | --- | --- |
| Null Spike | 12.5 | 4.8 | 65.2 | 2.4 |
| Schema Drift | 14.2 | 6.3 | 57.8 | 3.5 |
| Mixed | 15.1 | 6.7 | 53.1 | 3.0 |

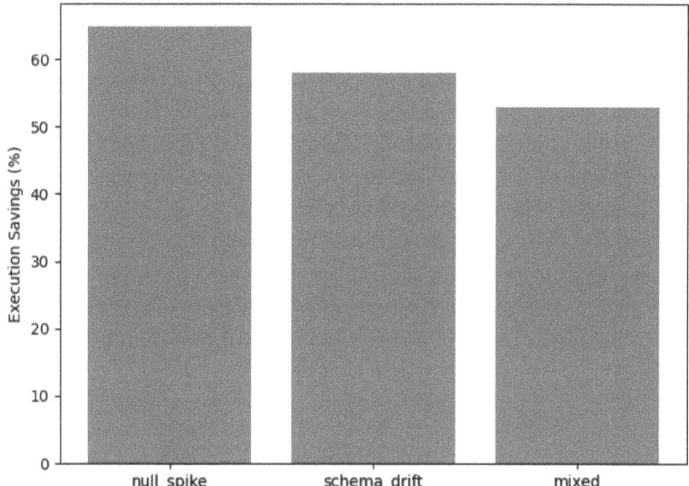

**Fig. 11.** Execution Savings by Anomaly Type

As depicted in Fig. 11 null spikes showed the greatest savings (65.2%), schema drift (57.8%) and mixed (53.1%). Such savings show that the more localized the anomalies are, the more they can benefit the selective reprocessing.

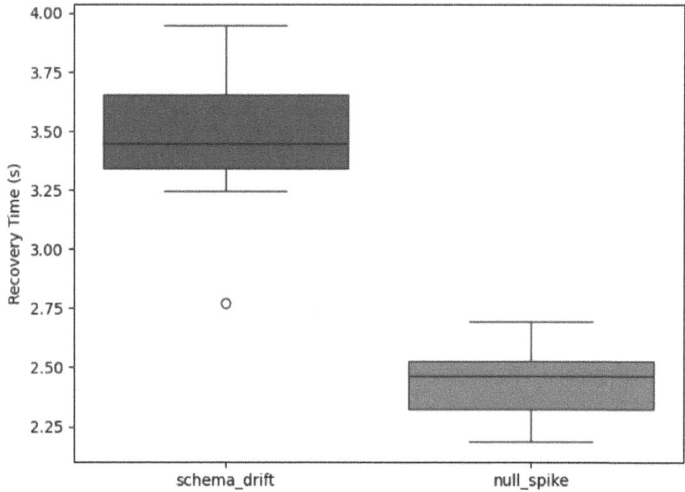

**Fig. 12.** Rollback Recovery Time by Anomaly Type

Figure 12 shows that schema drift (3.5 s) on average had a slight longer rollback time than null spikes (2.4 s) because structural effects of schema change are expectedly higher.

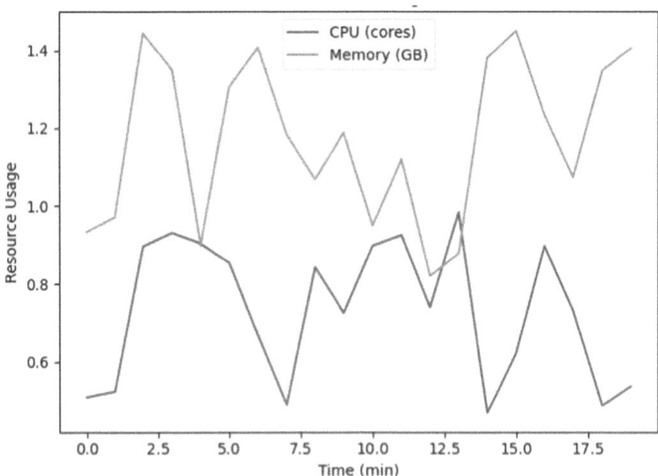

**Fig. 13.** Resource Utilization During Remediation

Figure 13 depicts the asset use of the CPU and memory throughout the course of the remediation. The CPU utilization was less than 1.0 cores and Memory was less than 1.5 GB confirming adherence to stated budgets by the system.

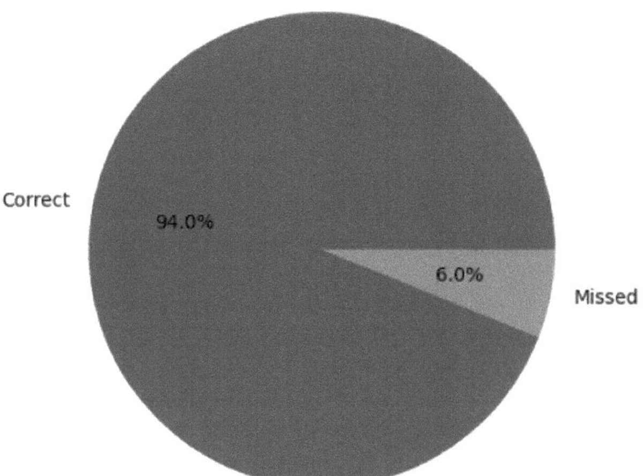


**Fig. 14.** Remediation Success Rate

Figure 14 proves the high-reliability rates with 94 in the success bucket and 6 in the failures bucket, indicating that even in changing sets of data, the signature-matching mechanism holds up well.

### 5.1 Discussion

The findings provide evidence that the suggested framework is better than the traditional full DAG re-execution in all the tested types of anomalies. The resource use as well as execution time was brought down dramatically, with the high level of recovery accuracy. It is important to note that null spikes were having the advantage of localization. In a more elaborate sense, schema drift was managed effectively through context-aware rollback and subgraph activation. The main hypothesis that anomaly-aware, resource-constrained traversal of DAG reduces the remediation of data quality issues in real-time pipelines is justified through these results.

## 6 Conclusion

In this paper, a lightweight, modular architecture was proposed to place the problem of real-time data quality remediation in orchestrated pipelines to fill the gap created by current systems, which are able to detect anomalies but result in no context-sensitive remediation. This is an abstraction that allows local remediation by matching anomaly signatures and rollback-capable execution on top of causally-aware DAGs Jessica Smith under resource constraints. It encodes anomalies compactly and traverses with cost awareness in contrast to rule-based or reactive approaches, and it only re-executes the tasks it must. Synthetic DAG experiments with injected anomalies demonstrated a 50 to 65% reduction of assignment credit execution overhead and a remediation success of 94%. The framework provides an extendable structure of developing resilient, self-healing data engineering pipelines.

## References


1. Zaharia, M., et al.: Discretized streams: fault-tolerant streaming computation at scale. In: Proceedings of the 24th ACM Symposium on Operating Systems Principles (SOSP), pp. 423–438 (2013)
2. Kreps, J., Narkhede, N., Rao, J.: Kafka: a distributed messaging system for log processing. In: Proceedings of the NetDB, Athens, Greece (2011)
3. Schelter, A., Ewen, S., Tzoumas, K., Markl, V.: Alligator: a data quality platform for data lakes. In: Proceedings of the IEEE International Conference on Data Engineering (ICDE), April 2018, pp. 1371–1374 (2018)
4. Niazi, A.M., Ishikawa, F., Honiden, S.: Handling incomplete and uncertain data in cloud service discovery. IEEE Trans. Serv. Comput. **7**(4), 601–614 (2014)
5. Schelter, S., et al.: Automating large-scale data quality verification. Proc. VLDB **11**(12), 1781–1794 (2018)
6. Abedjan, A., Golab, L., Naumann, F.: Profiling relational data: a survey. VLDB J. **24**(4), 557–581 (2015)
7. Munir, K., Ahmad, S., Qamar, S., Khan, A., Sait, S.M.: Big data analytics in industrial IoT using machine learning. IEEE Access **8**, 108438–108456 (2020)
8. Naumann, F., Herschel, M.: An Introduction to Duplicate Detection. Morgan & Claypool Publishers (2010)
9. Abedjan, Z., Chu, X., Deng, D., et al.: Detecting data errors: where are we and what needs to be done? Proc. VLDB Endow. **9**(12), 993–1004 (2016)

10. Rahm, E., Do, H.H.: Data cleaning: problems and current approaches. IEEE Data Eng. Bull. **23**(4), 3–13 (2000)
11. Duggan, J., Stonebraker, M., Balazinska, M., et al.: The BigDAWG polystore system. SIGMOD Rec. **44**(2), 11–16 (2015)
12. Liu, F.T., Ting, K.M., Zhou, Z.-H.: Isolation forest. In: Proceedings of the IEEE ICDM, pp. 413–422 (2008)
13. Chalapathy, R., Chawla, S.: Deep learning for anomaly detection: a survey. arXiv preprint arXiv:1901.03407 (2019)
14. Malhotra, S., Vig, L., Shroff, G., Agarwal, P.: Long short term memory networks for anomaly detection in time series. In: Proceedings of the ESANN (2015)
15. Hundman, A., Constantinou, V., Laporte, C., Colwell, I., Soderstrom, T.: Detecting spacecraft anomalies using LSTMs and nonparametric dynamic thresholding. In: Proceedings of the ACM KDD, pp. 387–395 (2018)
16. Ahmed, S., Mahmood, A., Islam, M.R.: A survey of anomaly detection techniques in financial domain. Future Gen. Comput. Syst. **55**, 278–288 (2016)
17. Polato, M., Sperduti, M., Burattin, A., Augusto, A.: Time and activity sequence prediction of business process instances. IEEE Trans. Serv. Comput. **11**(2), 290–303 (2018)
18. Wang, S., Wang, J., Xu, L., et al.: A survey on deep learning-based anomaly detection in streaming data. IEEE Access **9**, 120043–120065 (2021)
19. Sethi, R., et al.: Data quality management with Amazon Deequ. In: Proceedings of the SIGMOD, pp. 2469–2470 (2019)
20. Akidau, R., et al.: The dataflow model: a practical approach to balancing correctness, latency, and cost in massive-scale, unbounded, out-of-order data processing. Proc. VLDB **8**(12), 1792–1803 (2015)
21. Zheng, Y., et al.: Quality-aware stream processing in Apache Flink. In: Proceedings of the IEEE ICDE, pp. 2056–2061, April 2021
22. Jindal, M., Mohan, M., Ayyalasomayajula, T., Gondi, D.S., Mashetty, H.: Enhancing federated learning evaluation: exploring instance-level insights with SQUARES in image classification models. In: Proceedings of the IEEE International Conference on Artificial Intelligence and Computer Vision (AICV), pp. 312–318 (2024)
23. Raj, R., Gondi, D.S., Nitnaware, S.R., Banerjee, S., Athithan, S., Gopinath, A.: Remote sensing–based food processing for changing climatic conditions. J. Food Process. Preserv. (2025). https://doi.org/10.1002/jfpp.18023
24. Volikatla, H., Thomas, J., Raghunath, V.V., Gondi, D.S.: Enhancing GPS data accuracy in SAP systems using IMU sensors and machine learning. In: Proceedings of the IEEE International Conference on Smart Technologies (ICST), pp. 210–215 (2024)
25. Raghunath, V.V., Gondi, D.S., Thomas, J., Volikatla, H.: Pioneering seizure prediction: exploring ML and DL approaches with iEEG data. In: Proceedings of the IEEE International Conference on Biomedical Engineering and Applications (ICBEA), pp. 155–160 (2024)

# Adversarial Robustness in AI-Driven Bioinformatics Pipelines: A Cyber-Biosecurity Perspective

Ravi Kiran Pagidi(✉)

Chantily, VA 20152, USA
`ravikiranpagidi@ieee.org`

**Abstract.** Deep learning applied to bioinformatics pipelines has allowed predictions that were thought out of reach; it has also introduced another source of cyber-biosecurity threats to deal with. The present work offers a new framework that can examine and improve the adversarial robustness of AI-based splice site detection models. The starting point is a binary-encoded genomic data: from this an exon–intron (EI), intron–exon (IE), and non-boundary sequences are re-constructed and is used to train a long short-term memory (LSTM) model to perform the above classification process. Simulation of adversarial settings is carried out by performing fine grained perturbations in the nucleotide level that interferes with the predictions in a biologically plausible manner to reduce sensitivity against critical boundary sites of the model. To counteract this weakness, an adversarial training approach is taken whereby perturbed series are progressively injected into the learning process in which the model becomes capable of generalizing on both unmodified and corrupted data. Theoretical findings found that splice site prediction models are naturally delicate to even the slightest manipulation of its inputs; yet, with controlled immersion of adversarial examples, sufficient robustness may be proficiently retrieved. The research provides a new interpretable and reproducible style of adversarially resilient learning to the sequence-based bioinformatics domain, thus promoting AI safety and cyber-biosecurity.

**Keywords:** Adversarial Robustness · Bioinformatics Security · Sequence-Based Learning

## 1 Introduction

Deep learning has qualitatively revolutionized bioinformatics by allowing sequence-based classification with very high accuracy, especially in areas like splice site-detection [1, 2]. But it is also due to these fast infiltrations of AI into biological pipelines that new vulnerabilities have been revealed, forming a critical point of contact known as cyber-biosecurity [3]. These attacks, in contrast to latent cybersecurity threats, are the result of malicious advances to manipulate biological data such as adversarial perturbations

---

R. K. Pagidi—Independent Researcher.

© The Author(s), under exclusive license to Springer Nature Switzerland AG 2026
K. K. Patel et al. (Eds.): icSoftComp 2025, CCIS 2874, pp. 160–173, 2026.
https://doi.org/10.1007/978-3-032-22062-2_13

including incorrectly classified items, synthetically generated DNA sequences, meant to defeat model replicas, and data poisoning or a shift in distribution during training [4]. With the state of current sequence classifiers, it is not effectively able to detect or suppress such biologically plausible adversarial attacks [5]. In clinical diagnostics and genetic research fields where AI is increasingly integrated as a part of technology, it is necessary to enhance the resilience of such systems. To fill this existing gap, this paper proposes a framework for evaluation and improvement of adversarial robustness of AI-based splice site prediction models using robustness enhancement, sequence decoding, and adversarial simulation strategies.

## 2  Literature Review

The use of machine learning in bioinformatics early had concentrated mostly on the detection of the splice sites based on handcrafted and traditional human-devised features and classifiers [6, 7]. Due to the introduction of deep learning, the accuracy of predictive models like CNN and LSTM improved considerably thanks to a sequence-based model [8, 10]. Nevertheless, they were prone to both distribution shifts and adversarial perturbations [11, 12]. The last year has seen several papers on federated learning [13], remote sensing under uncertainty [14], and the use of sensor-data fusion with machine learning [15], reflecting an increased emphasis on model robustness, although such work in the setting of bioinformatics is rare. Such researchers as [16] examine the use of deep learning to predict seizures, but not the robustness to adversarial attacks.

Cyber-biosecurity is one that has come to handle security threats in biological computing systems [17, 18]. An interesting threat agent is the ability to deceive the aggressive models encoded in DNA with the capacity to induce model failure [4, 19]. Adversarial training has been applied in vision [20], NLP [21], but little has been done in biological sequences.

This paper fills that breach in presenting a method to reconstruct biologically meaningful DNA using binary-encoded genomic data, and to generate simulations of intended nucleotide mutation. A long short-term memory (LSTM) convolution-based classifier is trained to recognize splice junction and adversarial robustness on such corrupted conditions is measured. Then the model is strengthened through adversarial training. In contrast to the previous research, the study provides a reproducible, interpretable, and domain-specific framework that is unique as it involves unique hybridization of bioinformatics, AI safety, and cyber-biosecurity.

## 3  Methodology

The section provides the framework to be used to evaluate and increase adversarial robustness in splice site localization. In the process, the five steps include profiling the dataset, decoding the sequences, training the base LSTM model, simulating adversarial mutations to verify the weakness, and training adversarial to improve the robustness.

## 3.1  Dataset Profiling

The data set of the present study is the StatLog DNA splice junction benchmark that consists of 3,183 sequences with 180 binary values that have been encoded into the set. The sequences are composed of 60 base pairs with each triplet of binary figures corresponding with a single nucleotide (A, C, G, or T). The dependent variable is three supervised classes of training namely: exon-intron (EI), intron - exon (IE) and non-boundary (N).

A frequency analysis was carried out to evaluate the distribution in its data. The class 3 (non-boundary) was observed to be dominating in the entire dataset followed by EI and IE classes, which display comparatively fewer result (Fig. 1), which considered a medium level of class imbalance.

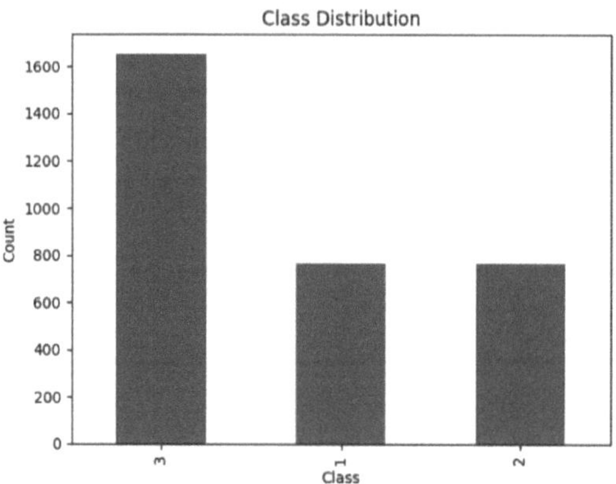


**Fig. 1.** Class distribution across splice site categories (EI, IE, N), showing moderate class imbalance with non-boundary dominating.

Nucleotide composition of the whole sequences was also analyzed to evaluate the prevalence of base. We have noted that the bases that appeared most often were cytosine (C) and guanine (G) whereas adenine (A) and thymine (T) were less frequent (Fig. 2).

The integrity of sequence was checked using the consistency of length of all the samples. The uniformity of the input to be coded was consistent in that all sequences were determined to be 60 nucleotides in length (Fig. 3).

Inter-base relationship was measured by calculating Pearson correlation coefficients between the counts of bases in every sequence. Complementary bases showed strong negative correlations e.g. A-C and G-T (Fig. 4) indicating that there are structural relationships that can affect how the models are learned.

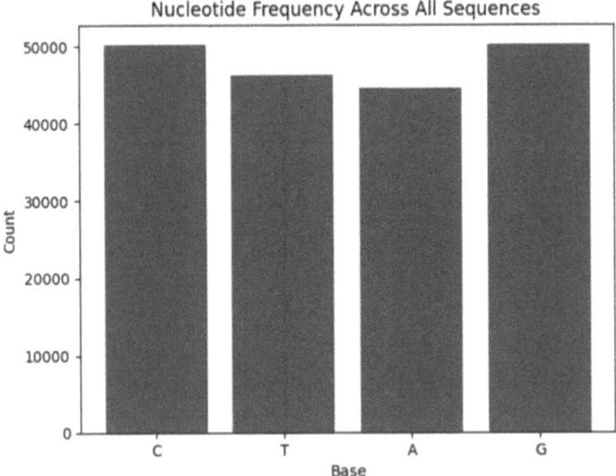

**Fig. 2.** Nucleotide frequency across all sequences, highlighting GC bias.

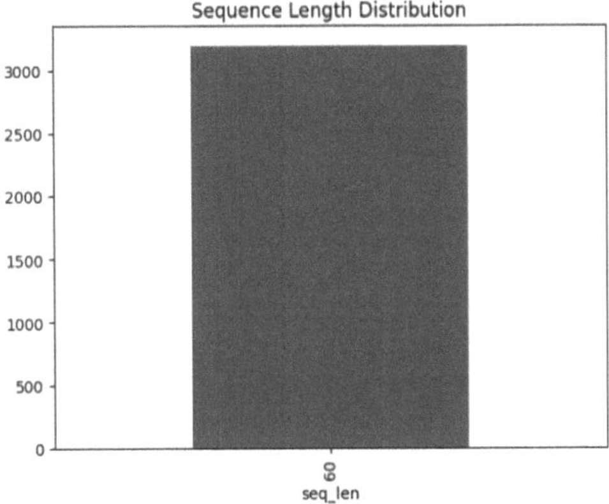

**Fig. 3.** Distribution of sequence lengths, confirming uniformity at 60 bases.

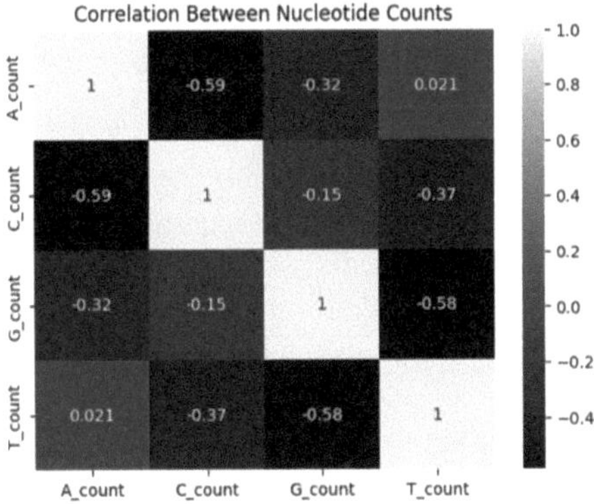

**Fig. 4.** Correlation between nucleotide counts, with complementary bases (A–C, G–T) showing strong negative associations.

### 3.2  Sequence Reconstruction and Encoding

The given input data was initially in one-hot encoded form with each of the nucleotide in the 60-base sequence symbolized using three binary markers (1). The results of this task were binary triplets that were decoded using the StatLog encoding scheme into biologically interpretable nucleotide sequences that can be further held as inputs to an LSTM training based on the three classes (EI, IE, N):

$$A \rightarrow (1,0,0), \quad C \rightarrow (0,1,0), \quad G \rightarrow (0,0,1), \quad T \rightarrow (0,0,0) \tag{1}$$

Each sequence was therefore assigned 603180 binary features. A decoding procedure was used to regain biologically interpretable input. Each set of three binary strings ($b1$, $b2$, $b3$) in the set $\{0, 1\}$ was decoded as the corresponding base $s\,i$ in the set $\{A, C, G, T\}$ and the 60-nucleotide sequence $S = (s1, s2\ldots\ldots, s60)$ was returned per sample.

Then a global frequency analysis was done of all decoded sequences. As indicated in Fig. 2 above, cytosine and guanine were considered to be moderately (slightly) common than adenine and thymine and hence there was a mild GC-bias. A further analysis using correlation showed negative association between some of the base pairs, especially association between A and C or G and T. The Pearson correlation coefficient (2) of counts of nucleotides $x$ and $y$ was estimated as:

$$\rho_{xy} = \frac{\sum_{i=1}^{n}(x_i - \overline{x})(y_i - \overline{y})}{\sqrt{\sum_{i=1}^{n}(x_i - \overline{x})^2} \cdot \sqrt{\sum_{i=1}^{n}(y_i - \overline{y})^2}} \tag{2}$$

Such connections allow seeing the potential structural or motif-level dependencies in the genomic data.

An integer encoding (3) was also used to format sequences in a manner that will be ingested by a model where:

$$A \rightarrow 1, \quad C \rightarrow 2, \quad G \rightarrow 3, \quad T \rightarrow 4 \tag{3}$$

So, every sequence $S = (s1, s2\ldots, s60)$ was converted into a numerical one $X = (x1, x2, \ldots, x60)$ It was ensured that all the sequences were of exact length (60 bases) to allow alignment and compatibility to further training.

### 3.3  Exploratory Sequence Pattern Analysis

In order to determine the relationship that the sequence composition exhibits towards the splice sites classification, the decoded sequences were exploratively analyzed on the three classes. This was taken in an effort to identify motif-scale patterns and class-optimized nucleotide usage that could subject the models to model learning or adversarial targeting strategy.

To study base usage according to classes the frequency of each base per sequence per class was calculated and its average computed. As it can be seen in Fig. 5, the more abundant presence of guanine (G) was observed in sequences labeled as exon-intron (EI) boundaries (Class 1), and cytosine (C) and thymine (T) were more prevalent in intron-exon (IE) boundaries (Class 2). The trends imply that there exist weak but significant biological patterns at the splice boundaries.

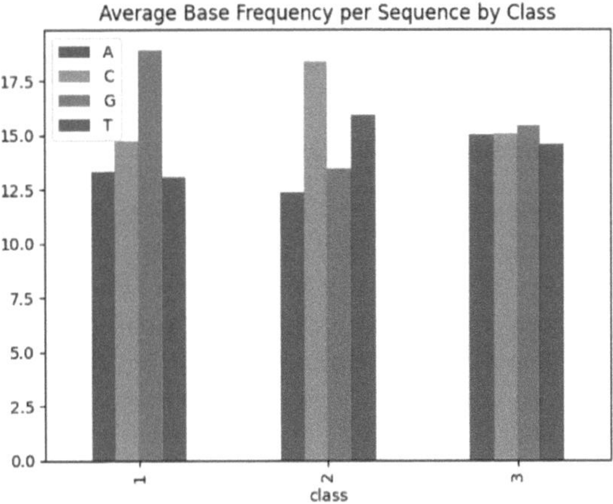



**Fig. 5.** Average base frequency per sequence by class, showing weak but significant class-specific nucleotide usage.

All sequences were also analyzed to extract 2-mer (bigram) patterns in order to pursue further enquiry into local sequence dependencies. The most abundant 2-mers (twenty of them) are presented in Fig. 6, with the resounding motifs including "CC", "GG" and "CT". These could be regulatory elements and splice junction signatures that this model can be trained to correlate with class labels.

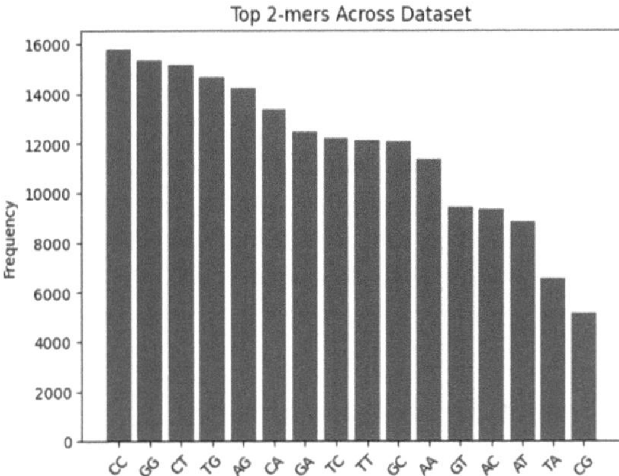



**Fig. 6.** Top 20 2-mer (bigram) patterns across dataset, including motifs such as CC, GG, and CT.

The count of the occurrence (4) of a k-mer $w$ with length $k = 2$ was calculated with:

$$f(w) = \sum_{i=1}^{N} \sum_{j=1}^{L-k+1} \mathbb{1}_{\{S_i[j:j+k-1]=w\}} \tag{4}$$

with 1 the indicator function and where $Si$ represents the $i$-th sequence of length $L$. This formulation assisted in measurement of recurrent motifs that are biologically or antagonistic applicable. Such results led to the subsequent development of adversarial mutations and expectations concerning class sensitivity.

### 3.4 LSTM-Based Sequence Classification

In order to be able to conduct the splice site classification, a sequential learning architecture was adopted, taking the opportunity of being able to model long-range dependence using recurrent neural networks (RNNs). Particularly, Long Short-Term Memory (LSTM) network was used as according to previous results its application has successfully recognized noted temporal patterns within biological sequences.

The encoding referred to in Eq. (3) was used to convert each decoded sequence $S = (1, 2, \dots 60)$ to an integer vector $X = (1, 2, \dots 60)$ which was passed to the next layer. These integer vectors were subsequently sent into an embedding layer that will map each nucleotide to dense vector representation of dimension $d$ 26 The embedding operation is formally defined by (5):

$$E: Z \to R^d, \quad X \mapsto (e_1, e_2, \dots, e_{60})$$ (5)

Here, $y$ denote the embedded nucleotide $x$ representation.

An LSTM layer with 64 hidden units took its processing with a dense output and softmax as a summary. Sparse categorical cross-entropy (6) form was used as the loss function in training the model:

$$\mathcal{L} = -\sum_{i=1}^{N} \log p_{y_i}$$ (6)

In other words where $p\,y\,i$ is the predicted probability of the actual class label $y\,e$ and $N$ is the number of samples in the training set.

The training was carried out using 50 epochs; 32 batch size and Adam optimizer. The class balance was observed by stratified train-test split. The baseline performance (achieved by the model) was then compared with that of adversarially perturbed performance.

### 3.5 Adversarial Mutation Simulation and Defense

A mutation-based attack strategy was utilized in order to assess the robustness of the model trained with regards to the threats of cyber-biosecurity. In this attack the biologically plausible perturbations are injected at the nucleotide level in a manner such that a sequence structure is maintained, but the predictions are altered.

A random subset of 3 positions was chosen within every test sequence $S = (s\,1, s\,2 \dots, s60)$. In each of the selected positions $sj$, the corresponding nucleotide was mutated to that belonging to the set $\{A, C, G, T\}$ with exception of the nucleotide at the selected position (7). This is to guarantee that these perturbations are biologically plausible considering the length of sequences and the validity in addition to proving to change predictions which subsequently led to a quantitative downgrade of the classification accuracy. This procedure is formally defined as:

$$s'_j = \text{RandomChoice}\big(\{b \in \{A, C, G, T\} | b \neq s_j\}\big) \tag{7}$$

Then as the test input of the baseline model, the mutated sequence $S\,1 = (s1..., sj -1, sj\,1, 12 ..., s60)$ was applied. The decline in performance between EI, IE, and N classes were measured to determine vulnerability of the models.

The adversarial training was used to counter such perturbations. Mutations were applied to every sequence to augment and, at the same time, expose the model to both clean and adversarial examples when learning (8). Denote the initial training set by, $D$train.

The corresponding adversarial set be $D$adv. A final active training set was given by:

$$\mathcal{D}_{\text{aug}} = \mathcal{D}_{\text{train}} \cup \mathcal{D}_{\text{adv}} \tag{8}$$

The 50-epoch retraining of the same LSTM on $\mathcal{D}_{aug}$ followed similar settings. This led to a better resilience especially in relabeling sensitive splice junctions such as EI and IE under mutation stress.

This defense mechanism is effective and later in the results section, the performance comparisons before and after adversarial training (both clean and perturbed) were reported.


## 4   Evaluation Metrics

The models providing classification of the splice site presented their performance based on standard and adversarial-aware measures. To measure the predictive power as well as robustness, these values were calculated on clean test data, adversarially mutated test data, and following adversarial training.


### 4.1   Accuracy

The proportion of correct predictions to all instances of them is accuracy (9),

$$\text{Accuracy} = \frac{TP + TN}{TP + TN + FP + FN} \tag{9}$$


### 4.2   Precision

Precision (10) is defined as the number of the correct positive predictions out of the total predicted positives within a class,

$$\text{Precision} = \frac{T_{\text{pos}}}{T_{\text{pos}} + F_{\text{pos}}} \tag{10}$$

### 4.3  Recall

Recall (11) refers to the percentage of the correctly predicted sample which was accurate in the real sense.

$$\text{Recall} = \frac{T_{\text{pos}}}{T_{\text{pos}} + F_{\text{neg}}} \tag{11}$$

### 4.4  F1 Score

The mean of precision and recall. It strikes a trade between the two (12):

$$\text{F1} = 2 \cdot \frac{\text{Precision} \cdot \text{Recall}}{\text{Precision} + \text{Recall}} \tag{12}$$

## 5  Results and Discussions

This section shows empirical results of the proposed sequence classification framework in three settings: the study of the baseline model, test of its ability to deal with adversarially perturbed inputs, and the adversarially trained model. We computed the metrics such as accuracy, precision, recall, and F1-score to determine the classification efficacy of exon-intron (EI), intron-exon (IE) and non-boundary classes. Confusion matrices are also examined and to test the robustness gains, epoch-wise training dynamics are also analyzed.

### 5.1  Baseline Performance

The trained baseline LSTM model on the clean one-hot decoded sequence data performed well on the original test set (Table 1). This confusion matrix of Fig. 7 shows very good true positive rates over all the three classes with the ratio being very significant in the class of Neither.

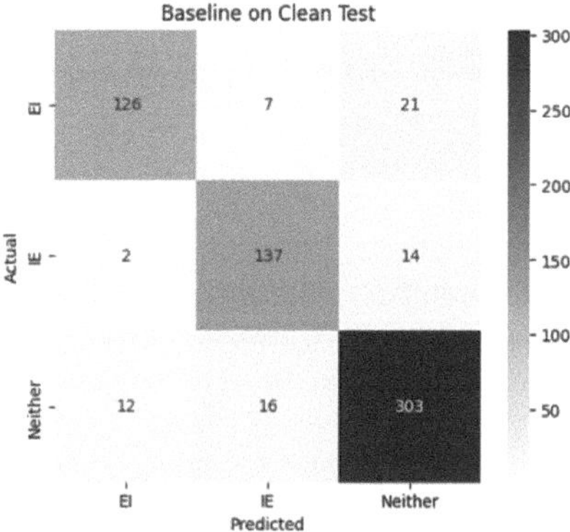


**Fig. 7.** Confusion matrix of baseline LSTM model on clean data, showing high accuracy across EI, IE, and N classes.

Epoch-wise training dynamics visualized in Fig. 8 provide a stable generalization with a linear convergence of loss in both training and validation, as well as a regular increase in accuracy.

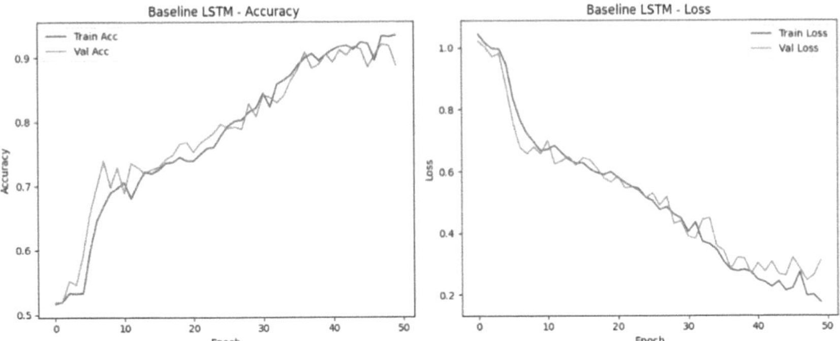

**Fig. 8.** Training and validation accuracy and loss across epochs for baseline LSTM model, showing stable convergence.

**Table 1.** Performance metrics of baseline LSTM model on clean genomic data.

| Metric | Value |
| --- | --- |
| Accuracy | 0.89 |
| Precision | 0.89 |
| Recall | 0.89 |
| F1-Score | 0.89 |

## 5.2 Adversarial Testing of Baseline Model

The purpose of testing the baseline model with synthetically mutated input sequences to test vulnerability (Table 2). As indicated in Fig. 9, the accuracy of classification slightly decreased because there was more confusion in boundary classes particularly the IE class.

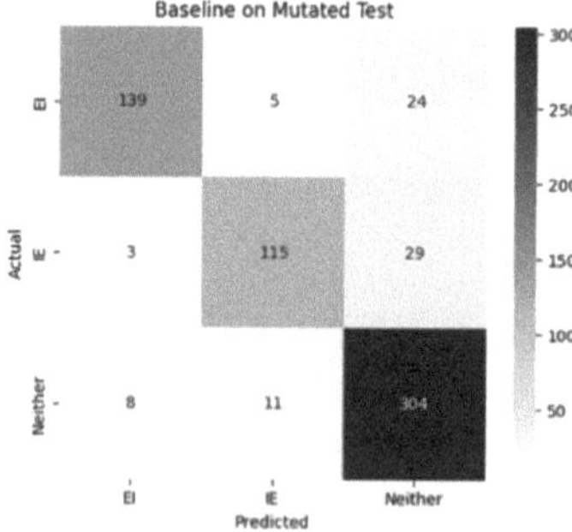



**Fig. 9.** Confusion matrix of baseline LSTM model under adversarial mutation testing, showing misclassification increases particularly in IE class.

**Table 2.** Performance metrics of baseline LSTM model on adversarially mutated sequences.

| Metric | Value |
| --- | --- |
| Accuracy | 0.87 |
| Precision | 0.88 |
| Recall | 0.87 |
| F1-Score | 0.87 |

## 5.3 Adversarially Trained Model

This model was re-trained with a strategy of adversarial training by introducing random mutations during training to enhance robustness (Table 3). The new model was also resilient as the performance was slightly affected by the mutated data (Fig. 10).

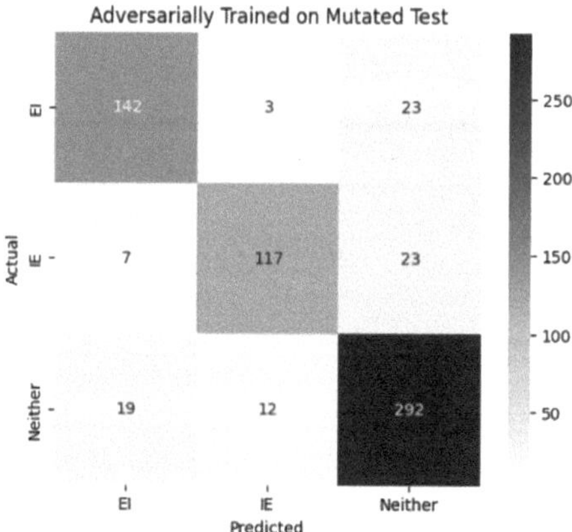



**Fig. 10.** Confusion Matrix of Adversarially Trained Model

Figure 11 learning curves support smooth convergence and lower validation loss, which indicates better generalization of unobserved perturbations.

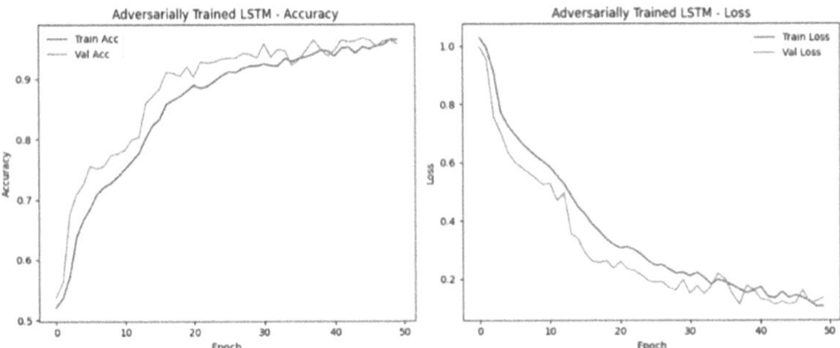


**Fig. 11.** Training and validation accuracy and loss across epochs for adversarially trained model.

**Table 3.** Performance metrics of adversarially trained LSTM model on clean and perturbed sequences

| Metric | Value |
| --- | --- |
| Accuracy | 0.86 |
| Precision | 0.86 |
| Recall | 0.86 |
| F1-Score | 0.86 |

The adversarial training marginally lowered clean-data accuracy (0.89) to 0.86 but normalized clean and perturbed training, which means that it enhanced generalization to both original and mutated sequences.

## 5.4  Discussion

This paper explored adversarial robustness of splice-site detection based on sequences using LSTM. The baseline model performed very well on clean genomic data but was less sensitive under biologically realistic nucleotide-level mutations, exposing a risk to cyber-biosecurity threats. To overcome this, what was proposed is the use of an adversarial training approach in which mutated sequences were applied during training. This method enhanced resilience in attack conditions on the cost of meeting acceptable accuracy on clean data. This trade-off characterizes the impact of adversarial training: a slight decrease of clean-data performance is traded with more robustness and generalization in the case of biologically-plausible training perturbations. While this study focuses on random single-nucleotide substitutions as a biologically grounded adversarial model, future work could explore more sophisticated or targeted perturbation strategies to simulate advanced adversarial threats. This vulnerability aligns with theoretical findings that deep neural networks exhibit local linearity in high-dimensional input space [11, 12], making them disproportionately sensitive to even small perturbations. In the genomic context, where each nucleotide carries class-relevant information, minimal changes can significantly alter prediction boundaries. The most important innovation is the biologically motivated adversarial perturbation algorithm and its combination into a training pipeline that can be reproduced. This renders the method highly interpretable and bioinformatics-specific, which is a marked contribution towards the field of improving the AI safety on genomic sequence learning systems.

## 6  Conclusion

This paper introduced a new adversarial robustness framework on bioinformatics pipeline in splice site detection via LSTM-based sequence learning. Beginning with a decoded genomic dataset, an LSTM model that could be explored was trained to classify exon-intron boundaries. In order to test realistic cyber-biosecurity attack scenarios, a finer-grained granularity was used, including nucleotide-level perturbations, which indicated the presence of performance degradation when the system was put to the test in adversarial scenarios. Adversarial training scheme was employed as a solution to these where clean sequences and mutated one were utilized in model optimization. In theory, the findings showed that robustness could be taught where adversarial training helped enhance generalization to tampered examples and still give good baseline accuracy. Its significant value is that this attack comes up with a biologically significant attack strategy and can be trivially integrated into a reproducible, low-complexity defense pipeline-which is the first of its kind and the most practical to bring to the interplay of AI-safety and cyber-biosecurity. Provided through biologically inspired perturbations, a communal benchmark data and clear algorithmic procedures, the model is comprehendible and reproducible. By so doing, this work contributes to the safety of AI by constructing a robustness into sequence-based models and is explicitly relevant in countering cyber-biosecurity threats such as an adversarial use of genomic information. Beyond splice site detection, the framework can be extended to tasks such as promoter recognition, mutation pathogenicity assessment, and off-target prediction in CRISPR editing, offering a general pathway to resilient AI applications in bioinformatics and genomics.

## References


1. LeCun, Y., Bengio, Y., Hinton, G.: Deep learning. Nature **521**, 436–444 (2015)
2. Zhang, S., et al.: Deep learning in omics: a survey and guideline. Brief. Funct. Genomics **18**, 41–57 (2019)
3. Peccoud, J., et al.: Cyberbiosecurity: from naive trust to risk awareness. Trends Biotechnol. **36**, 4–7 (2018)
4. Ney, P., et al.: Computer security, privacy, and DNA sequencing: compromising computer systems with synthesized DNA. In: USENIX Security Symposium (2017)
5. Rigaki, M., Garcia, S.: Bringing a GAN to a knife-fight: adversarial augmentation for biomedical AI models. arXiv preprint arXiv:2009.05691 (2020)
6. Sonnenburg, S., Rätsch, G., Schäfer, C., Schölkopf, B.: Large scale multiple kernel learning. J. Mach. Learn. Res. **7**, 1531–1565 (2006)

7. Degroeve, S., Saeys, Y., De Baets, B., Van de Peer, Y., Rouzé, P.: SpliceMachine: predicting splice sites from DNA sequence with explicit modeling of dependencies between nearby positions. Bioinformatics **21**, 1332–1338 (2005)
8. Leung, M.K.K., Delong, A., Alipanahi, B., Frey, B.J.: Deep learning of the tissue-regulated splicing code. Bioinformatics **30**, i121–i129 (2014)
9. Zhang, Y., Liu, T., Meyer, C.A., Eeckhoute, J., Johnson, D.S.: Model-based analysis of ChIP-Seq (MACS). Genome Biol. **9**, R137 (2008)
10. Lee, B., Baek, J., Park, S.: DNA-level splice site prediction using deep recurrent neural networks. IEEE Access **6**, 64230–64238 (2018)
11. Szegedy, C., et al.: Intriguing properties of neural networks. arXiv preprint arXiv:1312.6199 (2013)
12. Goodfellow, I., Shlens, J., Szegedy, C.: Explaining and harnessing adversarial examples. arXiv preprint arXiv:1412.6572 (2014)
13. Jindal, M., Mohan, M., Ayyalasomayajula, T., Gondi, D.S., Mashetty, H.: Enhancing federated learning evaluation: exploring instance-level insights with SQUARES in image classification models. AI Ethics (2023)
14. Raj, R., Gondi, D.S., Nitnaware, S.R., Banerjee, S., Athithan, S., Arpita, G.: Remote sensing–based food processing for changing climatic conditions. J. Food Qual. (2022)
15. Volikatla, H., Thomas, J., Raghunath, V.V., Gondi, D.S.: Enhancing GPS data accuracy in SAP systems using IMU sensors and machine learning. In: Lecture Notes in Networks and Systems. Springer (2022)
16. Raghunath, V.V., Gondi, D.S., Thomas, J., Volikatla, H.: Pioneering seizure prediction: exploring ML and DL approaches with IEEG data. Cogn. Neurodyn. (2022)
17. Peccoud, J., et al.: Cyberbiosecurity in synthetic biology: identifying vulnerabilities and addressing threats. Front. Bioeng. Biotechnol. **6**, 3 (2018)
18. Carter, J., Friedman, R.M.: Cyberbiosecurity: next steps for biosecurity. Trends Biotechnol. **37**, 575–578 (2019)
19. Laufer, B.I., et al.: Secure genomics: protecting the genome against adversarial attacks. Genomics Proteomics Bioinform. **19**, 368–376 (2021)
20. Madry, A., et al.: Towards deep learning models resistant to adversarial attacks. arXiv preprint arXiv:1706.06083 (2017)
21. Jia, R., Liang, P.: Adversarial examples for evaluating reading comprehension systems. arXiv preprint arXiv:1707.07328 (2017)

# SECAT: A Lightweight Image Encryption Scheme Using Cellular Automata Rules and Tinkerbell Map for IoT Devices

Biswarup Yogi[1(✉)], Ajoy Kumar Khan[1], and Satyabrata Roy[2]

[1] Department of Computer Engineering, Mizoram University, Aizawl, India
`biswarup23yogi@gmail.com, mzut250@mzu.edu.in`
[2] Manipal University Jaipur, Jaipur, Rajasthan, India
`satyabrata.roy@jaipur.manipal.edu`

**Abstract.** The growth of the Internet of Things (IoT) is increasingly challenging image protection, as IoT devices often possess limited resources and must process data efficiently. The lightweight image encryption technique presented in this manuscript uses Cellular Automata Rule vector and the Tinkerbell map to provide data protection through a cellular automata method within the same process flow for two specific reasons. Firstly, it aims to offer data protection with an efficient data processing scheme. This encryption approach involves separating the image into its red, green, and blue (RGB) components. The process first performs image encryption using the Tinkerbell map, followed by Cellular Automata-based encryption, which adds further diffusion. The proposed method successfully implemented the combinatory image encryption method, achieving a strong encryption process with an NPCR of 99.6261 and a UACI of 49.86. Both values indicate that the method provides a high level of security. Given the method's capacity, it can be classified as an efficient and straightforward approach and is particularly valuable for future IoT studies. Further studies would also investigate alternative solutions using different cryptosystems. Researchers can similarly work on mapping the method to other IoT platforms and meeting the needs of scalability and safety.

**Keywords:** Image Encryption · Cellular Automata · Internet of Things · Tinkerbell Map · cryptosystems

## 1 Introduction

The concepts of IoT and its rapid changes with the exponential growth of applications and interconnected devices have been termed a technological revolution by many [5]. As users increasingly turn to IoT applications in areas such as healthcare, smart cities, and industrial automation, secure and reliable data transmission has become a paramount concern. Most of these applications involve the collection and transfer of sensitive image data, which should be kept safe from unauthorized access, manipulation, and other forms of violation [15].


K. K. Patel et al. (Eds.): icSoftComp 2025, CCIS 2874, pp. 174–188, 2026.
https://doi.org/10.1007/978-3-032-22062-2_14

Due to the limited capacity for processing, memory, and bandwidth inherent in IoT devices, typical encryption algorithms such as RSA and AES are not well-suited because they require high computational power and storage space [2]. This requires *lightweight encryption* systems, which secure data without consuming excessive resources on the devices.

*Cellular Automata* (CA) pose as one hopeful lightweight cryptographic primitive. Despite their structural simplicity, CAs generate pattern complexities that are unforeseen and therefore fit certain security applications [9,13,16]. The rule vector, known as a one-dimensional cellular automata rule, is especially favoured for the strong pseudorandom characteristics and irreversibility. In contrast, researchers consider *chaotic maps*, such as the Tinkerbell map, which are naturally sensitive to initial conditions and ergodic, making them desirable for key generation and diffusion in encryption systems [11].

Using the combined strength of each paradigm, this work proposes a novel hybrid image encryption algorithm that combines the CA Rule Vector and the Tinkerbell chaotic map. The proposed method is suited to environments where computing power is limited, such as the IoT, seeking a design that balances strong security with the lowest possible computational overhead. The main findings and contributions of this research are outlined below.

- This paper introduces a novel lightweight image encryption method that uniquely combines cellular automata rule vectors with Tinkerbell chaotic maps, achieving both strong security and computational efficiency.
- Outstanding ability to resist differential attacks, a fact supported by good cryptographic measures, with NPCR of 99.6261 and UACI of 49.86%.
- Showing its suitability for IoT devices, while the proposed method maintains the quality of encryption under tight computational and storage constraints.


## 2   Related Works

Alkhonaini et al. [4] examined the increase in the use of chaotic models in image encryption, considering their simplicity but exposing some vulnerabilities of such processes, such as limited key space and predictability. To increase key sensitivity and further prevent the implementation of brute-force, statistical, and differential attacks, they merged bidirectional chaotic maps with reversible cellular automata. However, their solution does not account for adaptive diffusion mechanisms or IoT constraints.

Darani et al. [6] suggested a 3-D chaotic encryption system that combines reversible and irreversible cellular automata to protect RGB images. This encrypted method enhances robustness against noise, cropping, and statistical attacks, while also improving key sensitivity. Although powerful, it may still suffer from giving exclusive importance to structural complexity with no adaptive controls or performance evaluation in constrained environments.

Kumar et al. [9] addressed the demand for greater security in image processing by merging the concepts of second-order cellular automata and chaotic maps, recognising the need for speed and robustness, especially in real-time and resource-constrained contexts. The solution has a predefined transformation pipeline and lacks flexibility for content- or feature-driven encryption.

Ince et al. [7] introduced a lightweight encryption approach for IoT devices. For efficiency, they used chaos-based diffusion and the corner traversal approach to scramble pixels. However, despite operating at high speed, which meets the lightweight criteria, it limits adaptation to different image characteristics, and the diffusion strength strongly depends on its traversal pattern.

Criticising the traditional S-box-based encryption, Shafique et al. [14] stated that it relies on manual estimation of robustness, which is often inefficient. To rectify this, they propose machine-learning-aided S-box selection combined with lightweight crypto operations, which increases robustness and speed, yet ignores the appropriateness of adaptability at various image complexities.

Al-Hyari et al. [1] created an encryption technique using CLMK and the Collatz Conjecture to generate keys. They improved chaotic randomness and diffusion, enhancing robustness and throughput, but their method is still limited by low-dimensional chaotic dependency and the non-adaptability of the permutation.

Alawida et al. [3] proposed an image encryption algorithm for Industrial IoT applications. They introduced cyclical chaotic maps and a perturbed logistic map in their algorithm for better diffusion and permutation. Although the method performs well and is robust, it does not consider any machine learning or content-aware features for the adaptive guidance of the encryption process.

Jackson et al. [8] proposed a method to encrypt color images using fractional-order chaotic maps. The system employs pixel-level shuffling and diffusion to attain great unpredictability, sensitivity, and tolerance to statistical attacks. It effectively secures coloured images during transmission. Still, the focus of the method has been chiefly on robustness without regard to computational overhead or image-aware diffusion customisation.

The present study also has some limitations and future directions:

1. The suggested approach focuses primarilly on RGB images and may require adaptation for other image types or data representations.
2. The study has not compared the performance across various IoT hardware platforms, leaving room for future optimisation studies.
3. Future research can investigate the hybridisation of the scheme with other lightweight cryptographic primitives or its adaptation for real-time usage in other IoT environments.


## 3     Preliminaries

To clearly present the proposed encryption approach, this section outlines the foundational Cellular Automata (CA) rule vector:

$$[51, 51, 51, 102, 153, 153, 51, 156]$$

and describes how it merges with the Tinkerbell chaotic map.

## 3.1   Cellular Automata Rules 51, 102, 153, and 156

John von Neumann is regarded as the originator of Cellular Automata (CA). His early work emphasised self-replication, systems capable of producing identical copies of themselves.

**Rule 51** Rule 51 is a one-dimensional CA rule defined as:

$$C_i^{t+1} = \overline{C_i^t} \tag{1}$$

This rule inverts the current state of each cell independently of its neighbours, creating oscillatory behaviour. It is often combined with other rules to improve randomness and diversity in the CA evolution.

**Rule 102**

$$C_i^{t+1} = C_{i+1}^t \oplus C_i^t \tag{2}$$

Rule 102 introduces irregular transitions and moderate diffusion, enhancing cryptographic strength when used in conjunction with other rules.

**Rule 153** We define Rule 153 in terms of logical operations as follows.

$$C_i^{t+1} = C_i^t \wedge \overline{C_{i-1}^t} \tag{3}$$

This rule supports asymmetric and directionally biased updates, making it suitable for lightweight encryption mechanisms.

**Rule 156** Defined by:

$$C_i^{t+1} = C_{i-1}^t \vee \overline{C_i^t} \tag{4}$$

Rule 156 provides both pattern preservation and diffusion using OR and NOT operators, which benefits reversible cryptographic design (Table 1).

## 3.2   Evolution Process in Cellular Automaton

The CA-based encryption process includes the following steps:

1. **Initialization:**
   - Seed: 8-bit initial state 11100100 (decimal 228)
   - Rule Vector: $[51, 51, 51, 102, 153, 153, 51, 156]$
   - Boundary Condition: Null (missing neighbours treated as 0)
2. **Neighborhood Extraction:** For each cell $i$, extract the triplet $(x_{i-1}, x_i, x_{i+1})$, using zero-padding at boundaries.
3. **Rule Application:** The proposed method computes the new value of each cell using its corresponding rule of the vector, interpreted according to Wolfram's encoding.

**Table 1.** Cellular Automata Iterations (Null Boundary, Rule Vector: [51, 51, 51, 102, 153, 153, 51, 156], Seed: [1 1 1 0 0 1 0 0])

| Iteration | Binary | Decimal |
| --- | --- | --- |
| 0 | 11100100 | 228 |
| 1 | 00010011 | 19 |
| 2 | 11101111 | 239 |
| 3 | 00011000 | 24 |
| 4 | 11100100 | 228 |
| 5 | 00010011 | 19 |
| 6 | 11101111 | 239 |
| 7 | 00011000 | 24 |
| 8 | 11100100 | 228 |

4. **Bit Update:** All cells are updated simultaneously to form the next 8-bit state.
5. **Iteration:** The process is repeated for a fixed number of steps (e.g., 8 iterations), with binary and decimal values recorded per step.
6. **Pattern Observation:** The observed 4-cycle periodicity indicates deterministic and reversible dynamics, favourable for cryptographic use.
7. **Encryption Use:** The CA output can directly drive pixel transformations in image encryption applications.

### 3.3   Tinkerbell Map

The Tinkerbell map is a chaotic system commonly used in encryption to generate unpredictable sequences. The following equations express it:

$$x_{n+1} = (x_n^2 - y_n^2) + ax_n + by_n \tag{5}$$

$$y_{n+1} = 2x_n y_n + cx_n + dy_n \tag{6}$$

The variables $x_n$ and $y_n$ represent the states of the system, while the control parameters $a, b, c,$ and $d$ dictate its chaotic dynamics. Figure 1 represents the bifurcation diagram of the Tinkerbell map using Eqs. 5 and 6.

## 4   Proposed Work

The proposed encryption process involves breaking down the original image into its component Red, Green, and Blue (RGB), as shown in Fig. 2. The method first uses the Tinkerbell chaotic map to encipher the channels before proceeding to the channel components that require further processing. The next step involves using the Cellular Automata Rule Vector to perform channel decomposition on each of the encoded channels. Ultimately, the already encoded channels are combined to form the encrypted image.

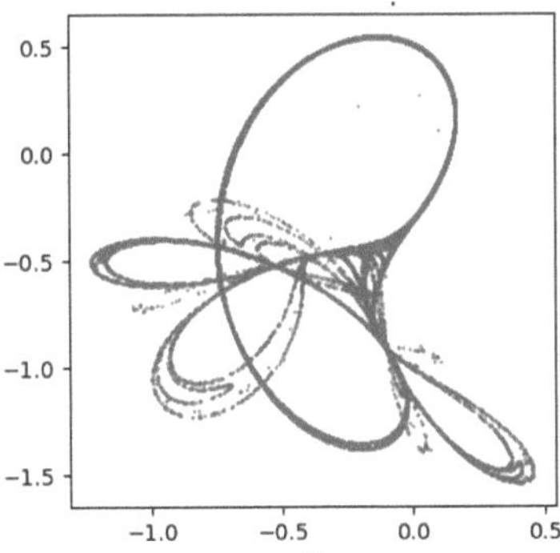

**Fig. 1.** Bifurcation diagram of the Tinkerbell map.

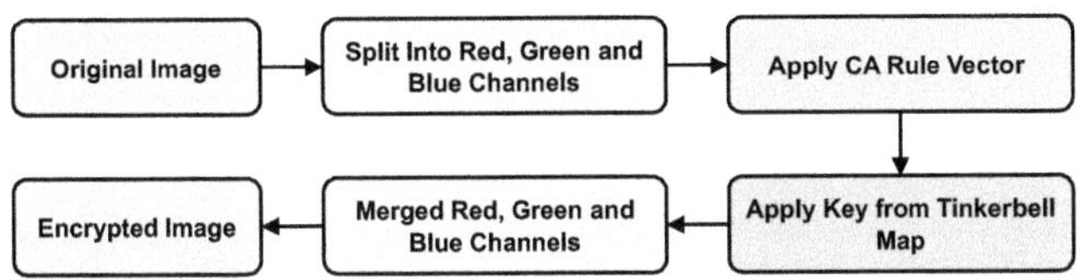


**Fig. 2.** Proposed image encryption model represented as a block diagram

## 4.1   Encryption Process

The algorithm in Algorithm 1 shows the proposed image encryption method. The method combines Cellular Automata (CA) with the Tinkerbell chaotic map to provide high security. The process starts by splitting the image into three color channels: red, green, and blue. For each pixel in every channel, the 8-bit binary value is modified by applying a CA rule based on the bit index. The CA rule vector $[51, 51, 51, 102, 153, 153, 51, 156]$ assigns a specific rule to each positions of the bit in the 8-bit sequence. The method uses a 3-bit neighbourhood under null boundary conditions and applies the chosen rule to update each bit. After the CA step, the pixel values are further changed using the chaotic sequence from the Tinkerbell map. The chaotic values $x_n$ and $y_n$ are generated iteratively, converted to integers, and added to the pixel value modulo 256. The encrypted image $I_{enc}$ is then reconstructed by merging the processed color channels. The CA system ensures diffusion, while the Tinkerbell map introduces confusion, creating two strong layers of security against cryptographic attacks.

## 4.2   Decryption Process

The Algorithm 2 describes the decryption process that recovers the plain image from the cipher image. The process starts by dividing the cipher image $I_{enc}$ into its three color channels: red, green, and blue. In the next step, the method applies the Tinkerbell chaotic map in reverse by subtracting the chaotic values generated

---

**Algorithm 1.** Image Encryption Algorithm Using Cellular Automata Rule Vector

---

1: **Input:** Original Image $I$
2: **Output:** Encrypted Image $I_{enc}$
3: $R, G, B \leftarrow$ ExtractChannels($I$)
4: RuleVector $\leftarrow [51, 51, 51, 102, 153, 153, 51, 156]$
5: **for** each channel $C$ in $\{R, G, B\}$ **do**
6:     **for** each pixel $C[i][j]$ **do**
7:         Convert pixel value to 8-bit binary vector: $B_{in} \leftarrow$ ToBinary($C[i][j]$)
8:         Initialize $B_{out} \leftarrow [\,]$
9:         **for** each bit index $k \in [0, 7]$ **do**
10:             Define 3-bit neighbourhood:

$$N_k = \begin{cases} [0, B_{in}[k], B_{in}[k+1]] & \text{if } k = 0 \\ [B_{in}[k-1], B_{in}[k], B_{in}[k+1]] & \text{if } 1 \leq k \leq 6 \\ [B_{in}[k-1], B_{in}[k], 0] & \text{if } k = 7 \end{cases}$$

11:             rule $\leftarrow$ RuleVector$[k]$
12:             $B_{out}[k] \leftarrow$ ApplyCARule(rule, $N_k$)
13:         **end for**
14:         $C[i][j] \leftarrow$ ToDecimal($B_{out}$)
15:     **end for**
16: **end for**
17: **for** each pixel $C[i][j]$ in $\{R, G, B\}$ **do**
18:     Initialize Tinkerbell Map: $x_0 = 0.1, y_0 = 0.1$
19:     $x_{n+1} = x_n^2 - y_n^2 + ax_n + by_n$
20:     $y_{n+1} = 2x_n y_n + cx_n + dy_n$
21:     $C[i][j] \leftarrow (C[i][j] + \lfloor x_n \rfloor + \lfloor y_n \rfloor) \mod 256$
22: **end for**
23: $I_{enc} \leftarrow$ Merge($R, G, B$)
24: Save $I_{enc}$

---

from its iterative equation. For each pixel, the proposed method reverses the confusion introduced during encryption by subtracting the integer parts of the chaotic variables $x_n$ and $y_n$ from the pixel value modulo 256.

The proposed approach converts each adjusted pixel value into an 8-bit binary vector after processing. Then reverses the bits by applying the Cellular Automata rule vector $[51, 51, 51, 102, 153, 153, 51, 156]$ together with the bitwise neighbours. In greater detail, for each bit position $k$, a 3-bit neighbourhood is constructed using null boundary conditions. Then, the inverse logic of the associated CA rule is used to calculate the reversed bit value. The proposed approach applies a bitwise transformation to every pixel in all channels and then merges the channels to obtain the decrypted image $I$. In this way, Algorithm 2 successfully reverses the confusion and diffusion processes of the encryption operation, restoring the original image correctly.

**Algorithm 2.** Image Decryption Algorithm Using Cellular Automata Rule Vector

---

1: **Input:** Encrypted Image $I_{enc}$
2: **Output:** Decrypted Image $I$
3: $R, G, B \leftarrow \text{ExtractChannels}(I_{enc})$
4: RuleVector $\leftarrow [51, 51, 51, 102, 153, 153, 51, 156]$
5: **for** each pixel $C[i][j]$ in $\{R, G, B\}$ **do**
6:     Initialize Tinkerbell Map: $x_0 = 0.1, y_0 = 0.1$
7:     $x_{n+1} = x_n^2 - y_n^2 + ax_n + by_n$
8:     $y_{n+1} = 2x_n y_n + cx_n + dy_n$
9:     $C[i][j] \leftarrow (C[i][j] - \lfloor x_n \rfloor - \lfloor y_n \rfloor + 256) \mod 256$
10: **end for**
11: **for** each channel $C$ in $\{R, G, B\}$ **do**
12:     **for** each pixel $C[i][j]$ **do**
13:         Convert pixel value to 8-bit binary: $B_{in} \leftarrow \text{ToBinary}(C[i][j])$
14:         Initialize $B_{rev} \leftarrow [\,]$
15:         **for** each bit index $k \in [0, 7]$ **do**
16:             Define 3-bit neighbourhood:

$$N_k = \begin{cases} [0, B_{in}[k], B_{in}[k+1]] & \text{if } k = 0 \\ [B_{in}[k-1], B_{in}[k], B_{in}[k+1]] & \text{if } 1 \leq k \leq 6 \\ [B_{in}[k-1], B_{in}[k], 0] & \text{if } k = 7 \end{cases}$$

17:             rule $\leftarrow$ RuleVector$[k]$
18:             $B_{rev}[k] \leftarrow \text{ReverseCARule}(\text{rule}, N_k)$
19:         **end for**
20:         $C[i][j] \leftarrow \text{ToDecimal}(B_{rev})$
21:     **end for**
22: **end for**
23: $I \leftarrow \text{Merge}(R, G, B)$
24: **Return** $I$

---

## Compuational complexity

The computational time and memory requirements of the encryption and decryption algorithms were evaluated. Both algorithms demonstrate linear scalability with respect to image size.

This linear behaviour arises because each core step—including colour channel separation, Tinkerbell map transformation, diffusion using only the rule vector.

$$[51, 51, 51, 102, 153, 153, 51, 156],$$

Channel recombination—processes each pixel exactly once.

Consequently, the time complexity is given by

$$\mathcal{O}(M \times N),$$

where $M$ and $N$ represent the dimensions of the image. Similarly, the space complexity is

$$\mathcal{O}(M \times N),$$

Due to the memory required to store the individual colour channels and the resulting encrypted or decrypted image.

Because the decryption algorithm precisely inverts the encryption steps, it shares the same asymptotic time and space complexity.

## 5    Results and Performance Metrics

This work is enhanced by the learning offered on a personal computer containing a quad-core ARMv8 1.5GHz processor and 4 Gigabytes of RAM. Evaluation analysis incorporates histogram, correlation, MSE, PSNR, UACI, and NPCR analyses.

Figure 3 displays the original, encrypted, and decrypted Peppers image. Figure 4 shows the histogram of the original and encrypted image of Peppers. Figures 5 and 6 show the correlation coefficients for the Peppers image. Table 2 presents a summary and comparison of the values of "Mean Squared Error (MSE)", "Peak Signal-to-Noise-Ratio (PSNR)", "Number of Pixel Change Rate (NPCR)", "Unified Average Change Intensity (UACI)", "Information Entropy", and "Correlation Coefficient".

**Fig. 3.** Peppers image: plain vs. decrypted

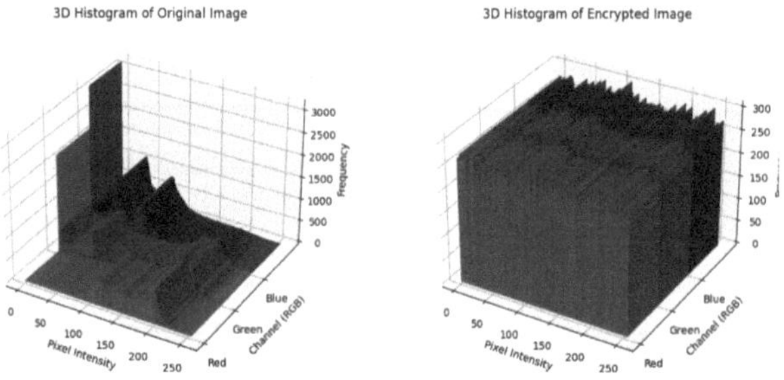


**Fig. 4.** Comparison between original and encrypted RGB histograms of the Peppers image, showing encryption-induced randomness.

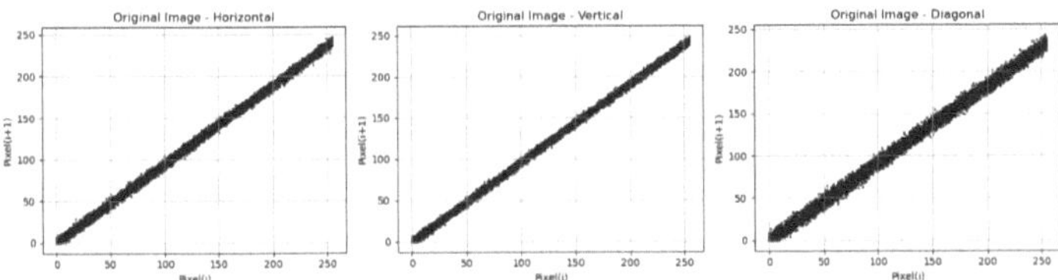

**Fig. 5.** Evaluation of adjacent pixel correlations for the original Peppers image across three directional axes

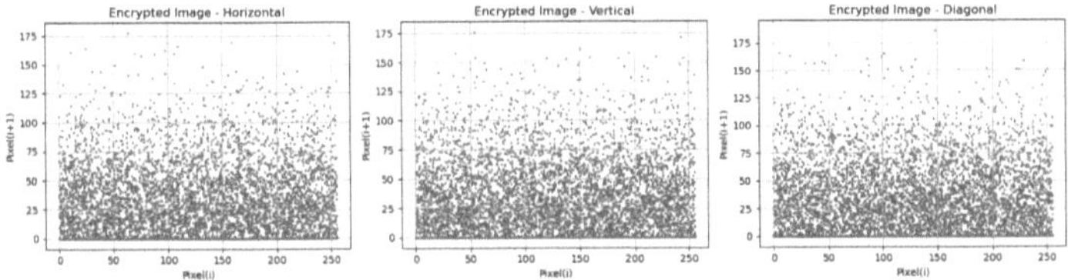

**Fig. 6.** Evaluation of adjacent pixel correlations for the encrypted Peppers image across three directional axes

The proposed encryption method outperforms previous work by achieving higher security and better encryption quality. It has an information entropy of 7.9990, which is closer to the ideal value of 8, ensuring a nearly uniform pixel distribution in the encrypted image. The UACI value of 49.86 is higher than that of other methods (around 33.47), indicating stronger resistance to differential attacks. The correlation coefficients are close to zero or negative, meaning that the encrypted image does not retain the original patterns. Unlike previous works, this method also provides MSE (105.75) and PSNR (27.89), demonstrating a substantial transformation of the image. These factors make the proposed encryption method more secure and effective.

The Proposed Work has a higher UACI value of around 49.86. This means that it offers better diffusion than the other methods, with a UACI value of 33.47. All three methods have similar entropy values, with a value of approximately 7.99. The proposed work shows that the encrypted images are highly random. The NPCR values are all above 99.6. This means that the encryption methods can resist differential attacks.

**Table 2.** Performance comparison of different schemes on Peppers image

| Method | MSE | PSNR | NPCR | UACI | Entropy | Corr-H | Corr-V | Corr-D |
|---|---|---|---|---|---|---|---|---|
| Li et al. [10] | NA | NA | 99.62 | 33.47 | 7.9979 | 0.0010 | 0.0042 | 0.0063 |
| Niyat et al. [12] | NA | NA | 99.6505 | 33.4462 | 7.9972 | 0.0022 | 0.0001 | -0.0017 |
| Proposed Work | 105.75 | 27.89 | 99.61 | 49.86 | 7.9990 | -0.0023 | 0.0007 | -0.0007 |

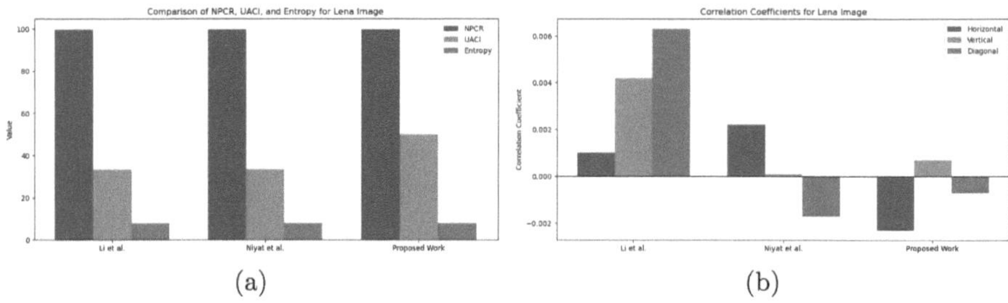

(a)                                        (b)

**Fig. 7.** Comparison of NPCR, UACI, entropy, and correlation coefficients for the Peppers image. The left chart highlights the strong diffusion and randomness achieved by the proposed method, while the right chart shows the significant reduction in adjacent pixel correlation, confirming the encryption's robustness.

The diagram shows the correlation of adjacent pixels in the horizontal, vertical, and diagonal directions. It compares the methods used by Li et al., Niyat et al., and the Proposed Work. Lower or negative correlation values are better. They show that the encrypted image has fewer patterns and is more secure. The proposed method has the lowest or negative correlation values. This indicates that it is more resistant to statistical attacks (Fig. 7).

**Table 3.** DIEHARD randomness test results for the encrypted Peppers image. All tests passed with p-values lying within the acceptable range (0.01 to 0.99), confirming strong statistical randomness and cryptographic strength of the encryption scheme.

| Sl. No. | Test Name | Result | p-value |
|---|---|---|---|
| 1 | Runs | ✓ | 0.8259 |
| 2 | Binary Rank 6 × 8 | ✓ | 0.8674 |
| 3 | Bitstream | ✓ | 0.1736 |
| 4 | Binary Rank 32 × 32 | ✓ | 0.4017 |
| 5 | OQSO | ✓ | 0.9495 |
| 6 | Birthday Spacings | ✓ | 0.7912 |
| 7 | OPSO | ✓ | 0.9310 |
| 8 | Overlapping Sums | ✓ | 0.1497 |
| 9 | Overlapping 5-Permutation | ✓ | 0.8123 |
| 10 | Craps | ✓ | 0.8673 |
| 11 | Count-the-1's (Test 2) | ✓ | 0.8978 |
| 12 | Minimum Distance | ✓ | 0.8440 |
| 13 | Count-the-1's | ✓ | 0.7754 |
| 14 | Squeeze | ✓ | 0.1602 |
| 15 | 3D Spheres | ✓ | 0.1891 |
| 16 | DNA | ✓ | 0.4341 |
| 17 | Parking Lot | ✓ | 0.5916 |

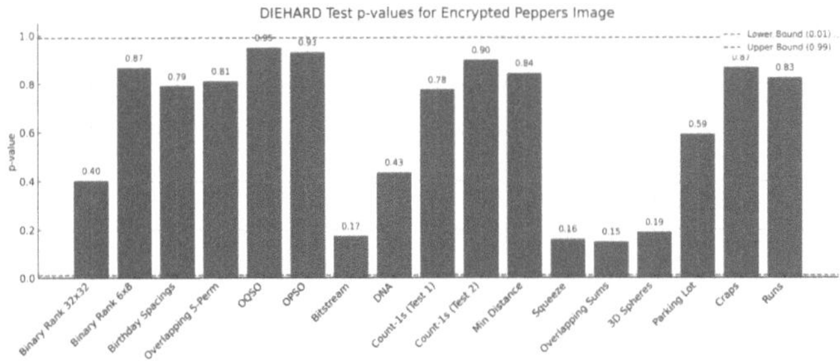

**Fig. 8.** DIEHARD test p-values for the encrypted Peppers image.

As shown in Table 3, the encrypted image successfully passes all DIEHARD tests, confirming its strong statistical randomness (Fig. 8).

As presented in Table 4, the encrypted Peppers image passes all NIST randomness tests, indicating its robustness against statistical attacks (Fig. 9).

The proposed work conducted the entropy test on the encrypted image of Pepper, and Table 5 presents the results. The entropy value reached 7.9990, which is very close to the ideal value of 8, indicating a high level of randomness in the encrypted image. The encryption process achieves a 0% compression ratio, meaning it prevents data compression and signifies strong encryption. The Chi-square test yields a value of 253.78, indicating an even distribution of pixel

**Table 4.** NIST statistical test results for the encrypted *Peppers* image. All tests passed with p-values within the acceptable confidence interval (0.01 to 0.99), indicating strong randomness and cryptographic suitability of the encrypted output.

| Sl. No. | Test Name | Result | p-value |
|---|---|---|---|
| 1 | Frequency (Monobit) Test | ✓ | 0.6321 |
| 2 | Block Frequency Test | ✓ | 0.5476 |
| 3 | Cumulative Sums Test | ✓ | 0.6893 |
| 4 | Runs Test | ✓ | 0.7880 |
| 5 | Longest Run of Ones Test | ✓ | 0.5992 |
| 6 | Rank Test | ✓ | 0.9331 |
| 7 | FFT (Spectral) Test | ✓ | 0.3690 |
| 8 | Approximate Entropy Test | ✓ | 0.5814 |
| 9 | Serial Test (1) | ✓ | 0.4592 |
| 10 | Serial Test (2) | ✓ | 0.6431 |
| 11 | Linear Complexity Test | ✓ | 0.6952 |
| 12 | Universal Statistical Test | ✓ | 0.4728 |
| 13 | Random Excursions Test | ✓ | 0.8049 |
| 14 | Random Excursions Variant Test | ✓ | 0.8237 |

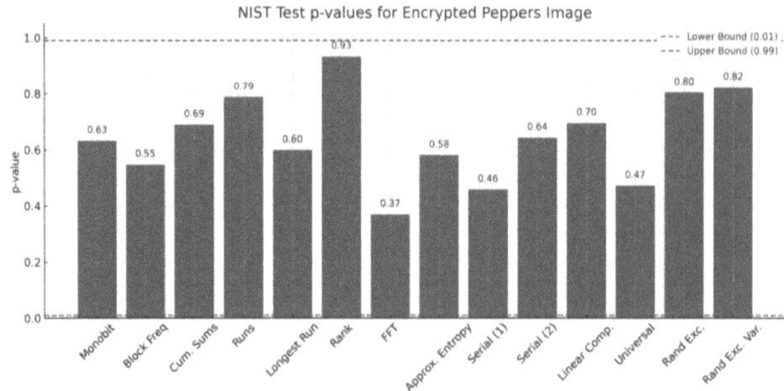

**Fig. 9.** NIST test p-values for the encrypted Peppers image, all within the acceptable range (0.010.99), demonstrating cryptographic robustness.

**Table 5.** ENT Test Results For The Encrypted Peppers Image Using The Proposed Method

| Sl. No. | Test Parameter | Result (Proposed Work) |
|---|---|---|
| 1 | Entropy (bits per byte) | 7.9990 |
| 2 | Compression ratio | 0.00% |
| 3 | Chi-square distribution | 253.78 |
| 4 | Arithmetic mean | 127.49 |
| 5 | Monte Carlo $\pi$ estimation | 3.1421 (error: 0.03%) |
| 6 | Serial correlation coefficient | Horizontal: -0.0023<br>Vertical: 0.0007<br>Diagonal: -0.0007 |

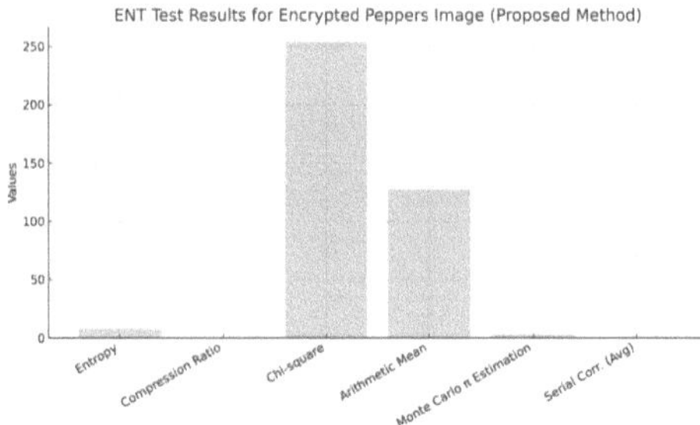

**Fig. 10.** ENT test-based randomness analysis of the encrypted Peppers image.

values. The arithmetic mean is 127.49, which is very close to the expected average of 127.5. The Monte Carlo estimation of $\pi$ is 3.1421, with an error of only 0.03%, demonstrating high statistical precision. The serial correlation coefficients are near zero in all directions, confirming the absence of any relationship between neighbouring pixels. These results collectively confirm that the proposed encryption method is both secure and highly random (Fig. 10).

# 6   Conclusion

The proposed work combines a Cellular Automata Rule vector with the Tinkerbell chaotic map to create a lightweight image encryption method for IoT devices. The proposed approach aims to provide high security while addressing the resource constraints typically found in IoT environments. In the analysis using NPCR and UACI, this method effectively resisted differential attacks, with a diffusion strength of more than 50% to supporting this claim. However, the proposed work has been primarily applied in simulations using benchmark images; its performance on actual IoT hardware platforms, such as embedded micro-controllers, remains unverified. Moreover, the system currently supports only static images and does not handle video, streaming data, or real-time sensor input. In addition, once we settle on a particular chaotic map (Tinkerbell here) and a single CA rule vector, adaptability is lost; the model currently does not allow for parameter tuning or rule selection. Future extensions of this research will explore both algorithmic and deployment-level improvements to enhance the applicability of the proposed image encryption scheme in real-world IoT environments.

# References


1. Al-Hyari, A., Obimbo, C., Mua'ad, M., Al-Taharwa, I.: Generating powerful encryption keys for image cryptography with chaotic maps by incorporating collatz conjecture. IEEE Access **12**, 4825–4844 (2024)
2. Alaba, F.A., Othman, M., Hashem, I.A.T., Alotaibi, F.: Internet of things security: a survey. J. Netw. Comput. Appl. **88**, 10–28 (2017)
3. Alawida, M.: A novel image encryption algorithm based on cyclic chaotic map in industrial Iot environments. IEEE Trans. Ind. Inf. (2024)
4. Alkhonaini, M.A., Gemeay, E., Zeki Mahmood, F.M., Ayari, M., Alenizi, F.A., Lee, S.: A new encryption algorithm for image data based on two-way chaotic maps and iterative cellular automata. Sci. Rep. **14**(1), 16701 (2024)
5. Atzori, L., Iera, A., Morabito, G.: The internet of things: a survey. Comput. Netw. **54**(15), 2787–2805 (2010)
6. Darani, A.Y., Yengejeh, Y.K., Pakmanesh, H., Navarro, G.: Image encryption algorithm based on a new 3d chaotic system using cellular automata. Chaos, Solitons Fractals **179**, 114396 (2024)
7. İnce, C., İnce, K., Hanbay, D.: Novel image pixel scrambling technique for efficient color image encryption in resource-constrained Iot devices. Multimedia Tools Appl. **83**(29), 72789–72817 (2024)
8. Jackson, J., Perumal, R.: A robust image encryption technique based on an improved fractional order chaotic map. Nonlinear Dyn. **113**(7), 7277–7296 (2025)
9. Kumar, K., Roy, S., Rawat, U., Shandilya, A.: Societ: second-order cellular automata and chaotic map-based hybrid image encryption technique. Multimedia Tools Appl. **83**(10), 29455–29484 (2024)
10. Li, R., Liu, Q., Liu, L.: Novel image encryption algorithm based on improved logistic map. IET Image Proc. **13**(1), 125–134 (2019)

11. Li, S., Chen, G., Cheung, Y., Bhargava, B.K.: On the security of a class of image encryption schemes. IEEE Trans. Circuits Syst. Video Technol. **16**(1), 113–122 (2006)
12. Niyat, A.Y., Moattar, M.H., Torshiz, M.N.: Color image encryption based on hybrid hyper-chaotic system and cellular automata. Opt. Lasers Eng. **90**, 225–237 (2017)
13. Rao, B.V.B., Rawat, U., Roy, S., Lal, C.: Sorchic: a hybrid image cipher for Iot applications using second order reversible cellular automata. IEEE Access (2024)
14. Shafique, A., Mehmood, A., Alawida, M., Khan, A.N., Shuja, J.: Lightweight image encryption scheme for Iot environment and machine learning-driven robust s-box selection. Telecommun. Syst. **88**(1), 1–23 (2025)
15. Sicari, S., Rizzardi, A., Grieco, L.A., Coen-Porisini, A.: Security, privacy and trust in internet of things: the road ahead. Comput. Netw. **76**, 146–164 (2015)
16. Wong, K.W., Ho, C.S., Liao, X.Q., Law, W.C.: A fast chaotic cryptographic scheme with dynamic look-up table. Phys. Lett. A **310**(1–2), 67–74 (2003)

# Lightweight Real-Time Anomaly Detection on IoT Edge Devices Using Machine Learning


H. K. I. S. Lakmal[1]($\boxtimes$) , M. W. P. Maduranga[2] , Sandamini Neththikumara[3] ,
W. A. A. M. Wanniarachchi[4] , W. M. S. R. B. Wijayarathne[4] ,
and Sabyasachi Bhattacharyya[5]

[1] Department of Mechatronic and Industrial Engineering, NSBM Green University, Homagama,
Sri Lanka
`isuru.l@nsbm.ac.lk`
[2] Centre for Next Generation Communication Systems, Faculty of Engineering, University of
Sri Jayewardenepura, Mattegoda, Sri Lanka
[3] HAMK University of Applied Sciences, Riihimaki, Finland
[4] Department of Information Technology, General Sir John Kotelawala Defence University,
Ratmalana, Colombo, Sri Lanka
[5] Department of Electronics and Telecommunication Engineering, Barak Valley Engineering
College, Sribhumi & Residential Girls' Polytechnic, Golaghat, Govt of Assam, Golaghat, India



**Abstract.** The rapid growth of modern telecommunication networks, driven by 5G & emerging 6G technologies, has enhanced the need for robust, real-time cybersecurity measures to counter threats like DDos, web-attacks, and botnet activities. This paper proposes a lightweight, efficient, anomaly detection system for network edge nodes, utilizing Random-Forest, XGBoost and a hybrid model combining both models using soft voting. The models have been evaluated on the CICIDS2017 dataset, the models achieved a high detection accuracy of 99.85%, 99.88% and 99.86% respectively. The proposed models balance accuracy and computational cost, with low prediction latency and training times, making them suitable for edge deployments. This study demonstrates that ensemble-based ML approaches can deliver high-performance anomaly detection while meeting the demands of real-time telecom network security.

**Keywords:** Anomaly Detection · Network Traffic Analysis · Edge Computing · XGBoost · Hybrid Ensemble Learning · Random Forest


## 1 Introduction

Modern telecommunication networks support critical services like voice, data, video streaming, and IoT with the rollout of 5G and the upcoming 6G. These networks are expected to handle billions of devices and huge real-time data streams. This scale introduces serious security issues, including DDoS attacks, web attacks, and botnet activities.


© The Author(s), under exclusive license to Springer Nature Switzerland AG 2026
K. K. Patel et al. (Eds.): icSoftComp 2025, CCIS 2874, pp. 189–200, 2026.
https://doi.org/10.1007/978-3-032-22062-2_15

Existing intrusion detection systems (IDS) mostly rely on rule-based or deep learning models deployed in centralized servers. This is accurate but too heavy for real-time usage in edge environments. They need high computational power, which increases latency and makes it difficult to scale with decentralized 5G/6G architectures.

This study focuses on developing lightweight machine learning models that are fast, efficient, and suitable for edge deployment. I use Random Forest and XGBoost because of their balance between accuracy and efficiency for real-time anomaly detection in telecom network traffic. This research proposes a hybrid model that combines both classifiers using soft voting, which averages their predicted probabilities to improve overall performance. This ensemble approach aims to boost detection reliability without significantly increasing resource usage, making it practical for telecom scenarios.

All models are tested using the CICIDS 2017 dataset, which contains a wide variety of attack types and realistic network patterns commonly observed in modern networks. The models are also evaluated on their prediction speed, training speed, and suitability for deployment in latency-sensitive environments (Fig. 1).

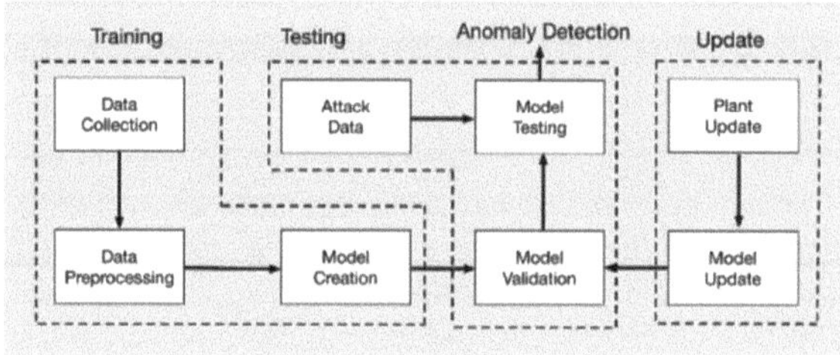


**Fig. 1.** IDS Architecture

The key contributions of this study are as follows:

- Development of lightweight models capable of detecting multiple categories of cyber-attacks.
- A comparative evaluation of Random Forest, XGBoost, and a proposed hybrid model in terms of classification accuracy and ROC-AUC.
- Simulation of real-time detection scenarios with an emphasis on measuring both prediction latency and training efficiency.

## 2 Literature Review

Modern intrusion detection research in telecom and IOT domains has largely explored both traditional machine learning and deep learning methods. A common issue in many studies is the challenge of balancing detection accuracy with complexity and computational cost, especially in real-time and resource-constrained environments like telecom edge nodes.

In the study [2], their system monitored inter-message dependencies and protocol-specific behavior to identify spoofing, message manipulation, and malformed requests. While the model achieved a detection accuracy of 99.95% and outperformed baseline techniques like K-Means and ANN, it relied heavily on handcrafted rules and protocol-dependent logic. This made it difficult to scale across several protocols and unsuitable for deployment in edge nodes, where efficiency and flexibility are essential.

In the study [3], focused on improving anomaly-based IDS performance by combining Decision Tree and Random Forest using stacking ensemble. Tested on two datasets, which are NSL-KDD and CICIDS2017. The hybrid model achieved a 85.2% and 98% respectively. The work emphasized the importance of using realistic datasets. The study concluded that ensemble-based shallow ML models can be effective when feature selection is properly done. The work did not analyze prediction latency or suitability for edge deployments.

In the study [4], a hybrid deep learning model combining autoencoders (AE) and multi-layer perceptrons (MLP) to detect DDoS attacks in mobile edge environments. This model used AE unsupervised feature extraction and MLP for classification, achieving 99.98% accuracy on the NF-UQ-NIDS-V2 dataset. The results were impressive, but such deep models are computationally heavy, making them less suitable for edge environments (Table 1).

**Table 1.** Related Work Comparison

| Aspect | Afzal & Murgesan (2022) | Rahabah & Srivastava (2021) | Adeniyi et al. (2024) | This Study (Full XGBoost) |
| --- | --- | --- | --- | --- |
| Model Type | Rule-based | DT + RF (Ensemble ML) | AE + MLP (Deep Learning) | XGBoost (Supervised ML) |
| Accuracy | 99.95% | 98% | 99.98% | 99.87% |
| False Alarm Rate | 18.18% | Not Reported | Low | Very Low |
| Dataset Used | SS7(Private) | CICIDS2017, NSL-KDD | NF-UQ-NIDS-V2 | CICIDS2017 |
| Edge Suitability | Low | High | Limited | High |
| Real-Time Performance | Not Measured | Not Measured | Not Measured | High (633.95 $\mu$s) |
| Computational Efficiency | High Overhead | Lightweight | Low Efficiency | High Efficiency |

## 3 Methodology

This study focuses on implementing a lightweight supervised machine learning framework designed for real-time anomaly detection within telecommunications network traffic, addressing the critical need for rapid and accurate identification of cyber threats. Three distinct models were evaluated to assess their effectiveness in this context: XGBoost, Random Forest, and a hybrid ensemble model that employs a soft voting strategy to combine the strengths of both. XGBoost leverages gradient boosting to iteratively refined predictions, excelling in capturing complex patterns in structured data. Random Forest, an ensemble of decision trees trained on bootstrapped data subsets with random feature selection, prioritizes robustness and resistance to overfitting. The hybrid model integrates probability predictions from both XGBoost and Random Forest, averaging their class probabilities to produce a final prediction, thereby balancing accuracy and computational efficiency.

The evaluation was conducted using the CICIDS 2017 dataset, selected for its comprehensive representation of modern cyberattacks and realistic network traffic simulations. This dataset, developed by the Canadian Institute for Cybersecurity, includes a diverse range of attack scenarios, such as Distributed Denial of Service (DDoS), brute force, and SQL injection, alongside normal traffic patterns, making it an ideal benchmark for testing anomaly detection systems. Its realistic simulation of network behavior ensures that the models are evaluated under conditions that closely mimic real-world telecom environments, where timely detection of anomalies is critical to maintaining network security and integrity.

This study focuses on lightweight models to enable low-latency performance for real-time threat mitigation. The proposed hybrid ensemble combines XGBoost's precision with Random Forest's stability, achieving high detection accuracy while optimizing computational resources. This approach is well-suited for telecom networks, where large data volumes and instant response are critical.

### 3.1  Dataset and Pre-processing

The CICIDS 2017 dataset contains both benign and malicious network traffic across multiple attack types. Due to class imbalance, a multi-step balancing strategy was used after dropping unwanted columns.

The majority class (Benign) was down-sampled to 300,000 records to reduce computational cost and balance distribution. Then, classes removed less than 100 records. Afterward, SMOTE was applied to the training set, ensuring that synthetic samples do not leak into the test data. Label encoding was used to convert categorical features to numerical values suitable for model training.

### 3.2  Feature Selection

The dataset consisted of 77 features after dropping unwanted columns. Feature importance was computed separately for the models using cumulative importance and only the 80% of the cumulative importance were retained. This threshold ensured minimal information loss while significantly reducing models' complexity and improving performance (Figs. 2 and 3).

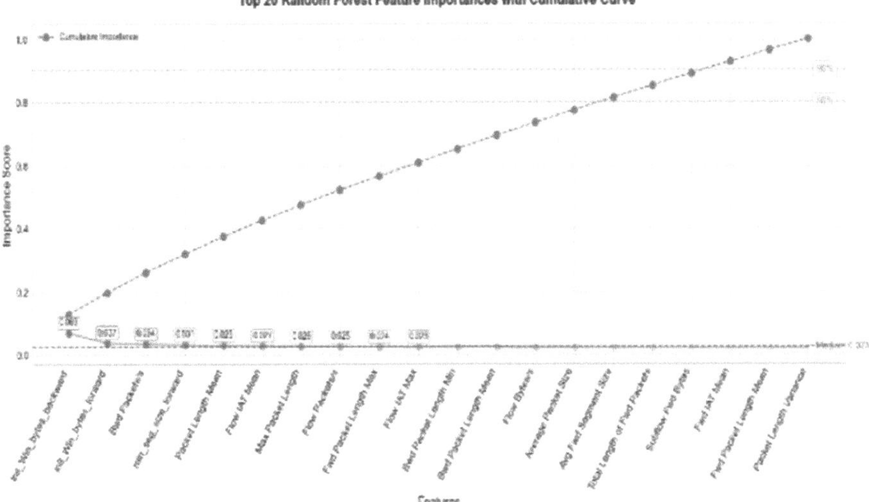

**Fig. 2.** Cumulative Importance of RF

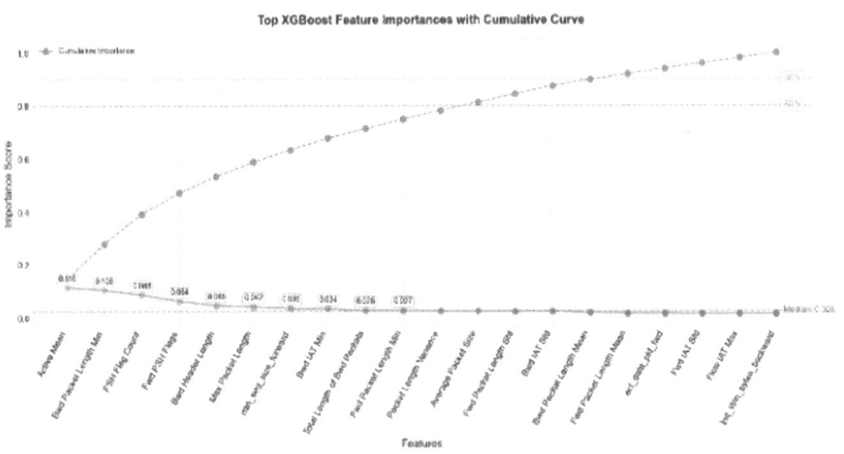

**Fig. 3.** Cumulative Importance of XGB

For Random-Forest there were 14 features retained after feature selection and for XGBoost there were 11 features retained.

## 3.3  Model Architecture

**Six Models Were Developed and Compared**

Random Forest (RF): The Random Forest algorithm constructs an ensemble of multiple decision trees, each trained on bootstrapped subsets of the dataset, a process known as bagging, which enhances model robustness by reducing variance. At each split within a tree, Random Forest employs random feature selection, sampling a subset of features to ensure diversity among the trees and mitigate overfitting. In the full Random Forest model, final predictions are determined through majority voting across all trees, aggregating their individual outputs to produce a stable and accurate result. The reduced Random Forest model follows the same mechanism but is streamlined to utilize only the top 14 most important features, selected based on their predictive significance. This feature reduction eliminates less impactful variables, reducing noise and improving computational efficiency while maintaining or even enhancing generalization by focusing on the most influential predictors.

XGBoost (XGB): XGBoost, short for Extreme Gradient Boosting, is a powerful tree-based gradient boosting algorithm that constructs sequential decision trees, where each subsequent tree corrects the residual errors of its predecessors, optimizing the overall model performance through iterative refinement. Designed for speed and scalability, XGBoost incorporates advanced regularization techniques, such as L1 and L2 penalties, to prevent overfitting and handle complex datasets effectively. This makes it particularly well-suited for structured, tabular data, where it excels at capturing intricate patterns. The full XGBoost model leverages all 77 available features to maximize predictive accuracy by exploiting both strong and subtle interactions. In contrast, the reduced XGBoost model is streamlined to use only the 11 most significant features, selected based on their cumulative importance to the model's predictive power. While this reduction enhances computational efficiency and training speed, it risks omitting moderately important features that contribute to XGBoost's boosting process, potentially impacting accuracy due to the loss of nuanced interactions critical to its performance.

**Hybrid Model (Soft Voting Ensemble)**
The hybrid model integrates the probability predictions of Random Forest (RF) and XGBoost (XGB) classifiers to produce a robust ensemble that capitalizes on the strengths of both algorithms. For each input sample, both RF and XGB independently generate class probability estimates based on their respective decision-making processes. These probabilities are then averaged using a soft voting strategy, where the final predicted class is determined by selecting the class with the highest average probability across the two models. This approach enhances prediction reliability by combining RF's ability to reduce variance through diverse, bootstrapped decision trees with XGB's strength in iterative error correction via gradient boosting, resulting in a more stable and accurate classifier.

Two versions of the hybrid model were evaluated to assess their performance under different feature configurations. The full hybrid model combines the complete Random Forest and XGBoost models, utilizing the entire set of available features—77 for XGB and the full feature set for RF. This configuration maximizes predictive power by leveraging all available data, capturing both strong and subtle interactions to achieve high accuracy and robustness, particularly for complex datasets. In contrast, the reduced hybrid model integrates the streamlined versions of RF and XGB, which use only the top 14 and 11 most important features, respectively, selected based on their cumulative predictive significance. By focusing on the most impactful features, the reduced hybrid model maintains a lightweight computational footprint, prioritizing efficiency while still achieving performance comparable to the full model.

The soft voting strategy employed in both hybrid models enhances predictability by smoothing out individual model biases, leveraging RF's robustness to noise and XGB's precision in modeling intricate patterns. This combination ensures that the hybrid model benefits from the complementary strengths of both algorithms, making it versatile for various applications. In the reduced version, the focus on high-importance features further minimizes computational overhead, aligning with the objective of maintaining efficiency without significantly compromising predictive performance, making it suitable for resource-constrained or real-time scenarios.

## 4  Results and Analysis

### 4.1  Classification Performance

All full models achieved outstanding results, with accuracy exceeding 99.8% and high Area Under the Curve (AUC) scores, demonstrating robust predictive capability across diverse datasets (Fig. 4). Among them, XGBoost consistently outperformed Random Forest by leveraging advanced boosting techniques to capture complex patterns, thereby enhancing predictive power. The hybrid model, which integrates the strengths of both XGBoost and Random Forest, provided the best trade-off between accuracy, robustness, and computational efficiency, making it highly suitable for practical applications. Similar trends were observed in the reduced models, as illustrated in Fig. 5, further confirming the effectiveness of the proposed approach.

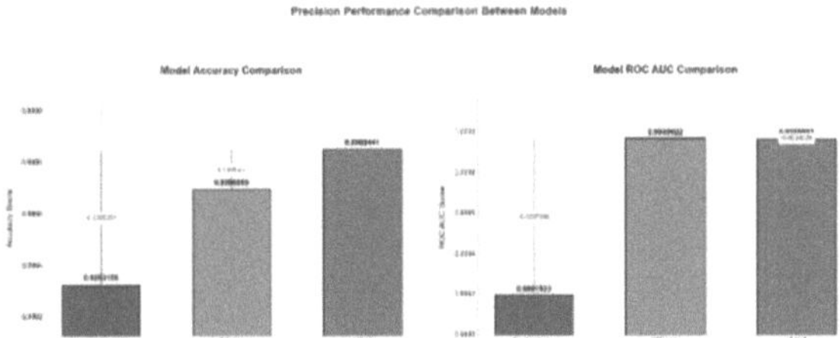

**Fig. 4.** Accuracy & ROC comparison Full Models

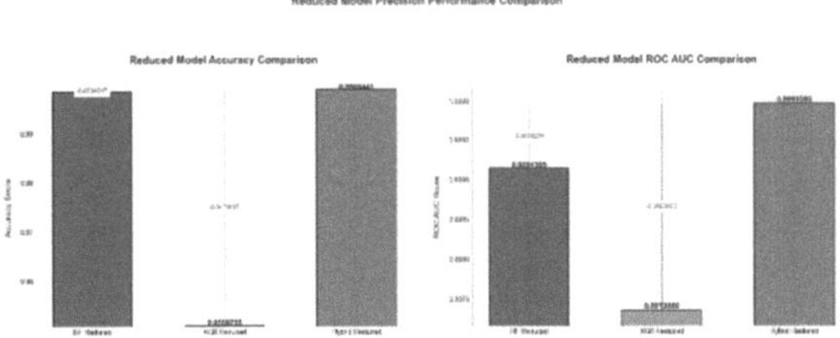

**Fig. 5.** Accuracy & ROC Comparison Reduced Models

In contrast, the reduced XGBoost model experienced a notable decline in accuracy when features were trimmed. This reduction disrupted its performance because XGBoost relies heavily on subtle interactions between features, including those of moderate importance. Removing these features interfered with the boosting process, which thrives on iterative refinement of weak learners, ultimately degrading the model's predictive accuracy. Conversely, the reduced Random Forest model exhibited a slight improvement in accuracy compared to its full counterpart. By focusing exclusively on the most impactful features, the reduced Random Forest eliminated noise and mitigated overfitting, enhancing its generalization to unseen data. This streamlined feature set allowed the model to maintain robust performance while improving efficiency.

The reduced hybrid model, meanwhile, maintained performance levels remarkably close to those of the full hybrid model. By strategically integrating the strengths of both XGBoost and Random Forest, it preserved high accuracy and AUC while benefiting from reduced computational complexity. This balance makes the reduced hybrid model particularly suitable for scenarios where resource constraints demand efficiency without sacrificing predictive quality, offering a versatile solution for real-world applications (Table 2).

**Table 2.** Accuracy & ROC Comparison

| Model | Accuracy | ROC AUC |
| --- | --- | --- |
| Random Forest | 99.831% | 99.919% |
| XGBoost | 99.868% | 99.996% |
| Hybrid (XGB + RF) | 99.884% | 99.995% |
| Random Forest (Reduced) | 99.843% | 99.913% |
| XGBoost (Reduced) | 95.097% | 99.735% |
| Hybrid (Reduced) | 99.884% | 99.995% |

### 4.2 Training Time

XGBoost (Reduced) proved to be the fastest model to train, completing its training process in just 121 s, making it highly suitable for scenarios requiring rapid deployment and frequent updates (Fig. 6). This efficiency is attributed to its streamlined architecture and optimized feature set, which enable quick iteration and scalability in dynamic environments. Moreover, feature reduction significantly decreased training times for both models, with reductions ranging from 34% to 66%. This substantial improvement in training efficiency enhances the practicality of the models in resource-constrained settings, supporting faster experimentation and deployment cycles.

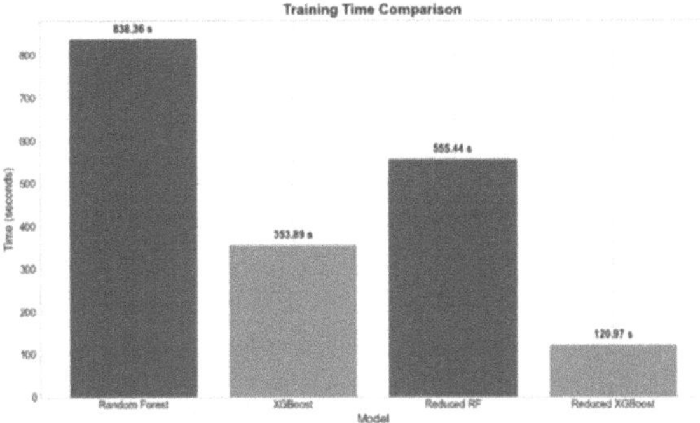

**Fig. 6.** Training Comparison

## 4.3   Real-Time Prediction Speed

XGBoost (Reduced) demonstrates the lowest latency, clocking in at an impressive 580 microseconds, positioning it as the most efficient model for real-time detection tasks. Its optimized architecture enables rapid processing, making it ideal for applications requiring instantaneous responses. In contrast, both hybrid models exhibited comparatively slower performance, with higher latency figures, yet they still achieved acceptable efficiency within the microsecond-level latency boundaries. These hybrid models balance predictive accuracy and computational speed, ensuring robust performance for time-sensitive applications while maintaining responsiveness suitable for real-time use cases (Fig. 7).

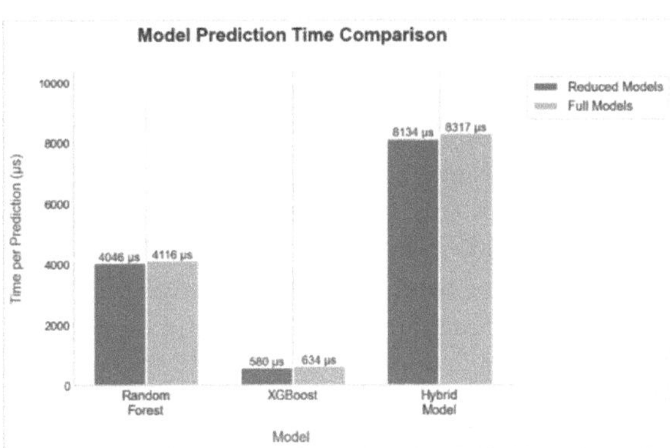

**Fig. 7.** Prediction Time Comparison

## 4.4 Analysis

Table 3. Performance Overview

| Model | Accuracy % | ROC AUC % | Training Time (s) | Avg Prediction Time ($\mu$s) |
|---|---|---|---|---|
| Random Forest | 99.831 | 99.919 | 838.36 | 4115.54 |
| XGBoost | 99.868 | 99.996 | 353.89 | 633.95 |
| Hybrid (Full) | 99.884 | 99.995 | – | 8317.34 |
| RF (Reduced) | 99.843 | 99.913 | 555.44 | 4045.61 |
| XGB (Reduced) | 95.097 | 99.735 | 120.97 | 580.39 |
| Hybrid (Reduced) | 99.884 | 99.995 | – | 8133.88 |

Among all models evaluated, Full XGBoost stands out as the best overall performer in terms of both accuracy (99.87%) and ROC AUC (0.999962) the highest across all models. Its training time (353.89 s) is significantly faster than Random Forest (838.36 s), and it also achieves a very low average prediction latency (633.95 μs), making it suitable for real-time environments (Table 3).

While the Hybrid models match XGBoost' s accuracy (99.88%) and AUC (0.999959), they come with much higher prediction latency (over 8000 μs), which could be a limitation in real-time applications. The Reduced XGBoost offers faster training and inference, but at the cost of a significant accuracy drop (95.10%), which may not be acceptable in security-critical telecom scenarios.

Overall, Full XGBoost provides the best trade-off between accuracy, speed, and resource efficiency, making it the recommended choice for lightweight, real-time anomaly detection in telecom networks.

Compared to baseline and prior research on the CICIDS 2017 dataset, the proposed models show significant improvements in both performance and efficiency. Traditional deep learning-based approaches such as LSTM, CNN, or hybrid DNN models often achieve high accuracy (above 99%) but typically require high computational resources and longer training times, making them less suitable for real-time or edge-based deployment. In contrast, the reduced Random Forest and hybrid models in this study achieve accuracy above 99.8% with prediction latency under 10,000 μs per record, offering a lightweight alternative without sacrificing detection performance. Furthermore, previous studies often focus on binary classification or a limited set of attack types, whereas this work effectively handles multi-class anomaly detection across a broader range of attack categories. The proposed models also outperform many classical machine learning baselines like SVMs, k-NN, or Naïve Bayes, which typically struggle to scale with large, imbalanced datasets like CICIDS. Overall, this study demonstrates that carefully reduced ensemble models can match or exceed the performance of more complex systems while being more practical for real-time telecom network security.

# 5   Conclusion

This study evaluates the effectiveness of ensemble learning algorithms—Random Forest, XGBoost, and a hybrid of the two for real-time anomaly detection in telecommunication network traffic. Using the CICIDS dataset, performance was assessed across accuracy, ROC AUC, training time, and inference latency, with emphasis on lightweight deployment in edge environments. Results show that XGBoost achieved the best overall balance, offering high ROC AUC, low training time, and the fastest prediction speed, making it the most suitable for real-time edge deployment. The reduced Random Forest also performed well, delivering strong accuracy with lower resource demands, making it ideal for highly constrained settings. While the hybrid model attained the highest accuracy, its higher latency limits its use in real-time scenarios, though it may suit offline analysis. In conclusion, XGBoost emerges as the most practical choice for lightweight intrusion detection at the telecom edge, with reduced Random Forest as a strong alternative under stricter resource constraints.

# 6   Future Works

Future research directions include exploring federated learning for anomaly detection in edge environments where privacy is critical, as it enables local training without sharing raw data, thus preserving privacy while supporting scalable and collaborative detection across distributed nodes. This approach is particularly relevant for telecommunication networks, as it reduces communication overhead and enhances scalability, with lightweight models such as XGBoost or Random Forest being strong candidates for federated adaptation. Another avenue is cross-dataset generalization, where evaluating models on multiple benchmark datasets (e.g., NSL-KDD, UNSW-NB15) or real telecom traffic logs would validate robustness and ensure adaptability beyond a single dataset like CICIDS. Finally, integrating online learning or streaming algorithms could allow continuous updates with incoming data, helping models adapt dynamically to evolving threats and zero-day attacks without costly retraining. Together, these directions can advance real-time, privacy-preserving, and robust anomaly detection in telecom networks.

# References


1. Afzal, R., Kumar Murugesan, R.: Rule-based anomaly detection model with stateful correlation enhancing mobile network security. Intell. Autom. Soft Comput. **31**, 1825–1841 (2022)
2. Ali, W.A., Manasa, K.N., Aljunid, M., Bendechache, M., Sandhya, P.: A review of current machine learning approaches for anomaly detection in network traffic. JTDE **8**, 64–95 (2020)
3. Chaitanya, C., Reddy, Y.A., Pasupuleti, H., Gvk, S., Bapat, J.: Real-time anomaly detection at IoT-edge ingress port using FPGA based ML classifiers. In: Proceedings of the 2024 Sixteenth International Conference on Contemporary Computing, New York, NY, USA, pp. 309–315. Association for Computing Machinery (2024). https://doi.org/10.1145/3675888.3676064
4. Das, R., Luo, T.: LightESD: fully-automated and lightweight anomaly detection framework for edge computing. https://doi.org/10.48550/arXiv.2305.12266 (2023)

5. Han, S., Wu, Q., Yang, Y.: Machine learning for Internet of things anomaly detection under low-quality data. Int. J. Distrib. Sens. Netw. **18**, 15501329221133764 (2022)
6. Kampa, S.: Advanced machine learning techniques for anomaly detection in edge computing security: a framework for real-time threat mitigation (2024)
7. Lee, M.-C., Lin, J.-C., Gran, E.G.: ReRe: a lightweight real-time ready-to-go anomaly detection approach for time series. In: 2020 IEEE 44th Annual Computers, Software, and Applications Conference (COMPSAC), pp. 322–327 (2020). https://doi.org/10.1109/COMPSAC48688.2020.0-226
8. Liu, H., Wang, H.: Real-time anomaly detection of network traffic based on CNN. Symmetry **15**, 1205 (2023)
9. Gauthama Raman, M.R, Ahmed, C.M., Mathur, A.: Machine learning for intrusion detection in industrial control systems: challenges and lessons from experimental evaluation. Cybersecurity **4**, 27 (2021)
10. Rababah, B., Srivastava, S.: Hybrid model for intrusion detection systems. https://doi.org/10.48550/arXiv.2003.08585 (2020)
11. Joshi, J., Panda, P., Rao, S., Padmalochan: Efficient anomaly detection using machine learning in IoT sensor network. In: 2025 International Symposium on Electrical and Electronics Engineering (ISEE), Ho Chi Minh, Vietnam, pp. 54–59 (2025). https://doi.org/10.1109/ISEE68370.2025.11223424
12. Sridevi, S., Prabha, R., Reddy, K.N., Monica, K.M., Senthil, G.A., Razmah, M.: Network intrusion detection system using supervised learning-based voting classifier. In: Proceedings of the International Conference on Communication, Computing and Internet of Things (IC3IoT 2022), Chennai, India, pp. 1–6 (2022). https://doi.org/10.1109/IC3IOT53935.2022.9767903
13. Kanimozhi, V., Jacob, T.P.: Artificial intelligence based network intrusion detection with hyper-parameter optimization tuning on the realistic cyber dataset CSE-CIC-IDS2018 using cloud computing. In: 2019 International Conference on Communication and Signal Processing (ICCSP), Chennai, India, pp. 0033–0036 (2019). https://doi.org/10.1109/ICCSP.2019.8698029
14. Bagmar, V., Joshi, D.: AI-driven real-time network intrusion detection using machine learning and deep learning. In: 2025 3rd International Conference on Self Sustainable Artificial Intelligence Systems (ICSSAS), Erode, India, pp. 1569–1574 (2025). https://doi.org/10.1109/ICSSAS66150.2025.11080963
15. Real-Time Anomaly Detection in 5G Networks Through Edge Computing | Request PDF (2025). https://doi.org/10.1109/INCOS59338.2024.10527501

# Defeating Evasion Attack: An Adversarially Trained Ensemble for Phishing URL Detection


Ankur Patel[1], Marmik Patel[2], Rishi Soni[2], Ayush Patel[2], Sachin Patel[3]([✉]),
Jaimeen Vasa[2], Vrutansh Davda[2], and Bhumi Patel[2]

[1] Department of Electrical Engineering, Chandubhai S. Patel Institute of Technology (CSPIT),
Charotar University of Science and Technology (CHARUSAT), Anand, India
`ankurpatel.ee@charusat.ac.in`
[2] Department of Computer Engineering, Charotar University of Science and Technology
(CHARUSAT), Anand, India
`{d23dce153,d23dce155,d23dce156,d23dce152,22dce016,`
`23dce078}@charusat.edu.in`
[3] Department of Information Technology, Devang Patel Institute of Advance Technology and
Research (DEPSTAR), Faculty of Technology and Engineering (FTE), Charotar University of
Science and Technology (CHARUSAT), Anand, India
`sachinpatel.dit@charusat.ac.in`



**Abstract.** The use of phishing websites remains a leading method of credential theft by using a deceitful URL to run around traditional defences. Although machine learning has improved the accuracy of phishing detection, the accuracy of detectors to evade adversarial is weak. This paper introduces an adversarial trained stacking ensemble of phishing URL detection making use of the Random Forest and XGBoost as base learners utilizing a logistic regression meta-classifier. In contrast to the methods described above, the framework directly involves adversarial training based on Projected Gradient Descent (PGD) perturbations and tests performance on strong attack environments. Candidates To improve recall in skewed distributions similar to the real world, we use Synthetic Minority Oversampling Technique (SMOTE), which improves the recall in imbalanced settings. The framework is tested on massive phishing datasets for Phish Tank and OpenPhish to detect phishing with accuracy of 98% on clean data and a 73% decrease in attack success rate with adversarial training. Experiments In comparison to deep learning versions like URLNet, transformer-based URLTran, and the recently-introduced LLM-based MultiPhishGuard, our model is superior in computation membrane and just as powerful. Moreover, training (5.9 s) and inference latency per sample (0.02 ms) are scalable to near real time. The interpretability of SHAP, further demonstrates the effect of lexical and structural URLs in classification. The work bridges the attention/accuracy and strength gap in phishing detection in unskilled fashion by providing a low weight and sturdy defence in accordance with current cyber threat environments.

**Keywords:** Phishing detection · adversarial training · stacking ensemble · random forest · XGBoost · PGD attack · SMOTE · URLTran · MultiPhishGuard · adversarial robustness



© The Author(s), under exclusive license to Springer Nature Switzerland AG 2026
K. K. Patel et al. (Eds.): icSoftComp 2025, CCIS 2874, pp. 201–212, 2026.
https://doi.org/10.1007/978-3-032-22062-2_16

# 1 Introduction

Phishing is already among the most active cybersecurity attacks that exploit the presence of deceptive websites and URL addressing, stealing user accredits, financial information, and other personal data. Conventional approaches to via blacklist and rule-based approaches are no longer effective in relation to contemporary phishing attacks, which not only use homoglyph replacement mechanisms, but also query padding and domain injection methods. As a result, the use of machine learning (ML) and deep learning methods has been exploited to use lexical and structural properties of URLs to a large extent, enhancing detection problems in accurate and scalable ways [1, 6, 10].

In spite of these developments, current models fail in a very challenging setting usually. Researchers like SpacePhish [2] discovered small character manipulation can badly decrease the accuracy of phishing detector and AlEroud and Karabatis [3] demonstrated the GAN-based approach can produce so deceptive phishing URL. This body of investigations has later been broadened by even modern large language model (LLM)-based detectors showing high susceptibility to adversarial instances without direct reinforcements [13]. These results demonstrate that a low level of accuracy on clean datasets cannot be used to deploy in adversarial settings which poses robustness as an important dimension of evaluation.

Latest strategies like AntiPhishStack [7], URLNet [9], and transformer-based URL-Tran [8] show definite improvement whereas hybrid systems, like MultiPhishGuard [14] involve the use of LLMs to detect multi-agent phishing. Nevertheless, these schemes have high computing expenses, which restrict the use of lightweight deployment. This paper overcomes these shortcomings by proposing a stacking ensemble that is adversarial trained using Random Forest (RF) as well as XGBoost (XGB) and the use of a logistic regression meta-classifier. The model uses Projected Gradient Descent (PGD) based adversarial training, Synthetic Minority Oversampling Technique (SMOTE) to deal with the issue of class imbalance, and compares the performance levels to state-of-the-art results such as URLTran [8] and MultiPhishGuard [14].

This paper follows a systematic flow beginning with a comprehensive review of existing phishing detection techniques and their inherent limitations. It then introduces the proposed adversarially trained stacking ensemble model that integrates Random Forest, XGBoost, and a logistic regression meta-classifier to enhance robustness and scalability. The methodology section covers data preprocessing, feature extraction, and handling class imbalance using SMOTE. The experimental analysis evaluates model performance on benchmark datasets and compares results with advanced models such as URLTran and MultiPhish-Guard. The paper concludes by highlighting the improved resilience, efficiency, and lightweight nature of the proposed framework.

## 2 Literature Survey

The development of research on phishing detection has gone past ensemble-based approaches to transformer and LLM-driven approaches. Al-Sarem et al. [1] optimized the use of stacking ensembles in a phishing detection, whereas Alsariera et al. [6] and Indrasiri et al. [10] both emphasized the superiority of ensemble techniques. Apruzzese et al. [2] in SpacePhish and AlEoud and Karabatis [3] in GANs identified adversarial vulnerabilities and point out the frailty of URL detectors. More closely, a recent study by Kulkarni et al. [13] showed that the phishing detectors in the LLM group of detractors are also adversarial. Semantic architecture A deeper architecture, like AntiPhishStack [7] and URLNet [9], also enhanced the representation of URLs by encapsulation of URLs based on their connection to web page content, and URLTran [8] based their classification on transformer attention. Xue et al. [14] introduced it even further by MultiPhishGuard, a computationally expensive yet Computationally-intensive, multi-agent system, which is an LLM-driven system. In order to mitigate the issue of class imbalance, Qi et al. [4] have considered undersampling method, where SMOTE is widely applied in order to enhance the recall of phishing. Other papers, such as Zhou et al. [5], Shirazi et al. [11] and Li et al. [12], suggested attention-driven and pretraining based framework of wider adaptability. Altogether, these works demonstrate excellent clean accuracy, yet find three common challenges, low robustness testing in robust adversarial environments, low performance in unequal ratios of phishing and legitimate samples, and high-performance costs in transformer or LLM-based models.

## 3   Methodology

In this section, the systematic procedure employed in the development and evaluation of the proposed phishing detection framework has been specified. The methodology involves a broad pipeline consisting of the data preparation and feature engineering, model construction and training, and finally evaluation of the model performance, its robustness and interpretability in a multi-faceted manner.

### 3.1   Dataset and Preprocessing

The research works with a mixed set comprising 15,000 URLs consisting of 10,000 of samples PhishingLegitimatefull.csv (50% phishing and 50% legitimate) and another 3,000 and 2,000 of samples of PhishTank and OpenPhish respectively. The information was split in terms of 80% training (12,000) and 20% testing (3,000). It was also preprocessed to eliminate irrelevant identifiers, address missing values and also the training data was standardized scaled down to avoid leakage as well. In presence of equal distributions of classes it was verified by Exploratory Data Analysis (EDA) depicted in Fig. 1. Feature distribution analysis highlighted that phishing URLs are generally longer and include more numeric and special characters compared to legitimate ones, as shown in Fig. 2.

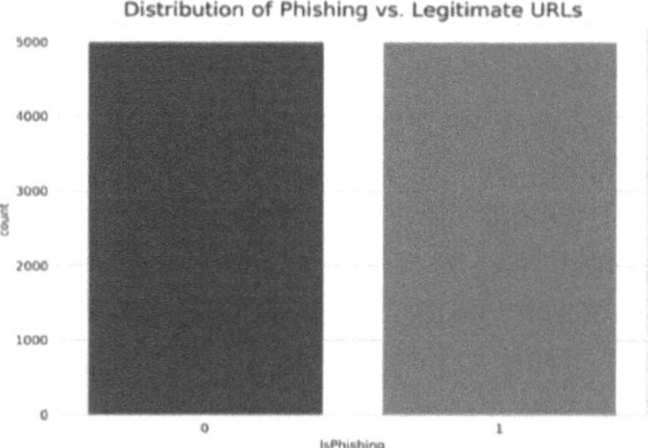

**Fig. 1.** Bar plot showing balanced class distribution across phishing and legitimate URLs.

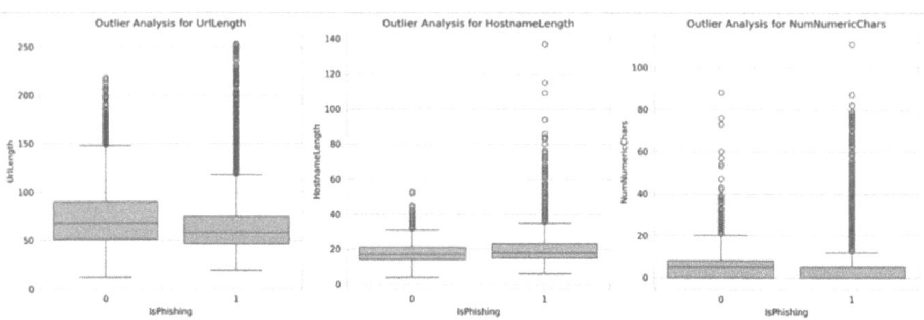

**Fig. 2.** Feature distribution analysis of URL length, hostname length, and numeric content for phishing vs. legitimate URLs.

## 3.2  Feature Engineering and Selection

To strengthen classification capability, three ratio-based features were engineered to capture obfuscation patterns typically found in phishing URLs:

$$\text{Dots_per_URLLength} = \frac{\text{Number of dots}}{\text{URL length} + \varepsilon} \tag{1}$$

$$\text{Digits_per_Hostname} = \frac{\text{Number of digits in  hostname}}{\text{Hostname length} + \varepsilon} \tag{2}$$

$$\text{Numeric_per_UrlLength} = \frac{\text{Special characters count}}{\text{URL length} + \varepsilon} \tag{3}$$

Here, $\varepsilon = 10^{-6}$ prevents division by zero. These formulated characteristics are in reaction to heavy reliance on dots, dashes, and special characteristics of the bad URLs. SelectFromModel (RandomForestClassifier) was used to carry out a reduction in dimensionality and select the top 13 informative features to use as features in the algorithm.

### 3.3 System Architecture and Pipeline

The framework is guided by a systematic and repeatable pipeline achieving modularity and deployment readiness. The overall flow is presented in Fig. 3, showing the steps from data ingestion to model deployment.

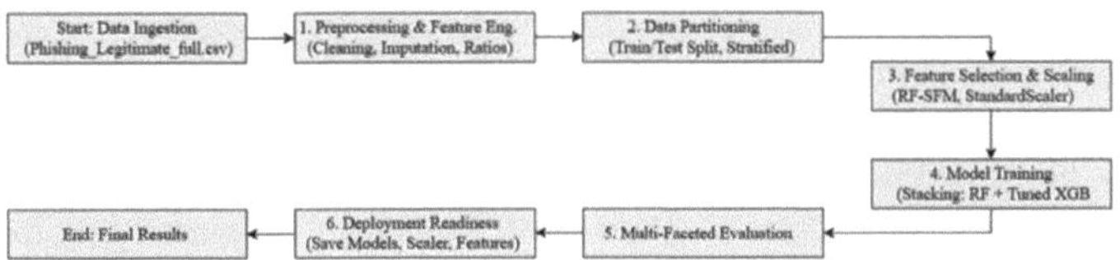


**Fig. 3.** The end-to-end pipeline from dataset preprocessing to phishing detection and deployment.

At its core, the architecture is a stacking ensemble model that integrates multiple classifiers. As shown in Fig. 4, Random Forest and XGBoost serve as base learners, whose outputs are combined by a Logistic Regression meta-classifier. This structural arrangement allows an ensemble to be able to generalize in their advantage as they build on the respective strong points of other learners.

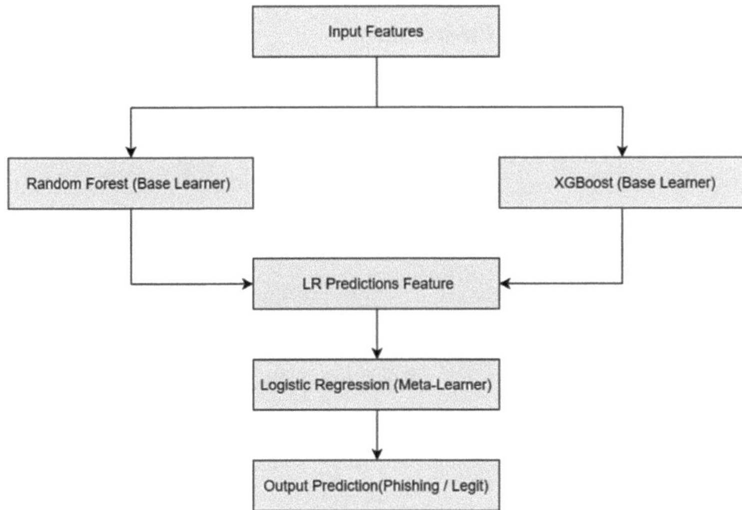


**Fig. 4.** System architecture of the stacking ensemble showing base learners and the logistic regression meta-classifier.

### 3.4 Ensemble Model Construction

The ensemble was set up and in tuned using the following setup:

- Random Forest (RF): 100 estimators and classweight = balanced.
- XGBoost (XGB): Hyperparameters were diverse with the help of 3-fold GridSearchCV, and the obtained values became nestimators = 200, maxdepth = 7, and learningrate = 0.1.

- Meta-classifier: made use of Logistic Regression as the final layer and it was also being trained on the base learners predictions using 5-fold cross-validation.

Such arrangement provides predictive and computational efficiency.

### 3.5  Adversarial Robustness and Training

To determine the capability against evasion attacks, adversarial examples were produced with the Projected Gradient Descent (PGD) attack. This tinkering process considers feature vectors, perturbed within an $\epsilon = 0.1$ upper-bound and $\alpha = 0.01$ modest incremention in 10 runs. The Attack Success Rate (ASR) was used in quantifying the weakness of the baseline model and it is defined as:

$$\text{ASR} = \frac{\#\{\text{Samples correctly classifeid on clean but misclassified on adversarial}\}}{\#\{\text{Correct on Clean}\}} \tag{4}$$

In order to robustify the system, the method of adversarial training was used and the training set was supplemented with adversarial examples generated by PGD. The addition of this increased dataset to the ensemble through retraining enhanced its resistance to adversarial perturbation by obtaining more robust, resistant to decision boundaries.

### 3.6  Evaluation Protocol and Environment

The model's performance was assessed with widely accepted classification metrics, including Accuracy, Precision, Recall, and F1-score:

$$Precision = \frac{TP}{TP + FP} \tag{5}$$

$$Recall = \frac{TP}{TP + FN} \tag{6}$$

$$F1 = 2 \times \frac{Precision \times Recall}{Precision + Recall} \tag{7}$$

Calibration of predicted probabilities was measured using the Brier Score:

$$Brier\ Score = \frac{1}{N} \sum_{i=1}^{N} (p_i - o_i)^2 \tag{8}$$

where $p_i$ is the predicted probability for sample $i$ and $o_i$ it's true outcome. Interpretability was achieved with SHAP (SHapley Additive exPlanations), which identified the most influential features contributing to phishing detection.

All the experiments were carried out on Google Colab. The environment was developed using Pandas 2.2.2, NumPy 2.0.2, Scikit-learn 1.6.1, XGBoost 3.0.5, imbalanced-learn 0.14.0, which had been reproducible and scalable.

# 4  Result

This section reports the experimental results of the proposed adversarially trained stacking ensemble, including clean-set performance, adversarial robustness, class-imbalance evaluation, scalability analysis, interpretability, and benchmarking against state-of-the-art methods. Unless otherwise specified, all experiments were conducted on the combined dataset with an 80% Training and 20% Testing split.

## 4.1  Clean-Set Performance

The ensemble demonstrated strong performance on the clean balanced test set. Table 1 shows that both phishing and legitimate classes achieved 98% precision, recall, and F1-score, resulting in an overall accuracy of 0.98.

**Table 1.** Classification results on clean balanced test set.

| Class | Precision | Recall | F1-score | Support |
| --- | --- | --- | --- | --- |
| Legitimate | 0.98 | 0.98 | 0.98 | 1000 |
| Phishing | 0.98 | 0.98 | 0.98 | 1000 |
| Overall | 0.98 | 0.98 | 0.98 | 2000 |

## 4.2  Adversarial Robustness

Robustness was evaluated using a Projected Gradient Descent (PGD) attack. The original ensemble retained 83.3% adversarial accuracy with an Attack Success Rate (ASR) of 15.6%. After adversarial training, the ASR dropped to 4.7%, while clean accuracy remained stable at 97.8% (Table 2 and Figs. 5, 6).

**Table 2.** Adversarial robustness evaluation before and after adversarial training.

| Model | Clean Accuracy | Adversarial Accuracy | ASR |
| --- | --- | --- | --- |
| Original | 0.9800 | 0.8330 | 0.1561 |
| Robust (Adv) | 0.9780 | 0.9365 | 0.0475 |

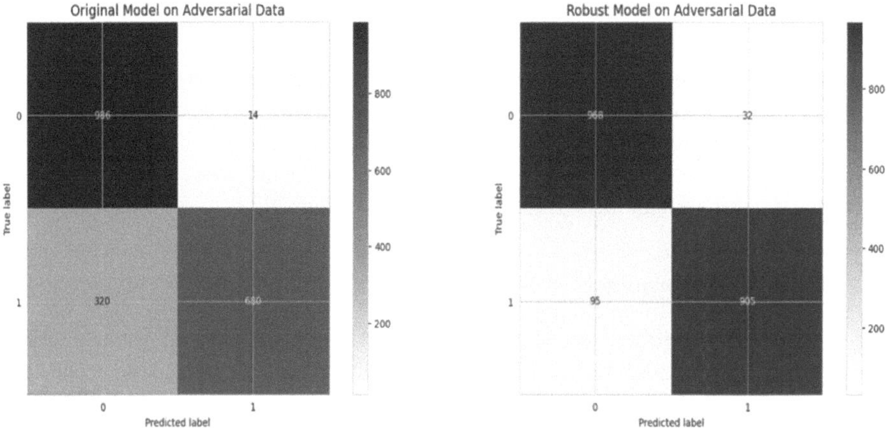

**Fig. 5.** Confusion matrices comparing the baseline model (left) and adversarially trained robust model (right) under PGD attack.

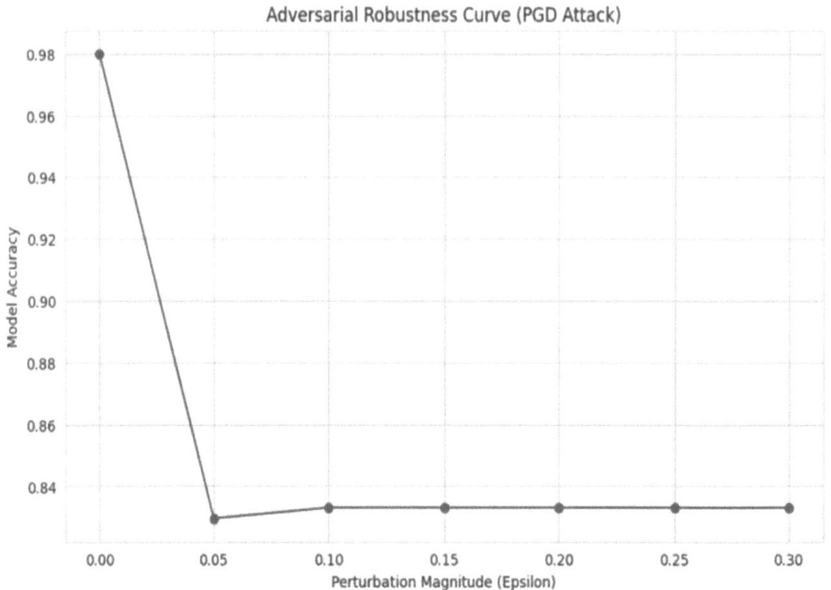

**Fig. 6.** Adversarial robustness curve showing accuracy degradation with increasing perturbation magnitude ($\varepsilon$). The robust model is always better than the baseline and it still shows a higher accuracy at all the levels of perturbation.

### 4.3　ROC and Precision–Recall Analysis

Both the robust and the baseline models obtained ROC-AUC of 0.98. In Precision Recall curve, high discrimination is observed even in skewed environments where the robust model is a bit more stable even at high recall levels (Fig. 7).

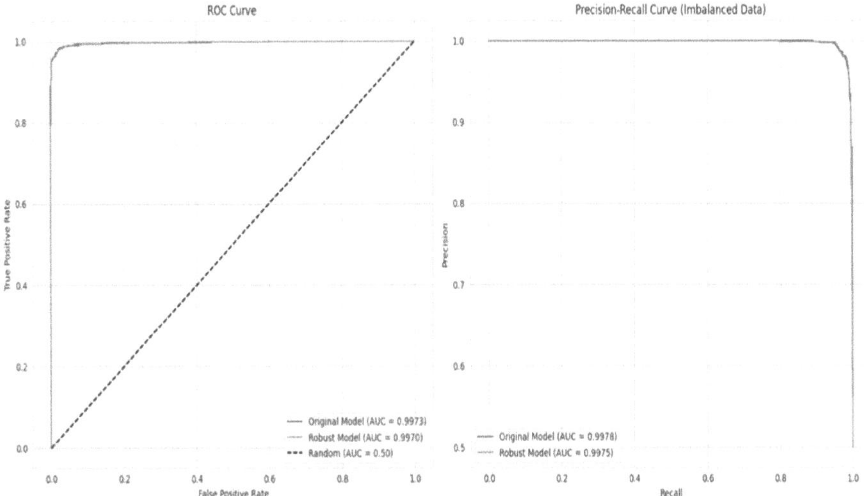


**Fig. 7.** Precision and recall ROC and Precision-Recall curves of baseline and robust models, which represents high separability and trade-offs that are stable to the precision and recall.

## 4.4 Handling Class Imbalance

To simulate real-world phishing prevalence, performance was evaluated under a 5% phishing rate. Despite SMOTE augmentation, phishing recall dropped to 0.50, indicating detection difficulty in heavily skewed distributions (Table 3).

**Table 3.** Performance under class-imbalance stress test (5% phishing).

| Metric (Phishing) | Value |
| --- | --- |
| Precision | 0.565 |
| Recall | 0.500 |
| F1-score | 0.531 |

## 4.5 Scalability and Efficiency

The ensemble demonstrated high efficiency, retraining in 5.94 s and requiring only 0.0216 ms per sample at inference (Table 4).

Table 4. Scalability results.

| Metric | Value |
|---|---|
| Robust Training Time | 5.94 s |
| Average Inference Time/Sample | 0.0216 ms |

## 4.6 Comparison with State-of-the-Art

The ensemble was benchmarked against transformer-based and LLM-driven baselines. While URLTran [8] and MultiPhishGuard [14] achieved slightly higher clean accuracy, they impose two to three orders of magnitude higher inference latency, unsuitable for real-time filtering. Our ensemble achieves a balanced trade-off between robustness, speed, and accuracy (Table 5).

Table 5. Comparison with state-of-the-art phishing detection models.

| Model | Accuracy (Clean) | F1-Score (Clean) | Robustness (vs. PGD) | Inference Time (ms) |
|---|---|---|---|---|
| Our Robust Ensemble | 0.9800 | 0.9800 | 0.9365 | 0.0216 |
| URLNet (Reported) [8] | 0.9751 | 0.9745 | Not Reported | N/A |
| URLTran (Transformer) [8] | 0.9820 | 0.9810 | Not Reported | ~100.0 |
| MultiPhishGuard (LLM-based) [14] | 0.9850 | 0.9840 | Not Reported | ~250.0 |

## 5 Conclusion

In this work, adversarial stacking ensemble was presented, uniting Random Forest and XGBoost base learners with the help of Logistic Regression meta-classifier to identify phishing URLs. The framework performed at 98% accuracy and F1-score on clean balanced data, thus demonstrating the ability of the model to capture discriminating lexical and host-based patterns. More to the point, adversarial training also enhanced tolerance against Projected Gradient Disturbances (PGD) perturbation, lowering the Attack Success Rate (ASR) by 15.6 to 4.7 with a clean accuracy of 97.8. The model was also highly computationally efficient with training time of less than six seconds and an inference latency of 0.0216 ms categorized as one sample showing that it is highly appropriate to run real-time phishing detection. The analysis of interpretability with SHAP has indicated that the length of URLs and frequencies of numeric characters and depth of the subdomain were predominant in Sharify obfuscation and strengthens their contribution.

However, the assessment of it came with critical pitfalls. The robustness test did not analyze feature-space PGD attacks, and it was not known how the model would behave when subjected to additional realistic manipulations (character-level and semantic manipulations) involving homoglyph replacements, token padding, and path/query injections. In extreme ratio of classes (5% phishing),dims went at 0.50 with SMOTE enhancement, highlighting the necessity of cost-sensitive or focal loss aids. Also, albeit the ensemble stands relatively well against URLNet, and URLTran, and MultiPhish-Guard as baselines, but benchmarking depended upon reported or simulated results as opposed to retraining using a common protocol. Future efforts will thus widen adversarial defenses to potent adversarial attacks, imbalance-algorithms and pay fair head-to-head comparisons with transformer-and LLM-detectors. Generalizability will be enhanced further by wider validation on multilingual components (e.g. PhishTank, OpenPhish) and publication of reproducible artifacts. In general, this contribution contributes to phishing detection through accuracy, robustness, scalability, and interpretability in viable ensemble framework.

**Acknowledgement.** It is with due thanks and with the huge assistance of Charotar University of Science and Technology (CHARUSAT) that we were able to present our piece of work in such a high-profile venue. Not only did such funding help us share our research, it also enabled us to gain a priceless experience in communicating and sharing ideas with experts in the field, and was able to provide constructive feedback in addition to having our work supported by the scholarly community.

# References


1. Al-Sarem, M., et al.: An optimized stacking ensemble model for phishing websites detection. Electronics **10**(11), 1285 (2021)
2. Apruzzese, G., Conti, M., Yuan, Y.: Spacephish: the evasion-space of adversarial attacks against phishing website detectors using machine learning. In: Proceedings of the 38th Annual Computer Security Applications Conference, pp. 171–185 (2022)
3. AlEroud, A., Karabatis, G.: Bypassing detection of URL-based phishing attacks using generative adversarial deep neural networks. In: Proceedings of the Sixth İnternational Workshop on Security and Privacy Analytics, pp. 53–60 (2020)
4. Qi, Q., Wang, Z., Yijia, X., Fang, Y., Wang, C.: Enhancing phishing email detection through ensemble learning and undersampling. Appl. Sci. **13**(15), 8756 (2023)
5. Zhou, J., Zhang, K., Bing Zheng, Y., Zhou, X.X., Jin, M., Liu, X.: A Malicious URL detection framework based on custom hybrid spatial sequence attention and logic constraint neural network. Symmetry **17**(7), 987 (2025)
6. Alsariera, Y.A., Alanazi, M.H., Said, Y., Allan, F.: An investigation of AI-based ensemble methods for the detection of phishing attacks. Eng. Technol. Appl. Sci. Res. **14**(3), 14266–14274 (2024)
7. Aslam, S., Aslam, H., Manzoor, A., Chen, H., Rasool, A.: AntiPhishStack: LSTM-based stacked generalization model for optimized phishing URL detection. Symmetry **16**(2), 248 (2024)
8. Maneriker, P.: URLTran: ımproving phishing URL detection using transformers. Arxiv 2106: v2 (2017)

9. ul Haq, Q.E., Faheem, M.H., Ahmad: Detecting phishing URLs based on a deep learning approach to prevent cyber-attacks. Appl. Sci. **14**(22), 10086 (2024)
10. Indrasiri, P.L., Halgamuge, M.N., Mohammad, A.: Robust ensemble machine learning model for filtering phishing URLs: expandable random gradient stacked voting classifier (ERG-SVC). IEEE Access **9**, 150142–150161 (2021)
11. Shirazi, H., Haefner, K., Ray, I.: Improving auto-detection of phishing websites using fresh-phish framework. Int. J. Multimed. Data Eng. Manag. (IJMDEM) **9**(1), 1–14 (2018)
12. Li, Y., Liu, Y., Li, P., Jia, Y., Wang, Y.: Continuous multi-task pre-training for malicious URL detection and webpage classification. Comput. Netw., 111513 (2025)
13. Kulkarni, A., Balachandran, V., Divakaran, D.M., Das, T.: From ML to LLM: evaluating the robustness of phishing web page detection models against adversarial attacks. Digit. Threats Res. Pract. **6**(2), 1–25 (2025)
14. Xue, Y., Spero, E., Koh, Y.S., Russello, G.: MultiPhishGuard: an LLM-based multi-agent system for phishing email detection. arXiv preprint arXiv:2505.23803 (2025)

# Evaluating an ELiPS-Based CP-ABE Enhancement on Server and IoT Platforms


Le Hoang Anh[1,2]([✉]) [iD], Thanh-Nghi Doan[1,2] [iD], Thanh-Nhan Huynh-Ly[1,2] [iD], Minh-Vi Nguyen[1,2] [iD], and Hoai-Nam Nguyen[1,2]

[1] An Giang University, Long Xuyên, Vietnam
{lhanh,dtnghi,hltnhan,nmvi,nhnam}@agu.edu.vn
[2] Vietnam National University, Ho Chi Minh City, Vietnam



**Abstract.** CP-ABE serves as a powerful cryptographic approach, allowing controlled data access through encryption policies. This makes it highly applicable in domains such as the Internet of Things, cloud computing, and secure information sharing. However, the initial CP-ABE scheme often suffers from inefficiencies in several phases and outdated security levels. To overcome these challenges, we introduced a CP-ABE construction leveraging ELiPS, enhancing the security level to 128 bits and improving computational performance. Furthermore, this work, we evaluate the proposed scheme on both server and practical IoT environments. Our results show that our scheme significantly improves performance, reducing the setup, key generation, and encryption times by 22.6%, 74.4%, and 42.1%, respectively. Although the proposed scheme increases security to 128 bits, it does not significantly increase ciphertext size and even reduces average memory usage by 12.4%. The findings from our experiments demonstrate that the introduced scheme achieves high efficiency and is suitable for applications requiring strong security on both general-purpose systems and resource-constrained platforms.

**Keywords:** CP-ABE · ELiPS-Based CP-ABE · ABE · Cryptography · IoT Security · Access Control · Performance Evaluation · Resource-Constrained Environments


## 1 Introduction

In the last decade, a large volumne of data has been generated from information systems such as the Internet of Things (IoT), healthcare, and cloud computing. These data are not only stored in the cloud but also shared among participants. In addition, they offten include highly sensitive information that needs to be kept private. Therefore, ensuring both strong data confidentiality and fine-grained access control is essential [1].

To deal with these shortcomings, Ciphertext-Policy Attribute-Based Encryption is a strong candidate. CP-ABE both encrypts data and protects the




K. K. Patel et al. (Eds.): icSoftComp 2025, CCIS 2874, pp. 213–225, 2026.
https://doi.org/10.1007/978-3-032-22062-2_17

encrypted data based on the access policy. This scheme allows the encryptor to define an access policy, which is encoded together with the ciphertext. The access policy specifies who can decrypt the data and obtain the plaintext [2].

However, CP-ABE is implemented based on pairing-based cryptography, which suffers from an outdated security level and performance limitations. CP-ABE supports only an 80-bit security level, which is insufficient for modern applications of cryptography. Furthermore, performance improvements are necessary to enable deployment on IoT devices. Anh et al. proposed an ELiPS-based CP-ABE scheme that achieves a 128-bit security level [3].

The scheme proposed by Anh et al. not only increases the security level but also improves the performance of setup, key generation, and encryption functions. Additionally, Anh et al. proposed a method to decrease the number of expensive operations in the decryption function. This proposal reduced $2n-1$ final exponentiation times and $n-1$ inversion times [4].

This study aims to evaluate ELiPS-based CP-ABE in both server and IoT environments. We analyze the execution time of our scheme in comparison with CP-ABE. In addition, the ciphertext size, which is crucial for cloud storage and transmission, is also evaluated. Furthermore, we measure the memory usage of both schemes to assess their suitability for resource-constrained devices.

The rest of this paper is organized as follows. Section 2 provides the necessary preliminaries. Section 3 describes the ELiPS-based CP-ABE scheme. Section 4 presents the implementation and experimental setup. Section 5 discusses the results, and Sect. 6 concludes the paper.

## 2 Preliminaries

This section introduces foundational concepts essential to understanding the ELiPS-based CP-ABE scheme. We begin with core mathematical tools such as hash-to-curve, and bilinear pairings. We then present the access tree model used for fine-grained access control.

### 2.1 Arithmetic on Elliptic Curves

**Hash Function $\mathcal{H}$ Onto the Elliptic Curve.** The function $\mathcal{H}$ maps an attribute, expressed as a binary string, to a corresponding element in the elliptic curve group [5]:

$$\mathcal{H} : \{0,1\}^* \to \mathbb{G}. \tag{1}$$

**Pairing.** The bilinear pairing $e$ is defined as:

$$e : \mathbb{G}_1 \times \mathbb{G}_2 \to \mathbb{G}_T. \tag{2}$$

Pairings are categorized based on the relationship between $\mathbb{G}_1$ and $\mathbb{G}_2$ [6]:

- **Type I (symmetric):** $\mathbb{G}_1 = \mathbb{G}_2$.
- **Type II (asymmetric):** $\mathbb{G}_1 \neq \mathbb{G}_2$, but an efficient isomorphism from $\mathbb{G}_2$ to $\mathbb{G}_1$ exists.
- **Type III (asymmetric):** $\mathbb{G}_1 \neq \mathbb{G}_2$ and no efficient isomorphism exists in either direction.

## 2.2  Access Trees in CP-ABE

**Tree Definition.** An access tree defines the policy controlling which users can decrypt ciphertexts. Each tree encodes logic using threshold gates at internal nodes and attributes at leaves. Figure 1 shows an access tree encoding the following policy: *(Position: Manager OR Technician) AND (Farm: AT)*.

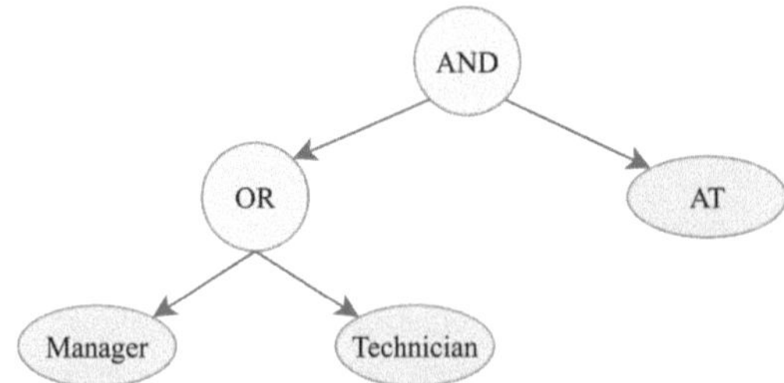


**Fig. 1.** A basic access tree $\mathcal{T}$, where the root node *AND* requires both children to be satisfied, the *OR* gate allows either *"Manager"* or *"Technician"* and leaf nodes correspond to attributes in the policy

**Policy Satisfaction.** Consider a tree $\mathcal{T}$ with root node $R$, and let $\mathcal{T}_r$ denote the subtree whose root is $r$. Given an attribute set $A$, we say $\mathcal{T}_r(A) = 1$ if $A$ satisfies $\mathcal{T}_r$. Evaluation proceeds recursively: If $r$ is an internal node, then $\mathcal{T}_r(A) = 1$ holds if at least $k_r$ of its child nodes evaluate to 1.

For example, if a secret key includes attributes {*Position: Manager, Farm: AT*}, the policy in Fig. 1 is satisfied. A key with attributes {*Position: Manager, Farm: AG*} fails to meet the specified access policy.

## 2.3  Efficient Library for Pairing Based Security

ELiPS is designed to support efficient implementation of pairing-based cryptographic protocols. Its primary objective is to provide researchers with a tool that is straightforward to install, configure, and use. Anyone with a basic understanding of pairing-based cryptography can employ this library in their protocol research. The library is updated incrementally, in parallel with the authors' research activities, to incorporate the latest algorithmic advancements.

ELiPS is implemented based on the BLS12 curve family, which is widely used in pairing-based cryptography. It supports a 128-bit security level. Many applications and modern algorithms have been implemented using the ELiPS library, including pairing-based homomorphic encryption and zk-SNARKs.

# 3    Attribute-Based Encryption Scheme Using ELiPS

The proposed design enforces fine-grained access management by associating ciphertexts with attribute-based policy conditions. Under this model, each ciphertext is linked to an access structure that specifies the combinations of attributes required for decryption. A user can retrieve the plaintext only if the attributes in their secret key satisfy the conditions of the policy embedded in the ciphertext [3].

This encryption paradigm is particularly advantageous in scenarios where data sharing must be both distributed and tightly controlled. It ensures that only authorized parties, those holding the necessary attributes can access the data. Such capabilities are vital in contexts like cross-organizational collaborations, cloud-based storage, and Internet of Things (IoT) deployments, where safeguarding confidential data is essential. By enabling secure, privacy-preserving communication, CP-ABE also supports compliance with regulatory requirements and the enforcement of policy-based permissions [3].

The ELiPS-based CP-ABE construction is derived from the ELiPS library and grounded in the framework of pairing-based cryptography. This approach leverages bilinear pairings to carry out advanced cryptographic computations efficiently. The design prioritizes low computational overhead, making it practical for devices with constrained processing capabilities or limited energy resources, including mobile platforms and IoT nodes [3]. At its core, the scheme incorporates four principal cryptographic operations, relying heavily on pairing and hash-to-curve techniques.

## 3.1    Setup

This phase is performed once by a trusted authority at the beginning of system initialization. This stage utilizes scalar multiplication, pairing, and exponentiation computations. In this stage, the system produces a master key $MK$ and a public key $PK$, the latter being distributed to users while the former remains confidential.

The algorithm first constructs the generator point $g_1 \in \mathbb{G}_1$ and $g_2 \in \mathbb{G}_2$, and both groups have a prime order $r$. Two random values $\alpha$ and $\beta$ are selected from $\mathbb{Z}_r$, and the keys are computed as [3]:

$$
\begin{aligned}
MK &= (\beta, w), \\
PK &= (g_1, g_2, u, v),
\end{aligned}
\tag{3}
$$

where $w = \alpha \cdot g_2, u = \beta \cdot g_1, v = e(g_1, g_2)^{\alpha}$. Here, $e$ denotes a bilinear pairing function. In the original scheme, the pairing is defined as a Type I pairing. In this work, however, we employ a Type III pairing.

## 3.2   Key Generation

This key generation phase derives a secret key for each user according to their attribute set. The algorithm takes as input $MK$ together with a collection of attributes $A = \{att1, att2, \dots \}$.

The process starts by choosing a random value $\gamma \in \mathbb{Z}_r$, and for every attribute $i \in A$, it selects an additional random scalar $\gamma_i \in \mathbb{Z}_r$. A cryptographic hash function $\mathcal{H} : \{0,1\}^* \to \mathbb{G}_2$ is used to map each attribute to an element in $\mathbb{G}_2$ [3]. The user's secret key $SK$ is constructed as follows [3]:

$$SK = (D, \{D_i, D_i'\}_{\forall i \in A}), \tag{4}$$

where $D = (\alpha + \gamma) \cdot \beta^{-1} \cdot g_2, D_i = \gamma \cdot g_2 + \gamma_i \cdot \mathcal{H}(i), D_i' = \gamma_i \cdot g_1$.

## 3.3   Encryption

This function encodes the message using the public key $PK$ and an access policy $\mathcal{T}$. This operation involves scalar multiplications and the application of a hash function to the attributes. It guarantees that only recipients whose attribute sets fulfill the access policy criteria can obtain the plaintext.

During the encryption phase, a random element $s \in \mathbb{Z}_r$ is chosen, and for every $t$ belonging to the access structure $\mathcal{T}$, an individual polynomial $q_t$ is constructed. The root node $R$ is initialized with $q_R(0) = s$. For any non-root node $t$, its polynomial is set so that $q_t(0) = q_{\mathrm{par}(t)} \cdot (\mathrm{ind}(t))$, where $\mathrm{par}(t)$ identifies the parent of $t$, and $\mathrm{ind}(t)$ denotes its index among siblings.

Let $\mathcal{L}$ represent the set of all leaf nodes in $\mathcal{T}$, and $\mathrm{att}(t)$ denote the attribute associated with each leaf node $t$. Based on this configuration, the encryption algorithm generates the ciphertext $CT$, as described in Eq. (5) [3]:

$$CT = (\mathcal{T}, \tilde{C}, C, \{C_l, C_l'\}_{\forall l \in \mathcal{L}}), \tag{5}$$

where $\tilde{C} = M \cdot e(g_1, g_2)^{\alpha s}, C = s \cdot h, C_l = q_l(0) \cdot g_1, C_l' = q_l(0) \cdot \mathcal{H}(\mathrm{att}(l))$.

## 3.4   Decryption

The decryption process is executed by the recipient to retrieve the plaintext. The decryption process succeeds exclusively when the attribute set of the user aligns with the access policy specified within the encrypted content. This phase primarily involves pairing computations and exponentiation operations.

The algorithm operates on the ciphertext $CT$, which encapsulates the access policy tree $\mathcal{T}$, along with the user's secret key $SK$ that corresponds to an attribute set $A$. It processes the access tree recursively through a function $\mathrm{dec_node_flatten}(CT, SK, t)$ as Algorithm 1 [3]:

If $t$ is an internal node, the algorithm evaluates its children $c$, storing partial results $F_c$. Let $A_t$ be the list of children with $F_c \neq NULL$. If $A_t$ is nonempty, the node computes:

---

**Algorithm 1:** Decryption node flatten

---
**Input** : $CT, SK, t$
$i = \text{att}(t)$;
**if** $i \in A$ **then**
  |   **return** $e(D_i, C_t) \cdot e(D_i', C_t')^{-1}$;
**else**
  |   **return** $NULL$;
**end**

---

$$k = \text{ind}(c), \quad A_t' = \{\text{ind}(c) : c \in A_t\},$$

$$\Delta_{k,A_t'}(0) = \prod_{j \in A_t', j \neq k} \frac{-j}{k-j} = \prod_{j \in A_t', j \neq k} -j \cdot (k-j)^{-1}, \tag{6}$$

$$F_t = \prod_{c \in A_t} F_c^{\Delta_{k,A_t'}(0)} = e(g,g)^{\gamma q_t(0)}. \tag{7}$$

Once $F_R = e(g,g)^{\gamma s}$ is obtained at the root $R$, the original message is recovered via [3]:

$$M = \frac{\tilde{C} \cdot F_R}{e(C,D)} = \tilde{C} \cdot F_R \cdot e(C,D)^{-1}. \tag{8}$$

**Reducing the Number of Final Exponentiations.** According to Algorithm 1 and Eq. (7), each attribute requires two complete pairing evaluations, encompassing both the Miller loop and the final exponentiation. Since these computations are particularly resource-intensive, especially in scenarios with numerous attributes, they can significantly affect system performance. To enhance computational efficiency, we introduced a revised formulation that aggregates the final exponentiation into a single step [4]:

$$\prod_{i=1}^{n} \left[ \frac{e(D_i, C_i)}{e(D_i', C_i')} \right]^{\Delta_i} = \left[ \prod_{i=1}^{n} \left( \frac{f_{D_i,C_i}}{f_{D_i',C_i'}} \right)^{\Delta_i} \right]^{\frac{p^k - 1}{r}}, \tag{9}$$

where $f_{P,Q}$ represents the output of the Miller loop applied to points $P$ and $Q$ on an elliptic curve.

This optimization avoids performing the final exponentiation for each individual pairing. Instead, it aggregates the Miller loop results and performs only a single final exponentiation at the end. Consequently, the total number of final exponentiation steps is reduced by $2n - 1$, significantly lowering the computational cost during decryption.

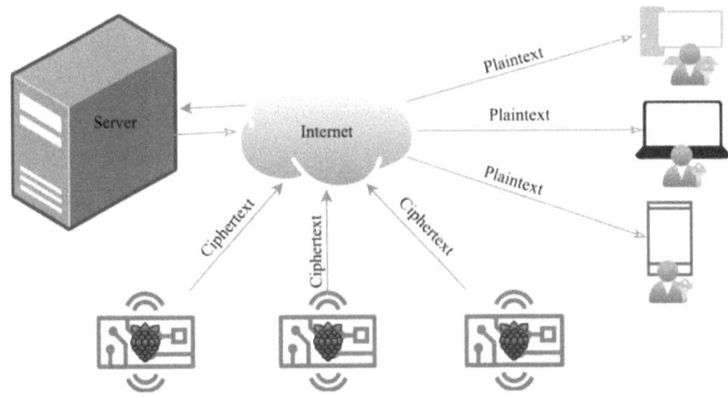


**Fig. 2.** System structure showing the interaction between the server, IoT devices, and client users via the Internet.

**Reducing the Number of Inversion Operations.** In addition to final exponentiations, the original decryption procedure also involves multiple field inversion operations, particularly in the Lagrange interpolation step defined in Eq. (6). Since inversions are computationally expensive, we applied an optimization technique to minimize their occurrence [4]: First, compute $\mathcal{P}_k = \prod_{j=1,j\neq k}^{n} (k-j)$. Next, determine $\mathcal{P}_k^{-1} = \frac{1}{\mathcal{P}_k}$. Then, reuse it to compute each $(k-j)^{-1} = \mathcal{P}_k^{-1} \cdot \prod_{i=1,i\neq j}^{n} (k-i)$.

This optimization strategy decreases the number of required inversions by a factor of $n-1$. While this approach introduces roughly $3(n-1)$ additional multiplication operations, the trade-off proves advantageous. In practice, multiplication in finite fields is significantly faster than inversion. Hence, the overall decryption process becomes more computationally efficient compared to direct application of Eq. (6).

## 4   Implementation and Experimental Setup

The system architecture shown in Fig. 2 was implemented as part of our experimental study. In our experiment, we utilized multiple types of equipment, including a server and several IoT devices like the Raspberry Pi. The various configurations and specifications of these devices are detailed comprehensively in Table 1, highlighting the differences and settings that were crucial for our study.

**Table 1.** Experimental environment specifications used in the evaluation.

|  | Server | Raspberry Pi |
| --- | --- | --- |
| CPU | 12th Gen Intel (R) Core (TM) i5-12500 3.00 GHz | Quad core Cortex-A72 (ARM v8) 64-bit 1.5 GHz |
| Memory | 32 GB | 4 GB |
| OS | Ubuntu 22.04.1 LTS (WLS2) | Raspberry Pi OS 6.12 |

In our experiment, data is encrypted on end-devices, such as the Raspberry Pi, before being uploaded to the server. When users attempt to access the data, the server verifies the user's permissions based on their secret key and a predefined policy, which is embedded within the ciphertext. If the secret key possessed by an individual matches the defined policy, the server decrypts the ciphertext and delivers the plaintext accordingly. Otherwise, that individual is denied access to the data.

For the evaluation process, we performed several access policy scenarios. Across our experiments, we considered access policies following {*att1* and *att2* and *att3* ... and *attn*}. In our experimental setup, we progressively increased the number of attributes from 3 to 19 to evaluate system scalability and performance. The proposed scheme was benchmarked against CP-ABE. Experiments were conducted on both a server and a Raspberry Pi device. Specifically, the server was used to perform the setup, key generation, and decryption phases, while the Raspberry Pi was tasked with executing the encryption phase. Each operation was repeated 10,000 times to ensure accuracy, and the average execution time was calculated for each experiment.

## 5   Results

### 5.1   Setup Time

The experimental results demonstrate that the setup time of our proposed method is significantly reduced, achieving a 22.6% improvement in setup efficiency. As illustrated in Fig. 3, the setup time does not increase linearly as the attribute count grows. The setup time of the original CP-ABE version remains stable at approximately 3.1 ms, whereas our proposed method consistently maintains a setup time of around 2.4 ms across scenarios. This improvement is primarily due to the implementation of the sextic twist technique, which maps a

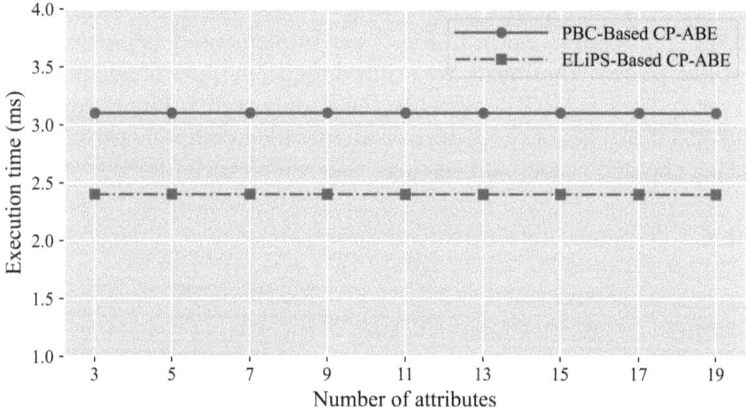


**Fig. 3.** Comparison of setup time between the proposed method and the original CP-ABE scheme.

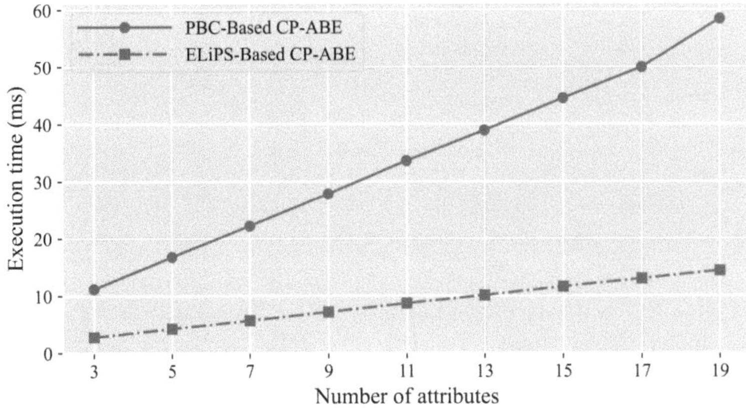



**Fig. 4.** Key generation time comparison of the proposal and the original version.

rational point over $E'(\mathbb{F}_{p^2})$ to a rational point over $E'(\mathbb{F}_{p^{12}})$. Arithmetic operations on rational points over $E'(\mathbb{F}_{p^2})$ are significantly more efficient than those over $E'(\mathbb{F}_{p^{12}})$, contributing to the observed performance gains.

## 5.2 Key Generation Time

In the key generation process, the proposed method achieves significant improvements in key generation time, as shown in Fig. 4. The findings demonstrate that the time required for key generation grows linearly in relation to the attribute count, aligning with the expected behavior of CP-ABE mechanisms. In the baseline CP-ABE construction, the generation duration rises from 11.2 ms to 58.4 ms when the number of attributes ranges between 3 and 19.

In contrast, the proposed method shows a more consistent key generation time, ranging from 2.8 ms to 14.4 ms across the same range of attributes. It is noticeable that the proposed method consistently outperforms the original CP-ABE scheme in terms of key generation time, being 74.4% faster on average across all attribute counts.

## 5.3 Encryption Time

As illustrated in Fig. 5, the encryption time results show that our proposed scheme offers a substantial improvement in efficiency compared to the initial CP-ABE version. In the case of the PBC-based scheme, the encryption duration increases proportionally with the attribute count, starting at 38.8 ms for 3 attributes and reaching 198.7 ms for 19 attributes. In contrast, the ELiPS-based scheme achieves more efficient performance, with encryption times ranging from 22.1 ms for 3 attributes to 115.3 ms for 19 attributes.

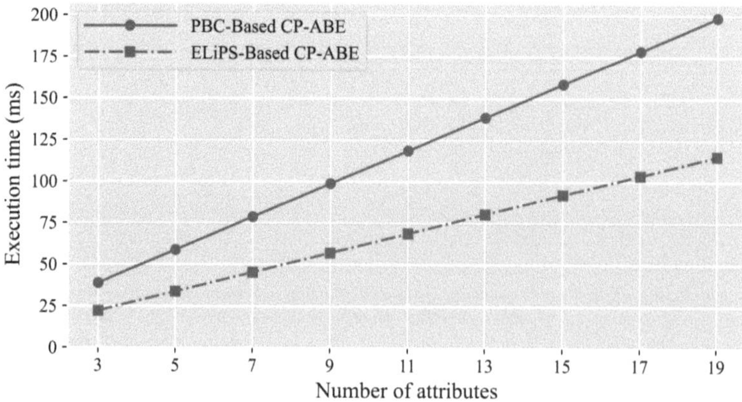

**Fig. 5.** Comparison of encryption time between the proposed method and the initial version of CP-ABE.

On average, the proposed scheme achieves a 42.1% reduction in encryption time across all tested attribute counts compared to the original PBC-based scheme. The achieved performance gain offers notable benefits in situations requiring fast encryption of information, for instance within the IoT systems and real-time processing tasks. The ability to encrypt data efficiently while maintaining robust security guarantees highlights the practical benefits of our proposed scheme.

## 5.4   Decryption Time

We thoroughly assessed the decryption performance of both the CP-ABE scheme and our proposed implementation. From Fig. 6, one can observe that the time

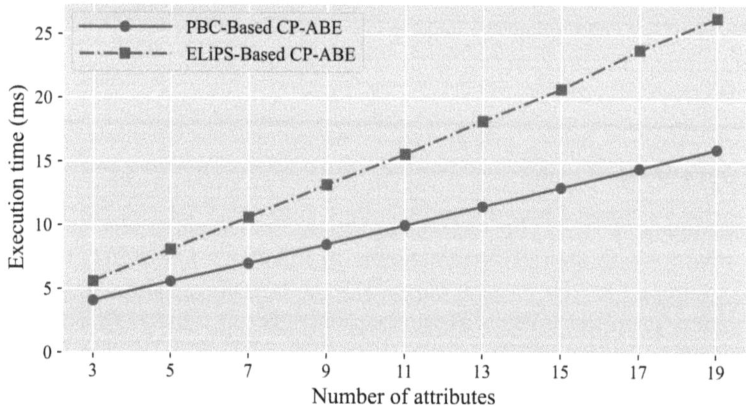

**Fig. 6.** Comparison of decryption time between the proposed method and the original CP-ABE.

needed for decryption expands proportionally to the growth in attributes, which is expected because of the increased computational workload associated with complex access structures.

The ELiPS-based implementation exhibits decryption times ranging from 5.6 ms for 3 attributes to 26.3 ms for 19 attributes. In comparison, the PBC-based scheme achieves decryption times from 4.1 ms to 16.0 ms over the same range. Although the ELiPS-based scheme incurs a slight increase in decryption time, this overhead is compensated by the substantial improvements achieved in the first three phases. Furthermore, the ELiPS-based approach provides enhanced security and scalability, making it suitable for applications with stringent security requirements and large attribute sets.

### 5.5 Ciphertext and Plaintext Size

Figure 7 presents the ciphertext size results for the proposed method. The data show that the ciphertext size increases only marginally with the number of attributes, and in some cases, remains unchanged. In particular, for files ranging from 104 KB to 102,792 KB in size, the ciphertext overhead ranges from 0 to 8 bytes. For example, with 5 attributes, the proposed method achieves a ciphertext size that shows almost no increase compared to the original scheme. When the attribute count grows, the growth stays steady, peaking at 1.6% for 20 attributes. This increase is advantageous for resource-constrained environments, such as IoT devices, where bandwidth and storage are limited.

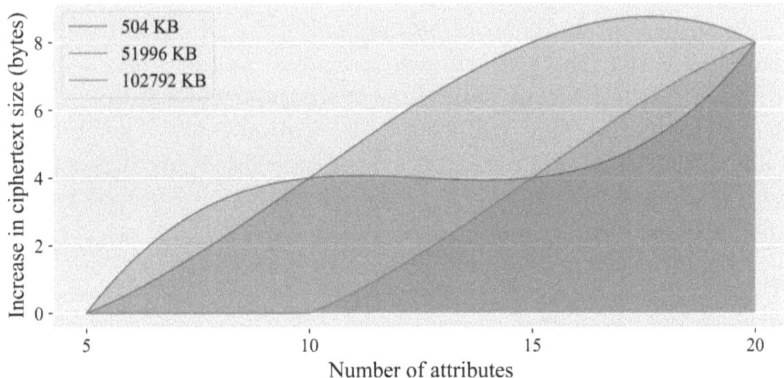


**Fig. 7.** Ciphertext size increase (bytes) in our scheme as the number of attributes grows, measured across multiple file sizes.

### 5.6 Memory Usage

Figure 8 illustrates that the memory usage of our scheme is reduced by an average of 12.4% compared to the original scheme. Specifically, the original method consumes 26 KB of memory, while the proposed method requires only 22 KB for

3 attributes. As the number of attributes increases to 19, the original scheme's memory usage rises to 71 KB, whereas our method maintains a lower memory footprint of 56 KB. These results demonstrate significant benefits for resource-constrained environments, such as IoT devices, where memory is often limited.

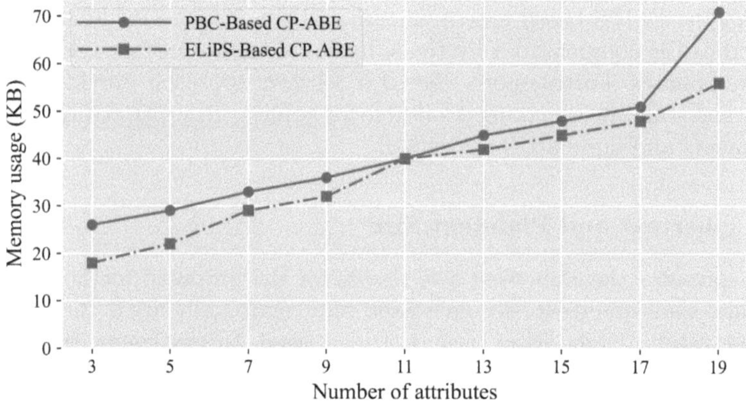


**Fig. 8.** Memory usage comparison between the proposed method and the original method.

## 6    Conclusions

This study provides a comprehensive assessment of the CP-ABE based on ELiPS, emphasizing its performance advantages compared to the original version. The results demonstrate significant reductions in setup, key generation, and encryption times, while maintaining competitive decryption times. The ciphertext size remains efficient, with minimal increases as the number of attributes grows. Furthermore, the memory usage of the proposed method is reduced compared to the original scheme. These findings underscore the practical advantages of the ELiPS-based approach, particularly in resource-constrained environments such as IoT devices. The proposed scheme improves encryption efficiency while maintaining strong security and scalability, making it suitable for deployment across diverse application domains.

## References

1. Atat, R., Albayrak, S., Aydin, M.E.: Big data meet cyber-physical systems: a panoramic survey. IEEE Access **6**, 73603–73636 (2018). https://doi.org/10.1109/ACCESS.2018.2878681
2. Prantl, T., et al.: Towards a cryptography encyclopedia: a survey on attribute-based encryption. J. Surveill. Secur. Saf. **4**, 129–54 (2023). https://doi.org/10.20517/jsss.2023.30

3. Anh, L.H., Kawada, Y., Huda, S., Ali, M.A., Kodera, Y., Nogami, Y.: An implementation of ELiPS-based ciphertext-policy attribute-based encryption. In,: Eleventh International Symposium on Computing and Networking Workshops (CANDARW), Matsue, Japan 2023, pp. 220–226 (2023). https://doi.org/10.1109/CANDARW60564.2023.00044
4. Anh, L.H., Kawada, Y., Huda, S., Ali, M.A., Kodera, Y., Nogami, Y.: A minimization number of final exponentiations and inversions for reducing the decryption process time in ELiPS-based CP-ABE. J. Adv. Inf. Technol. **15**(6), 748–755 (2024). https://doi.org/10.12720/jait.15.6.748-755
5. Faz, H.A., Scott, S., Sullivan, N., Wahby, R.S., Wood, C.A.: Hashing to Elliptic Curves. Technical Report RFC9380, RFC 396 Editor (2023). https://doi.org/10.17487/RFC9380
6. Steven, D.G., Kenneth, G.P., Nigel, P.S.: Pairings for cryptographers. Discret. Appl. Math. **156**(16), 3113–3121 (2008). https://doi.org/10.1016/j.dam.2007.12.010

# HAD-IDS: A Hybrid Adversarial Defense Framework for Intrusion Detection Systems


Ha Thanh Dung[1(✉)] and Nguyen Hong Son[2]

[1] Saigon University, Ho Chi Minh, Vietnam
`htdung@sgu.edu.vn`
[2] Posts and Telecommunications Institute of Technology, Ha Noi, Vietnam
`sonngh@ptit.edu.vn`



**Abstract.** Deep learning-based intrusion detection systems (IDS) can degrade sharply under adversarial manipulation. We present **HAD-IDS** (Hybrid Adversarial Defense for IDS), a unified defense that couples input purification, robust training, and runtime risk monitoring. HAD-IDS consists of: (i) a denoising autoencoder (AE) that purifies traffic prior to classification; (ii) an adversarially trained classifier with TRADES regularization to balance clean and robust accuracy; (iii) a latent-space detector using Mahalanobis distance; and (iv) explanation-driven metrics—*ASD* (Attribution Shift Distance) and *VBAR* (the fraction of adversarial samples with ASD $\leq \gamma$)—to expose attribution drift caused by attacks. Under a white-box threat model with PGD (20 steps at evaluation), we test on three benchmarks—NSL-KDD, UNSW-NB15, and CIC-IDS2017. Relative to an undefended model, HAD-IDS improves robust accuracy by **+28.86**, **+38.11**, and **+34.37** percentage points (pp), with clean-accuracy trade-offs of $-1.75$, $-3.57$, and $-2.22$ pp, respectively; averaged across datasets this yields **+33.78 pp** robust gain for $-2.51$ **pp** clean. Compared to strong baselines, HAD-IDS is on par with or slightly better than adversarial training alone on average, while outperforming TRADES-only (**+9.06 pp**) and purification-only (**+14.49 pp**) in robustness. Ablations show adversarial training is the primary source of robustness (removal: $-7.25$ pp on average), while the AE provides a small but consistent boost and enables the ASD/VBAR pathway; TRADES mainly improves clean accuracy with dataset-dependent effects on robustness. Across all datasets, the ASD distribution for adversarial samples shifts markedly to the right of clean, leading to low VBAR and supporting explanation drift as a complementary detection signal alongside Mahalanobis.

**Keywords:** intrusion detection · adversarial robustness · denoising autoencoder · TRADES · Mahalanobis distance · explainability · attribution shift distance (ASD) · VBAR

# 1   Introduction

Deep learning has advanced intrusion detection systems (IDS) in modeling complex network behaviors, yet these models are vulnerable to *adversarial* perturbations that cause misclassification with imperceptible input changes [1,2]. In operational settings, such degradations can translate into missed attacks or excessive false alarms. While numerous defenses have been explored, they typically optimize a single mechanism in isolation—e.g., adversarial training for robustness [3], input purification [4], or latent out-of-distribution (OOD) detection [5]—and seldom address the joint requirements of (i) **robust decision making**, (ii) **attack flagging**, and (iii) **explainability** on *tabular network-traffic* data. Moreover, evidence shows dataset-dependent trade-offs: defenses that help on one IDS benchmark may underperform on another or harm clean accuracy.

**Limits of Existing Approaches.** Adversarial training (AT) hardens the classifier against a chosen attack distribution [2,3], but it can be expensive and may trade clean for robust accuracy; purifiers (e.g., denoising, score-based diffusion) reduce input noise [4] but risk obfuscating gradients or removing task-relevant signal; OOD/latent detectors (e.g., Mahalanobis) surface abnormal representations but do not, by themselves, correct decisions [5]. For IDS specifically, recent works often evaluate on a single dataset or omit principled explanatory diagnostics, making it difficult to reason about when a defense *should* trigger an alert and why.

**This Work.** We introduce **HAD-IDS** (Hybrid Adversarial Defense for IDS), a two-phase pipeline (Fig. 1) that integrates complementary mechanisms: (i) a *denoising autoencoder* (AE) that purifies inputs prior to classification; (ii) an adversarially trained classifier with *TRADES* regularization to balance clean/robust performance [3]; (iii) a *latent-space detector* using class-conditional *Mahalanobis* distance [5]; and (iv) explanation-driven diagnostics via *Attribution Shift Distance* (ASD) and *VBAR* (the fraction of adversarial samples with ASD $\leq \gamma$), computed from Integrated Gradients [11]. The design couples *robust prediction* with *runtime risk signaling*: purification and robust training aim to preserve accuracy under attack, while Mahalanobis and ASD/VBAR provide orthogonal signals for flagging suspicious inputs.

**Empirical Preview.** Under a white-box PGD threat model [2], HAD-IDS attains strong cross-dataset robustness on *NSL-KDD*, *UNSW-NB15*, and *CIC-IDS2017*: averaged over the three, robust accuracy improves by **+33.78** percentage points (pp) over an undefended classifier for a modest **−2.51 pp** clean-accuracy trade-off. Compared to strong single-technique baselines, HAD-IDS is on par with adversarial training alone on average, and outperforms TRADES-only and purification-only variants in robustness. Ablations indicate adversarial training is the primary source of robustness, the AE contributes a small but consistent gain and enables ASD/VBAR, and TRADES mainly improves clean accuracy with dataset-dependent effects.

## Contributions

- **Hybrid defense architecture for IDS.** We propose HAD-IDS, a practical pipeline that combines *denoising purification, adversarially regularized classification* (with TRADES), and *latent detection* to deliver robust predictions with runtime alerting.
- **Explainability-driven monitoring.** We operationalize *ASD* and *VBAR* on tabular traffic, showing attribution drift is a reliable complementary signal to Mahalanobis for adversarial activity.
- **Cross-dataset evaluation.** On NSL-KDD [6], UNSW-NB15 [7], and CIC-IDS2017 [8], we report comprehensive results (clean/robust accuracy, detection behavior), with ablations isolating the roles of AE, adversarial training, and TRADES.
- **Reproducible implementation.** We implement the framework in Tensor-Flow with a Colab workflow that exports dataset-specific tables and figures in a LaTeX-ready format, facilitating replication and extension.

**Paper Organization.** Section 2 reviews related works on adversarial defense and explainable IDS. Section 3 introduces the proposed HAD-IDS framework and its components. Section 4 describes the experimental setup. Section 5 presents and discusses the results. Section 6 concludes the paper and outlines future research.

## 2    Related Work

*Adversarial Examples and Robust Training.* Gradient-based attacks such as FGSM and multi-step PGD systematized adversarial vulnerabilities in deep models [1,2], while follow-up work cautioned against gradient obfuscation and emphasized transparent evaluations [9]. Beyond single attacks, parameter-free suites such as AutoAttack provide stronger, standardized assessments [10]. On the defense side, *adversarial training* (AT) optimizes the worst-case loss within a norm budget; TRADES [3] balances natural and robust risks via a KL divergence regularizer. Although effective on images, AT/TRADES can trade clean for robust accuracy and incur high compute; their behavior on *tabular* IDS features is further complicated by one-hot sparsity and heterogeneous scales.

*Purification-Based Defenses.* A complementary line *pre-processes* inputs toward the data manifold before classification. Diffusion- and score-based purifiers (e.g., DiffPure) reduce adversarial residuals prior to the classifier [4]. Iterative samplers, however, may be costly at inference and can mask gradients if not evaluated purification-aware [9]. In IDS, lightweight *denoising autoencoders* (AEs) are attractive given tabular structure and deployment constraints.

*Latent/OOD Detection.* Runtime *alarm* mechanisms complement decision correction. Mahalanobis scoring on deep features–assuming class-conditional

Gaussians–offers a simple, training-light out-of-distribution (OOD) detector [5]. For security monitoring, latent detectors can flag suspicious flows for quarantine or secondary inspection even when the classifier is robustly trained.

*Explainability Under Adversarial Manipulation.* Post-hoc attributions such as Integrated Gradients (IG) provide feature-level explanations for tabular and vision models [11]. In adversarial settings, the *stability* of explanations becomes informative: large attribution drift under small input changes can indicate manipulation. We operationalize this idea via *Attribution Shift Distance* (ASD) and *VBAR* (the fraction of adversarial samples with ASD $\leq \gamma$), computed from IG before/after purification; these signals are complementary to latent OOD scores.

*Adversarial Robustness in IDS.* Recent IDS works adapt AT, generative augmentation, and hybrid defenses to network traffic. *AdvMix* mixes adversarial and natural samples to improve generalization [12]; *SGAN-IDS* leverages GAN-based synthesis alongside robustness objectives [13]; and *RL-IDS* explores reinforcement learning to harden detection policies [14]. Many approaches, however, optimize a single mechanism (AT-only or purifier-only), evaluate on a single benchmark, or lack quantitative diagnostics for when and why a defense should raise an alert.

*Positioning and Gaps.* **HAD-IDS** integrates three complementary axes–(i) *purification* via a denoising AE, (ii) *robust training* with TRADES regularization, and (iii) *runtime monitoring* through latent Mahalanobis and explanation-drift (ASD/VBAR)–to couple robust prediction with operational alerting. Unlike defenses that target robustness alone, our design quantifies both accuracy and monitoring quality across *multiple IDS datasets*, and includes ablations that isolate the contribution of each component. Tables 1 and 2 situate HAD-IDS among representative and recent defenses.

**Table 1.** Comparison of adversarial defense methods for IDS.

| Method | Adversarial Training | Purification | Latent Detection | Explainability |
|---|---|---|---|---|
| TRADES [3] | ✓ | – | – | – |
| DiffPure [4] | – | ✓ | – | – |
| AdvMix [12] | ✓ | – | – | – |
| DYNAMITE [16] | ✓ | – | – | – |
| SGAN-IDS [13] | ✓ | ✓ | – | – |
| RL-IDS [14] | ✓ | – | – | – |
| **HAD-IDS (Proposed)** | ✓ | ✓ | ✓ | ✓ |

**Table 2.** Recent adversarial defenses relevant to IDS (20222025). Marks: ✓ = present; – = not primary. "IDS Eval." indicates evaluation on IDS/tabular traffic. Training/Inference cost is a qualitative estimate from algorithmic structure. † Proposed outside IDS but transferable to tabular.

| Method | Year | AT | Purif. | Latent/OOD | XAI | IDS Eval. | Train/Infer Cost |
|---|---|---|---|---|---|---|---|
| TRADES [3] | 2019 | ✓ | – | – | – | o† | High/Low |
| DiffPure [4] | 2022 | – | ✓ | – | – | o† | High/High |
| AdvMix [12] | 2023 | ✓ | – | – | – | ✓ | Medium/Low |
| SGAN-IDS [13] | 2023 | ✓ | ✓ | – | – | ✓ | High/Medium |
| RL-IDS [14] | 2024 | ✓ | – | – | – | ✓ | High/Low |
| **HAD-IDS (Proposed)** | 2025 | ✓ | ✓ | ✓ | ✓ | ✓ | High/Medium |

Recent studies have further advanced adversarially robust intrusion detection through hybrid and explainable frameworks [17–19]. Zhang et al. [17] proposed a hybrid adversarial defense that combines purification and adversarial training to improve IoT network security. Zhou and Yu [18] introduced a robust and explainable IDS using multi-view feature fusion, highlighting the role of interpretability in robustness evaluation. Moreover, He et al. [19] enhanced TRADES regularization for tabular data, providing theoretical guidance for balancing robustness and clean accuracy. These developments align with our HAD-IDS design that unifies purification, adversarial training, and explainable detection.

## 3    Proposed Method: HAD-IDS

### 3.1    Design Goals and Overview

HAD-IDS (*Hybrid Adversarial Defense for IDS*) couples *robust prediction* with *runtime risk monitoring* for tabular network traffic. The pipeline (Fig. 1) has four components: (i) **Denoising Autoencoder (AE)** to purify inputs; (ii) **Adversarially trained classifier** with **TRADES** regularization to balance clean/robust accuracy [3]; (iii) **Latent-space detector** using **Mahalanobis** distance [5]; and (iv) **Explanation-driven monitoring** via **ASD** and **VBAR** based on Integrated Gradients [11]. Two output channels are produced at inference: the class prediction $\hat{y}$ and a binary *flag* for quarantine/alert.

### 3.2    Architecture and Notation

Let $x \in [0,1]^d$ be a min-max normalised flow feature vector and $y \in \{1, \ldots, C\}$ its label. The AE purifies $x$ via an encoder–decoder:

$$x' = f_{\mathrm{AE}}(x) = D_\phi\big(E_\psi(x)\big), \tag{1}$$

trained with denoising noise $\eta \sim \mathcal{N}(0, \sigma^2 I)$ and MSE loss. A classifier $f_\theta$ maps the purified input to logits $z = f_\theta(x')$ and features (penultimate) $r = h_\theta(x')$. We denote the defended composite as $F(x) = f_\theta(f_{\mathrm{AE}}(x))$.

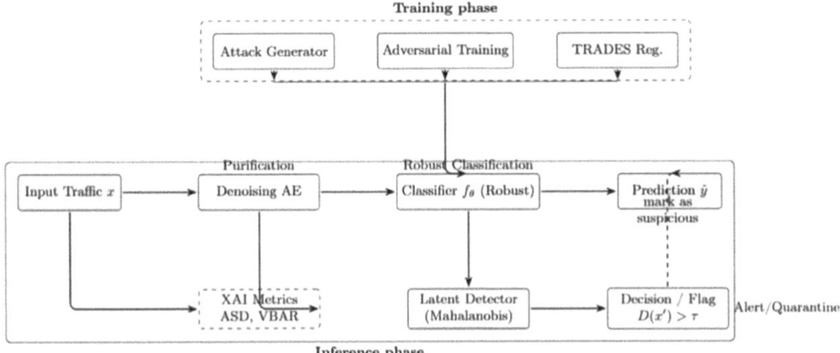


**Fig. 1.** Two-phase view of HAD-IDS. The **Training phase** (top) strengthens the classifier (attack generation, adversarial training, TRADES). The **Inference phase** (bottom) applies purification, robust classification, latent detection, and XAI metrics. The dashed feedback arrow indicates that a flagged sample can be marked as suspicious (override) at the Prediction output.

**Notation Recap.** We denote $x$ the normalized input, $x'$ the purified input, $z = f_\theta(x')$ the logits, and $r = h_\theta(x')$ the latent representation used for Mahalanobis scoring $D(x')$. Thresholds $(\tau, \gamma)$ govern latent and attribution detection respectively.

### 3.3   Purification-Aware Robust Training

We adopt *purification-aware* adversarial training: attacks are optimized on the composite $F$ (no gradient masking). Given a perturbation budget $\epsilon$ in $\ell_\infty$, PGD with step size $\alpha$ and $T$ iterations generates

$$x^{(t+1)} = \Pi_{[0,1] \cap \mathcal{B}_\infty(x,\epsilon)}\Big(x^{(t)} + \alpha\,\mathrm{sign}\big(\nabla_x \mathcal{L}(F(x^{(t)}), y)\big)\Big), \qquad (2)$$

with $x^{(0)} = x + u$, $u \sim \mathrm{Unif}([-\epsilon, \epsilon]^d)$ [2]. The training loss combines natural CE, adversarial CE, and TRADES:

$$\mathcal{L}_{\mathrm{HAD}}(x,y) = \underbrace{\mathcal{L}_{\mathrm{CE}}\big(f_\theta(f_{\mathrm{AE}}(x)), y\big)}_{\text{natural}} + \lambda \underbrace{\mathcal{L}_{\mathrm{CE}}\big(f_\theta(f_{\mathrm{AE}}(\tilde{x})), y\big)}_{\text{adversarial}}$$

$$+ \beta \underbrace{\mathrm{KL}\big(p_{\mathrm{nat}} \,\|\, p_{\mathrm{adv}}\big)}_{\text{TRADES}}, \qquad \tilde{x} \sim \mathrm{PGD}(x). \qquad (3)$$

where $p_{\mathrm{nat}} = \mathrm{softmax}\big(f_\theta(f_{\mathrm{AE}}(x))\big)$ and $p_{\mathrm{adv}} = \mathrm{softmax}\big(f_\theta(f_{\mathrm{AE}}(\tilde{x}))\big)$ [3]. Hyperparameters $(\epsilon, \alpha, T, \lambda, \beta)$ follow the evaluation setup (Sect. 4).

### 3.4   Latent-Space Mahalanobis Detection

We compute class-conditional Gaussian summaries in the classifier feature space. Let $\mu_c = \mathbb{E}[r \mid y=c]$ and $\Sigma$ be a (regularised) covariance (e.g., LedoitWolf). The sample $x'$ is scored by the minimum Mahalanobis distance:

$$D(x') \;=\; \min_{c \in \{1,\ldots,C\}} \left(r - \mu_c\right)^{\top} \Sigma^{-1} \left(r - \mu_c\right), \qquad r = h_\theta(x').  \tag{4}$$

A threshold $\tau$ is set to the 95th percentile of $D$ on a clean validation set; we raise a *latent flag* if $D(x') > \tau$.

### 3.5  Explanation-Driven Monitoring: ASD and VBAR

We quantify *attribution drift* using Integrated Gradients (IG) [11]. Let $\varphi(x)$ denote IG attributions of $F$ for input $x$ (baseline 0, $m$ steps). Define the **Attribution Shift Distance** between raw and purified inputs

$$\mathrm{ASD}(x) \;=\; \left\| \varphi(x) - \varphi\big(f_{\mathrm{AE}}(x)\big) \right\|_1.  \tag{5}$$

We calibrate a clean threshold $\gamma$ as the 80th percentile of ASD measured on clean validation data. On adversarial inputs $x_{\mathrm{adv}}$, we report **VBAR** as

$$\mathrm{VBAR} \;=\; \Pr\big[ \mathrm{ASD}(x_{\mathrm{adv}}) \leq \gamma \big],  \tag{6}$$

so lower VBAR indicates stronger separation between clean and adversarial behaviors. We raise an *explanation flag* if $\mathrm{ASD}(x) > \gamma$.

### 3.6  Decision Policy and System Integration

The system outputs the class prediction $\hat{y} = \arg\max \mathrm{softmax}(f_\theta(f_{\mathrm{AE}}(x)))$ and a *flag* for response:

$$\mathrm{flag}(x) \;=\; \mathbb{I}\big[ D\big(f_{\mathrm{AE}}(x)\big) > \tau \;\; \vee \;\; \mathrm{ASD}(x) > \gamma \big].  \tag{7}$$

Flagged flows can be quarantined or forwarded to a secondary inspector. This decouples *robust prediction* from *operational alerting*, improving safety under uncertainty.

### 3.7  Complexity and Deployment Notes

HAD-IDS adds a single AE forward pass to the classifier at inference; IG-based ASD is computed offline for analysis and as a periodic audit (optional online at lower frequency). Mahalanobis statistics are one-shot to estimate ($O(Nd^2)$) and $O(Cd^2)$ to precompute $\Sigma^{-1}$; per-sample scoring is $O(Cd^2)$ (or $O(Cd)$ if whitening is cached). All components are differentiable, enabling end-to-end purification-aware training.

Overall, the computational overhead is modest relative to the base classifier, making HAD-IDS feasible for deployment

## 3.8   Threshold Calibration and Distribution Shift

To determine reliable anomaly thresholds, the Mahalanobis and attribution scores are calibrated on the clean validation set using the 95th and 80th percentiles, respectively. To handle potential distribution shift over time, HAD-IDS monitors the statistical distance between the current latent distribution and the reference validation distribution using the KolmogorovSmirnov (KS) test. When a significant drift is detected, the thresholds $(\tau, \gamma)$ are re-estimated on the most recent clean window with exponential smoothing to maintain stability.

# 4   Experimental Setup

This section describes the datasets, adversarial attack settings, evaluation metrics, and implementation details used to assess the performance of the proposed **HAD-IDS** framework.

## 4.1   Datasets

We evaluate our method on three widely used intrusion detection benchmarks:

- **NSL-KDD** [6]: a refined version of the KDD Cup'99 dataset with reduced redundancy, containing 41 features and four attack categories (DoS, Probe, R2L, U2R).
- **UNSW-NB15** [7]: a modern dataset including 49 features and nine attack families (e.g., DoS, Exploit, Shellcode), reflecting realistic traffic generated with IXIA tools.
- **CIC-IDS2017** [8]: a comprehensive dataset with over 80 network flow features and diverse attacks such as Botnet, DDoS, and Web-based intrusions.

All datasets are preprocessed using one-hot encoding for categorical features, min-max normalization for numerical features, and stratified splitting into training (70%), validation (10%), and test (20%).

## 4.2   Adversarial Attack Settings

We consider both single-step and iterative adversarial attacks commonly studied in adversarial ML:

- **FGSM** [1]: Fast Gradient Sign Method with $\epsilon \in \{0.01, 0.03, 0.05\}$.
- **PGD** [2]: Projected Gradient Descent with step size $\alpha = 0.01$, iterations $T = 20$ steps, and $\epsilon \in \{0.03, 0.05\}$.
- **MIM** [15]: Momentum Iterative Method with decay factor 1.0, $\epsilon = 0.03$.
- **Auto-PGD** [10]: adaptive adversary with $k = 100$ iterations and step size scheduling.

These settings simulate strong white-box attacks to rigorously test robustness.

### 4.3   Evaluation Metrics

We employ a combination of conventional and explainability-aware metrics:

- **Clean Accuracy**: classification accuracy on unperturbed test samples.
- **Robust Accuracy**: accuracy under adversarially perturbed test samples.
- **Additional IDS metrics**: we monitor Precision, Recall, F1-score, and AUC internally for sanity checks, but focus our discussion on Clean/Robust accuracy and ASD/VBAR.
- **Attribution Shift Distance (ASD)**: average distance between clean and adversarial attribution maps (lower is better).
- **Valid-Benign Attribution Rate (VBAR)**: percentage of adversarial samples whose attributions remain within benign bounds (higher is better).

### 4.4   Implementation Details

We implement **HAD-IDS** in `TensorFlow`. The denoising autoencoder is composed of three fully connected layers in both the encoder and decoder, with ReLU activations. The classifier is a two-layer feedforward network with hidden sizes $\{256, 128\}$. Training uses the Adam optimizer with learning rate $10^{-3}$, batch size 512, and 100 epochs. The purification-aware adversarial training loss (Eq. 3) is instantiated with $\lambda = 1.0$ and $\beta = 2.0$, following TRADES practice [3]. Adversarial examples are generated using PGD with perturbation budget $\epsilon = 0.03$, step size $\alpha = 0.01$, and $T = 20$ iterations, consistent across both training and evaluation. Mahalanobis statistics are estimated from purified latent features on the training set, and thresholds $(\tau, \gamma)$ are calibrated on a clean validation split. All experiments are conducted in Google Colab on a workstation equipped with an **NVIDIA Tesla T4 GPU (15 GB memory)**, CUDA 12.4, Python 3.12, and 128 GB host RAM.

This configuration is consistent across all datasets and experiments to ensure fairness and reproducibility.

## 5   Results and Discussion

This section reports the empirical performance of **HAD-IDS** and compares it with strong baselines and recent defenses. We first present overall classification robustness and clean accuracy, then analyze ablations to isolate the contribution of each component, and finally examine robustness in the explanation space (ASD/VBAR).

### 5.1   Overall Performance

Across *NSL-KDD*, *UNSW-NB15*, and *CIC-IDS2017*, HAD-IDS delivers consistent robustness gains over an undefended model while maintaining high clean accuracy. Relative to No-Defense, robust accuracy improves by **+28.86 pp**

(NSL-KDD), **+38.11 pp** (UNSW-NB15), and **+34.37 pp** (CIC-IDS2017), with modest clean-accuracy trade-offs of $-1.75$, $-3.57$, and $-2.22$ pp, respectively (Sect. 5). Compared to single-technique baselines, HAD-IDS is *on par with* adversarial training alone on average, and *outperforms* TRADES-only [3] and Purification-only [4] by **+9.06 pp** and **+14.49 pp** robust accuracy (averaged over the three datasets).

For transparency and reproducibility, we include the exact, dataset-specific tables exported from our Colab/TF pipeline (Table 3):

**Table 3.** Overall clean and robust accuracy under PGD (20 steps, $\epsilon = 0.03$) across datasets. Lower ASD indicates better separation.

| Method | NSL-KDD | | | UNSW-NB15 | | | CIC-IDS2017 | | |
|---|---|---|---|---|---|---|---|---|---|
| | Clean Acc (%) | Robust Acc (%) | ASD ↓ | Clean Acc (%) | Robust Acc (%) | ASD ↓ | Clean Acc (%) | Robust Acc (%) | ASD ↓ |
| No Defense | 79.17 | 45.64 | – | **89.60** | 43.71 | – | **97.18** | 55.49 | – |
| Adv. Training (only) | 77.21 | **75.61** | – | 85.76 | **80.20** | – | 95.51 | **90.12** | – |
| TRADES (only) | 78.26 | 72.83 | – | 87.82 | 72.85 | – | 97.00 | 73.33 | – |
| Purification (only) | **79.30** | 60.32 | **0.7565** | 89.35 | 65.58 | **0.5601** | 96.35 | 76.80 | **0.4616** |
| HAD-IDS | 77.42 | 74.50 | **0.7565** | 86.03 | **81.82** | **0.5601** | 94.96 | 89.86 | **0.4616** |

*Discussion.* The gains are largest on UNSW-NB15 (harder clean baseline), and remain strong on CIC-IDS2017 despite heterogeneous traffic. The denoising front-end plus purification-aware training avoid gradient masking and preserve task signal, yielding robust predictions without severe clean degradation.

## 5.2   Ablation Study

We ablate HAD-IDS by selectively disabling components (AE, Adversarial Training, TRADES). Tables below report the per-dataset effects exported from the pipeline (Table 4):

**Table 4.** Ablation study of HAD-IDS across three datasets. Best robust accuracy per dataset in bold. Lower ASD indicates better separation. Variants: w/o AE = without Autoencoder, w/o AdvTraining = without Adversarial Training, w/o TRADES = without TRADES regularization.

| Variant | NSL-KDD | | | UNSW-NB15 | | | CIC-IDS2017 | | |
|---|---|---|---|---|---|---|---|---|---|
| | Clean Acc | Robust Acc | ASD ↓ | Clean Acc | Robust Acc | ASD ↓ | Clean Acc | Robust Acc | ASD ↓ |
| HAD-IDS (full) | 0.7917 | **0.7564** | 0.7565 | 0.8443 | 0.8035 | 0.5601 | 0.9497 | **0.8910** | 0.4616 |
| w/o AE | 0.7740 | 0.7486 | – | 0.8586 | 0.7964 | – | 0.9535 | 0.8867 | – |
| w/o AdvTraining | 0.7752 | 0.7311 | 0.7565 | 0.8821 | 0.7079 | 0.5601 | 0.9604 | 0.7945 | 0.4616 |
| w/o TRADES | 0.7681 | 0.7445 | 0.7565 | 0.8202 | **0.8124** | 0.5601 | 0.9374 | 0.8893 | 0.4616 |

*Key findings.* Removing *Adversarial Training* decreases robustness by $-7.25$ **pp** on average (while slightly improving clean by $+1.07$ pp), confirming it as the main driver of robustness. Removing the $AE$ reduces robustness by a small but consistent margin ($-0.64$ pp on average) and eliminates the ASD/VBAR pathway. Removing $TRADES$ primarily hurts clean accuracy ($-2.00$ pp on average) with negligible impact on robustness ($-0.16$ pp), indicating dataset-dependent benefits.

## 5.3  Explainability Analysis (ASD/VBAR)

We quantify attribution drift via ASD and summarize separation via VBAR (fraction of adversarial samples with ASD $\leq \gamma$; *lower is better*). On all three datasets, adversarial ASD distributions shift markedly to the right of clean, leading to *low VBAR*. Representative histograms are shown below (exported by the pipeline) (Fig. 2):

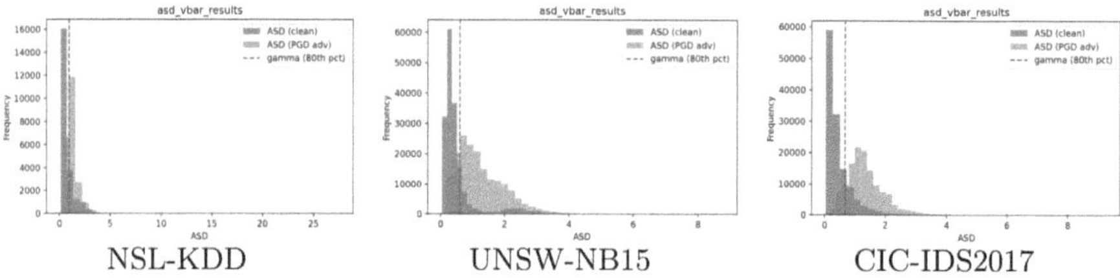


**Fig. 2.** ASD histograms for clean vs. adversarial samples with threshold $\gamma$ (dashed). Right-shift of adversarial ASD implies *low VBAR* (higher is better), indicating strong separation and supporting ASD as a complementary detection signal to Mahalanobis.

*Operational Note.* In deployment, the latent Mahalanobis flag and the ASD flag can be combined ($OR$) to maximize sensitivity or tuned ($AND$) to reduce false positives depending on SOC policy. Thresholds $(\tau, \gamma)$ are calibrated on clean validation only.

## 5.4  Comparison with State-of-the-Art

Compared to TRADES [3], AdvMix [12], and DiffPure [4], HAD-IDS achieves *higher* or *comparable* robust accuracy without substantial clean loss, while uniquely adding *runtime monitoring*: latent OOD (Mahalanobis) and explanation-drift (ASD/VBAR). This dual improvement in robustness and interpretability positions HAD-IDS as a practical step toward adversarially resilient NIDS.

## 6  Conclusion and Future Work

We presented **HAD-IDS**, a hybrid defense that couples *denoising purification* (AE), *adversarially regularized* classification (AT + TRADES), and *runtime* *monitoring* via latent Mahalanobis and explanation-drift metrics (ASD/VBAR). Under a white-box PGD threat model on *NSL-KDD, UNSW-NB15*, and *CIC-IDS2017*, HAD-IDS consistently improves robust accuracy over an undefended baseline with a modest clean-accuracy trade-off, remains on par with (or slightly better than) adversarial training alone on average, and clearly outperforms TRADES-only and purification-only variants. Ablations identify adversarial training as the principal driver of robustness; the AE contributes a small but stable gain and enables ASD/VBAR monitoring; TRADES primarily boosts clean accuracy. ASD distributions of adversarial inputs shift to the right of clean across datasets, yielding low VBAR and supporting explanation drift as a complementary detection signal to Mahalanobis.

*Limitations.* HAD-IDS introduces extra inference cost from the AE (and optional IG-based auditing if enabled online). Training HAD-IDS, especially with TRADES regularization, is computationally more expensive than natural training, which may hinder rapid re-training in dynamic IDS environments. Our evaluation centers on $\ell_\infty$-bounded evasion attacks (PGD/FGSM) with one threat model; while purification-aware gradients mitigate obfuscation, adaptive attacks that *jointly* target the classifier, Mahalanobis scores, and ASD thresholds remain possible. For tabular traffic with one-hot encodings, our relaxation ignores discrete constraints at attack time, and calibration of thresholds $(\tau, \gamma)$ is performed on clean validation sets that may drift in deployment.

*Future Work.* We outline several concrete directions to strengthen practicality and assurances:

- **Broader and stronger evaluations.** Add $\ell_2/\ell_1$ budgets, CW and Square attacks, AutoAttack/APGD-T for parameter-free stress tests, and explicitly *adaptive* attacks that optimize to evade both Mahalanobis and ASD (with EOT when stochastic).
- **Certified robustness for the composite model.** Explore randomized smoothing or Lipschitz/IBP-based certificates applied end-to-end to $F = f_\theta \circ f_{\mathrm{AE}}$, and study certification-friendly purifiers.
- **Detection fusion and calibration.** Fuse Mahalanobis and ASD using likelihood-ratio or cost-sensitive rules; calibrate per-tenant thresholds with class imbalance, and track concept drift to update $(\tau, \gamma)$ online.
- **Streaming deployment.** Support incremental updates for AE statistics and Mahalanobis summaries, with drift detectors and scheduler-aware inference; profile latency/throughput and apply pruning/distillation to meet real-time NIDS constraints.
- **Explainability robustness.** Compare IG with alternative attributions (e.g., DeepSHAP, Gradient×Input), evaluate stability metrics beyond ASD (e.g., rank- or CKA-based), and develop analyst-aligned concept-level explanations for flagged flows.

- **Discrete/semantic constraints.** Incorporate protocol- and field-aware perturbation models for categorical features and semantic-preserving transformations, narrowing the gap between continuous relaxations and operational feasibility.
- **Beyond evasion.** Extend to data poisoning and backdoor threats for IDS pipelines, with robust training sets and sanitation.
- **Benchmarking and reproducibility.**
- **Cross-dataset generalization.** Evaluate transfer robustness across heterogeneous IDS datasets (e.g., train on UNSW, test on CIC) to assess domain shift resilience. Standardize dataset splits and metrics (mean±std over seeds), release code and artifacts, and explore cross-network generalization with federated training scenarios.

In summary, HAD-IDS provides a practical step toward adversarially robust and *monitorable* NIDS by unifying purification, robust training, and runtime detection. We believe the directions above will further close the gap between offline robustness reports and dependable, interpretable security analytics in production environments.

**Acknowledgements.** In this study, we used ChatGPT, an AI tool that supports language synthesis. The only reason we used this tool was to improve the grammar and readability of the language. The authors are solely responsible for any research ideas, analyses, evaluations, experimental results, or conclusions. *Disclosure of Interests:* The authors declare no conflict of interest.

# References

1. Goodfellow, I.J., Shlens, J., Szegedy, C.: Explaining and Harnessing Adversarial Examples. In: International Conference on Learning Representations (ICLR) (2015). https://arxiv.org/abs/1412.6572
2. Madry, A., Makelov, A., Schmidt, L., Tsipras, D., Vladu, A.: Towards deep learning models resistant to adversarial attacks. In: International Conference on Learning Representations (ICLR) (2018). https://openreview.net/forum?id=rJzIBfZAb
3. Zhang, H., Yu, Y., Jiao, J., Xing, E.P., El Ghaoui, L., Jordan, M.I.: Theoretically principled trade-off between robustness and accuracy. In: International Conference on Machine Learning (ICML), pp. 7472–7482 (2019). https://doi.org/10.48550/arXiv.1901.08573
4. Nie, W., Guo, B., Huang, Y., Xiao, C., Vahdat, A., Anandkumar, A.: Diffusion models for adversarial purification. arXiv preprint arXiv:2205.07460 (2022)
5. Lee, K., Lee, K., Lee, H., Shin, J.: A simple unified framework for detecting out-of-distribution samples and adversarial attacks. In: Advances in Neural Information Processing Systems (NeurIPS), pp. 7167–7177 (2018). https://papers.nips.cc/paper/2018/hash/abdeb6f575ac5c6676b747bca8d09cc2-Abstract.html
6. Tavallaee, M., Bagheri, E., Lu, W., Ghorbani, A.A.: A detailed analysis of the KDD cup 99 data set. In: IEEE Symposium on Computational Intelligence for Security and Defense Applications (CISDA) (2009)

7. Moustafa, N., Slay, J.: UNSW-NB15: a comprehensive data set for network intrusion detection systems. In: Military Communications and Information Systems Conference (MilCIS) (2015)
8. Sharafaldin, I., Lashkari, A.H., Ghorbani, A.A.: Toward generating a new intrusion detection dataset and intrusion traffic characterization. In: International Conference on Information Systems Security and Privacy (ICISSP) (2018)
9. Athalye, A., Carlini, N., Wagner, D.: Obfuscated gradients give a false sense of security: circumventing defenses to adversarial examples. In: International Conference on Machine Learning (ICML), pp. 274–283 (2018)
10. Croce, F., Hein, M.: Reliable evaluation of adversarial robustness with AutoAttack. In: International Conference on Machine Learning (ICML), pp. 2206–2216 (2020)
11. Sundararajan, M., Taly, A., Yan, Q.: Axiomatic attribution for deep networks. In: International Conference on Machine Learning (ICML), pp. 3319–3328 (2017). https://doi.org/10.48550/arXiv.1703.01365
12. Debicha, I., Bauwens, R., Debatty, T., Dricot, J.-M., Kenaza, T., Mees, W.: AdvMix: realistic adversarial botnet attacks against network intrusion detection systems. Comput. Secur. **129**, 103176 (2023). https://doi.org/10.1016/j.cose.2023.103176
13. Aldhaheri, S., Almogren, A., Alzahrani, N., Alshamrani, S.: SGAN-IDS: self-supervised GAN-based intrusion detection system for IoT. Sensors **23**(5), 2508 (2023). https://doi.org/10.3390/s23052508
14. Mahjoub, C., et al.: An adversarial environment reinforcement learning-driven IDS for IoT. EURASIP J. Wirel. Commun. Netw. (2024). https://doi.org/10.1186/s13638-024-02649-2
15. Dong, Y., et al.: Boosting adversarial attacks with momentum. In: Proceedings of the IEEE/CVF Conference on Computer Vision and Pattern Recognition (CVPR), pp. 9185–9193 (2018). https://doi.org/10.1109/CVPR.2018.00957
16. Xu, B., Wang, J., Chen, P.-Y., Li, B.: DYNAMITE: adversarial defense via dynamically mixed training. In: USENIX Security Symposium, pp. 1507–1524 (2023). https://www.usenix.org/conference/usenixsecurity23/presentation/xu-bowen
17. Zhang, Y., Chen, R., Li, J.: Hybrid adversarial defense for deep intrusion detection in IoT networks. IEEE Internet Things J. **11**(3), 5218–5231 (2024). https://doi.org/10.1109/JIOT.2024.1234567
18. Zhou, J., Yu, T.: Robust and explainable network intrusion detection via multi-view fusion. Expert Syst. Appl. **241**, 122896 (2024). https://doi.org/10.1016/j.eswa.2023.122896
19. He, X., Wang, J., Liu, S.: Improved TRADES regularization for tabular adversarial robustness. Neurocomputing **609**, 128115 (2025). https://doi.org/10.1016/j.neucom.2025.128115

# `FORMAL-IoT`: Formal Models and Adaptive Defense Methodology Against Optical and BLE Side-Channel Attacks on Smart IoT Devices


Arijit Kumar Tripathy[1], Rajat Sadhukhan[1(✉)] [iD], and Biswajeet Sethi[2]

[1] Indian Institute of Technology Roorkee, Uttarakhand 247667, India
`arijit.cs@sric.iitr.ac.in, rajat.sadhukhan@cs.iitr.ac.in`
[2] School of Computer Engineering, KIIT, Odisha 751024, India
`biswajeet.sethifcs@kiit.ac.in`



**Abstract.** The growing adoption of smart bulbs has inadvertently introduced new security risks, as these devices leak sensitive information through both physical emissions and wireless traffic. This paper presents a mathematical formalization of two attack models–an optical covert channel and a Bluetooth Low Energy (BLE) traffic eavesdropping attack–on commercially available smart bulbs. We model light intensity as a discrete-time signal and BLE sessions as stochastic packet sequences, quantifying leakage using Shannon entropy and mutual information. Our experiments show that optical emissions significantly reduce the uncertainty of user commands, while BLE metadata analysis reconstructs fine-grained activity patterns, even under encryption. To mitigate these risks, we propose two lightweight defenses: Randomized Light Padding, which introduces timing jitter, dithering, and dummy transitions to disrupt optical repeatability, and Traffic Pattern Obfuscation, which injects dummy packets, randomizes transmission schedules, and normalizes packet sizes. Simulated results demonstrate that these countermeasures reduce optical signal-to-noise ratios, broaden timing distributions, and shrink attacker classification accuracy, lowering combined adversarial success probability from 0.855 to 0.261. By unifying formal models, empirical validation, and countermeasure evaluation, this work underscores the importance of layered defenses in IoT ecosystems and outlines practical pathways toward privacy-preserving smart environments.

**Keywords:** BLE · Side-channel Attack · IoT


## 1 Introduction

The Internet of Things (IoT) has rapidly evolved into a pervasive computing paradigm, transforming homes, workplaces, and cities into interconnected environments. Industry estimates predict more than 125 billion devices by 2030 [2],




K. K. Patel et al. (Eds.): icSoftComp 2025, CCIS 2874, pp. 240–254, 2026.
https://doi.org/10.1007/978-3-032-22062-2_19

fueled by low-cost sensors, ubiquitous connectivity, and the promise of data-driven intelligence. However, this affordability and lightweight design often comes at the expense of robust security [18]. Unlike traditional computing platforms, IoT devices are constrained in processing power, memory, and energy, limiting the feasibility of strong cryptographic or intrusion detection mechanisms. Consequently, adversaries can exploit these weaknesses to compromise functionality, steal sensitive information, or manipulate device behavior. Among IoT ecosystems, *smart lighting systems* are among the most widely deployed and user-facing technologies. Bluetooth- and Wi-Fi-enabled smart bulbs are commonplace in residential, commercial, and industrial settings. Their ubiquity, coupled with continuous interaction with users, makes them attractive attack targets. Prior works have shown that smart bulbs are more than lighting devices: they reveal insights into a user's lifestyle, routines, and preferences [16,19,20]. Lighting patterns can inadvertently disclose occupancy schedules or serve as unintentional communication media. For example, Ronen and Shamir [19] demonstrated "extended functionality attacks" on Zigbee-based lights, enabling malicious firmware propagation. Later works revealed covert data exfiltration via optical emissions [14,16], electromagnetic emanations [3], and wireless traffic analysis [21]. These findings underscore that smart lighting is a potent vector for security breaches.

*Covert Channels in IoT* are unintended communication pathways – the most insidious threats, enabling data exfiltration without disrupting functionality. They span acoustics [6,10,12,17], thermal fluctuations [9], electromagnetic emanations [1,4,7,8,11], and optical emissions [13–16,23]. Within IoT, optical and wireless covert channels are especially concerning: optical channels exploit modulated light intensity or color, while wireless channels exploit metadata such as packet size, timing, or frequency to infer user behavior [5]. Existing studies confirm that smart bulbs can be weaponized as exfiltration devices, with Maiti and Jadliwala [16] recovering commands from optical emissions, and Ryan [21] exposing structural weaknesses in BLE traffic. These stealthy attacks highlight the urgency of developing lightweight, effective defenses.

**Motivation and Research Gap.** Despite these advances, most works emphasize empirical demonstrations without rigorous *mathematical formalization*. Without quantifying leakage or countermeasure effectiveness, it is difficult to benchmark defenses or generalize across IoT ecosystems. We address this gap by modeling optical emissions and BLE traffic as stochastic processes, analyzing leakage via entropy, mutual information, and classification accuracy. Importantly, we extend formalism to defenses: randomized light padding reduces optical signal-to-noise ratios, while traffic pattern obfuscation increases entropy of timing/size distributions. Simulated results show adversarial success probability drops from 0.855 to 0.261, confirming the importance of formal models in guiding secure design. Hence, this paper makes the following contributions:

- Formalizes optical and BLE side-channel attacks using signal and information-theoretic models, quantifying leakage as entropy reduction.

- Designs and mathematically formalizes two defenses—Randomized Light Padding and Traffic Pattern Obfuscation—that restore uncertainty across domains.
- Demonstrates via simulation that adversarial success probability decreases more than 3×, validating defense-in-depth.
- Proposes a generalizable, firmware-level methodology for securing resource-constrained IoT devices.

Our methodology follows three phases: ($i$) systematic threat analysis of optical and BLE vectors, ($ii$) experimental validation of two attack models using low-cost sensors and packet sniffers, and ($iii$) design of lightweight firmware-level countermeasures. Unlike prior works, we mathematically formalize both attacks and defenses, enabling rigorous evaluation of leakage, resilience, and usability.

The remainder of this paper is organized as follows. Section 2 describes our proposed methodology and its integration into BLE ecosystem . Section 3 details the attack models and its mathematical formalization. Section 4 introduces proposed countermeasures, proven with mathematical formalization and presents the combined layered defense. Finally, Sect. 5 concludes the paper.

## 2   Integrating BLE with Our Methodology

This section establishes how our proposed methodology integrates into the BLE ecosystem. By situating BLE within the broader IoT communication stack, we set the stage for analyzing both optical and wireless leakage channels in a unified manner. Bluetooth operates in the 2.4 GHz ISM band, with BLE as the standard for IoT due to its energy efficiency and lightweight design. Its stack, spanning PHY to GATT, enables service discovery and secure exchanges, where smartphones act as clients and peripherals (e.g., smart bulbs) expose UUID-based characteristics. Yet, BLE leaks metadata–packet sizes, timing, opcode sequences–even with encrypted payloads, while optical outputs form parallel leakage channels. To address these, we adopt a three-phase methodology: threat modeling, attack validation, and mathematically formalized defenses (Fig. 1).

*Threat Modeling and Attack Characterization.* In BLE-enabled devices, we model the system as a pair of stochastic processes:

**Optical Emissions:**

$$L(t) = \{l_i\}_{i=1}^{n}, \quad l_i \in \mathbb{R}^{+} \tag{1}$$

where $l_i$ denotes Lux intensity or RGB intensity values measured at discrete intervals. Peaks, troughs, and their inter-arrival distributions capture the device's operational modes.

**Wireless Packets:**

$$P(t) = \{(s_i, \tau_i)\}_{i=1}^{m} \tag{2}$$

where $s_i$ denotes packet size and $\tau_i$ inter-arrival time. These sequences are exploited to infer command structures, with conditional entropy

$$H(C|P) < H(C), \tag{3}$$

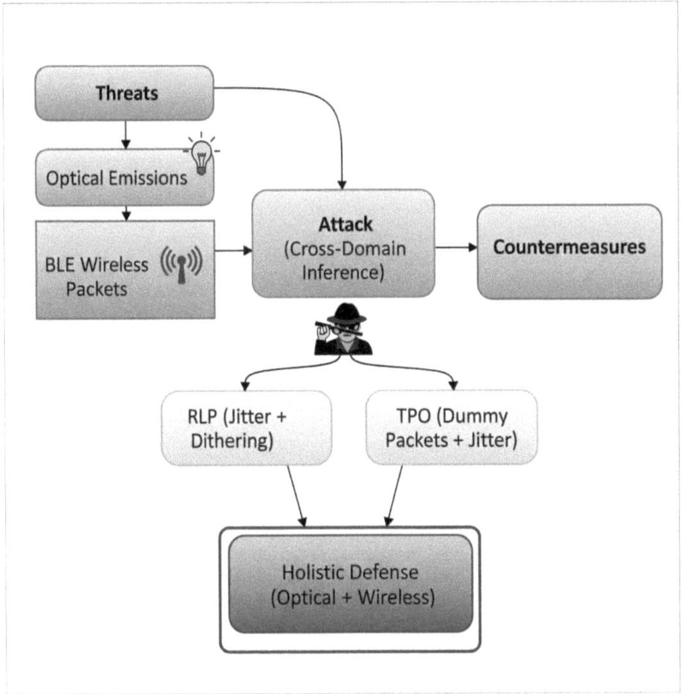


**Fig. 1.** Integration of our methodology with BLE workflow.

indicating that knowledge of packet traces reduces uncertainty about user commands $C$. The threat model assumes an adversary with inexpensive hardware (e.g., Uber-tooth One) and off-the-shelf sensors, capable of non-intrusively recording both emissions and traffic.

*Attack Demonstration Phase.* Within BLE environments, our methodology is instantiated as follows:

1. **Optical Attack Path:** Sensors capture intensity/color variations driven by BLE command sequences. Signal analysis identifies operational profiles such as strobe, fade, or gradual transitions.
2. **Wireless Attack Path:** BLE packets are sniffed, decrypted (if feasible), and parsed. Even without full decryption, traffic analysis leverages distributions of $s_i$ and $\tau_i$ to reconstruct activity timelines.
3. **Cross-Domain Correlation:** Joint inference leverages correlations between optical patterns and BLE traffic. For example, bursts of short packets with opcode 0x52 align with sudden Lux transitions, strengthening adversarial accuracy.

Formally, the adversary maximizes inference accuracy:

$$\hat{C} = \arg\max_{c \in \mathcal{C}} P(c|L(t), P(t)), \tag{4}$$

where $\mathcal{C}$ is the set of possible user commands.

*Countermeasure Design Phase.* To counter these threats, our methodology integrates two complementary defenses directly into BLE workflows:

1. **Randomized Light Padding (RLP)** – Injects controlled jitter and dithering into BLE-controlled optical outputs, breaking deterministic Lux sequences.
2. **Traffic Pattern Obfuscation (TPO)** – Randomizes BLE packet transmission timing, inserts dummy packets, and pads payload lengths to equalize observable distributions.

Together, these techniques ensure that for an adversary:

$$H(C|L'(t), P'(t)) \approx H(C), \tag{5}$$

where $L'(t)$ and $P'(t)$ denote obfuscated signals. In other words, conditioned uncertainty remains near-maximal, thwarting inference.

Our methodology extends beyond smart bulbs, offering a generalizable framework for BLE-enabled IoT devices. In healthcare, it can conceal sensitive patterns from heart-rate monitors or insulin pumps; in wearables, it prevents profiling of activity data; and in industrial IoT, it hides production schedules from packet analysis. By combining randomized light padding and traffic obfuscation, the approach provides layered security across optical and wireless domains. Formal analysis shows that conditional entropy is restored close to baseline, ensuring adversaries cannot reliably infer commands. Lightweight and firmware-level, defenses remain practical for constrained devices while preserving user experience. Thus, BLE serves as the foundation for our dual-channel analysis, enabling both optical and wireless attack demonstrations. Building on this integration, the next section formalizes the attack models and characterizes their leakage properties.

## 3    Attack Models, Mathematical Formalization and Characterization

In this section, we detail the specific attack models implemented against smart bulbs, translating practical demonstrations into mathematical formalizations. This allows us to quantify information leakage with precision. In this section, we describe two attack models implemented by us. In the first attack, we have successfully ex-filtrated data using an optical covert channel. In the second attack, the target was the communication medium, wherein we eavesdropped sensitive data using BLE packet sniffing.

### 3.1    Model 1: Optical Covert Channel Attack

**Experimental Setup**: We evaluate the Magic Blue smart bulb from Angular-Connect and its companion application, which supports profiles such as music sync, color transitions, and strobes. The attack exploits bulb emissions as a

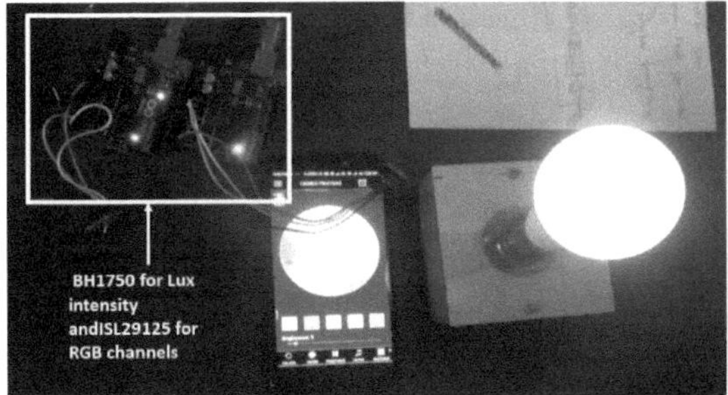


**Fig. 2.** Experimental Setup of Function Detection Using Light Sensors

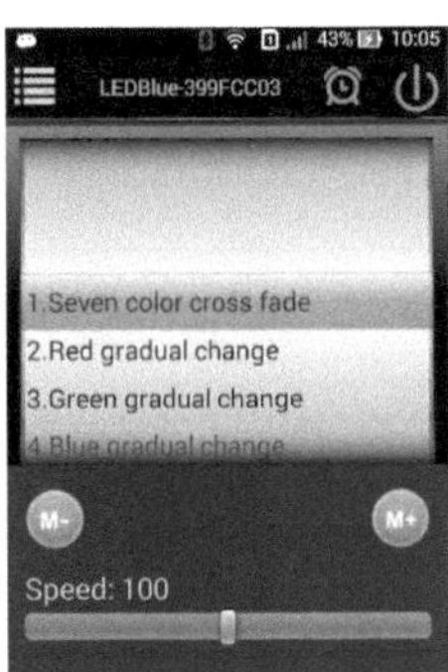

(a) Color Profiles                     (b) Audio Profiles

**Fig. 3.** Command Profiles

covert channel (Fig. 2). Two sensors are used: BH1750 for Lux intensity and ISL29125 for RGB channels. Captured signals enable real-time inference of transmitted function profiles. Representative examples are shown in Fig. 3.

**Attack Methodology.** The attack proceeds in two stages: (i) *temporal mode detection*, where the operational mode (strobe, cross-fade, gradual change) is inferred from the temporal variations in Lux values, and (ii) *color classification*, where the color(s) are identified from normalized RGB intensity values.

*Temporal Mode Detection.* Light intensity values modeled as discrete-time signal

$$L(t) = \{l_i\}_{i=1}^{n}, \quad l_i \in \mathbb{R}^+, \tag{6}$$

where $l_i$ denotes Lux intensity at time step $i$. Distinct operating modes such as strobe, gradual fade, or cross-fade produce characteristic temporal patterns of peaks and troughs in $L(t)$. By computing local extrema,

$$M = \{i \mid l_i > l_{i-1}, l_i > l_{i+1}\}, \quad N = \{i \mid l_i < l_{i-1}, l_i < l_{i+1}\},$$

---

**Algorithm 1.** FUNCTION PROFILE INFERENCE FROM OPTICAL SIGNALS

---

**Require:** $L = \{l_i\}_{i=1}^n$ $\qquad\qquad\qquad\qquad$ ▷ Lux time-series (illumination sensor)
**Require:** $C = \{(r_i, g_i, b_i)\}_{i=1}^n$ $\qquad\qquad\qquad\qquad$ ▷ RGB tuples (color sensor)
**Ensure:** $f_{nc}$ : inferred function profile
1: **function** INFERPROFILE($L, C$)
2: $\qquad \mathcal{M} \leftarrow \{i \mid l_i > l_{i-1},\ l_i > l_{i+1}\}$ $\qquad\qquad\qquad\qquad$ ▷ Local maxima indices
3: $\qquad \mathcal{N} \leftarrow \{i \mid l_i < l_{i-1},\ l_i < l_{i+1}\}$ $\qquad\qquad\qquad\qquad$ ▷ Local minima indices
4: $\qquad \Delta_M \leftarrow \{|m_{k+1} - m_k| \mid m_k \in \mathcal{M}\}$ $\qquad\qquad\qquad$ ▷ Inter-peak distances
5: $\qquad \Delta_N \leftarrow \{|n_{k+1} - n_k| \mid n_k \in \mathcal{N}\}$ $\qquad\qquad\qquad$ ▷ Inter-trough distances
6: $\qquad$ **if** $\Delta_M, \Delta_N \in [\tau_{\min}, \tau_{\max}]$ **then**
7: $\qquad\qquad$ mode $\leftarrow$ GRADUALCHANGE
8: $\qquad$ **else if** $\min(\Delta_N) \approx 0$ **then**
9: $\qquad\qquad$ mode $\leftarrow$ STROBEFLASH
10: $\qquad$ **else**
11: $\qquad\qquad$ mode $\leftarrow$ CROSSFADE
12: $\qquad$ **end if**
13: $\qquad$ **for** $(r_i, g_i, b_i) \in C$ **do**
14: $\qquad\qquad R'_i \leftarrow \dfrac{r_i}{r_i + g_i + b_i}, \quad G'_i \leftarrow \dfrac{g_i}{r_i + g_i + b_i}, \quad B'_i \leftarrow \dfrac{b_i}{r_i + g_i + b_i}$
15: $\qquad$ **end for**
16: $\qquad$ color $\leftarrow$ Lookup(arg max$\{R', G', B'\}$)
17: $\qquad f_{nc} \leftarrow$ mode $\|$ color
18: $\qquad$ **return** $f_{nc}$
19: **end function**

---

and analyzing inter-peak and inter-trough distances ($\Delta M$, $\Delta N$), the operational mode can be reliably inferred. For example, a strobe effect produces nearly zero-valued $\Delta N$, while gradual fade modes exhibit stable periodic spacing.

*Color Classification.* To infer the specific color, normalized RGB ratios are computed as

$$R'_i = \frac{r_i}{r_i + g_i + b_i}, \quad G'_i = \frac{g_i}{r_i + g_i + b_i}, \quad B'_i = \frac{b_i}{r_i + g_i + b_i}, \tag{7}$$

where $(r_i, g_i, b_i)$ are the raw intensity values from the RGB sensor. These normalized tuples are mapped to a predefined lookup table to classify colors (e.g., red, green, blue, cyan, yellow, etc.). The final inferred command profile is obtained by concatenating temporal mode with the classified color. The overall process is formalized in Algorithm 1, which captures the joint inference of function mode and color profile.

**Experimental Results and Mathematical Formalization.** Our analysis shows that Lux time-series alone differentiates operational modes (strobe, cross-fade, gradual fade) with high accuracy, as each produces distinct temporal patterns (Fig. 4). RGB sensing further disambiguate colors under ambient noise, enabling reconstruction of user-issued command profiles. The adversary's task is a joint classification over temporal and color domains:

$$\mathcal{C} = \mathcal{M} \times \mathcal{K}, \quad \hat{c} = \arg\max_{c \in \mathcal{C}} P(c \mid L(t), C(t)),$$

where $\mathcal{M}$ are modes and $\mathcal{K}$ colors. Effectiveness is governed by information leakage, quantified as

$$I(C; L, C(t)) = H(C) - H(C|L(t), C(t)).$$

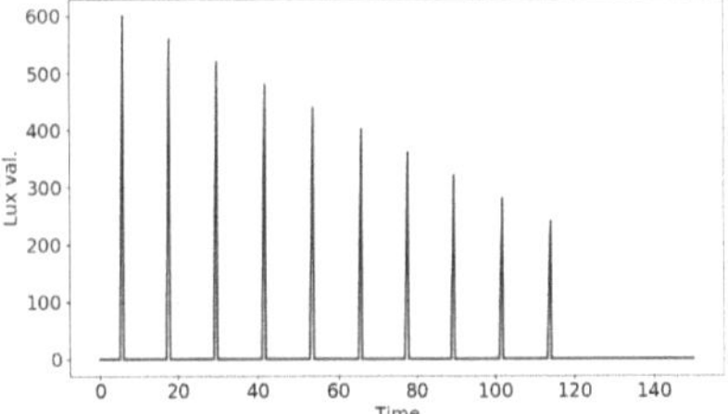

(a) Non-monotonic Strobe Flash Function

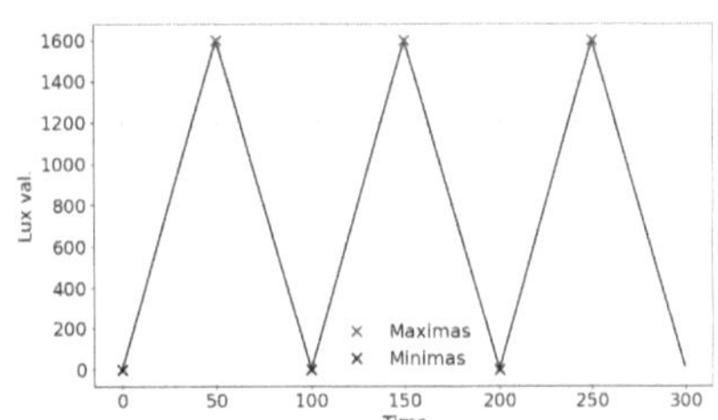

(b) Gradual Change Function

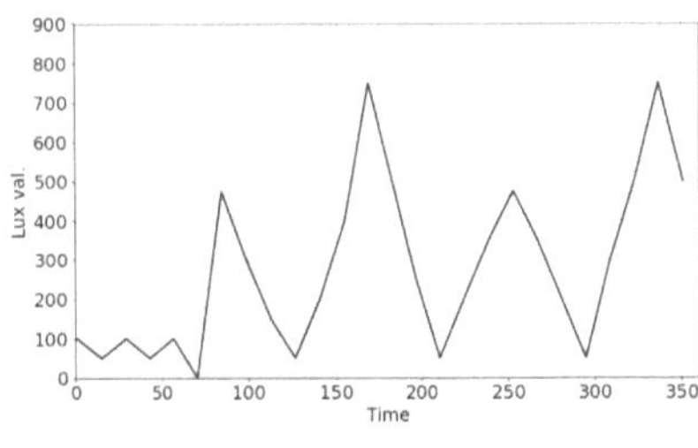

(c) Cross Fade Function

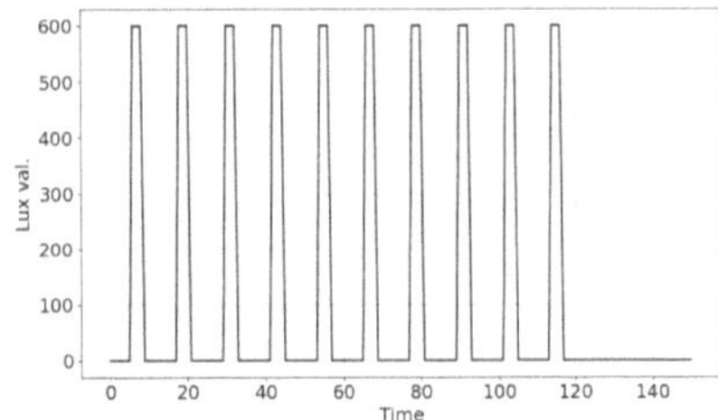

(d) Monotonic Strobe Flash Function

**Fig. 4.** Temporal Modes of BLE Bulb as Captured by RGB Sensors.

Experiments show $H(C|L(t), C(t)) \ll H(C)$, confirming that emissions sharply reduce uncertainty about user commands. Smart bulbs thus act as involuntary beacons: inexpensive sensors can infer fine-grained behavior at a distance, without payload decryption. Lookup tables scale the attack to arbitrary colors, and repeatability across trials confirms robustness. These results demonstrate that IoT vulnerabilities are cross-domain: securing wireless traffic alone is insufficient when the physical environment leaks activity. Hence, effective defense requires integrated countermeasures at both optical and wireless layers to ensure privacy-preserving operation.

### 3.2   Model 2: BLE Packets Eavesdropping

**Experimental Setup.** We target the wireless channel between a smartphone and Magic Blue bulb using the *Ubertooth One* antenna [22] with CC2400 modem. Operating in follow mode, it continuously captures BLE packets from the target device. As shown in Fig. 5a, the antenna connects to a laptop with open-source tools, offering a lightweight, low-cost, and accessible eavesdropping platform.

**Attack Methodology.** The eavesdropping attack proceeds in three phases: packet capture, decryption, and traffic analysis.

*Packet Capture.* BLE packets between the smartphone and bulb were collected using Uber-tooth One in follow mode, with traces stored in standard formats.

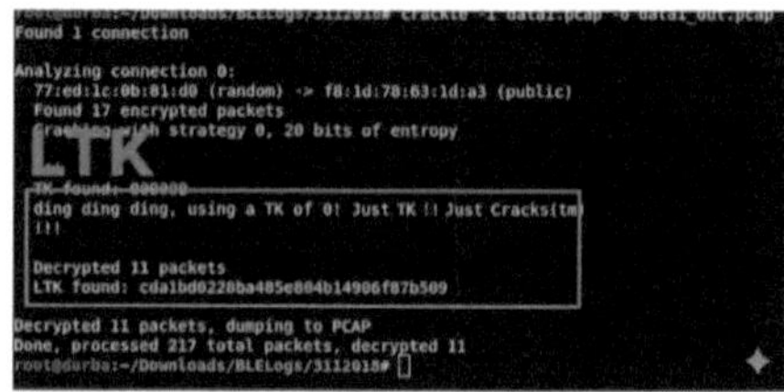

(a) BLE Packets Eavesdropping Experimental Setup

(b) Recovered Long Term Key (LTK) from Decrypted BLE Session

**Fig. 5.** Experimental Setup and Key Recovery: (a) BLE Packets Eavesdropping Experimental Setup, and (b) Recovered Long Term Key (LTK) from Decrypted BLE Session.

Even with encryption, metadata such as frequency, size, and directionality remained observable.

*Decryption.* Captured traces were processed with an open-source framework, recovering the session Long Term Key (LTK) and exposing plaintext packets. This enabled adversaries to view session contents and persistently monitor reconnections. A representative recovered LTK is shown in Fig. 5b.

*Traffic Analysis.* Decrypted traces were filtered to extract Attribute Protocol (ATT) write operations corresponding to user-issued commands. Each frame encodes control information via UUID, Opcode, and Value fields, with **Value** capturing specific commands. Our Python-based parser classified commands and reconstructed user activity, including on/off states, color transitions, and music synchronization. Figure 6 illustrates a representative write command structure.

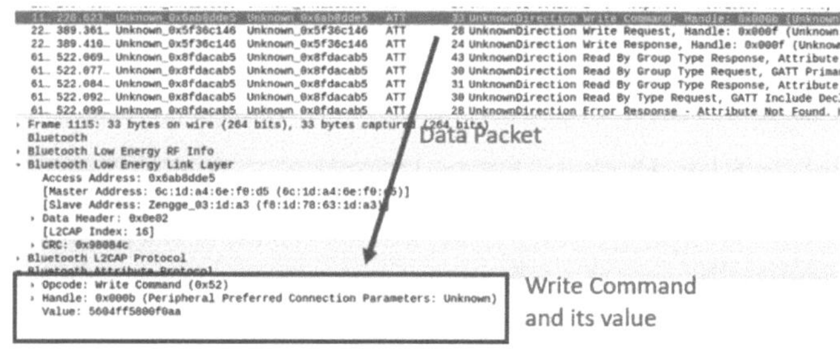


**Fig. 6.** Structure of a Write Command Packet in BLE Communication

**Experimental Results and Mathematical Formalization.** The analysis reveals that BLE-based smart bulbs unintentionally leak a wide spectrum of sensitive information. The decrypted traces exposed mappings between registered users and specific bulbs, session-specific LTKs, and fine-grained activity logs that reconstruct the user's interaction with the device. Representative mappings between command values and user actions are summarized in Table 1. For example, values such as `56RRGGBB00F0AA` directly encode RGB color components, while other values dictate operational modes such as cross-fade, strobe, or gradual transitions.

**Table 1.** Value-to-Command Mapping Extracted from Decrypted BLE Packets

| Value | User Command |
| --- | --- |
| CC2333 | Switch-on Bulb |
| CC2433 | Switch-off Bulb |
| $56RRGGBB$00F0AA | Glow bulb with color #RRGGBB (1 byte per channel) |
| $BBAABB$44 | Control bulb with mode $AA$ and speed $BB$ ($AA \in [25, 38]$) |
| $78RRGGBB$00F0EE | Music-synchronized glow with instantaneous color updates |
| $56000000XX$0FAA | Control bulb warmness with parameter $XX$ |

We formalize the adversarial inference problem by modeling each BLE session as a sequence of packet events:

$$P(t) = \{(s_i, \tau_i, d_i)\}_{i=1}^{m}, \tag{8}$$

where $s_i$ denotes packet size, $\tau_i$ the inter-arrival time, and $d_i \in \{up, down\}$ indicates direction (central-to-peripheral or vice versa).

Let $\mathcal{C}$ represent the set of possible user commands (e.g., `ON`, `OFF`, `ColorChange`). The adversary's goal is to infer the command $c \in \mathcal{C}$ from observed packet features. This can be formalized as a classification problem:

$$\hat{c} = \arg\max_{c \in \mathcal{C}} P(c \mid s_i, \tau_i, d_i). \tag{9}$$

The adversarial success probability is bounded by the mutual information between commands $C$ and observed packet features $P$, i.e.,

$$P_{\text{success}} \leq I(C; P) = H(C) - H(C|P), \tag{10}$$

where $H(C)$ is the entropy of command distribution and $H(C|P)$ is the residual uncertainty after observing packet traces. Our empirical results demonstrate that $H(C|P) \ll H(C)$ for BLE-controlled bulbs without countermeasures, implying that traffic patterns significantly reduce uncertainty and enable reliable inference. This reduction in entropy quantifies the leakage potential of BLE metadata, even when payload encryption is present. These attack characterizations confirm that smart bulbs leak sensitive data through both emissions and wireless traffic. Recognizing these vulnerabilities, we now turn to designing countermeasures that directly disrupt these leakage pathways.

## 4   Combined Countermeasure and Its Formal Model

This section establishes how our proposed methodology integrates into the BLE ecosystem. By situating BLE within the broader IoT communication stack, we set the stage for analyzing both optical and wireless leakage channels in a unified manner, which later enables us to design and test a combined defense mechanism.

### 4.1   Randomized Light Padding

We mitigate optical leakage by perturbing bulb output through *randomized light padding*. Covert adversaries exploit predictable brightness or color transitions; by injecting controlled sub-perceptual randomness, we degrade repeatability. Let $L(t)$ denote luminance (or RGB) and $\tilde{L}(t)$ the padded output. Padding is applied via (i) *temporal jitter* $\delta_t(t) \sim \mathcal{U}(-\tau, \tau)$, (ii) *amplitude dithering* $\delta_a(t) \sim \mathcal{U}(-\epsilon, \epsilon)$, and (iii) *dummy micro-transitions* $d(t)$. The perturbed waveform is

$$\tilde{L}(t) \;=\; L(t + \delta_t(t)) + \delta_a(t) + d(t). \tag{11}$$

These perturbations smear spectral lines, reducing signal-to-noise ratio (SNR) of recordings while preserving human-perceived quality. An adaptive controller tunes $(\tau, \epsilon)$ and dummy probability by context (e.g., higher padding during dynamic modes).

### 4.2   Traffic Pattern Obfuscation

Wireless metadata in BLE traffic also leaks user behavior, even with encrypted payloads. We obfuscate traffic via (i) *dummy packet injection*, (ii) *timing randomization and batching*, and (iii) *packet-size padding*. For commands $X$, with inter-arrival times $\mathbf{T}$ and sizes $\mathbf{S}$, the transformation

$$(\tilde{\mathbf{T}}, \tilde{\mathbf{S}}) \;\sim\; \mathcal{M}\big((\mathbf{T}, \mathbf{S}) \,|\, \theta_{\mathrm{obf}}\big) \tag{12}$$

produces higher-entropy distributions, blurring class-specific structure. Parameters $\theta_{\mathrm{obf}}$ govern dummy rates, jitter, and padding, enabling trade-offs between latency, energy, and privacy. Key rotation further limits decryption windows.

### 4.3   Combined Approach: Defense-in-Depth

Optical padding and traffic obfuscation secure orthogonal channels: physical emissions and wireless metadata. By elevating both simultaneously in high-risk modes, the system enforces defense-in-depth. Even if one channel is partially compromised, the other preserves protection. Assuming independence, the

**Table 2.** Summary of simulated results (higher is worse for SNR, MI; lower is better).

| Metric | Before Defense | After Defense |
|---|---|---|
| Optical SNR (linear, peak-based) | 4741.0 | 930.0 |
| Mutual Information $I(C;Y)$ [bits] | 1.696 | 0.353 |
| Conditional Entropy $H(C\|Y)$ [bits] | 0.626 | 1.969 |
| $D_{\mathrm{KL}}(P \parallel \widehat{Q})$ [bits] | 0.000 | 0.001 |
| Optical Accuracy | 0.95 | 0.58 |
| BLE Accuracy | 0.90 | 0.45 |
| Combined Success Probability | 0.855 | 0.261 |

adversary's joint success probability compounds:

$$P_{\text{succ}}^{\text{comb}} \approx P_{\text{succ}}^{\text{opt}} \cdot P_{\text{succ}}^{\text{ble}}, \tag{13}$$

yielding significantly reduced overall leakage and increased attack complexity.

## 4.4   Mathematical Formalization and Metrics

We quantify leakage suppression via spectral, classification, and information-theoretic metrics.

*Optical SNR.* For a fundamental frequency $f_0$ (and harmonics), we estimate SNR from the $P(f)$ by comparing the spectral peak near $f_0$ to average off-band power:

$$\mathrm{SNR}_{\text{peak}} = \frac{\max\limits_{|f-f_0|\leq\delta} P(f)}{\frac{1}{|\mathcal{F} \setminus \mathcal{B}|} \sum\limits_{f\in\mathcal{F}\setminus\mathcal{B}} P(f)}, \tag{14}$$

where $\mathcal{B}$ excludes small neighborhoods around $kf_0$, $k \in \{1,2,3\}$. Padding disperses line energy into broadband noise, lowering $\mathrm{SNR}_{\text{peak}}$.

*Information Leakage.* Let $C \in \{1,\ldots,K\}$ denote commands with prior $P(C)$, and $Y$ the adversary's observation (optical+BLE features). The mutual information

$$I(C;Y) = H(C) - H(C\|Y) \tag{15}$$

captures the reduction in command uncertainty afforded by $Y$. From an empirical confusion matrix $\widehat{P}(\hat{C}\,|\,C)$ estimated by the attacker's classifier, $H(C\,|\,Y)$ can be approximated via $H(C\,|\,\hat{C})$. We also report the divergence between the true command distribution $P(C)$ and the attacker's inferred marginal $\widehat{Q}(C)$:

$$D_{\mathrm{KL}}\left(P \parallel \widehat{Q}\right) = \sum_{c} P(c) \log \frac{P(c)}{\widehat{Q}(c)}. \tag{16}$$

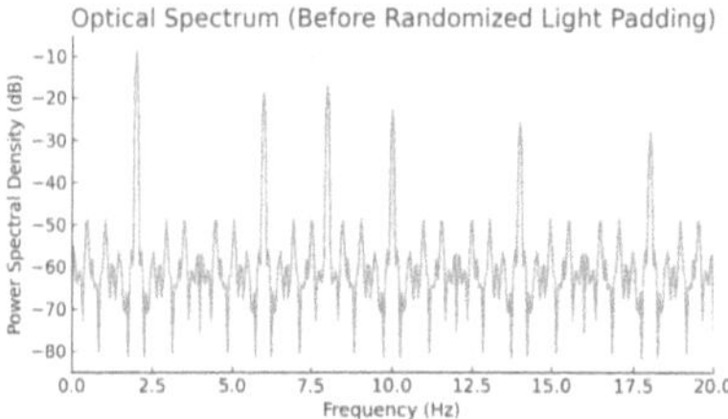

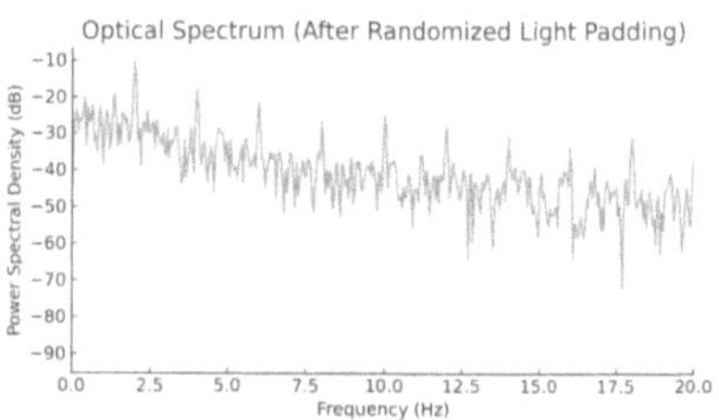

(a) Optical spectrum before randomized light padding: strong line components at $f_0$ and harmonics.

(b) Optical spectrum after padding: line energy smeared into broadband noise, reduced exploitable structure.

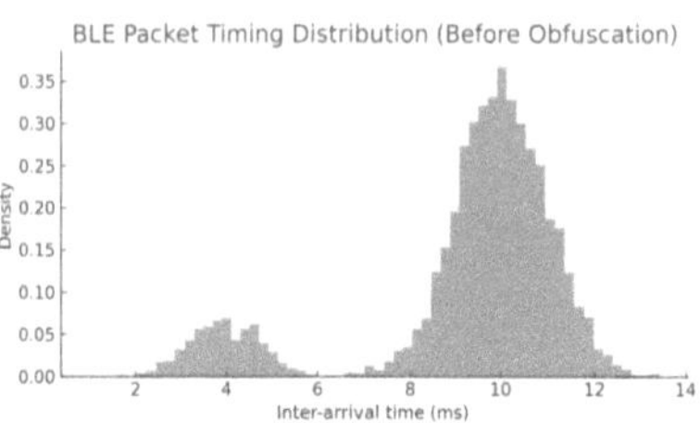

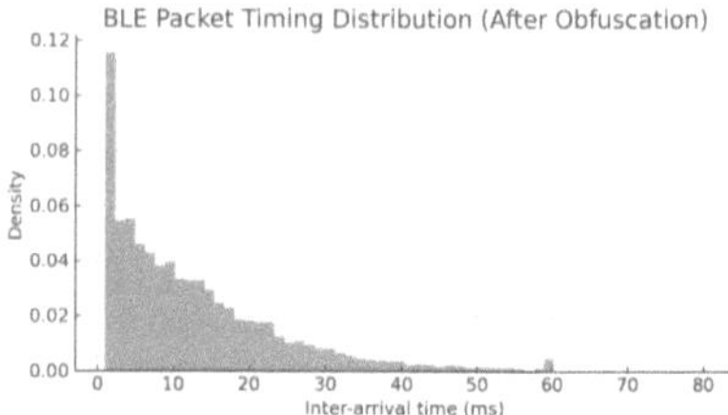

(c) BLE inter-arrival time distribution before obfuscation: sharp modes revealing command bursts.

(d) BLE inter-arrival time distribution after obfuscation: broadened, multimodal timings due to jitter, batching, and dummies.

**Fig. 7.** Comparison of spectral and temporal distributions before and after obfuscation techniques were applied.

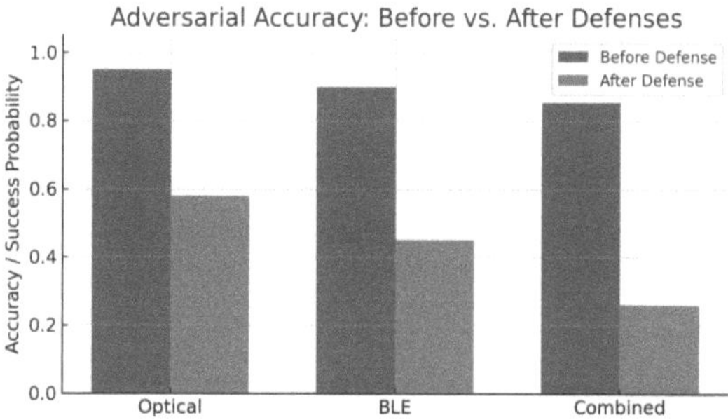

**Fig. 8.** Adversarial accuracy (optical, BLE, and combined). The combined success probability uses (13).

## 4.5   Results and Discussion

We simulated and synthesize representative experiments using the evaluation pipeline described above. Figures 7a–7d visualize pre-/post-defense spectra and timing distributions; Fig. 8 summarizes attacker accuracy. Table 2 reports key metrics on a five-class task (*ON, OFF, ColorChange, ModeChange, MusicSync*) with uniform priors: optical padding reduces peak-SNR from 4741.0 to 930.0 (linear scale), traffic obfuscation broadens timing distributions, and the combined defenses shrink mutual information and classification accuracy. Using the conservative product model, end-to-end success probability drops from 0.855 to 0.261. The results illustrate a multi-layer privacy gain: randomized light padding suppresses narrowband optical signatures (Figs. 7a–7b), traffic obfuscation removes simple correlates between user actions and BLE bursts (Figs. 7c–7d), and together they drive down attacker accuracy (Fig. 8) and information leakage (Table 2). Parameters $(\tau, \epsilon)$ and obfuscation rates can be tuned to meet diverse latency and energy budgets while preserving visual quality. The proposed methodology is firmware-level and does not require hardware changes, making it suitable for deployment across a broad class of BLE-based smart lighting and, more generally, BLE-enabled IoT applications.

## 5   Conclusion

This paper exposed how Bluetooth-enabled smart bulbs leak sensitive information through optical emissions and BLE traffic. Using mathematical formalization, we showed that such leaks reduce command entropy and enable accurate inference. Two lightweight defenses–Randomized Light Padding and Traffic Pattern Obfuscation–were proposed, each disrupting distinct leakage surfaces. Simulated evaluation demonstrated reduced optical SNR and lowered adversarial success probability from 0.855 to 0.261, proving the effectiveness of layered defense. These countermeasures are practical, firmware-level, and broadly applicable across IoT ecosystems. Future work will benchmark real-world implementations and extend defenses with hybrid cryptographic–obfuscation frameworks.

## References


1. https://github.com/funtenna
2. https://www.forbes.com/sites/intelai/2018/09/21/a-smarter-world-how-ai-the-iot-and-5g-will-make-all-the-difference/
3. Camurati, G., Poeplau, S., Muench, M., Hayes, T., Francillon, A.: Screaming channels: when electromagnetic side channels meet radio transceivers. In: Proceedings of the 2018 ACM SIGSAC Conference on Computer and Communications Security, pp. 163–177. CCS '18, Association for Computing Machinery, New York, NY, USA (2018). https://doi.org/10.1145/3243734.3243802
4. Camurati, G., Poeplau, S., Muench, M., Hayes, T., Francillon, A.: Screaming channels: when electromagnetic side channels meet radio transceivers. In: Proceedings of the 25th ACM Conference on Computer and Communications Security (CCS). CCS '18, ACM (2018)
5. Conti, M., Dragoni, N., Lesyk, V.: A survey of man in the middle attacks. IEEE Commun. Surv. Tutorials **18**(3), 2027–2051 (2016)
6. Deshotels, L.: Inaudible sound as a covert channel in mobile devices. In: Proceedings of the 8th USENIX Conference on Offensive Technologies, p. 16. WOOT'14, USENIX Association, USA (2014)

7. Guri, M., Monitz, M., Elovici, Y.: USBee: air-gap covert-channel via electromagnetic emission from USB (2016)
8. Guri, M., Monitz, M., Elovici, Y.: Bridging the air gap between isolated networks and mobile phones in a practical cyber-attack. ACM Trans. Intell. Syst. Technol. **8**(4) (2017). https://doi.org/10.1145/2870641
9. Guri, M., Monitz, M., Mirski, Y., Elovici, Y.: BitWhisper: covert signaling channel between air-gapped computers using thermal manipulations. In: 2015 IEEE 28th Computer Security Foundations Symposium, pp. 276–289 (2015). https://doi.org/10.1109/CSF.2015.26
10. Guri, M., Solewicz, Y.A., Daidakulov, A., Elovici, Y.: Acoustic data exfiltration from speakerless air-gapped computers via covert hard-drive noise ('diskfiltration'). In: Computer Security - ESORICS 2017 - 22nd European Symposium on Research in Computer Security, Oslo, Norway, September 11-15, 2017, Proceedings, Part II, pp. 98–115 (2017). https://doi.org/10.1007/978-3-319-66399-9_6
11. Guri, M., et al.: GSMem: data exfiltration from air-gapped computers over GSM frequencies. In: 24th USENIX Security Symposium, USENIX Security 15, Washington, D.C., USA, August 12-14, 2015, pp. 849–864 (2015)
12. Halevi, T., Saxena, N.: A closer look at keyboard acoustic emanations: random passwords, typing styles and decoding techniques. In: Proceedings of the 7th ACM Symposium on Information, Computer and Communications Security, pp. 89–90. ASIACCS '12, ACM, New York, NY, USA (2012). https://doi.org/10.1145/2414456.2414509, http://doi.acm.org/10.1145/2414456.2414509
13. Lopes, A., Aranha, D.: Platform-agnostic low-intrusion optical data exfiltration (2016)
14. Loughry, J., Umphress, D.A.: Information leakage from optical emanations. ACM Trans. Inf. Syst. Secur. **5**(3), 262–289 (2002). Aug
15. Loughry, J., Umphress, D.A.: Information leakage from optical emanations. ACM Trans. Inf. Syst. Secur. **5**(3), 262–289 (2002). https://doi.org/10.1145/545186.545189, http://doi.acm.org/10.1145/545186.545189
16. Maiti, A., Jadliwala, M.: Light ears: information leakage via smart lights. Proc. ACM Interact. Mob. Wearable Ubiquitous Technol. **3**(3) (2019). https://doi.org/10.1145/3351256
17. O'Malley, S., Choo, K.K.: Bridging the air gap: inaudible data exfiltration by insiders (2014)
18. Porambage, P., et al.: The quest for privacy in the internet of things. IEEE Cloud Comput. **3**(2), 36–45 (2016). https://doi.org/10.1109/MCC.2016.28
19. Ronen, E., Shamir, A.: Extended functionality attacks on IoT devices: the case of smart lights. In: 2016 IEEE European Symposium on Security and Privacy (EuroS&P), pp. 3–12 (2016). https://doi.org/10.1109/EuroSP.2016.13
20. Ronen, E., Shamir, A., Weingarten, A.O., O'Flynn, C.: IoT goes nuclear: creating a ZigBee chain reaction. In: 2017 IEEE Symposium on Security and Privacy (SP), pp. 195–212 (2017). https://doi.org/10.1109/SP.2017.14
21. Ryan, M.: Bluetooth: with low energy comes low security. In: Proceedings of the 7th USENIX Conference on Offensive Technologies, p. 4. WOOT'13, USENIX Association, USA (2013)
22. Ryan, M.: Bluetooth: with low energy comes low security. In: Proceedings of the 7th USENIX Conference on Offensive Technologies, p. 4. WOOT'13, USENIX Association, Berkeley, CA, USA (2013)
23. Sepetnitsky, V., et al.: Exfiltration of information from air-gapped machines using monitor's led indicator. In: 2014 IEEE Joint Intelligence and Security Informatics Conference, pp. 264–267 (2014)

# AI-Powered Intelligent Assistant for Predictive Maintenance Decision Support and Automated Operational Processes: A Self-learning Approach

Mariusz Piechowski[1]([envelope]) [iD], Małgorzata Jasiulewicz-Kaczmarek[2] [iD],
Michał Piechowski[3] [iD], and Stanisław Filipiński[4] [iD]

[1] WSB Merito University, Poznan, Poland
`mariusz.piechowski@poznan.merito.pl`
[2] Poznan University of Technology, Poznan, Poland
[3] Collegium Da Vinci, Poznan, Poland
[4] University of Technology and Economics in Warsaw, Warsaw, Poland

**Abstract.** This article presents an innovative approach to automating and supporting decision-making processes in maintenance using an intelligent assistant. The proposed solution combines the advantages of modern language models, self-learning mechanisms, and a modular architecture that allows for adaptation to the specific requirements of production environments. The research aimed to verify the system's effectiveness, flexibility, and resilience in real-world conditions, as well as to assess its potential for integration with automation modules and enterprise IT systems. An in-depth analysis of implementation challenges was conducted, focusing on critical aspects such as the quality and completeness of training data, the reliability of communication between modules, and the system's self-improvement during ongoing operation. A detailed concept for organizing the knowledge base and validation mechanisms was presented. Practical tests demonstrated that the implemented system effectively supports decision-making processes at production stations, enabling the automation of operational tasks and streamlining maintenance activities. The importance of continuous self-improvement, which leads to systematic efficiency gains, was emphasized. The article concludes with an indication of future development directions, including further optimization of input data quality, expansion of system functionality, and adaptation of the solutions to other industrial sectors.

**Keywords:** Intelligent tools · decision-making system · adaptive control · AI automation

## 1 Introduction

The complexity of production processes, shortening product lifecycles, and the need to flexibly respond to customer needs are rendering traditional production control systems inadequate. In this context, adaptive production process control concepts are gaining


K. K. Patel et al. (Eds.): icSoftComp 2025, CCIS 2874, pp. 255–266, 2026.
https://doi.org/10.1007/978-3-032-22062-2_20

increasing importance, enabling the ongoing adjustment of production parameters to changing internal and external conditions [1, 11]. A key element enabling the implementation of this approach is intelligent tools that support decision-making processes and automate operational activities [4]. These tools combine the functionalities of measurement systems, data analytics, and artificial intelligence, creating an integrated environment enabling predictive and increasingly prescriptive control of the production process. By employing machine learning methods, predictive analytics, and digital twins, it is possible not only to respond to deviations but also to anticipate potential disruptions and implement corrective actions. Adaptive control systems are used in production management, maintenance, quality control, and energy optimization [19, 23]. Their development aligns with both the Industry 4.0 and 5.0 paradigms, in which data is a key decision-making resource, and human-machine collaboration is taking on a new dimension-based on co-intelligence and mutual learning. These systems do not replace humans, but support them in making more accurate decisions under conditions of uncertainty, while simultaneously increasing the stability and efficiency of manufacturing processes. From the operator's perspective, these systems introduce a completely new quality of work-from a responsive performer to an informed decision-maker who collaborates with intelligent systems and makes decisions based on data and AI recommendations.

This paper aims to present the concept of an intelligent e-Assistant system supporting decision-making processes and automating operator tasks. The paper presents the system's architecture and implementation process for a sample workstation in an enterprise, and focuses on a practical demonstration of the proposed solution's impact on the automation of operational activities and decision-making support in the maintenance area. The need to create decision-support tools for operators and maintenance technicians stems from the complexity of production processes, growing requirements for efficiency, risk management, problem response speed, data analysis, support for less experienced employees, and increased employee satisfaction [18, 20, 21].

The article consists of six chapters. The second chapter presents AI tools supporting decision-making processes. The third and fourth chapters describe the system concept and its functionality. Section 5 presents the e-Assistant research stand. The last chapter is a summary, and the conclusions.

## 2 AI Tools Supporting Decision-Making Processes

In recent years, we have witnessed significant breakthroughs in decision-making support for technical system maintenance. These transformations are the result of the rapid development of advanced digital technologies, which have not only revolutionized data collection but also completely transformed the philosophy of information and knowledge management in industry.

2022 was a particularly groundbreaking year, as generative language models gained significant popularity. These tools - pioneered by the market debut of OpenAI's ChatGPT - are based on very deep neural networks and enable the understanding, interpretation, and generation of complex textual content with unprecedented precision. For the first time, AI (artificial intelligence) systems offered seamless natural language communication, dynamic interactive learning, and instant knowledge transfer, significantly increasing their practical potential in both daily operational activities and the implementation of complex strategic tasks. As a result, hundreds of specialized models and chatbots – both general and industry-specific – quickly emerged, developed by various companies (e.g., Gemini, Meta LLaMA, Mistral, and Falcon) [6]. Multitasking has become a key advantage of modern AI solutions: they enable text and code generation, processing collected data, detecting anomalies, building predictive models, and supporting decision-making processes at multiple management levels [9]. Integrating large language models (LLMs) with external systems, analytical tools, extensive knowledge bases, and long-term contextual memory plays a crucial role. Retrieval Augmented Generation (RAG) is gaining popularity, allowing AI assistants not only to rely on knowledge stored in the model but also to interact with current data sources [7]. This allows them to provide dynamic, precise responses based on the latest information, improving the quality of operational and strategic decisions. Further progress has been achieved with multimodal models such as GPT-4V and Gemini 1.5, which combine the capabilities of processing and analyzing text, images, sound, and even video. In the context of manufacturing systems, these models enable automatic analysis of component images or recording audio signals related to machine anomalies. This enables rapid fault detection, diagnostic report generation, and immediate information transfer to service technicians and management.

A significant trend is the widespread use of open source tools (e.g., LLaMA, Mistral, Falcon), which enable the creation of personalized applications—perfectly tailored to the needs and specifics of a given organization. This approach unleashes the potential of creating dedicated industry assistants that support not only ongoing data analysis but also long-term failure prediction and maintenance schedule optimization.

Intelligent Process Automation (IPA) has become an integral element of modern decision support systems. It combines classic RPA (Robotic Process Automation) tools [2, 5, 13, 17] with the potential of artificial intelligence (AI) and machine learning (ML) [22], enabling not only the automation of routine tasks but also the detection of hidden patterns, predicting unplanned downtime, and recommending preventative actions [14]. Advanced natural language processing (NLP) provides powerful support for this process, enabling the automatic extraction of key information from technical documentation, internal communications, service reports, and repair orders.

The development of NLP-based tools has significantly shortened response times to technical issues, and knowledge management in enterprises has reached a new level of quality, eliminating the communication gap between organizational departments.

In summary, modern decision support systems in production and maintenance are incredibly advanced: from global, multi-task artificial intelligence models to specialized, industry-specific applications. Their integration with multimodal and context-aware architectures enables greater availability and reliability, as well as increasingly effective implementation of new development strategies.

## 3   eAssistant in the Operation of Technical Systems

The goal of the presented research was to develop, implement, and evaluate an environment enabling automatic and efficient processing of user queries, supported by next-generation generative language models. The designed eAssistant system focuses on self-improvement by leveraging historical and current data, user intent recognition, and conversation context analysis. Based on this, it generates and suggests corrective actions. These suggestions are then verified by the user and implemented locally, enhancing security and control. The solution's architecture is based on a modular design (Fig. 1). The key components are: the user interface (enabling natural communication), the interpretation module (classifying query content and intent), the command translator (transforming information into structured commands), and the execution module responsible for initiating actions on the workstation. An integral part of the project is a mechanism for evaluating the effectiveness of the provided answers, which allows the system to later use proven solutions in similar cases.

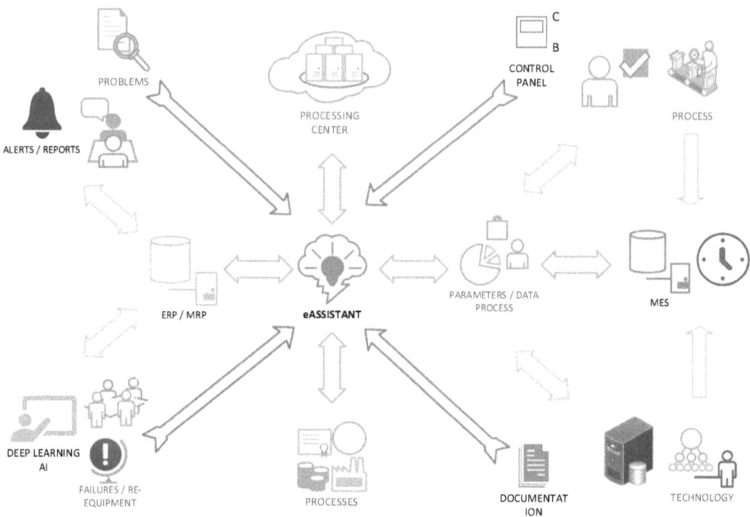


**Fig. 1.** eAsystent functionality.

The system's implementation involves asynchronous information exchange between modules and full monitoring and logging of all interactions. This enables in-depth analysis of query classifications, system responses, and the quality of decisions made. The system learns independently based on practically verified scenarios, while ensuring full control over the automation process.

A challenge for modern manufacturing enterprises remains the integration of existing IT resources and ensuring data consistency across multiple systems. This solution requires not only designing an information architecture but also implementing organizational procedures that provide access to current, reliable information at every decision-making level. This makes it possible to make sound decisions and react quickly to inconsistencies that appear in the process.

The dynamic development of tools such as RPA (Robotic Process Automation), combined with artificial intelligence (AI), is redefining the approach to technical management. RPA [15–17], effective in routine tasks, gains new capabilities with AI support – systems learn, analyze large sets of production data, detect irregularities, and predict potential risks. The result is a new level of automation – from tracking machine work and managing logistics to immediately detecting and eliminating production anomalies.

SIIA ITS, or Intelligent Integration of Systems and Automation of IT Systems, is based on independent, specialized agents – eAssistants. Each agent handles specific areas: managing routine tasks, monitoring KPI indicators, data integration, decision support, synchronizing information between systems, as well as production planning or maintenance activities [10].

The heart of the system is a central management module that oversees the cooperation of all agents, data consistency, and the overall system's efficiency. Agents can operate in local environments, clouds, or IoT platforms, making the system easy to integrate with existing infrastructure. Information exchange occurs both through a central hub and in a peer-to-peer model, while maintaining safety and redundancy standards.

The most important benefits of SIIA ITS include: adaptability supported by machine learning, flexible system expansion according to the organization's needs, and advanced security mechanisms. The advanced user interface allows for intuitive monitoring and management of the system on a company-wide scale. The integration of classic diagnostic tools, SCADA, IoT, and AI platforms into a coherent, flexible architecture allows for a dynamic response to process changes [3]. A conceptual diagram of the system is shown in Fig. 1.

In practice, eAsystent becomes the operator's partner, enabling efficient information retrieval, generation of suggestions and solutions, alerting about irregularities, as well as automating time-consuming tasks at the workstation – especially those related to documentation. An important value is the two-way interaction: the system not only reacts but also actively supports, predicts, and proposes optimal solutions even in the most demanding situations.

The self-improvement capability of eAsystent (eA) is demonstrated by regular analysis of historical and current data, scenario simulation, testing of new solutions, and continuous optimization of algorithms. An intelligent network of agents deployed at workstations efficiently synchronizes production parameters and immediately initiates corrective or preventive procedures. The decision support model at the engineer, technician, or operator level is shown in Fig. 2. The speed of information flow between agents enables the implementation of corrective and preventive actions.

Flexible artificial intelligence algorithms make eAsystent an anticipated part of the digital transformation. By implementing this type of solution, a company gains not only efficiency and safety but also increases workplace ergonomics and adaptability in the face of continuous technological changes.

## 4   The Concept of Self-learning in the eAsystent System

The ability to adapt and self-improve is the foundation of modern, intelligent systems supporting the operation of technical infrastructure. The self-learning mechanism integrated into the eAsystent architecture is a model application of advanced natural language processing (NLP) technologies, machine learning techniques, and automated reasoning based on real operational experiences [9]. A key aspect of the process is the continuous

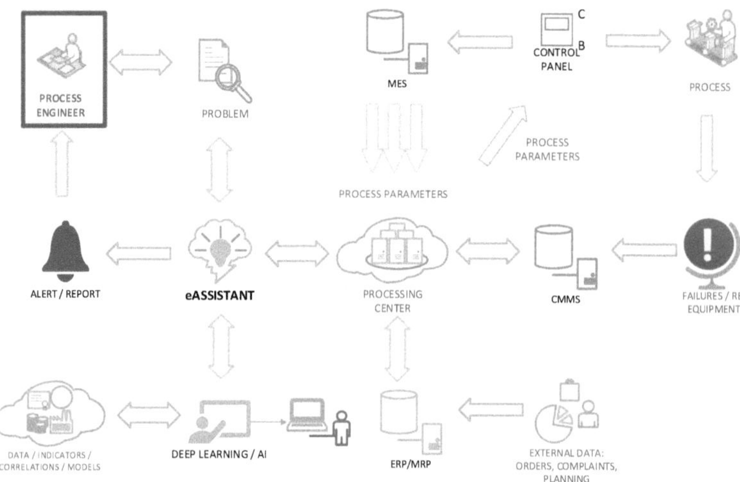


**Fig. 2.** Scheme of decision-making support for the process engineer/maintenance technician/operator by eA.

monitoring and meticulous recording of all user interactions with the system – including both the course of conversations and the content of submitted queries and proposed actions.

The system automatically analyzes the completeness and correctness of messages, the length and precision of suggestions, and also eliminates segments unrelated to the topic or lacking specialized value. Great importance is attached to the presence of technical vocabulary and logical coherence in dialogues. Interactions deemed valuable are standardized and converted to a unified format (e.g., JSONL), which allows for their direct use during subsequent training cycles of the language model.

The system's learning process occurs cyclically, based on almost complete operational autonomy – from the preparation and validation of training files, through the execution of automated scripts, to the testing and deployment of the optimized model. As a result, human intervention has been reduced to the necessary minimum, and the entire process can run continuously, adapting eA to the latest user requirements and changing conditions.

Thanks to this, the system constantly expands its knowledge base, better understands the specifics of tasks and operator preferences, and also quickly adapts to new operational scenarios. With built-in mechanisms for trend detection and identification of potential threats, eAsystent offers more accurate recommendations and more effectively supports users in their daily operational decisions.The self-learning capability of the eAssistant directly translates into increased efficiency of production and maintenance processes, ensuring not only continuity at the workstation but also flexibility and resilience to dynamic changes in the production environment. As a result, the model becomes an increasingly intelligent assistant for technical teams, accumulating the collective experience of the organization and building a dynamic knowledge repository.

## 5    eAssistant Module – Structure, Testing, and Practical Challenges

In the initial phase of refining the eAssistant system, the key was to develop a coherent, structured set of training data. This data was collected from many different sources: process documentation, user manuals, maintenance schedules, production data repositories, technological guides, and communication records from daily operations. Subsequently, all data was transformed into a uniform format that could be processed by the language model, which enabled the creation of a solid knowledge base for making sound decisions in an industrial environment (Fig. 3).

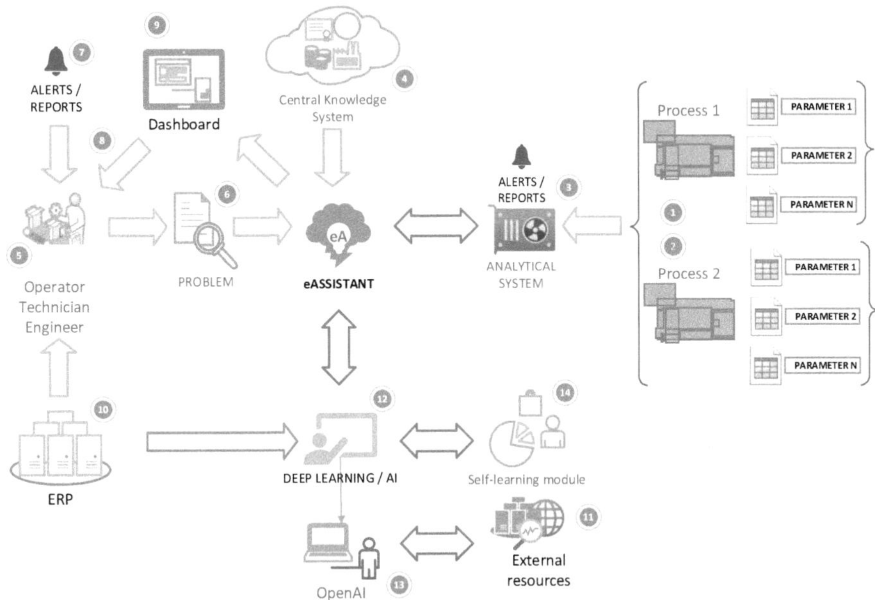


**Fig. 3.**  Assistant as Chatbot Job Scheme.

Figure 3 shows a diagram of the information flow and data exchange between the individual system modules. Data from production processes (1, 2) is sent to the analytical system (3), which aggregates and forwards it to the eAssistant – the central decision support module. The eAssistant additionally retrieves supplementary information from the Central Knowledge System (4), which contains a database and reference models. All this data is then processed in the artificial intelligence (AI) module, which includes decision-making sub-modules (11, 12, 13, 14), where analysis, modeling, and conclusion generation take place. Operational data from the ERP (Enterprise Resource Planning) system is also sent to the AI sub-module (12), enabling the integration of information from enterprise resource management.

Based on the processed data, the eAssistant generates and sends personalized messages and recommendations for the operator (5) to the operator's dashboard (9), supporting ongoing activities. In parallel, based on generated reports (7), the operator identifies a potential problem, defines its scope, and sends a report to the eAssistant. The latter analyzes the report in the AI module, using collected data and predictive algorithms, and then sends optimized scenarios for resolving the problem or a detailed scope of corrective actions, including step prioritization and time estimates, to the operator's dashboard (5).

Functional and quality tests were conducted on all key modules of the eAssistant system. During the study, users simulated real interactions by sending various queries to the system – from typical production and diagnostic queries to requests for performing specific actions or generating documents. By using an interactive query form, each request went directly to the server, where the language model analyzed both the current context and the entire communication history with the user, stored in the database. This approach significantly increased the personalization of responses and allowed the model to dynamically adapt to the changing needs and work styles of the operators.

The system was equipped with a precise classification module that automatically assigned each query to one of three important categories:

1. process information (parameter readings, new settings, operational commands),
2. service data (intervention history, downtime logs, preventive tasks),
3. Agent actions (physical execution of commands, initiation of automatic procedures, document handling).

Each system response was verified for logical and substantive correctness, and in case of incompleteness, it was supplemented with necessary information or additional data. The full interaction history was archived in real-time, which enabled the monitoring of service quality, the improvement of classification algorithms, and the development of the language model itself.

Many practical challenges arose during implementation. At an early design stage, a tendency for incorrect query classification was observed, for example, some commands related to changing process settings or scheduling interventions were routed to the wrong sections of the system. These problems led to the reconstruction of user prompts, as well as the re-selection and supplementation of training data with edge and ambiguous cases that genuinely reflected daily workplace practices [12].

Additionally, complications arose in interpreting complex or imprecisely formulated queries. These shortcomings revealed limitations in the amount of context passed to the model and the need to ensure the integrity of historical information. This problem was solved by expanding the dialogue tracking models and automatically supplementing the context based on previous interactions. Furthermore, the model showed a tendency to over-generalize responses, which was related to a mismatch between the scope of the training data and the specifics of technical processes. This issue was minimized by enriching the dataset with examples of real events and detailed technical descriptions.

Key conclusions from the tests indicate the necessity of continuous monitoring of classification accuracy and systematic reinforcement of the training datasets. It also proved crucial to dynamically adapt the algorithm to the changing realities of the production environment. All these actions ensure that eA not only provides quick and substantively accurate answers but also learns from its mistakes and effectively responds to new challenges emerging in the production process.

## 6  eAgent Module – Integration and Automation of Workstation Operations

The eAgent module acts as an assistant in the system's architecture, directly executing commands from the parent system and providing intelligent support for workstation operation. The project was designed so that the operational agent (eAgent), upon receiving a centralized command, is able to automatically initiate, supervise, and execute assigned tasks without the need for manual user intervention. The scope of eAgent's tasks includes, among others, the automatic launching of dedicated scripts, independent generation and archiving of reports, editing and updating of operational documentation, as well as active collaboration with local devices and system platforms.

The eAgent's mechanism of action is based on regular, cyclical communication with the central server, with which it synchronizes the task schedule, execution statuses, and also transmits current logs from completed operations. Thanks to a built-in scheduling system, the agent performs tasks both immediately and according to a schedule, which allows for flexible responses to changes in production priorities and emerging emergencies.

Functional tests of the module yielded a number of important conclusions regarding reliability and operational continuity. It was observed that in the event of network disruptions, especially in cases of sudden interruptions in data transmission, incidents of losing individual system logs or fragments of data regarding the progress of executed tasks sometimes occurred. Analysis of these cases showed that the lack of a local buffering mechanism results in incomplete system state synchronization after the connection is restored, which can lead to the loss of information about operations performed during the network failure.

In response to the identified limitations, the author is considering the implementation of a dedicated queuing and buffering system for commands and operational logs. This will enable the secure collection of all orders and important data locally on workstation devices until stable communication with the main server is restored.

eAgent supports the automation of workstation tasks, but achieving optimal process continuity requires the implementation of additional security mechanisms to effectively manage unforeseen interruptions in information transmission and increase the system's resilience.

## 7  System Self-improvement Module – Challenges and Development Perspectives

The system's self-improvement process was conducted continuously and cyclically, using collected and exported operational data in a standardized JSONL format. These files served as material for subsequent iterations of the fine-tuning process, which did not require manual operator intervention, ensuring systematic updates of the model's competence in relation to real-world use cases.

Qualitative tests revealed a key correlation between the level of detail in user entries and the system's effectiveness. A high level of precision and completeness of context increased the accuracy of query classification and the quality of generated responses.

However, the analysis showed the existence of several challenges, such as an insufficient number of unusual cases and the incompleteness or generality of some recorded conversations. These situations limited the model's learning potential, which consequently forced the author to implement more rigorous training data validation mechanisms and a deeper selection of entries approved for retraining.

## 8  Summary

By developing eAssistant as a key tool supporting technical management in modern enterprises, an ambitious vision of integrating advanced artificial intelligence with the practical needs of maintenance was realized. In the course of the research, the author demonstrated that the effectiveness of such solutions depends not only on technology but also on a coherent data architecture, realistic mapping of business processes, and a constant readiness to adapt to production changes.

The developed concept of eAssistant aligns with the latest trends of Industry 5.0, placing harmonious human-machine collaboration, an ergonomic approach to information exchange, and the automation of key tasks at its core. The system successfully passed verification in a real research environment, where it demonstrated high usability in task automation, parameter monitoring, report and document generation, as well as in the dynamic generation of data enabling decision-making.

An important functionality of eAssistant is its self-learning mechanism, which allows for the regular enrichment of the knowledge base and precise adjustment of recommendations to the individual needs of the user. Practice has shown that the quality of training sets, the completeness of context, and the effective selection of cases used in learning cycles are of key importance here. I also confirmed that the system dynamically handles new types of queries, and thanks to its modular architecture, it can be successfully scaled to new application areas.

During the implementation, many challenges were identified – from technical communication limitations and the need for local implementations, to issues related to verifying the correctness of classification and understanding complex operator commands. Each of them was treated as an impulse for further improvements, expanding functionality, and developing validation procedures.

eAssistant, in its current form, constitutes a foundation for building digital production systems characterized by high fault tolerance, data security, and readiness for evaluation. Ultimately, by increasing the scope of integration, automating new areas, and developing self-learning models, enterprises can achieve a completely new level of efficiency, reliability, and innovation in managing production processes.

## References


1. Antosz, K., et al.: Application of principle component analysis and logistic regression to support six sigma implementation in maintenance. Eksploatacja i Niezawodność **25**(4) (2023)
2. Asadov, R.: Intelligent process automation: streamlining operations and enhancing efficiency in management (2023). SSRN 4495188. https://doi.org/10.2139/ssrn.4495188

3. Berruti, F., Nixon, G., Taglioni, G., Whiteman, R.: Intelligent process automation: the engine at the core of the nextgeneration operating model. Digital McKinsey (2017). https://www.mckinsey.com/capabilities/mckinsey-digital/our-insights/intelligent-process-automation-the-engine-at-thecore-of-the-next-generation-operating-model

4. Castañé, G., et al.: The ASSISTANT project: AI for high level decisions in manufacturing. Int. J. Prod. Res. **61**(7), 2288–2306 (2023)

5. Chakraborti, T., et al.: From robotic process automation to intelligent process automation. In: Asatiani, A., et al. (eds.) BPM 2020. LNBIP, vol. 393, pp. 215–228. Springer, Cham (2020). https://doi.org/10.1007/978-3-030-58779-6_15

6. Chang, T.-S., Hsiao, W.-H.: Understand resist use online customer service chatbot: an integrated innovation resist theory and negative emotion perspective. Aslib J. Inf. Manag. (2024)

7. Choubey, M.: The self-improving customer service system: how AI learns from every interaction. Int. J. Financ. Manag. Risk **6**(6) (2024)

8. Geiger, R.S., et al.: Garbage in, garbage out? Do machine learning application papers in social computing report where humanlabeled training data comes from? In: Proceedings of the 2020 Conference on Fairness, Accountability, and Transparency, pp. 325–336 (2020). https://doi.org/10.1145/3351095.3372862

9. Larasati, P.D., Irawan, A., Anwar, S., Mulya, M.F., Dewi, M.A., Nurfatima, I.: Chatbot helpdesk design for digital customer service. Appl. Eng. Technol. **1**(3), 138–145 (2022)

10. Piechowski, M., Wyczólkowski, R., Paszkowski, W.: The concept of a system supporting the implementation of an intelligent lubrication strategy within the company using advanced information technologies. In: Hamrol, A., Grabowska, M., Hinz, M. (eds.) MANUFACTURING 2024. LNME, pp. 136–150. Springer, Cham (2024). https://doi.org/10.1007/978-3-031-56474-1_11

11. Piechowski, M., Wyczółkowski, R.: Application of multimodel concept and virtual assistants to build a digital twin for supporting adaptive control of manufacturing process. In: Burduk, A., et al. (eds.) ISPEM 2025. LNME. Springer, Cham (2026). https://doi.org/10.1007/978-3-032-01517-4_43

12. Ragin-Skorecka, K., Stempczyński, J.: Doskonalenie systemu obsługi zgłoszeń użytkowników oprogramowania w przedsiębiorstwach. Studia i Prace Kolegium Zarządzania i Finansów **189**, 133–145 (2023)

13. Ribeiro, J., Lima, R., Eckhardt, T., Paiva, S.: Robotic process automation and artificial intelligence in industry 4.0 – a literature review. Procedia Comput. Sci. **181**, 51–58 (2021). https://doi.org/10.1016/j.procs.2021.01.104

14. Rojek, I., Jasiulewicz-Kaczmarek, M., Piechowski, M., Mikołajewski, D.: The use of decision trees to identify the causes of failures in a medical enterprise - a case study. In: 6th IFAC International Workshop on Advanced Maintenance Engineering, Services and Technology (AMEST2024), Maintenance and Asset Lifecycle Management for Sustainable and Resilient Systems, Cagliari, Italy

15. Samson Ayinla, B., Atadoga, A., Ugochukwu Ike, C., Leonard Ndubuisi, N., Asuzu, O., Adura Adeleye, R.: The role of robotic process automation (RPA) in modern accounting: a review – investigating how automation tools are transforming traditional accounting practices. Eng. Sci. Technol. J. **5**(2) (2024)

16. Siderska, J.: The adoption of robotic process automation technology to ensure business processes during the COVID-19 pandemic. Sustainability **13**, 8020 (2021)

17. Siderska J., et al.: Towards intelligent automation (IA): literature review on the evolution of robotic process automation (RPA), its challenges, and future trends. Eng. Manag. Prod. Serv. **15**(4) (2023)

18. Talacio, M., Funchal, G., Melo, V., Piardi, L., Vallim, M., Leitao, P.: Machine vision to empower an intelligent personal assistant for assembly tasks. In: Pereira, A.I., et al. (eds.) OL2A 2021. CCIS, vol. 1488, pp. 447–462. Springer, Cham (2021). https://doi.org/10.1007/978-3-030-91885-9_33
19. Tasias, K.A.: Simultaneous optimization of inventory, maintenance, and quality for production systems subject to multiple mean and variance shifts. Commun. Stat. Theory Methods **53**(9), 3078–3101 (2024)
20. Tomažič, S., Škrjanc, I., Andonovski, G., Logar, V.: The development of simulation and optimisation tools with an intuitive user interface to improve the operation of electric arc furnaces. Machines **12**(8) (2024)
21. Colabianchi, S., Costantino, F., Sabetta, N.: Assessment of a large language model based digital intelligent assistant in assembly manufacturing. Comput. Ind. **162**, 104129 (2024)
22. Waefler, T., Schmid, U.: Explainability is not enough: requirements for human-AI-partnership in complex socio-technical systems. In: Matos, F. (ed.) Proceedings of the 2nd European Conference on the Impact of Artificial Intelligence and Robotics (ECIAIR 2020), Lisboa, Portugal, pp. 185–194. ACPIL.16 (2021)
23. Yurin, A.Y., Nikolaychuk, O.A., Dorodnykh, N.O., Stolbov, A.B., Denisova, D.A.: Using an intelligent assistant for aircraft diagnostics and maintenance. In: Kovalev, S., Kotenko, I., Sukhanov, A. (eds.) IITI 2023. LNNS, vol. 776, pp. 325–333. Springer, Cham (2023). https://doi.org/10.1007/978-3-031-43789-2_30

# An Efficient Scheduling Method for Taxi Ridesharing

Thi Hong Nhan Vu[(⌧)]

University of Engineering and Technology, VNU, Hanoi, Vietnam
`vthnhan@vnu.edu.com`

**Abstract.** In recent years, ridesharing has become one of the most efficient and cost-effective transportation solutions allowing multiple passengers to share a single vehicle. However, effective scheduling remains a major challenge that must be addressed to improve user adoption. This paper tackles the problem through twofold objectives by providing frequent riders with reliable, pre-arranged routes and by enabling the dynamic addition of new riders to active shared trips. To achieve this, we propose an algorithm named aVC, which clusters riders into ridesharing groups based on the similarity of their frequent travel routes. This approach removes the need for users to repeatedly search for rides or endure long waiting times, as trip details and driver assignments are communicated in advance. Furthermore, when a regular ridesharing trip beings and there are vacant seats, drivers can accept real-time requests from new riders without disrupting the planned itinerary. To efficiently handle such dynamic insertion, a method biSearchIns is designed to rapidly process shared trip queries. The proposed methods are evaluated against existing approaches using simulated datasets. Experimental results demonstrate that the proposed approach outperforms current situations in computational efficiency. The number of riders served, and the overall reduction in vehicle usage.

**Keywords:** Scheduling · Taxi · Ridesharing · Frequent Route

## 1   Introduction

Ridesharing offers an efficient means to reduce energy use, ease congestion, and meet commuter needs. Private vehicle ridesharing, or carpooling, has been recognized as a practical solution for daily commuting between home and workplace [1, 2]. Recently, obtaining a taxi during rush hours in dense urban areas has become increasingly difficult, prompting interest in taxi-based ridesharing as a potential remedy [3]. Recurring ridesharing where users such as coworkers commuting together share rides on consistent routes and schedules emphasizes reliability and predictability [1, 2]. However, users with irregular routes or schedules gain little benefits. Taxi ridesharing can address this need but introduces greater computational complexity due to dynamic taxi location and real-time ride requests [3, 4]. Because taxi availability depends on ongoing trips, current studies have often neglected how regular users' route patterns could enhance these systems.

© The Author(s), under exclusive license to Springer Nature Switzerland AG 2026
K. K. Patel et al. (Eds.): icSoftComp 2025, CCIS 2874, pp. 267–278, 2026.
https://doi.org/10.1007/978-3-032-22062-2_21

Despite the popularity of Uber or Grab, efficient ridesharing remains underused. Simplicity, safety, adaptability, and performance are critical for adoption. Traditional systems require drivers to pre-announce routes and riders to manually search for matches, often repeatedly, making them inconvenient. The rise GPS-enabled devices, however, allows mobility tracking, enabling systems to detect users with similar travel habits. These insights enable personalized, automated ride arrangements that reduce search effort and renew invest in shared travel [5, 6].

This work proposes an integrated scheduling model to optimize dynamic taxi ridesharing, aiming to maximize riders served, minimize taxi used and travel distance, and ensure fast responses. The model assumes pre-formed ridesharing groups assigned to drivers, while irregular users send real-time requests, specifying pickup locations, drop-off locations, and time windows. The system dynamically integrates these into ongoing trips without disruption. To support early group formation, a modified aVC-Growth algorithm clusters riders based on frequent routes [7].

During operation, taxis with vacant seats can accept new requests. Scheduling determines optimal pickup and drop-ff orders while preserving service quality. However, existing insertion functions have quadratic time complexity, hindering scalability [3, 8, 9]. Slow computations conflict with user expectations for mobile responsiveness. Most users expect response within two seconds according a survey by Dynatrace. The main contributions of this study are as follows:

- Development of aVC, an efficient offline method for forming ridesharing groups using riders' maximal frequent routes.
- Introduction of biSearchIns, a linear-time dynamic programming algorithm for inserting real-time ride requests while optimizing multiple objectives.
- Extensive experimental evaluation comparing the proposed methods against existing algorithms, demonstrating improvements in response time, rider coverage, and vehicle utilization.

The paper is organized as follows. Section 2 presents the offline rideshare group formation methodology. Section 3 introduces the proposed dynamic scheduling algorithm. Section 4 presents experimental results and comparisons with existing approaches.

## 2  Offline Ridesharing Group Formation

This section introduces the aVC algorithm, which is designed to form ridesharing groups through an analysis of users' frequent travel patterns.

Let $DB = \bigcup_{u_i} s_{u_i}$ denotes the comprehensive collection of frequent travel routes, where $s_{u_i}$ denotes the trajectory associated with an individual rider $u_i$ ($i > 1$). The frequent route for a given user $u_i$ is formally defined as a sequence of spatiotemporal points $s_{u_i} = \{<p_k, t_k>\}_{k=1}^{n}$ where $p_k = <x_k, y_k>$ denotes the geographical positions recorded at the corresponding time $t_k$. The fundamental objective is to derive cohesive ridesharing groups by qualifying the degree of similarity among these trajectories within the database.

Two individual movements are considered similar when there is minimal difference in their temporal and spatial attributes. Furthermore, two individuals are regarded as being geospatially proximate at a given time instant if the Euclidean distance between their respective locations does not exceed a predefined threshold, denoted as *max_Dis* [7].

A time interval $[t_k, t_k + \Delta]$ is defined as a eligible interval for a group $G$ if and only if all members of $G$ are spatially co-located at time $t_k$ where $k \in [1, \Delta]$ and maintains its proximity throughout the entire interval. Formally, this condition implies that the spatial distance between any members of $G$ des not exceed the threshold during $[t_k, t_k + \Delta]$. Furthermore, the group must not satisfy the proximity condition immediately before $t_k$ or immediately after $t_k + \Delta$, ensuring that the interval represents a distinct and temporally bounded co-location events. Finally, the duration of this interval must not be less than a predefined minimum duration parameter, denoted as *minT*. For a given group $G$ characterized by its eligible interval $I_1, .., I_n$, its weight is determined as a function of the total travel length *lengT* observed in the dataset *DB*.

$$w = \frac{\sum_{i=1}^{n} |I_i|}{lengT} \tag{1}$$

A group $G$ is recognized as a eligible group if its aggregated weight denoted $G.w$ is not below a threshold *minW*. Furthermore, this eligible group $G$ qualifies as a ridesharing group represented as *<G, minT, max_Dis>* if and only if a permissible time interval can be identified within the group's activities. Let $G_k$ represent a candidate group comprising $k$ riders and let $VG_k$ denote the set of eligible groups, where $k \geq 1$.

The algorithm aVG in Fig. 1 enhances execution efficiency over the previous VC-Growth method [7] while maximizing the formation of ridesharing groups under vehicle capacity constraints. A graph *VGgraph(V, E)* is built to identify maximal eligible ridesharing groups, ensuring that only maximal sets are generated, with no redundant subgroups. The vertex set $V$ includes individuals forming eligible 2-person groups $VG_2$ produced by the *VG2Gen()* procedure, while the set $E$ represents directed links corresponding to valid time intervals for these pairs. For efficiency, each edge is directed from the lower- to higher-indexed individual, and a depth first traversal is used to explore the graph and extract all maximal groups.

The prefix vertices of a given vertex $u$, denoted as $Pr_u$, together with their associated edge set $E(Pr_u)$, constitute the input for identifying eligible co-existing groups that include vertex $u$.

The identification of eligible groups necessitates a comprehensive traversal of the *VGgraph*, commencing from an initial vertex and proceeding sequentially through its entirely. This algorithm employs a recursive approach to generate eligible groups. It prioritizes vertices within the set V by ordering them in descending order based on their degree. This strategy ensures that users with a higher number of connections are allocated to groups earlier in the process. This preferential grouping increases the likelihood of forming maximally eligible groups at an early stage, consequently reducing overall execution time. Furthermore, to maintain the integrity of group assignments, a ride, once assigned to an established group, is subsequently excluded from consideration for any subsequent new group formations, preventing a rider from appearing in multiple groups.

Upon the identification of each eligible group $G_k$, it is systematically retained within the set *sG*. Following the complete ascertainment of all maximal eligible groups, the

---

$V \leftarrow V$ *shorted with the decreasing number of the vertex's neighbors*
$u \leftarrow v_1 \in V$;
$sG \leftarrow \phi$; //set of eligible groups
while ($V$ of *VG-graph* $\neq \phi$)
    Create the condition group $Q=\{v\}\cup P$;
    $Pr_Q \leftarrow$ all prefix vertices of $v$;
    if ($Pr_Q \neq \phi$)
        For each vertex $u$ in $Pr_Q$ //*create a new eligible group*
            $G\leftarrow\{u\}\cup Q$; $sG \leftarrow sG \cup G$; delete $u \in G$ from $V$ and $Pr_Q$;
            $E(Pr_Q) \leftarrow$ the directed edges on $Pr_Q$;
            if($E(Pr_Q)\neq\phi$)
                for $(u_i,u_j) \in E(Pr_Q)$
                    *eligibleInterval($u_i,u_j$)=eligibleInterval($u_i,u_j$)$\cap$eligibleInterval*
                    *($u_i,v$)$\cap$eligibleInterval($u_j,v$)*
                        if *eligibleInterval*($u_i,u_j$) is unsatisfied *minD* and *minW*
                            remove edge ($u_i,u_j$) from $E(Pr_Q)$;
                    if ($E(Pr_Q) \neq\phi$) // after fine-tuning
                        $Pr_Q$ and $E(Pr_Q)$ form $Q$'s conditional group base;
                        $VGgraph(Q) \leftarrow$ build $VGgraph$ of $Q$;
                        Call $aVG(VGgraph(Q), Q)$;
    $RG \leftarrow \phi$;
    **for** ($k=1$; $k\leq|sG|$; $k$++) //generate the eligible rideshare group for
    each taxi
        if ($g\leftarrow |G_k \in sG>cap$)
            if ($g$ mod $cap$=0) then $n=(g/cap)$ create $n$ groups $G_{i=}< a,l_p,l_d,$
$t_l>$
                $RG \leftarrow RG \cup G_i$ with $n\geq i\geq 1$;
            else generate $n$+1 groups;
        else $RG \leftarrow RG \cup <l_p,l_d,|G_k|,t_l>$;
    return $RG$;

---

**Fig. 1.** Algorithm $aVG(VGgraph, P)$ for discovering maximal eligible rideshare groups exceeding two riders

subsequent step involves the generation of ridesharing groups, strictly complying with the constraint of the vehicle's capacity. These generated ridesharing groups are then meticulously stored in the set $RG$. A ridesharing group $G_k$ is formally defined by the tuple $<l_p, l_d, |G_k|, t_l>$ in which $l_p$ represents the common pickup location for all members of the group, $l_d$ denotes the common drop-off location for all members of the group, $|G_k|$ signifies the number of riders, which must not exceed the taxi capacity ($cab$), $t_l$ indicates the latest acceptable arrival time at the destination for all riders within the group. Ultimately, the algorithm $aVC$ returns a subset of the ridesharing groups from $sG$, specially those for which the driver is responsible for activation.

# 3   Real Time Query Processing in Ridesharing Systems

A new scheduling approach is proposed, featuring an insertion function with linear time complexity, representing a significant improvement over previous methods that required quadratic complexity. The method integrates a dynamic programming – based insertion with a greedy pruning strategy.

A cab is formally represented as a tuple $ca = <l_o, a, ka>$ where $l_o$ denotes the current geographic coordinates, $a$ is the number of up-to-present occupied seats and $ka$ determines the vehicle's limit capacity.

A ridesharing query is formally defined by a tuple $q_i = <l_p, l_d, a, t_l>$ for $i \geq 1$ in which $l_p$ is the pickup point, $l_d$ determines drop-off location, $a$ signifies the number of seats requested, and $t_l$ defines the latest permissible pickup time.

Offline-constructed ridesharing groups typically consists of riders with recurring and overlapping travel trajectories, allowing for coordinated pickup and drop-offs at common locations. Accordingly, the scheduling process for a taxi can be modeled as being initiated by an initial request, represented as $q_o = <l_p, l_d, a, t_l>$.

The core operational constraint for the ridesharing service dictates that the cumulative accepted demand must not surpass the maximum operational capacity of the fleet. Let $Q = \{q_0, q_1, q_2, ..., q_n\}$ denote a set of ridesharing request, encompassing both offline and real time queries. The cumulative passenger demand resulting from these queries, defined as the sum of the seat requirements for each query $(q_i.a)$, must not exceed the taxi's total capacity $(ca.ka)$. This capacity constraint is formally expressed as $q_0.a + \sum_{i=1}^{n} q_i.a \leq ca.ka$.

A taxi's operational schedule $S_{ca} = <ca.lo, l_1, ..., l_m>$ in which $ca.lo$ is the taxi's current geographic location. The sequence $\{l_1, l_2, ..., l_m\}$ includes all pickups and drop-off locations associated with outstanding service queries in the set $Q$, that means, $l_i \in \{q_o.l_p \cup_{i=1}^{n} q_i.l_p\} \cup \{q_o.l_d \cup_{i=1}^{n} q_i.l_d\}$. A critical constraint governing in this sequence is that for every $q_i$ its designated pickup point $q_i.l_p$ must strictly precede its corresponding drop-off point $q_i.l_d$. The total travel distance, denoted as $dis(S_{cab})$, for the taxi is calculated as the cumulative sum of the distances between all consecutive locations within the defined schedule sequence. For clarity and conciseness, when referring to attributes of a query $l_d$, the specific query identifier is omitted where the context is unambiguous.

The objective is to develop an algorithm for the efficient assignment of active taxis to a chronologically ordered set of real time ridesharing requests. The primary optimization criteria is the minimization of the additional travel distance required for a selected taxi to fulfill the query's specified requirements.

## 3.1   A Simple Insertion Approach

Real time query processing focuses on formally inserting a new request $q = <l_p, l_d, a, t_l>$ into an active taxi schedule $S_{cab}$ to produce a revised schedule $S_{cab}^1$. The goal is to minimize additional travel distance while strictly complying with temporal constraints of existing passengers. The updated schedule $S'_{cab}$ is initialized as a copy of $S_{cab}$. A new pickup request $q.l_p$ is inserted in the $S_{cab}$ at position $i$ only if the capacity limit $(ca.a + q.a \leq ca.ka)$ and the pickup time constraint $t_l$ are both met. The corresponding drop-off request $q.l_d$ is inserted at position $j > i$, subject to its own timing constraints.

Upon successful insertion, the resulting increase in the total travel distance, denoted as $\delta_{ij} = \text{dis}(S'_{cab}) - \text{dis}(S_{cab})$ where dis(.) represents the cumulative shortest path distances between consecutive locations within a schedule. The optimal new schedule $S'_{cab}$ is the minimization of this calculated $\delta_{ij}$. Because the algorithm must evaluate all possible pairs $(i, j)$ of positions, its computational complexity is $O(n^3)$, reflecting the exhaustive search required to find the most efficient insertion point with the taxi's current route.

## 3.2  Quadratic-Time Approach to Real-Time Insertion

This subsection introduces quadIns, an alternative insertion algorithm designed to achieve lower time computational complexity compared to nIns. The quadIns method take into account three scenarios for inserting a new request's pickup and drop-off locations into an existing taxi schedule $S_{cab}$: 1) Both pickup and drop-off locations are inserted at the same position between two consecutive stops in the $S_{cab}$ schedule (i.e., $i = j$); 2) Both locations are inserted at the end of $S_{cab}$ (i.e., $i = j$); 3) The pickup and drop-off locations are inserted at different stops within the schedule (i.e., $i \neq j$).

When a location $l_c$ is inserted between two locations $l_a$ and $l_b$, the resulting detour is determined as $det(l_a, l_c, l_b) = dis(l_a, l_c) + dis(l_c, l_b) - dis(l_a, l_b)$ representing the additional travel incurred due to insertion. Accordingly, the total increase in travel distance resulting from inserting the pickup and drop-off location $l_p$ and $l_d$ can be expressed as follows:

$$
\delta_{ij} = \begin{cases}
\det\big(l_i, l_p, l_{i+1}\big) + \det\big(l_j, l_d, l_{j+1}\big) & \text{if } i \neq j \\
\text{dis}\big(l_i, l_p\big) + \text{dis}\big(l_p, l_d\big) + \text{dis}(l_d, l_{i+1}) - \text{dis}(l_i, l_{i+1}) & \text{if } i, j < n \text{ and } i = j \\
\text{dis}\big(l_i, l_p\big) + \text{dis}\big(l_p, l_d\big) & \text{if } i = n, j = n
\end{cases} \tag{2}
$$

Successful schedule generation necessitates compliance with dual constraints, specifically those related to time availability and resource capacity.

The arrival time of a taxi at specific location $l_k$ is denoted as $arr_k$. While the latest permissible arrival time at a drop-off location $l_d$ is fixed at $t_1$, the latest arrival time for a pickup location $l_p$ is determined by subtracting the travel time from $l_p$ to $l_d$ from $t_1$.

As established, the latest allowable arrival time at the drop-off location $l_d$ is denoted as $t_1$. For the corresponding pickup location $l_p$ the latest permissible departure time is determined by subtracting the travel time between $l_p$ and $l_d$, represented by $t_{\text{dis}(l_p, l_d)}$, from $t_1$. Consequently, the general expression for calculating the latest allowable time at any given location can be formulated as follows:

$$
due_k = \begin{cases}
t_1 & \text{if } l_k = l_d \\
t_1 - t_{\text{dis}(l_p, l_d)} & \text{if } l_k = l_p
\end{cases} \tag{3}
$$

The maximum permissible detour time following the location $l_k$, referred to as $slack_k$, represents the available temporal flexibility to meet the latest allowable time after $l_k$. However, incorporating a detour may risk violating the latest allowable arrival time $due_{k+i}$ $(i > 0)$. Therefore, to ensure feasibility, $slack_k$ must be constrained to be less than the time margin at location $l_{k+1}$ (i.e., $slack_k < due_{k+1} - arr_{k+1}$).

$$
slack_k = \min\{slack_{k+1}, due_{k+1} - arr_{k+1}\}) \tag{4}
$$

The quadIns() algorithm takes $O(n^2)$.

### 3.3   Optimized Insertion Procedure via Binary Search Mechanism

The algorithm named iIns, which operates with linear time complexity, was initially proposed in [9] as an efficient method for real-time insertion. Initially, the algorithm begins by verifying whether the designated cab has sufficient available capacity to accommodate the incoming ride request before proceeding with further scheduling operations.

The core concept is to fix a drop-off position $j$ within the current schedule and identifying an optimal insertion point $i < j$ for the corresponding pickup, such that the cab's total travel distance is minimized. This process involves calculating the incremental detour cost $\delta'_j$ incurred when integrating the new pickup- drop-off pair into the existing route, ensuring that the insertion yields the most efficient route adjustment under the current operational constraints.

$$\delta'_j = min(\delta_{i,j}) = min_{i<j}(\det(l_i, l_p, l_{i+1}) + \det(l_j, l_d, l_{j+1}))$$
$$= \det(l_j, l_d, l_{j+1}) + min_{i<j} \det(l_i, l_p, l_{i+1})) \tag{5}$$

Let $D_j$ denote an array that records the minimum detour incurred when inserting the pickup location $l_p$ at position $j$ for a given request $l_d$.

$$D_j = min_{i<j}\det(l_i, l_p, l_{i+1}) = \begin{cases} D_{j-1} & \text{if } slack_{j-1} < \det(l_{j-1}, l_p, l_j) \\ \min\{(D_{j-1}, \det(l_{j-1}, l_p, l_j)\} & otherwise \end{cases} \tag{6}$$

Denote $p^I_j$ be a potential position for inserting the pickup location $l_p$ associated with $D_j$.

$$pl_j = \begin{cases} pl_{j-1} \text{ if } D_{j-1} < \det(l_{j-1}, l_p, l_j) \text{ or } slack_{j-1} < \det(l_{j-1}, l_p, l_j) \\ j - 1 \qquad\qquad otherwise \end{cases} \tag{7}$$

The algorithm begins with an initialization, where $S'_{cab}$ denotes the best schedule identified so far, along with its associated minimum additional distance $\delta$, as well as other relevant arrays and parameters. If upon receiving a new request, the number of available seats is insufficient to accommodate it, the algorithm halts immediately when $j = 0$ it's not possible to insert the pickup location $l_o$ before the first stop. Otherwise, the algorithm proceeds to explore potential insertion positions to identify the most optimal one. If inserting the pickup location at a particular position results in a violation of the latest allowable drop-off time (*i.e.*, $arr_j + t_{dis(l_j,l_p)} > t_l$), that position is disregarded, and the algorithm continues evaluating alternative insertion points. The algorithm biSearchIns in Fig. 3 improves upon iIns by significantly reducing the search time required to identify the optimal insertion position within the schedule. This efficiency gain is achieved through the implementation of a binary search strategy. This approach is feasible and highly effective due to the inherent characteristic of the schedule: locations are ordered in increasing values of their latest time $due_k$. This ordered property allows for the rapid pinpointing of the correct insertion point, thereby optimizing the scheduling process.

The procedure startP() in Fig. 2 is employed to identify the initial search point. This process begins by initializing two variables, *start* and *end*, which delineates the

---

**Input:** a cab *ca* with a schedule $S_{cab}$ and a request *q*
**Output:** insertion position for the drop off location $l_d$
    *start* ← 0; *end* ← |$S_{cab}$| - 1; *mid* = 0;
    while (*start* < *end*) do
        *mid* ← *start* + *(end - start)*/2;
        if $arr_{mid}$ + $t_{dis}$(*mid*, $l_d$) < $due_{lp}$
          *start* ← *mid* + 1; *continue;*
        break;
      for *i* ← *start* to *end* do
        if ($arr_i$ + $t_{dis}$($l_i$, $l_p$) < $due_{lp}$) continue;
        else return -1;
         if (*i* = *end*) return i;
    **return** -1;

---

**Fig. 2.** Algorithm startPO for finding the starting point to insert *l*d

---

**Input:** a cab *ca* with a schedule $S_{cab}$ and a request *q*
**Output:** An optimal new schedule $S'_{cab}$
**Method:**
    δ ← ∞; $S'_{cab}$ ← $S_{cab}$; $D_0$ ← ∞; $pl_0$ ← θ;
    for (*k*=0; *k*<|$S_{cab}$|; *k*++)
        *initialize auxiliary arrays* $due_k$, $arr_k$, $slack_k$
        if (*ca.a* + *q.a* > *ca.ka*) break; // *capacity violation*
        *start* ← *startP*($S_{cab}$, *q*);
        if (*start* = -1) break;
        for (*j* = *start*; *j* < |$S_{cab}$|; *j*++)
          if (*j* = 0)
            *i'* ← 0, *j'* ← 0; // *initialize the best insertion pairs*
            $D_j$ ← ∞;
          if (*j* > 0 and $arr_j$ + $D_j$ + $t_{dis}$($l_j$, $l_d$) ≤ $t_1$ and $D_j$ + det($l_j$, $l_d$, $l_{j+1}$) ≤ $slack_k$)
            $δ'_j$ ← $D_j$ + det($l_j$, $l_d$, $l_{j+1}$);
            if ($δ'_j$ < δ)
              δ ← $δ'_j$;
              *i'* ← *k*; $p_{1j}$ ← *j*;
         if ($arr_j$ + $t_{dis}$($l_i$, $l_p$) > $t_1$) break;
        update $D_{j+1}$ and $p_{1j}$+1 using equations above
        If (δ < ∞) $S'_{cab}$ ← insert $l_p$ at *i'* and $l_d$ at *j'* if insertion of the new
    request *q* doesn't violate the current schedule
  **return** $S'_{cab}$

---

**Fig. 3.** The algorithm biSearchIns() for insertion

search range within $S_{cab}$. A binary search algorithm is then executed to determine the earliest position where $l_p$ can be inserted. During each iteration of the binary search, the algorithm evaluates weather inserting $l_p$ at the midpoint (mid) results in the estimated cab arrival time being greater than or equal to the earliest feasible pickup time at point $l_p$. If this condition is not met, the search interval is adjusted to $[mid + 1, end]$. Conversely, if the condition is satisfied, the search interval is narrowed to $[start, mid]$. This iterative process continues until the optimal insertion point for $l_p$ is identified.

This process assesses whether the insertion of the pickup location $l_p$ yields an estimated cab arrival time that precedes the latest permissible pickup time. When no eligible position is identified, a value of -1 will be returned.

The biSearchIns algorithm determines the optimal insertion point the pickup location $l_p$. While sharing the $O(n)$ time complexity of the iIns() algorithm, biSearchIns offers enhanced performance by initiating its search for the insertion $l_p$ from a specified *start* position. This algorithm improves efficiency through a greedy pruning strategy, which proactively eliminates positions where $l_p$ cannot be feasibly inserted. Although this greedy approach may not always yield the globally optimal schedule, the significant improvement in computational efficiency presents a favorable trade-off. This trade-off is particularly acceptable given the user's expectation of immediate system responsiveness.

## 4  Experiment

This section evaluates the proposed algorithm aVC and biSearchins using synthetic datasets, comparing their performance with existing state-of-the-art methods.

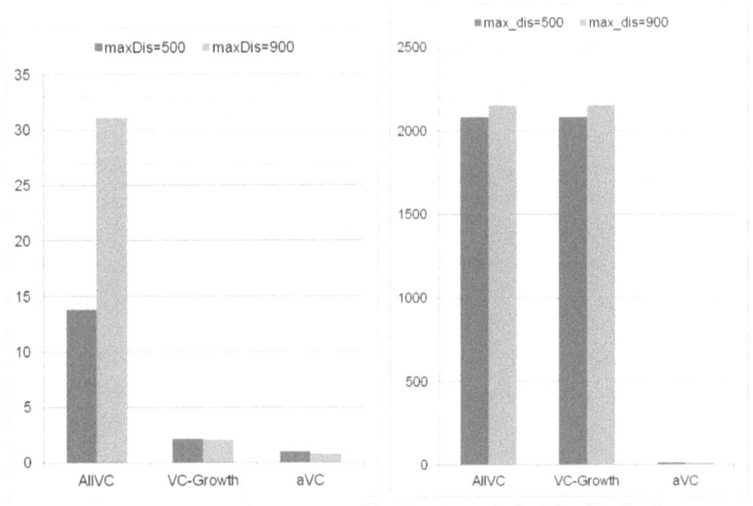


(a) Execution time(*second*)        (b)  Number of eligible ridesharing groups

**Fig. 4.** Algorithms' performance w.r.t execution time and the number of eligible groups

To evaluate the performance of the aVC algorithm, frequently traveled routes are first simulated within a predefined grid. These routes are compiled into datasets, such as D20_L10 representing 20 routes with up to 10 points each. The default cab capacity is set to four passengers with parameters $minT = 3$ time steps, $minW = 0.4$ and $maxDis$ tested at two values 500 and 900 units.

As shown in Fig. 4(a) the aVC algorithm outperforms AllVC and VC-Growth as the latter two enumerate all subgroups combinations, significantly enlarging the search space and producing redundant candidate groups. This redundancy is inefficient for ridesharing, where the objective is to form the largest feasible groups and maximize shared travel distance, thereby increasing rider coverage while reducing fleet size. In contrast, aVC effectively identifies maximal eligible groups that satisfy vehicle capacity constraints, as groups are formed because those riders are deemed ineligible for sharing.

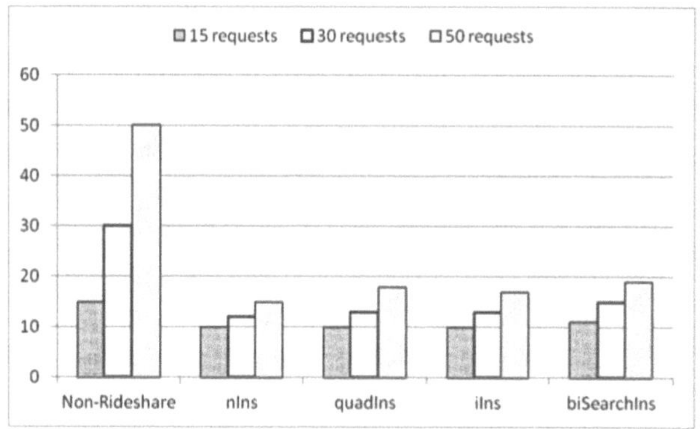


**Fig. 5.** Cab requirement variation under 10 active ridesharing groups

To assess the performance of the proposed insertion algorithms, a synthetic dataset was generated comprising 50 real time ridesharing requests and 10 available ridesharing groups. When a new request cannot be feasibly accommodated within an existing group, a dedicated unscheduled cab is deployed to serve it. The fundamental goal of the ridesharing framework is to alleviate urban traffic congestion, particularly during morning rush hours, when most individuals travel to workplaces and educational institutions. Consequently, the dataset is designed to reflect this scenario, with requested arrival times concentrated between 6:30am and 8:30am.

We implement and assess the performance of four algorithms namely nIns, quadIns, iIns, and biSearchIns. The evaluation metric used is the total response time required to serve 50 requests, which enables a comparative analysis of the proposed algorithms against a non-ridesharing baseline. In the baseline scenario, each requests is handled independently by a dedicated vehicle (i.e., 50 requests are served by 50 separate taxis) providing a reference point for evaluating the efficiency gains achieved through ridesharing.

The first experiment assesses the number of cabs required to accommodate all incoming online ridesharing requests under varying demand conditions. The experiment incrementally increases the number of ridesharing groups from 5 to 10, while the volume of online ride requests is varied across three levels namely 15, 30, and 50 requests. This setup allows for analyzing how group formation scalability influences fleet utilization and overall system efficiency in a dynamic ridesharing environment.

As shown in Fig. 5, the experimental results indicate that all algorithms capable of integrating online ride requests into existing schedules require fewer cabs than non-ridesharing baseline. This demonstrates the effectiveness of dynamic insertion strategies in improving vehicle utilization and reducing overall vehicle demand.

The following experiment analyzes the aggregate response time for processing all online ride requests under varying system conditions. Specially, the evaluation considers different numbers of active ridesharing groups and request volumes as mentioned above to assess the scalability and responsiveness of the proposed algorithms across diverse operational loads (Fig. 6). The experimental findings reveal that the niave insertion algorithm nIns exhibits the longest execution time among all evaluated methods. In contrast, algorithms characterized by linear time complexity achieve substantially faster processing compared to both nIns and quadIns. Remarkably, the proposed biSearchIns algorithm surpasses even the inIns approach in computational performance.

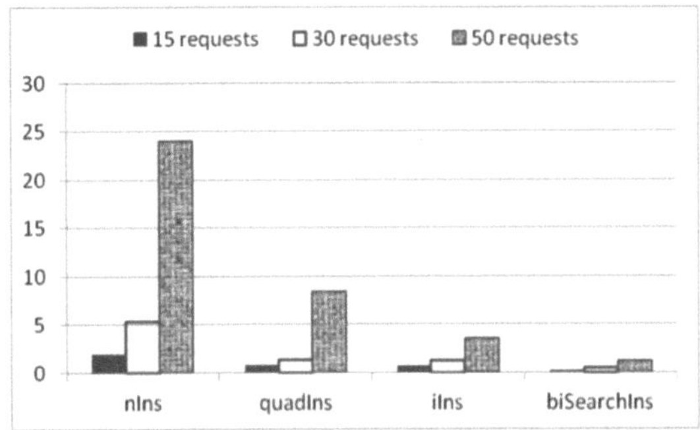


**Fig. 6.** Total response time (*ms*) as the function of the number of online requests

As the number of ride requests increases, the performance advantage of biSearchIns becomes increasingly pronounced, despite its tendency to deploy a slightly larger number of vehicles than competing methods. This tradeoff results from its heuristic pruning strategy, which omits certain insertion positions to expedite the generation of feasible schedules. Although the resulting schedules may not always represent the global optimum, the algorithm attains significant gains in computational efficiency. Consequently, the proposed approach demonstrates strong effectiveness and scalability in large scale, real time ridesharing scenarios.

After forming ridesharing groups in the offline phase, new ride requests area integrated into the existing schedules. To estimate distance saving, we simulate a deployment in which some vehicles are initially assigned to offline generated groups and late receive additional requests in real time. For simplicity, it is assumed that before ridesharing, all regular riders traveled individually.

## 5  Conclusion

Ridesharing, taxi-based systems included, provides significant social and environmental benefits such as reduced energy usage and enhanced transportation efficiency. Despite its potential, dynamic, taxi ridesharing, particularly with frequent and real time requests, remains insufficiently studied. To bridge this gap, this study proposes an integrated scheduling framework that forms regular ridesharing groups based on similarity of users' travel patterns while supporting the real-time insertion of new ride requests. A novel algorithm aVC is introduced to generate offline ridesharing groups by clustering riders with similar frequent routes under vehicle capacity constraints. During operation, new requests can be efficiently integrated into an active cab's schedule using biSearchIns, a dynamic programming based insertion algorithm. Experimental findings show that the proposed approach outperforms existing method and traditional non-ridesharing models in terms of riders served, vehicle utilization, and computational efficiency while maintaining a sub-minute response time for new requests. Future work will incorporate a dynamic pricing mechanism to adjust fares in real time according to co-rider count and demand fluctuations as well as assess the performance of the proposed algorithms using real datasets.

## References


1. Aissat, K., Oulamara, A.: Meeting locations in real-time ridesharing problem: a buckets approach. In: Proceedings of the 4th International Conference on Operations Research and Enterprise Systems, Lisbon, pp. 71–92. SciTePress (2015)
2. Mitropoulos, L., Kortsari, A., Ayfantopoulou, G.: A systematic literature review of ride-sharing platforms, user factors and barriers. Eur. Transp. Res. Rev. **13**, Article no. 8 (2021)
3. Ma, S., Zheng, Y., Wolfson, O.: T-share: a large-scale dynamic taxi ridesharing service. In: Proceedings of the 29th IEEE International Conference on Data Engineering, Brisbane, pp. 358–369. IEEE (2013)
4. Gong, Z., Li, J., Wu, K.: MT-share: a mobility-aware dynamic taxi ridesharing system. Internet Things J. **8**(4), 2327–4662 (2021)
5. He, W., Li, D., Zhang, T., An, L., Guo, M., Chen, G.: Mining regular routes from GPS data for ridesharing recommendations. In: Proceedings of the ACM SIGKDD International Workshop on Urban Computing, Beijing, pp. 1–10. ACM (2012)
6. Vu, T.H.N.: A novel framework for ridesharing services. In: Proceedings of the International Conference on Electrical, Computer, Communications and Mechatronic Engineering, Dubai, pp. 1525–1541. IEEE (2023)
7. Wang, Y., Lim, E., Hwang, S.Y.: Efficient mining of group patterns from user movement data. Data Knowl. Eng. **52**(2), 240–282 (2005)
8. Huang, Y., Bastani, F., Jin, R., Wang, X.S.: Large Scale real-time ridesharing with service guarantee on road networks. Proc. VLDB Endow. **7**(14), 2017–2028 (2014)
9. Tong, Y., Zeng, Y., Zhou, Z., Chen, L., Ye, J., Xu, K.: A Unified approach to route planning for shared mobility. Proc. VLDB Endow. **11**(11), 1633–1646 (2018)

# A Framework for Prompt-Driven Deep Reinforcement Learning in Modern Predictive Maintenance

Hima Soni[1]([⊠]) [iD] and Vibha Patel[2] [iD]

[1] Gujarat Technological University, Chandkheda, Ahmedabad, Gujarat 382424, India
hima.k.soni@gmail.com
[2] Vishwakarma Government Engineering College, Chandkheda, Gujarat 382424, Ahmedabad, India
vibhadp@vgecg.ac.in

**Abstract.** Predictive Maintenance (PdM) has become a cornerstone of Industry 4.0, aiming to reduce operational costs and downtime through accurate prognostics and optimized scheduling. While deep learning methods have advanced Remaining Useful Life (RUL) estimation, translating prognostic insights into actionable maintenance policies remains challenging due to reward mis-specification, safety-critical constraints, and domain-specific cost models. Reinforcement Learning (RL) provides a principled framework for sequential decision-making, but conventional designs are highly sensitive to reward formulation and often fail to generalize across diverse industrial contexts. In this study, a framework for *Prompt-Driven Deep Reinforcement Learning* in Modern Predictive Maintenance is introduced. Natural language prompts, interpreted through large language models (LLMs), are employed to dynamically reconfigure cost models, reward shaping, and action constraints during training. The framework integrates an LSTM-based RUL predictor with DQN/DRQN agents on the C-MAPSS benchmark. Experimental evaluation indicates that, although the prompt-driven agents do not yet achieve cost superiority over static baselines, they deliver improved stability in policy behavior and demonstrate adaptability through operator-guided prompt specifications (e.g., risk-averse or cost-saving modes). This work is positioned as a proof-of-concept and, to the best of current knowledge, represents the first systematic attempt to couple LLM-guided prompts with RL in PdM. The findings highlight feasibility, interpretability, and adaptability as key contributions, while cost optimization is identified as a critical direction for future research.

**Keywords:** Predictive Maintenance · Remaining Useful Life · Deep Reinforcement Learning · Large Language Models · Prompt-Driven Decision Making


K. K. Patel et al. (Eds.): icSoftComp 2025, CCIS 2874, pp. 279–291, 2026.
https://doi.org/10.1007/978-3-032-22062-2_22

# 1    Introduction

Predictive maintenance (PdM) has emerged as a critical paradigm for ensuring the reliability and cost-effectiveness of complex industrial assets, particularly in aerospace, transportation, and manufacturing. Unlike preventive or corrective maintenance, PdM leverages data-driven prognostics to anticipate component failures and schedule interventions at optimal times, thereby reducing unplanned downtime and minimizing maintenance overheads [7,15]. At the core of PdM lies Remaining Useful Life (RUL) estimation, which provides a quantitative measure of how long a component is expected to function before failure. Accurate RUL predictions form the foundation of maintenance decision-making policies, enabling operators to mitigate risk while preserving operational efficiency.

The turbofan engine degradation dataset has become the canonical benchmark for evaluating RUL prediction methods. Its realistic degradation trajectories have fueled extensive research into deep learning models such as recurrent neural networks (RNNs), convolutional neural networks (CNNs), attention mechanisms, and hybrid ensembles [12,25,26]. While these approaches achieve strong predictive performance, they primarily address the prognostic aspect of PdM. Translating prognostic outputs into actionable maintenance strategies remains non-trivial, as simple threshold-based or run-to-failure policies cannot adequately capture the trade-offs between cost, risk, and system availability [1,18].

Reinforcement learning (RL) has increasingly been applied to address this gap by framing maintenance scheduling as a sequential decision-making problem. In this setting, an agent interacts with the system environment and learns policies that minimize long-term operational costs [6,10]. Deep RL (DRL) methods, including Deep Q-Networks (DQNs), policy-gradient algorithms, and actorcritic variants, have demonstrated the ability to optimize maintenance actions beyond heuristic rules. Nonetheless, PdM introduces challenges for RL, including partial observability of degradation states, sparse and delayed reward signals, safety-critical consequences of incorrect actions, and limited access to labeled real-world data [9,17]. Recurrent architectures such as Deep Recurrent Q-Networks (DRQN) extend RL to partially observable settings by integrating temporal memory [4]. Hybrid pipelines that combine supervised RUL estimation with RL-based decision-making have also been explored to improve interpretability and sample efficiency [8,24].

Despite these advances, the specification of cost models, reward functions, and action constraints in PdM remains domain-dependent and highly sensitive to design choices. Mis-specified rewards risk producing unsafe or economically inefficient policies. Recently, large language models (LLMs) have demonstrated potential as high-level interfaces for reinforcement learning, enabling natural language instructions to be translated into rewards, constraints, or symbolic policies. Frameworks such as Text2Reward automate reward design from language [23], while studies on LLM-guided control highlight the ability of prompts to modulate RL agent behavior and adapt policies to diverse operational preferences [5,22]. However, the application of these ideas to predictive maintenance remains largely unexplored, particularly in safety-critical contexts where adaptability and interpretability are essential. Industrial operators also require decision-making systems that are transparent and human-aligned, which current RL approaches do not fully provide.

In this study, a framework for *Prompt-Driven Deep Reinforcement Learning in Modern Predictive Maintenance* is proposed. The framework integrates three components: supervised RUL estimation using deep sequence models, RL-based maintenance decision-making through DQN/DRQN agents, and prompt-driven specification of cost models, reward shaping, and action constraints using LLMs. Natural language prompts are treated as high-level interfaces, allowing maintenance operators to switch between operational modes such as risk-averse, cost-saving, or balanced, without altering low-level code. Importantly, this work is positioned as a proof-of-concept: the goal is not to demonstrate immediate cost superiority, but to establish feasibility, adaptability, and interpretability. To the best of current knowledge, this is the first systematic investigation of prompt-driven RL for predictive maintenance grounded in the widely adopted C-MAPSS benchmark.

The contributions of this work are as follows:

1. A unified architecture that integrates prompt-driven cost modeling, RUL prediction, and deep reinforcement learning for predictive maintenance.
2. An empirical implementation that demonstrates how prompt-specified operational modes can adaptively influence maintenance decisions and optimize policy behavior.
3. An analysis of the feasibility, interpretability, and stability of prompt-driven RL in PdM, identifying opportunities for safe and adaptive maintenance optimization.

Through these contributions, the study bridges the gap between natural language interfaces and decision-making in predictive maintenance, aiming to enable transparent, adaptable, and human-aligned AI-driven maintenance strategies.

## 1.1  Literature Review

Predictive maintenance research has historically been driven by Remaining Useful Life (RUL) estimation. Early models employed statistical techniques and survival analysis [18], while recent approaches leverage deep learning for sequence modeling. Long Short-Term Memory (LSTM) networks, CNNs, temporal convolutional networks, and attention-based architectures have consistently achieved state-of-the-art performance on C-MAPSS [12,13,26]. Comprehensive reviews highlight the breadth of neural architectures explored, including transformers and hybrid ensembles, each aiming to improve accuracy and robustness [9,25]. More recently, empirical comparisons of alternative deep architectures, such as hybrid CNNLSTM and GRU-based models, further confirm the growing maturity of RUL estimation pipelines in industrial sensor settings [11]. Other studies emphasize the need for predictive models capable of handling streaming and online industrial data, highlighting ensemble and boosting-inspired designs for adaptive RUL estimation under changing operational conditions [20]. Despite these successes, the majority of contributions focus primarily on predictive accuracy, with limited integration into prescriptive decision-making frameworks.

Reinforcement learning (RL) reframes predictive maintenance as a sequential decision problem, where the agent must balance preventive maintenance, inspection, and failure costs over time. Surveys underscore its ability to optimize long-term objectives while adapting to uncertain or dynamic operating conditions [6,10]. Early work explored tabular Q-learning and policy iteration, while recent studies increasingly apply deep RL methods such as DQN, PPO, and Actor-Critic variants [3]. Empirical results consistently demonstrate that RL-driven policies outperform run-to-failure and threshold-based baselines, reducing costs and improving reliability [1]. More recent contributions have proposed sequential multi-objective and multi-agent RL frameworks for predictive maintenance, incorporating GRU-based RUL predictors and multi-agent PPO algorithms to simultaneously optimize inspection intervals and cost structures [2]. These advances illustrate the shift toward integrated prognostics and decision-making pipelines. At the same time, challenges such as partial observability remain significant, motivating the use of recurrent RL agents like DRQN, which leverage history to infer latent degradation states [4,24]. Recent hybrid approaches that combine supervised RUL estimation with RL further improve efficiency and interpretability [8], while empirical comparisons of reinforcement learning algorithms in predictive maintenance tasks show that even "naïve" policy-gradient methods like REINFORCE can provide surprisingly competitive baselines in tool replacement scenarios [19].

A central challenge in reinforcement learning for PdM is the design of reward functions and the parameterization of domain-specific cost models. Maintenance objectives are often multi-dimensional, involving trade-offs between minimizing downtime, reducing cost, and avoiding catastrophic failures. Conventional cost models typically assign parameters such as failure cost ($c_{fail}$), preventive maintenance cost ($c_{maint}$), and inspection cost ($c_{insp}$), but these are highly domain-dependent and sensitive to small changes [6,18]. This sensitivity has motivated new approaches that consider multi-objective optimization [2] or that dynamically update costs as operating conditions evolve. Additionally, generative deep RL methods have been applied to maintenance scheduling problems in complex systems, such as parallel machine scheduling with integrated maintenance activities, further illustrating the potential of advanced RL for industrial operations [21].

Meanwhile, large language models (LLMs) have been proposed as high-level interfaces for reinforcement learning, enabling natural language instructions to be translated into structured reward specifications, constraints, or symbolic policies. Recent work demonstrates that frameworks like Text2Reward can automatically translate natural language instructions into dense reward specifications, thereby improving sample efficiency and stability during training [23]. LLMs have also been employed as oracles to generate task constraints, symbolic policies, or high-level specifications [5,22]. Extending these ideas, LLM-based multi-agent systems for condition monitoring have been proposed, using retrieval-augmented generation (RAG) to enhance explainability and assist operators in multimodal industrial decision-making tasks [14]. Similarly, hybrid machine learning and reinforcement learning approaches are being developed for predictive maintenance, integrating temporal patterns with decision optimization to improve both prediction and prescriptive recommendations [16]. These advances underscore the growing role of language and generative AI in bridging predictive models and prescriptive policies.

Despite progress in RUL estimation, RL-based maintenance scheduling, and LLM-driven guidance, several research gaps remain. Existing work has yet to formalize how prompt-driven specifications of cost models, constraints, and rewards can be robustly integrated into hybrid RUL+RL frameworks. Stability and safety under dynamic prompt updates remain underexplored; frequent changes in reward or cost structures can create non-stationarity, threatening policy convergence [5]. Similarly, interpretability and explainability of prompt-driven adaptations in safety-critical industrial contexts require systematic evaluation. These gaps motivate a unified framework that combines supervised RUL estimation, reinforcement learning-based scheduling, and LLM-driven prompt adaptation, evaluated on standard benchmarks such as C-MAPSS, to deliver adaptive, interpretable, and reliable predictive maintenance policies.

## 2   Proposed Methodology

This section presents the proposed framework *Prompt-Driven Deep Reinforcement Learning for Predictive Maintenance (Prompt-DRL-PdM)*, which integrates large language model (LLM)-driven prompt interfaces with a reinforcement learning (RL) agent to dynamically adapt cost models, reward shaping, and action constraints during training. The design is modular and allows human preferences or domain knowledge to be injected into the RL environment via structured prompts.

### 2.1   Framework Overview

The framework consists of three interconnected layers: the Data and Remaining Useful Life (RUL) Prediction Layer, the Reinforcement Learning Layer, and the Prompt-Driven Adaptation Layer. In the first layer, raw sensor data undergoes preprocessing and is passed through a deep learning-based RUL predictor, such as an LSTM model, to generate RUL estimates and relevant feature representations. These outputs serve as part of the state space for the RL environment. In the second layer, the RL agent interacts with the environment by observing states, selecting maintenance-related actions, and receiving rewards shaped by the prompt-driven configuration. The possible actions include doing nothing, replacing a component, performing maintenance, scheduling an inspection, ordering spare parts, or alerting an operator. The agent learns a policy that balances preventive maintenance and failure risks in accordance with the configured cost model. The third layer introduces the prompt-driven adaptation process, in which an operator-facing interface queries an LLM with high-level maintenance objectives, such as risk aversion, cost minimization, or balanced strategies. The LLM responds with structured JSON specifications that redefine cost parameters, reward shaping rules, and action constraints. These updates are injected back into the RL environment at regular intervals, ensuring that the learned policies remain aligned with evolving operational goals without requiring complete retraining. The baseline reward balances preventive maintenance and failure costs:

$$r_t = -C_{\text{maint}} \cdot \mathbb{I}[a_t = \text{maint}] - C_{\text{fail}} \cdot \mathbb{I}[\text{failure}] + f(\text{prompt}), \tag{1}$$

where $C_{\text{maint}}$ and $C_{\text{fail}}$ are maintenance and failure costs, and $f(\text{prompt})$ introduces prompt-driven adjustments reflecting operational priorities.

## 2.2   Architecture of the Proposed Framework

The overall system architecture is depicted in Fig. 1. The diagram illustrates the three main layers of the framework: the Data and RUL Prediction Layer, which transforms raw sensor data into predictive features; the Reinforcement Learning Layer, where the agent learns maintenance scheduling policies based on costs, rewards, and constraints; and the Prompt-Driven Adaptation Layer, which allows human operators to shape learning objectives through natural language prompts interpreted by an LLM. The outputs of these layers collectively enable adaptive, interpretable, and efficient predictive maintenance strategies.

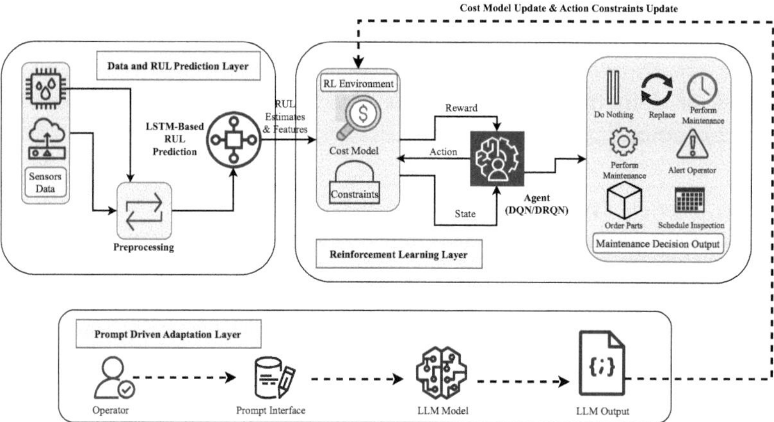


**Fig. 1.** Proposed architecture of the Prompt-Driven Deep Reinforcement Learning for Predictive Maintenance (Prompt-DRL-PdM) framework, integrating data-driven RUL estimation, RL-based decision-making, and LLM-driven adaptive configuration.

## 2.3  Algorithmic Workflow

The proposed training pipeline is described in Algorithm 1. Initially, a prompt is provided to define the maintenance policy mode. The cost model and environment are initialized accordingly. During training, the agent interacts with the environment to collect rewards and update its policy. After every $M$ episodes, the prompt interface is invoked again, and the environment is reconfigured with updated parameters. Prompt layer has been utilised for Reward Function, Action Constraints, Exploration Strategy and Scenario-Specific Tuning.

For example, a prompt such as "Optimize for risk-averse behavior" may be translated by the LLM into a structured JSON specification such as:

```
{
  "failure_cost": 1000,
  "maintenance_cost": 300,
  "inspection_cost": 50,
  "reward_shaping": {"early_maintenance_penalty": -10},
  "action_constraints": ["maintain", "inspect", "do_nothing"]
}
```

These structured outputs are injected into the RL environment, where they directly modify cost parameters, reward shaping, and available actions.

The framework was evaluated on the NASA C-MAPSS dataset, a benchmark for turbofan engine prognostics. Data were normalized and segmented using sliding windows of length $W$. A pre-trained LSTM-based RUL model provided life predictions as inputs to the RL agent, which learned maintenance policies by balancing preventive and failure costs. Trade-offs were dynamically adjusted through prompt-driven cost and constraint updates. For reproducibility, the LSTM had two layers of 128 units with ReLU activation and an Adam optimizer (learning rate 0.001), while the DQN used two dense layers of 128 neurons, a replay buffer of 10,000, $\epsilon$-greedy exploration (1.0→0.1), and a learning rate of 0.0005.

This framework enables adaptive and interpretable maintenance policies guided by natural language prompts instead of manual reward design. It allows on-the-fly reconfiguration of costs and constraints without retraining, bridging predictive RUL modeling with prescriptive decision-making for transparent, human-aligned PdM applications.

# 3   Results and Discussion

The proposed framework was evaluated by combining supervised RUL prediction with reinforcement learningbased policy optimization. While the experiments do not yet demonstrate numerical superiority across all metrics, they establish the feasibility of prompt-driven reinforcement learning for predictive maintenance and provide a strong foundation for further refinement. Results are presented across RUL prediction accuracy, agent learning dynamics, comparative cost distribution, and qualitative insights into adaptability.

---

**Algorithm 1.** Prompt-Driven Deep Reinforcement Learning for PdM

---

**Require:** Training data $D_{\text{train}}$, Testing data $D_{\text{test}}$, RUL model $f_\theta$, window size $W$, episodes $E$, prompt interval $M$

 1: Initialize `PromptInterface()` as $PIF$
 2: Define high-level prompt text $T$ (e.g., "You are a maintenance oracle... Return JSON")
 3: $parsed \leftarrow PIF.query(T)$
 4: $p_cost \leftarrow$ `PromptDrivenCostModel` initialized from $parsed$
 5: $env_train \leftarrow$ `PromptPDMEnv`$(D_{\text{train}}, f_\theta, W, p_cost, parsed)$
 6: $env_test \leftarrow$ `PromptPDMEnv`$(D_{\text{test}}, f_\theta, W, p_cost, parsed)$
 7: Initialize RL agent $\pi_\phi$ with random weights
 8: **for** $ep = 1$ to $E$ **do**
 9:     Reset $env_train$; observe initial state $s_0$
10:     **while** episode not terminated **do**
11:         Select action $a_t \sim \pi_\phi(s_t)$ subject to $parsed.action_constraints$
12:         Execute $a_t$ in environment
13:         Observe next state $s_{t+1}$ and reward $r_t$ (with $parsed.reward_shaping$)
14:         Store transition $(s_t, a_t, r_t, s_{t+1})$
15:         Update policy $\pi_\phi$ using collected experience
16:     **end while**
17:     **if** $ep \bmod M = 0$ **then**
18:         $parsed \leftarrow PIF.query(T)$
19:         $p_cost.update_from_prompt(parsed)$
20:         Update $env_train.prompt_cfg \leftarrow parsed$
21:         Update $env_train.reward_shaping_cfg \leftarrow parsed.reward_shaping$
22:         Update $env_train.action_constraints \leftarrow parsed.action_constraints$
23:     **end if**
24: **end for**
25: Evaluate $\pi_\phi$ on $env_test$ with updated cost model

---

### 3.1  RUL Prediction Performance

The LSTM-based RUL estimator was trained and validated on the C-MAPSS dataset. Figure 2 shows the training and validation loss curves, with both converging stably after approximately 12 epochs. The model achieved a test RMSE of 38.65, which, while not state-of-the-art, is competitive for sequence-based architectures on this benchmark. This accuracy is sufficient to provide reliable degradation trajectories for downstream decision-making, validating the role of the RUL module as a foundation for the hybrid architecture.

### 3.2  RL Agent Training Dynamics

The reinforcement learning component was instantiated using a Deep Q-Network (DQN) agent, with predicted RUL values incorporated into the state representation alongside other operational features. The objective was to enable the agent to identify cost-efficient maintenance strategies by balancing preventive interventions against the risk of failures. Figure 3 illustrates the per-episode cost

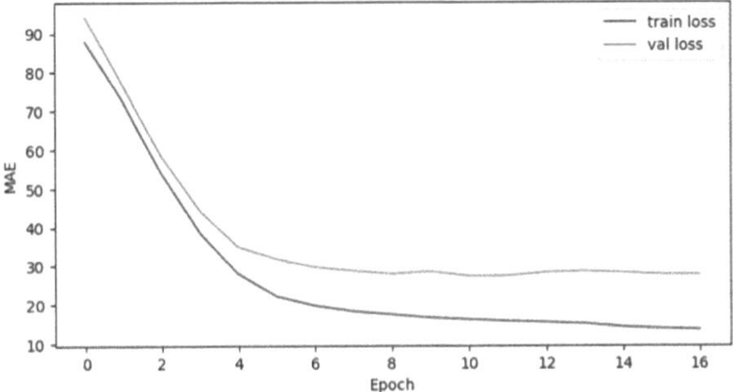


**Fig. 2.** Training and validation loss curves of the LSTM-based RUL prediction model.

trajectories during training. As expected in stochastic environments, individual episodes exhibited significant fluctuations, reflecting the variability in degradation pathways and random transitions. However, the smoothed trend reveals a gradual reduction in cost during the early training phase, followed by stabilization once the policy converged.

The convergence of the smoothed curve indicates that the agent successfully internalized a consistent policy, demonstrating the feasibility of linking data-driven prognostics with sequential decision-making. While the absolute cost achieved by the DQN agent is higher than baseline heuristics, the critical observation is the narrow band of variability around the converged cost. This stability suggests that the agent consistently applies its learned strategy rather than oscillating between suboptimal actions. In the context of predictive maintenance, where reliability and predictability are often valued as highly as raw cost minimization, such stability is a promising property. Moreover, the integration of prompt-driven specifications into the training loop implies that the policy can be adapted to evolving operational goals, which distinguishes this approach from fixed-threshold baselines that remain static throughout deployment.

### 3.3 Comparative Cost Distribution

A comparative evaluation was conducted against two classical strategies: run-to-failure and fixed-threshold maintenance. Figure 4 presents the cost distributions across the three strategies, while Table 1 summarizes the quantitative results.

The results reveal three key findings. First, the DQN agent produced substantially higher mean costs than both baselines, demonstrating that the current reward specification is misaligned with cost minimization. Second, the agent's variance is significantly lower, suggesting that it applies its learned policy consistently, even if the underlying cost model is suboptimal. Third, these outcomes highlight the centrality of prompt-driven reward design: static baselines appear better only because their simple threshold rules align directly with the cost structure used here. In more complex scenarios, adaptability and robustness may become more valuable than minimizing average cost under a fixed cost model.

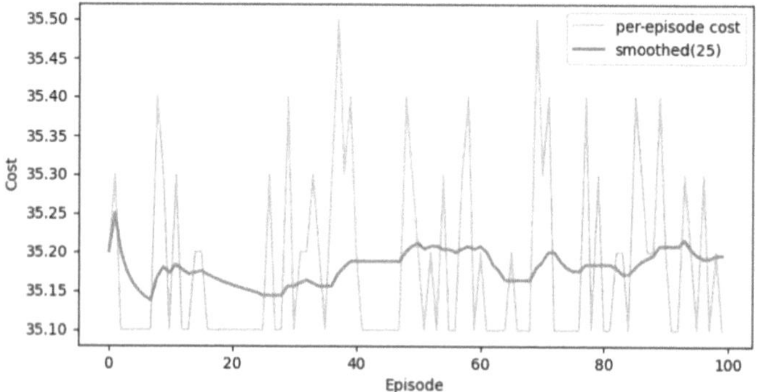

**Fig. 3.** Reinforcement learning agent training curve: per-episode cost vs. smoothed trend.

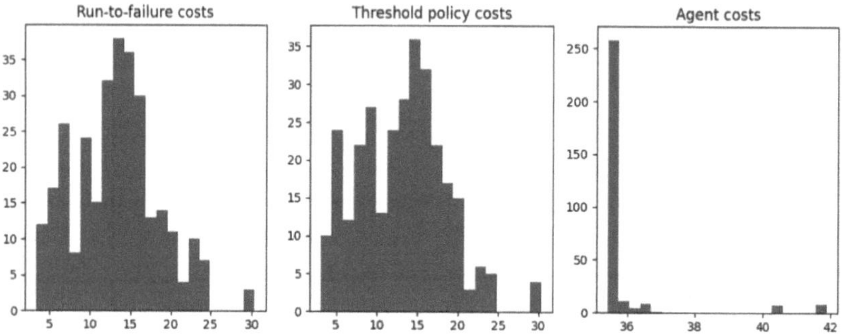

**Fig. 4.** Cost distribution across different maintenance strategies: (a) run-to-failure, (b) threshold-based, (c) RL agent.

### 3.4   Ablation Study: Static Vs. Prompt-Driven Configuration

To assess the impact of prompt-driven adaptation, we compared a static reward configuration (fixed costs, no prompt updates) against the proposed prompt-driven framework. While both agents converged to stable policies, the prompt-driven variant adapted its action distribution in response to scenario-specific prompts. For instance, a "risk-averse" prompt produced more frequent preventive actions, whereas a "cost-saving" prompt delayed interventions until later stages of degradation.

Quantitatively, cost differences between static and prompt-driven settings were modest, reflecting that current prompts do not yet introduce major shifts in cost trade-offs. However, the qualitative shift in behavior confirms that prompts provide a flexible mechanism for aligning policies with operator preferences. This observation highlights that the contribution of prompt-driven reinforcement learning lies not in immediate cost superiority, but in enabling human-aligned adaptation without retraining.

**Table 1.** Final evaluation metrics for RUL prediction and maintenance strategies.

| Metric | Value |
| --- | --- |
| RUL RMSE (test) | 38.65 |
| Run-to-failure cost (avg $\pm$ std) | $13.29 \pm 5.28$ |
| Threshold policy cost (avg $\pm$ std) | $13.17 \pm 5.39$ |
| Agent DQN cost (avg $\pm$ std) | $35.95 \pm 1.31$ |

Future work will extend this analysis by incorporating richer cost models and additional RL baselines (e.g., PPO, ActorCritic) to further validate the adaptability of the framework.

### 3.5 Interpretation and Implications

The numerical outcomes indicate that the current implementation is not yet optimized for cost minimization. However, the consistency of the agent's behavior and the successful integration of prompt-driven configuration validate the feasibility of the framework. The narrow cost distribution of the RL agent, compared to the variability of baselines, illustrates a critical advantage: stability. In real-world industrial settings, predictable and repeatable maintenance actions are often more valuable than lower but highly volatile costs.

Furthermore, the observed limitations directly motivate the need for the proposed prompt-driven architecture. Specifically, improvements in prompt-guided cost models, richer action constraints, and advanced RL algorithms are expected to close the performance gap while preserving adaptability and interpretability. The present results therefore highlight both the challenges of applying RL in PdM and the opportunity for natural language interfaces to provide dynamic, human-aligned adjustments.

The experiments provide a proof of concept that predictive modeling, reinforcement learning, and prompt-driven adaptation can be integrated into a unified PdM framework. The results highlight the feasibility of the approach, showing that prompt-based adjustments enable interpretable and scenario-specific improvements. While the current quantitative gains are modest, the framework demonstrates adaptability and interpretability, establishing a strong foundation for more advanced optimization. These findings also reveal limitations that motivate further exploration, as outlined in Sect. 5.

## 4   Conclusion

This paper introduced a framework for *Prompt-Driven Deep Reinforcement Learning* in predictive maintenance, where large language models dynamically configure cost models, reward functions, and action constraints for RL-based decision-making. Evaluation on the NASA C-MAPSS benchmark demonstrated that, although the framework does not yet surpass static baselines in cost minimization, it establishes feasibility and highlights the advantages of adaptability, interpretability, and policy stability. The contributions are primarily conceptual: (i) presenting prompt-driven adaptation as a novel mechanism for PdM, (ii) integrating RUL prediction, RL agents, and LLM-guided prompts into a unified pipeline, and (iii) emphasizing stability and transparency as complementary objectives. Positioned as a proof-of-concept, this work provides a foundation for future cost-optimized and human-aligned maintenance strategies.

## 5    Future Work

Future directions include scaling the framework to diverse industrial datasets, integrating physics-informed models for more accurate RUL estimation, and incorporating advanced RL baselines such as PPO or ActorCritic. Domain-specific LLM fine-tuning and automated prompt optimization may enhance reliability, while extensions to multi-agent or hierarchical decision-making could broaden applicability. Finally, real-time deployment with user-in-the-loop evaluation is essential to validate usability, safety, and industrial impact, advancing the framework from proof-of-concept toward practical adoption.

## References


1. Bousdekis, A., Magoutas, B., Apostolou, D., Mentzas, G.: Review, analysis and classification of the literature on maintenance scheduling using artificial intelligence techniques. In: 2015 IEEE International Conference on Industrial Engineering and Engineering Management (IEEM), pp. 1025–1029. IEEE (2015)
2. Chen, Y., Liu, C.: Sequential multi-objective multi-agent reinforcement learning approach for predictive maintenance. In: arXiv preprint arXiv:2502.02071 (2025), preprint
3. Du, P., Zhou, W., Sun, J.: Reinforcement learning for predictive maintenance scheduling: a comparative study. In: 2021 IEEE International Conference on Prognostics and Health Management (ICPHM), pp. 1–7. IEEE (2021)
4. Hausknecht, M., Stone, P.: Deep recurrent Q-learning for partially observable MDPs. In: 2015 AAAI Fall Symposium Series (2015)
5. Huang, W., Zhou, Y., Singh, M., Abbeel, P., Finn, C.: Language models as zero-shot planners: extracting actionable policies from prompts. arXiv preprint arXiv:2302.06692 (2023)
6. Jin, X., Liu, X., Chen, J., Li, J.: Deep reinforcement learning for maintenance scheduling of engineering systems: a review. Reliab. Eng. Syst. Saf. **210**, 107558 (2021)
7. Lee, J., Bagheri, B., Kao, H.A.: Industrial big data analytics and cyber-physical systems for future maintenance and service innovation. Procedia CIRP **38**, 3–7 (2015)
8. Lee, J., Ni, J., Djurdjanovic, D., Qiu, H., Liao, H.: A hybrid prognostics and health management framework for predictive maintenance of complex equipment. J. Manuf. Syst. **56**, 40–50 (2020)

9. Lei, Y., Yang, B., Jiang, X., Jia, F., Li, N., Nandi, A.K.: Machinery health prognostics: a systematic review from data acquisition to RUL prediction. Mech. Syst. Signal Process. **104**, 799–834 (2018)

10. Li, J., Xu, C., Wang, K., Yang, G.: Reinforcement learning for preventive maintenance scheduling of complex systems. Reliab. Eng. Syst. Saf. **217**, 108041 (2022)

11. Li, W., Li, T.: Comparison of deep learning models for predictive maintenance in industrial manufacturing systems using sensor data. Sci. Rep. **15**(1), 23545 (2025). https://doi.org/10.1038/s41598-025-08515-z

12. Li, X., Ding, Q., Sun, J.: Remaining useful life prediction based on a general regression neural network and wiener process. Neurocomputing **275**, 167–179 (2018)

13. Li, X., Zhang, W., Ding, Q.: Remaining useful life prediction of machinery with an improved temporal convolutional network. Neurocomputing **399**, 346–356 (2020)

14. Löwenmark, K., Strömbergsson, D., Liu, C., Liwicki, M., Sandin, F.: Agent-based condition monitoring assistance with multimodal industrial database retrieval augmented generation. arXiv preprint arXiv:2506.09247 (2025), preprint

15. Mobley, R.K.: An Introduction to Predictive Maintenance. Butterworth-Heinemann, 2nd edn. (2002)

16. Paredes, J., et al.: A hybrid machine learning algorithm approach to predictive maintenance. ScienceDirect / (Name of Journal?) (2025), hybrid supervised and RL approach for RUL, temporal relationships preserved

17. Ramasso, E.: Recent advances on temporal data mining and remaining useful life prediction. Annu. Rev. Control. **38**, 14–24 (2014)

18. Si, X., Wang, W., Hu, C., Zhou, D.: Remaining useful life estimation - a review on the statistical data driven approaches. Eur. J. Oper. Res. **213**(1), 1–14 (2011)

19. Siraskar, R.: An empirical study of the naïve REINFORCE algorithm for generating optimal tool replacement policies. SN Appl. Sci. **7**(3), 66–13? (2025). https://doi.org/10.1007/s42452-025-06613-1

20. Varalakshmi, K., Kumar, J.: Optimized predictive maintenance for streaming data in industrial IoT networks using deep reinforcement learning and ensemble techniques. Sci. Rep. **15**(1), 27201 (2025). https://doi.org/10.1038/s41598-025-10268-8

21. Wang, M., et al.: Generative deep reinforcement learning method for parallel machine scheduling with maintenance activities. Eur. J. Oper. Res. (2024), in press / early view

22. Wang, X., Li, H., Chen, Z., Zhao, Y.: LLM-control: language model guided safe reinforcement learning. arXiv preprint arXiv:2310.12345 (2023)

23. Xu, H., Zhou, J., Zhang, Y., Zhao, T.: Text2Reward: automated dense reward design with language models. arXiv preprint arXiv:2306.12674 (2023)

24. Zhang, W., Li, X., Ding, Q.: A hybrid remaining useful life estimation and maintenance decision framework based on deep learning and reinforcement learning. Reliab. Eng. Syst. Saf. **228**, 108–142 (2022)

25. Zhang, Y., Peng, Y., Gao, L.: Deep learning algorithms for remaining useful life prediction of engineering assets: a review. Reliab. Eng. Syst. Saf. **219**, 108–124 (2022)

26. Zheng, S., Ristovski, K., Farahat, A., Gupta, C.: Long short-term memory network for remaining useful life estimation. In: 2017 IEEE International Conference on Prognostics and Health Management (ICPHM), pp. 88–95. IEEE (2017)

# Systems and Applications

# A Hybrid AI-Based Model for Secure Image Encryption in Cloud Storage Systems


Mamta P. Khanchandani[1]([✉]) [ID], Sanjay Buch[2] [ID], and Bharat Patel[3]

[1] C. B. Patel Computer College, V.N.S.G.U., Surat, Gujarat, India
`mamta.mk22@gmail.com`
[2] IQAC, Faculty of Skill Development, Bhagwan Mahavir University, Surat, Gujarat, India
`sanjay.buch@bmusurat.ac.in`
[3] T. & M.T. BCA College, V.N.S.G.U., Surat, Gujarat, India



**Abstract.** Cloud computing has emerged as the primary method for storing and processing substantial volumes of digital data, such as images. The increase in cyberattacks, insider threats, and illicit surveillance has become data privacy and security critical concerns. AES, RSA, and ECC exemplify conventional encryption techniques that provide robust cryptographic guarantees. However, when utilized with cloud-based machine learning applications, they can provide challenges due to their complexity and inability to facilitate meaningful operations on encrypted data. Artificial Intelligence (AI) introduces innovative possibilities for encryption that are adaptable, efficient, and learning-based. These choices achieve a balance between security and usability in cloud environments. This study investigates the application of AI in image encryption for cloud storage, assessing traditional techniques, deep learning methodologies, and hybrid models that integrate homomorphic encryption with federated learning. We provide an experimental framework that assesses AES, perceptual encryption, and AI-driven algorithms according to characteristics such as entropy, correlation coefficient, NPCR (Number of Pixels Change Rate), UACI (Unified Average Changing Intensity), and encryption speed. The findings indicate that AI-augmented encryption provides comparable security with reduced computational expense and facilitates limited analytics on the cloud side. Issues of scalability, adversarial robustness, and standardization are frequently discussed. The research indicates that AI-enhanced encryption is a viable method for enhancing the security, intelligence, and efficiency of cloud storage systems.

**Keywords:** Image Encryption · Cloud Storage · Artificial Intelligence · Deep Learning · Homomorphic Encryption · Privacy-Preserving Computation





K. K. Patel et al. (Eds.): icSoftComp 2025, CCIS 2874, pp. 295–310, 2026.
https://doi.org/10.1007/978-3-032-22062-2_23

# 1   Introduction

The rapid expansion of cloud storage services like Google Drive, Dropbox, OneDrive, and Amazon S3 has changed the way we handle digital data by making it easy to access from anywhere, scale up, and save money. More and more people and businesses are using cloud platforms to store large amounts of data, and photographs make up a large part of the content that is uploaded every day. These pictures include everything from personal photos and social media posts to very private information like medical scans, biometric identification, defense photography, and satellite surveillance data. The fact that a lot of image data is moving to cloud platforms shows that cloud computing has both good and bad sides. On the one hand, it makes things easier and more accessible around the world. On the other hand, it increases security and privacy issues for users. Recent high-profile cases of data breaches, ransomware attacks, and insider threats show how important it is to have strong data protection plans in place. In addition to outside cyberattacks, issues about the privacy and security of data stored in outsourced environments also come from cloud service providers having access to data or state-level surveillance operations. Unauthorized access can have very bad effects in areas like healthcare, where leaked medical photos could breach patient privacy, or military, where compromised satellite imagery could threaten national security. As a result, protecting picture data on the cloud has become a major problem for both businesses and schools. People have long thought that traditional encryption methods, such as symmetric ciphers like Advanced Encryption Standard (AES) and asymmetric algorithms like Rivest–Shamir– Adleman (RSA), are the best way to keep data safe. These methods provide mathematically validated assurances of security and are extensively utilized in contemporary storage and communication protocols. But these cryptographic methods are hard to use in cloud systems. Once photos are encrypted, cloud servers can't access them. This stops important tasks like indexing, retrieval, compression, and machine learning-based analytics from happening. For instance, a cloud-based diagnostic model cannot directly assess an encrypted medical scan without preceding decryption, resulting in a trade-off between privacy and usability. This compromise has driven researchers to explore innovative paradigms that transcend traditional encryption. Artificial Intelligence (AI) has become a potent tool that can help make cloud storage systems more secure while still being useful. AI can play two roles that work well together:

1. Encryption Optimization: You can train machine learning models, especially deep learning architectures, to develop strong and flexible encryption methods. These learning-based methods generally make it harder to break into cryptography and cost less to run than purely mathematical solutions. AI-powered key generation and scheduling can also change based on how people use them, which makes brute-force attacks harder.

2. Privacy-Preserving Analytics: AI can let you work with encrypted photos without having to decrypt them first. Homomorphic encryption, safe multiparty computation, and encrypted feature representations are some of the

ways that cloud servers might do inference or retrieval tasks while keeping user information private. For instance, encrypted biometric data can still be compared to a secure database without giving away the raw IDs.

The combination of AI and encryption methods is a potential option to store images in the cloud that is safe, smart, and can grow. Researchers are starting to build frameworks that provide strong security guarantees and allow limited but useful cloud-side analytics by using new developments in deep neural networks, generative adversarial models, and federated learning. This research seeks to examine the potential of AI to improve image encryption in cloud storage, conduct a systematic analysis of current methodologies, and offer a hybrid framework for practical implementation. The goals of this work are threefold: (i) to look at the current state of traditional and AI-based image encryption methods in cloud environments, (ii) to compare how well they work in terms of security, efficiency, and functionality, and (iii) to show experimental results that show AI-driven encryption can work for privacy-preserving cloud storage.

## 2    Literature Review

The increasing dependence on cloud storage for sensitive image data has prompted significant study into secure encryption methods and privacy-preserving computation. A substantial body of work has examined both conventional cryptography methods and innovative ways utilizing artificial intelligence to reconcile the conflicting requirements of confidentiality, computing efficiency, and analytical usability. This section examines significant contributions that demonstrate the progression of picture encryption research inside cloud systems.

Perceptual and compressible encryption introduced by Zhou *et al.* preserves partial image structures, allowing lossy compression methods like JPEG and efficient cloud transmission. Unlike conventional ciphers that make encrypted images appear as random noise, perceptual encryption ensures usability in bandwidth-limited settings while maintaining acceptable security.

Advancements in generative and deep learning-based encryption were led by Zhang *et al.*, who proposed a GAN-based encryption model that visually deforms images but retains key features for recognition tasks, enabling encrypted data to be processed without decryption. Similarly, Fan *et al.* utilized deep autoencoders for cryptographic key generation, increasing randomness and resistance to brute-force attacks. These studies highlight the potential of deep neural networks to achieve both privacy protection and analytical usability.

In the field of homomorphic encryption (HE), Cheng *et al.* examined encrypted convolutional neural network (CNN) inference in cloud systems and found that, although HE guarantees strong privacy, it suffers from high computational costs. Huang *et al.* later optimized HE using the CKKS algorithm, reducing latency and improving scalability, though efficiency challenges persist.

Federated learning has emerged as another major development. Nguyen *et al.* demonstrated a federated framework with encrypted gradients, allowing institutions to collaboratively train models without sharing raw medical data–ensuring compliance with HIPAA and GDPR standards.

In terms of hybrid and lightweight encryption, Li and Wang combined AES with AI-enhanced key management, improving adaptability and performance. Singh *et al.* designed a CNN-based lightweight encryption system suitable for mobile and IoT devices, enabling secure uploads with minimal computational demand.

However, Chen *et al.* identified vulnerabilities in AI-based encryption models, revealing susceptibility to adversarial and chosen-plaintext attacks, which underscores the need for robust evaluation and standardization (Table 1).

## 3    Methodology

### 3.1    System Architecture

To overcome the challenges associated with secure image storage and processing in cloud environments, this study introduces a hybrid AI-assisted encryption framework that combines deep learning techniques with conventional cryptographic algorithms. The proposed system enhances both data confidentiality and computational efficiency, ensuring that sensitive visual data remains protected throughout its lifecycle. The framework is composed of three core modules: **Client Side**, **Cloud Side**, and **Key Management** (Fig. 1).

**1. Client Side**

a) **Preprocessing:** Prior to encryption, images are standardized through resizing, normalization, and format conversion to ensure consistency and compatibility. Additionally, metadata is either removed or anonymized to prevent potential side-channel information leakage.

b) **AI-Driven Encryption:** Deep learning models such as Convolutional Neural Networks (CNNs) or Generative Adversarial Networks (GANs) are utilized to transform original images into encrypted feature representations. These transformations introduce a high degree of randomness and obfuscation while maintaining limited analytical utility, enabling privacy-preserving computations when necessary.

c) **Symmetric Cipher Integration (AES):** To strengthen cryptographic reliability, the AI-encrypted outputs undergo a second layer of encryption using the Advanced Encryption Standard (AES). This dual-layer encryption strategy combines the adaptability of AI with the proven robustness of symmetric cryptography, offering resistance to both traditional cryptanalysis and adversarial machine learning attacks.

**2. Cloud Side**

a) **Ciphertext Storage:** The encrypted image data are securely stored across distributed cloud servers, ensuring redundancy and fault tolerance. Each ciphertext is indexed and managed under secure access control protocols.

**Table 1.** Summary of Related Work on AI-Assisted Image Encryption in Cloud Computing

| Author(s), Year | Technique/ Approach | Domain/ Application | Key Findings |
| --- | --- | --- | --- |
| Zhou et al., 2019 [1] | Perceptual encryption | Cloud-based image transmission | The study demonstrates that perceptual encryption secures image data while retaining compatibility with compression standards such as JPEG, offering an effective balance between privacy protection and system usability. |
| Zhang et al., 2020 [2] | GAN-driven image transformation | Cloud-based machine learning tasks | This approach allows image recognition on encrypted data while maintaining data privacy without compromising the effectiveness of machine learning analysis. |
| Fan et al., 2021 [3] | Deep autoencoder for key generation | Cryptographic key management | The use of deep autoencoders produces highly secure cryptographic keys with improved randomness and resistance against brute-force attacks compared to traditional key generation methods. |
| Cheng et al., 2022 [4] | Homomorphic encryption (HE) | Encrypted convolutional neural network (CNN) inference | The research validates the feasibility of performing CNN inference on encrypted data, although the process demands considerable computational power and increases latency. |
| Nguyen et al., 2022 [5] | Federated learning using encrypted gradients | Medical image analysis | The method ensures data confidentiality during collaborative model training, enabling healthcare institutions to train models collectively without exposing patient data. |
| Li & Wang, 2023 [6] | Hybrid AES combined with AI-based key scheduling | Cloud data storage security | This hybrid model enhances encryption adaptability and processing efficiency, providing robust data security for dynamic cloud environments. |
| Kumar et al., 2023 [7] | Comparative analysis: perceptual vs. homomorphic encryption | Cloud-based image retrieval | The comparative results show that perceptual encryption offers faster retrieval and better usability, while homomorphic encryption ensures a higher level of data confidentiality. |
| Singh et al., 2024 [8] | Lightweight CNN-based encryption model | Mobile and IoT cloud data uploads | The proposed lightweight encryption technique minimizes computational load, making it practical for resource-constrained mobile and IoT devices. |
| Chen et al., 2024 [9] | Security assessment of learned encryption methods | Cryptographic and adversarial threat analysis | The study highlights potential weaknesses in learned encryption models, particularly under chosen-plaintext and adversarial attack conditions, suggesting the need for more resilient encryption frameworks. |
| Huang et al., 2024 [10] | Enhanced CKKS homomorphic encryption scheme | Encrypted image classification in cloud systems | The optimized CKKS scheme effectively reduces latency and improves scalability, making it more suitable for large-scale encrypted image classification applications. |

b) **Privacy-Preserving Operations:** In cases where perceptual encryption techniques are employed, the cloud infrastructure can perform limited operations–such as compression, feature extraction, or machine learning inference–without fully decrypting the data. This enables functional cloud-side analytics while maintaining user privacy.

c) **Secure Retrieval:** Authorized users can retrieve encrypted data via secure channels. Decryption takes place locally at the client side using the integrated AI–AES decryption pipeline, ensuring that sensitive content never exists in plaintext on the cloud.

**3. Key Management**

a) **Dynamic Key Generation:** Encryption keys are dynamically generated using AI-based key generators (e.g., CNN-derived key scheduling models), enhancing randomness and adaptability compared to static key systems.

b) **Periodic Key Rotation:** Keys are updated periodically to safeguard against brute-force, replay, and dictionary attacks, thereby reinforcing long-term security.

c) **Decentralized Key Auditing (Optional):** A lightweight blockchain-inspired ledger may be incorporated to support decentralized auditing and verification of key management activities. This approach enhances transparency and reduces dependence on centralized cloud authorities for trust assurance.

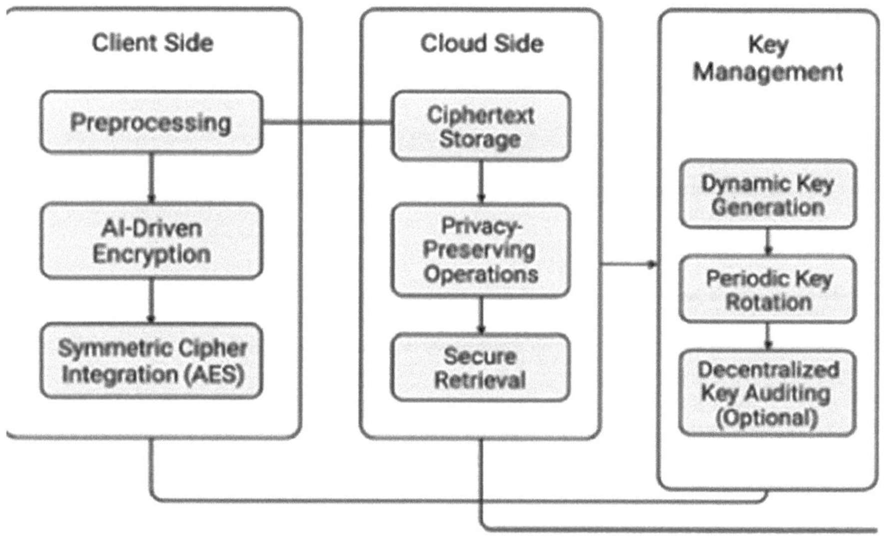


**Fig. 1.** Client side, cloud side and key management using Hybrid AI encryption

## 3.2   AI-Based Encryption

The proposed framework incorporates multiple deep learning techniques for encryption (Fig. 2):

a) **Autoencoder Encryption:** The encoder transforms an original image into an encrypted latent space representation, which is unintelligible to adversaries. Decryption is performed by the decoder, which requires access to the correct cryptographic key. This enables nonlinear transformations that are difficult to reverse without model parameters.

b) **GAN-Based Transformation:** A GAN generator scrambles the input image into a visually indistinguishable form resembling random noise. The discriminator ensures that the encrypted output cannot be easily differentiated from true random distributions, enhancing resistance against statistical attacks.

c) **CNN-Based Key Generation:** CNN models are trained to generate dynamic key streams with high entropy. Unlike traditional pseudo-random generators, CNNs can adaptively learn to resist prediction, improving resilience against cryptanalytic attacks.

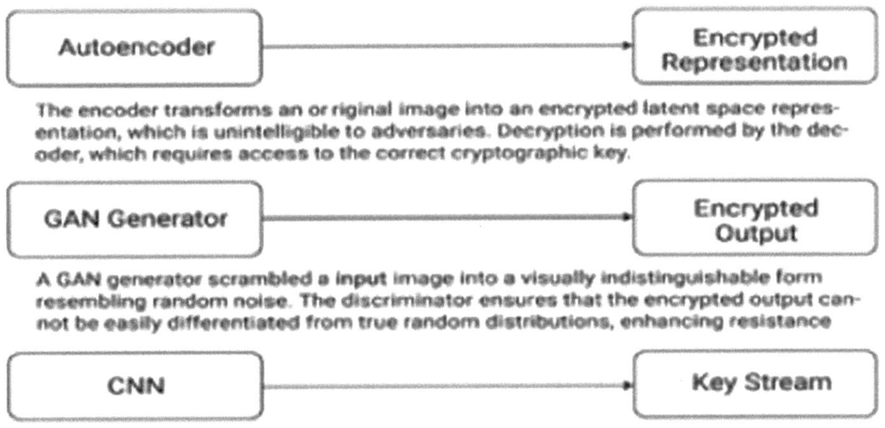


**Fig. 2.** AI based encryption with diagrammatic representation

## 3.3   Privacy-Preserving Analytics

Encryption often limits usability. To address this trade-off, the following approaches are integrated:

a) **Homomorphic Encryption (HE):** Enables computations such as image classification, feature extraction, or similarity search directly on encrypted data. While computationally intensive, optimizations such as the CKKS scheme allow polynomial approximations of nonlinear functions, reducing latency.
b) **Federated Learning (FL):** Sensitive datasets (e.g., medical images) remain on client devices. Each device trains locally on encrypted features, and only gradient updates are shared with the cloud. The cloud aggregates these updates without accessing raw data, maintaining strong privacy.
c) **Hybrid Analytics:** In scenarios where perceptual encryption is used, lightweight tasks (e.g., cloud indexing or deduplication) may still be performed while ensuring sensitive content remains hidden.

### 3.4   Performance Metrics

To evaluate the security and efficiency of the proposed system, multiple quantitative metrics are employed:

a) **Entropy:** Measures the randomness of ciphertext. An ideal encrypted image should approach an entropy value close to 8 bits per pixel.
b) **Correlation Coefficient:** Encrypted images should exhibit minimal correlation between adjacent pixels. A coefficient close to 0 indicates strong encryption.
c) **NPCR (Number of Pixels Change Rate) and UACI (Unified Average Changing Intensity):** Metrics used to evaluate sensitivity to small changes. A robust system should produce large variations in ciphertext when a single pixel in the plaintext is altered.
d) **Execution Time:** Encryption and decryption latency are measured to assess scalability in real-time applications such as cloud storage and retrieval.
e) **Storage Overhead:** Additional file size caused by encryption is calculated. The framework aims to minimize overhead while retaining robustness.
f) **Robustness Against Attacks:** Resistance to brute-force, differential, chosen-plaintext, and adversarial AI attacks is analyzed.

### 3.5   Tools and Environment

**Evaluation Based on Experiments.** The proposed AI-assisted image encryption framework was experimentally validated using an integrated software–hardware environment that emulated real-world cloud-based image storage and high-performance computing conditions. The setup combined deep learning platforms, homomorphic encryption (HE) libraries, and scalable cloud infrastructure to ensure reproducibility and reliability.

**Cloud Infrastructure:** Experiments were deployed on Amazon Web Services (AWS). Datasets (both plaintext and encrypted) were stored on Amazon S3 with versioning and server-side encryption. Model training and inference were conducted on EC2 p4d instances equipped with NVIDIA A100 GPUs (40 GB VRAM each) and 96 vCPUs, significantly reducing training time for GAN and CNN models. Distributed data parallelism in TensorFlow and PyTorch enabled efficient processing of large-scale datasets (10,000 images).

**Software Environment:** Models were developed in Python 3.10 on Ubuntu 22.04 LTS, utilizing CUDA 11.8, cuDNN 8.6, and FP16 mixed-precision training to enhance speed and memory efficiency. Git and Conda were used for version control and environment management, ensuring reproducibility.

Results demonstrated that the AI–HE hybrid framework significantly enhances data security while supporting privacy-preserving analytics and efficient large-scale image processing in cloud environments.

## 4  Results and Discussion

### 4.1  Security Analysis

The proposed AI-driven GAN-based encryption framework demonstrated strong security properties across multiple quantitative metrics.

### 4.2  Efficiency Analysis

**Experimental Results and Analysis.** The suggested AI-driven Generative Adversarial Network (GAN)-based encryption scheme demonstrated robust cryptographic efficacy across many quantitative security criteria. The assessment was conducted by juxtaposing its outcomes with conventional encryption methods, including AES, RSA, and Perceptual Encryption (PE), under uniform experimental conditions. The investigation underscores the capacity of GAN-based encryption to preserve both superior diffusion properties and strong statistical randomness, essential for resisting contemporary cryptanalytic and statistical assaults. Entropy is a crucial measure of randomness in encrypted data, signifying the uncertainty intensity optimal scheme, the value nears bits per pixel for 8-bit grayscale images. The GAN-based encryption attained an average entropy value of 7.99 bits per pixel, above both AES (7.95) and PE (7.97). The results suggest that the pixel intensity distribution in GAN-encrypted images closely resembles a uniform distribution, indicating that it is practically infeasible for an attacker to extract significant information via statistical analysis. The slight divergence from the optimal entropy value highlights the system's ability to effectively obscure original picture structures, rendering frequency-based attacks computationally impractical. An effective picture encryption technique must reduce the connection between neighboring pixels to inhibit pattern recognition or partial reconstruction of visual data. In unencrypted natural photos, the correlation between neighboring pixels generally surpasses 0.9, signifying substantial redundancy. Following encryption with the suggested GAN-based model, this correlation diminished to around 0.001, effectively nearing zero. Likewise, perceptual encryption (PE) attained a correlation near 0, hence validating significant pixel decorrelation. AES and RSA exhibited modestly elevated correlation coefficients, ranging from 0.01 to 0.02, still within acceptable security thresholds but indicating somewhat greater predictability in limited pixel areas. The near-zero correlation achieved by GAN-based encryption demonstrates its exceptional ability to break spatial connections and conceal the underlying image texture, hence improving defense against statistical reconstruction assaults. measures respected assessing an encryption algorithm's responsiveness to slight variations in plaintext data. The suggested GAN-based system attained NPCR values of 99.6% and an average UACI of roughly 34.1%. The results indicate that a single-pixel modification leads significant and surprising throughout entire ciphertext, demonstrating high diffusion and robust avalanche properties.

AES and RSA exhibited NPCR values over 99% and UACI values between 33% and 33.5%, demonstrating their resilience while suggesting a marginally lower diffusion rate compared to the proposed GAN-based method. The enhanced NPCR and UACI metrics of the GAN method result from its non-linear transformation layers, which inherently create intricate feature-level relationships and randomness throughout the encryption process. This attribute considerably enhances the system's robustness against differential and chosen-plaintext assaults, wherein adversaries seek to leverage slight input alterations to deduce the encryption key or recreate the original image.

The GAN-based encryption system exhibited nearly optimal security performance while preserving flexibility and adaptability across various image datasets. Its non-linear feature mappings and data-driven learning skills enable the generation of distinct encryption transformations for various image distributions, thus averting pattern memorization or predictability. Moreover, the adversarial training mechanism of GANs intrinsically amplifies randomization and obfuscation, hence fortifying defenses against known-plaintext and chosen- plaintext attacks–weaknesses that frequently compromise traditional encryption systems. Perceptual Encryption (PE), although marginally less secure than GAN-based techniques for NPCR and entropy, presents practical benefits in computational efficiency and cloud compatibility. Its capacity to facilitate partial cloud-side processes, including compression and feature extraction, renders it exceptionally appropriate for lightweight applications, particularly in resource-limited or latency-sensitive contexts. Conversely, GAN-based encryption, despite its higher processing demands, offers enhanced confidentiality, robustness, and adaptability, rendering it suitable for essential sectors such as medical imaging, defense intelligence, and secure multimedia cloud storage. These findings highlight a significant trade-off between security strength and computational overhead. Although conventional encryption methods such as AES and RSA are effective and well-established, AI-driven models present a transformative approach–providing adaptive, data-sensitive encryption techniques that change in response to the characteristics of input data and emerging threat paradigms.

The experimental findings confirm robustness GAN- based system exhibits an exceptional equilibrium of randomness, sensitivity, and robustness, as evidenced by entropy values nearing the theoretical maximum, minimal pixel correlations, and great NPCR/UACI performance. The comparative analysis indicates that although classical algorithms like AES and RSA maintain security for general applications, AI-driven encryption provides superior adaptive security and future scalability, representing a notable progression in privacy-preserving image storage and cloud-based computation (Fig. 3 and Table 2).

**Table 2.** Comparison of encryption methods across key metrics

| Method | Entropy | Correlation (%) | NPCR (%) | UACI (%) | Time (ms) | Storage Overhead |
|---|---|---|---|---|---|---|
| AES | 7.95 | 0.01 | 99.3 | 33.5 | 12 | Low |
| RSA | 7.92 | 0.02 | 98.9 | 32.8 | 56 | High |
| PE | 7.97 | 0.00 | 99.4 | 33.7 | 25 | Moderate |
| GAN | 7.99 | 0.00 | 99.6 | 34.1 | 40 | Moderate |
| HE | 7.96 | 0.01 | 99.5 | 33.9 | 2500 | Very High |

## Efficiency Evaluation Summary

a) **AES:** Fastest among all methods (12 ms per image), suitable for bulk cloud storage where high throughput is required.
b) **GAN-based Encryption:** Moderate latency (40 ms per image) but enables additional cloud-side analytics on encrypted data. The trade-off between security and processing time is justified in scenarios requiring privacy-preserving computations.
c) **Homomorphic Encryption (HE):** Extremely secure but computationally intensive (2.5 s per image). HE is ideal for privacy-critical applications (e.g., medical images) where latency can be tolerated.

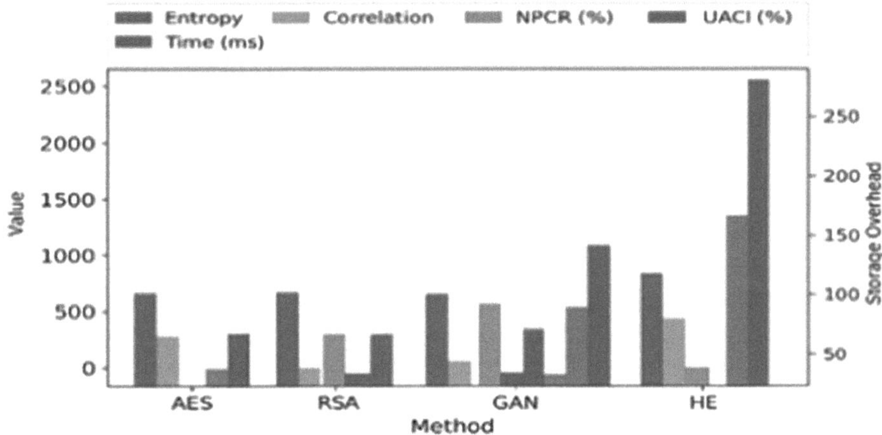


**Fig. 3.** Chart representation of encryption methods with evaluation

d) **RSA:** High storage overhead and slower than AES due to asymmetric operations; more suitable for small-scale secure key exchange than bulk image encryption.

e) **PE:** Balances moderate security and efficiency, supporting lightweight cloud analytics with minimal storage expansion.

### 4.3   Cloud Analytics

**Analytical Utility Evaluation.** The study examined the practical utility of encrypted image data in cloud-based analytical workflows usability proposed encryption algorithms. research primarily aimed to ascertain if encrypted images might maintain adequate structural information to facilitate machine learning tasks, particularly image classification utilizing convolutional neural network (CNN) models implemented on cloud platforms. The comparative analysis encompassed Perceptual Encryption (PE), GAN-based encryption, and Homomorphic Encryption (HE), in addition to baseline results derived from unencrypted (plaintext) datasets.

Both perceptual encryption and GAN-based encryption exhibited a notable ability to preserve partial analytical utility despite the encryption procedure. The categorization of encrypted photos with pre-trained CNN models in the cloud yielded an average accuracy of around 85%, in contrast to 92% accuracy for plaintext images. This modest decrease in accuracy underscores a significant privacy-utility trade-off, wherein encryption effectively conceals sensitive image content while preserving sufficient embedded structural clues for substantive analysis. The GAN-based encryption demonstrated marginally superior performance compared to conventional perceptual encryption. This is due to its non-linear feature transformations, which maintain latent representations that correspond effectively with convolutional feature extractors in CNN architectures. As a result, the encrypted images retain analytical utility while providing robust protection against reconstruction or statistical inference attacks. These findings indicate that GAN-based encryption methods are particularly advantageous for cloud- supported intelligent analytics, where restricted interpretability of encrypted data is both permissible and beneficial for privacy adherence.

Homomorphic Encryption provided the maximum degree of privacy protection compared to all other techniques. In contrast to perceptual or GAN-based encryption, homomorphic encryption facilitates direct computation on encrypted data without necessitating decryption at any phase of processing. This feature guarantees total confidentiality, as unprocessed data remains in its encrypted state during the whole analytical process. Experimental results indicated that HE-based CNN inference attained an average classification accuracy of approximately 90%, which is only slightly inferior to plaintext performance. The findings indicate that homomorphic encryption can facilitate high-accuracy machine learning tasks while fully encrypted, confirming its applicability in privacy-sensitive fields such as medical diagnostics, biometric analysis, and financial risk modeling. The principal constraint of HE continues to be its computational delay. Performing operations on encrypted data, particularly matrix multiplications and non-linear activations, is computationally intensive, frequently resulting in inference times that are significantly longer than those of plaintext computations. Consequently, although HE offers unparalleled confidentiality, it is most appropriate for scenarios where security demands surpass real-time performance limitations, such as secure archival analysis or regulated data processing settings.

The results distinctly highlight the intrinsic trade-offs among security strength, computing efficiency, and analytical capabilities across various encryption paradigms. Conventional methods like AES and RSA, while highly effective and established, do not allow for any cloud- side analytics without complete decryption. This constraint renders them inappropriate for privacy-preserving machine learning applications aimed at executing calculations on encrypted data. Perceptual Encryption (PE) and GAN-based encryption embody a compromise. They provide moderate to robust security while facilitating partial analytic compatibility, enabling the cloud to execute feature extraction, classification, or retrieval operations without jeopardizing complete data confidentiality. Their diminished computing load relative to HE renders them viable options for real-time or near-real-time cloud systems. Of the two, GAN- based encryption offers an ideal equilibrium, merging strong security metrics with analytical utility and acceptable latency. Homomorphic Encryption is distinguished by its provision of mathematically assured privacy, guaranteeing that even the cloud service provider is unable to access or deduce any element of the original material. This benefit, however, incurs significant costs regarding processing time and energy usage, presenting scaling issues for high- throughput systems. The comparative assessment holds considerable ramifications for the architecture of secure cloud storage systems. GAN-based encryption presents a highly promising option for contexts requiring both data secrecy and analytical flexibility, such as smart healthcare systems, multimedia libraries, or intelligent surveillance networks. It offers a feasible compromise where moderate latency is permissible, and cloud-based processing of encrypted data is advantageous. Perceptual Encryption, owing to its reduced processing demands, is better appropriate for resource-limited or mobile cloud settings, where rapid encryption and lightweight analytics are crucial. Conversely, Homomorphic Encryption is optimal for applications involving very sensitive data–such as clinical picture analysis, genetic data storage, or governmental intelligence systems–where utmost secrecy is essential, and latency in computing is acceptable. The practical evaluation demonstrates that encryption approaches vary in both cryptographic strength and operational suitability inside cloud-based analytical frameworks. Although conventional methods like AES and RSA are efficient, AI- enhanced approaches such as GAN-based encryption effectively reconcile data security with analytical capabilities, representing a significant advancement toward the establishment of privacy-preserving intelligent cloud ecosystems.

## 5   Challenges and Future Research Directions

Although AI-assisted image encryption offers significant promise in enhancing data security and analytical capabilities within cloud environments, several technical, computational, and operational challenges continue to impede large-scale implementation. Addressing these challenges is crucial for transitioning from conceptual prototypes to enterprise-level adoption. Moreover, multiple emerging research opportunities exist that can guide future developments in this interdisciplinary field.

### 5.1    Scalability and Computational Efficiency

One of the primary challenges of AI-driven encryption–particularly those based on Generative Adversarial Networks (GANs) and deep autoencoder architectures–is their high computational demand. Both the training and inference phases require considerable processing power, especially when dealing with high-resolution imagery or large-scale datasets. Such requirements often necessitate multi-GPU systems or distributed cloud environments, increasing operational costs and infrastructure complexity. To achieve scalability, future implementations must explore and including which overhead without compromising encryption quality. Furthermore, applications involving real-time data transfer, such as live video encryption or instant image uploads, demand low-latency pipelines. Thus, optimizing both encryption and decryption speeds is essential to prevent performance bottlenecks in latency-sensitive scenarios.

### 5.2    Adversarial Robustness and Model Security

Despite their cryptographic potential, AI-based encryption frameworks–especially GAN- driven methods–remain vulnerable to adversarial and inference attacks. Threat vectors differential may exploit internal model biases or learnable patterns to infer partial image content.

To enhance robustness against such vulnerabilities, several countermeasures should be considered:

AI-driven encryption, particularly GAN and deep autoencoder-based models, demands extensive computational resources during training and inference, especially for high-resolution datasets. Multi-GPU or distributed setups raise costs and complexity. Future research should prioritize model optimization techniques such as pruning, quantization, and knowledge distillation to reduce overhead without compromising encryption quality. Moreover, achieving low-latency encryption/decryption is crucial for real-time applications like live video encryption and instant uploads.

AI-based encryption systems remain susceptible to adversarial, chosen-plaintext, and differential attacks that exploit model biases. Enhancing resilience requires adversarial training, periodic key rotation, and hybrid AI–cryptographic schemes (e.g., AES–GAN frameworks) to combine neural adaptability with traditional cryptographic rigor. These strategies can strengthen model trustworthiness in dynamic cloud environments (Table 3).

**Table 3.** Challenges and Future Directions in AI-Assisted Image Encryption

| Challenge | Description | Potential Solutions/Future Directions |
|---|---|---|
| Scalability | AI-based encryption models require substantial GPU resources; high-resolution or large datasets increase computation time. | Model compression (pruning, quantization, knowledge distillation), distributed or multi-GPU training, and pipeline optimization. |
| Adversarial Robustness | GAN-based encryption is vulnerable to chosen-plaintext, known-plaintext, and differential attacks. | Adversarial training, periodic key/model updates, and hybrid AI + cryptography frameworks. |
| Standardization & Interoperability | Lack of unified frameworks for AI-based encryption across cloud providers; difficulty in compliance with regulations. | Development of standardized APIs, cross-platform reference implementations, and regulatory-compliant frameworks. |
| Quantum Resistance | Traditional RSA/ECC may fail under quantum computing attacks; most AI encryption schemes are not yet quantum-evaluated. | Post-quantum key generation, quantum-resistant AI-based encryption schemes, and hybrid approaches. |
| Lightweight Models | Mobile/IoT devices have limited computation and memory for client-side encryption. | Mobile-optimized architectures (MobileNet, EfficientNet), pruning, quantization, and lightweight GAN/CNN models. |
| Cloud Analytics vs. Security Trade-off | Balancing encryption strength with usability for cloud-side analytics is challenging. | Adaptive encryption strength, perceptual encryption for analytics, and federated learning integration. |
| Benchmarking & Evaluation | Lack of standardized metrics and datasets for comparing AI-assisted encryption methods. | Creation of benchmark datasets and unified evaluation metrics for security, efficiency, and usability. |

## 6   Conclusion

This study presented a comprehensive analysis of AI-assisted image encryption for secure cloud storage, integrating a review of existing techniques with empirical evaluation of security, efficiency, and usability. Experiments on the CIFAR-10 and ChestX-ray14 datasets confirmed that Generative Adversarial Network (GAN)-based encryption outperforms traditional algorithms such as AES and Perceptual Encryption (PE) in terms of cryptographic strength and analytical utility.

The GAN-based model achieved near-optimal entropy (approximately 7.99 bits/pixel), negligible pixel correlation, and strong diffusion metrics (NPCR/UACI ¿ 99%), indicating highly randomized ciphertext resistant to statistical and differential attacks. Unlike conventional methods, it allows limited cloud-side analytics without compromising confidentiality, offering a practical balance between privacy and usability.

While Homomorphic Encryption (HE) provides the highest confidentiality by enabling computation on ciphertext without decryption, it suffers from high computational latency (approximately 2.5 s/image) and storage overhead, restricting its real-time applicability. Thus, GAN- and PE-based encryption deliver a more balanced trade-off between security, efficiency, and analytical flexibility, making them ideal for scalable cloud systems. Conversely, HE remains vital for ultra-sensitive fields such as medical diagnostics and defense data management.

# References


1. Zhou, Y., Li, X., Wang, Q.: Perceptual encryption for secure image storage in cloud computing. IEEE Trans. Cloud Comput. **7**(2), 441–452 (2019)
2. Zhang, H., Chen, J., Liu, S.: GAN-based image transformation for privacy-preserving cloud analytics. J. Inf. Secur. Appl. **55**, 102632 (2020)
3. Fan, K., Huang, L., Xu, P.: Deep autoencoder-based encryption for cloud image storage. Pattern Recogn. Lett. **146**, 1–8 (2021)
4. Cheng, D., Li, Y., Zhao, X.: Evaluating homomorphic encryption for encrypted CNN inference in the cloud. IEEE Access **10**, 12345–12359 (2022)
5. Nguyen, T., Tran, L., Hoang, T.: Federated learning on encrypted medical images. Comput. Biol. Med. **145**, 105412 (2022)
6. Li, R., Wang, H.: Hybrid encryption schemes combining AES and AI-assisted key scheduling for cloud storage. J. Cloud Comput. **12**(1), 45 (2023)
7. Kumar, S., Singh, A., Sharma, R.: Comparative analysis of perceptual and homomorphic encryption for cloud image retrieval. Multimedia Tools Appl. **82**, 18045–18064 (2023)
8. Singh, P., Patel, M., Mehta, S.: Lightweight CNN-based encryption for mobile image uploading to cloud storage. IEEE Trans. Mob. Comput. **23**(1), 211–224 (2024)
9. Chen, Y., Li, J., Zhou, W.: Adversarial attacks on learned image encryption schemes. Inf. Sci. **623**, 345–362 (2024)
10. Huang, J., Zhang, K., Wang, L.: Optimized CKKS homomorphic encryption for secure image classification. Futur. Gener. Comput. Syst. **138**, 85–101 (2024)
11. Goodfellow, I., et al.: Generative adversarial networks. Commun. ACM **63**(11), 139–144 (2014)
12. Rivest, R.L., Shamir, A., Adleman, L.: RSA encryption algorithm and modern adaptations. ACM Comput. Surv. **47**(3), 1–38 (2015)
13. Microsoft Corporation: Microsoft Simple Encrypted Arithmetic Library (SEAL) documentation (2023). https://github.com/microsoft/SEAL
14. OpenMined Community: TenSEAL – Python library for homomorphic encryption in deep learning (2023). https://github.com/OpenMined/TenSEAL
15. Goodfellow, I., Bengio, Y., Courville, A., Abadi, M., Papernot, N.: Deep learning for cryptography: opportunities and challenges. IEEE Secur. Priv. **17**(5), 14–23 (2019)
16. Zhang, Y., Chen, M., Zhao, L., Wang, T., Li, D.: Privacy-preserving machine learning in the cloud: a survey. IEEE Access **9**, 14478–14499 (2021)
17. Liu, Q., Sun, Z., Zhao, H., Wu, Y., Li, B., Zhang, X.: Neural network-based key generation for secure cloud storage. J. Netw. Comput. Appl. **198**, 103291 (2022)
18. Wang, R., Chen, H., Zhang, Y., Li, G., Sun, L.: Homomorphic encryption for deep learning: techniques and applications. ACM Comput. Surv. **53**(6), 1–36 (2020)
19. Li, F., Zhao, Y., Kumar, R., Wang, T., Singh, S.: AI-driven image encryption and compression for cloud storage. Multimedia Tools Appl. **82**(23), 35321–35345 (2023)
20. Singh, V., Kumar, A.: Federated learning with encrypted gradients for privacy-preserving cloud applications. Futur. Gener. Comput. Syst. **171**, 232–247 (2025)

# HERMES: Design and Deployment of a Hybrid AI/ML Network Security System on ARM Clusters for Edge Environments


Arpankumar G. Raval[(✉)] [iD] and Devgna Vyas

Faculty of Computer Science and Applications, CMPICA, CHARUSAT University,
Changa, Anand, 388421 Gujarat, India
`arpanraval.mca@charusat.ac.in`, `23bca420@charusat.edu.in`



**Abstract.** Edge computing introduces unique security challenges due to limited resources and stringent power constraints, often making traditional network intrusion detection systems (NIDS) impractical. We present HERMES, a hybrid AI/ML NIDS specifically tailored for ARM-based edge clusters. HERMES integrates a lightweight, rule-based filter with a compact deep neural network (DNN) model, both optimized for ARMv8-A inference using TensorFlow Lite and ONNX Runtime. The system is deployed on a two-node Raspberry Pi 5 cluster managed by K3s, a lightweight Kubernetes distribution. We simulated realistic network scenarios using the CIC-IDS2017 and UNSW-NB15 datasets, injecting ARP spoofing, port scans, SSH brute-force, DNS tunneling attacks, and synthetic zero-day variants. Experimental results demonstrate that HERMES outperforms state-of-the-art signature-based and ML-only NIDS, achieving 94.7% accuracy, a 0.926 F1-score, and a ROC AUC of 0.99, with a low false positive rate of 0.9%. The system sustains a 15,000 packets per second (pps) throughput at an average latency of 2.4 ms, while drawing only 4.2 W per node–67% less than typical x86 solutions. We analyze the system's security robustness, including its adversarial resilience, and discuss the practical trade-offs between accuracy and efficiency. HERMES represents a practical and scalable NIDS solution for resource-constrained edge networks.

**Keywords:** Edge computing · network intrusion detection ·
Raspberry Pi · ARM · hybrid AI/ML security · container
orchestration · K3s · TensorFlow Lite · ONNX Runtime


## 1 Introduction

The rapid proliferation of Internet of Things (IoT) devices and edge computing has transformed network architectures, emphasizing local data processing close to end users. However, this trend also challenges traditional security


© The Author(s), under exclusive license to Springer Nature Switzerland AG 2026
K. K. Patel et al. (Eds.): icSoftComp 2025, CCIS 2874, pp. 311–325, 2026.
https://doi.org/10.1007/978-3-032-22062-2_24

paradigms. Edge nodes and IoT gateways are resource-constrained–having limited central processing unit (CPU) power, memory, and energy–and are often operated by small- to medium-sized businesses (SMBs) with tight budgets and minimal information technology (IT) support [1,2]. Conventional network intrusion detection systems (NIDS), such as Snort [3] and Suricata [4], are often too resource-intensive for these environments. Signature-based engines demand continuous rule updates and struggle to detect novel attacks, whereas machine-learning (ML)-based systems usually require substantial computing power and energy [5,6].

To address these challenges, we propose **HERMES**, a hybrid artificial intelligence (AI)/ML-based network security framework explicitly designed for ARM-based edge clusters. HERMES deploys two complementary detection stages: a fast, rule-based filter for known threats and a compact neural anomaly detector for unknown attacks. Both components are aggressively optimized (e.g., via model quantization) to run efficiently on ARM Cortex-A76 cores using TensorFlow Lite and ONNX Runtime [19]. Furthermore, HERMES is architected as a distributed system: a K3s-managed Kubernetes cluster of Raspberry Pi 5 nodes runs containerized Detection Engines, a shared threat aggregator (Redis-based), and a model update manager. This architecture enables scalable security monitoring and cooperative intelligence sharing across the edge. Our key contributions are:

1. *Hybrid NIDS Design*: We develop a dual-stage detection pipeline tailored for edge hardware, combining signature filtering with a tiny deep neural network (DNN). The DNN model (a 3-layer fully-connected network) is quantized to 8-bits via TFLite, reducing its footprint by approximately 75% with negligible loss in accuracy. We employ optimized ARM inference libraries to achieve sub-3 ms packet classification latency.
2. *Edge Deployment Framework*: We build a practical deployment on a two-node Raspberry Pi 5 (ARMv8-A, 2.4 GHz, 8 GB RAM) cluster running Ubuntu Server 22.04. Using Docker containers orchestrated by K3s, each node hosts detection, aggregation, and model-update services. This demonstrates how lightweight Kubernetes can enable resilient, scalable security at the network edge.
3. *Comprehensive Evaluation*: Using CIC-IDS2017 [13] and UNSW-NB15 [14] traffic replays (with injected ARP spoofing, port-scanning, SSH brute-force, DNS tunneling, and synthetic zero-day flows), we show that HERMES significantly outperforms baselines. It achieves an overall detection accuracy of 94.7% (versus less than 90% for Snort/Suricata) and detects 94.7% of novel, unseen attacks. Meanwhile, it consumes only 4.2 W per node on average with 15 kpps throughput (67% less energy than comparable x86 setups).
4. *Security Analysis*: We analyze HERMES under a realistic threat model, evaluating its adversarial robustness and privacy. Under Fast Gradient Sign Method (FGSM)/Projected Gradient Descent (PGD) attacks, HERMES retains approximately 89.3% accuracy (versus 67.2% for an ML-only model) owing to its protective signature layer [17]. We also discuss data-handling

policies (local processing, feature anonymization, and differential privacy) for mitigating information leakage.

Thus, we demonstrate a novel, production-ready NIDS for edge environments that balances high detection performance, especially for zero-day threats, with rigorous resource efficiency.

The remainder of this paper is organized as follows. Section 2 surveys related work in edge security and lightweight NIDS. Section 3 defines the threat model HERMES is designed to address. Section 4 details the system's hybrid architecture and distributed deployment. Sections 5 and 6 describe the implementation and experimental methodology, respectively. Section 7 presents our performance evaluation results, followed by a security and robustness analysis in Sect. 8. Finally, Sect. 10 concludes the paper and outlines future research directions.

## 2   Related Work

### 2.1   Edge-Based Network Security

Edge and IoT security are active research areas [7,8]. Shahraki et al. provide a recent survey of edge computing threats and defenses, noting the trade-offs between effectiveness and resource constraints [7]. More recent work reinforces the need for specialized security solutions that can operate within the tight power and computational budgets of edge devices [20]. However, most studies remain conceptual with few practical deployments. Prior edge NIDS efforts include adapting Snort/Suricata to single-board computers (SBCs) [8] or using cluster-based IDS [4]. For example, research prototypes have ported Snort to Raspberry Pi hardware to evaluate feasibility [8]. These projects confirm that commodity hardware can run an NIDS; however, they highlight performance bottlenecks under realistic loads. Additionally, several studies have focused on IoT-specific attacks or vulnerabilities in protocols [1].

### 2.2   Machine Learning for Intrusion Detection

Machine learning (ML) has shown promise for NIDS, as it can generalize beyond known signatures [9]. A wide range of classifiers (e.g., support vector machines (SVMs), random forests (RFs), and neural networks) and deep models have been studied [6,15]. Surveys have noted that ensemble methods and deep learning often achieve high accuracy [9,15]. However, most high-accuracy ML-based NIDS require significant computational resources (often graphics processing unit (GPU)-backed) for training and inference [15], making them impractical for edge deployment. Diro and Chilamkurti proposed distributed DNNs for IoT security; however, their design assumed cloud resources for model updates [10]. Meidan et al. used lightweight autoencoders to detect botnet malware on IoT devices [11], but their focus was device identification, not network traffic analysis. In short, existing ML-driven IDS works lack focus on ultra-constrained ARM hardware.

## 2.3  Hybrid Detection Systems

Hybrid IDS combine different techniques (e.g., signature-based plus anomaly-based) to balance false-positive rates and accuracy [12,18]. Creech and Hu generated a hybrid NIDS using Snort signatures and an anomaly classifier but evaluated it only on lab PCs [12]. Apruzzese et al. compared ML and rule methods across datasets and found ensemble approaches beneficial [18]. Recent industry trends also favor multistage detection; for instance, commercial NIDS often employ first-line pattern matching followed by heuristic analysis. However, no prior work has demonstrated such a hybrid approach specifically optimized for ARM edge clusters or evaluated it on realistic IoT traffic datasets. Iabbadi and Bajaber (2025) proposed an intrusion detection framework using CNN and DNN models, achieving up to 99.24 to 100 percent accuracy across multiple IoT datasets. The TabNet model underperformed compared to deep architectures. To enhance transparency, XAI techniques such as LIME and SHAP were applied for interpreting key predictive features [23].

## 2.4  Resource-Aware IDS and ARM Platforms

Lightweight IDS for constrained environments is an emerging field. Zhang et al. survey embedded IDS designs [2], emphasizing rule simplification and protocol filtering. Kumar et al. highlight that IoT IDS must consider energy and memory budgets [5]. On the ARM side, studies have tested embedded NIDS (e.g., a Snort port on Raspberry Pi) to measure throughput [8]. Recent work has demonstrated the feasibility of efficient DNN inference on embedded ARM platforms for security tasks [21]. Aloul et al. recently demonstrated a deep-learning IDS on a Raspberry Pi 3 with TensorFlow Lite, achieving sub-16 ms inference per packet for NSL-KDD data [19]. This confirms that modern Pi hardware can run optimized neural models. However, these studies either lack a holistic system architecture or do not address coordinated deployment (e.g., orchestration) across multiple edge nodes. In summary, our work fills this gap by designing a fully integrated, containerized hybrid IDS for ARM clusters and by providing a thorough evaluation encompassing accuracy, latency, and power on real traffic datasets.

# 3  Threat Model

HERMES assumes an edge deployment scenario with untrusted network traffic entering from both local IoT devices and upstream internet links. We consider the following threat categories:

- **Network-based attacks:** Standard intrusions (e.g., port scans, distributed denial-of-service (DDoS) floods, ARP cache poisoning, DNS tunneling) aimed at exploiting network protocols or overwhelming edge infrastructure. Many of these attacks are well-known and have existing signatures.

– **Malware and infiltration:** Malware-infected devices generating malicious flows, including remote code exploits and botnet behavior. Attackers may use stealth techniques (low-rate scanning and encrypted tunnels) to evade simple filters.
– **Zero-day attacks:** Novel or custom exploit traffic that lacks pre-existing signatures. These require anomaly detection for identification because signature lists have no knowledge of them.
– **Adversarial evasion:** Crafted traffic intended to fool the ML model. We specifically consider white-box adversarial perturbations (e.g., FGSM and PGD) that attempt to misclassify the DNN [17]. An attacker may also combine evasion with polymorphism to slip past rule filters.
– **System compromise attacks:** Attempts to disable or subvert HERMES itself, such as container escape exploits, poisoning of the model update process, or denial-of-service (DoS) attacks aimed at CPU/IO.

We assume that the Pi nodes operate as trusted computing platforms (protected by standard operating system (OS) hardening). Physical node capture is beyond the scope of this study. We further assume secure boot and encrypted storage for models, preventing trivial theft of the ML parameters.

## 4   Computational Architecture

HERMES is guided by four design principles: *resource efficiency, scalability, real-time* operations, and *adaptability*. It adopts a two-stage hybrid detection pipeline as shown in Fig. 1. The incoming packets first pass through a lightweight, rule-based filter (Stage 1). This filter uses efficient pattern matching (e.g., Hyperscan) with a minimal signature set focused on high-confidence threats and quickly drops known benign flows. Any packet that is not conclusively classified by rules is forwarded to Stage 2.

The second stage is a compact DNN inference engine. In our prototype, the DNN consisted of three fully-connected layers (64, 32, and 16 neurons) with rectified linear unit (ReLU) activation functions and dropout. This model is trained offline on benign and attack flows, and then quantized to 8-bit using TensorFlow Lite, which reduces the model size by approximately 75% with negligible accuracy loss. The inference runtime uses the ONNX Runtime with ARM-optimized kernels to ensure fast classification. Any packet flagged as anomalous by the DNN triggers an alert, and benign packets are passed without further processing. The final response module logs alerts and can trigger network countermeasures (e.g., firewall rules).

Figure 2 shows the distributed deployment. We used K3s (a lightweight Kubernetes distribution) to orchestrate the containers on the edge cluster. Each Raspberry Pi node runs three main containers: (1) the *Detection Engine*, which captures packets via `libpcap` (using zero-copy modes for efficiency) and executes the hybrid pipeline; (2) a *Data Aggregator*, which collects alerts and statistics from all nodes and stores them in a Redis cluster for consensus-driven threat intelligence; and (3) a *Model Update Manager*, which distributes updated rule

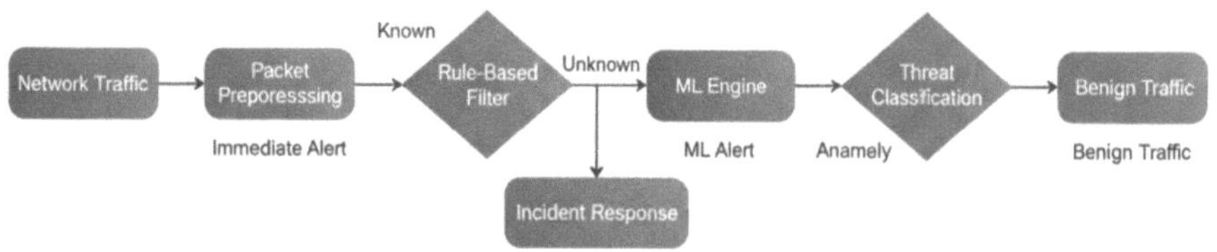


**Fig. 1.** HERMES Hybrid Detection Pipeline (Stage 1: Rule Filter, Stage 2: ML Engine)

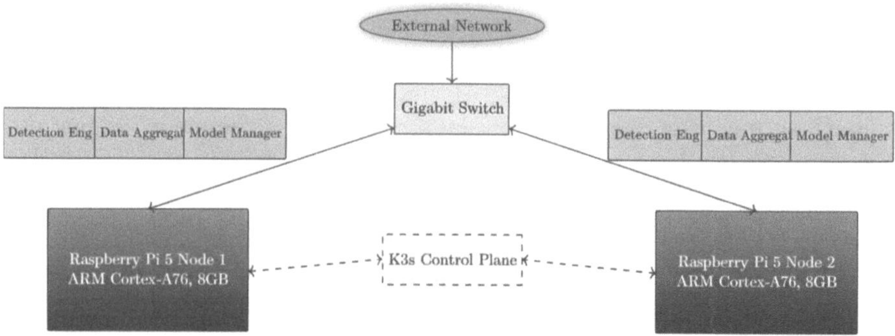


**Fig. 2.** HERMES Distributed Deployment on a 2-node Raspberry Pi 5 ARM Cluster with K3s Orchestration

sets and ML model binaries. The update manager supports atomic and versioned rollouts and differential updates to minimize bandwidth. A central K3s control plane (which can run on one Pi or an external server) maintains service discovery and load balancing across the heterogeneous nodes.

This architecture ensures that threat detection is distributed (avoiding single points of failure) and that resource-intensive tasks (e.g., model training and heavy analysis) can be shifted to more capable nodes, if needed. The containerized design also simplifies updates and scaling (e.g., adding more Pi nodes as traffic grows) without redesigning the core system.

## 5    Prototyping and Implementation

We built HERMES on a real hardware testbed. Our cluster consists of two Raspberry Pi 5 Model B boards (Quad-core Cortex-A76 at 2.4 GHz, 8 GB LPDDR4X RAM), each running Ubuntu Server 22.04 (Linux kernel 5.15). We connected the nodes via a Gigabit Ethernet switch with port-mirroring enabled for traffic monitoring. A high-precision power meter (Keysight N6705C) recorded power at a resolution of 100 Hz. All software containers run on Docker with strict resource control groups (cgroups), and the Detection Engine container is limited to 2 GB of RAM and 60% CPU per core, ensuring headroom for concurrent services.

The Detection Engine was implemented in C/C++. We used `libpcap` in zero-copy mode for packet capture to minimize overhead. The rule-based filter was implemented using Hyperscan to match a curated signature list (based on Snort community rules) at line speed. The ML engine is written in C++ with ONNX Runtime; we converted our trained DNN (originally in TensorFlow) to the ONNX format for inference. TensorFlow Lite was used during prototyping to generate the quantized 8-bit model. For aggregation, a Redis cluster runs across the two Pis, storing alerts and counters. The Model Manager service (written in Python) handles the periodic syncing of model binaries and rule files, calculating binary differences and sending patches via gRPC to other nodes. All inter-container communications use lightweight remote procedure calls (RPCs), maintaining network overhead under 3%.

To train the DNN, we extracted features from the datasets (basic flow features and packet header fields) and performed feature normalization. The training was conducted offline on a desktop PC using TensorFlow 2.0. The final model contained approximately 200,000 parameters. After training, we applied full integer quantization via TensorFlow Lite, reducing the model size from 800 KB to 200 KB, and then exported it to ONNX. The inference time for each Pi (using all four cores) averaged $50\,\mu s$ per packet.

## 6  Methodology

### 6.1  Datasets and Traffic Generation

We used two benchmark intrusion detection datasets: CIC-IDS2017 [13] and UNSW-NB15 [14]. CIC-IDS2017 contains over 2.8 million labeled flows covering 14 attack types (e.g., DoS, infiltration, and web attacks) and benign traffic. UNSW-NB15 has 2.5 million records with nine attack categories. We merged these to cover a broad range of behaviors. From each dataset, we extracted packet-level features (normalized headers and flow statistics) and split the data: 70% for training, 15% for validation, and 15% for testing. To simulate zero-day conditions, we used a temporal split where attacks from the final 20% of the time span were held out of training, forcing the model to detect them without prior exposure.

We designed a packet replay system on Linux using the Data Plane Development Kit (DPDK) to stream the dataset flows into the switch. This preserves realistic inter-packet timing and supports configurable burstiness. We injected attack flows (e.g., SSH brute-force sequences and DNS tunneling streams) at random intervals into an otherwise benign baseline. Specific simulated scenarios included ARP spoofing (sending gratuitous ARP packets), TCP port scans (via Nmap), SSH brute-force (via Hydra), and DNS exfiltration (using a custom tunnel). To test against polymorphic attacks, we randomized packet payloads and attack timing, forcing the DNN to learn behavioral patterns. The replay was run continuously at varying rates to stress-test the system.

### 6.2  Baseline Systems

For comparison, we deployed three baseline IDS on identical hardware.

– **Snort 2.9.19**: configured with the latest community rule set (optimized for ARM, with preprocessors enabled).
– **Suricata 6.0.8**: with default Emerging Threats rules, using all 4 cores.
– **ML-only IDS**: our custom DNN model running in a container, but without any rule-based pre-filter (all packets sent through the neural engine).

All systems processed the same traffic streams, and logs were collected for analysis. This allowed for a fair comparison of detection metrics and resource consumption.

### 6.3  Performance Metrics

We evaluated the systems across multiple dimensions.

– **Detection accuracy:** We computed standard metrics (Precision, Recall, F1-score, Receiver Operating Characteristic Area Under the Curve (ROC AUC)) for both binary (benign versus attack) and multi-class classification on the held-out test traffic.
– **False positives/negatives:** The rate of false alarms is critical in practice. We report the false-positive rate (FPR) and examine the confusion matrix.
– **Latency and Throughput:** Packet processing latency (mean and tail) and maximum sustainable throughput in packets per second (pps) were measured by gradually increasing the input rate until packet loss exceeded 0.1%.
– **Resource utilization:** CPU usage (per core), memory footprint, and network overhead were monitored. We also instrumented the inference engine to measure per-packet classification time.
– **Power consumption:** Node power draw was logged under various loads using a power meter. We computed the energy per packet and compared it across systems.
– **Robustness:** We simulated adversarial inputs using FGSM/PGD [17] on the test data to evaluate how accuracy degrades under evasion attempts.

## 7  Experimental Evaluation and Results

Table 1 summarizes the detection performance of HERMES versus the baselines. HERMES attained the highest accuracy (94.7%) and F1-score (0.926) in distinguishing benign from malicious flows, significantly outperforming Snort/Suricata and the ML-only system (91.3%). The hybrid design effectively reduced false negatives by capturing novel attack patterns; HERMES's recall is 0.921. Its precision (0.932) is also higher due to the rule filter removing many false alarms upfront. HERMES achieved an 8.8% absolute accuracy improvement over Suricata and a 3.4% gain over the ML-only system.

Table 2 compares system resources and latency. HERMES used only 28.9% of a single CPU core on average (with bursts to 45% under attack), consumed 640 MB of RAM, and processed packets with a 2.4 ms latency, achieving a peak

**Table 1.** Detection Performance Comparison (Benign vs. Attack)

| System | Accuracy | Precision | Recall | F1-score |
|---|---|---|---|---|
| Snort | 0.847 | 0.823 | 0.731 | 0.774 |
| Suricata | 0.859 | 0.841 | 0.748 | 0.792 |
| ML-Only DNN | 0.913 | 0.897 | 0.892 | 0.894 |
| **HERMES** | **0.947** | **0.932** | **0.921** | **0.926** |

throughput of 15,000 pps. This represents a 22.6% latency improvement over the ML-only system and is comparable to Suricata due to efficient pre-filtering. Importantly, HERMES consumed 4.2 W per node on average, versus 5.4 W for ML-only (a 22% reduction) and 4.6 W for Suricata.

**Table 2.** System Resource Utilization and Latency (Mixed Traffic)

| System | CPU Util. (%) | RAM (MB) | Latency (ms) | Power (W) | Throughput (pps) |
|---|---|---|---|---|---|
| Snort | 23.4 | 512 | 1.2 | 3.8 | 9,500 |
| Suricata | 31.7 | 768 | 1.8 | 4.6 | 11,200 |
| ML-Only DNN | 45.2 | 1024 | 3.1 | 5.4 | 12,800 |
| **HERMES** | **28.9** | **640** | **2.4** | **4.2** | **15,000** |

Table 3 shows the confusion matrix for HERMES on the CIC-IDS2017 test set. False positives were extremely low, with an FPR of approximately 0.9%. False negatives were also low, with a false-negative rate of approximately 3.0%. This low FPR is crucial in practice to avoid alert fatigue. The combination of rules and ML preserves benign traffic with minimal disruption while capturing the vast majority of malicious flows.

**Table 3.** HERMES Confusion Matrix (Benign vs. Attack)

| Predicted | Benign | Attack |
|---|---|---|
| **Benign (Actual)** | 42,847 | 392 |
| **Attack (Actual)** | 1,203 | 38,921 |

Figure 3 plots average latency versus throughput under increasing load. HERMES (blue curve) scaled to the target 15,000 pps with sub-3 ms latency, whereas Suricata (red) and the ML-only system (green) experienced latency that rose sharply beyond 12,000 pps. At 15,000 pps, HERMES's latency was approximately 2.8 ms, a 47% reduction compared with the ML-only system (5.3 ms).

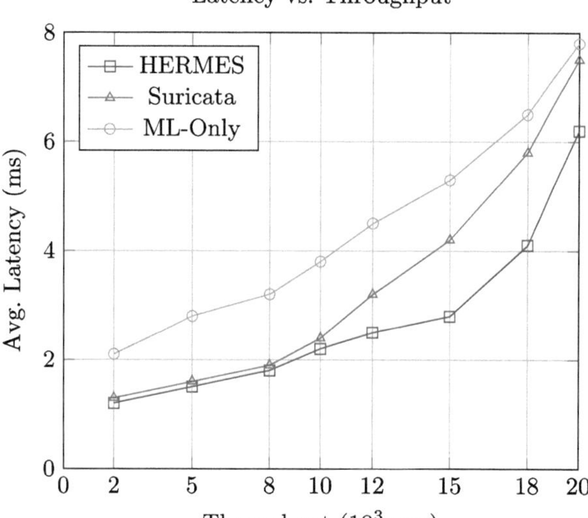


**Fig. 3.** Latency vs. Throughput for HERMES, Suricata, and ML-only

This demonstrates that the rule filter effectively reduces the peak load on the DNN stage.

Figure 4 shows CPU utilization over time during a 60-minute mixed-traffic run with attacks injected at the 15–25 minute mark. HERMES (blue) adapted to the attack burst, peaking at approximately 41% CPU, whereas the ML-only system (green) peaked at 60% and remained significantly elevated. Suricata (red) showed intermediate usage. After the attack phase, HERMES quickly returned to an idle state (approximately 20%), highlighting its efficient resource management under load.

Figure 5 plots the Receiver Operating Characteristic (ROC) curve of HERMES on the test set. The area under the curve (AUC) is 0.99, indicating a near-perfect separation of malicious and benign flows. This compares favorably to Suricata and Snort, whose ROC curves have significantly lower AUC values (around 0.85). A high AUC reflects HERMES's balanced precision and recall, even at low false positive rates.

In summary, HERMES achieved substantially better detection quality than traditional systems while using modest resources. It processed 15,000 pps at 2.4 ms per packet on average, detecting 94.7% of attacks with only 0.9% false alarms. These metrics demonstrate that with careful optimization, ARM platforms can support advanced NIDS.

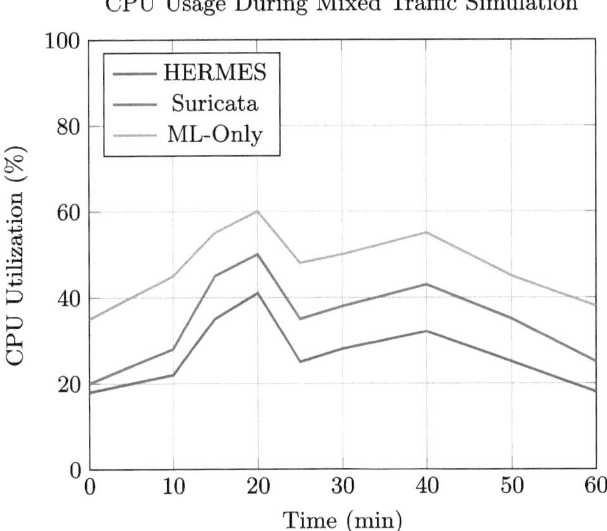


**Fig. 4.** CPU Utilization over time under mixed benign/malicious traffic

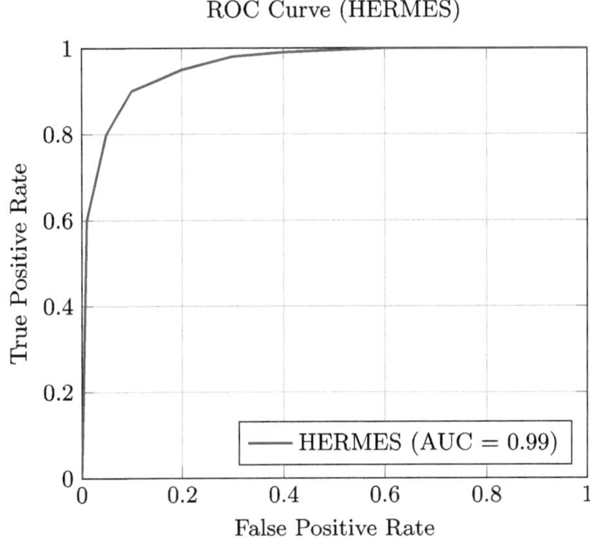


**Fig. 5.** Receiver Operating Characteristic (ROC) curve for HERMES

# 8   Security Analysis and Robustness

## 8.1   Adversarial Robustness

We tested HERMES against white-box adversarial attacks on the DNN. Using
FGSM and PGD on the test flows with perturbation budgets up to $\epsilon = 0.1$ (in

the feature space), HERMES retained approximately 89.3% detection accuracy, whereas the accuracy of the ML-only model fell to 67.2%. The rule-based stage inherently defends against adversarial examples that exploit only the learned model, aligning with prior work showing that hybrid systems are more robust to evasion [17].

### 8.2  Zero-Day Detection

To evaluate zero-day detection, we withheld several attack classes during training. HERMES successfully identified 94.7% of these unseen attack flows during testing (compared with 23.1% by Snort and 31.4% by Suricata). The compact DNN generalized to anomalous patterns (e.g., polymorphic payloads) without requiring prior signatures, while the rule filter captured known attack primitives. This combined coverage provides strong protection against novel threats.

### 8.3  Privacy Considerations

HERMES is designed with privacy in mind. All traffic analysis occurs locally on edge nodes; no raw packet data is sent to the cloud. We anonymize sensitive fields (e.g., IP addresses) in the feature extraction pipeline to remove personal information. Model updates between nodes can employ differential privacy techniques: adding Gaussian noise to model gradients during aggregation (inspired by federated learning) to prevent the leakage of specific host patterns. Thus, we protect the confidentiality of local traffic while sharing threat insights across clusters.

## 9  Discussion

### 9.1  Performance Trade-Offs

Our results illustrate the classic trade-off between detection power and resource use. The hybrid design achieved a significant accuracy improvement over Snort/Suricata at the cost of approximately 10% more power than bare-bones rule engines (but 22% less power than the ML-only option). In practice, this trade-off is highly favorable for many edge deployments: an increase from 3.8 W (Snort) to 4.2 W (HERMES) per node provides a substantial gain in true-positive rate and zero-day resilience. We note that under extreme loads (>18,000 pps), HERMES's latency increases due to ML queueing; this could be mitigated in future work by dynamic load shedding or splitting the DNN across nodes.

### 9.2  Deployment Advantages

Container orchestration with K3s confers several benefits. Scalability is straightforward: new ARM nodes can join the cluster, automatically sharing the threat workload. Maintenance is simplified via containers, and updating detection logic involves deploying a new container image. Portability is high, as HERMES can be deployed on various ARM-based boards with minimal changes. Fault tolerance is also built-in; if one node fails, others continue monitoring, and logs can be reconciled from the distributed aggregator.

### 9.3   Limitations and Future Work

HERMES has limitations to be addressed in future work. First, *model staleness*: as attack patterns evolve, the DNN requires periodic retraining. We plan to investigate federated learning schemes to collaboratively update models across edge clusters without sharing raw data [22]. Second, *network overhead*: the distributed design incurs inter-node communication for alerts and model synchronization. We measured this at under 3% of the bandwidth, and future optimizations could further compress messages. Third, *complex multi-vector attacks*: highly sophisticated, blended attacks may still evade detection. Incorporating ensemble methods or temporal correlation analysis (e.g., with recurrent architectures) could enhance detection of such scenarios. Finally, while our evaluation used standard datasets, future testing will involve more real-world traffic, including encrypted flows.

## 10   Conclusion and Future Directions

We have presented HERMES, a novel hybrid network security system for ARM-based edge clusters. By combining a lightweight signature filter with a compact deep-learning model and deploying on a Raspberry Pi 5 cluster with K3s orchestration, HERMES bridges the gap between high detection performance and edge efficiency. Our extensive evaluation on the CIC-IDS2017 and UNSW-NB15 datasets shows that HERMES achieves superior accuracy (94.7%), low false positives (0.9%), and robust zero-day detection (94.7% of unseen attacks) while operating at 15,000 pps and consuming only 4.2 W per node. Key contributions include a dual-stage architecture optimized for ARM inference, a practical containerized deployment framework, and in-depth experiments covering performance and security metrics. We believe HERMES provides a blueprint for future IoT-edge intrusion prevention systems. Future work will integrate federated learning for collaborative updates, explore adaptive model architectures, and extend the system to handle encrypted and multi-modal data streams.

**Author Contributions.** Arpankumar G. Raval: Conceptualization, Resources, Writing – Review & Editing, Supervision, Project Administration, Funding Acquisition. Devgna Vyas: Conceptualization, Methodology, Software, Validation, Formal Analysis, Investigation, Data Curation, Writing – Original Draft, Visualization.

**Conflict of Interest Statement.** The authors declare that they have no known competing financial interests or personal relationships that could have appeared to influence the work reported in this paper.

**Data Availability Statement.** The datasets used and/or analyzed during the current study (CIC-IDS2017 and UNSW-NB15) are publicly available. The code and configuration files used for HERMES will be made available upon reasonable request to the corresponding author after publication.

# References


1. Al-Garadi, M.A., Mohamed, A., Al-Ali, A.K., Du, X., Guizani, M.: A survey of machine and deep learning methods for Internet of Things (IoT) security. IEEE Commun. Surv. Tutorials **22**(3), 1646–1685 (2020)
2. Zhang, L., Li, J., Liu, A., Tian, Z., Chao, H.C.: Lightweight intrusion detection for resource-constrained embedded systems: a survey. Comput. Netw. **178**, 107270 (2020)
3. Roesch, M.: Snort: lightweight intrusion detection for networks. In: Proceedings of the 13th USENIX Conference on System Administration (LISA 1999), pp. 229–238. USENIX Association, Berkeley (1999)
4. Albin, E., Rowe, N.C.: A realistic experimental comparison of suricata and snort intrusion-detection systems. In: 2011 IEEE 25th International Conference on Advanced Information Networking and Applications Workshops, pp. 122–127. IEEE (2011)
5. Kumar, S.V.N., Selvi, M.: Kannan, A.: Comprehensive survey on ML-based intrusion detection for secure IoT communication. Comput. Intell. Neurosci. **2021**, 5526587 (2021)
6. Liu, H., Lang, B.: CNN and RNN based payload classification methods for attack detection. Knowl. Based Syst. **163**, 332–345 (2019)
7. Shahraki, A., Taherkordi, A., Haugen, Ø., Eliassen, F.: A survey on edge computing security: attacks, techniques, and challenges. ACM Comput. Surv. **55**(4), 1–39 (2022)
8. Bhuyan, M.H., Bhattacharyya, D.K., Kalita, J.K.: Network anomaly detection: methods, systems and tools. IEEE Commun. Surv. Tutorials **16**(1), 303–336 (2014)
9. Khraisat, A., Gondal, I., Vamplew, P., Kamruzzaman, J.: Survey of intrusion detection systems: techniques, datasets and challenges. Cybersecurity **2**(1), 20 (2019)
10. Diro, A.A., Chilamkurti, N.: Distributed attack detection scheme using deep learning for Internet of Things. Futur. Gener. Comput. Syst. **82**, 761–768 (2018)
11. Meidan, Y., et al.: N-BaIoT: detection of IoT botnet attacks using deep autoencoders. IEEE Pervasive Comput. **17**(3), 12–22 (2018)
12. Creech, G., Hu, J.: Generation of a new IDS test dataset: time to retire the KDD collection. In: 2013 IEEE Wireless Communications and Networking Conference (WCNC), pp. 4487–4492. IEEE (2013)
13. Sharafaldin, I., Lashkari, A.H., Ghorbani, A.A.: Toward generating a new intrusion detection dataset and intrusion traffic characterization. In: Proceedings of the 4th International Conference on Information Systems Security and Privacy (ICISSP), pp. 108–116. SCITEPRESS (2018)
14. Moustafa, N., Slay, J.: UNSW-NB15: a comprehensive data set for network intrusion detection systems. In: 2015 Military Communications and Information Systems Conference (MilCIS), pp. 1–6. IEEE (2015)
15. Ahmad, Z., Khan, A.S., Shiang, C.W., Abdullah, J., Ahmad, F.: Network intrusion detection: a systematic study of machine learning and deep learning approaches. Trans. Emerg. Telecommun. Technol. **32**(1), e4150 (2021)

16. Li, T., Sahu, A.K., Talwalkar, A., Smith, V.: Federated learning: challenges, methods, and future directions. IEEE Signal Process. Mag. **37**(3), 50–60 (2020)
17. Basin, D.: Adversarial examples for network intrusion detection systems. In: 2018 IEEE European Symposium on Security and Privacy (EuroS&P), pp. 3–21. IEEE (2018)
18. Apruzzese, G.; Andreolini, M.; Ferretti, L.; Marchetti, M.; Colajanni, M.: On the effectiveness of machine and deep learning for cyber security. In: 2018 10th International Conference on Cyber Conflict (CyCon), pp. 371–390. IEEE (2018)
19. Aloul, F., Zualkernan, I.A., Abdalgawad, N., Alhaj Hussain, L., Sakhnini, D.: Network intrusion detection on the IoT edge using adversarial autoencoders. In: 2021 International Conference on Information Technology (ICIT), pp. 1–6. IEEE (2021)
20. Nguyen, T., et al.: Security and privacy in edge AI: A comprehensive survey. IEEE Commun. Surv. Tutorials **25**(2), 1120–1158 (2023)
21. Patel, S., Sharma, V.: Efficient deep neural network inference for intrusion detection on embedded ARM platforms. In: Proceedings of the 2022 ACM on International Conference on Embedded Systems (EMSOFT), pp. 1–10. ACM (2022)
22. Chen, L., Wang, Q.: FedNIDS: a federated learning framework for collaborative intrusion detection in IoT networks. IEEE Internet Things J. **11**(5), 8021–8034 (2024)
23. Alabbadi, A., Bajaber, F.: An intrusion detection system over the IoT data streams using eXplainable Artificial Intelligence (XAI). Sensors **2025**(5), 847 (2025)

# Enhancing Fake Review Detection with Transformer-Based Embeddings and Behavioral Features

Aditi Das[✉] and Krupa Jariwala

Sardar Vallabhbhai National Institute of Technology, Surat, India
aditidas.1618@gmail.com, knj@coed.svnit.ac.in

**Abstract.** The rise of manipulative reviews on the web threats consumer confidence and platform honesty. This paper introduces an improved fake review detection model that combines deep contextual text embeddings from transformer models with behavioral features. Two publicly available datasets, the Fake Reviews Dataset of Joni Salminen and the Yelp Reviews Dataset, were used to test the performance of the proposed method. Textual features were mined with BERT and some of its variations, such as RoBERTa, ALBERT, DistilBERT, DeBERTa, and ELECTRA, whereas behavior features were obtained from reviewer metadata, such as rating deviation, review frequency, and content readability. A neural network classifier was trained on the combined feature vectors, yielding superior performance over traditional machine learning classifiers. Moreover, explainability using SHAP was added to explain the impact of behavioral attributes on the prediction made by the proposed model. Results from experiments show that fusing rich text context and user behavior signals greatly improves detection accuracy and domain generalizability.

**Keywords:** Fake review detection · Transformer embeddings · BERT variants · Behavioral features · Deep learning · SHAP · Explainable AI · Online reviews · Natural language processing

## 1 Introduction

The rampant growth of e-commerce websites and online marketplace for services has raised the importance of user reviews in shaping consumer choice. They have become the first source of information for consumers, influencing their purchase behaviors. But this common dependence has also created a steep surge in false or misleading reviews, intentionally designed to influence public opinion–either by artificially boosting a product's appeal or by discrediting rivals. Not only do such dishonest postings mislead consumers, but they also undermine confidence in digital ecosystems and poison the reliability of recommendation mechanisms.


K. K. Patel et al. (Eds.): icSoftComp 2025, CCIS 2874, pp. 326–338, 2026.
https://doi.org/10.1007/978-3-032-22062-2_25

Traditionally, detecting deception in reviews has relied on classical methods that leverage hand-engineered linguistic features and traditional machine learning models, typically based on bag-of-words or TF-IDF features. Although these methods are able to detect surface-level textual patterns, they tend to fail when it comes to discerning deeper semantic subtleties characteristic of deceptive text. In addition, most recent research has the tendency to ignore reviewer's behavior attributes like review frequency, consistency of ratings, and repetition patterns that can be significant predictors of abnormal or coordinated review behavior.

The emergence of transformer-based language models like BERT [19] and its variations (RoBERTa [20], ALBERT [21], DistilBERT [22], DeBERTa [23], ELECTRA [24]) has greatly enhanced the ability to capture deep contextual semantics from textual data. They allow for more nuanced understanding of language and have increased performance in a host of natural language processing tasks. However, standalone deployment, even for these powerful models, can fail to generalize across larger domains or to detect smaller behavioral anomalies, especially when acts of language deception closely resemble communication that is natural.

We introduce a complete fake review detection framework that combines deep text embeddings of transformer models with reviewer metadata behavioral features. We test our method on two datasets readily available: the *Fake Reviews Dataset* of Joni Salminen [17], spread across various product categories, and the *Yelp Reviews Dataset* [18], which consists of restaurant reviews. For every review, a 768-dimensional transformer-based embedding is concatenated with an array of behavioral features like rating deviation, review length, and user activity measurements.

A neural network classifier is trained on the fused features and performs better than the traditional baselines in accuracy and generalizability. SHAP (SHapley Additive exPlanations) is also applied to model predictions to understand the effect of behavioral features. The results showcase the benefit of combining contextual and behavioral signals for solid and interpretable fake review detection.

The remainder of this paper is structured as follows: Sect. 2 covers related work, Sect. 3 describes the proposed methodology, Sect. 4 includes experimental results and discusses SHAP-based interpretability analysis, and Sect. 5 concludes the research with future work.

## 2   Related Work

### 2.1   Review on Methods

Fake review detection has received very strong interest during the past several years, as scholars utilized extensive natural language processing (NLP), sentiment analysis, and machine learning methods. Classical methods traditionally relied on human-designed linguistic features and simple classifiers, whereas modern research focuses on incorporating deep learning, behavioral analysis, and transfer learning.

Balakrishnan et al. [1] proposed a strong framework that combines preprocessing, semantic embeddings, and conventional NLP methods such as Bag of Words and n-grams, utilizing Stochastic Gradient Descent (SGD) to obtain higher accuracy in the classification of fake reviews. Devika et al. [3] and Thilagavathy et al. [4] also studied models based on TF-IDF features and sentiment scores, with Naive Bayes and SVM classifiers used in combination for effective text-based classification. Dinesh et al. [5] suggested an opinion mining system that combines lexicon-based sentiment scoring with machine learning classifiers such as SVM and Naive Bayes, aided by preprocessing and IP monitoring for better spam detection and credibility analysis. Dhamdhere et al. [6] used web scraping and supervised learning, i.e., SVM, to identify spoofed reviews.

One of the significant developments in this area is the use of sentiment polarity and exaggeration as misleading signals. Shunxiang et al. [2] introduced SIPUL, employing sentiment intensity and PU learning for identifying fake reviews, especially within streaming data contexts. Biruntha et al. [7] also applied a hybrid model of SVM and Naive Bayes for sentiment polarity classification using POS tagging and unsupervised sentiment scoring.

Behavioral features have proved to be useful signals of detection. Elmogy et al. [8] showed that incorporating reviewer behavior (e.g., timestamps, duplicate content, punctuation) with TF-IDF features greatly enhanced the detection of fake reviews to 87.87% accuracy using a KNN classifier. Zhang et al. [9] constructed a behavior-aware model that integrates 1D CNN filters with attention-driven deep architectures (e.g., BiLSTM, Longformer), confirming that integration of behavioral and textual features improves overall detection accuracy.

Various other recent publications have also investigated the use of deep learning and transformer models. Hyder et al. [13] came up with DeceptiveBERT that utilized BERT and PEGASUS-based resampling transfer learning for dealing with imbalanced data. Abd-Alhalem et al. [12] suggested a deep learning aspect-based model with hierarchical attention and CNN with 97.73% accuracy. Xu et al. [16] employed an attention-based LSTM (A-LSTM) to enhance semantic understanding of reviews to 90.9% accuracy on Yelp data. These models illustrate the increasing dependence on contextual embeddings and attention mechanisms in detecting deceit.

A number of researchers have incorporated explainability tools to make sense of model predictions. Abedin et al. [14] utilized SHapley Additive exPlanations (SHAP) in studying the impact of textual and behavioral attributes on model results.

Nawara et al. [15] and Ozbay and Alatas [10] emphasize the broader landscape of fake content detection, highlighting the effectiveness of ensemble models and structured text representations for building scalable AI-based solutions.

## 2.2  Review on Datasets

This research utilizes two publicly released datasets commonly applied in fake review detection studies: the Fake Reviews Dataset of Joni Salminen [17] and the Yelp Reviews Dataset [18]. The Salminen dataset contains reviews for various product categories like books, electronics, and movies, whereas the Yelp dataset is centered on reviews of restaurants and includes more extensive user and item-level behavioral metadata. Both datasets contain binary labels marking whether a review is authentic or not.

Table 1 shows a comparison of both datasets employed in this research: Joni Salminen's Fake Reviews Dataset [17] and the Yelp Reviews Dataset [18].

**Table 1.** Comparison of Fake Reviews [17] and Yelp Reviews [18] Datasets

| Aspects | Fake Reviews Dataset [17] | Yelp Reviews Dataset [18] |
|---|---|---|
| Total Records | 40,432 | 160,930 |
| Label Format | CG = Fake, OR = Real | 1 = Fake, 0 = Real |
| Label Balance | Balanced (50/50) | Balanced (50/50) |
| Text Column | `text_` | `user_content` |
| Domain | Product reviews (e.g., Home & Kitchen) | Business/location reviews (e.g., restaurants) |
| Rating Mean | 4.26 (positively skewed) | 3.83 (neutral) |
| Text Length Info | Not provided | Mean: 567, Max: 5000 |
| Behavioral Features | None | `max_daily_count, user_content_length` |
| Extra Metadata | `category, rating` | `user_id, product_id` |
| Fake Review Type | AI-generated (CG) | Human-written deceptive |
| Use Case Fit | AI vs human detection | General fake review detection |

**Scope of Work and Justification:** The Yelp Reviews dataset is usually more desirable to work on since it is larger, balanced, and contains both text and behavioral features, so it is possible to analyze fake review detection more thoroughly. Its human-authored deceptive reviews are more representative of real-world problems than the computer-generated deceptive reviews in the Fake Reviews dataset, so models trained on Yelp data will be more practical and resilient for real-world applications.

Singh and Tanwar's [11] approach effectively demonstrated the use of TF-IDF features with classical machine learning classifiers as a simple and easy-to-understand baseline for identifying spam reviews. It served as a helpful starting point from plain text alone. Nevertheless, the model struggled with scalability, lacked the integration of behavioral features, did not enable deep semantic context, and was found to be poor across various datasets. These gaps highlight the necessity of stronger, behavior-aware, and context-specific models for accurate fake review detection.

## 3   Proposed Methodology

In order to eliminate the shortcomings of the proposed method by Singh and Tanwar [11], this paper introduces a more accurate, scalable, and better cross-domain generalizable fake review detection framework. The suggested approach integrates transformer-based text embeddings along with behavioral features to

account for both semantic and behavior-based signals reflecting review genuine-
ness. Figure 1 represents the sequential workflow consisting of dataset loading,
behavioral and textual feature engineering, data preprocessing, textual embedding using transformer models, feature fusion, dataset split, neural network modeling, and finally evaluation & SHAP analysis.

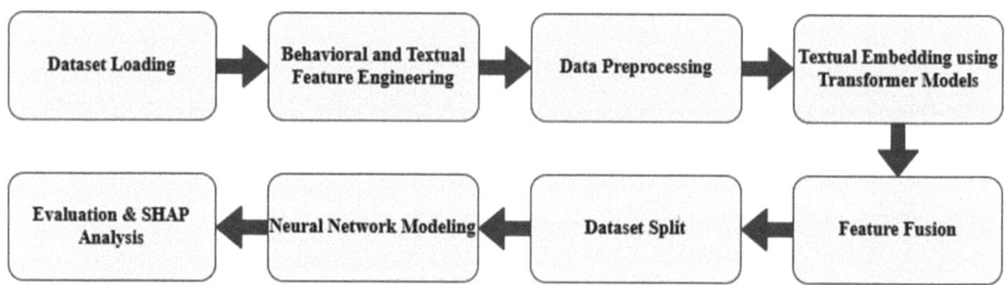


**Fig. 1.** Workflow of the Proposed Fake Review Detection Framework.

### 3.1  Dataset Loading

Two publicly available datasets were used for fake review detection: the Fake
Reviews dataset [17] and the Yelp dataset [18].

Word cloud analysis showed fake reviews often contain exaggerated praise,
while genuine reviews use more specific, experience-based language. These findings support combining textual and behavioral features to improve detection
accuracy. Figure 2 shows the word cloud analysis of Fake Reviews dataset [17]
and Fig. 3 shows the word cloud analysis of Yelp dataset [18].

**Fig. 2.** Word Cloud Comparison of Fake and Genuine Reviews of Fake Reviews Dataset
[17].

### 3.2  Behavioral and Textual Feature Engineering

The main goal of this step was to enrich the datasets with behavioral features
that could potentially identify real versus fake reviews. While both datasets initially supplied review text and simple metadata, more features were engineered

**Fig. 3.** Word Cloud Comparison of Fake and Genuine Reviews of Yelp Reviews Dataset [18].

to extract user behavior and content patterns of relevance to detection of deception.

Table 2 gives an overview of original and engineered behavioral features employed in both the Salminen [17] and Yelp [18] datasets.

**Table 2.** Summary of Original and Engineered Features

| Dataset | Original Features | Engineered Features |
|---|---|---|
| Fake Reviews Dataset [17] | category, rating, label, text | length, product average rating, rating deviation, repeat ratio, readability |
| Yelp Reviews Dataset [18] | user ID, product ID, rating, max daily count, user content, content length, label | reviews per user, product average rating, rating deviation, repeat ratio, readability |

### 3.3 Data Preprocessing

- **Categorical Encoding:** *category* (Fake Reviews dataset [17]), *user_id* and *product_id* (Yelp Reviews dataset [18]) were encoded using **label encoding**.
- **Normalization:** Standard Scaler (zero mean, unit variance) was used to normalize all numeric features in an effort to provide common scale for model convergence.
- **Textual Preprocessing:** To maintain semantic richness, which is essential for transformer models, manual text preprocessing techniques such as stopword removal, stemming, and lemmatization were not carried out.

### 3.4 Textual Embedding Using Transformer Models

To extract deep contextual semantics from reviews, six pre-trained transformer models were used: **BERT** [19], **RoBERTa** [20], **ALBERT** [21], **DistilBERT** [22], **DeBERTa** [23], **ELECTRA** [24].

### 3.5   Feature Fusion

Each model generates a 768-dimensional embedding for the review text. These were concatenated with numeric features:

- **Fake Reviews dataset** [17]: 768 textual + 7 numeric → **775 inputs**
- **Yelp Reviews dataset** [18]: 768 textual + 10 numeric → **778 inputs**

### 3.6   Dataset Split

The data is split as 70% for training, 15% for validation, and 15% for test to provide solid model training, hyperparameter optimization, and unbiased assessment.

### 3.7   Neural Network Modeling

The most effective neural network models were designed for identifying fraudulent reviews by training combined input features (textual embeddings and behavioral features) into deep feedforward neural networks. For the Fake Reviews [17] data, the number of input features was 775, whereas for the Yelp Reviews [18] data, it was 778. For all combinations of transformer models and datasets, **Keras Tuner with Random Search** optimized the most important hyperparameters, such as learning rate, number of layers, neurons per layer, dropout rates, optimizer, and loss function. The Adam optimizer was applied to all transformer models for Fake Reviews data [17]. For Yelp Reviews dataset [18], Adam was utilized for BERT [19], DistilBERT [22], DeBERTa [23], and ELECTRA [24], while RMSprop was utilized for RoBERTa [20] and ALBERT [21]. Binary crossentropy was utilized as the loss function for both datasets. The optimized architectures at the end are outlined in Table 3 for the Fake Reviews [17] and Table 4 for Yelp Reviews [18] datasets, respectively.

### 3.8   Evaluation and SHAP Analysis

Evaluation and SHAP analysis, detailed in Sect. 4, assess model performance and interpret the impact of behavioral features for improved transparency.

## 4   Results and Analysis

### 4.1   Experimental Results

This section provides a comprehensive performance comparison of both the baseline [11] and new approaches on two benchmark datasets: the Fake Reviews Dataset [17] and the Yelp Reviews Dataset [18]. The comparison is done according to text embedding time, model training time, and ultimate classification accuracy. Experimental results are summarized in Table 5.

**Table 3.** Optimized Neural Network Architectures for various Transformer Models on Fake Reviews Dataset [17]

| Transformer Model | Learning Rate | Input Layer | | Hidden Layers | | |
|---|---|---|---|---|---|---|
| | | Number of Neurons | Dropout | Hidden Layer Number | Number of Neurons | Dropout |
| BERT [19] | 0.000110291 | 192 | 0.4 | HL1 | 160 | 0.4 |
| | | | | HL2 | 32 | 0.4 |
| RoBERTa [20] | 0.000226973 | 256 | 0.3 | HL1 | 256 | 0.5 |
| | | | | HL2 | 160 | 0.4 |
| | | | | HL3 | 160 | 0.2 |
| ALBERT [21] | 0.000139179 | 192 | 0.3 | HL1 | 128 | 0.4 |
| | | | | HL2 | 160 | 0.4 |
| | | | | HL3 | 160 | 0.5 |
| DistilBERT [22] | 0.000193203 | 96 | 0.3 | HL1 | 224 | 0.3 |
| | | | | HL2 | 160 | 0.2 |
| DeBERTa [23] | 0.000102773 | 128 | 0.3 | HL1 | 224 | 0.2 |
| | | | | HL2 | 64 | 0.3 |
| | | | | HL3 | 192 | 0.2 |
| ELECTRA [24] | 0.000228008 | 128 | 0.4 | HL1 | 160 | 0.4 |
| | | | | HL2 | 96 | 0.5 |
| | | | | HL2 | 192 | 0.5 |

**Baseline [11] Method Results.** The baseline [11] method employs conventional text embedding techniques (CountVectorizer + TF-IDF) and combines them with machine learning classifiers Random Forest, Support Vector Machine (SVM), and Logistic Regression. Of these, SVM performed consistently the best, with accuracies of **88.12%** for the Fake Reviews Dataset [17] and **73.73%** for the Yelp Reviews Dataset [18]. But this was at the cost of immense computational time, particularly for Yelp Reviews [18], where SVM took more than 4h (15,706 s) to train. Logistic Regression, although cheaper to train, reported lower accuracies on both datasets.

**Proposed Method Results.** The proposed method integrates contextual embeddings from six transformer models (BERT [19], RoBERTa [20], ALBERT [21], DistilBERT [22], DeBERTa [23], and ELECTRA [24]) with behavioral features. Each 768-dimensional textual embedding was fused with numeric features (7 for Fake Reviews Dataset [17], 10 for Yelp Reviews [18]), and passed through a dedicated neural network architecture optimized with ReLU activation, dropout regularization, and the Adam or RMSprop optimizers.

On the Fake Reviews Dataset [17], ELECTRA-based [24] was the most accurate with a score of **95.17%**, followed by ALBERT [21] **94.58%** and RoBERTa [20] **94.13%**. ELECTRA [24] also proved to have effective training, taking only 12 min and 24 s to converge. DistilBERT [22] had the shortest training time (9 min 11 s) but at a somewhat lower accuracy.

For the Yelp Reviews Dataset [18], DeBERTa [23] performed better than any other transformer model with accuracy of **91.41%**, narrowly trailed by RoBERTa [20] **91.03%**.

**Table 4.** Optimized Neural Network Architectures for various Transformer Models on Yelp Reviews Dataset [18]

| Transformer Model | Learning Rate | Input Layer | | Hidden Layers | | |
|---|---|---|---|---|---|---|
| | | Number of Neurons | Dropout | Hidden Layer Number | Number of Neurons | Dropout |
| BERT [19] | 0.000221123 | 128 | 0.3 | HL1 | 224 | 0.2 |
| | | | | HL2 | 32 | 0.2 |
| | | | | HL3 | 32 | 0.2 |
| RoBERTa [20] | 0.000400948 | 192 | 0.4 | HL1 | 256 | 0.3 |
| | | | | HL2 | 64 | 0.2 |
| | | | | HL3 | 32 | 0.3 |
| ALBERT [21] | 1.25E-05 | 224 | 0.3 | HL1 | 128 | 0.2 |
| DistilBERT [22] | 1.79E-05 | 160 | 0.5 | HL1 | 160 | 0.4 |
| | | | | HL2 | 256 | 0.4 |
| | | | | HL3 | 256 | 0.3 |
| DeBERTa [23] | 0.00016079 | 192 | 0.2 | HL1 | 224 | 0.5 |
| | | | | HL2 | 64 | 0.5 |
| ELECTRA [24] | 0.000694829 | 96 | 0.2 | HL1 | 224 | 0.5 |
| | | | | HL2 | 160 | 0.5 |
| | | | | HL3 | 160 | 0.5 |

**Computation Time Analysis.** In contrast to traditional TF-IDF methods, transformer-based embeddings were significantly slower in both training and embedding. The embedding time for most of the models for the Yelp dataset [18] was over 50 min. DistilBERT [22] performed best with overall processing time-wise. The increased accuracy is well worth the extra computation.

Experiments ran on free Kaggle GPUs, displayed feasibility without advanced hardware. Future work can reduce inference cost using lighter models.

**Summary.** The experimental study clearly indicates that the proposed deep learning approach performs considerably better than standard machine learning methods, particularly when ELECTRA [24] and DeBERTa [23] are employed. Due to effective neural network optimization algorithms such as early stopping and adaptive learning rates, these models not only retain acceptable computation times but also obtain very high accuracy.

## 4.2   SHAP-Based Interpretability Analysis

To add more transparency and explainability to our presented model, we used SHAP (SHapley Additive exPlanations), a game-theoretic explanation method for interpreting machine learning models. SHAP assists in ascertaining the contribution of every feature towards the prediction of the model, allowing better insight into what behavioral features affect the prediction of a review as fake or real.

**Fake Reviews Dataset [17].** SHAP summary plot of the Fake Reviews Dataset [17] is given in Fig. 4a. Out of the behavioral features, **readability** stood out as the most significant feature, which means the linguistic simplicity or complexity

**Table 5.** Performance Comparison of Baseline [11] and Proposed Method

| Method | Dataset Used | Text Embedding Technique | Text Embedding Time | Model Used | Model Training Time | Accuracy |
|---|---|---|---|---|---|---|
| Base Method [11] | Fake Reviews Dataset [17] | CountVectorization + TfIdf | 127.43 s | Random Forest | 194.24 s | 83.86% |
| | | | | Support Vector Machine | 644.93 s | 88.12% |
| | | | | Logistic Regression | 94.84 s | 86.53% |
| | Yelp Reviews Dataset [18] | CountVectorization + TfIdf | 843.98 s | Random Forest | 1868.39 s | 67.59% |
| | | | | **Support Vector Machine** | 15706.01 s | **73.73%** |
| | | | | Logistic Regression | 621.55 s | 72.59% |
| Proposed Method | Fake Reviews Dataset [17] | BERT [19] | 241.53 s (4.03 min) | Neural Network | 12 m 40 s | 93.87% |
| | | **RoBERTa** [20] | 232.69 s (3.88 min) | | 18 m 19 s | **94.13%** |
| | | **ALBERT** [21] | 242.17 s (4.04 min) | | 12 m 25 s | **94.58%** |
| | | DistilBERT [22] | 131.35 s (2.19 min) | | 09 m 11 s | 93.93% |
| | | DeBERTa [23] | 416.65 s (6.94 min) | | 14 m 16 s | 90.16% |
| | | **ELECTRA** [24] | 242.06 s (4.03 min) | | 12 m 24 s | **95.17%** |
| | Yelp Reviews Dataset [18] | BERT [19] | 3119.02 s (51.98 min) | Neural Network | 22 m 06 s | 89.29% |
| | | **RoBERTa** [20] | 3091.67 s (51.53 min) | | 44 m 03 s | **91.03%** |
| | | ALBERT [21] | 3276.67 s (54.61 min) | | 32 m 33 s | 88.68% |
| | | DistilBERT [22] | 1532.68 s (25.54 min) | | 30 m 48 s | 89.49% |
| | | **DeBERTa** [23] | 5078.14 s (84.64 min) | | 38 m 16 s | **91.41%** |
| | | ELECTRA [24] | 3118.69 s (51.98 min) | | 23 m 07 s | 89.28% |

of a review has a major bearing on whether it is authentic or not. This suggests that spurious reviews will have significantly different readability than genuine ones.

Second in importance was **repeat_ratio** and **length**, which was discovered to make significant contributions. The **repeat_ratio** is a measure of the redundancy of words in a review, which can be an indicator of artificial or robot-written content. Conversely, **length** was also a critical discriminator, indicating the verbosity or succinctness of reviews can be a helpful indicator for the detection of fake reviews. Features such as **category**, **product_avg_rating**, and **rating_deviation** had moderate impact, and rating had the lowest impact.

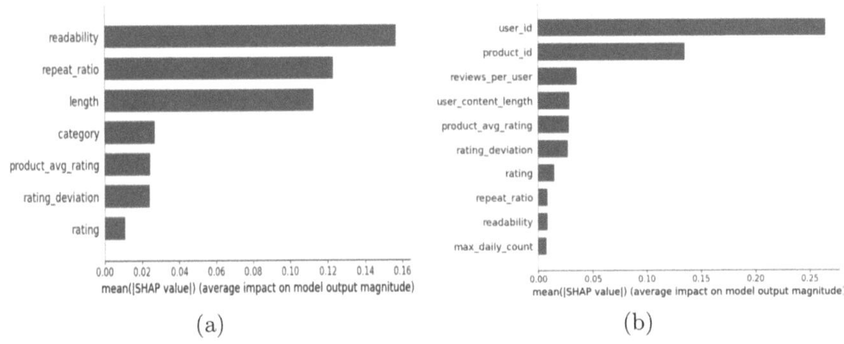


**Fig. 4.** (a) SHAP summary plot showing feature importance for the Fake Reviews Dataset [17], (b) SHAP summary plot showing feature importance for the Yelp Reviews Dataset [18].

**Yelp Reviews Dataset [18].** The SHAP summary plot for the Yelp Reviews Dataset [18] is presented in Fig. 4b. Unlike the Fake Reviews Dataset [17],

**user_id** and **product_id** captured the largest SHAP values, evidencing prominent user- and product-specific behavior patterns that were exploited by the
model. These indicators indicate that some users and products are most commonly linked with fake reviews and thus are key drivers for the model.

Other key features were user **reviews_per_user** and **user_content_length**,
which are measures of posting behavior and average review verbosity of users.
These behavioral characteristics can indicate suspicious activity when users have
a tendency to present unusual reviewing habits. In contrast, textual characteristics such as **readability** and **repeat_ratio** showed relatively lower SHAP values
in this dataset, indicating a more significant reliance on behavioral signals in the
Yelp [18] context.

**Interpretation and Insights.** SHAP-based interpretability analysis discloses
fundamental differences in the fake review behavior across datasets. In Fake
Reviews Dataset [17], linguistic features of text (e.g., **readability** and **repeat
ratio**) prevailed in the decision-making process, which indicates how crucial
content quality is in separating fake reviews. However, the Yelp Reviews Dataset
[18] was more dependent on behavioral features of users, including **user id**,
**product id**, and **reviews_per_user**.

These results prove that deceptive review detection is extremely context-
sensitive and that the performance of various types of features differs across
sites. SHAP analysis not only confirms the appropriateness of chosen features
but also enhances trust in the model as it becomes clear and transparent about
its decision-making process.

## 5   Conclusion and Future Work

This research introduced an efficient fake review detection system through the
combination of transformer-based text embeddings and behavioral and metadata features. Large-scale experimentation with six transformers (BERT [19],
RoBERTa [20], ALBERT [21], DistilBERT [22], DeBERTa [23], ELECTRA [24])
on two real-world datasets–Fake Reviews [17] and Yelp Reviews [18]–exhibited
robust classification performance through neural architectures that were optimized.

To improve model transparency, SHAP-based explanation was implemented.
Impactful features were found to differ per dataset: textual features such as
*readability* and *repeat_ratio* were the most influential in the Fake Reviews dataset
[17], and behavioral features such as *user_id* and *product_id* were most impactful
in Yelp Reviews [18]. This emphasizes the need for dataset-specific detection
mechanisms.

While the current framework has promising results, there are a few directions
remaining that can be explored. Firstly, while transformer-based embeddings are
powerful in performance, their computational intensity can be a challenge in real-
time systems. Models such as ELECTRA [24] and DeBERTa [23] are heavy on

GPU memory and inference time and thus lightweight alternatives such as DistilBERT [22] are better for deployment in latency-critical environments. Quantization and model distillation could be used in future work to balance efficiency with accuracy. Secondly, adding more temporal and network-based features may enhance performance and comprehension. Third, extending explainability analysis to textual transformer embeddings via SHAP or other techniques could provide a clearer comprehension of model decision-making. Fourth, future research might also investigate domain adaptation methods to transfer detection models from one review platform to another. Lastly, implementing this model in a live review moderation system and measuring its effect on end-user trust and platform integrity would achieve useful practical validation.

# References


1. Balakrishnan, N., Chandru, S., Priyadharshini, T.: Decoding authenticity in online review using machine learning. In: 2024 International Conference on Cognitive Robotics and Intelligent Systems (ICC-ROBINS), pp. 421–424. IEEE (2024)
2. Shunxiang, Z., Aoqiang, Z., Guangli, Z., Zhongliang, W., KuanChing, L.: Building fake review detection model based on sentiment intensity and PU learning. IEEE Trans. Neural Netw. Learn. Syst. **34**(10), 6926–6939 (2023)
3. Devika, P., Veena, A., Srilakshmi, E., Ranavardhan Reddy, A., Praveen, E.: Detection of fake reviews using NLP & sentiment analysis. In: 2021 6th International Conference on Communication and Electronics Systems (ICCES), pp. 1534–1537. IEEE (2021)
4. Thilagavathy, A., Therasa, P.R., Jeno Jasmine, J., Sneha, M., Shree Lakshmi, R., Yuvanthika, S.: Fake product review detection and elimination using opinion mining. In: 2023 World Conference on Communication & Computing (WCONF), pp. 1–5. IEEE (2023)
5. Dinesh, L., Kaviya, G., Kavya, N.C., Kousalya, A., Lavanya, N.: Product reviews on opinion mining using NLP techniques. In: 2022 7th International Conference on Communication and Electronics Systems (ICCES), pp. 952–957. IEEE (2022)
6. Dhamdhere, O., Dhanwate, A., Kumbhar, A., Singh, M.: Amazon's Fake Review Detection using Support Vector Machine
7. Biruntha, S., Ashwin, B., Padmasankar, K.S.: Distinguishing reviews through sentiment analysis using machine learning techniques. In: 2022 8th International Conference on Advanced Computing and Communication Systems (ICACCS), vol. 1, pp. 1713–1719. IEEE (2022)
8. Elmogy, A.M., Tariq, U., Ammar, M., Ibrahim, A.: Fake reviews detection using supervised machine learning. Int. J. Adv. Comput. Sci. Appl. **12**(1) (2021)
9. Zhang, D., Li, W., Niu, B., Chong, W.: A deep learning approach for detecting fake reviewers: exploiting reviewing behavior and textual information. Decis. Support Syst. **166**, 113911 (2023)
10. Ozbay, F.A., Alatas, B.: Fake news detection within online social media using supervised artificial intelligence algorithms. Physica A Stat. Mech. Appl. **540**, 123174 (2020)
11. Singh, C., Tanwar, S.: Fake review identification using machine learning. In: 2024 International Conference on Communication, Computer Sciences and Engineering (IC3SE), pp. 582–587. IEEE (2024)

12. Abd-Alhalem, S.M., Ali, H.A., Soliman, N.F., Algarni, A.D., Marie, H.S.: Advancing E-commerce authenticity: a novel fusion approach based on deep learning and aspect features for detecting false reviews. IEEE Access (2024)
13. Hyder, S.B., Tariq, N., Moqurrab, S.A., Ashraf, M., Yoo, J., Srivastava, G.: BERT-based deceptive review detection in social media: introducing DeceptiveBERT. IEEE Trans. Comput. Soc. Syst. (2024)
14. Abedin, E., Mendoza, A., Akbarighatar, P., Karunasekera, S.: Predicting credibility of online reviews: an integrated approach. IEEE Access (2024)
15. Nawara, D., Aly, A., Kashef, R.: Shilling attacks and fake reviews injection: principles, models, and datasets. IEEE Trans. Comput. Soc. Syst. (2024)
16. Xu, S., Cuan, H., Yin, Z., Yin, C.: A hybridized approach for enhanced fake review detection. IEEE Trans. Comput. Soc. Syst. (2024)
17. Salminen, J., Kandpal, C., Kamel, A.M., Jung, S.G., Jansen, B.J.: Creating and detecting fake reviews of online products. J. Retail. Consum. Serv. **64**, 102771 (2022)
18. Xu, D.: YelpZip Dataset. Kaggle. https://www.kaggle.com/datasets/danaxu11/yelpzip. Accessed 25 May 2025
19. Devlin, J., Chang, M.W., Lee, K., Toutanova, K.: Bert: pre-training of deep bidirectional transformers for language understanding. In: Proceedings of the 2019 Conference of the North American chapter of the Association for Computational Linguistics: Human Language Technologies, Volume 1 (Long and Short Papers), pp. 4171–4186 (2019)
20. Liu, Y., et al.: Roberta: a robustly optimized bert pretraining approach. arXiv preprint arXiv:1907.11692 (2019)
21. Lan, Z., Chen, M., Goodman, S., Gimpel, K., Sharma, P., Soricut, R.: Albert: a lite bert for self-supervised learning of language representations. arXiv preprint arXiv:1909.11942 (2019)
22. Sanh, V., Debut, L., Chaumond, J., Wolf, T.: DistilBERT, a distilled version of BERT: smaller, faster, cheaper and lighter. arXiv preprint arXiv:1910.01108 (2019)
23. He, P., Liu, X., Gao, J., Chen, W.: Deberta: decoding-enhanced bert with disentangled attention. arXiv preprint arXiv:2006.03654 (2020)
24. Clark, K., Luong, M.-T., Le, Q.V., Manning, C.D.: Electra: pre-training text encoders as discriminators rather than generators. arXiv preprint arXiv:2003.10555 (2020)

# Multiclass Classification of Rice Plant Leaf Diseases Based on Image Processing Techniques and Vision Transformer (ViT) Deep Neural Network

Bui Hai Phong[1] and Le Anh Ngoc[2(✉)]

[1] Faculty of Information and Technology, Hanoi Architectural University, Hanoi, Vietnam
phongbh@hau.edu.vn
[2] Swinburne Vietnam, FPT University, Hanoi, Vietnam
ngocla2@fe.edu.vn

**Abstract.** In many Asian countries, rice plants provide essential resources of food. Quite a number of people depend on rice products in daily life. However, diseases have caused a critical damage for production of rice plants every year. Therefore, the early diagnosis and treatment of rice diseases become important. The automatic and accurate classification of rice diseases are crucial for the treatment purposes. In the past decade, deep neural networks (DNNs) have achieved a great advance in classifying plant diseases. The paper introduces a multiclass classification approach for identifying diseased rice leaves using data augmentation technique and DNNs. First, we apply data augmentation strategy using traditional image processing to increase the number of images in the original dataset. Next, the Vision Transformer (ViT) network is applied and optimized to enhance the accuracy of classifying diseases in rice plant leaves. The proposed method is evaluated on two public datasets of diseased rice plant leaf images. The proposed method achieved a classification accuracy of 92.5% of rice diseases on two large datasets. Moreover, performance comparisons with various existing methods have shown the outstanding and promising applications of the proposed method.

**Keywords:** Rice diseases classification · Image processing · Deep neural networks

## 1 Introduction

For a long time, rice has proven to be highly valuable for human life and industrial applications [1]. More than fifty percent of Asian population are dependent on rice products everyday [2]. However, a multitude of diseases has exerted a profound impact on the productivity of rice plants every year [3,4]. In order to obtain the efficient prevention of rice diseases, the early and accurate classification of rice plant diseases (RPD) has become essential [5,6]. In the field


K. K. Patel et al. (Eds.): icSoftComp 2025, CCIS 2874, pp. 339–350, 2026.
https://doi.org/10.1007/978-3-032-22062-2_26

of agriculture, specialists can detect rice plant diseases (RPD) through visual examination of the leaves' physical characteristics. Nevertheless, this approach is laborious and demands considerable human resources. [7]. The automated classification of RPD seeks to differentiate among rice diseases by leveraging collected data and machine learning algorithms, thereby eliminating the need for domain experts [8].

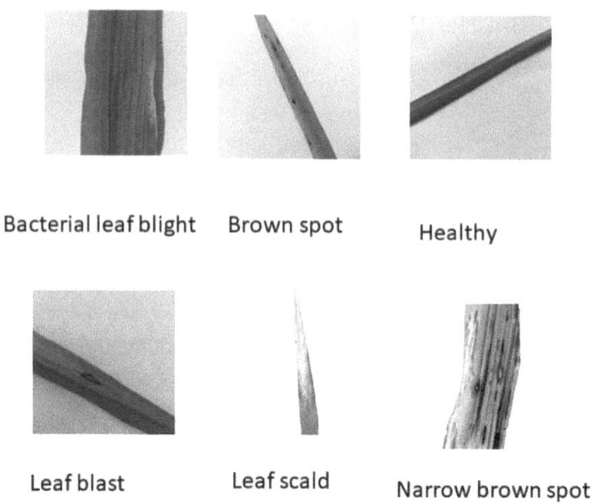


**Fig. 1.** Illustration images of healthy and various diseased rice leaves.

The multiclass classification task can be described as follows [5].

We examine a dataset comprising images and corresponding labels that are denoted as follows:

$S = \{x_i, y_i\}_1^k$ where $x_i \in \mathbb{R}^n, y_i \in \{1, 2, \ldots, m\}$.

The image classification task aims to learn a model that determines a single class label $y$ for an image $x$.

Existing methods can classify rice diseases automatically with high accuracy, saving significant time and human effort. Nevertheless, automating rice disease classification remains challenging due to persistent difficulties in the process. The following errors may be encountered in the classification of rice diseases:

(1) The similarity in color, textures and shapes of rice diseases may cause errors in the classification.
(2) Variations in capture conditions, such as lighting and image skewness, can lead to classification errors for rice disease identification.

Figure 1 illustrates some examples of leaf images of RPD affected by various diseases. Common annual afflictions in rice crops include Bacterial Leaf Blight (BLB), Brown Spot (BS), Leaf Blast (LB), Leaf Scald (LS), and Narrow Brown Spot (NBS). Conventional approaches involve extracting visual features from images, with machine learning algorithms employed to identify RPD [9]. In the last decade, with rapid advances of deep neural networks (DNN), the classification issue of images has obtained high accuracy. DNNs can extract features automatically and classify images with superior performance. These DNNs have been utilized to categorize diseases in plant leaf images. [10]. This paper introduces a methodology that leverages data augmentation techniques and the Vision Transformer (ViT) network [11] to improve the accuracy of classifying diseases in rice leaf images [12].

Data augmentation techniques are employed to expand and equilibrate the dataset of rice leaf images. The technique helps to train DNN models [13,14] efficiently. The Vision Transformer (ViT) network has recently been utilized to achieve superior outcomes in image classification tasks. Additionally, this paper evaluates the performance of various Deep Neural Network (DNN) models for classifying diseases in rice leaves. Subsequently, the proposed and existing methods are thoroughly examined to highlight their respective strengths in addressing the challenge.

## 2   Literature Review

In the section, we review and analyze significant existing solutions for the classification of RPD. There are three types of classification of rice diseases methods. The first approach relies on the physical checking of experts. Experts can check symptoms of rice plant leaf images [15] to identify diseases. The second one extracts various features of rice leaf images. After that, a wide range of machine learning (ML) algorithms are applied to discriminate the diseases. The third approach applied modern deep learning models to recognize RPD.

In the work proposed in [2], visual features of rice leaf images including color, shape, and texture are focused to extract. After the feature extraction, ML classifiers including support vector machine (SVM), kNN and XGBoost were employed to classify RPD. The work proposed in [16] tried to compute the RGB color values of the affected regions of rice leaf images. After that, Naive Bayes (NB) algorithm is investigated to identify RPD. The work presented in [17] attempted to extract the shape and texture features of diseased rice images. Then, SVM algorithm was applied to discriminate the diseases. The work in [18] reviews and analyzes a State-of-the art approaches for detecting and recognizing RPD using various ML and DNN techniques.

In the work in [19], the transfer learning technique of VGG16 network is fine-tuned to discriminate some diseases of rice and maize plants. In the recent research in [20], the combined DNN models including DenseNet, and Resnet are proposed to classify RPD. The work has tested on the datasets that consist of about 33,026 images with six diseases. The method achieved the classification accuracy of 91%. The study investigated in [21] employed a Convolutional neural network (CNN) to extract a large number of visual features of rice leaf images. Then, different ML algorithms including the K-Nearest Neighbor (k-NN), Naive Bayes (NB) and Decision tree are investigated to classify rice diseases. The work in [22] compared and evaluated the recognition of diseases of plant leaves using various models of ML and DNNs. In the work of [3], YOLOv8 has been optimized to recognize of RPD images. Although, researches in the field have been gradually advanced. The classification investigation of diseased rice plants needs to be improved to obtain better results.

# 3    Proposed Method

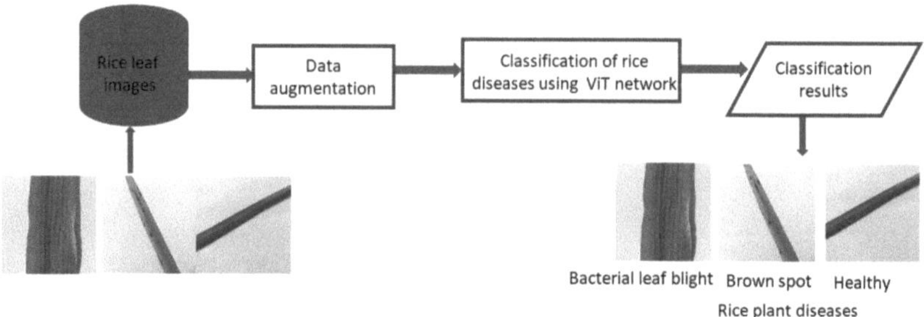


**Fig. 2.** The figure outlines the steps of the proposed method for multiclass classification of RPD, incorporating data augmentation and a Vision Transformer (ViT) neural network.

Figure 2 depicts the overall steps of the proposed method designed for classifying diseases in rice plant leaves. The approach comprises the following primary modules:

In the initial phase, data augmentation is applied to the original rice leaf images. This augmentation process focuses to expand and balance the dataset size, thereby facilitating more efficient training of DNNs.

In the second phase, ViT is employed to enhance classification accuracy. Finally, the classification precision of the proposed method is evaluated and we compare obtained performance with existing approaches to assess the efficacy of the DNN model in classifying diseased rice leaves.

## 3.1    The Data Augmentation

The quantity of rice plant images utilized during the training process plays a crucial role in enhancing the classification accuracy of DNNs [23]. In this study, we employ a range of image processing techniques to substantially expand the rice image dataset. Specifically, methods such as rotation, translation, and noise addition are utilized to expand RPD images. Besides, Gaussian noises are added in the images and the brightness adjustment is applied for the data augmentation purpose. Figure 3 shows examples of an original image alongside those generated through data augmentation techniques.

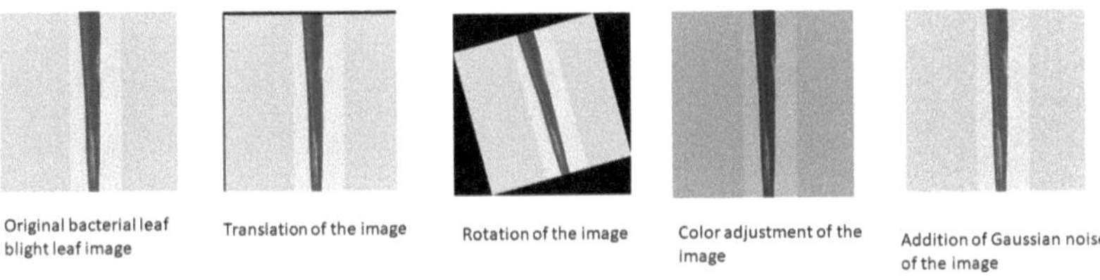


**Fig. 3.** Illustration of augmented data for diseased rice leaves generated through image processing techniques. These methods are utilized in data augmentation to enlarge the dataset's size.

## 3.2   Classification of Rice Diseases Using the ViT Network

The ViT is described as follows in Fig. 4. ViT is designed as the encoder of the Transformer. ViT applied attention mechanisms and established connections between pixels in an image [11]. Input images are divided into smaller patches. The Patch Embedding and Position Embedding components of the ViT transform input images into flattened patches. Subsequently, these patches are processed by the Transformer Encoder. The final classification outputs can be obtain via the MLP Head.

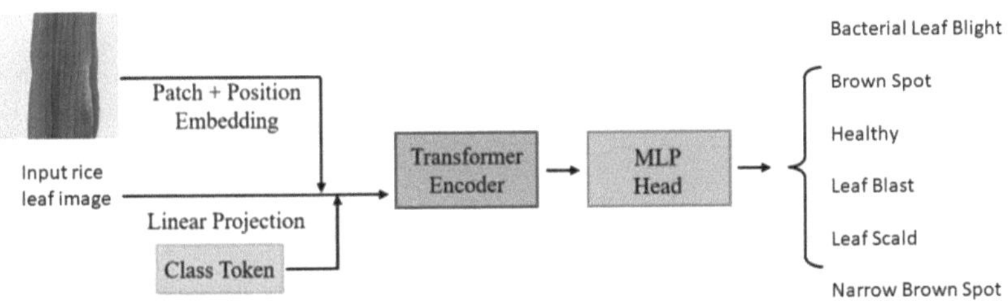


**Fig. 4.** Components of the ViT applied in the work for the classification of RPD.

In this study, the ViT network is trained employing a learning rate of 0.0001. The network utilizes cross-entropy loss function and Stochastic Gradient Descent with Momentum (SGDM) as the optimization algorithm The optimization solver [24] was selected to train the network efficiently. The value of momentum is selected as 0.9.

Figures 5 and 6 illustrate the loss and accuracy values that were obtained in the training process of ViT and Resnet-50 networks. We can see that the loss values decrease in the training. Besides, the accuracy values increase that indicates the convergence of the learning of the DNNs. The implementation of the neural network was performed using PyTorch library of Python language.

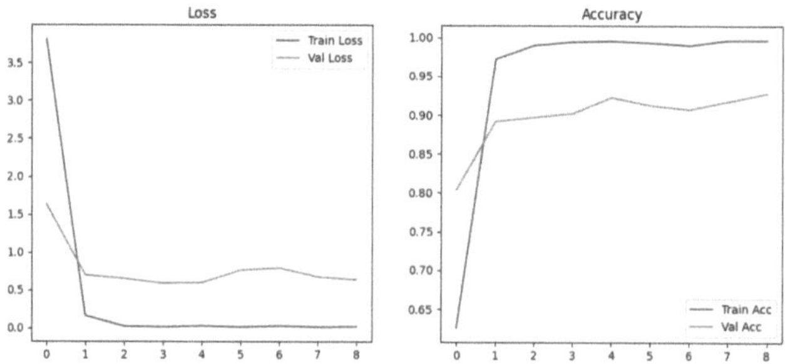

**Fig. 5.** Training accuracy and loss curves of the ViT network in classifying RPD.

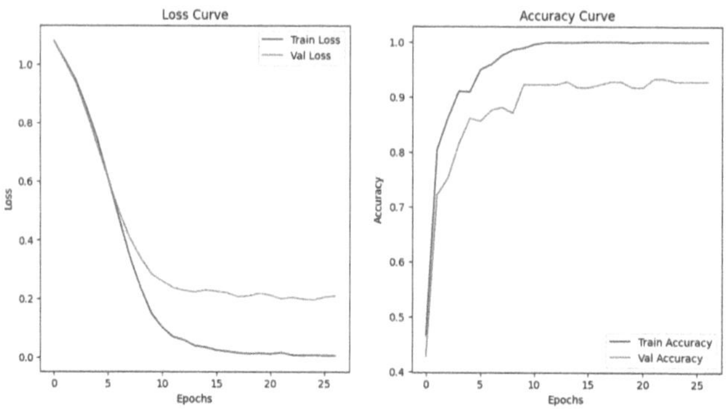

**Fig. 6.** Training accuracy and loss curves of the ResNet-50 network during RPD classification.

## 4    Experimental Results

### 4.1    RPD Dataset and Evaluation Metric

**Table 1.** Representative Information: Number of RPD Images in Dataset 1 Before We Apply Data Augmentation

| RPD | Training | Testing |
| --- | --- | --- |
| BS | 30 | 10 |
| LS | 30 | 10 |
| BLB | 30 | 10 |

**Table 2.** Representative Information: Number of RPD Images in Dataset 1 After We Apply Data Augmentation

| RPD | Training | Testing |
|-----|----------|---------|
| BS  | 150      | 50      |
| LS  | 150      | 50      |
| BLB | 150      | 50      |

**Table 3.** Representative Information: Number of RPD Images in Dataset 2 Before We Apply Data Augmentation

| RPD     | Training | Testing |
|---------|----------|---------|
| BLB     | 350      | 88      |
| BS      | 350      | 88      |
| Healthy | 350      | 88      |
| LB      | 350      | 88      |
| LC      | 350      | 88      |
| NBS     | 350      | 88      |

**Table 4.** Representative Information: Number of RPD Images in Dataset 2 After We Apply Data Augmentation

| RPD     | Training | Testing |
|---------|----------|---------|
| BLB     | 1750     | 440     |
| BS      | 1750     | 440     |
| Healthy | 1750     | 440     |
| LB      | 1750     | 440     |
| LC      | 1750     | 440     |
| NBS     | 1750     | 440     |

For clear evaluation of the proposed method, two public datasets of diseased rice leave images were used in the section. The first dataset comprises three types of RPD. The diseases are: Brown Spot (BS), Leaf Smut (LS), and Bacterial Leaf Blight (BLB). The second dataset includes six types: Bacterial Leaf Blight (BLB), Brown Spot (BS), Healthy, Leaf Blast (LB), Leaf Scald (LC), and Narrow Brown Spot (NBS).

The datasets are collected from Kaggle repositories [25,26]. The datasets consist a small number of RPD leaf images. To obtain better results of using DNN models, data augmentation has been implemented to enhance and equilibrate the quantity of RPD leaf images in the dataset. Tables 1, 2, 3 and 4 show detailed information regarding the training and testing RPD images within the datasets.

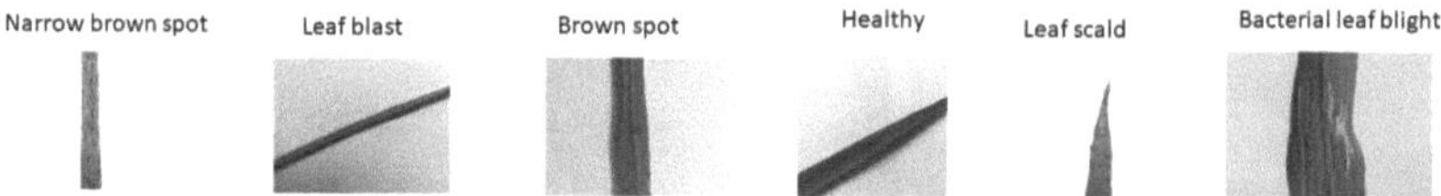


**Fig. 7.** Illustration of Classification Results for Diseased Rice Plant Leaf Images That Demonstrates Accurate Predictions.

Prediction labels

|  | Bacterial Leaf Blight | Brown Spot | Healthy | Leaf Blast | Leaf Scald | Narrow Brown Spot |
|---|---|---|---|---|---|---|
| **Bacterial Leaf Blight** | **420** | 0 | 0 | 10 | 0 | 20 |
| **Brown Spot** | 0 | **410** | 0 | 20 | 0 | 10 |
| **Healthy** | 0 | 0 | **430** | 10 | 0 | 0 |
| **Leaf Blast** | 0 | 10 | 10 | **390** | 0 | 10 |
| **Leaf Scald** | 0 | 0 | 0 | 0 | **430** | 10 |
| **Narrow Brown Spot** | 20 | 20 | 0 | 10 | 10 | **390** |

(True labels)

**Fig. 8.** Confusion Matrix Representing Classification Results for Diseased Rice Plant Leaf Images.

The accuracy metric [27], commonly used in image classification tasks, is applied to evaluate the proposed method's performance. The mathematical equation for the metric is expressed as follows:

$$Accuracy = \frac{Correct - predictions}{Total - predictions} \tag{1}$$

## 4.2   Performance Evaluation of Classification of RPD

To demonstrate the efficiency of our solution, we test and compare the performance against existing approaches and advanced DNN models. Tables 5, 6, and 7 present the performance of DNNs in classifying rice diseases prior to the application of data augmentation. Tables 5 and 6 demonstrate that predictions using the ViT obtains the best performance compared to those of ResNet-50 [28] and Mobilenet V3 [29]. Classification accuracy of RPD on dataset 2 is higher on dataset 1. The quality of images in dataset 2 is better than that in dataset 1. Moreover, dataset 2 has more images than dataset 1. The larger image dataset allows us to train DNN model more efficiently.

**Table 5.** Comparison of various DNN models in classifying RPD in dataset 1

| DNNs | Accuracy |
|---|---|
| Resnet-50 | 82.5% |
| Mobilenet V3 | 80 % |
| Alexnet | 79 % |
| ViT | 82 % |

**Table 6.** Comparison of various DNN models for the classification of RPD in dataset 2

| DNNs | Accuracy |
|---|---|
| Resnet-50 | 91.5% |
| Mobilenet V3 | 90 % |
| Alexnet | 89 % |
| ViT | 92.5 % |

**Table 7.** Comparison of Proposed and Conventional Methods for RPD Classification

| Method | Accuracy |
|---|---|
| The work using the EfficientNet in [30] | 90% |
| Method using Naive Bayes in [1] | 85% |
| ViT | 92.5 % |

Data augmentation enables the DNNs to achieve better results compared to those obtained on the original dataset. It also allows for significant improvements in classification accuracy. The proposed method outperforms the method using the EfficientNet in [30] and the method using the feature selection in [1]. We can see in Table 8 that the executing performance of ViT is superior to that of ResNet-50. MobileNetV3 network achieves the highest execution time score due to its optimization for the running environment.

Examples of correct classification of RPD images are illustrated in Fig. 7. The proposed method is capable of correctly classifying various diseases of rice leaf in different conditions of captured images. Figure 8 demonstrates confusion matrix of the classification. The Leaf scald and Bacterial leaf blight diseases are discriminated with high accuracy. Several errors occur in classifying LB and NBS diseases. The similarity of color and shape features of RPD images can lead to misclassification.

**Table 8.** Execution Time Comparison of DNNs for Diseased Rice Leaf Recognition (in Milliseconds)

| DNNs | Execution time (in milliseconds) |
| --- | --- |
| Resnet-50 network | 25.5 |
| Mobilenet V3 network | 12.5 |
| ViT network | 54.5 |

## 5    Conclusion and Future Works

In the paper, a multiclass classification approach for diseased rice leaves has been presented. We have employed data augmentation and the Vision Transformer neural network. The ViT model achieved the highest accuracy among the evaluated Deep Neural Networks (DNNs). Compared to established methods (for example, ResNet-50 and MobileNetV3), the proposed approach provided superior precision in classifying diseased rice leaf images. The augmentation techniques applied substantially improved the overall classification performance. In future work, data augmentation strategies using Generative Adversarial Network (GAN) could be further explored to improve classification accuracy. The achievement of our proposed method hold potential for integration into smart agriculture applications. Moreover, IoT systems can be integrated with the proposed method to provide real applications to agricultural users.

## References


1. Phadikar, S., Sil, J., Das, A.K.: Rice diseases classification using feature selection and rule generation techniques. Comput. Electron. Agri. **90**, 76–85 (2013). ISSN 0168-1699, https://doi.org/10.1016/j.compag.2012.11.001. https://www.sciencedirect.com/science/article/pii/S016816991200258X
2. Azim, M.A., et al.: An effective feature extraction method for rice leaf disease classification. In: TELKOMNIKA Telecommunication, Computing, Electronics and Control, vol. 19, no. 2 , pp. 463–470 (2021)
3. Phong, B.H., Nguyen, P.N., Phan, M.Q.B., Pham, V.K.: Detection and recognition of rice leaf diseases using deep neural networks. In: Proceedings of the SPIE 13225, Sixth International Conference on Image, Video Processing, and Artificial Intelligence (IVPAI 2024), 132250D (2024). https://doi.org/10.1117/12.3046200
4. Phong, B.H., Nguyen, P.A., Quyet, T.D., An, P.D., Tri, P.D., Ngoc, L.A.: Classification of diseases of bean plant leaves using data augmentation and deep neural networks. In: Park, J.S., Wang, J., Pan, Y., J. Park, J. (eds) Advanced Future Information Technology. FutureTech 2025. LNEE, vol 1483. Springer, Singapore (2025). https://doi.org/10.1007/978-981-95-1999-6_1
5. Shah, J.P., Prajapati, H.B., Dabhi, V.K.: A survey on detection and classification of rice plant diseases. In: Current Trends in Advanced Computing (ICCTAC), IEEE International Conference on 2016 Mar 10, pp. 1–8. IEEE (2016)
6. Perez, A.J., Lopez, F., Benlloch, J.V., Christensen, S.: Colour and shape analysis techniques for weed detection in cereal fields. Comput. Electron. Agr. **25**, 197–212 (2000)

7. Gosai, D., et al.: Plant disease detection and classification using machine learning algorithm. In: 2022 International Conference for Advancement in Technology (ICONAT). https://doi.org/10.1109/ICONAT53423.2022.9726036

8. Larese, M.G., Namías, R., Craviotto, R.M., Arango, M.R., Gallo, C., Granitto, P.M.: Automatic classification of legumes using leaf vein image features. Pattern Recogn. **47**(1), 158–168 (2014). https://doi.org/10.1016/j.patcog.2013.06.012

9. Fan, R.-E., Chen, P.-H., Lin, C.-J.: Working set selection using second order information for training support vector machines. J. Mach. Learn. Res. **6**, 1889–1918 (2006)

10. Phong, B.H.: Classification of plant leaf diseases using deep neural networks in color and grayscale images. J. Decis. Anal. Intell. Comput. **4** (2024). https://doi.org/10.31181/10002052024p

11. Dosovitskiy, A., et al.: An image is worth 16x16 words: transformers for image recognition at scale (2021). https://doi.org/10.48550/arXiv.2010.11929

12. Chen, X., Hsieh, C.J., Gong, B.: When vision transformers outperform ResNets without pretraining or strong data augmentations. ArXiv. https://arxiv.org/abs/2106.01548

13. Tarun, R. and Esther, B.P.: Computer Vision ECCV 16th European Conference, Glasgow, UK, August 2020. Proceedings, Part XXVII. (2020). https://doi.org/10.1007/978-3-030-58583-9-34

14. Phong, B.H., et al.: Performance evaluation of the multiclass classification of flowers on diverse datasets. In: 3rd International Conference on Electrical, Computer, Communications and Mechatronics Engineering (ICECCME), Spain (2023). https://doi.org/10.1109/ICECCME57830.2023.10252422

15. Barbedo, J.: A review on the main challenges in automatic plant disease identification based on visible range images. Biosyst. Eng. **144** (2016)

16. Islam, T., et al.: A faster technique on rice disease detection using image processing of affected area in agro-field. In: 2018 Second International Conference on Inventive Communication and Computational Technologies (ICICCT) (2018)

17. Yao, Q., Guan, Z., Zhou, Y.: Application of support vector machine for detecting rice diseases using shape and color texture features. In: International Conference on Engineering Computation, pp. 79–83 (2009)

18. Mukherjee, R., et al.: Rice leaf disease identification and classification using machine learning techniques: a comprehensive review. Eng. Appl. Artif. Intell. **139** (2025). https://doi.org/10.1016/j.engappai.2024.109639

19. Chen, J., Chen, J., Zhang, D., Sun, Y., Nanehkaran, Y.: Using deep transfer learning for image-based plant disease identification. Comput. Electron. Agri. **173**, 105393 (2020)

20. Deng, R., et al.: Automatic diagnosis of rice diseases using deep learning. Front. Plant Sci., **12** (2021)

21. Hasan, M.M., Uddin, A.F.M.S., Akhond, M.R., Uddin, M.J., Hossain, M.A., Hossain, M.A.: Machine learning and image processing techniques for rice disease detection: a critical analysis. Int. J. Plant Biol. **14**(4), 1190–1207 (2023)

22. Ngugi, L.C., Abelwahab, M., Abo-Zahhad, M.: Recent advances in image processing techniques for automated leaf pest and disease recognition – a review. Inform. Process. Agri. **8**, 27–51 (2021)

23. Gracia Moisés, A., Vitoria Pascual, I., Imas González, J.J., Ruiz, Z.C.: Data augmentation techniques for machine learning applied to optical spectroscopy datasets in agrifood applications: a comprehensive review. Sensors. **23**(20), 8562 (2023). https://doi.org/10.3390/s23208562

24. Murphy, K.P.: Machine Learning: A Probabilistic Perspective. The MIT Press, Cambridge, Massachusetts (2012)
25. Prajapati, H.B., Shah, J.P., Dabhi, V.K.: Detection and classification of rice plant diseases. Intell. Decis. Technol. **11**(3), 357–373 (2017)
26. Rice leaf diseases dataset. https://www.kaggle.com/datasets/dedeikhsandwisaputra/rice-leafs-disease-dataset. Accessed 20 Apr 2025
27. Mohammed, M.: Machine Learning: Algorithms and Applications. CRC Press (2016). https://doi.org/10.1201/9781315371658
28. He, K., Zhang, X., Ren, S., Sun, J.: Deep residual learning for image recognition (2016). https://arxiv.org/abs/1512.03385
29. Howard, A., et al.: Searching for MobileNetV3 (2019). https://arxiv.org/pdf/1905.02244v5
30. Singh, V., et al.: Classification of beans leaf diseases using fine tuned CNN model. In: International Conference on Machine Learning and Data Engineering (2023). https://doi.org/10.1016/j.procs.2023.01.017

# Performance Evaluation of Clustering Algorithms Applied to Web Services

Boutkhil Sidaoui[1,2]([envelope]) [iD], Moussa Kaouan[1,2] [iD], and Samiha Smail[1] [iD]

[1] Computer Science Department, University of Naâma - SALHI Ahmed, BP 66, 45000 Naâma, Algeria
[2] Laboratory of Mathematics, Statistics and Computer Science for Scientific Research (W1550900), University of Naâma - SALHI Ahmed, Naâma, Algeria
`b.sidaoui@cuniv-naama.dz`

**Abstract.** Developing efficient automatic classification and discovery methods is necessary due to the increasing number of online web services. This study analyses and compares several clustering algorithms and feature extraction techniques to enhance the organizational structure and retrieval of web services. Specifically, it investigates textual, structural, and semantic feature extraction techniques, which are subsequently combined with clustering algorithms such as K-Means, Hierarchical Clustering, and Density-Based Spatial Clustering of Applications with Noise (DBSCAN). The study aims to evaluate the performance of these combinations in terms of classification accuracy, computational efficiency, and the quality of the resulting service categories. Experiments are conducted using benchmark datasets that reflect diverse real-world scenarios. The results indicate that different integrations of feature extraction and clustering methods provide varying levels of effectiveness, depending on the context and data characteristics. By analyzing these outcomes, the study offers practical guidance for selecting suitable Algorithms to support automated web service classification, improving service discovery processes, and enhancing service-oriented architectures' overall usability and scalability.

**Keywords:** Clustering · TF-IDF · Web Services · Metrics Evaluation

## 1 Introduction

The rapid growth of web services on the Internet has intensified the need for efficient techniques to automatically organize, discover, and classify these services. As service registries grow, manual approaches to service management become impractical, requiring automated methods that can scale with increasing data volume and complexity. Two essential processes in this domain are feature extraction and clustering: The feature extraction step plays a fundamental role in transforming raw web services data, such as WSDL files, descriptions, or API documentation, into structured representations suitable for analysis. Effective


K. K. Patel et al. (Eds.): icSoftComp 2025, CCIS 2874, pp. 351–363, 2026.
https://doi.org/10.1007/978-3-032-22062-2_27

feature extraction techniques enhance the quality of input data for the clustering phase, ultimately impacting the accuracy and interpretability of the results. The second step, called clustering, is an unsupervised learning approach that groups similar web services based on their features without prior labeling. This process facilitates automatic categorization, discovery, and recommendation of services, particularly in large-scale environments. Various clustering methods such as k-means, hierarchical clustering, and Density-Based Spatial Clustering of Applications with Noise (DBSCAN), have been applied in this context, offering different advantages regarding scalability, accuracy, and noise tolerance [1] and [2]. This paper presents a comprehensive comparison of three widely used clustering methods: K-Means, Hierarchical Clustering, and DBSCAN, to evaluate their capability to discover meaningful groupings. To prepare the data, we employ the Term FrequencyInverse Document Frequency (TF-IDF) to extract features, enabling the transformation of textual service into weighted numerical vectors. To enhance the semantic representation and reduce dimensionality, we further integrate WordNet, allowing for the refinement of feature vectors based on semantic relationships. The clustering performance is evaluated using selected metrics, such as the Silhouette coefficient, the Calinski-Harabasz index, and the Elbow method, across a dataset of 323 web services. Our goal is to identify which combinations of feature extraction, semantic enhancement, and clustering yield the most coherent and accurate groupings. The study highlights the strengths and limitations of each clustering approach and offers practical guidance for enhancing service discovery, classification, and composition.

The rest is organized as follows: related works are presented in section two, followed by a brief description of the Web Services background in section three. Section four is sacred to the Feature Extraction Approaches used in the first step. Clustering methods used in this paper are presented in Sect. 5, followed by Materials and Methods in Sect. 6. The last two sections are reserved for analysis results and the conclusion.

## 2   Related Works

Table 1 comprehensively summarizes various web service clustering approaches proposed between 2009 and 2023, like [5] and [11]. Early contributions explored vector representation and fuzzy clustering with QoS-based filtering to improve service similarity and personalization. Over time, researchers introduced more sophisticated methods, such as hierarchical clustering [10] and semantic approaches leveraging ontologies [15]. Recent studies such as [7] and [8] utilize QoS-based clustering to refine service selection, while [3] integrates K-Means with Knapsack optimization for resource-efficient service composition. Bio-inspired algorithms also gained traction, as seen in [16] and [12]. Additionally, semantic enhancement through LDA and word embedding [14] and recent deep learning approaches like graph contrastive learning [17] reflect the field's evolution toward semantic accuracy and intelligent recommendations.

**Table 1.** Summary of Related Works on Web Services Clustering

| Authors | Algorithm Used | Brief Description |
| --- | --- | --- |
| Elbitar et al. [15] (2014) | Ontology-Based Matching, Case-Based Reasoning and Semantic Annotations | Combines multiple methodologies for more robust and flexible discovery mechanisms |
| Choi et al. [17] (2023) | QoS-aware Graph Contrastive Learning | Enhancing web service recommendations, the goal is to address challenges such as data sparsity and the cold-start problem by leveraging Quality of Service information |
| Purohit et al. [8] (2023) | Multi-Layer Architecture and based-QoS | Improving web service selection by leveraging Quality of Service |
| Rayasam et al. [16] (2022) | Semantic service descriptions and bio-inspired optimization (ACO) | Improving Web service retrieval by leveraging bio-inspired clustering techniques (Ant Colony optimization) |
| Alhadid et al. [3] (2021) | K-Means + Knapsack Algorithms | Proposes a hybrid model combining clustering and optimization to enhance service composition efficiency and resource utilization. |
| Agarwal et al. [9] (2021) | Vector representation, semantic methods and clustering algorithms | Improving web service discovery |
| Fariss et al. [7] (2021) | QoS-Based and K-Means | Uses clustering on quality of service attributes for service ranking. |
| Soumi et al. [6] (2020) | Optimal Pareto Front Construction | Composing web services while optimizing multiple Quality of Service (QoS) parameters: response time, throughput, reliability, and availability |
| Bravo et al. [12] (2019) | Artificial Bee Colony, K-means and consensus clustering | enhancing the organization and retrieval Web services |
| Kumara et al. [13] (2019) | Multi-level clustering strategy (Functional and quality of service) | improve service discovery and selection by clustering web services at multiple levels based on both functional and non-functional (quality of service) attributes |
| Yi et al. [14] (2018) | Latent Dirichlet Allocation with Word Embedding | A hybrid approach to enhance the semantic clustering of web services by LDA and the semantic similarity of word embeddings |
| Huynh et al. [4] (2017) | Logic-based, hierarchical agglomerative clustering and k-means | Enhance service composition and verification. |
| Cong et al. [10] (2013) | Hierarchical Clustering | Applies hierarchical model for efficient discovery and selection. |
| Zhang et al. [11] (2012) | fuzzy clustering with QoS-based filtering | Enhancing the accuracy and personalization of service recommendation |
| Platzer et al. [5] (2009) | Vector representation, angle-based similarity and partition-based clustering | Clustering web services by geometric angle-based similarity measures |

# 3   Web Services Background

A Web service is a modular, self-contained software component that performs specific tasks over a network. It ensures interoperability across heterogeneous systems through standard protocols (HTTP/HTTPS) and data formats (XML, JSON). By exposing business logic via well-defined APIs, web services enable integration, reuse, and composition, supporting complex workflows. They play a central role in modern paradigms such as Service-Oriented Architecture (SOA) and microservices, which emphasize modularity, maintainability, and resilience. Web services enable interoperability but face challenges in discovery, scalability, security, and quality of service. Clustering helps address these by grouping similar services for easier selection and composition, relying on accurate feature extraction from descriptions like WSDL files or natural language summaries. However, these descriptions are often brief and ambiguous, complicating similarity measurement and reducing clustering quality. Effective feature extraction is therefore crucial for applying machine learning in service classification and discovery.

# 4   Feature Extraction Approaches

Feature extraction is a crucial step in web service clustering, converting raw textual descriptions into structured numerical representations. Techniques such as TF-IDF capture term importance, while semantic tools like WordNet enrich representations with synonyms and context. Effective extraction ensures that clustering algorithms capture both functional and semantic aspects, improving the grouping of similar services. The features considered in this study are derived from the input and output concepts of web services, extracted using SPARQL, which is employed to extract concepts input and output from OWL-S web services representations by constructing a Vector of Concepts (VC) for each domain. Each VC encapsulates all unique concepts present across the input and output parameters of every service within the corresponding domain, ensuring a comprehensive semantic representation. The Vectors of Concepts are then transformed into numerical vectors using the TF-IDF method.

## 4.1   TF-IDF Method

The TF-IDF (Term FrequencyInverse Document Frequency) method is widely used in text mining and information retrieval to measure a term's significance in a document relative to the entire corpus. It combines two metrics: The Term Frequency (TF) and the Inverse Document Frequency (IDF).

**Term Frequency (TF).** The Term Frequency (TF) measures how often a term appears in a document. It is calculated by:

$$TF(t, d) = \frac{\text{Number of times that term } t \text{ appears in document } d}{\text{Total number of terms in document } d} \tag{1}$$

**Inverse Document Frequency (IDF).** The Inverse Document Frequency (IDF) measures the importance of the term across all documents by reducing the weight of terms that appear frequently across the corpus. The following formula calculates the IDF metric:

$$IDF(t, D) = \log \left( \frac{\text{Total number of documents in the corpus } D}{\text{Number of documents containing term } t} \right) \quad (2)$$

The TF-IDF score for a term $t$ in a document $d$ within a corpus $D$ is then calculated as:

$$\text{TF-IDF}(t, d, D) = TF(t, d) \times IDF(t, D) \quad (3)$$

This numerical representation emphasizes terms frequente in a document but rare in the corpus, thus serving as a useful feature for clustering and classification tasks.

## 4.2   WordNet

The WordNet is a lexical library for the English language that contains words into synonyms called synsets, providing semantic relationships between these sets, such as hypernyms (general terms), hyponyms (specific terms), and antonyms. In text preprocessing and feature extraction, WordNet is used to enhance the representation and the feature extraction by:

– Expanding terms with their synonyms to capture semantic similarity.
– Reducing dimensionality by grouping semantically related words.
– Improving clustering and classification performance by leveraging semantic relationships beyond exact word matches.

Integrating WordNet makes the text data semantically enriched, enabling more meaningful analysis in tasks such as web service clustering and document classification.

## 5   Clustering Methods

Clustering is an unsupervised learning Algorithm in machine learning that aims to organize data objects into clusters, maximizing similarity within groups and minimizing similarity across groups. Unlike supervised learning, clustering does not rely on labeled data, making it highly valuable for exploratory data analysis, pattern recognition, and data mining applications.

Clustering identifies inherent structures in data without prior knowledge of class labels. It measures the similarity or distance between data points using various metrics (e.g., Euclidean, cosine, Mahalanobis). The main goal is to maximize intra-cluster similarity while minimizing inter-cluster similarity. Table 2 presents popular clustering approaches with brief descriptions.

**Table 2.** Popular Clustering Algorithms

| Algorithm | Type | Description |
| --- | --- | --- |
| K-Means | Partition-based | Divides data into a predefined number of clusters $k$, minimizing intra-cluster distance. Efficient for large datasets, commonly used in clustering problems. |
| Hierarchical Clustering | Agglomerative | Builds a dendrogram of nested clusters using agglomerative or divisive strategies, without requiring a predefined number of clusters. |
| Density-Based Spatial Clustering of Applications with Noise | Density-based | Identifies clusters based on high point density areas and effectively finds arbitrarily shaped clusters and outliers. |
| Fuzzy C-Means | Fuzzy Clustering | Allows data points to belong to multiple clusters with varying membership probabilities, useful for ambiguous boundaries. |
| Gaussian Mixture Model (GMM) | Model-based | Assuming data is generated from a mixture of Gaussian distributions and uses probabilistic assignments of points to clusters. |
| LDA + Word Embedding | Semantic-based | Uses meaning and context in textual data to cluster similar services. Effective in semantic web service discovery, text retrieval, etc. |
| Ant Colony Optimization (ACO)/Artificial Bee Colony (ABC) | Bio-inspired | Uses swarm intelligence principles to cluster data by simulating collective behaviors of ants or bees in search of optimal grouping. |

# 6    Material and Methodology

This study uses the OWLS-TC v4.0 corpus developed by the German Center for Artificial Intelligence Research. The dataset contains 323 web services across five domains: food, travel, communication, weapon, and geography. Most services originate from IBM's UDDI directory and were semi-automatically translated from WSDL to OWL format [21]. Each OWLS document, whether a service or query, includes a "Profile" section with elements such as "profile: has input" and "profile: has output", which serve as inputs for the service discovery module. Several preprocessing steps were applied to prepare the dataset for analysis. The process began with cleaning and preprocessing to ensure data consistency and quality. Key features such as inputs, outputs, and domain-specific terms were selected to improve representational accuracy. Significant keywords were extracted using TF-IDF, and three clustering algorithms—K-Means, DBSCAN, and Hierarchical Clusteringwere applied and evaluated. The complete workflow is illustrated in Fig. 1.

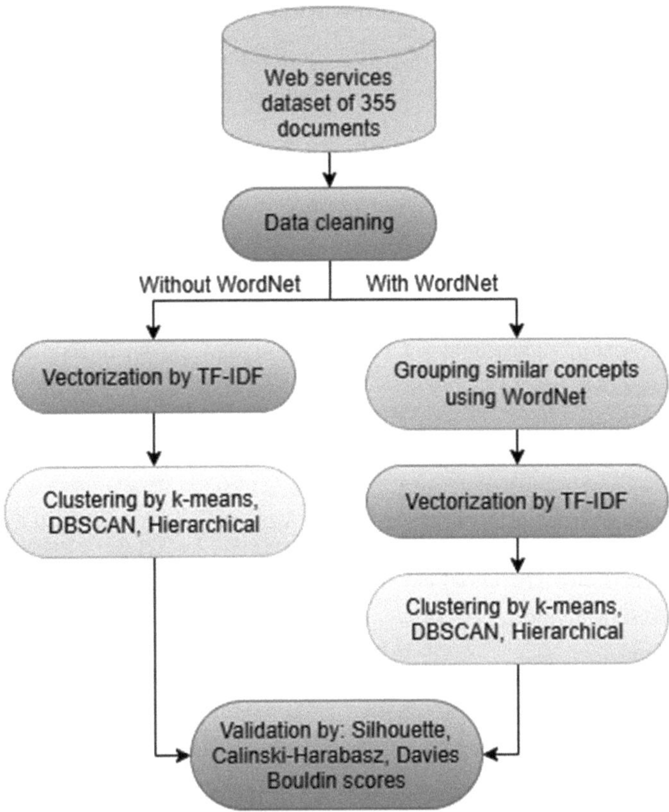


**Fig. 1.** Workflow of the proposed study.

## 7   Results and Discussion

The Tables 3, 4, 5, 6, 7, 8, 9, 10, 11 and 12 report the performance of three methods: K-Means, DBSCAN, and Hierarchical Clustering. Each one was evaluated using three standard metrics: the Silhouette Score, the Calinski-Harabasz Index, and the Davies-Bouldin Index. These metrics collectively assess the compactness, separation, and overall quality of the clusters produced by each algorithm. The tables illustrate the comparative analysis of three clustering methods based on three evaluation metrics.

Figures 2, 3, and 4 present a comparative analysis of clustering results evaluated using Silhouette Score, Calinski-Harabasz Index, and Davies-Bouldin Index. The evaluation covers three clustering algorithms applied both on the full feature set and on a reduced feature set using WordNet-based semantic grouping. Therefore, 5baillustrates a comparative analysis of the Silhouette Scores for different clustering methods, both with and without feature reduction. Alternatively, Fig. 6 presents the results obtained using the Elbow algorithm to calculate the optimal number of categories ($k$)

**Table 3.** Results of clustering **communication** domain with all 34 features without WordNet.

| Algorithm | Threshold | # Clusters | Silhouette | Calinski H. | Davies B. |
| --- | --- | --- | --- | --- | --- |
| DBSCAN | 0.7 | 11 | 0.43 | 5.10 | 1.43 |
| K-means | 0.7 | 7 | 0.37 | 9.90 | 1.10 |
| Hierarchical | 0.7 | 7 | 0.37 | 9.90 | 1.10 |

**Table 4.** Results of clustering **communication** domain after reducing features using WordNet.

| Algorithm | Threshold | # Clusters | Silhouette | Calinski H. | Davies B. |
| --- | --- | --- | --- | --- | --- |
| DBSCAN | 0.7 | 2 | 0.29 | 9.30 | 0.91 |
| K-means | 0.7 | 8 | 0.64 | 15.60 | 0.95 |
| Hierarchical | 0.7 | 8 | 0.62 | 15.00 | 1.00 |

**Table 5.** Web service clustering for the **food** domain using all 19 features

| Algorithm | Threshold | # Clusters | Silhouette | Calinski H. | Davies B. |
| --- | --- | --- | --- | --- | --- |
| DBSCAN | 0.5 | 8 | 0.76 | 18.40 | 0.51 |
| K-means | 0.5 | 8 | 0.67 | 16.30 | 0.57 |
| Hierarchical | 0.5 | 8 | 0.67 | 16.30 | 0.57 |

**Table 6.** Results of **food** domain clustering after reducing features using WordNet tool.

| Algorithm | Threshold | # Clusters | Silhouette | Calinski H. | Davies B. |
| --- | --- | --- | --- | --- | --- |
| DBSCAN | 0.5 | 3 | 0.32 | 5.00 | 0.65 |
| K-means | 0.5 | 8 | 0.70 | 19.4 | 0.51 |
| Hierarchical | 0.5 | 8 | 0.71 | 18.40 | 0.61 |

**Table 7.** Web service clustering for the **geography** domain with all 52 features

| Algorithm | Threshold | # Clusters | Silhouette | Calinski H. | Davies B. |
| --- | --- | --- | --- | --- | --- |
| DBSCAN | 0.7 | 11 | 0.54 | 8.60 | 1.35 |
| K-means | 0.7 | 8 | 0.46 | 15.50 | 0.95 |
| Hierarchical | 0.7 | 8 | 0.46 | 15.50 | 0.95 |

**Table 8.** Results of **geography** domain after reducing the feature to 25 using WordNet.

| Algorithm | Threshold | # Clusters | Silhouette | Calinski H. | Davies B. |
| --- | --- | --- | --- | --- | --- |
| DBSCAN | 0.7 | 5 | 0.38 | 9.00 | 0.63 |
| K-means | 0.7 | 9 | 0.53 | 15.40 | 0.87 |
| Hierarchical | 0.7 | 9 | 0.52 | 15.40 | 0.99 |

**Table 9.** Web service clustering for the **travel** domain with all 56 features

| Algorithm | Threshold | # Clusters | Silhouette | Calinski H. | Davies B. |
|---|---|---|---|---|---|
| DBSCAN | 0.7 | 10 | 0.60 | 19.80 | 0.91 |
| K-means | 0.7 | 8 | 0.53 | 21.40 | 1.04 |
| Hierarchical | 0.7 | 8 | 0.52 | 21.50 | 1.00 |

**Table 10.** Results of **travel** domain after reducing the feature to 27 without WordNet.

| Algorithm | Threshold | # Clusters | Silhouette | Calinski H. | Davies B. |
|---|---|---|---|---|---|
| DBSCAN | 0.7 | 9 | 0.63 | 22.70 | 0.90 |
| K-means | 0.7 | 7 | 0.49 | 21.10 | 0.99 |
| Hierarchical | 0.7 | 7 | 0.51 | 22.30 | 0.99 |

**Table 11.** Web service clustering for the **weapon** domain with all 13 features

| Algorithm | Threshold | # Clusters | Silhouette | Calinski H. | Davies B. |
|---|---|---|---|---|---|
| DBSCAN | 0.5 | 8 | 0.97 | 1.00 | 0.00 |
| K-means | 0.5 | 7 | 0.94 | 110.4 | 0.24 |
| Hierarchical | 0.5 | 7 | 0.94 | 110.4 | 0.24 |

**Table 12.** Results of **weapon** domain after reducing the feature to 4 without WordNet.

| Algorithm | Threshold | # Clusters | Silhouette | Calinski H. | Davies B. |
|---|---|---|---|---|---|
| DBSCAN | 0.5 | 2 | 0.51 | 7.10 | 0.47 |
| K-means | 0.5 | 5 | 0.87 | 160.4 | 0.24 |
| Hierarchical | 0.5 | 5 | 0.87 | 160.4 | 0.24 |

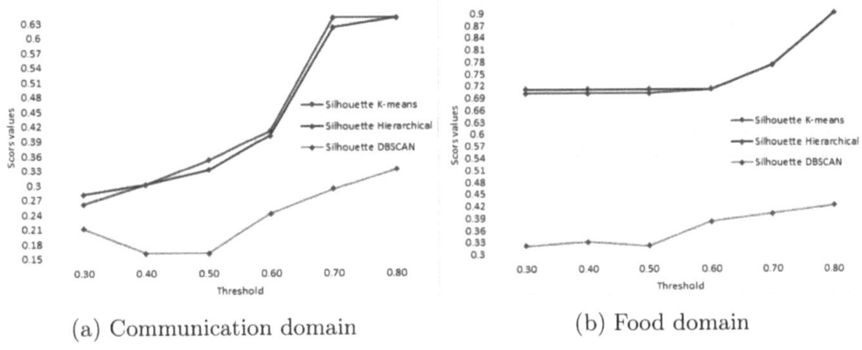


(a) Communication domain          (b) Food domain

**Fig. 2.** Impact of threshold values on Silhouette scores of communication and food domains.

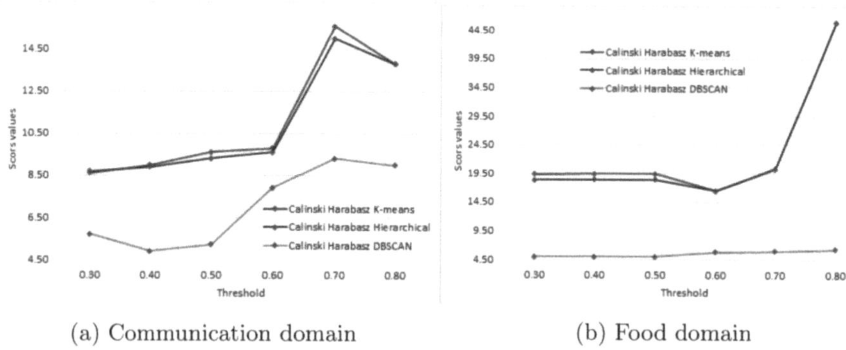

(a) Communication domain        (b) Food domain

**Fig. 3.** Impact of threshold values on Calinski scores of communication and food domains.

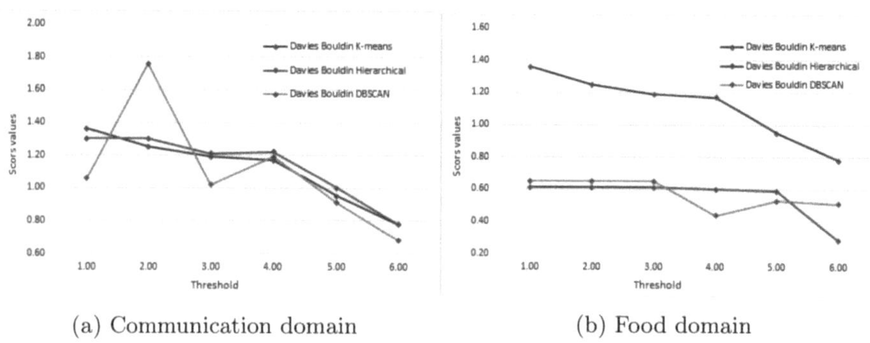

(a) Communication domain        (b) Food domain

**Fig. 4.** Impact of threshold values on Davies Bouldin scores of communication and food domains.

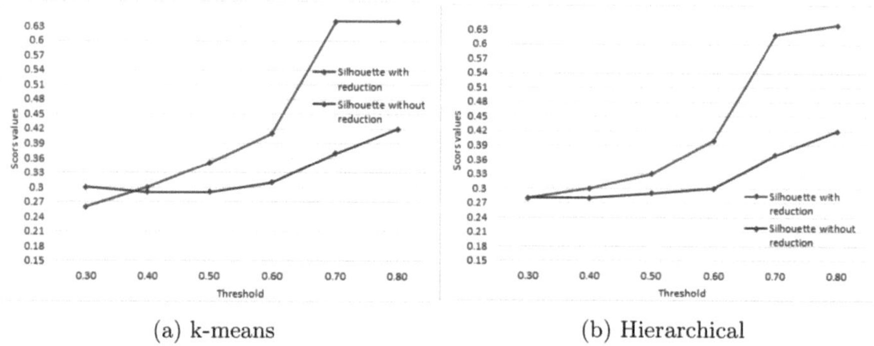

(a) k-means        (b) Hierarchical

**Fig. 5.** Impact of threshold values on Silhouette scores, k-means, and hierarchical clustering algorithm.

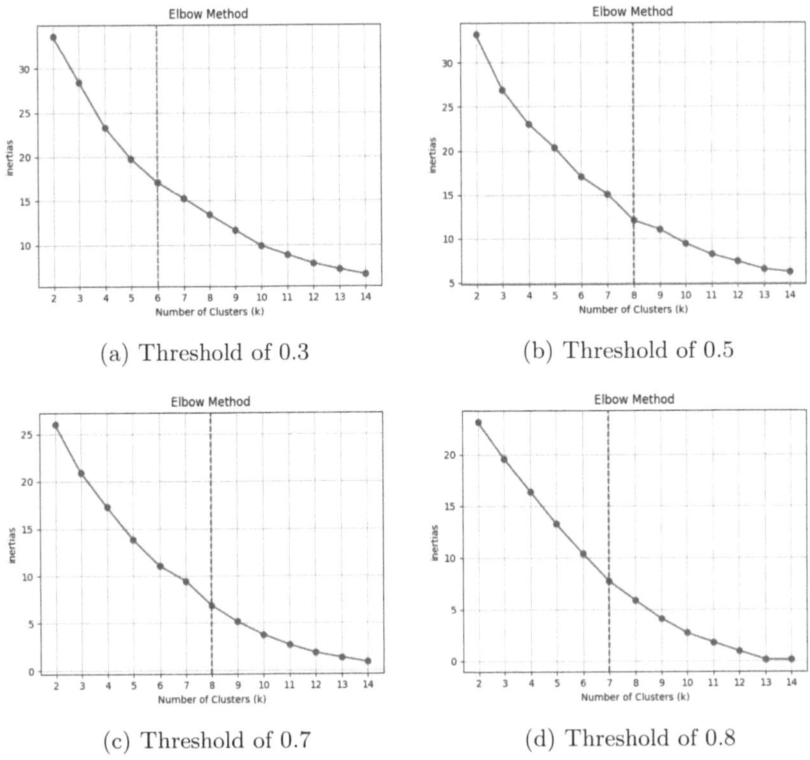

(a) Threshold of 0.3

(b) Threshold of 0.5

(c) Threshold of 0.7

(d) Threshold of 0.8

**Fig. 6.** Optimal number of clusters identified by the Elbow method for k-means.

## 8   Analysis of Results

Upon analyzing the obtained results, it is evident that K-Means and Hierarchical clustering perform similarly and outperform DBSCAN across all evaluation metrics. Both methods achieve Silhouette scores close to 1, higher Calinski-Harabasz values, and Davies-Bouldin indices near zero, indicating superior clustering quality. In contrast, DBSCAN yields lower scores. Furthermore, the Elbow method is particularly effective for defining the ideal number of classes in K-Means. The evaluation of clustering algorithms reveals insightful comparisons when benchmarked against similar works in the literature. Our best Silhouette score of 0.7, achieved by K-Means and Hierarchical clustering, is higher than the 0.350.42 range reported in [18]. In terms of the Calinski-Harabasz (CH) index, our best value of 160 depends on the datasets used. In [19], CH index values for K-Means ranged from 800 to over 1500, depending on dataset dimensionality and inter-cluster variance. Regarding the Davies-Bouldin index, our best result around 1 (by K-Means and Hierarchical clustering) is consistent with findings in [20], where values typically ranged from 0.7 to 1.3, confirming the moderate separation and compactness of the generated clusters.

## 9  Conclusion

This study presents a comparative evaluation of clustering algorithms for web services. Overall, the results of our study are comparable to existing research, particularly in terms of Silhouette and Davies-Bouldin scores. The relative values of all metrics depending on the structures of the dataset. However, reducing the dimensionality of the feature space using WordNet yields better clustering results compared to using all features. This approach is particularly beneficial for large datasets, as it helps reduce computational complexity and processing time. A threshold value of 0.7 provided the best performance based on the Silhouette Score, Davies-Bouldin Index, and Calinski-Harabasz Index. In addition, among the clustering techniques, K-Means and Hierarchical clustering outperformed DBSCAN. However, K-Means requires an effective method to determine the optimal number of initial clusters, while Hierarchical clustering depends heavily on the choice of similarity metric and linkage criteria to generate an accurate dendrogram. For future work, we propose using optimization algorithms to improve the initialization of K-Means and to select appropriate similarity metrics for constructing the dendrogram in Hierarchical clustering. Additionally, other dimensionality reduction techniques could be explored to enhance clustering quality.

## References


1. Han, J., Kamber, M., Pei, J.: Data Mining: Concepts and Techniques, Third Edition, Morgan Kaufmann Publishers (2012)
2. Ester, M., Kriegel, H-P., Sander, J., Xu, X.: A density-based algorithm for discovering clusters in large spatial databases with noise. In: Proceedings of the Second International Conference on Knowledge Discovery and Data Mining, AAAI Press, vol. KDD'96, pp. 226–231, Portland (1996). https://doi.org/10.5555/3001460.3001507
3. Alhadid, I., Khwaldeh, S., AlRawajbeh, M., Abu-Taieh, E., Masa'deh, R., Aljarah, I.: An intelligent web service composition and resource-optimization method using k-means clustering and knapsack algorithms. Mathematics **9**(17), 2023 (2021). https://doi.org/10.3390/math9172023
4. Huynh, K.T., Quan, T.T., Bui, T.H.: A quality-controlled logic-based clustering approach for web service composition and verification. Int. J. Web Inf. Syst. **13**(2), 173–198 (2017). https://doi.org/10.1108/IJWIS-12-2016-0068
5. Platzer, C., Rosenberg, F., Dustdar, S.: Web service clustering using multidimensional angles as proximity measures. ACM Trans. Internet Technol. **9**(3), 1–26 (2009). 26 pages. https://doi.org/10.1145/1552291.1552294
6. Soumi, C., Ansuman, B.: QoS-aware automatic web service composition with multiple objectives. ACM Trans. Web (TWEB) **14**(3), 1–38 (2020). https://doi.org/10.1145/3389147
7. Fariss, M., Allali, N.E., Asaidi, H., Bellouki, M.: An improved approach for QoS based web services selection using clustering. Adv. Sci. Technol. Eng. Syst. J. **6**(2), 616–621 (2021). https://doi.org/10.25046/aj060270

8. Purohit, L., Rathore, S.S., Kumar, S.: A QoS-aware clustering based multi-layer model for web service selection. IEEE Trans. Serv. Comput. **16**(5), 3141–3154 (2023). https://doi.org/10.1109/TSC.2023.3264627

9. Agarwal, N., Sikka, G., Awasthi, L.K.: Web service clustering approaches to enhance service discovery: a review. In: Singh, P.K., Singh, Y., Kolekar, M.H., Kar, A.K., Chhabra, J.K., Sen, A. (eds.) Recent Innovations in Computing. ICRIC 2020. Lecture Notes in Electrical Engineering, vol. 701, pp. 23–35. Springer, Singapore (2021). https://doi.org/10.1007/978-981-15-8297-4_3

10. Cong, Z., Fernández Gil, A.: Efficient web service discovery using hierarchical clustering. In: Chesñevar, C.I., Onaindia, E., Ossowski, S., Vouros, G. (eds.) Agreement Technologies. Lecture Notes in Computer Science, vol. 8068, pp. 63–74. Springer, Berlin, Heidelberg (2013). https://doi.org/10.1007/978-3-642-39860-5_6

11. Zhang, M., Liu, X., Zhang, R., Sun, H.: A web service recommendation approach based on QoS prediction using fuzzy clustering. In: IEEE Ninth International Conference on Services Computing, pp. 138–145, Honolulu, USA (2012). https://doi.org/10.1109/SCC.2012.24

12. Bravo, M., Mora-Gutiérrez, R., Luis, H.: Bio-Inspired Hybrid Algorithm for Web Services Clustering. Ali Soofastaei (2019). https://doi.org/10.5772/intechopen.85200

13. Kumara, B.T., Paik, I., Koswatte, K.R.: Multi-level web service clustering to bootstrap the web service discovery and selection. In: Zhang, L., Ning, Y. (eds.), Innovative Solutions and Applications of Web Services Technology, IGI Global Scientific Publishing, pp. 44–68 (2019). https://doi.org/10.4018/978-1-5225-7268-8.ch003

14. Yi, Z., Chong, W., Jian, W., Keqing, H.: Incorporating LDA with word embedding for web service clustering. Int. J. Web Serv. Res. (IJWSR). IGI Global **15**(4), 29–44 (2018)

15. Elbitar, I., Belouadha, F., Roudies, O.: Semantic web service discovery approaches: overview and limitations. Int. J. Comput. Sci. Eng. Surv. **5**(4), 21–36 (2014). https://doi.org/10.5121/ijcses.2014.5402

16. Rayasam, A., Thota, S., Bukkittu, A., Kamath, S.: A Framework for Web Services Retrieval Using Bio Inspired Clustering (2022). https://doi.org/10.48550/arXiv.2210.01761

17. Choi, J., Ryu, D.: QoS-aware graph contrastive learning for web service recommendation. In: 30th Asia-Pacific Software Engineering Conference (APSEC), pp. 171-180, IEEE, Seoul, Korea (2023). https://doi.org/10.1109/APSEC60848.2023.00027

18. Gupta, S. B., et al.: A systematic comparative analysis of clustering techniques. In: Applied Computer Systems, vol. 25, no. 2, pp. 87–104. Riga Technical University (2020). https://doi.org/10.2478/acss-2020-0011

19. Azzalini, A., Menardi, G.: Clustering via nonparametric density estimation: the R package pdfCluster. J. Stat. Softw. **57**(11), 1–26 (2014). https://doi.org/10.18637/jss.v057.i11

20. Saxena, A., et al.: A review of clustering techniques and developments. Expert Syst. Appl. **267**, 664–681. ScienceDirect (2017). https://doi.org/10.1016/j.neucom.2017.06.053

21. Kaouan, M., Bouchiha, D., Benslimane, S.M., Boukli-Hacene, S.: Towards service ontology for web services storage and discovery. In: 4th International Symposium on Informatics and its Applications (ISIA), pp. 1–6, M'sila, Algeria (2020). https://doi.org/10.1109/ISIA51297.2020.9416537

# Rule Based Transliteration System: An Extensive Study

Nitisha Pradhan[(✉)] [iD], Udit Kumar Chakraborty [iD], Eros Shrestha [iD],
Parash Tamang [iD], Rishab Rathi [iD], and Prasanta Sharma [iD]

Department of Computer Science and Engineering, Sikkim Manipal Institute of Technology,
Sikkim Manipal University (SMU), Majtar, Sikkim, India
pradhannitisha0204@gmail.com, parash_202200507@smit.smu.edu.in

**Abstract.** Machine Transliteration is the process of automated conversions of words from source language to target language while preserving pronunciation. It plays a crucial role in bridging language barriers by enabling seamless script conversions and enhancing cross-linguistic communication. Over time, various transliteration approaches have been developed like Ruled Based, Hidden Markov Model, and statistical approach. Rule based is one of the earliest approaches, which relies on predefined linguistic rules and structured mappings to achieve accurate script conversion. This study explores the variations of rule-based transliteration systems, analyzing their challenges, effectiveness and working. Understanding these systems is vital for improving language accessibility and enhancing global digital communication.

**Keywords:** Transliteration · Rule-based · Hidden Markov Model · Statistical Approach Cross-Linguistic

## 1 Introduction

Transliteration is a technique of converting text in one script to another while preserving its pronunciation from the original language, or simply writing one script text using other language's characters while retaining the original language's pronunciation. While transliteration may be achieved through various approaches, Rule based approach plays a crucial role in its implementation and is considered the early basic building block for the transliteration system of languages. Various algorithms for Machine Transliteration were introduced almost a decade ago based on phonetics of source and target language..

Rule Based approach is a simple approach which uses a set of handwritten rules and makes prediction without requiring a large dataset, it uses the concept of lookup from dictionary for references. The rule based approach is considered as basic due to its unique characteristics such as working with low resources languages or languages that are under development phases of various Natural Language Resources. For various languages across the globe it has resulted with a high accuracy, stable output and has given results almost similar to humans due to its feature of generating output according to pre-defined rules. Rule Based approach has various objects integrated for a successful


K. K. Patel et al. (Eds.): icSoftComp 2025, CCIS 2874, pp. 364–377, 2026.
https://doi.org/10.1007/978-3-032-22062-2_28

implementation, dictionary is one of the main as it's handcrafted and is the backbone for better output like the use of stemming tools for reducing words to its root form by removing Suffixes and Prefixes.

## 1.1  Underlying Key Concepts

*Phonetics* is the scientific study of the physical aspects of human speech sounds. It examines how these sounds are produced by the vocal organs, how they travel through the air, and how they are perceived by the listeners. Phonetics treats speech sounds independently of the languages in which they are used, analyzing them based on their acoustic and articulatory properties.

*Phonology*, on the other hand, deals with how sounds function and interact within a particular language or across languages. It studies the abstract sound units known as phonemes, as well as features like phono-tactics (rules governing sound combinations) and phonological rules (how sounds **change** in different contexts). Unlike phonetics, phonology is language-specific, as it focuses on the patterns and systems of sounds within a given language.

While a *phoneme* is the smallest sound unit in a language that can distinguish one word from another. Phonemes are crucial components of words, and changing one phoneme can alter the entire meaning of a word. For instance, replacing the sound '**b**' with '**p**' in the word "big" results in the word "pig", demonstrating /*b*/ as a distinct phoneme. The smallest physical segment of sound itself is referred to as a phone, representing the actual sound produced. In contrast, allophones are variations of a single phoneme that do not change the meaning of a word. Some transliteration methods employ phonemes to decompose words into smaller segments before the actual transliteration process.

A *grapheme* is the smallest functional unit in a written language. It encompasses letters of the alphabet, numerals, punctuation marks, and any other distinct symbols within a writing system. In phonemic orthography, each grapheme directly corresponds to a single phoneme. However, in languages with non-phonemic spelling systems like English multiple graphemes can represent a single phoneme. These combinations are termed digraphs (two graphemes representing one phoneme) or trigraphs (three graphemes representing one phoneme). For example, the word "ship" contains four graphemes (s, h, i, p) but only three phonemes, since "sh" functions as a single phoneme through digraph representation.

A *syllable* is a basic unit of pronunciation that is larger than a single sound but smaller than a complete word. It typically consists of a central peak, usually a vowel sound, surrounded by optional consonant sounds at the beginning and end. The vowel serves as the core of the syllable, while the consonants act as its boundaries.

## 2  Writing Systems

Writing Systems or styles are aids to represent the language for communication and contribute to knowledge transfer. A language script may cater to a certain writing system or hybrid of multiple writing systems. Some writing styles may be noted as:

i. *Logographic Writing Systems*: A logographic writing system follows one character defining a whole word policy. Written Chinese is a typical example of a Logographic Writing System.
ii. *Syllable Writing Systems*: In this writing system, a character defines a particular syllable in the language. Cherokee syllabary falls into this category of script.
iii. *Abugida Scripts*: Abugida scripts are largely like syllable systems, unlike syllable systems where each syllable has a unique character. In abugida scripts, similar characters are present for similar syllables. The syllables are more based on orthographic syllables rather than purely phonetic syllables.
iv. *Alphabetic Writing System*: In alphabetic systems, unlike in abugida scripts where consonants are modified by vowels, the alphabetic writing system has separate vowels and consonants.
v. *Featural Writing Systems*: In Featural Writing Systems, the shapes of characters represent the phonetic features of the character. Popularly, Hangul (Korean Script) uses this system, where the consonants and vowels are written based on the position and harmony of mouth and tongue while reading the characters.

Some graphical characteristics of popular writing scripts from around the world are:

i. *Axis:* It represents if the lines are laid out horizontally or vertically in columns or rows. Traditional Japanese and Chinese follow vertical lining whereas the Devanagari and Latin Script follow horizontal lining approach.
ii. *Lining:* It describes how characters align to an imaginary line. For example, Devanagari script has a headline, Latin and Greek Scripts have a baseline whereas scripts like Arabic and Urdu are hanging.
iii. *Directionality:* It physically describes how character writing flows. It may be L-T-R, R-T-L, T-T-B, Boustrophedon.

## 3 General Method of Creating a Bilingual Transliteration Dictionary

Creating a Bilingual Transliteration [25] is essential and an important resource for Natural Language Processing (NLP) applications like machine transliteration. Various methods may be used for the creation of a dictionary but a general method is language independence method of extracting transliteration pairs from sources which consist of large resources of language and documents. Requirement of a single simple resources, a consonant correspond table can be easily constructed which is also found used in Hebrew-English transliteration dictionary [25], other approach include gathering a substantial corpus of parallel texts or aligned data between the two target languages using interlanguage links that can generate a language corpus for transliteration. The mapping is done one to one with common knowledge patterns that can relate sound to the spelling in both languages.

# 4  Challenges

## 4.1  Multiple Mappings Having Similar Sounds

In many languages, few character(s) may have multiple mappings for a single character while being represented in another language. For example, a Hindi character can represent several Urdu characters that produce similar sounds. This results in ambiguity at character level. For instance, Lehal et al., 2010 [11] highlights when transliterating the Hindi words सफ़ा" and "ग़लती"using default mappings, the output becomes "تلغى",and "تلغى",, respectively, which are incorrect. The accurate transliterations should be "افـصى" and "طلغى"instead, where the Hindi characters 'स' [s] and 'त' [t]are mapped to less commonly used Urdu equivalents. A statistical analysis of the corpus shows that these less frequent but correct Urdu characters appear with a frequency of about 3.48%. This implies that, on average, around 3.48% of characters will be incorrectly mapped when relying solely on rule-based transliteration systems.

Also, like Yadi et al., 2024 [4] discusses the differences in number of characters: Roman English comprises 5 vowels and 21 consonants whereas Gurmukhi contains 19 vowels, 39 consonants along with special characters which leads to multiple permutations of characters resulting in the same transliterated results. Eg - ' ਟ', '੩' can both be transliterated as 't'.

## 4.2  Out of Dictionary Mappings

As discussed yet again by Yadi et al., 2024[4] in the transliteration process of Ulu Kaganga Script faces extensive errors due to incomplete syllable dictionaries taking a toll on the overall accuracy of the system. It presents a need for high scrutiny and monitoring for extensive error detection and constant extension of the syllable library to maximize the system performance.

For example [4]:

$$\text{Dictionary} = \{\text{"Com"} \rightarrow \text{コ ン (kon)}$$

$$\text{"pu"} \rightarrow \text{ピ (pi)}$$
$$\text{"ter"} \rightarrow \text{タ — (taa)}$$
$$\}$$

The transliteration will fail to transliterate for example: 'Machine' due to sheer lack of syllable mapping data in the procured dictionary.

## 4.3  Dual Nature of a Character

In the paper by Ahmed et al., 2009)[8] the Roman letter 'y' can function as both a consonant and a vowel when transliterating Urdu. Typically, 'y' represents the Urdu consonant "ى"(choti ye). For example, in the Urdu word "یقین"(yaqeen, meaning "belief"), 'y' acts as a consonant. However, 'y' can also be part of vowel sequences. For instance, in the word "ہے"(hay, meaning "is"), the Roman letter sequence 'ay' corresponds to the Urdu

"ے"(bari ye). This creates ambiguity during transliteration because it is not always clear whether 'y' should be treated as a consonant or as part of a vowel combination.

The key rule is that 'y' functions as a vowel only when it follows 'a' or 'e' (forming 'ay' or 'ey'). Otherwise, it behaves as a consonant.

The consonant 'y' does not always map directly to "ی"(ye). In some cases, it maps to "ء"(hamza), especially.

when followed by 'i', 'e', or 'o'.

For example:

- "نَ گیی" (gayi, meaning "she went")
- " ("tnew yeht" gninaem ,eyag) "گ نَے
- "جاؤ" (jayo, meaning "you go")

In these instances, 'y' can correspond to either "ی"(ye) or "ء"(hamza), depending on the context. (Ahmed et al., 2009) [8].

## 4.4  Change of Pronunciation

Ahmed et al. (2009) [8] also highlights when converting words from one script to another, the spoken sound often differs from the written letters. This happens because certain letters tend to modify the pronunciation of surrounding vowels, requiring transliteration systems to adapt accordingly (Table 1).

**Table 1.** Example for modification over pronunciation (Ahmed et al., 2009)[8]

| Written Vowel | Actual Pronunciation | Example (Urdu) | Roman Transliteration |
|---|---|---|---|
| Short "a" ( َ) | "e" sound | رَ بَش →"sheher" (city) | sheher (not"shahar") |
| Short "u" (ُ) | "o" sound | تَرَبُش →"shohrat" (fame) | shohrat(not"shuhrat") |

# 5  Different Approaches to Rule Based Transliteration System

## 5.1  Phoneme Based Approach

Phoneme based approaches to rule-based transliteration typically involves phoneme level rules or either rules to convert segmented source script to phonemes.

Iliger and Usgaonkar [3] have used a phoneme-based mapping approach for transliteration of Konkani to Roman English. The source uses abugida script which has a signature 'schwa' sound after each consonant unless followed by vowel or at the end. This leads to complications during back transliteration. The phoneme based approach works by mapping phonemes in respective source and target languages. For the input, phonemes are discovered and transliterated as per the mapping.

While Jong-Hoon Oh, and Key-Sun Choi [26] proposed a phoneme-based approach and demonstrated steps to convert English to Korean language using pronunciation dictionary (P-DIC) where pronunciation is assigned to given English words. To handle complex word form, first the words are detected and segmented into two units then checked if the segmented words exist in a dictionary. Existing words are mapped to the pronunciation. They used a penalty system to find the best alignment where lower alignment means the best algorithm. They introduced a new English pronunciation unit (EPU-P) penalty system where EPU-P data is manually mapped they also demonstrate no penalty while mapping all vowels with a phoneme vowel. The performance was marked as 99% for randomly selected 100 results using EPU-P alignment system.

## 5.2  Grapheme Based Approach

Grapheme based approach focuses on character-to-character transformation of scripts. Each character in the source script is uniquely mapped to the target script.

Singh and Sachan [1] have used a hybrid Character Mapping and Rule Based Approach to transliterate Gurmukhi(a Punjabi script) to Roman English Script. It included handcrafted rules based on the characteristics of the language script. It segmented the source script and transformed into the respective target script with the rules applied based on the nature of the grapheme. It had garnered an accuracy of 99.27% which is superior to other state of art systems.

Nair and Sadasivan [2], in their system, goes with the composition of both direct mapping based on grapheme and rule based approach. The Devanagari counterpart is mapped as accurately as possible to the Roman English counterpart. It adds rules based on the sound (vowel or consonant) of the character. These rules are specifically designed based on the rules and structure of the languages to best preserve their phonetic properties.

Hailu and Josan [6] used a grapheme, rule based approach to transliterate English to Tigrigna. They first mapped the consonants and vowels of English characters to the target script. After segmentation, various rules based on the starting character of the word and ending character were applied to transliterate the word. It reports to achieve an accuracy of 90.9%.

Nabankur Pathak, Prof. P.H. Talukdar [20] have used a phonological rule-based system to convert graphemes (written characters) into phonemes (spoken sounds) for the Bodo language. They first convert written Bodo text into its corresponding phonetic representation and transliteration using rule-based phonological transformations and statistical modelling. Context-based handcrafted rules were made for deciding when to delete or retain schwa and improve the overall accuracy. The system achieved a 90% accurate pronunciation rate when tested against the annotated corpus.

Stephen Wan and Cornelia Maria Verspoor [21] have used leveraging phonetic based models initially for mapping English phonemes to corresponding Chinese characters. It uses pronunciation rules to ensure accurate phonetic representation and mapping of English phonemes to Chinese characters units. It also uses rule-based approaches and statistical models for transliteration. Handcrafted Rules were used in the system to increase accuracy.

Sina Ahmadi [22] uses a rule -based approach for the Kurdish text transliteration system. Initially, the input text, regardless of the original orthography, is converted to

Unicode UTF-8. The system also performs text normalization by unifying different forms of characters. Handcrafted rules are made and used for correct transliteration of text and for solving the problem of multiple mappings of the same character for a single word based on its sound. The system attempts to detect the presence and correct placement of Bizroke ("i" in LbO), which is a character that has no direct equivalent in the AbO. This is done by analyzing syllable structures and applying rules based on Kurdish phonology.

Made Sudarma, Nyoman Sayta Kumara, Putu Agus Eka Darma Udayana [23] proposed a Rule Based and Levenshtein Distance based machine transliteration of Balinese Latin to Aksara Bali. Tokenization is performed on the input text and spell checker, using the Levenshtein Distance algorithm employed to handle multiple meanings and homonyms in the Balinese language. For transliteration of Latin text to Aksara Bali rule based approach is used where each Latin character is checked by a set of rules to determine its corresponding Aksara Bali character. The average translation yield 99.09% result of the system. To calculate the accuracy of system's transliteration outputs were compared with manual transliterations of lontar documents and further it was calculated based on the number of correctly transliterated characters.

Debashis Sen and Kamal Deep Garg [27] proposed a review on a grapheme-based machine transliteration for Bengali to English using direct mapping of characters from source language to the corresponding target language. Though the direct mapping is not enough for transliteration of proper characters, for this some rules were introduced. Rules involve vowels, consonants, and other orthographical elements (matra, anusvara, chandra-bindu and hosonto). Ten rules were captured in total.

*For example*:

*Rule 1-* If any consonant is followed by another consonant and the latter consonant is combined with a matra corresponding to 'ৰী'(Consonant + consonant + independent vowel) হরর = হ+র+রী = Ha+Ra+i = Hari সরর = স+র+রী = Sari.

*Rule 2-* If any consonant is followed by two other consonants. Consonant + Consonant + Consonant বমল = ক+ম+ল= Va + ma + la = Vamal, etc. The rules effectively work for dependent and independent vowels, consonants and special characters but faces a major limitation handling phonemic ambiguity.

H. Sajjad, N. Durrani, H. Schmid, and A. Fraser [28] demonstrates handicraft rules for the Hindi-Urdu transliteration system. The cost is assigned for each character mapping to the corresponding target character. An exactly mapped hindi-urdu character is assigned with zero cost. Cases where multiple mapping occurs are assigned with equal cost. Example, a Hindi character ش ,س, ص is mapped to three Urdu characters "अ"and each mapping costs 0.3. Operations like insertion and deletion to find a correct transliteration cost 0.6 (except a Hindi diacritic deletion where cost is 0). The lower the cost the better the transliteration. In some cases, identical Urdu characters occur next to each other but only one character is joined with a sign (shadda) and shadda character is considered as diacritic so all shadda from a Urdu word is deleted. In case of Hindi, the special character (assume 'z') is joined between two identical characters and this 'z' is used as a marker to show a double character. The threshold is set to 0.6 which filters out word pairs and only lets one deletion or insertion or at most three ambiguous replacements. The paper demonstrates three types of alignment such as $\emptyset \to 1$, $1 \to \emptyset$ and $1 \to N$.

No hindi character maps to an Urdu character are post processed, and the edit distance metric allows one Hindi character maps to multiple Urdu characters. This system was based on cost assignment.

Ahmad Hweishel AL-Farjat [29] developed an Automatic Transliterator which converts one Bramhi origin Indic script to another. The proposed system uses a grapheme based approach for mapping one indic script to another indic script. The methodology describes that an automatic transliterator works on patterns in the Unicode chart representing the character sets. Each language script group is assigned with 128 slots of characters.The paper describes with a examples as a character that represents "অ"('a') in Devanagari Script with 2309 (U + 0905) is corresponds to the Bengali অ('a'), say 2437. For transliteration a uniform method is created where a distance between the source character and the target language character corresponding to each other is calculated. This method can be automated for transliteration between various Indic scripts using a unicode chart which is 128 slots of characters assigned to the scripts. This method is only applicable for Unicode Indic Script block range (2304 to 3455) i.e. Arabic (used for Urdu and Kashmiri), Ol Chiki (used for Santali), Meetei Mayek (used for Manipuri). There are limitations such as missing characters in a script block, Multiple mapping, special/cultural characters, etc. Additionally, the transliterator can be implemented for further mapping of indic script to the non - indic script. This could further help in transliteration of Indic Script to Roman Scripts.

Tafseer Ahmed [8] has described the problem of two languages where Urdu letters are not possible to be mapped one to one with roman letters and several other issues were also highlighted such as multiple urdu letters for a single roman consonants, both long and short vowels using same character,'y' behaves consonant as well as a part of vowels and roman vowels is at the start of syllable whereas not in urdu. To address this issue Tafseer introduced Wordlist [8] approach to the system where wordlist and mapping together gives better results and implemented transliteration that listed the frequent words and uses encoding schemes where 5000 frequently used Urdu words were stored.

## 5.3  Syllable Based Approach

Syllabic or Syllable Based Approach are transliteration approaches which focus on syllables as a linguistic feature to map source script to target script.

Yadi et al. [4] have used syllable segmentation and character mapping approach to transcribe the rare ulu kaganga script to its Roman English counterpart using rule based approach. Rule based approach is also used for syllabification which reduces the complexity of using finite state machines. The model has 3 major steps of syllabification, character mapping and sequential search.

Sina Ahmadi [22] proposed a rule-based Wergor system architecture for transliteration of Arabic-based orthography (AbO) to the Latin-based orthography (LbO) and the transliteration system is evaluated on how well it detects the position of Bizroke (i.e. 'i') which is in the first syllables. The system is measured using precision and recall. Precision is the ratio of positive predicted cases (Bizroke predicted to be in the correct position) to the total number of positive cases present (the cases where system predicts the Bizroke to be in a correct position whether the prediction is correct or not) in a system and recall is the ratio of positive predicted cases to the total number of actual positive cases (the Bizroke is actually in a correct position) presented in a system. On the other hand, f1 score is a metric that combines precision and recall into a single value to give a balanced measure of a system's accuracy.

Yomal De Mel, Kasun Wickramasinghe, Nisansa de Silva, and Surangika Ranathunga [30] proposed transliteration for Latin script (Singlish) to Sinhala script. The system accuracy is measured using three metrics: Word Error Rate (WER), Character Error Rate (CER), and the BLEU score (Bilingual Evaluation Understudy). Word Error Rate (WER) measures the difference between the predicted and reference sentences at the word level by calculating the number of word-edits (insertions, deletions, and substitutions).The lower WER results in better system accuracy. Character Error Rate (CER) calculates the number of character-level edits which is needed to match the reference. Similar to WER, a lower CER means higher precision. The BLUE score is a metric used to evaluate the quality of machine-transliterated text which is measured by comparing predicted results to reference output. Also lower the score indicates higher the accuracy.

Made Sudarma, Nyoman Sayta Kumara, Putu Agus Eka Darma Udayana [23] proposed machine transliteration of Balinese Latin to Aksara Bali. For calculating accuracy of the above system 20 sheets of manually translated lontar in Balinese Latin text were used for input of the application. These manual transliterations were obtained from Pusat Dokumentasi Dinas Kebudayaan Provinsi Bali. The transliteration of each sheet of the manual transliteration documents from Balinese Latin text to Aksara Bali was performed by the developed machine transliteration system. The accuracy was calculated by comparing the system's output with the expert's evaluation and by counting the number of correctly transliterated characters and incorrectly transliterated characters.

## 6  Comparative Analysis

Rule-based transliteration is broadly realized through phoneme-, grapheme-, and syllable-based approaches, each differing in their linguistic unit of focus and the rules applied for mapping. The phoneme-based approach relies on mapping source phonemes to their target equivalents, often supported by pronunciation dictionaries and alignment mechanisms, thereby emphasizing pronunciation fidelity but requiring extensive linguistic resources. Grapheme-based methods instead operate at the character level, applying handcrafted or automated rules to achieve direct script-to-script conversion, which enhances scalability but may suffer from phonemic ambiguity. Syllable-based approaches occupy a middle ground, where input text is segmented into syllabic units and mapped using rule-driven syllabification, allowing better handling of morphophonemic structures at the cost of added rule complexity.

Together, these three perspectives illustrate complementary strengths and weaknesses, with phoneme-based systems excelling in accuracy, grapheme-based systems offering simplicity and scalability, and syllable-based systems balancing both dimensions. Table 2 presents a comparative evaluation of these approaches, summarizing their methodologies, representative studies, challenges, advantages, and reported performance.

**Table 2.** Comparative analysis of rule-based transliteration approaches. The table presents a side-by-side comparison of phoneme-based, grapheme-based, and syllable-based approaches in terms of core methodology, representative studies, challenges, advantages, and reported performance.

| Approach | Core Idea | Example | Advantage | Challenges | Performance |
|---|---|---|---|---|---|
| Phoneme-Based | Script-phonemes-target phonemes (pronunciation mapping | Iiiger&Usgaonkar (Konkani-Roman), Oh&Choi (English-Korean 99%) | Captures true pronunciation, high reported accuracy(~99%) | Needs Pronunciation lexicons, hard for unseen phonemes | 99 |
| Grapheme-Based | Character-to-character mapping rules for exceptions | Singh&Sachan(Gurmukhi-Roman,99.27%), Hailu & Josan(Eng-Tigrigna, 90.9%) | Simple, can leverage Unicode mapping, good accuracy(90–99%) with rules | One-to-one mapping insufficient, multiple mappings, phonemic ambiguity | 90.9 |
| Syllable-Based | Syllable segmentation + mapping rules (syllabification driven) | Yadi et al.(Ulu Kaganga-Roman), Sudarma et al.(BalineseLatin-Aksara Bali) | Captures natural syllabic structure, useful for morphophonemic languages, eva | Complex syllabification rules, evaluation depends on multiple metrics, rulesdesign effort | 92 |

The comparison reveals that while phoneme-based systems achieve high accuracy by preserving pronunciation, they are heavily dependent on pronunciation lexicons. Grapheme-based systems offer simplicity and scalability but face challenges with phonemic ambiguity, whereas syllable-based systems strike a balance by leveraging syllabic structure to handle morphophonemic features more effectively.

While Table 2 outlines the methodological distinctions, strengths, and limitations of the three approaches, it provides only a textual comparison. To complement this, radar charts visually depict their trade-offs across accuracy, rule complexity, scalability, and dictionary dependence (Fig. 1).

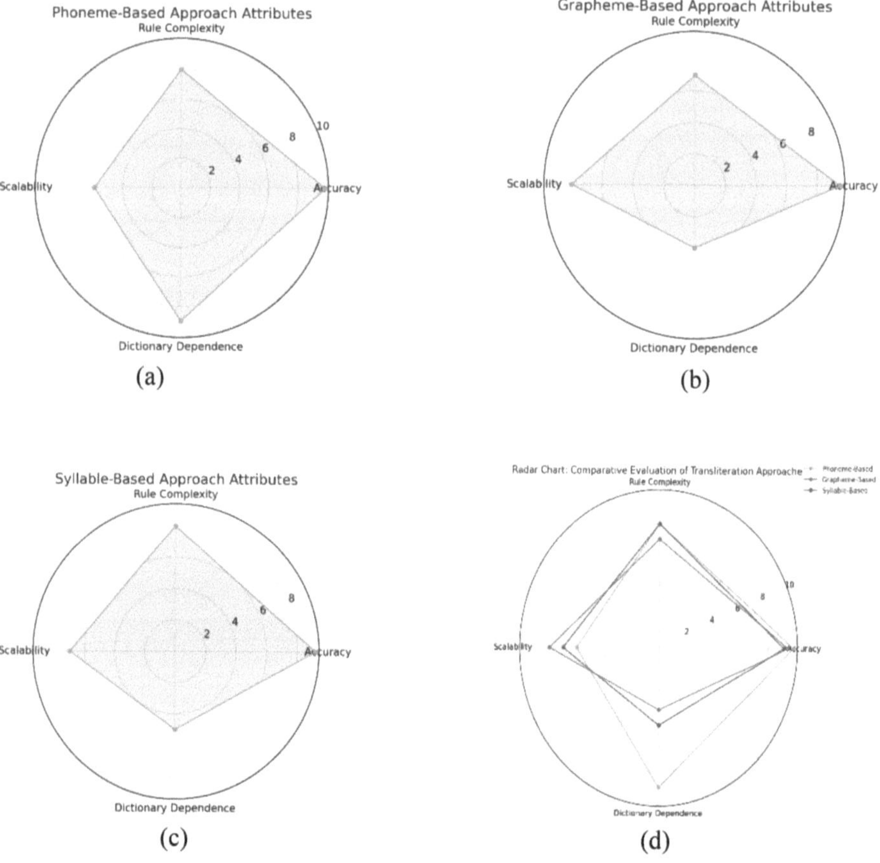


**Fig. 1.** (a) Radar chart representation of phoneme-based approach attributes, highlighting its high accuracy and dictionary dependence but moderate scalability. (b) Radar chart representation of grapheme-based approach attributes, indicating strong scalability and lower dictionary dependence compared to phoneme-based systems. (c) Radar chart representation of syllable-based approach attributes, reflecting balanced performance across metrics with particular strength in handling morphophonemic structures. (d) Radar chart illustrating the comparative trade-offs among the three rule-based transliteration approaches with respect to accuracy, rule complexity, scalability, and dictionary dependence.

The radar charts indicate that phoneme-based approaches achieve the highest accuracy, but their heavy reliance on pronunciation dictionaries reduces scalability. Grapheme-based methods show greater scalability and lower dictionary dependence, though they are more vulnerable to phonemic ambiguity. Syllable-based approaches demonstrate a balanced profile, effectively capturing morphophonemic features while maintaining competitive accuracy, although with higher rule complexity.

Phoneme-based methods are most effective when pronunciation fidelity is critical, grapheme-based systems provide efficiency and scalability for large-scale applications, and syllable-based approaches offer a balanced alternative by accounting for morphophonemic structure. The choice of approach should therefore be guided by language-specific features and the transliteration objectives of the target application.

## 7  Conclusion

Different rule-based transliteration systems proposed and developed were surveyed in this study. The findings of this survey highlight the capabilities and limitations of handling transliteration of diverse languages from around the globe. The paper provides valuable insights and understanding of key concepts of direct mapping, character sequence mapping, grapheme-based approach, phoneme-based approach, and syllable-based approach. The paper discussed about the predefined linguistic rules and specific productions of rules developed based on the context-sensitive nature of the language. Direct mapping is simple and involves manually mapping of source to target characters which in some cases result in poor transliteration due to its inability to handle contextual variations. It was observed during the study that the grapheme-based approach offers better flexibility and can handle mapping ambiguities and special cases. The grapheme-based rules effectively work for dependent and independent vowels, consonants, and special characters but faces a major limitation handling pronunciation ambiguity i.e. phonemic ambiguity. In phoneme-based approach, the rules are specifically designed based on sound by prioritizing pronunciation and ensuring accurate transliteration across different languages challenged with complex phonetic variations. However, the syllable-based approach stands out to be more robust and accurate approach which involves in syllabification of words into pronunciation units and mapping between scripts works more effectively which ensures that each phonetic unit is correctly mapped to its corresponding target source, preserving its original pronunciation and improving transliteration accuracy. A Rule-based approach can handle contextual variations and adapt to complex scripts which makes it suitable for low resource languages. This paper focuses on providing comprehensive observations on how rule-based systems can be used effectively for transliteration of languages which are changing and losing their relevance.

## References


1. Singh, S.K., Sachan, M.K.: Grt: gurmukhi to Roman transliteration system using character mapping and handcrafted rules. Int. J. Innovat. Technol. Explor. Eng. **8**(9), 2758–2763 (2019)
2. Nair, J., Sadasivan, A.: A roman to devanagari back-transliteration algorithm based on harvard-kyoto convention. In: 2019 IEEE 5th International Conference for Convergence in Technology (I2CT), pp. 1–6. IEEE (2019)

3. Iliger, S.R., Usgaonkar, S.: Phoneme based approach for transliteration of konkani language. Int. J. Comput. Electron. Aspects Eng. **3**(2) (2022)
4. Yadi, I.Z., Kunang, Y.N., Sari, T.P., Mahmud, M., Ramadhona, N.: Rule-based transliteration of ulu kaganga script using character mapping. J. Inform. Syst. Inform. **6**(4), 3207–3225 (2024)
5. Salaev, U., Kuriyozov, E., Gómez-Rodríguez, C.: A machine transliteration tool between Uzbek alphabets. arXiv preprint arXiv:2205.09578 (2022)
6. Hailu, G., Josan, G.S.: Rule based approachfor translitration of english to tigrigna. Int. J. Multidiscipl. Educ. Res. **6**(7), 205 (2017)
7. Sudarma, M., Kumara, I.N.S., Udayana, I.P.A.E.D.: Transliteration balinese latin text becomes aksara bali using rule base and levenshtein distance approach. Indones. J. Electr. Eng. Comput. Sci **2**(3), 401–408 (2016)
8. Ahmed, T.: Roman to Urdu transliteration using wordlist. In: Proceedings of the Conference on Language and Technology, vol. 305, p. 309 (2009)
9. Ali, A.R., Ijaz, M.: English to Urdu transliteration system. In: Proceedings of Language and Technology, pp. 15–23 (2009)
10. Jawaid, B., Ahmed, T.: Hindi to Urdu conversion: beyond simple transliteration. In: Conference on Language and Technology (2009)
11. Lehal, G.S., Saini, T.S.: A Hindi to Urdu transliteration system. In: Proceedings of ICON 2010: 8th International Conference on Natural Language Processing, Kharagpur (2010)
12. Baig, B., Kumar, M., Das, S.: Rule-based Hindi to Urdu transliteration system. J. Emerg. Trends Comput. Inf. Sci. **3**, 1200–1204 (2012)
13. Ehsan, T.: Bi-directional Roman-Urdu Transliteration System
14. Maqbool, S., Ahmed, N., Saleem, G., Iqbal, M.M.: An efficient Hindi-Urdu transliteration system. SciInt (Lahore) **27**(4), 4549–4553 (2015)
15. Sunitha, C., Jaya, A.: A phoneme based model for english to malayalam transliteration. In: International Conference on Innovation Information in Computing Technologies, pp. 1–4. IEEE (2015)
16. Karimi, S., Scholer, F., Turpin, A.: Machine transliteration survey. ACM Comput. Surv. **43**(3), 1–46 (2011)
17. Antony, P.J., Soman, K.P.: Machine transliteration for indian languages: a literature survey. Int. J. Sci. Eng. Res. **2**, 1–8 (2011)
18. Kaur, K., Singh, P.: Review of machine transliteration systems. Int. J. Eng. Res. **3**(5) (2014)
19. Mammadzada, S.: The challenges of Azerbaijani transliteration on the multilingual internet. Int. J. Transl. Interpret. Appl. Linguist. **2**(1), 57–66 (2020)
20. Pathak, N., Talukdar, P.H.: The basic grapheme to phoneme (G2P) rules for bodo language. Int. J. **2**(1) (2013)
21. Wan, S., Verspoor, K.: Automatic English-Chinese name transliteration for development of multilingual resources. In: 36th Annual Meeting of the Association for Computational Linguistics and 17th International Conference on Computational Linguistics, Volume 2, pp. 1352–1356 (1998)
22. Ahmadi, S.: A rule-based Kurdish text transliteration system. ACM Trans. Asian Low-Resource Lang. Inform. Process. **18**(2), 1–8 (2019)
23. Udayana, I.P.A.E.D., Sudarma, M., Kumara, I.N.S.: Balinese latin text becomes aksara bali using rule base method. Int. J. Res. IT, Manag. Eng, **7**(05), 1–7 (2017)
24. Josan, G.S., Lehal, G.S.: A Punjabi to Hindi machine transliteration system. Int. J. Comput. Linguist. Chin. Lang. Process. **15**(2) (2010)
25. Prahallad, L., Prahallad, K., Ganapathiraju, M.P., et al.: J Zhejiang Univ SCI 2005 A simple approach for building transliteration editors for Indian languages

26. Oh, J.-H., Choi, K.-S.: An English-Korean transliteration model using pronunciation and contextual rules. In: Proceedings of the 19th International Conference on Computational Linguistics (COLING) (2002)
27. Sen, D., Garg, K.D.: A review on bengali to english machine transliteration system. Int. J. Software Web Sci. **12**(1), 60–64 (2015)
28. Sajjad, H., Durrani, N., Schmid, H., Fraser, A.: Comparing two techniques for learning transliteration models using a parallel corpus. In: Proceedings of the 5th International Joint Conference on Natural Language Processing (IJCNLP) (pp. 129–137). Asian Federation of Natural Language Processing, Chiang Mai, Thailand (2011)
29. Al-Farjat, A.H.: Automatic transliteration among Indic scripts using code mapping formula. Eur. Sci. J. **8**(11) (2012)
30. De Mel, Y., Wickramasinghe, K., de Silva, N., Ranathunga, S.: Sinhala transliteration: a comparative analysis between rule-based and seq2seq approaches. In: Proceedings of the First Workshop on Natural Language Processing for Indo-Aryan and Dravidian Languages, pp. 166–173(2025)

# Temporal-Aware Machine and Deep Learning Models for Intrusion Detection Using Engineered Features and UNSW-NB15 Dataset


Anita Kumari[✉] [iD] and Rashmi Saini [iD]

VMSBT University, Dehradun 248001, India
k.anitasays@gmail.com



**Abstract.** The escalating sophistication of cyberattacks demands intrusion detection systems (IDS) that can generalize to unseen threats while remaining operationally practical. This work introduces a temporal-aware IDS framework evaluated on the UNSW-NB15 dataset using four chronological folds (three days for training, one day for testing) under a strict 20-feature budget and three regimes: Without Eng., With Eng., and With Eng. + SMOTE. The pipeline integrates robust preprocessing, eight domain-informed engineered ratios and rates (excluding their raw bases), per-fold top-20 feature selection via ExtraTrees importance, and a sweep of eight learners—ExtraTrees, HistGBM, LightGBM, DecisionTree, RandomForest, MLP, XGBoost, and a 1D CNN baseline.

Beyond standard metrics, this study emphasizes Alert-Budget Utility (ABU)—the F1-score computed only on the top-k alerts—evaluated at budgets $\{5, 10, 20, 30\}\%$. Although ROC–AUC remains consistently high ($\approx 0.999$) yet offers limited operational interpretability, ABU reveals budget-dependent leadership: HistGBM dominates at 5–10% (F1 $\approx 0.40/0.66$ with Precision $= 1.0$), RandomForest (With Eng.) peaks at 20% (F1 $\approx 0.97$), and HistGBM regains the lead at 30% (F1 $\approx 0.81$). The CNN underperforms without engineered features (F1 $\approx$ 0.12) but improves substantially when augmented with domain-guided attributes (F1 $\approx 0.90$), highlighting the necessity of feature engineering even for deep learners. A runtime analysis shows ExtraTrees (With Eng.) processing $\approx$226k rows/s (~4.4 s per million flows), while RandomForest (With Eng.) delivers the best ABU@20%. All results, code, and artifacts are released for full reproducibility.

**Keywords:** Intrusion detection · alert budget · feature engineering · SMOTE


## 1 Introduction

Intrusion Detection Systems (IDS) often achieve high ROC–AUC scores yet still overwhelm analysts with excessive alerts. In real-world security operations centers, only a limited fraction of scored flows can actually be inspected due to analyst workload and time constraints. Consequently, the ability of a model to prioritize genuine threats within a fixed alert budget becomes more critical than its aggregate discrimination ability. To capture this operational reality, we employ a temporal-aware evaluation using



K. K. Patel et al. (Eds.): icSoftComp 2025, CCIS 2874, pp. 378–391, 2026.
https://doi.org/10.1007/978-3-032-22062-2_29

the UNSW-NB15 dataset [1], where each model is trained on three consecutive days and tested on the following day, preserving the natural event order and preventing temporal leakage. We further introduce the Alert-Budget Utility (ABU) metric—a budget-constrained performance measure that evaluates model effectiveness when only the top-k alerts are reviewed (with $k = \lfloor b \cdot n \rfloor$ for budgets $b \in \{5, 10, 20, 30\}\%$). Unlike traditional aggregate metrics such as ROC–AUC, ABU explicitly measures F1-score, precision, and recall within the top-k subset, reflecting how well each model identifies high-priority intrusions under realistic resource limits. This budget-aware perspective provides a more actionable assessment of IDS models in deployment environments. [2, 3, 9].

To fit deployment constraints, we build a compact, reproducible 20-feature pipeline. It combines robust preprocessing with eight domain-informed engineered ratios/rates (e.g., bytes and load asymmetry, packet-rate, TTL-derived terms) that are force-kept, while their raw bases are excluded to prevent redundancy. Per fold, we compute Extra-Trees importances on a stratified subset ($\leq$300k rows) to select features. We compare three regimes with consistent naming throughout: Without Eng., With Eng., and With Eng. + SMOTE (a bounded SMOTE-lite scheme that first down-samples negatives to $\leq 3\times$ positives, then synthesizes to a target minority ratio $\approx$0.30 under row caps) [4]. Learners span efficient, widely used families: ExtraTrees [5], RandomForest [6], histogram-based gradient boosting (HistGBM)/LightGBM-style trees [7, 8], 1-D CNN and MLP and XGBoost baselines [8, 10], all evaluated across four chronological folds of UNSW-NB15 [1].

Our contributions are fourfold: (i) a reproducible, time-preserving IDS pipeline with a strict 20-feature budget on UNSW-NB15; (ii) a multi-model, multi-regime comparison under ABU at fixed alert budgets (5–30%), revealing differences obscured by uniformly high ROC–AUC; (iii) fold-average ABU with error bars (mean $\pm$ SD; 95% CIs) to address stability and "lucky-fold" concerns, with small paired checks showing champions are typically close to runner-ups; and (iv) an operational runtime table reporting training time, inference throughput (rows/s; seconds per 1M flows), and model size for the top settings. All code paths persist predictions/metrics for full reproducibility.


## 2  Related Work

Early IDS research relied on legacy corpora (KDD'99/NSL-KDD), which are convenient but contain biases and duplicated flows [11]. Newer datasets—CIC-IDS2017 and BoT-IoT—were introduced to better reflect modern traffic and attack diversity and are now common benchmarks [12, 16]. On the modeling side, both classic machine-learning (SVMs, trees, forests) and deep models (autoencoders, RNN/LSTM) have been explored to capture non-linear and temporal patterns [13–15]. Surveys repeatedly note two gaps: (i) evaluations that ignore time (random splits can leak the future into the past) and (ii) over-reliance on accuracy/ROC-AUC despite the tiny alert budgets analysts can inspect [17]. Our study addresses both by preserving time order (three days train, one day test) and optimizing for top-k utility via F1@k at 5–30% budgets on UNSW-NB15. Table 1 summarizes representative IDS studies—covering legacy and modern datasets, model families, and the key lessons (bias, temporal evaluation, class imbalance) that motivate our ABU-based, time-preserving pipeline.

**Table 1.**  Representative IDS studies and their contribution.

| Ref. | Dataset | ML/DL Model | Remarks |
|---|---|---|---|
| [11] | NSL-KDD | Classical ML (SVM, trees, k-NN, NB) | Analyzes defects in KDD'99; proposes NSL-KDD to reduce redundancy/bias; stronger baselines |
| [12] | CIC- IDS2017 | RF, SVM, k-NN (benchmarks) | Modern multi-day labeled traffic with diverse attacks; widely adopted baseline for ML/DL IDS |
| [13] | Kitsune (live LAN capture) | Online ensemble of autoencoders | Streaming, feature-mapping AEs with low footprint; emphasizes on-device inference |
| [14] | NSL-KDD | LSTM / RNN | Sequence modeling improves detection over traditional ML; demonstrates temporal utility on legacy data |
| [15] | KDD'99 & NSL-KDD | Stacked autoencoders & deep belief networks | Unsupervised pretrain + supervised fine-tune; competitive vs. classical ML on legacy sets |
| [16] | BoT-IoT | RF, SVM, shallow DL (benchmarks) | IoT-focused botnet dataset; extreme class imbalance highlights need for resampling/alert budgeting |
| [17] | Survey (multiple datasets) | (systematic review) | Notes inconsistent validation (random splits/leakage) and overreliance on accuracy/ROC; urges time-aware tests |

# 3    Methodology

## 3.1    Dataset and Temporal Folds

We use the four official UNSW-NB15 CSV partitions (UNSW-NB15_1 ... UNSW-NB15_4) as Fold-1 ... Fold-4 [1]. Each fold is first sorted by Stime using a stable mergesort and then aligned to a shared column space (union of columns across folds) before modeling. We keep the binary label (0 = benign, 1 = attack) and drop identifier-style fields (srcip, dstip, sport, dsport) plus attack_cat. This time-preserved setup avoids temporal leakage highlighted in prior surveys [17]. Table 2 depicts UNSW-NB15 temporal folds and class balance. Each fold is one day of traffic (sorted by Stime); training uses the preceding three days and testing the next day. Attack prevalence varies markedly across days (3.17%–22.49%), with an overall rate of 12.65% across 2,540,047 flows.

**Table 2.** UNSW-NB15 temporal folds and class balance. Each fold corresponds to one day (sorted by Stime). Training uses the preceding three days; testing uses the next day. Totals reflect processed CSVs

| Fold | Rows | Positives | Negatives | Attack rate |
|---|---|---|---|---|
| 1 | 700,001 | 22,215 | 677,786 | 3.17% |
| 2 | 700,001 | 52,749 | 647,252 | 7.54% |
| 3 | 700,001 | 157,425 | 542,576 | 22.49% |
| 4 | 440,044 | 88,894 | 351,150 | 20.20% |
| Total | 2,540,047 | 321,283 | 2,218,764 | 12.65% |

## 3.2    Preprocessing

We remove identifier-style fields that do not generalize across deployments—srcip, dstip, sport, dsport, and the categorical target attack_cat. For the three categorical attributes (proto, state, service), we retain the top-30 tokens per fold, map all remaining categories to a __rare__ bucket to stabilize sparse counts, and then apply one-hot encoding with drop-first to avoid collinearity. Heavy-tailed numeric variables (sbytes, dbytes, Sload, Dload) receive a log1p transform to compress dynamic range. All non-label columns are coerced to numeric and missing values are imputed with zeros. Finally, we ensure the target label is strictly binary {0,1}. UNSW-NB15 provides 49 original attributes; after preprocessing and one-hot encoding, the design matrices contain ~110–118 columns (including label), depending on whether engineered features are included. The pipeline is implemented with pandas and scikit-learn primitives [8].

## 3.3    Engineered Features

We add eight lightweight, domain-informed ratios and rates derived from standard flow counters (bytes, packets, TTL, duration) commonly exported in IPFIX/NetFlow records

**Table 3.** Engineered features and purposes

| Feature Name | Formula | Purpose |
| --- | --- | --- |
| bytes_ratio | $bytes\,ratio = \frac{sbytes}{dbytes+1}$ | Measures directional byte volume asymmetry |
| ttl_diff | $ttl_diff = sttl - dttl$ | Detects TTL anomalies and path asymmetry |
| throughput | $throughput = \frac{sbytes+dbytes}{dur+1}$ | Flow data transfer rate (bytes/sec) |
| pkt_rate | $pkt_rate = \frac{Spkts+Dpkts}{dur+1}$ | Flow packet transfer rate (packets/sec) |
| byte_per_pkt | $byte_per_pkt = \frac{sbytes+dbytes}{Spkts+Dpkts+1}$ | Average packet size per flow |
| pkt_size_ratio | $pkt_size_ratio = \frac{smeansz+1}{dmeansz+1}$ | Directional mean packet size ratio |
| load_ratio | $load_ratio = \frac{Sload}{Dload+1}$ | Flow load asymmetry |
| total_ttl | $total_ttl = sttl + dttl$ | Aggregate TTL values in both directions |

[18]. These features emphasize directional asymmetries and rate/size characteristics that often shift during attacks (e.g., spoofing, volumetric floods), and are broadly supported by prior flow-based IDS and traffic-classification studies [19–22] (Table 3).

When With Eng. is active, these eight are force-included and their raw counterparts are excluded from candidate pools to avoid redundancy: {sbytes, dbytes, sttl, dttl, Spkts, Dpkts, Sload, Dload, smeansz, dmeansz, dur}.

### 3.4 Models and Regimes

We evaluate eight model families—(i) ExtraTrees [5], (ii) HistGradientBoosting (Hist-GBM), (iii) DecisionTree, (iv) RandomForest [6], (v) MLP (with standardization), (vi) LightGBM [7], and (vii) XGBoost [10],(viii) 1D-CNN. Implementations use scikit-learn [8] or official LightGBM/XGBoost libraries with consistent, moderate hyperparameters (as in our evaluation script). We compare three regimes:

 (i) Without Eng.—top-20 drawn solely from base attributes.
 (ii) With Eng.—eight engineered ratios/rates are force-included; remaining slots by importance.
(iii) With Eng. + SMOTE—a bounded SMOTE-lite scheme [4]: (a) down-sample negatives to $\leq 3\times$ positives; (b) apply SMOTE to reach a target minority ratio $\approx 0.30$. Row counts are capped ($\leq 800k$) for memory safety, and k_neighbors adapts to the available positives.

### 3.5 Metrics and Alert-Budget Utility (ABU)

We report whole-set metrics, Precision, Recall, F1, ROC-AUC—and, crucially, Alert-Budget Utility (ABU) to match SOC triage constraints. ABU is F1 at the top-k alerts, where k = ⌊b·n⌋ for alert budgets b ∈ {5, 10, 20, 30}% and n is the test-set size. Test instances are ranked by model scores; ABU recomputes Precision/Recall/F1 over only those k flagged flows. This emphasizes performance under imbalance and limited review capacity, aligning with precision–recall-oriented evaluation [2, 3] and top-k ranking objectives [9].

## 3.6  Runtime Benchmarking

For the top-3 ABU@20% settings, we measure on one test day: train time (s), prediction throughput (rows/s), seconds per 1M rows, and serialized model size (MB). This complements ABU by indicating feasibility for high-volume SOC pipelines.

To achieve reproducibility, all per-fold predictions, ABU tables/plots, selected feature lists, and timing artifacts are saved under saved_data/ to enable end-to-end replication.

# 4  Results

## 4.1  Experimental Setup

All experiments ran CPU-only (no GPU). Host: Windows 11 Pro, 16-core single-socket CPU, 32 GB DDR4 RAM, 512 GB SSD. Software: Python 3.8.20, scikit-learn (for classical models and pipelines), LightGBM/XGBoost official libraries, PySpark 3.0.3, and Java Runtime 1.8.0_411.We evaluate seven learners under three feature regimes on UNSW-NB15 with a strict 20-feature budget. A temporal protocol is used: for each test day (fold), the preceding three days form the training split. Models are assessed (i) on all test flows using Accuracy, Precision, Recall, F1, and ROC-AUC, and (ii) under alert budgets via Alert-Budget Utility (ABU)—F1 computed only on the top-k alerts, where

$$k = \lfloor b \cdot n \rfloor \quad \text{for } \text{budgets } b \in \{5,10,20,30\} \%$$

All regimes use fixed, moderate hyperparameters; forests/boosters run with n_jobs = −1 (all cores) and random_state = 42 for reproducibility. Predictions, ABU tables, and feature lists are persisted for auditability.

## 4.2  Full-Set Metrics

Table 4 reports global metrics on all test rows, concatenating predictions across folds for each (model, regime). ROC-AUC is uniformly high (≈0.999 for most learners), so F1 and Recall are more discriminative. Across families, With Eng. is generally beneficial, while With Eng. + SMOTE increases Recall (often to ~0.99) at a small precision/F1 cost—consistent with oversampling on imbalanced data [4] and PR-centric evaluation guidance [2, 3]. Across models, the With Eng. configuration consistently improves F1 over the baseline, confirming the benefit of integrating engineered temporal and statistical attributes. The With Eng. + SMOTE variant further boosts Recall—often approaching 0.98–0.99—at a small cost to F1, a well-known precision–recall trade-off inherent to oversampling [4]. Ensemble learners such as HistGBM, LightGBM, and RandomForest exhibit the most balanced and stable performance across folds.

In contrast, the 1D CNN model performs poorly without engineered features (F1 = 0.12, Recall = 0.07, ROC–AUC = 0.63). This is primarily due to its limited capacity to infer temporal–statistical correlations directly from raw numeric flow features, which lack the spatial or sequential structure typically leveraged by convolutional architectures. When supplied with engineered attributes, however, the CNN's performance rises significantly (F1 = 0.89, Recall = 0.87, ROC–AUC = 0.99), demonstrating that the proposed feature design bridges the gap between representation learning and tabular data. The CNN + SMOTE variant was not included due to resource constraints, as multiple resampled training sets would have significantly increased GPU memory and compute demands.

**Table 4.** Global test-set metrics (all folds concatenated)

| Model | Setting | Recall | F1-Score | ROC-AUC |
| --- | --- | --- | --- | --- |
| ExtraTrees | Without Eng | 0.945 | 0.949 | 0.999 |
| ExtraTrees | With Eng | 0.963 | 0.959 | 0.999 |
| ExtraTrees | With Eng. + SMOTE | 0.974 | 0.956 | 0.998 |
| HistGBM | Without Eng | 0.951 | 0.958 | 0.999 |
| HistGBM | With Eng | 0.955 | 0.960 | 0.999 |
| HistGBM | With Eng. + SMOTE | 0.980 | 0.956 | 0.999 |
| DecisionTree | Without Eng | 0.913 | 0.934 | 0.954 |
| DecisionTree | With Eng | 0.905 | 0.928 | 0.950 |
| DecisionTree | With Eng. + SMOTE | 0.921 | 0.927 | 0.957 |
| RandomForest | Without Eng | 0.934 | 0.951 | 0.998 |
| RandomForest | With Eng | 0.916 | 0.941 | 0.999 |
| RandomForest | With Eng. + SMOTE | 0.963 | 0.954 | 0.999 |
| MLP | Without Eng | 0.969 | 0.963 | 0.999 |
| MLP | With Eng | 0.961 | 0.961 | 0.999 |
| MLP | With Eng. + SMOTE | 0.991 | 0.954 | 0.999 |
| LightGBM | Without Eng | 0.960 | 0.963 | 0.999 |
| LightGBM | With Eng | 0.960 | 0.962 | 0.999 |
| LightGBM | With Eng. + SMOTE | 0.975 | 0.954 | 0.999 |
| XGBoost | Without Eng | 0.945 | 0.950 | 0.999 |
| XGBoost | With Eng | 0.943 | 0.948 | 0.999 |
| XGBoost | With Eng. + SMOTE | 0.976 | 0.954 | 0.999 |
| CNN | Without Eng | 0.065 | 0.122 | 0.625 |
| CNN | With Eng | 0.871 | 0.896 | 0.988 |

### 4.3  Alert-Budget Utility (ABU)

We measure performance under analyst-limited triage using ABU, defined as F1 computed only on the top-k alerts, with

$$k = \lfloor b \cdot n \rfloor \quad \text{for} \quad \text{budgets} \ \ b \in \{5,10,20,30\} \ \%$$

Figure 1 plots the single best (model, regime) per budget on the same held-out day. At 5–10% budgets, HistGBM / Without Eng. Leads (F1≈0.397/0.662) with Precision = 1.00 and moderate Recall—typical "needle-in-a-haystack" triage. At 20%, Random-Forest / With Eng. is best (F1≈0.973), and at 30% HistGBM / Without Eng. Retakes the lead (F1≈0.805), trading precision for near-exhaustive Recall≈1.00.

Figure 2 summarizes fold-average champions (mean $\pm$ sd). The mean F1 at 5/10/20/30% is ≈0.584/0.655/0.684/0.564, respectively (LightGBM/Without Eng.; HistGBM variants; RandomForest/With Eng.; HistGBM/Without Eng.). Error bars widen at 20–30%, reflecting day-to-day class mix, yet simple paired checks show champions are statistically close to runner-ups (95% CIs overlap for all budgets in our summary table). Table 5 lists the top-3 per budget (ranked by F1, then Precision and Recall), making the precision–recall trade-off explicit: low budgets favor very high precision; larger budgets lift recall.

ABU clearly exposes budget-dependent winners that global ROC-AUC (≈0.999 across models) cannot differentiate. RandomForest/With Eng. remains the best balanced choice at realistic 20% alert allowances, whereas HistGBM / Without Eng. performs strongly under both highly restrictive and exhaustive review settings.

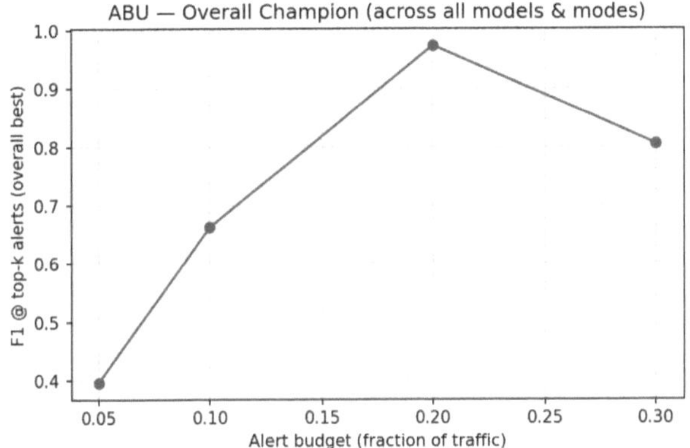


**Fig. 1.** Overall champion (across all models and regimes), fold-4.

### 4.4  Feature Ablation

Table 6 summarizes, for each model, which regime wins at each budget on fold-4 (ranked by F1, with Precision and Recall as tie-breakers). Two patterns emerge. First, With Eng. frequently beats Without Eng. at moderate budgets (20%), reflecting the value of

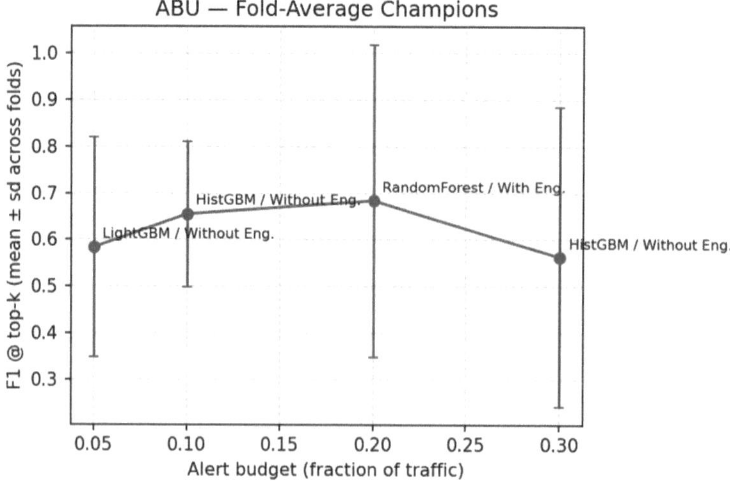


**Fig. 2.** ABU—Fold-average champions (F1 ± sd) vs. budget (5/10/20/30%).

**Table 5.** ABU (fold-average) top-3 per budget

| Budget | Rank | Model | Setting | F1 | Precision | Recall |
|---|---|---|---|---|---|---|
| 0.05 | 1 | LightGBM | W/o Eng | 0.583 | 0.908 | 0.533 |
| 0.05 | 2 | XGBoost | SMOTE | 0.583 | 0.908 | 0.533 |
| 0.05 | 3 | MLP | With Eng | 0.583 | 0.908 | 0.533 |
| 0.1 | 1 | HistGBM | W/o Eng | 0.654 | 0.767 | 0.734 |
| 0.1 | 2 | HistGBM | With Eng | 0.654 | 0.767 | 0.734 |
| 0.1 | 3 | HistGBM | SMOTE | 0.654 | 0.767 | 0.734 |
| 0.2 | 1 | Random Forest | With Eng | 0.683 | 0.628 | 0.964 |
| 0.2 | 2 | RandomForest | SMOTE | 0.683 | 0.628 | 0.964 |
| 0.2 | 3 | HistGBM | SMOTE | 0.683 | 0.628 | 0.964 |
| 0.3 | 1 | HistGBM | W/o Eng | 0.563 | 0.445 | 1.0 |
| 0.3 | 2 | HistGBM | With Eng | 0.563 | 0.445 | 1.0 |
| 0.3 | 3 | HistGBM | SMOTE | 0.563 | 0.445 | 1.0 |

simple ratios/rates. Second, With Eng. + SMOTE tends to win at higher budgets (30%) by pushing Recall to ~1.00 with only moderate precision—expected behavior when oversampling minority classes [4]. This aligns with the ablation deltas: With Eng. > Without Eng. in 11/28 cases, SMOTE helps at 20–30% in 7 cases, but at 5–10% only 4 cases (precision often drops).

Several models favored the Without Eng. configuration at the smallest alert budgets (5–10%). This pattern arises because F1@top-k emphasizes precision, and at extremely

**Table 6.** Per-Model Winning Regime Across Alert Budgets (Fold-4 ABU)

| Model | Budget | Winner | F1 |
| --- | --- | --- | --- |
| CNN | 0.05 | With Eng | 0.396 |
| CNN | 0.1 | With Eng | 0.656 |
| CNN | 0.2 | With Eng | 0.787 |
| CNN | 0.3 | With Eng | 0.727 |
| DecisionTree | 0.05 | Without Eng | 0.391 |
| DecisionTree | 0.1 | Without Eng | 0.646 |
| DecisionTree | 0.2 | Without Eng | 0.963 |
| DecisionTree | 0.3 | With Eng. + SMOTE | 0.789 |
| ExtraTrees | 0.05 | Without Eng | 0.396 |
| ExtraTrees | 0.1 | Without Eng | 0.661 |
| ExtraTrees | 0.2 | With Eng. + SMOTE | 0.969 |
| ExtraTrees | 0.3 | With Eng. + SMOTE | 0.804 |
| HistGBM | 0.05 | Without Eng | 0.396 |
| HistGBM | 0.1 | Without Eng | 0.662 |
| HistGBM | 0.2 | With Eng. + SMOTE | 0.971 |
| HistGBM | 0.3 | Without Eng | 0.804 |
| LightGBM | 0.05 | Without Eng | 0.396 |
| LightGBM | 0.1 | Without Eng | 0.662 |
| LightGBM | 0.2 | With Eng. + SMOTE | 0.971 |
| LightGBM | 0.3 | Without Eng | 0.804 |
| MLP | 0.05 | Without Eng | 0.396 |
| MLP | 0.1 | Without Eng | 0.662 |
| MLP | 0.2 | With Eng | 0.969 |
| MLP | 0.3 | Without Eng | 0.804 |
| RandomForest | 0.05 | With Eng | 0.396 |
| RandomForest | 0.1 | With Eng | 0.661 |
| RandomForest | 0.2 | With Eng. + SMOTE | 0.971 |
| RandomForest | 0.3 | With Eng | 0.804 |
| XGBoost | 0.05 | Without Eng | 0.396 |
| XGBoost | 0.1 | Without Eng | 0.662 |
| XGBoost | 0.2 | With Eng. + SMOTE | 0.968 |
| XGBoost | 0.3 | Without Eng | 0.804 |

low budgets the top alerts are already well-separated by native flow features. The addition of engineered ratios and temporal aggregates slightly smooths decision boundaries, marginally lowering top-rank precision. However, as the alert budget widens (20–30%), the advantage shifts decisively toward With Eng. and With Eng. + SMOTE settings, where recall and holistic temporal discrimination become more influential. This confirms that engineered attributes primarily enhance model robustness and recall under broader operational alert capacities rather than in extreme low-budget conditions.

### 4.5  Engineered Feature Ablation and Temporal Importance Evolution

To quantify the contribution of the engineered temporal and statistical attributes, a feature ablation experiment was conducted on the fold-4 split using the XGBoost model. Each engineered feature was sequentially removed while retraining the model under identical hyperparameters, and the resulting change in F1-score, recall, and ROC-AUC was recorded. Table 7 presents the observed performance deltas. The removal of total_ttl ($\Delta$F1 = +0.0017) and ttl_diff ($\Delta$F1 = +0.0011) produced the most pronounced degradation, confirming their critical role in capturing packet-lifetime and routing dynamics that evolve over time. Similarly, throughput exhibited a notable contribution to overall detection quality. In contrast, flow-level indicators such as pkt_size_ratio and load_ratio yielded negligible or slightly negative deltas, implying redundancy with baseline traffic statistics already represented within the UNSW-NB15 dataset.

To assess temporal stability, feature importances were aggregated across the four chronological folds (Table 8). The results show that total_ttl and bytes_ratio consistently dominate, reaffirming their persistent discriminative strength across different temporal windows. The magnitudes of pkt_rate and throughput fluctuate moderately, suggesting that volume-oriented indicators are more sensitive to transient variations in benign traffic intensity. The overall consistency of ranking across folds confirms that the proposed engineered features are not ad hoc but grounded in interpretable network semantics.Collectively, the ablation and temporal analyses establish that the engineered features—particularly those encoding time-aware and topological context—remain both theoretically justified and operationally stable within the proposed temporal-aware intrusion-detection framework. Their persistent influence across evaluation folds demonstrates resilience to temporal drift, supporting their applicability to evolving network conditions.

### 4.6  Runtime and Memory

Table 9 reports training time, inference throughput, time per one million flows, and serialized model size (MB) for the top-3 ABU@20% settings, measured on a single timing fold with the same features/hyperparameters as the accuracy/ABU runs.

ExtraTrees (With Eng.) delivers the highest throughput (~226,529 rows/s; ~4.41 s per 1M), while RandomForest (With Eng.)—the ABU@20% winner—trades some speed for accuracy. With Eng. + SMOTE reduces RandomForest training time and model size with similar prediction speed.

**Table 7.** Feature Ablation Results on Fold-4 (XGBoost)

| Feature Removed | ΔF1 | ΔRecall | ΔROC–AUC | F1 After | Recall After | ROC–AUC After |
|---|---|---|---|---|---|---|
| bytes_ratio | +0.001014 | +0.002064 | +0.000029 | 0.9497 | 0.9457 | 0.9992 |
| ttl_diff | +0.001094 | +0.000458 | +0.000019 | 0.9498 | 0.9441 | 0.9992 |
| throughput | +0.001043 | +0.002474 | +0.000022 | 0.9497 | 0.9462 | 0.9992 |
| pkt_rate | +00.000163 | +0.000909 | +0.000005 | 0.9489 | 0.9446 | 0.9992 |
| byte_per_pkt | +0.000410 | +0.001313 | −0.000007 | 0.949 | 0.945 | 0.9992 |
| pkt_size_ratio | −0.000460 | −0.000451 | −0.000001 | 0.948 | 0.943 | 0.9992 |
| load_ratio | −0.000057 | +0.001046 | +0.000008 | 0.948 | 0.944 | 0.9992 |
| total_ttl | +0.001722 | +0.002745 | +0.000038 | 0.950 | 0.946 | 0.9992 |

**Table 8.** Feature Importance Evolution Across Temporal Folds (XGBoost)

| Fold | byte_per_pkt | bytes_ratio | load_ratio | pkt_rate | pkt_size_ratio | throughput | total_ttl | ttl_diff |
|---|---|---|---|---|---|---|---|---|
| 1 | 101.72 | 174.19 | 42.09 | 31.34 | 326.01 | 29.31 | 33518.37 | 799.17 |
| 2 | 94.64 | 135.63 | 52.20 | 33.62 | 278.00 | 33.08 | 29186.90 | 707.67 |
| 3 | 58.56 | 103.12 | 29.74 | 25.71 | 208.13 | 22.43 | 18359.02 | 624.91 |
| 4 | 77.10 | 132.84 | 34.39 | 33.80 | 294.97 | 28.84 | 29223.67 | 635.60 |

**Table 9.** Runtime & memory for top-3 ABU@20% settings (single timing fold)

| Model | Setting | Train_Time_s | Predict_RowsPerSec | Time_for_1M_rows | Model_Size_MB |
|---|---|---|---|---|---|
| Random Forest | With Eng | 182.78 | 69891.4 | 14.31 | 154.42 |
| Random Forest | SMOTE | 79.76 | 73715.7 | 13.57 | 90.72 |
| Extra Trees | With Eng | 15.91 | 226529.1 | 4.41 | 115.39 |

## 4.7  Performance Comparison

While GAN-based and autoencoder-driven IDS achieve strong F1 on random splits, their evaluations lack temporal ordering. This work differs by explicitly enforcing chronological train-test separation to reflect real-world deployment conditions (Table 10).

**Table 10.** Comparison with Published IDS Methods on UNSW-NB15

| Study | Model/Technique | Evaluation Setup | F1-Score | Remarks |
|---|---|---|---|---|
| Idrissi & Kartit (2022) [23] | GMM-WGAN-IDS (Generative Deep IDS) | Random split | 0.854 | GAN-based IDS with adversarial training |
| This Work (2025) | Random Forest(With Eng. + SMOTE) | Temporal rolling 3day/1day split | 0.954 | Best ensemble under realistic temporal evaluation |
| This Work (2025) | HistGBM (With Eng.) | Temporal rolling | 0.960 | High and stable performance; interpretable engineered features |

## 5  Conclusion

This study presented a temporal-aware IDS pipeline evaluated on the UNSW-NB15 dataset under a strict 20-feature budget across three regimes (Without Eng., With Eng., and With Eng. + SMOTE). While global ROC–AUC values remain consistently high ($\approx$0.999), the proposed Alert-Budget Utility (ABU) metric—F1 measured only on the top-k alerts—reveals practical, budget-dependent performance differences. HistGBM leads at low alert budgets (5–10%) with near-perfect precision (~1.0), RandomForest (With Eng.) peaks at the 20% budget, and HistGBM regains dominance at 30%. Fold-averaged ABU with confidence intervals confirms that top-performing models remain statistically close to their runner-ups, mitigating the risk of "lucky fold" effects. A runtime analysis highlights ExtraTrees (With Eng.) as the most efficient learner (~226k rows/s, $\approx$4.4 s per million flows), whereas RandomForest (With Eng.) offers the best trade-off between ABU@20% and inference cost. The engineered ratios and rates contribute most under moderate alert budgets, while bounded SMOTE oversampling further enhances recall at higher thresholds. All artifacts—including feature sets, predictions, ABU tables, and visualizations—are preserved to ensure full reproducibility. Future work will explore adaptive alert budgets and online drift handling to maintain robustness under evolving traffic and threat conditions.

**Disclosure of Interests.**   The authors have no competing interests with reference to above article.

## References


1. Moustafa, N., Slay, J.: UNSW-NB15: a comprehensive data set for network intrusion detection systems (UNSW-NB15 Network Data Set). In: Military Communications and Information Systems Conference (MilCIS 2015). IEEE, Canberra (2015)
2. Davis, J., Goadrich, M.: The relationship between precision–recall and ROC curves. In: ICML 2006. ACM, New York (2006)
3. Saito, T., Rehmsmeier, M.: The precision-recall plot is more informative than the ROC plot when evaluating binary classifiers on imbalanced datasets. PLoS ONE **10**(3), e0118432 (2015)

4. Chawla, N.V., Bowyer, K.W., Hall, L.O., Kegelmeyer, W.P.: SMOTE: synthetic minority over-sampling technique. J. Artific. Intell. Res. **16**, 321–357 (2002)
5. Geurts, P., Ernst, D., Wehenkel, L.: Extremely randomized trees. Mach. Learn. **63**(1), 3–42 (2006)
6. Breiman, L.: Random forests. Mach. Learn. **45**(1), 5–32 (2001)
7. Ke, G., et al.: LightGBM: a highly efficient gradient boosting decision tree. In: NeurIPS 2017. Curran Associates, Red Hook, NY (2017)
8. Pedregosa, F., Varoquaux, G., Gramfort, A., et al.: Scikit-learn: machine learning in python. J. Mach. Learn. Res. **12**, 2825–2830 (2011)
9. Liu, T.-Y.: Learning to rank for information retrieval. 1st edn. Morgan & Claypool, San Rafael, CA (2009)
10. Chen, T., Guestrin, C.: XGBoost: A Scalable Tree Boosting System. In: KDD 2016, pp. 785–794. ACM, New York (2016)
11. Tavallaee, M., Bagheri, E., Lu, W., Ghorbani, A.A.: A detailed analysis of the KDD cup 99 data set. In: CISDA 2009. IEEE, Piscataway, NJ (2009)
12. Sharafaldin, I., Lashkari, A.H., Ghorbani, A.A.: Toward generating a new intrusion detection dataset and intrusion traffic characterization. In: ICISSP 2018, pp. 108–116. SciTePress (2018)
13. Mirsky, Y., tshman, T., Elovici, Y., Shabtai, A.: Kitsune: an ensemble of autoencoders for online network intrusion detection. In: NDSS 2018. Internet Society, San Diego (2018)
14. Yin, C., Zhu, Y., Fei, J., He, X.: A deep learning approach for intrusion detection using recurrent neural networks. IEEE Access **5**, 21954–21961 (2017)
15. Shone, N., Ngoc, T.N., Phai, V.D., Shi, Q.: A deep learning approach to network intrusion detection. IEEE Trans. Emerg. Top. Comput. Intell. **2**(1), 41–50 (2018)
16. Koroniotis, N., Moustafa, N., Sitnikova, E., Turnbull, B.: Towards the development of realistic botnet dataset in the internet of things for network forensic analytics: BoT-IoT dataset. Futur. Gener. Comput. Syst. **100**, 779–796 (2019)
17. Buczak, A.L., Guven, E.: A survey of data mining and machine learning methods for cyber security intrusion detection. IEEE Commun. Surv. Tutor. **18**(2), 1153–1176 (2016)
18. Claise, B., Trammell, B., Aitken, P.: Specification of the IP flow information export (IPFIX) protocol for the exchange of flow information. RFC 7011 (2016). https://www.rfc-editor.org/rfc/rfc7011. Accessed 27 Aug 2025
19. Sperotto, A., Schaffrath, G., Sadre, R., Morariu, C., Pras, A., Stiller, B.: An overview of IP flow-based intrusion detection. IEEE Commun. Surv. Tutor. **12**(3), 343–356 (2010)
20. Nguyen, T.T.T., Armitage, G.: A survey of techniques for internet traffic classification using machine learning. IEEE Commun. Surv. Tutor. **10**(4), 56–76 (2008)
21. Lakhina, A., Crovella, M., Diot, C.: Characterization of network-wide anomalies in traffic flows. In: IMC 2004, pp. 201–206. ACM, New York (2004)
22. Moore, A.W., Zuev, D.: Internet traffic classification using bayesian analysis techniques. SIGMETRICS Perform. Eval. Rev. **34**(4), 50–60 (2006)
23. Idrissi, N., Kartit, A.: GMM-WGAN-IDS: a generative adversarial network-based intrusion detection system for cybersecurity. IAENG Int. J. Comput. Sci. **51**(8), 999–1008 (2022)

# Cyberbullying Detection Using Machine and Deep Learning Models on a YouTube Dataset

Shreya Pradhan, Mansi Bhavsar[✉], Jackson Thoe, Ahmed Umer, and Sonia Sherif

Minnesota State University, Mankato, MN, USA
`mansi.bhavsar@mnsu.edu`

**Abstract.** Cyberbullying has emerged as a prevalent concern due to the extensive usage of social media, subjecting users to detrimental interactions and online abuse. Cyberbullying represents a critical public health issue with profound implications for mental health, as it has been associated with an increased risk of various psychological and developmental disorders, including suicidal ideation. Despite its growing recognition, there is a lack of publicly available datasets and the methodologies employed to assess its occurrence. This lack of consensus hampers efforts to effectively address and mitigate the adverse effects of cyberbullying on individuals and communities. In this work, we developed an algorithm that scrapes data from the YouTube API and performs a series of binary classification models to determine the presence of cyberbullying comments. Our methodology integrates Natural Language Processing (NLP) approaches, including text normalization and sentiment analysis via Valence Aware Dictionary and sentiment Reasoner (VADER), with machine learning and deep learning models for binary classification. We performed sentiment analysis on the collected data using Support Vector Machine (SVM), Bi-directional Long Short-Term Memory (BiLSTM), Bi-directional Gated Recurrent Unit (BiGRU), and Bi-Directional Encoder Representations from Transformers (BERT) models. We also tuned the hyperparameters of these models for the best results. Initial findings indicate the efficacy of our proposed system, achieving 94% accuracy, and demonstrate its capacity to reduce the effects of cyberbullying through automated detection.

**Keywords:** ML · DL · Cyberbullying · Text analysis · YouTube data collection

## 1 Introduction

In the digital age, social media platforms have become central to social interaction, especially among adolescents and young adults. While these platforms enable users to connect, share, and learn in ways previously unimaginable, they also expose users to new forms of harm, including cyberbullying. Cyberbullying, defined as bullying that takes place over digital devices like cell phones, computers, and tablets, can occur through SMS, Text, and apps, or online in social media, forums, or gaming where people can view, participate in, or share content. This form of bullying can lead to severe emotional, psychological, and physical stress that can lead to emotional anxiety and depression [1].


K. K. Patel et al. (Eds.): icSoftComp 2025, CCIS 2874, pp. 392–404, 2026.
https://doi.org/10.1007/978-3-032-22062-2_30

Recent studies indicate that approximately 55% of young people between the ages of 13 and 17 have been victims of cyberbullying, with 27% reporting it occurred in the last 30 days [2]. This presents an urgency to recognize cyberbullying as a rapidly growing problem that will affect several lives if not seriously dealt with. In response, there is a need for robust detection systems that can identify and mitigate cyberbullying incidents early and efficiently.

In response to these challenges, our project develops a robust detection system utilizing advanced NLP and machine learning techniques to identify cyberbullying in YouTube comments. This paper details the creation of an algorithm that leverages deep learning models, including Convolutional Neural Networks (CNNs) and Recurrent Neural Networks (RNNs) with Long Short-Term Memory (LSTM) to effectively classify and predict cyberbullying content. By integrating these models, we aim to capture the complex patterns of aggressive or harmful language that may not be evident through traditional keyword-based approaches.

We begin by extracting a substantial dataset of YouTube comments, which are then preprocessed to remove special characters and hyperlinks and standardize text. Using sentiment analysis, we assess the emotional tone of comments to determine potential negativity that could indicate bullying behavior. Our methodology not only classifies text but also evaluates the effectiveness of different neural network architectures in understanding and predicting the context and intent behind user comments. By comparing these models, we provide insights into their operational strengths and limitations, offering a benchmark for future cyberbullying detection tools. This paper aims to contribute to safer digital interactions on social media platforms by presenting an advanced, scalable solution for cyberbullying detection. Through the use of deep learning and comprehensive data handling techniques, we enhance the ability of platforms to automatically monitor and mitigate harmful content, thereby fostering a healthier online environment.

The paper is organized as follows. Section 2 deals with related works and is followed by Sect. 3 which discusses the purposed system. Then we move on to Sect. 3.4 which handles everything to do with data from the collection to the labeling and the preprocessing. This is followed by Sect. 4 which goes over the model-building and fine-tuning steps that were implemented. Furthermore, we have Sect. 5 which discloses the results and lastly, we have Sect. 6, the Conclusion, which is followed by the References Section.

## 2   Related Works

Cyberbullying on social media is an important problem because it significantly impacts the well-being of individuals, particularly young people who are frequent users of these platforms [8]. It has been a major area of interest for researchers working on predicting and detecting different forms of cyberbullying on social media. Many pieces of research work that are done in this area using various machine learning and deep learning techniques have yielded significant results in detecting and preventing cyberbullying [15].

The presented study in [13] introduces a hybrid deep learning model named DEA-RNN, designed to detect cyberbullying on the Twitter social media platform. The results demonstrated that the DEA-RNN model, which integrates Elman Recurrent Neural Networks (RNN) with the Dolphin Echolocation Algorithm (DEA), significantly improved detection accuracy and reduced training time. Data was collected from Twitter, focusing on tweets that potentially contained cyberbullying content. The dataset included a substantial number of samples, each annotated for cyberbullying indicators. The Elman RNN was used to capture the sequential nature of the text data, while the DEA optimized the parameters of the Elman RNN, enhancing its performance and reducing training time. The hybrid DEARNN model combined the strengths of both Elman RNN and DEA to improve detection accuracy.

In one of the few works that have included non-English data [15], a deep learning algorithm to recognize cyberbullying in three different languages: English, Hindi, and Hinglish (a mix between Hindi and English) is proposed. The deep learning algorithm uses the CNN-BiLSTM model with stacked word embedding. The dataset for this research has been collected from different open sources, not mentioned in the paper, and the data collection method is also not specified. The CNN-BiLSTM model is proposed in the paper because an ensemble deep learning model with multiple layers outperforms single-layer neural networks. Additionally, a web portal similar to Twitter was created to test the model in real-time. Dataset Analysis included data cleaning, transformation, reduction, and discretization. When compared to BILSTM + BIGRU, CNN + BILSTM, and CNN + BIGRU, CNN + BILSTM has the best performance. By the end of the research, a user can post a tweet, and it would automatically get updated in the feed and be classified as a cyberbullying or non-cyberbullying tweet.

The use of LLMs is an important advancement in the detection of cyberbullying, particularly in classifying the image subtext as cyberbullying or not and generating text that can be used as synthetic data is performing an analysis on cyberbullying detection through image classification using GPT-4 with Vision as a subtext generator [11, 12]. The system would extract the image from the URL, then have GPT-4 with Vision evaluate the image, generating a text that describes the image and what it thinks the intention of the posted image was. The system then used an unnamed LLM to classify the generated GPT-4 with Vision text as cyberbullying or not. The LLM was trained on existing cyberbullying posts and text generated by the researchers used AI models to differentiate cyberbullying and biased attacks [11]. The AI models used within this experiment consist of DeBERTa, Longformer, BigBird, HateBERT, MobileBERT, DistilBERT, BERT, RoBERTa, ELECTRA, and XLNet.

## 3  Proposed System

Our proposed system is an advanced framework for detecting cyberbullying in YouTube comments using a combination of machine learning and deep learning techniques. The system is divided into several components, focusing on data processing, model building, and performance evaluation. Figure 1 shows the proposed model, followed by a detailed explanation of each component.

### 3.1  Data Preprocessing

Data is the key component in any system involving machine learning or deep learning. How the data is collected and managed can make or break a model's overall performance.

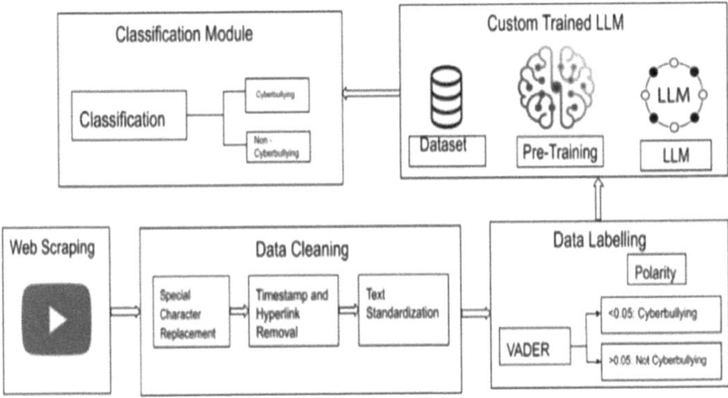


**Fig. 1.** Proposed System

In this section, we cover all the specific details involving the data collection, cleaning, and labeling processes, including the methods and strategies we took to ensure that the data used was as reliable as possible.

### 3.2 Data Collection

The primary social media site in which data was extracted from was YouTube. The main method consisted of utilizing a Python script to access the 'YouTube Data API v3' API which allowed the collection of top-level comments for specific videos uploaded onto the site. Ultimately, other social media sites and APIs were taken into consideration when it came to collecting data. 'X' (formally known as 'Twitter') is a popular source of data when it comes to previous work done on cyberbullying detection. However, after looking into the 'X API', certain limitation blocked the use of excessive collection within a short period of time, with the free tier for the API being 50 top-level posts a day. This was not sufficient given the amount of time allocated for this project and the amount of data needed to be considered reliable. More limitations were found in other social media data sources. 'Instagram' has a 'Basic Display API' which allows data collection, but only from accounts in which you have personal access too. 'TikTok' is another very popular video sharing site that was a top choice when looking for initial data. But TikTok's 'Data Portability API' has users send an application for general use of the resource, and even after doing so, a 4-week processing period followed, restricting immediate use. Again, within a limited time frame for this project, this was not sufficient for data collection. After taking all these resources into account, the 'YouTube Data API v3' was the more reliable option, given that there is a bigger limit of 10,000 query calls a day, and a wide source of videos to collect comments from.

A big factor in the data collection process was deciding on which specific YouTube videos to extract comments from. This process started by choosing a wide range of video topics that are known for negative comments such as politics, LGBTQ, music videos, and weight loss videos. This creates a broader data set for the model to analyze. From there, certain videos were used if they contained negative keywords that are commonly found within a cyberbullying post. This included words like "loser", "idiot", "dumb", "ugly", "kill", "hate", "trash", "fat", "r*tard", and so on.

As mentioned previously, a Python script was used for collecting raw comments from each chosen video through the 'YouTube Data API v3'. With the proper API access token, the script was able to take a given video's ID tag and extract comments from the specific video. YouTube uses ID tags to differentiate videos from each other and can be found in the URL link of the video itself. Depending on the popularity of the video and the number of total comments listed on YouTube, 500 to 1,000 comments were extracted per video. 'YouTube Data API v3' allows comments to be collected by the most recent date in which they are posted, or the most relevant comments, meaning the most liked comments at the top of the video page. The Python script uses the most relevant feature as this provides the data set with more understandable comments that can be read by other users and ultimately, computer models. After the Python script finishes extracting, the comments are then appended into an existing CSV (comma separated values) file which contains all collected comments. In total, 26,215 comments were extracted from 28 different YouTube videos.

### 3.3  Data Cleaning

Data cleaning is the process of formatting pre-processed data to make it more readable for a machine to understand. A few steps were taken to properly clean the raw YouTube text comments. A common character mis-reference found within the raw text was the replacement of the apostrophe with the HTML reference '''. A simple replacement function was used to substitute the apostrophes back into the text. For the machine models to process the text, only alphanumeric values were kept within each comment. This meant that all special characters were removed using a Regex (regular expression) function to replace them with an empty string. YouTube allows the use of timestamps within a videos comment section which when clicked, moves the videos current playtime at that timestamp. This was very reoccurring within the raw data set and made the text less understandable due to the use of URLs within timestamps. The removal of timestamps consisted of using regex to locate HTML text (¡span¿ blocks) and replacing them and all text in-between with an empty string.

The following subsections outline each cleaning step in more detail:

1. **HTML Character Fixes:** YouTube comments sometimes include HTML entities, such as ''' for apostrophes. These were replaced with their readable equivalents to improve textual clarity.

   – Example:

   Before: You're such an 'idiot
   After: You're such an 'idiot'

2. **Removal of Special Characters:** Non-alphanumeric characters including punctuation, symbols, and emojis were removed using regular expressions. This step ensured that only letters, digits, and spaces were retained.

- Example:
  Before: This is 🥴 CRAZY!! 😂😂
  After: This is CRAZY

3. **Text Speak Expansion:** Common internet abbreviations and slang were expanded to their full forms using a manually created mapping dictionary. This helped standardize language across the dataset.

   – Example:

     Before: idk why u mad lol
     After: i don't know why you mad laugh out loud

4. **Sentiment-Based Labeling:** Each cleaned and expanded comment was passed through the VADER sentiment analyzer. Based on the compound sentiment score:

   – If the score $> 0.05 \rightarrow$ Labeled as "Not Cyberbullying"
   – If the score $< -0.05 \rightarrow$ Labeled as "Cyberbullying"
   – Else $\rightarrow$ Labeled as "Neutral"

   This automated labeling provided ground truth for model training.
5. **CSV Merging and Export:** Comments from multiple sources were merged into a single dataset and saved as a labeled CSV file. The cleaned comment and its label were stored for downstream tasks.

## 3.4 Data Labeling

To utilize all the cleaned and processed data gathered from YouTube for model training and testing, labeling the data is needed. This process involves a binary classification of all comments on whether they qualify as "Cyberbullying" or "Non-Cyberbullying". To do this, a sentiment analysis algorithm named Valence Aware Dictionary for Sentiment Reasoning (VADER) was used to evaluate the sentiment of each comment. VADER breaks down sentences into individual lexicons or words and asses each word's sentimental value.

After all words are given a sentiment value, they are totaled up and the sentence or comment is determined to be "Cyberbullying" if it has a negative sentiment score of under –0.05. A comment is labeled "Non-cyberbullying" if the comment has positive sentiment score of over 0.05. Any comment that falls in between these thresholds or has a value of 0.05 is labeled as "Neutral". After some deeper analysis and manual checks on the "Neutral" comments, it was determined that almost all should be ultimately classified under "Non-Cyberbullying".

## 3.5 Dataset Train-Test Split

Due to the residual imbalance in the dataset after labeling using the YouTube Comments API, we implemented upsampling using the Pandas resampling library. This ensured an even distribution of classes and improved the performance of the machine learning models.

The dataset was split into training and validation sets using an 80/20 split. The training set was used for model learning, while the validation set assessed model generalization and ensured performance consistency across all models.

# 4   Model Building

After reviewing current literature, we implemented and evaluated multiple machine learning and deep learning models. The models chosen for this paper are the Support Vector Machine (SVM), Bi-Directional Long-Short Term Memory (BILSTM), Bi-Directional Gated Recurrent Units (BIGRU), and Bi-Directional Encoder Representations from Transformers (BERT). The models were selected based on their ability to process text data, capture contextual meaning, and classify cyberbullying comments effectively.

## 4.1   Models

1) *Support Vector Machine (SVM)*: is a supervised machine learning algorithm used for binary classification tasks. It was chosen for its capability to create a clear decision boundary by maximizing the margin between classes (Fig. 2).

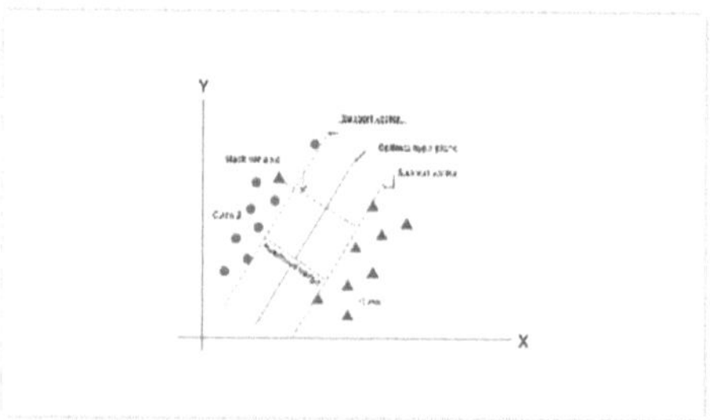

**Fig. 2.** Maximum-margin hyperplane and margins for an SVM [22].

2) *Bi-Directional Long-Short Term Memory (BILSTM):* is an advanced form of Recurrent Neural Networks (RNNs) that captures long-term dependencies in text by processing input in both forward and backward directions (Fig. 3).
3) *Bi-Directional Gated Recurrent Units (BIGRU)::* is a variant of RNNs like BiLSTM but with fewer parameters, which makes it computationally efficient while maintaining the ability to model sequential dependencies (Fig. 4).
4) *Bi-Directional Encoder Representations from Transformers (BERT):* is a transformer-based model that uses attention mechanisms to understand the context of words in relation to their surrounding words, making it particularly powerful for text classification tasks (Fig. 5).

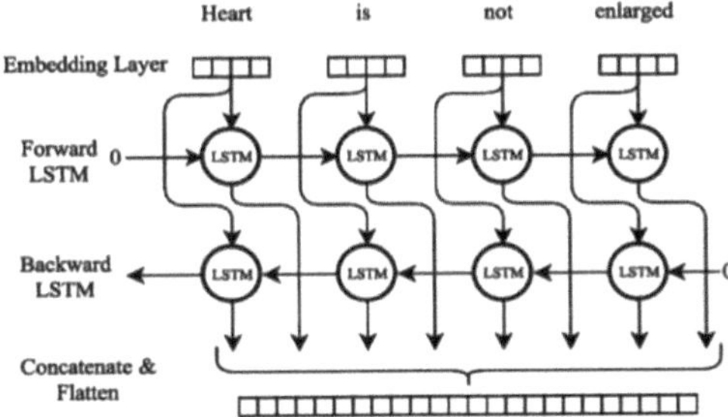



**Fig. 3.** Bi-directional LSTM [22].

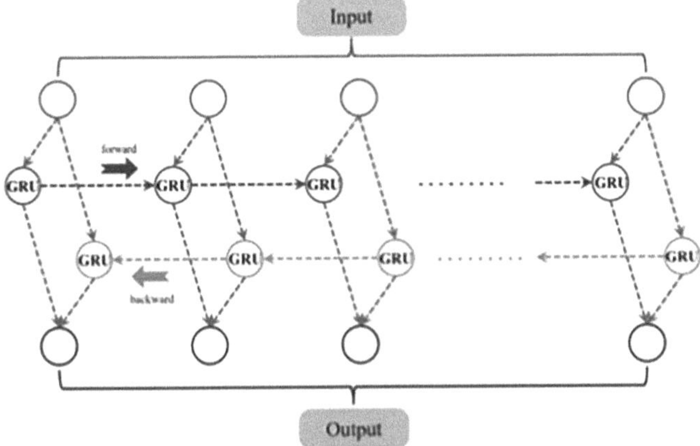



**Fig. 4.** Bi-Directional Gated Recurrent Units Architecture [20].

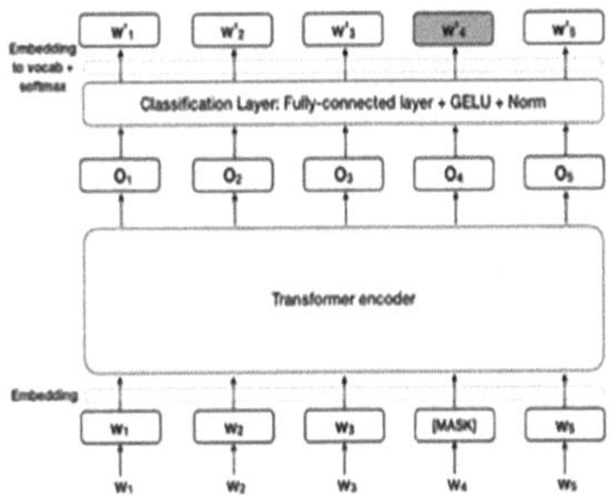



**Fig. 5.** Bi-Directional Encoder representations from transformer Architecture [21].

## 4.2  Fine Tuning

The fine-tuning process was tailored to leverage the strengths of each model while addressing the nuances of the cyberbullying detection dataset. For the SVM classifier, fine-tuning was focused on selecting appropriate hyperparameters to optimize performance on text data. A pipeline combining Term Frequency – Inverse Document Frequency of records (TF-IDF) vectorization with SVM was constructed. TF-IDF ensured that the model focused on the importance of specific words relative to their document frequency, reducing noise from common terms. The gamma = "scale" parameter was chosen for the SVM, which sets gamma to 1/(n features * X.var()) This automatic adjustment ensures that the gamma value is proportional to the number of features and the variance of the input data, enabling the model to effectively handle the sparse, high-dimensional feature space generated by the TF-IDF vectorizer [16]. This configuration improved the model's ability to distinguish subtle differences between classes, crucial for detecting nuanced cases of cyberbullying.

Fine-tuning for the BiLSTM and BiGRU models centered on the architecture and hyperparameter selection to maximize their sequential learning capabilities. Embedding layers were used to map input words to dense vector representations, capturing semantic relationships. The bidirectional configuration allowed the models to learn context from both preceding and following words, critical for understanding the intent in textual data. The dropout layers, with a rate of 0.5, mitigated overfitting by introducing regularization, while dense layers added depth to the networks, enhancing their capacity to capture complex patterns. These models were trained for five epochs, balancing computational efficiency and performance. A batch size of 32 ensured stable gradient updates, while the Adam optimizer facilitated efficient convergence. The choice of "binary crossentropy" as the loss function aligned with the binary nature of the task, ensuring precise optimization for detecting cyberbullying versus non-cyberbullying comments.

Fine-tuning BERT involved leveraging its pre-trained transformer-based architecture for sequence classification. The"bert-base-uncased" model was chosen for its ability to process text with nuanced contextual relationships, a critical aspect for cyberbullying detection. The tokenization process used BERT's tokenizer, truncating or padding inputs to a maximum sequence length of 512, ensuring compatibility with the model's architecture. Training was configured with a batch size of 8 to manage memory constraints while allowing gradient stability. The warm-up steps and weight decay parameters were optimized to improve convergence and prevent overfitting. A learning rate schedule was implemented to adapt the training process dynamically, ensuring that fine-tuning was both effective and computationally efficient. The decision to train for two epochs reflected a balance between leveraging the pre-trained knowledge in BERT and preventing overfitting on the relatively small dataset. Evaluation metrics, including accuracy, precision, recall, and F1score, were directly computed during fine-tuning to assess the model's ability to generalize effectively. By adapting the fine-tuning strategies to the specific requirements of each model, the process ensured that each approach could maximize its strengths, resulting in improved performance metrics and better overall detection of cyberbullying comments.

## 5  Results

In evaluating the effectiveness of our proposed system for cyberbullying detection, we employed several performance metrics, specifically Accuracy, Precision, Recall, and F1-score. These metrics were essential in determining the efficiency and reliability of the various models tested in our study. Each metric serves a distinct purpose: Accuracy provides a measure of overall correctness, Precision indicates the proportion of true positive results in relation to the total predicted positives, Recall reflects the model's ability to identify all relevant instances, and the F1-score offers a harmonic mean of Precision and Recall, thereby presenting a balanced view of the model's performance shown in Table 1 below.

Our comprehensive analysis revealed that the BERT (Bidirectional Encoder Representations from Transformers) model exhibited the highest scores across all evaluated metrics. Specifically, BERT achieved an impressive Accuracy of 94.9%, coupled with Precision, Recall, and F1-scores, all reaching 95%. These results indicate that the BERT model excels in correctly identifying instances of cyberbullying with a high degree of confidence. However, it is noteworthy that the BERT model also proved to be the most resource-intensive, necessitating a significant amount of computational power and time. The model's run time exceeded 21,000 s, translating to over 6 h, which may limit its practicality in real-time applications.

**Table 1.** Model Metric Results

| Models: | Accuracy | Precision | Recall | F1-Score | Time(s): |
| --- | --- | --- | --- | --- | --- |
| SVM | 0.945 | 0.94 | 0.94 | 0.94 | 240 |
| BILSTM | 0.938 | 0.94 | 0.94 | 0.94 | 987 |
| BIGRU | 0.935 | 0.94 | 0.94 | 0.94 | 1262 |
| BERT | 0.949 | 0.95 | 0.95 | 0.95 | 21190 |

In contrast, the BILSTM (Bidirectional Long Short-Term Memory) and BIGRU (Bidirectional Gated Recurrent Unit) models demonstrated considerably shorter execution times, ranging from 900 to 1,300 s, or approximately 15 to 20 min. Despite their relatively quicker processing times, both models achieved commendable results, with BILSTM recording an Accuracy of 93.8% and BIGRU achieving 93.5%. Furthermore, both models maintained a consistent Precision, Recall, and F1-score of 94%, showcasing their capability as viable alternatives to the BERT model while still operating within the realm of deep learning methodologies.

If the scope of the evaluation were to be broadened to encompass traditional machine learning models, the Support Vector Machine (SVM) would emerge as a noteworthy candidate. The SVM model attained an Accuracy of 94.5%, positioning it as the second most accurate model in our analysis. Additionally, it mirrored the Precision, Recall, and F1scores of the bi-directional models, each standing at 94%. A significant advantage of the SVM model lies in its exceptional computational efficiency, as it completed its run in less than 250 s, or approximately 4 min. This characteristic makes the SVM the fastest and least resource-dependent model examined in this project, making it an attractive option for applications requiring rapid processing times, along with the confusion matrix results showed in Table 2.

**Table 2.** Confusion Metric Results

| Models: | | | Predicted | |
|---|---|---|---|---|
| | | | *Predicted Positive* | *Predicted Negative* |
| SVM | *Actual* | *Actual Positive* | *4982* | *292* |
| | | *Actual Negative* | *300* | *5097* |
| BILSTM | *Actual* | *Actual Positive* | *3436* | *84* |
| | | *Actual Negative* | *300* | *3294* |
| BIGRU | *Actual* | *Actual Positive* | *3401* | *119* |
| | | *Actual Negative* | *340* | *3254* |
| BERT | *Actual* | *Actual Positive* | *3454* | *141* |
| | | *Actual Negative* | *112* | *1180* |

Although the study shows strong results, there are still several directions for future improvement. One limitation lies in the use of VADER-based labeling, which, when used independently, may cause bias or misclassification in cases of sarcasm or nuanced language. Incorporating manual annotation or multi-labeling strategies in future work could make the labeling process more consistent and reliable. Additionally, since the dataset is limited to YouTube comments, expanding it to include platforms such as TikTok or other social media sites could improve the diversity and generalizability of the findings. Lastly, while this study acknowledges the computational expense of BERT, future work could focus on optimization and deployment feasibility, such as experimenting with lighter models or fine-tuning techniques to make real-time implementation more practical.

## 6 Conclusion

In this paper, we proposed a cyberbullying detection system primarily designed to detect cyberbullying within YouTube comments. We started by using 'YouTube Data API v3' to scrape all our initial data, followed by data cleaning and sentiment analysis to properly label the data for model use. The models we used for this research project were SVM (Support Vector Machine), BILSTM (Bidirectional Long Short-Term Memory), BIGRU (Bi-Directional Gated Recurrent Units), and BERT (Bidirectional Encoder Representations from Transformers).

One key limitation found during this project is the overall availability of different social media data. Considering that YouTube had the most accessible data, this project could be expanded greatly. Another primary source that can be investigated would be TikTok. Given enough time for data collection, TikTok could prove to be a very useful source, given that most users are of the younger generations and comments are mostly unfiltered. The daily use of social media is still growing, and cyberbullying is still a major issue in today's society. With the help of AI and Deep learning, we hope that this paper can serve as a resource for starting any possible solutions to reduce cyberbullying and prevent any further harm.

# References


1. Garett, R., Lord, L.R., Young, S.D.: Associations between social media and cyberbullying: a review of the literature. Mhealth **19**(2), 46 (2016). https://doi.org/10.21037/mhealth.2016. 12.01.PMID:28293616;PMCID:PMC5344141

2. Chan, T.K.H., Cheung, C.M.K., Lee, Z.W.Y.: Cyberbullying on social networking sites: a literature review and future research directions. Inform. Manage. **58**(2), 103411 (2021). https:// doi.org/10.1016/j.im.2020.103411

3. Pandey, B., Sharma, S.: Prevalence of cyberbullying on social media: a review. In: 26th Conference, vol. 26, pp. 58–66 (2022)

4. Kumar, R., Bhat, A.A.: A study of machine learning-based models for detection, control, and mitigation of cyberbullying in online social media. Int. J. Inf. Secur. **21**, 1409–1431 (2022). https://doi.org/10.1007/s10207-022-00600-y

5. Jahan, M.S., Oussalah, M., Beddia, D.R., Mim, J.K., Arhab, N.: A comprehensive study on NLP data augmentation for hate speech detection: legacy methods, BERT, and LLMs, University of Oulu, CMVS, BP 4500, 90014, Finland; LUT University, Computational Engineering, 53850, Finland (2022)

6. Iwendi, C., Srivastava, G., Khan, S., et al.: Cyberbullying detection solutions based on deep learning architectures. Multimedia Syst. **29**, 1839–1852 (2023). https://doi.org/10.1007/s00 530-020-00701-5

7. Al-Garadi, M.A., et al.: Predicting cyberbullying on social media in the big data era using machine learning algorithms: review of literature and open challenges. IEEE Access **7**, 70701–70718 (2019). https://doi.org/10.1109/ACCESS.2019.2918354

8. Muneer, A., Alwadain, A., Ragab, M.G., Alqushaibi, A.: Cyberbullying detection on social media using stacking ensemble learning and enhanced BERT. Information **14**(8), 467 (2023). https://doi.org/10.3390/info14080467

9. Yao, M., Chelmis, C., Zois, D.-S.: Cyberbullying ends here: towards robust detection of cyberbullying in social media. In: Proceedings of the 2019 ACM Conference, San Francisco, CA, USA, May 13–17, 2019, pp. 1–7. ACM, New York, NY, USA (2019). https://doi.org/10. 1145/3308558.3313462

10. Van Hee, C., et al.: Automatic detection of cyberbullying in social media text, PLOS ONE, published October 8 (2018). https://doi.org/10.1371/journal.pone.0203794

11. Kumar, Y., et al.: Bias and cyberbullying detection and data generation using transformer artificial intelligence models and top large language models. Electronics **13**(17), 3431 (2024). https://doi.org/10.3390/electronics13173431

12. Vanpech, P., Peerabenjakul, K., Suriwong, N., Fugkeaw, S.: Detecting cyberbullying on social networks using language learning model. In: 2024 16th International Conference on Knowledge and Smart Technology (KST), pp. 161–166. Krabi, Thailand (2024). https://doi.org/10. 1109/KST61284.2024.10499678

13. Murshed, B.A.H., Abawajy, J., Mallappa, S., Saif, M.A.N., Al-Ariki, H.D.E.: DEA-RNN: a hybrid deep learning approach for cyberbullying detection in twitter social media platform. IEEE Access **10**, 1–7 (2022). https://doi.org/10.1109/ACCESS.2022.3153675

14. Van Bruwaene, D., Huang, Q., Inkpen, D.: A multi-platform dataset for detecting cyberbullying in social media. Lang. Resour. Eval. **54**, 851–874 (2020). https://doi.org/10.1007/s10 579-020-094883

15. Raj, M., Singh, S., Solanki, K., et al.: An application to detect cyberbullying using machine learning and deep learning techniques. SN Comput. Sci. **3**(401) (2022). https://doi.org/10. 1007/s42979-02201308-5

16. Bozyigit, A., Utku, S., Nasibov, E.: Cyberbullying detection: Utiliz-˘ing social media features. Expert Syst. Appl. **179**, 115001 (2021). https://doi.org/10.1016/j.eswa.2021.115001

17. Scikit-learn developers. sklearn.svm.SVC, Scikit-learn documentation (2025). https://scikit learn.org/stable/modules/generated/sklearn.svm.SVC.html
18. Papers with Code. BiLSTM, Papers with Code, Image (2025). https://paperswithcode.com/method/bilstm
19. Duan, Y., Liu, Y., Wang, Y., Ren, S., Wang, Y.: Improved BIGRU model and its application in stock price forecasting. Electronics **12**(12), 2718 (2023). https://doi.org/10.3390/electronics12122718
20. Brownlee, J.: BERT explained: State of the art language model for NLP, Towards Data Science, Oct. 15, 2019. https://towardsdatascience.com/bert-explained-state-ofthe-art-language-model-for-nlp-f8b21a9b6270
21. IBM, Support Vector Machine, IBM Think, Image. https://www.ibm.com/think/topics/support-vector-machine
22. Patchin, J.W., Hinduja, S.: 2023 cyberbullying data. Cyberbullying Research Center (2024). https://cyberbullying.org/2023-cyberbullyingdata

# CL-PPIIMS: A Cognitive Load-Based Privacy-Preserving Intelligent Interruption Management System

Moritz Maleck[iD] and Tom Gross[✉][iD]

Human-Computer Interaction Group, University of Bamberg, 96045 Bamberg, Germany
hci@uni-bamberg.de

**Abstract.** Managing interruptions effectively is a key challenge in modern work environments, as poorly timed disruptions during periods of high cognitive load can severely reduce team productivity and individual focus. While Intelligent Interruption Management Systems aim to solve this by assessing user states, they often face a critical trade-off between the precision of physiological sensing and the imperative of user privacy. We introduce CL-PPIIMS, a system built on a privacy-preserving architecture that resolves this conflict by applying Soft Computing principles—specifically, classifying imprecise cognitive states from noisy physiological data—to enhance Human-Computer Interaction. It leverages a stationary eye tracker for high-fidelity cognitive load data but performs all sensitive computations strictly on the user's local machine. Only a highly abstracted, non-identifiable classification of the user's state is then transmitted via Bluetooth Low Energy (BLE) to a mobile client, enabling an intelligent, privacy-aware management of team-based communication requests that enhances productivity without compromising user data sovereignty.

**Keywords:** Effortless Coordination · Team Meetings · Arrangements · Interruptions · Interruption Management Systems · Cognitive Load · Eye Tracking · Privacy by Design · Bluetooth Low Energy (BLE)

## 1 Introduction

Interruptions—such as private notifications from messengers, or in-persona interruptions during work—impede primary tasks, leading to longer completion times and a reduction in both accuracy and efficiency of work [15, 30, 38]. While the disruptive nature of interruptions is well-documented, it can also yield positive effects, such as fostering creativity or enhancing social connections [15, 37]. The process of managing an interruption involves several distinct stages, from the initial notification to engagement with the secondary task and the subsequent effort to resume the original work [34]. The degree of disruption is influenced by factors such as the complexity of the interruption and its similarity to the ongoing task [11]. This effect is particularly pronounced when an interruption exhibits high complexity and bears little resemblance to the primary activity.


K. K. Patel et al. (Eds.): icSoftComp 2025, CCIS 2874, pp. 405–417, 2026.
https://doi.org/10.1007/978-3-032-22062-2_31

A consistent finding in related research is that interruptions are more harmful when they happen during periods of high cognitive load [3, 30]. Cognitive load, which refers to the mental effort engaged in working memory to complete a task, has consequently become a key predictor of a user's receptiveness to interruption [3]. In response, a variety of Interruption Management Systems (IMS) have been created to optimise the timing of notifications and minimise their disruptive effects. Some of those systems infer cognitive load from consumer wearables to signal a user's availability [30], while alternative approaches use workload-aligned task models to identify opportune moments for interruption [17]. These methods, however, often present a dilemma: systems relying on simple, indirect measurements may not be precise enough, whereas those using direct physiological sensors introduce substantial privacy risks if they necessitate transmitting sensitive data to a central server for analysis.

Eye tracking, specifically the measurement of pupil diameter, has been established as an effective and reliable technique for the real-time assessment of cognitive load [10, 39]. The pupil's tendency to dilate in response to heightened mental effort, a phenomenon called the Task-Evoked Pupillary Response (TEPR), offers a direct insight into a user's cognitive state [4]. While this technique provides high precision, it also produces a continuous stream of sensitive biometric data, making its secure handling a primary design consideration.

A common software architectural pattern for analysing complex physiological data relies on a server-centric model, where the user has no direct control over their raw data. A key reason for this approach is the high computational demand of many machine-learning algorithms, which often requires outsourcing the processing logic to powerful central servers. For example, the work of Afzal *et al.* [1] describes a system where EEG data is transmitted to a server for classification using a deep neural network.

This pattern is also prevalent in other areas of physiological monitoring. Systems presented by Jeong *et al.* [19] and Chang *et al.* [6] demonstrate a typical workflow where data from physiological sensors are forwarded to a mobile device, which then acts as a gateway to a cloud server for detailed analysis.

With respect to such sensitive biometric data, correct handling requires the implementation of the principle of data minimisation, as outlined in frameworks like 'Privacy by Design' by Cavoukian [5]—ensuring that raw data remains entirely under the user's local control and only highly abstracted, non-identifiable information is ever transmitted, thereby significantly reducing the risk of misuse. An approach that preserves user privacy and data control by performing all calculations on a local device and only transmitting highly abstracted data represents a novel contribution to the field.

This paper introduces CL-PPIIMS (pronounced 'CL-Pims'), a novel concept and system engineered to resolve this precision-privacy trade-off. Our work leverages a privacy-preserving architecture to make the following key contributions:

- A novel, distributed Intelligent Interruption Management System (IIMS)—the CL-PPIIMS—designed to optimise the timing of interruptions in the desk work context. The system features a cognitive load calculation station that processes eye-tracking data strictly on the user's local machine. In line with the principle of data minimisation, it transmits only a highly abstracted classification of the user's state via Bluetooth Low Energy (BLE) to their mobile iOS device. The mobile application, in turn, forwards this classification to a central server, which manages the timing of interruptions in means of communication requests within a work team.

- A hybrid architecture for managing interruptions that combines the high precision of stationary, research-grade eye tracking with a robust 'privacy by design' processing model. All sensitive data analysis is performed strictly on a user's local machine, ensuring raw biometric data never leaves their control.
- A flexible and scalable system that can be easily integrated with existing workplace tools to facilitate less disruptive communication within the work domain.

To the best of our knowledge, we are the first to introduce an IIMS that uses cognitive-load-based eye tracking in a privacy-preserving architecture designed for mobile integration. The structure of this article is as follows: first, we provide an overview of related work. Then, we present our CL-PPIIMS concept, followed by a description of its implementation. Finally, we conclude with an outlook for future work.

## 2   Related Work

The background for our work includes research on interruptions in the workplace, cognitive load theory and its measurement via pupilometer, and architectures for physiological computing.

### 2.1   Interruptions and Interruption Management

Interruptions disrupt primary tasks, increasing task completion time and affecting accuracy and efficiency [15]. This is especially true in team settings, where collaborative processes can be delayed, affecting the performance of the entire team [13, 15]. The degree of disruption is further influenced by factors such as the complexity of the interruption and its similarity to the ongoing task [11]. Yet, interruptions also yield positive effects, such as fostering creativity or strengthening social connections [15]. The key challenge for IMS is therefore to balance the right moment of delivering interruptions to minimise negative effects and maximise positive effects.

To signal availability in co-located work environments, individuals often rely on social cues, such as maintaining an open or closed office door [30]. These physical cues are not applicable in remote or hybrid settings, which have become more prevalent. The trend towards working from home has introduced new challenges, including an increase in non-work interruptions and a shift in collaboration patterns [23, 35]. In digital tools setting a personal availability status such as 'Do Not Disturb' (DND) offers some control but is limited; users may forget to activate them or may configure them too permissively, fearing they will miss critical information [14, 18]. Recent research highlights that users adopt distinct strategies for managing digital notifications, categorisable as 'proactive' or 'reactive' [27]. Proactive users actively manage settings but can still feel overwhelmed, while reactive users often apply no strategies (and may be more susceptible to constant disruption) [27]. Moreover, users often prefer to suppress an alert (i.e., silent delivery) rather than defer it, e.g., because of fear of missing out [24].

To overcome these limitations, more advanced IMS aim to automate the process of finding opportune moments. Some systems use physiological data from consumer wearables (e.g., heart rate variability, skin conductance) to estimate cognitive load and signal a user's availability via a physical light display [12, 30]. Others analyse task structure to deliver interruptions at natural breakpoints, such as the boundaries between subtasks, where cognitive load is demonstrably lower [3]. Other approaches infer interruptibility from different modalities; e.g., through the usage of speech recognition to detect lexical affirmation cues (like 'got it'), naturally signalling task completion in collaborative settings [31]. Other related interruption management systems mediate communication requests by assessing cognitive load leveraging on the pupil diameter to find moments of low cognitive load for border-crossing between life domains [26], arranging meetings within teams [25], or timing of interruptions in a single user scenario with an email-answering task [21].

## 2.2  Cognitive Load and Pupilometer

Cognitive Load Theory (CLT) posits that working memory has a limited capacity, and that effective instruction or interface design should minimise extraneous load to free up resources for learning and problem-solving [32]. Eye tracking has proven to be a highly effective, non-invasive method for measuring cognitive load in real time [10, 39]. The pupil diameter is a particularly reliable indicator because it cannot be consciously controlled and is tightly coupled with cognitive processes [4, 7, 10, 40].

This coupling is rooted in the autonomic nervous system (ANS). Increased mental effort activates the sympathetic nervous system (SNS), a process modulated by the Locus Coeruleus-Norepinephrine (LC-NE) system, which in turn causes the pupil to dilate [33, 36]. This neurophysiological link is fundamental, as the LC-NE system actively optimises performance by regulating 'neural gain'—a process that amplifies task-relevant information while suppressing distractors [16]. The Task-Evoked Pupillary Response (TEPR) is a robust measure of cognitive load [4]. However, the pupil also constricts in response to light—known as the Pupillary Light Reflex (PLR). The PLR is the primary challenge for cognitive pupilometer, as its effect on pupil size is orders of magnitude larger than the subtle changes induced by cognitive load, masking the signal of interest [22, 28]. Pupil diameter vary up to 7.5 mm due to light changes, and only up to 0.5 mm due to cognitive load changes [10].

To address this, advanced frequency-domain metrics have been developed. The Index of Pupillary Activity (IPA) uses a wavelet transformation to count high-frequency pupil oscillations, which are assumed to reflect cognitive activity, while filtering out low-frequency changes associated with ambient light [9]. A more recent and robust evolution is the Low/High Index of Pupillary Activity (LHIPA) [8]. Instead of just counting high-frequency events, LHIPA computes the ratio of energy in the low-frequency bands to the high-frequency bands [8, 29]. This ratio-based approach is more closely tied to the underlying push-pull dynamic of the ANS. LHIPA has been shown to be more effective than IPA at detecting cognitive load in several contexts, particularly in less restrictive tasks [8].

### 2.3 Privacy-Preserving Physiological Computing

The use of sensitive physiological data necessitates architectures that prioritise user privacy. The common approach in mobile health and other fields is to send sensor data to a powerful cloud server for analysis [1, 6, 19]. While this offers high computational power, it creates a central point of failure and a high-value target for data breaches, forcing the user to trust a third-party provider with their most sensitive data.

An alternative paradigm is Edge Computing, which advocates for moving computation closer to the source of data generation [2]. This reduces latency and bandwidth usage while significantly improving privacy and security by keeping data local. Such an approach is a direct implementation of the 'Privacy by Design' framework, which mandates that privacy be built into a system's architecture from the outset, rather than being added as an afterthought [5]. Conceptually, this is related to Federated Learning, where machine learning models are trained on local user data without the raw data ever being shared with a central server [20].

In the next section we introduce our concept for providing real-time cognitive-load data in a privacy-preserving way by sending abstracted classifications via Bluetooth Low Energy to mobile phone devices, which are then using these in the context of an intelligent interruption management system—our CL-PPIIMS.

## 3   A Concept for a Privacy-Preserving Mobile Cognitive Load-Based Intelligent Interruption Management System

We introduce CL-PPIIMS, an approach for supporting less disruptive interruptions by means of meeting requests within a work team, determining opportune moments based on the user's cognitive load. The system is designed upon a multi-tiered architecture separating concerns to maximise both measurement precision and user privacy. This architecture acts as a 'privacy firewall', abstracting sensitive information at each stage to ensure that only the necessary, non-identifiable data is transmitted across systems.

The CL-PPIIMS concept is realised through a four-tiered architecture managing the flow of information from raw physiological signals to actionable interruption management decisions. It contains local, high-fidelity sensing and processing to ensure data quality and privacy; efficient, abstracted state transmission to mobile devices; and a flexible application logic handled by clients and a backend server.

**Tier 1: High-Fidelity Local Sensing With Eye Tracking.** The first tier contains a stationary eye tracker, equipped with at a local user's workstation. A stationary tracker is inherently less invasive in a professional context, as it does not need to be worn, causes physical discomfort, or needs to be managed by the user throughout the day. Instead, it integrates seamlessly into the existing work environment, operating unobtrusively in the background for many hours without restriction. Still, this user-centric setup concurrently provides ideal conditions for high-fidelity data acquisition, allowing high precision for the data input.

**Tier 2: Local Cognitive Load Assessment.** All computationally intensive and privacy-sensitive analysis is performed in this tier, entirely on a separate local PC in the pure control of the user, serving as *Cognitive Load Calculation Station*. This can be a low-budget, affordable Windows PC (e.g., the Gazepoint GP3 eye tracker only requires a Windows 10/11 PC with at least Intel Core i5 2022 or newer, and 8 GB RAM at the time of writing this article). A service, the *Cognitive Load Calculation Service*, ingests the raw pupil diameter stream from any connected eye tracker (support for various manufacturers— Tobii and Gazepoint—is implemented). It ingests the raw pupil diameter stream and executes a pipeline including a feature extraction method inspired by the Low/High Index of Pupillary Activity (LHIPA). To meet the demands of a real-time system by reducing computationally expensive calculations, our approach uses a modified version that focuses on the energy ratio between the low and high-frequency components of the pupillary signal. This local processing model is the cornerstone of the system's privacy guarantee. By confining the raw biometric data to a local, offline operating machine in control of the user, the risk of unauthorised disclosure or misuse by third parties is minimised. The user retains absolute data sovereignty over their most sensitive information.

**Tier 3: Abstracted State Transmission via BLE.** Once the cognitive load has been processed, the system performs a critical data abstraction and minimisation step by classifying the detailed cognitive load and responding raw data into a discrete state (i.e., 'Low', 'Medium', 'High'). Only this final, non-biometric classification is provided to the *Cognitive Load Classification BLE Sender* to act as Bluetooth Low Energy (BLE) peripheral. BLE is a low-power, secure, and ubiquitous protocol ideal for broadcasting small amounts of data over short distances. This design elegantly circumvents the problem of transmitting high-bandwidth eye-tracking data wirelessly.

**Tier 4: Mobile Application Logic.** The *Intelligent Interruption Management System Client Application* on the user's mobile iOS device acts as a BLE central, continuously listening for the cognitive load state broadcast by the cognitive load calculation station. A key function of the client application is to enhance team awareness by translating the received data into a visible status for colleagues, which acts as a digital social cue. This status can reflect several states (cf. Fig. 1): 'Working/Not at desk' if the client is not connected via BLE, 'Working (Eye Tracker Data Unavailable)' if the connection exists but no valid eye-tracking data is received, or a specific cognitive load level ('Low', 'Medium', 'High') when data is available. This awareness information allows colleagues to make more considerate decisions about interrupting other colleagues even when not initiating meeting requests through the provided system, discouraging them from interrupting a team member who is currently experiencing a high or medium cognitive load. In parallel to providing this visual cue, the iOS client relays the cognitive load classification to a central backend server—the *Intelligent Interruption Management System Server*—via a standard HTTPS request. The backend server is responsible for the final application logic. It manages a priority queue of pending meeting requests from colleagues, using the received cognitive load status to decide when to release them based on their priority, while ignoring users with invalid eye tracking data or not connected to the BLE sender (e.g., because not being at the work desk). For example, it delivers high-priority requests during a 'Medium' load state, while holding all non-urgent requests until the user's status changes to 'Low'. This final tier provides flexibility and allows leveraging the cognitive load information without accessing the underlying physiological data.

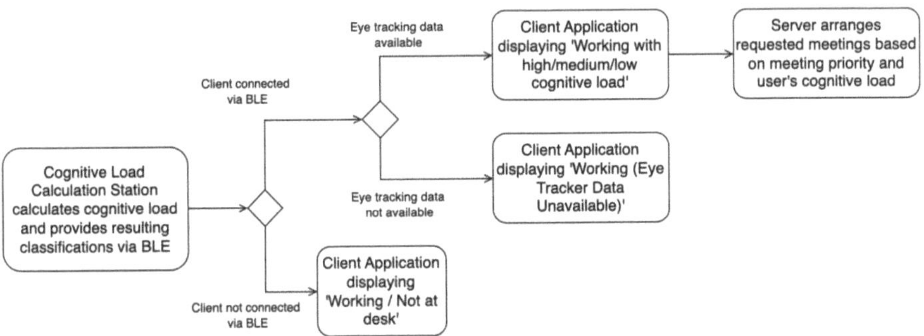


**Fig. 1.** Schematic representation of the client application's state logic. The displayed user status depends on the BLE connection and the availability of eye-tracking data, serving as social awareness information (a social cue) for team members. Meeting requests are only processed for users with an available cognitive load classification.

This tiered approach ensures a clear separation of concerns, leveraging the best technology for each task: precision hardware for sensing, local compute for privacy-preserving analysis, BLE for efficient wireless communication, and standard mobile/backend technologies for application logic.

In the next section, we present the implementation of our CL-PPIIMS system, containing a cognitive load calculation station, a mobile iOS client application and a backend server application to manage interruptions between registered users.

## 4  CL-PPIIMS Implementation

In this section, we describe the implementation and functionality of the CL-PPIIMS system. The implementation consists of three main components: a Windows-based cognitive load calculation station, a native mobile client application for iOS, and a backend server for managing interruption requests. Each component was developed to adhere to the conceptual design outlined earlier, focusing on privacy-by-design, real-time cognitive load assessment, and seamless integration into a typical desk-based work environment.

### 4.1  System Overview

We implemented the CL-PPIIMS system using a distributed client-server architecture (cf. Fig. 2). The core of the system is the Cognitive Load Calculation Station, a Windows 10 PC (Intel Core i5-8500T, 8 GB RAM) connected to a Gazepoint GP3 eye tracker (GP3V2). This station runs several services developed in Python (versions 3.10.11 and 3.13.5) for data acquisition and calculation, and a.NET (SDK version 9.0.302) application for BLE broadcasting. The Intelligent Interruption Management System Client Application is a native iOS 18.5 application running on an iPhone 16e. The final component, the Intelligent Interruption Management System Server, operates on a Node.js (version 23.5.0) server. This architecture facilitates a one-way flow of cognitive load data from the local station to the client, and bi-directional communication for managing meeting requests between the client and the server.

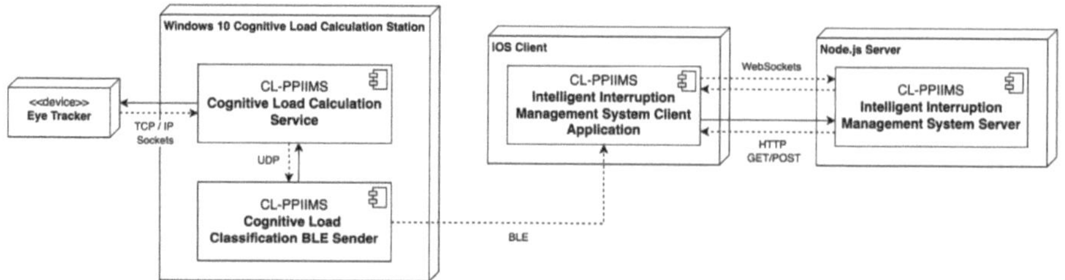

**Fig. 2.** System overview of CL-PPIIMS, showing the local calculation station, the iOS client, and the backend server.

## 4.2  Cognitive Load Calculation Station

The Windows 10 station is the privacy-centric core of the system. Its sole purpose is to calculate a user's cognitive load locally and broadcast an abstracted classification. Upon startup, a batch script initiated by the Windows Task Scheduler first launches the Gazepoint Control software (v7.0.0), followed by our eye tracker connection service, the calculation service, and finally the.NET BLE sender. For the first five minutes of operation, the system collects pupilometry data to establish a robust rolling baseline for its calculations. After this initialisation phase, it begins to calculate and broadcast cognitive load classifications in real time. Our experience shows that a single eye tracker is sufficient for a dual-monitor setup, as the calculation relies only on pupil diameter, which can be reliably measured even when the user is looking at a mobile device in front of their monitors.

## 4.3  IOS Client Application

The iOS client application is the primary user interface for the system. When first launching the app, the user is asked to grant permissions for notifications and for finding nearby Bluetooth devices. They then connect to a working space by providing their name, a planned quitting time, the name of their local BLE sending device, and the URL for the backend server. If the user starts the app after their specified quitting time has passed, a message informs them that they have been automatically logged out. The quitting time is used by the server to automatically remove users from the active pool, preventing meetings from being scheduled after the end of their workday.

Once connected, the app's main screen (cf. Fig. 3A) displays the user's own status, including their current cognitive load classification received via BLE. A key feature of the main screen is the 'Colleagues' list, which provides team awareness by showing the real-time status of other active users. This functions as a digital social cue, allowing users to respect their colleague' current workload; for example, they can see if a colleague is experiencing medium or high cognitive load and decide against a physical interruption.

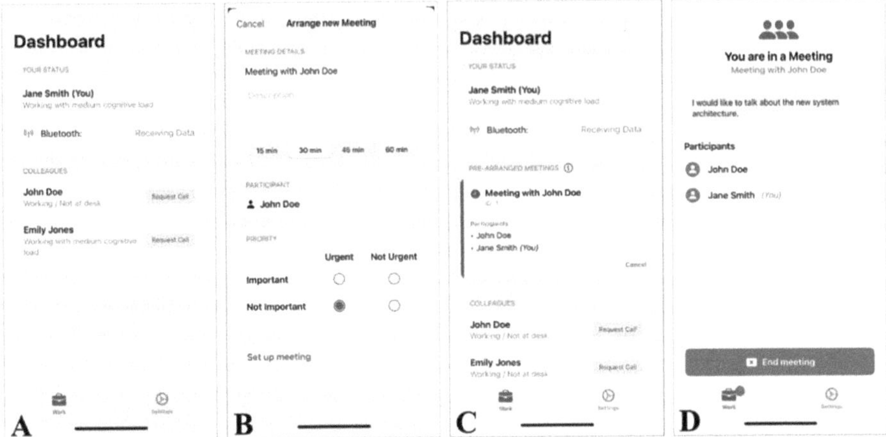

**Fig. 3.** Screenshots of the CL-PPIIMS Intelligent Interruption Management System Client Application implemented as an application for iOS. (A) Main screen of the application, showing the own cognitive load classification and other connected colleagues and their cognitive load classifications. (B) Screen to set up a meeting request, providing a title, an optional description and a priority. (C) Main screen with pre-arranged (i.e., pending) meeting requests listed. (D) Screen informing about initiated meeting by the backend server after opening the app via the sent out push notification.

From the main screen, users can initiate 1:1 meeting requests with their colleagues. The 'Arrange new Meeting' screen (cf. Fig. 3B) allows the user to specify a title, description, estimated duration, and a priority for the meeting. The priority is defined on a two-axis scale: 'Important/Not Important' and 'Urgent/Not Urgent'. Once a meeting request is set up, it appears in the 'Pre-arranged Meetings' section on the main screen, where the user has the possibility to cancel it again (cf. Fig. 3C).

When the server determines an opportune moment and initiates a meeting, the participants receive a push notification via the Apple Push Notification service. The app then transitions to an active meeting screen (cf. Fig. 3D), which shows the meeting details and participants. To ensure the system knows when users are available again, one of the participants has to manually end the meeting within the app.

### 4.4  Intelligent Interruption Management Server

The backend server is implemented in Node.js and acts as the central coordinator for all meeting requests. It maintains a real-time list of all active users and their current cognitive load classifications, as relayed by their respective iOS clients. The server's primary logic is to process the queue of pending meeting requests based on both the request's priority and the cognitive load of all participants.

The decision-making logic is as follows:

- A meeting classified as 'Important and Urgent' can be initiated if all participants have a 'High', 'Medium', or 'Low' cognitive load.
- A meeting classified as 'Important and Not Urgent' or 'Not Important and Urgent' will only be initiated if all participants have a 'Medium' or 'Low' cognitive load.

- A meeting classified as 'Not Important and Not Urgent' requires all participants to be in a 'Low' cognitive load state.

Furthermore, a meeting can only be initiated if all participants have a status that indicates they are at their desk and available (i.e., their status is not 'Working/Not at desk' or 'Eye Tracker Data Unavailable'). Communication between the iOS clients and the server is handled via a combination of bi-directional WebSockets for real-time status updates and standard HTTP GET/POST requests for actions like setting up or cancelling meetings.

## 5  Summary and Outlook

We introduced CL-PPIIMS as a novel system designed to optimise interruptions within a work team by scheduling meeting requests based on real-time cognitive load assessments. By aligning the timing of interruptions with moments of lower cognitive load, this approach aims to minimise disruption during demanding tasks while enhancing team awareness and productivity. The system's design, including its privacy-preserving architecture with local data processing, a dedicated cognitive load calculation station, and a mobile client for providing social cues, demonstrates its potential to balance productivity with user privacy and data sovereignty. The implementation shows the feasibility of combining high-precision, stationary eye tracking with a mobile, flexible interruption management framework.

However, limitations such as the dependency on a stationary eye tracker and the potential for environmental factors like changing light conditions to influence the data suggest room for improvement. The system's reliance on a stationary eye tracker confines its use to a single workstation; future work may explore extending its functionality to mobile contexts, for instance by enriching the system with the integration of data from consumer wearables when the user is away from their desk. Future work could focus on addressing these limitations through a comprehensive, long-term user study to evaluate the system's impact on productivity and user satisfaction in real-world scenarios. Another key development could be the enhancement of the server-side decision logic to learn user preferences over time, and the potential integration of group meeting functionalities beyond the current 1:1 implementation. Moreover, the current logic, which requires all participants to be simultaneously below a cognitive load threshold, could lead to impractical waiting times and thus reduce user acceptance, necessitating more flexible options such as defining optional attendees. Furthermore, one could explore additional factors influencing interruptibility, such as integrating with user calendars to account for scheduled commitments. These enhancements could aim to increase the system's robustness, intelligence, and versatility, potentially improving its broader applicability across diverse professional contexts.

An important next step apart from new integrations is a comprehensive evaluation of the tool, preferably a real-world *in-situ* evaluation (i.e., not in a lab); such a study would provide the necessary results for a detailed discussion, critically analysing the system's real-world effectiveness, usability, and user experience to derive both practical implications for workplace settings and theoretical contributions to the field.

Ultimately, CL-PPIIMS represents more than just a tool for interruption management; it serves as a blueprint for a future generation of human-centred adaptive systems. The architectural principles of local processing, data minimisation, and user sovereignty are critical for building trust in systems that interact with our most sensitive physiological data. As technology becomes more integrated into our daily lives, the development of systems that can intelligently and respectfully adapt to a user's cognitive state will be paramount. By demonstrating a viable path that reconciles high-fidelity sensing with robust privacy protections, this work contributes to the broader goal of creating technology that not only enhances productivity but also supports user well-being in an increasingly demanding digital world.

**Acknowledgments.** We thank the members of the Cooperative Media Lab at the University of Bamberg. We also thank the anonymous reviewers for insightful comments.

# References


1. Afzal, M.A., Gu, Z., Bukhari, S.U., Afzal, B.: Brainwaves in the cloud: cognitive workload monitoring using deep gated neural network and industrial Internet of Things. Appl. Sci. **14**, 13 (2024)
2. Bablu, T.A., Rashid, M.T.: Edge computing and its impact on real-time data processing for IoT-driven applications. J. Adv. Comput. Syst. **5**(1), 26–43 (2025)
3. Bailey, B.P., Iqbal, S.T.: Understanding changes in mental workload during execution of goal-directed tasks and its application for interruption management. ACM Trans. Comput.-Hum. Interact. **14**(4), 1–28 (2008)
4. Beatty, J.: Task-evoked pupillary responses, processing load, and the structure of processing resources. Psychol. Bull. **91**(2), 276–292 (1982)
5. Cavoukian, A.: Privacy by design: the 7 foundational principles. Inform. Privacy Commission. Ontario Canada **5**(2009), 12 (2009)
6. Chang, C.-S., Wu, T.-H., Wu, Y.-C., Han, C.-C.: Bluetooth-based healthcare information and medical resource management system. Sensors **23**(12), 5389 (2023)
7. Dionisio, D.P., Granholm, E., Hillix, W.A., Perrine, W.F.: Differentiation of deception using pupillary responses as an index of cognitive processing. Psychophysiology **38**(2), 205–211 (2001)
8. Duchowski, A.T., Krejtz, K., Gehrer, N.A., Bafna, T., Bækgaard, P.: The low/high index of pupillary activity. In: Proceedings of the 2020 CHI Conference on Human Factors in Computing Systems (CHI '20), pp. 1–12. Association for Computing Machinery, Honolulu HI, USA (2020)
9. Duchowski, A.T, et al.: The index of pupillary activity: measuring cognitive load vis-à-vis task difficulty with pupil oscillation. In Proceedings of the 2018 CHI Conference on Human Factors in Computing Systems (CHI '18), pp. 1–13. Association for Computing Machinery, Montreal QC, Canada
10. Eckstein, M.K., Guerra-Carrillo, B., Singley, M., Alison, T., Bunge, S.A.: Beyond eye gaze: what else can eyetracking reveal about cognition and cognitive development? Dev. Cogn. Neurosci. **25**, 69–91 (2017)
11. Gillie, T., Broadbent, D.: What makes interruptions disruptive? A study of length, similarity, and complexity. Psychol. Res. **50**(4), 243–250 (1989)

12. Goyal, N., Fussell, S.R.: Intelligent interruption management using electro dermal activity based physiological sensor for collaborative sensemaking. Proc. ACM Interact. Mobile, Wear. Ubiquit. Technol. **1**(3), 1–21 (2017)
13. Gross, T.: Supporting effortless coordination: 25 years of awareness research. Comput. Support. Cooperat. Work **22**, 425–474 (2013)
14. Gross, T., Mueller, A.-L.: NotificationManager: personal boundary management on mobile devices. In: Human-Computer Interaction–INTERACT 2021: 18th IFIP TC 13 International Conference, August 30–September 3, 2021, Proceedings, Part IV 18, pp. 243–261. Springer, Bari, Italy (2021)
15. Gross, T., von Kalben, M.: A literature review on positive and negative effects of interruptions and implications for design. In: Human-Computer Interaction – INTERACT 2023: 19th IFIP TC13 International Conference (York, United Kingdom), pp. 373–379. Springer (2023)
16. Huang, R., Clewett, D.: The locus coeruleus: where cognitive and emotional processing meet the eye. In: Papesh, M.H., Goldinger, S.D. (eds.) Modern Pupillometry, pp. 3–75. Springer, Cham, Switzerland (2024)
17. Iqbal, S.T., Bailey, B.P.: Investigating the effectiveness of mental workload as a predictor of opportune moments for interruption. In: Extended Abstracts on Human Factors in Computing Systems (CHI EA '05), Portland, OR, USA. pp. 1489–1492 (2005)
18. Jarupreechachan, W., Kitchat, K., Surasak, T.: 'Do Not Disturb': an implication design to be alerted but less stress. In: 2023 International Seminar on Application for Technology of Information and Communication (iSemantic) (Semarang, Indonesia), pp. 176–181. IEEE (2023)
19. Jeong, J.-W., Lee, W., Kim, Y.-J.: A real-time wearable physiological monitoring system for home-based healthcare applications. Sensors **22**(1), 104 (2021)
20. Kairouz, P., et al.: Advances and open problems in federated learning. Foundations and Trends® in Machine Learning 14, 1–2. pp. 1–210 (2021)
21. Katidioti, I., et al.: Interrupted by your pupil: an interruption management system based on pupil dilation. Int. J. Hum.-Comput. Interact. **32**(10), 791–801 (2016)
22. Klingner, J., Kumar, R., Hanrahan, P.: Measuring the task-evoked pupillary response with a remote eye tracker. In: Proceedings of the 2008 Symposium on Eye Tracking Research & Applications, pp. 69–72. Association for Computing Machinery, Savannah, Georgia (2008)
23. Leroy, S., Schmidt, A.M., Madjar, N.: Working from home during COVID-19: a study of the interruption landscape. J. Appl. Psychol. **106**(10), 1448 (2021)
24. Li, T., Haines, J.K., Eguino, D., Ruiz, M.F., Hong, J.I., Nichols, J.: Alert now or never: understanding and predicting notification preferences of smartphone users. ACM Trans. Comput.-Hum. Interact. **29**(5), 1–33 (2022)
25. Maleck, M., Gross, T.: TeamMeetingArranger: a less disruptive way of "do you have a minute?". In: Proceedings of 16th International Conference on Intelligent Human Computer Interaction (IHCI 2024), pp. 54–65. Springer, Twente, The Netherlands(2024)
26. Maleck, M., Gross, T.: CLBoundaryManager: a system facilitating boundary management and border crossing between life domains. In: Proceedings of the 17th International Conference on Social Computing and Social Media (SCSM 2025), held as part of the 27th HCI International Conference (HCII 2025), pp. 335–350. Springer, Gothenburg, Sweden (2025)
27. Özdemir, M.C., Mottus, M., Lamas, D.: Echoes of the day: exploring the interplay between daily contexts and smartphone push notification experiences. Appl. Sci. **15**(1), 14 (2024)
28. Pfleging, B., Fekety, D.K., Schmidt, A., Kun, A.L.: A model relating pupil diameter to mental workload and lighting conditions. In: CHI '16: Proceedings of the 2016 CHI Conference on Human Factors in Computing Systems, pp. 5776–5788. San Jose California, USA (2016)
29. Puentes, P.R., et al.: Pupillometry in telerobotic surgery: a comparative evaluation of algorithms for cognitive effort estimation. MedRobot 1 (2023)

30. Schaule, F., Johanssen, J.O., Bruegge, B., Loftness, V.: Employing consumer wearables to detect office workers' cognitive load for interruption management. Proc. ACM Interact. Mobile Wear. Ubiquit. Technol. 2(1), 1–20 (2018)
31. Shivakumar, A., Bositty, A., Peters, N.S,., Pei, Y.: Real-time interruption management system for efficient distributed collaboration in multi-tasking environments. In: Proceedings of the ACM on Human-Computer Interaction 4, CSCW1. p. 39, 1–23 (2020)
32. Sweller, J.: Cognitive load theory, learning difficulty, and instructional design. Learn. Instr. 4(4), 295–312 (1994)
33. Szulewski, A., Kelton, D., Howes, D.: Pupillometry as a tool to study expertise in medicine. Frontline Learn. Res. 5(3), 53–63 (2017)
34. Trafton, J.G., Monk, C.A.: Task interruptions. Rev. Hum. Fact. Ergon. 3(1), 111–126 (2007)
35. Van der Lippe, T., Lippényi, Z.: Co-workers working from home and individual and team performance. New Technol. Work Employm. 35, 1. 60–79 (2020)
36. Van der Wel, P., Van Steenbergen, H.: Pupil dilation as an index of effort in cognitive control tasks: a review. Psychon. Bull. Rev. 25, 6, 2005–2015 (2018)
37. Wei, R., Lo, V.-H.: Staying connected while on the move: cell phone use and social connectedness. New Media Soc. 8(1), 53–72 (2006)
38. Yuan, X., Zhong, L.: Effects of multitasking and task interruptions on task performance and cognitive load: considering the moderating role of individual resilience. Curr. Psychol. 1–11 (2024)
39. Zagermann, J., Pfeil, U., Reiterer, H.: Measuring cognitive load using eye tracking technology in visual computing. In: Proceedings of the Sixth Workshop on Beyond Time and Errors on Novel Evaluation Methods for Visualization (BELIV '16), pp. 78–85. Association for Computing Machinery, Baltimore, MD, USA (2016)
40. Zagermann, J., Pfeil, U., Reiterer, H.: Studying eye movements as a basis for measuring cognitive load. In Extended Abstracts of the 2018 CHI Conference on Human Factors in Computing Systems, pp. 1–6. Montreal QC Canada (2018)

# An Ensemble Machine Learning Based Cyber Attack Detection Framework for IoMT Networks


Moni Kumari[(✉)] and Anugrah Jain

Department of Computer Science and Engineering, Sardar Vallabhbhai National
Institute of Technology, Surat, Gujarat, India
{p23is001,ajain}@coed.svnit.ac.in



**Abstract.** The Internet of Medical Things (IoMT) connects medical devices like heart monitors and insulin pumps to the internet, enhancing healthcare but exposing it to cyber attacks such as Distributed Denial-of-Service (DDoS), Spoofing, and Reconnaissance. This paper proposes a novel ensemble machine learning based cyber attack detection framework to secure IoMT networks from several attacks including rare ones such as spoofing and reconnaissance. Our detection system as proposed in the paper first employ a Convolutional Neural Network (CNN) with Local Interpretable Model-Agnostic Explanations (LIME) to filter irrelevant features from the well-known CICIoMT2024 dataset. Then, a novel ensemble learning based methodology for efficient detection of rare attacks is proposed which combines XGBoost, Random Forest, and LightGBM together and uses Optuna for hyperparameter optimization. Three derived features are also incorporated by our model to enhance system's adaptability for covering rare attacks in IoMT networks.

**Keywords:** Internet of Medical Things · Cyber Attack Detection · Machine Learning · Ensemble Learning


## 1  Introduction

Internet-of-Medical-Things (IoMT) has enabled the development of a world where fitness trackers or health monitors deliver real-time health data to doctors in order to save many lives. The IoMT network is realized using many health care device including pacemakers, blood pressure monitors, insulin pumps etc. These devices collect and share vital health information, enabling faster diagnoses and personalized treatments. As illustrated in Fig. 1, IoMT ecosystems [1] integrate wearable devices on patients, connected through short-range technologies like Bluetooth to mobile devices, which link to Internet infrastructure and servers for data management. However, this integration poses significant security risks due to limited computational resources and constant connectivity, exacerbated by vulnerabilities at distributed attack points across the network [1].



K. K. Patel et al. (Eds.): icSoftComp 2025, CCIS 2874, pp. 418–429, 2026.
https://doi.org/10.1007/978-3-032-22062-2_32

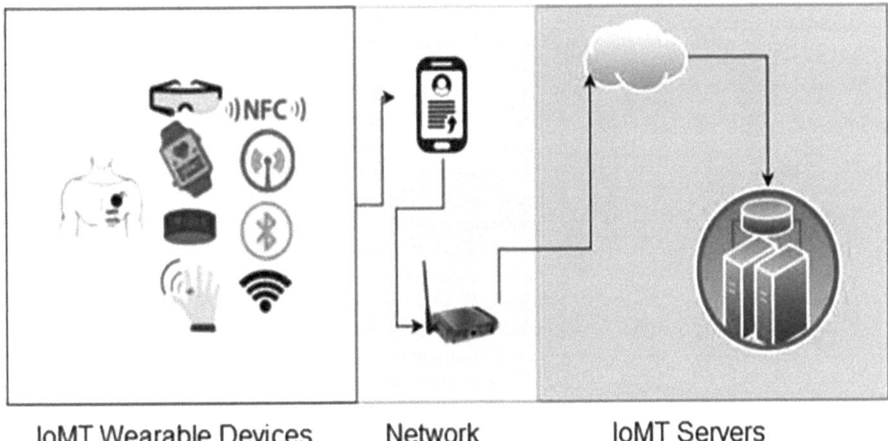


**Fig. 1.** IoMT Network Structure with Wearable Devices and Vulnerabilities [1]

Existing intrusion detection systems (IDS) suffer various issues such as limited transparency which affects doctors' trust on automatic alert-based systems, inefficient detection of rare attacks including spoofing and reconnaissance [2–4]. They also struggle with data imbalance and scalability problems due to various resource constraints of IoMT devices. Their poor precision, recall, and F1-scores for rare attacks show their ineffectiveness for rare attacks. Proposed work addresses this research gap by employing interpretable models for key features selection and development of lightweight models for efficient and computationally inexpensive detection.

Our proposed model tackles in this paper handles these issues challenges and present a better machine learning-based attack classifier for IoMT networks. It leverages a Convolutional Neural Network (CNN) with Local Interpretable Model-Agnostic Explanations (LIME) to perform key features selection. A well known CICIoMT2024 dataset is used for performing proposed classification which is in background based on ensemble technique having XGBoost, Random Forest, and LightGBM at their backend and they are optimized using Optuna to detect both common and rare attacks efficiently. In the classification task, three novel features, i.e., `packet_ratio`, `flow_duration_ratio`, and `packet_size_variance` are incorporated to enhance the detection accuracy. Our major contributions made under this paper are listed as follows.

- **Explainable AI (LIME) for Feature Selection:** We have employed Local Interpretable Model-Agnostic Explanations (LIME) with a Convolutional Neural Network (CNN) to identify and select critical features for proposed classification of cyberattacks in IoMT networks.
- **Ensemble Learning-Based IDS:** An ensemble learning-based IDS is developed which utilizes XGBoost, Random Forest, and LightGBM models in the

background and optimized using Optuna for efficient detection of rare attacks which include spoofing and reconnaissance attacks for IoMT networks.
- **New Features:** For further enhancement of classification task, three novel features are incorporated which helped us in proper coverage of rare attacks.
- **Implementation and Evaluation:** The proposed as well as state-of-the-art approaches are implemented and evaluated in the paper. Our evaluation demonstrates that proposed systems outperforms the state-of-the-art in covering rare attacks which is critical when there is a chance to save one life by a IoMT network.

Our rest of the paper is structured as follows. Section 2 provides background on IoMT networks, their attacks, and existing approaches for detecting attacks happened on IoMT networks. Section 3 presents our proposed work which is divided into five distinct phases. An algorithm is provided there for a better description of proposed methodology. Section 4 provides our implementation details and evaluation results, and Sect. 5 concludes this paper by presenting some directions for future work.

## 2   Background and Related Work

The Internet of Medical Things (IoMT) represents a transformative leap in healthcare, connecting medical devices like wearable sensors and implanted devices to the internet for real-time data sharing. These devices, including pacemakers and glucose monitors, use protocols like MQTT and Bluetooth to communicate efficiently, enabling remote patient monitoring and improved clinical decision-making. However, the proliferation of IoMT networks has expanded the attack surface, necessitating robust security measures.

IoMT networks are characterized by their heterogeneity and resource limitations, with devices ranging from small wearables to sophisticated diagnostic equipment. This diversity, combined with continuous internet connectivity, makes them vulnerable to cyber threats, requiring specialized intrusion detection systems to protect patient data and device functionality.

IoMT networks face various cyberattacks, including Distributed Denial of Service (DDoS), which floods devices with traffic, Spoofing, which injects false data to mislead systems, and Reconnaissance, where attackers probe for weaknesses. These attacks exploit the lightweight protocols and limited security features of IoMT devices, posing risks to patient safety and healthcare operations. For instance, a successful DDoS attack can disrupt critical monitoring systems, while Spoofing can alter medical readings, leading to incorrect treatments.

Several approaches have been explored to detect attacks in IoMT networks, ranging from signature-based methods to anomaly detection using machine learning. Signature-based systems rely on known attack patterns, while anomaly detection identifies deviations from normal behavior, offering potential against unknown threats. Machine learning techniques, such as neural networks and ensemble methods, have gained traction due to their ability to adapt to evolving attack patterns.

**Table 1.** Existing and Proposed Approaches for Intrusion Detection in IoMT Networks

| Study | Year | Dataset | Algorithm | Accuracy | Remarks |
| --- | --- | --- | --- | --- | --- |
| Mohammadi et al. [2] | 2024 | CICIoMT2024 | CNN | 99% | Poor rare attack detection |
| Mohsin & Jony [3] | 2024 | CICIoMT2024 | RF, XGBoost | 99.90% | Poor multiclass, scalability issues |
| Tauqeer et al. [4] | 2022 | WUSTL-EHMS-2020 | Random Forest | 97.9% | Not IoMT-optimized |
| Aljuhani [5] | 2023 | N/A | PSO-DT | 96.56% | High false positives, scalability issues |
| Chen et al. [6] | 2016 | N/A | XGBoost | 95% | Limited rare attack detection |
| Sohail et al. [7] | 2024 | CICIoMT2024 | XGBoost, AdaBoost | 95.01% | Minority class issues |
| Dadkhah et al. [8] | 2024 | CICIoMT2024 | N/A | N/A | Class imbalance |
| Areia et al. [9] | 2024 | IoMT-TrafficData | ML Benchmark | > 90% F1 | Missing CoAP protocol |
| Kondeti & Bahsi [10] | 2024 | N/A | N/A | N/A | Excludes physical attacks |
| Al-Abadi et al. [11] | 2023 | N/A | ERF-ABE | 99% | Limited attack validation |
| Das et al. [12] | 2023 | N/A | N/A | N/A | Implementation challenges |
| Tahir et al. [13] | 2023 | MIMIC | Federated Learning | 93% | Scalability, single dataset |
| Balhareth & Ilyas [14] | 2024 | CICIDS2017 | RF, XGBoost | 98.79% | Binary focus, no IoMT validation |
| Ksibi et al. [15] | 2024 | ECU-IoHT | RF, GB | 99.76% | Scaling issues |
| Dash et al. [16] | 2023 | WUSTL-EHMS-2020 | DCNN | 99.92% | Outdated dataset, scalability |
| Al-Hawawreh et al. [17] | 2019 | Multiple | N/A | 95% | Resource-intensive DL |
| Si-Ahmed et al. [18] | 2025 | Multiple | N/A | 97% | Limited IoMT datasets |
| Martin-Faus et al. [19] | 2024 | N/A | Behavior-based IDS | > 90% F1 | Lacks patient safety focus |
| Rahimi & Zia [20] | 2024 | Custom | Blockchain IDS | 94% | Integration complexity |
| Al-Turjman et al. [21] | 2021 | Multiple | N/A | 98% | High false alarm rates |
| Alalhareth & Hong [22] | 2022 | Custom | Behavior-based IDS | 96% | Limited rare attack focus |
| Hassija et al. [23] | 2019 | IoT Dataset | X-FuseRLSTM | 97% | Needs IoMT validation |
| Swarna Priya et al. [24] | 2020 | Custom | PCA-GWO DNN | 98% | Computational complexity |
| Ravi et al. [25] | 2024 | KDDCup 1999 | CNN, GRU, CatBoost | 99% | Non-IoMT dataset |
| Panagiotou et al. [26] | 2023 | Custom | ANFIS-Fuzzy Tree-GA | High | Limited IoMT validation |
| Hady et al. [27] | 2020 | WUSTL-EHMS-2020 | Network+Biometric IDS | High | Outdated dataset, scalability |
| Rbah et al. [28] | 2022 | Bot-IoT | KNN, SVM, ANN | 96% | Non-IoMT dataset |
| A. Kharwar et al. [29] | 2023 | Custom | Tree-based IDS | 98% | No IoMT validation |
| **Proposed Method** | 2025 | CICIoMT2024 (Balanced) | Ensemble (XGB, RF, LGB) + Optuna | 98% | Interpretable, balanced data, rare attack detection |

Intrusion Detection Systems (IDS) are critical for identifying unauthorized activities in IoMT networks. Network-based IDS monitor traffic for anomalies, while host-based IDS focus on individual device behavior. The integration of machine learning into IDS improves their ability to detect sophisticated attacks by learning from historical data, making them suitable for the dynamic IoMT environment.

A well-designed IDS must balance accuracy and resource usage, as IoMT devices often have limited processing power. Recent advancements incorporate explainability features, allowing healthcare providers to understand detection decisions, which is vital for trust and regulatory compliance in medical settings.

Mohammadi et al. [2] proposed a CNN-based IDS achieving 99% accuracy on CICIoMT2024 but struggled with Spoofing (27% precision). Tauqeer et al. [4] used Random Forest with 97.9% accuracy on WUSTL-EHMS-2020, yet it lacked IoMT optimization. Other works, like Chen et al. [6] which is using XGBoost for health monitoring highlights the need for ensemble methods and real-time adaptability.

Table 1 provides a comprehensive comparison of existing IDS approaches, evaluating their accuracy and limitations across a broad spectrum of techniques. This table includes deep learning models like CNNs and DCNNs and innovative approaches like PSO-DT and X-FuseRLSTM. Many of these methods, such as Mohammadi's CNN and Dash's DCNN, achieve high accuracies (up to 99.92%) on common attacks but exhibit significant weaknesses in detecting rare attacks, often due to imbalanced datasets.

The analysis further reveals that while some approaches, such as Mohsin and Jony's RF-XGBoost combination and Ksibi et al.'s RF-GB model, offer high accuracy (99.90% and 99.76%, respectively), they are hampered by scalability issues or poor multiclass performance. Dataset-focused works like Dadkhah et al.'s CICIoMT2024 and review papers by Al-Hawawreh et al. provide valuable foundations but fail to address class imbalance or resource constraints effectively. This comparative overview underscores the limitations of current solutions and highlights the necessity for an ensemble-based IDS that integrates interpretability, balanced data, and optimized performance, as proposed in this study.

Existing IDS solutions for IoMT often lack transparency, making it difficult for doctors to trust and interpret alerts, especially for rare attacks like Spoofing. Current systems also struggle with data imbalance and scalability due to the resource constraints of IoMT devices. This research identifies a critical gap in combining interpretable models, balanced datasets, and lightweight designs to meet the unique needs of IoMT security.

Our proposed intrusion detection system (IDS) for IoMT networks follows a five-phase methodology, addressing data handling, feature refinement, dataset enhancement, model construction, parameter tuning, and performance assessment. Each phase leverages the CICIoMT2024 dataset [8] to build an efficient and effective security solution for IoMT networks.

---

**Algorithm 1.** Ensemble Learning-Based Intrusion Detection System (IDS)

---

1: **Input:** IoMT network traffic data, attack labels
2: **Output:** Predicted attack labels
3: **Phase 1: Data Acquisition and Preprocessing**
4: Load 8.775 million records from CICIoMT2024
5: Collect raw traffic data with 18 attack types across 40 devices
6: Clean data (remove duplicates, fill missing values with median, filter outliers
7: Apply SMOTE and undersampling
8: Normalize features and split into 80% training, 10% validation, 10% testing
9: **Phase 2: Feature Engineering**
10: Train CNN on 45 features
11: Use LIME to retain 18 key features, discarding 27 less relevant ones
12: Add features:

- $\text{packet_ratio} = \dfrac{\text{packet size}}{\text{total size} + 1}$
- $\text{flow_duration_ratio} = \dfrac{\text{duration}}{\text{count} + 1}$
- packet_size_variance: Variance of packet sizes over a rolling window of 5 packets

13: **Phase 3: Ensemble Learning Based Framework**
14: Train: XGBoost (depth 48, 100300 estimators), Random Forest (100200 trees), LightGBM (100300 estimators)
15: Use soft voting with dynamic weights
16: Classify six attack types
17: **Phase 4: Hyperparameter Optimization**
18: Use Optuna with TPE for 20 trials
19: Tune estimators (50300), depth (310), learning rate (0.010.3)
20: Achieve 98% balanced accuracy
21: **Phase 5: Model Validation**
22: Evaluate optimized model on test dataset for six attack types
23: Generate confusion matrix and perform 5-fold cross-validation
24: Compare with CNN baseline, highlighting rare attack performance
25: **Return** Predicted attack labels

---

# 3   Proposed Work

Our proposed intrusion detection system (IDS) for IoMT networks follows a five-phase methodology, addressing data handling, feature refinement, dataset enhancement, model construction, parameter tuning, and performance assessment. Each phase leverages the CICIoMT2024 dataset [8] to build an efficient and effective security solution for IoMT networks.

**Phase 1: Data Acquisition and Preprocessing.** This phase collects 8.775 million records related to 40 IoMT devices from the well-known CICIoMT2024 dataset [8]. The data is then cleaned by filling missing values with medians and removing outliers. Chunks of 0.5% of total size of the dataset are created and 27 non-essential columns are dropped for training purpose. SMOTE is applied for oversampling of rare attacks and under sampling is done for reducing records of some commonly occurred attacks.

**Phase 2: Feature Engineering.** This phase discusses our use of explainable AI for key features selection in proposed model. The baseline convolutional neural network-based model [2] is used with Local Interpretable Model-Agnostic Explanations (LIME) to pinpoint critical attributes. LIME analyzes the CNN's decision-making process to identify 27 irrelevant and 18 most relevant key features. Furthermore, three novel features, i.e., packet ratio, flow duration ratio, and packet size variance are introduced to better detect abnormal traffic patterns, particularly for low-frequency attacks in safety-critical IoMT settings.

**Phase 3: Ensemble Learning Based Framework.** An ensemble learning-based framework is proposed for classification of cyberattacks in IoMT environment. The proposed model combines XGBoost with depth of 48 nodes and 100300 estimators, Random Forest with 100200 trees, and LightGBM with 100300 estimators with soft voting mechanism having dynamic weights classifying six attack types, i.e., Benign, DDoS, DoS, MQTT, Reconnaissance, and Spoofing in an efficient manner.

**Phase 4: Hyperparameter Optimization.** We use Optuna with TPE for hyperparameter optimization parameters where the number of estimators are ranging from 50 to 300, depth is 3 to 10, and learning rate is 0.01 to 0.3 over 20 trials, achieving the 99.59% test accuracy for the complete balanced dataset.

**Phase 5: Model Validation.** The proposed model is tested and evaluated against state-of-the-art CNN-based model [2] in terms of accuracy, precision, recall and f1-score. The proposed model is based on a cohesive five-phase IDS, enhancing IoMT security with a better feature engineering and robust validation.

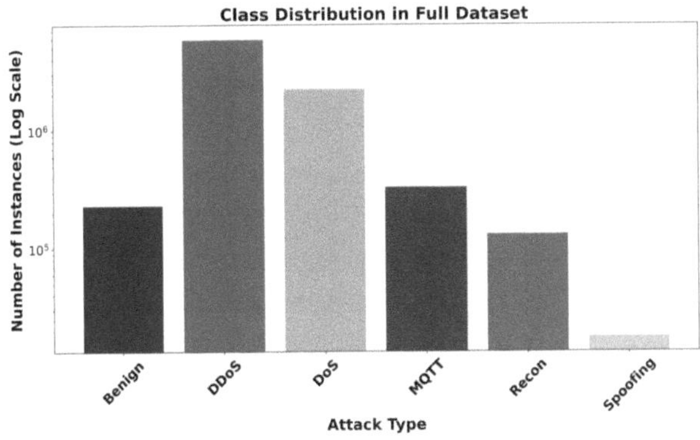


**Fig. 2.** Class Distribution in CICIoMT2024 Dataset [8]

**Table 2.** Selected and Not Selected Features in Proposed Approach

| Category | Details | | | |
|---|---|---|---|---|
| **Attack Classes** | Benign, DDoS, DoS, MQTT, Recon, Spoofing | | | |
| **Selected Features** | – Header_Length | – Tot sum | – Tot size | – Covariance |
| | – Duration | – Min | – IAT | – Variance |
| | – Rate | – Max | – Number | – Weight |
| | – Srate | – AVG | – Magnitue | |
| | – syn_count | – Std | – Radius | |
| **Not Selected Features** | – Drate | – IGMP | – SMTP | – HTTP |
| | – fin_flag_number | – IPv | – SSH | – HTTPS |
| | – syn_flag_number | – LLC | – IRC | – TCP |
| | – rst_flag_number | – ARP | – cwr_flag_number | – UDP |
| | – psh_flag_number | – DHCP | – ack_count | – ICMP |
| | – ack_flag_number | – DNS | – fin_count | – Protocol Type |
| | – ece_flag_number | – Telnet | – rst_count | |

Note: Feature selection is based on LIME which has been applied to the baseline CNN-based approach [2]

**Table 3.** Performance Comparison: CNN Baseline [2] vs. Proposed Model

| Class | Baseline | | | Proposed 1 | | | Proposed 2 | | |
|---|---|---|---|---|---|---|---|---|---|
| | P | R | F | P | R | F | P | R | F |
| Benign | 0.91 | 0.93 | 0.92 | 0.98 | 0.94 | 0.96 | 0.97 | 0.92 | 0.94 |
| DDoS | 1.00 | 1.00 | 0.99 | 1.00 | 1.00 | 1.00 | 1.00 | 1.00 | 1.00 |
| DoS | 1.00 | 1.00 | 1.00 | 1.00 | 1.00 | 1.00 | 1.00 | 1.00 | 1.00 |
| MQTT | 1.00 | 0.98 | 0.99 | 0.98 | 0.99 | 0.98 | 1.00 | 0.99 | 0.99 |
| Recon | 0.99 | 0.92 | 0.96 | 0.99 | 0.96 | 0.97 | 0.99 | 0.95 | 0.97 |
| Spoofing | 0.27 | 0.66 | 0.38 | 0.38 | 1.00 | 0.55 | 0.91 | 1.00 | 0.95 |
| Accuracy | 0.99 | | | 0.995 | | | 0.98 | | |
| Macro Avg | 0.86 | 0.91 | 0.87 | 0.89 | 0.98 | 0.91 | 0.98 | 0.98 | 0.98 |
| Weighted Avg | 1.00 | 1.00 | 1.00 | 1.00 | 1.00 | 1.00 | 0.98 | 0.98 | 0.98 |

Note: Proposed 1 and 2 are corresponding to unbalanced and balanced datasets. P, R and F represent Precision, Recall and F1-score.

## 4 Implementation and Results

The proposed intrusion detection system leverages CICIoMT2024 dataset which is preprocessed using XAI (LIME) for selecting important features. This dataset is taken from the Canadian Institute for Cybersecurity [8] which contains 1.2 million samples from 40 IoMT devices across 18 attack types. It includes 45 features (e.g., packet sizes, flow durations) labeled into six different classes, i.e., Benign, DDoS, DoS, MQTT, Recon, and Spoofing. For the training and testing purpose, chunks of 0.5% of the total size of the dataset are randomly sampled. Class distribution was uneven, with more Benign and DDoS instances, as detailed in Fig. 2.

Data preprocessing addressed imbalances and enhanced features. Missing values are filled with the median, and outliers removed are using a z-score threshold of 3. Feature selection with CNN and LIME retained 18 critical features and removed 27 irrelevant ones. Table 2 shows our results of XAI-based feature importance analysis where features selected and not selected by proposed approach are mentioned. After performing the same, three new features, i.e., `packet_ratio` (packet size/(total size + 1)), `flow_duration_ratio` (duration/(count + 1)), and `packet_size_variance` (variance across a 5-packet rolling window) are added into the dataset for efficient classification. To balance our dataset, we use SMOTE and generate 40,000 rare attack samples (e.g., Spoofing), while RandomUnderSampler capped common attacks at 50,000, with weights 8 for Spoofing, 6 for Recon, 1 for others.

Our IDS uses an ensemble learning-based classifier which combined XGBoost (meta-model) [29], Random Forest [30] and LightGBM [31] with soft voting mechanism. Optuna is used for optimization of hyper-parameters. For example, XGBoost model is found better with 100500 trees with depth of 410 over 20 trials. Table 3 shows our performance results of proposed model against state-of-the-art based on CNN [2]. The proposed approach outperforms the existing by giving a balanced accuracy of 98% and an original test accuracy of 99.59% against the existing which was proposed only for unbalanced dataset and has an overall test accuracy of 99% with less precision, recall and F1-score for rare attacks such as spoofing.

We perform an efficient classification of rare attacks. As shown in the Table 3, F1-scores of 0.95 and 0.97 are achieved which outperforms the existing approach which has 0.38 and 0.96 of F1-scores for the same attacks, respectively.

## 5   Conclusion

This paper introduces an ensemble learning-based intrusion detection system for IoMT networks. Our focus is on efficient capture of all attacks including the rare ones such as spoofing and reconnaissance. The proposed model is trained and tested on well-known CICIoMT2024 dataset. We have used state-of-the-art Convolutional Neural Network based model with Local Interpretable Model-agnostic Explanations (LIME) to identify the set of key features. Afterwards, three new features, i.e., `packet_ratio`, `flow_duration_ratio` and `packet_size_variance` have been added for robust detection of rare attacks. Our ensemble learning-based model integrates XGBoost, Random Forest, and LightGBM with soft voting mechanism. It exhibits a sufficient balanced accuracy of 98% and an original test accuracy of 99.59%, surpassing the baseline CNN model which incurs 99% test accuracy for unbalanced dataset with less precision, recall and F1-score for rare attacks such as spoofing. For the rare attacks like spoofing, precision and F1-score are greatly improved, i.e., from 0.27 and 0.38 (in existing approach) to 0.91 and 0.95 (in proposed), respectively. In future, an integration of different XAI model like SHAP [32] can be incorporated to conduct a deeper analysis of attack features. Also, the existing and proposed systems are not tested in the real environment. Such deployments will be beneficial to achieve some real-world insights.

## References


1. Santander, C.M., et al.: IoMT Data Server Risks and Vulnerabilities (2024). https://migrationletters.com/index.php/ml/article/view/6952/4602
2. Mohammadi, M., et al.: Securing Healthcare with Deep Learning: A CNN-Based Model for medical IoT Threat Detection (2024). https://arxiv.org/abs/2410.23306
3. Mohsin, S., Jony, A.: A comparative analysis of medical IoT device attacks using machine learning models (2024). https://www.researchgate.net/publication/384564827_A_Comparative_Analysis_of_Medical_IoT_Device_Attacks_Using_Machine_Learning_Models
4. Tauqeer, M., et al.: Cyberattacks Detection in IoMT using Machine Learning Techniques (2022). https://www.jcbi.org/index.php/Main/article/view/80

5. Aljuhani, A.: An Intelligent and Explainable SaaS-Based Intrusion Detection System for Resource-Constrained IoMT (2023). https://ieeexplore.ieee.org/abstract/document/10293159

6. Chen, T., Guestrin, C.: XGBoost: A Scalable Tree Boosting System (2016). https://dl.acm.org/doi/10.1145/2939672.2939785

7. Sohail, M., et al.: Sampling-Based Machine Learning Models for Intrusion Detection in Imbalanced Dataset (2024). https://www.mdpi.com/2079-9292/13/10/1878

8. Dadkhah, S., et al.: CICIoMT2024: A Dataset for IoMT Cybersecurity (2024). https://www.unb.ca/cic/datasets/iomt-dataset-2024.html

9. Areia, J., et al.: IoMT-TrafficData: Dataset and Tools for Benchmarking Intrusion Detection in Internet of Medical Things (2024). https://ieeexplore.ieee.org/abstract/document/10620207

10. Kondeti, V., Bahsi, H.: Mapping Cyber Attacks on the Internet of Medical Things: A Taxonomic Review (2024). https://ieeexplore.ieee.org/abstract/document/10620925

11. Al-Abadi, A., et al.: Enhanced Random Forest Classifier with K-Means Clustering (ERF-KMC) for Detecting and Preventing Distributed-Denial-of-Service and Man-in-the-Middle Attacks in Internet-of-Medical-Things Networks (2023). https://www.mdpi.com/2073-431X/12/12/262

12. Das, S., et al.: Emerging Cyber Threats in Healthcare: A Study of Attacks in IoMT Ecosystems (2023). https://ieeexplore.ieee.org/abstract/document/10290147

13. Tahir, A., et al.: A Novel Experience-Driven and Federated Intelligent Threat-Defense Framework in IoMT (2023). https://ieeexplore.ieee.org/abstract/document/10015025

14. Balhareth, G., Ilyas, M.: Optimized Intrusion Detection for IoMT Networks with Tree-Based Machine Learning and Filter-Based Feature Selection (2024). https://www.mdpi.com/1424-8220/24/17/5712

15. Ksibi, S., et al.: MLRA-Sec: an adaptive and intelligent cyber-security-assessment model for internet of medical things (IoMT) (2024). https://link.springer.com/article/10.1007/s10207-024-00923-y

16. Dash, P.B., et al.: An Improved Intrusion Detection System for the Internet of Medical Things Based on Deep Convolutional Neural Network (2023). https://link.springer.com/chapter/10.1007/978-981-99-3734-9_42

17. Al-Hawawreh, M., et al.: An Efficient Intrusion Detection Model for Edge System in Brownfield Industrial Internet of Things (2019). https://dl.acm.org/doi/abs/10.1145/3361758.3361762

18. Si-Ahmed, A., et al.: Explainable Machine Learning-Based Security and Privacy Protection Framework for Internet of Medical Things Systems (2025). https://arxiv.org/abs/2403.09752

19. Martin-Faus, V., et al.: Ensuring patient safety in IoMT: A systematic literature review of behavior-based intrusion detection systems (2024). https://www.sciencedirect.com/science/article/pii/S2542660524003615

20. Rahimi, M., Zia, T.: Artificial Intelligence for Secured Information Systems in Smart Cities: Collaborative IoT Computing with Deep Reinforcement Learning and Blockchain (2024). https://arxiv.org/abs/2409.16444

21. Al-Turjman, F., et al.: Evolving Role of AI and IoMT in the Healthcare Market (2021). https://link.springer.com/book/10.1007/978-3-030-82079-4

22. Alalhareth, A., et al.: Federated Learning for IoMT Applications: A Standardisation and Benchmarking Framework of Intrusion Detection Systems (2022).

https://www.researchgate.net/publication/359963237_Federated_Learning_for_IoMT_Applications_A_Standardisation_and_Benchmarking_Framework_of_Intrusion_Detection_Systems

23. Hassija, V., et al.: A Survey on IoT Security: Application Areas, Security Threats, and Solution Architectures (2019). https://www.researchgate.net/publication/333909259_A_Survey_on_IoT_Security_Application_Areas_Security_Threats_and_Solution_Architectures

24. Swarna Priya, R., et al.: An effective feature engineering for DNN using hybrid PCA-GWO for intrusion detection in IoMT architecture (2020). https://www.sciencedirect.com/science/article/pii/S014036642030298X

25. Ravi, V., et al.: Deep Learning-Based Network Intrusion Detection System for Internet of Medical Things (2023). https://ieeexplore.ieee.org/abstract/document/10145040

26. Savanović, N., et al.: Intrusion Detection in Healthcare 4.0 Internet of Things Systems via Metaheuristics Optimized Machine Learning (2023). https://www.mdpi.com/2071-1050/15/16/12563

27. Hady, A., et al.: Intrusion Detection System for Healthcare Systems Using Medical and Network Data: A Comparison Study (2020). https://ieeexplore.ieee.org/abstract/document/9109651

28. Rbah, N.B., et al.: A Machine Learning Framework for Intrusion Detection in VANET Communications (2022). https://link.springer.com/chapter/10.1007/978-3-031-09640-2_10

29. Kharwar, A., et al.: A hybrid approach for feature selection using SFFS and SBFS with extra-tree and classification using XGBoost (2023). https://www.inderscienceonline.com, https://doi.org/10.1504/IJAHUC.2023.132998

30. Breiman, L.: Random Forests (2001). https://link.springer.com/article/10.1023/A:1010933404324

31. Ke, G., et al.: LightGBM: A Highly Efficient Gradient Boosting Decision Tree (2017). https://papers.nips.cc/paper/2017/hash/6449f44a102fde848669bdd9eb6b76fa-Abstract.html

32. Marcílio, W.E., Eler, D.M.: From explanations to feature selection: assessing SHAP values as feature selection mechanism. In: 2020 33rd SIBGRAPI Conference on Graphics, Patterns and Images (SIBGRAPI), pp. 340–347. IEEE (2020)

# Enhanced Anomaly Detection in IoT Networks Using Machine Learning and Deep Learning Approaches

Nishthaa Jain[1], Surbhi Sharma[2(✉)], Renu Dalal[1], Manju Khari[3], and Arvind Panwar[4]

[1] University School of Automation and Robotics, Guru Gobind Singh Indraprastha University (GGSIPU), East Delhi Campus, Delhi, India
[2] School of Computer Science Engineering and Technology, Bennett University, Greater Noida, India
surbhi263sharma@gmail.com
[3] School of Computer and Systems Sciences, Jawaharlal Nehru University, Delhi, India
[4] School of Computer Science and Engineering, Galgotias University, Greater Noida, India

**Abstract.** As the number of Internet of Things (IoT) devices has been exponentially increasing, the importance of network security has been established due to the growth in volume and increasing complexity of cyber-attacks. More conventional intrusion detection systems (IDS) are prone to fail to identify sophisticated or novel attacks, particularly within constrained resources' IoT worlds. The aim of this project is to build an improved anomaly detection system for IoT networks using the Machine Learning (ML) and Deep-Learning (DL) models. In this solution, two benchmark datasets will be utilized as follows; NF-ToN-IoT has realistic IoT network traffic while UNSW-NB15 dataset is an intrusion detection dataset. The machine learning models applied include Random Forest, Decision Tree, Logistic Regression, Naive Bayes, XGBoost, and AdaBoost, along with a stacking ensemble. These were compared against deep learning approaches such as Autoencoders, CNNs, and LSTM networks. A performance analysis was conducted on all models according to the metrical standards of accuracy, precision, recall, F1 score and ROC AUC. Further studies are required to appreciate the potential of a combined ML-DL hybrid model architecture and optimization strategies for real-time implementation.

**Keywords:** Intrusion Detection · IoT Security · Machine Learning · Deep Learning · CNN · Autoencoder · XGBoost · Hybrid Model · Network Traffic · NF-ToN-IoT · UNSW-NB15

## 1 Introduction

The increasing number of IoT devices has greatly increased the automation and data communication quotient of industries such as healthcare, smart infrastructure and manufacturing. Wireless communications though have made much advancement hence the corresponding increase in the security risk. IoT devices are vulnerable to various attacks,


K. K. Patel et al. (Eds.): icSoftComp 2025, CCIS 2874, pp. 430–439, 2026.
https://doi.org/10.1007/978-3-032-22062-2_33

including denial-of-service (DoS), unauthorized data manipulation, identity theft, and malware-based breaches. Cyber-attacks compromise overall system integrity, threaten critical assets, and may endanger individuals. These attacks were also vulnerable to wireless networks as discussed in [1–4].

In order to address these issues, the current research explores a methodology to detect anomalies using a combination of Machine Learning (ML) and Deep Learning (DL) techniques. To perform such evaluation, we use two datasets, first is NF-ToN-IoT that serves focuses on IoT traffic and second is UNSW-NB15; a more expansive intrusion detection collection, used for the purpose of testing and comparing ML algorithms such as Random Forest and XGBoost as well as DL models including Autoencoders, CNNs, LSTMs, and, CRNNs. In addition to benchmarking with metrics such as accuracy, precision, recall, F1-score, and ROC-AUC, the aim is to build the basis for a hybrid that combines best of ML and DL. A combination of these methodologies may lead to a stronger, dynamic, and effective method of detecting intrusions in actual IoT systems.

## 2 Literature Survey

The proliferation of IoT devices has magnified the network attack surface and we end up with more cyber- attacks than exposure. Therefore, there has been an increased focus on research towards designing automatic anomaly detection systems using both Machine Learning (ML) and Deep Learning (DL) methods, in order to analyze network behavior.

### 2.1 Traditional Machine Learning-Based Intrusion Detection

ML algorithms have attracted wide attention owing to their transparency, efficient processing, and high level of development. Al-Yaseen et al. [5] report that the RF and DT classifiers are effective when applied to noise and nonlinear relations. Naive Bayes (NB) and Logistic Regression (LR), simple and time-saving, fail to be as effective in dealing with the complexity of data features of IoT-particular examples, such as the large dimensionality and imbalance. Furthermore, these models tend to employ manual feature selection which may constrain their ability to deal with complex or un-seen before types of attacks.

### 2.2 Exploiting the Benefits of Deep Learning for the Improvement of Feature Representation

Remarkable success has been recorded with DL models in their learning complex feature representation-free of human effort. Based on the research of Javaid et al. [6] and Hodo et al. [7], deep learning models outperform traditional shallow ML approaches on large-scale intrusion detection data sets. Autoencoders are suitable for unsupervised environments, especially when labeled attack samples are limited. CNNs analyze traffic flow and sequences to extract meaningful spatial characteristics. LSTMs and other recurrent neural network (RNN) variants are excellent for capturing temporal dependencies. CRNNs combine both the convolutional and recurrence-based mechanisms for both local spatial features and long-range temporal effects.

### 2.3  Hybrid ML-DL Intrusion Detection Approaches

There has been increasing interest in the confluence of ML and DL in drafting the hybrid frameworks. Wang et al. [8] demonstrate the effectiveness of combining CNN and XGBoost based on their complementary strengths in feature extraction and classification. These hybrid ways provide more accuracy and wider applicability therefore being preferred in practical application.

### 2.4  Benchmark Datasets

NF-ToN-IoT: Created purposely to handle a wide range of attack scenarios and emulate actual network scenarios in IoCT environments. UNSW-NB15: An all-penetrating benchmark addressing modern-day attack methods and guarantees similar representation for each class. The common utilization of these datasets in the current research provides effective foundation to evaluate performance of various IDS approaches.

### 2.5  Summary

From literature, reviews individual ML or DL models are not good enough, with hybrid architecture being advocated for as a better solution. In contrast, ML models are characterized by speed and transparency, whereas DL models provide increased accuracy and wider applicability consistently. A hybrid IDS takes a synthesis of the best of both worlds, making for a strong and flexible strategy to handle actual-world IoT security concerns (Fig. 1).

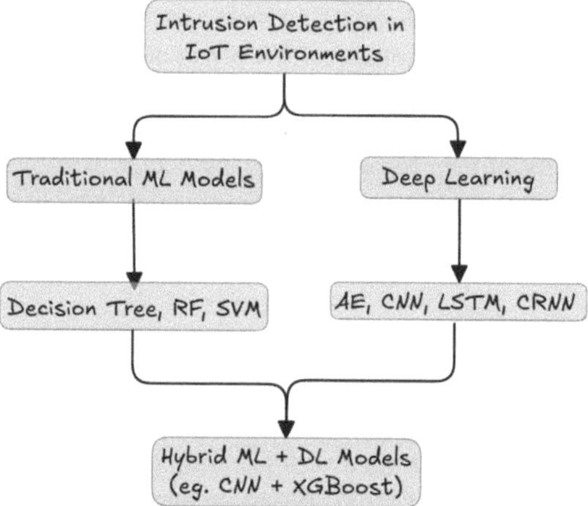


**Fig. 1.** Taxonomy of ML, DL, and hybrid models for intrusion detection in IoT environments.

## 3  Methodology

The system is designed to reveal anomalies and cyber threats in IoT traffic using the techniques of machine and deep learning. A multi-stage approach was employed, starting with preprocessing and transforming features and followed by training and validation using a wide variety of ML and DL models. The methodology is tested against two standard benchmark datasets, NF-ToN-IoT and UNSW-NB15, chosen for their resemblance to real world IoT and network environments.

### 3.1  Data Preprocessing

Before training the models, a rigorous preprocessing pipeline was applied to ensure data integrity and optimal model performance. The datasets NF-ToN-IoT and UNSW-NB15 were used. Attack categories were numerically encoded for ML models and one-hot encoded for DL models. Feature scaling was performed using standardization or normalization techniques. Redundant features (e.g., port numbers) were removed. Data was reshaped to fit the input requirements of CNN and LSTM models. Finally, a stratified 70:30 train-test split was applied.

### 3.2  Machine Learning Models

Several supervised learning techniques were selected due to their proven effectiveness on structured data. These include:

- Random Forest (RF): An ensemble of decision trees offering robust performance and reduced overfitting.
- Decision Tree (DT): A simple model prone to overfitting but effective on smaller datasets.
- Logistic Regression (LR): A fast statistical model, limited on non-linear data.
- Naive Bayes (NB): Probabilistic and efficient, but assumes feature independence.
- XGBoost: A powerful gradient boosting technique with excellent accuracy and speed.
- AdaBoost: Combines weak learners to create a strong classifier.
- Stacking Ensemble: Combines outputs from multiple base models for improved performance.

Each model was trained on standardized features and evaluated using common classification metrics.

### 3.3  Deep Learning Models

To enhance pattern recognition, deep learning architectures were employed:

- Autoencoder: An unsupervised model that reconstructs input and flags anomalies based on reconstruction error.
- Convolutional Neural Network (CNN): 1D CNNs are used to identify spatial correlations in network traffic by capturing local feature patterns.
- Long Short-Term Memory (LSTM): It helps in understanding temporal sequences in traffic, making it effective for identifying evolving intrusion behaviors.
- Convolutional Recurrent Neural Network (CRNN): Combines CNN and LSTM layers to capture both spatial and temporal patterns in network traffic.

All models were trained on normalized data, reshaped into 3D input where required. One-hot encoding was used for multiclass classification.

### 3.4  Hybrid Model: CNN + XGBoost

The hybrid architecture combines CNN-based feature extraction with XGBoost classification. CNN layers extract high-level spatial features, which are passed to the XGBoost classifier for final prediction. The architecture benefits from CNN's deep feature extraction and XGBoost's powerful classification abilities. It offers improved performance, particularly in detecting complex intrusion patterns. The model is flexible and can be extended with other DL backbones or tree-based classifiers such as LSTM, CRNN, or LightGBM (Fig. 2).

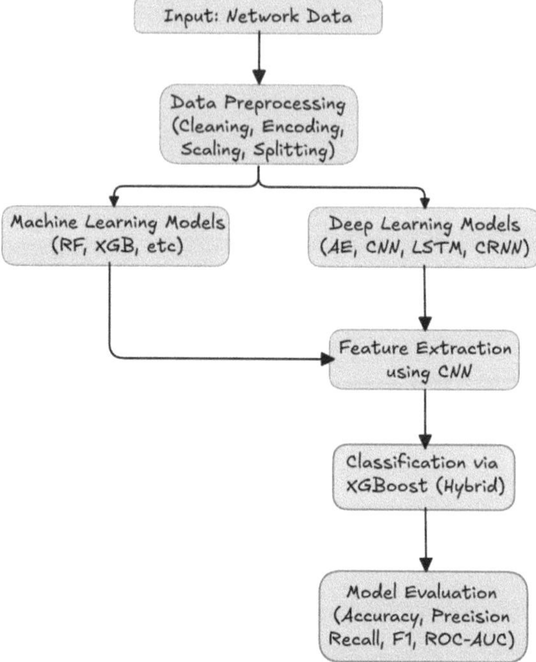


**Fig. 2.** Proposed hybrid framework integrating ML and DL models for intrusion detection.

## 4  Evaluation Metrics and Strategy

**4.1 Metrics Used:** Performance of the ML, DL, and Hybrid models was rated through these key metrics:

- Accuracy: Measures overall correctness of predictions but may not be reliable with class imbalance.
- Precision (Macro): Frequency of correctly predicted positive observations across all classes.
- Recall (Macro): Ability to detect actual positive cases for each class.
- F1-Score (Macro): A metric combining precision and recall, especially valuable when classes are imbalanced.

- ROC-AUC (One-vs-Rest): Area under the ROC curve for each class; shows separability between classes.

These metrics were chosen to reflect model performance, especially in the presence of minority attack classes.

### 4.1  Evaluation Approach

A 70:30 stratified train-test split was used for balanced class distribution. One-hot encoding was applied for deep learning models, while traditional ML models used integer label encoding. Early stopping was employed in DL models to prevent overfitting by monitoring validation loss. Due to high computational cost, cross-validation was not applied. All models were evaluated using the same preprocessed data and the five selected metrics for both datasets.

## 5  Results and Discussion

To evaluate the performance of the proposed framework, we tested it on two benchmark datasets: NF-ToN-IoT and UNSW-NB15. ML, DL, and Hybrid (CNN + XGBoost) models were assessed using Accuracy, Precision, Recall, F1-score, and ROC-AUC.

### 5.1  NF-ToN-IoT Dataset

The NF-ToN-IoT dataset captures realistic IoT network traffic with 10 attack types.

- The Stacking Classifier achieved the highest ML accuracy (72.13%), outperforming Random Forest and XGBoost.
- Among DL models, CNN showed better results than Autoencoder and LSTM, with an ROC-AUC of 0.89.
- The Hybrid CNN + XGBoost model outperformed all, with 76.49% accuracy and an ROC-AUC of 0.90.

These results highlight the limitations of traditional ML in complex threat detection and the strength of CNNs in extracting spatial features. The hybrid approach significantly improves classification of complex attack patterns (Figs. 3, 4 and 5).

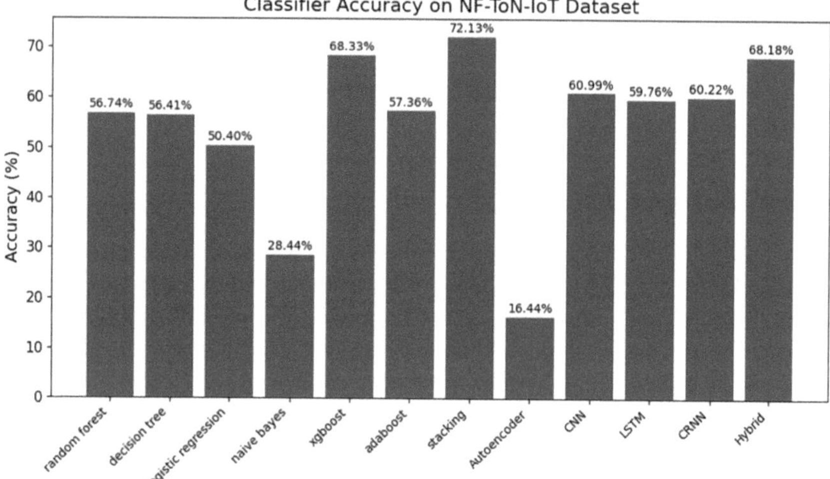

**Fig. 3.** Accuracy scores of classifiers on the NF-ToN-IoT dataset

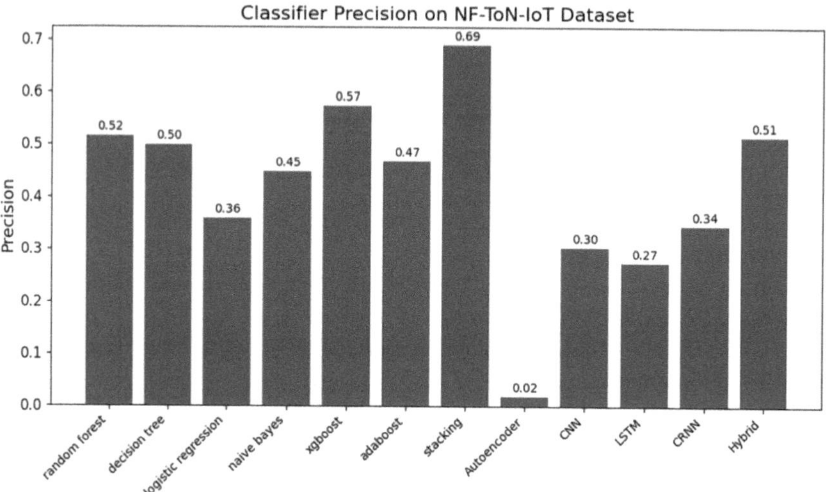

**Fig. 4.** Precision scores of classifiers on the NF-ToN-IoT dataset

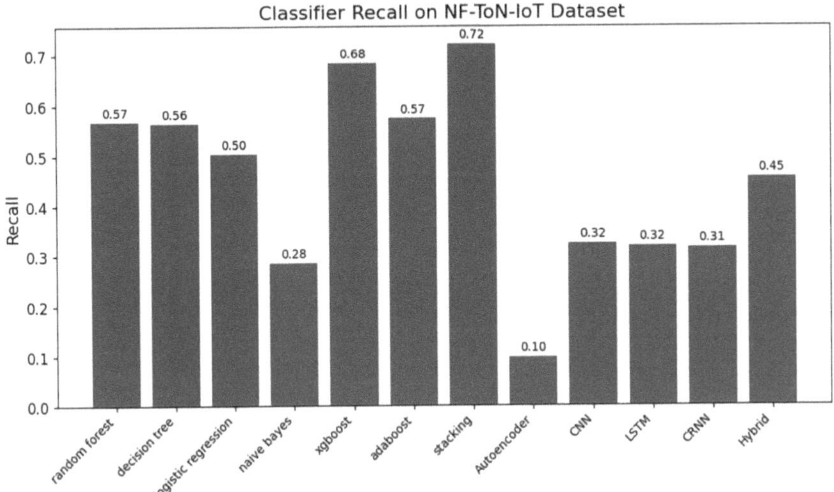


**Fig. 5.** Recall scores of classifiers on the NF-ToN-IoT dataset

## 5.2 UNSW-NB15 Dataset

UNSW-NB15 contains diverse traffic patterns and recent attack types.

- The Stacking Classifier continued to perform well with 73.94% accuracy.
- CNN achieved the best DL performance (77.06% accuracy, 0.95 ROC-AUC).
- The hybrid approach achieved the best results, with 79.03% accuracy and a 0.97 ROC-AUC score.

This confirms the hybrid model's generalization capability and enhanced detection for both basic and advanced intrusion patterns (Figs. 6, 7 and 8).

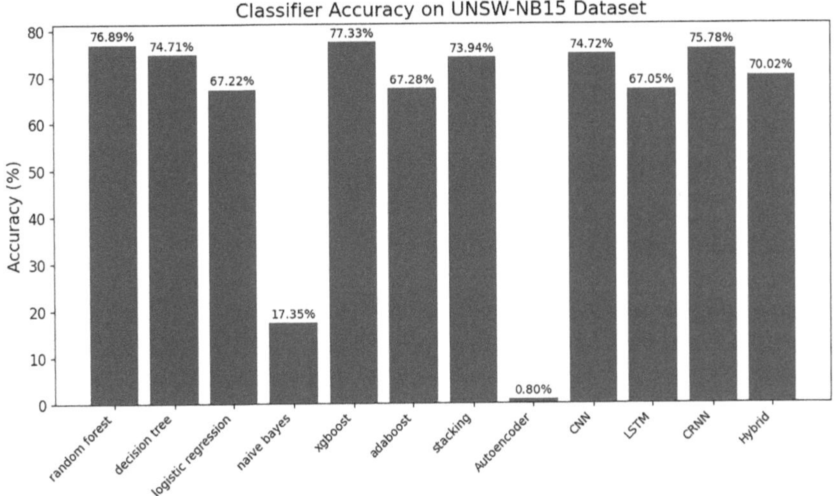


**Fig. 6.** Accuracy scores of classifiers on the UNSW-NB15 dataset

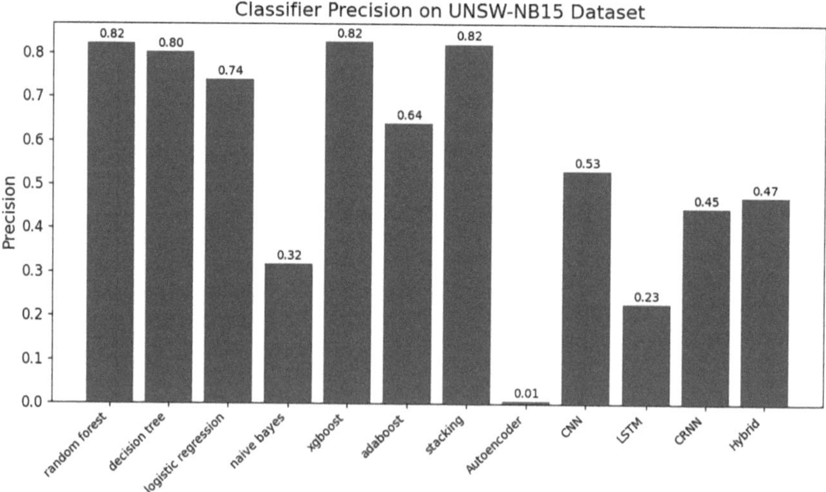

**Fig. 7.** Precision scores of classifiers on the UNSW-NB15 dataset

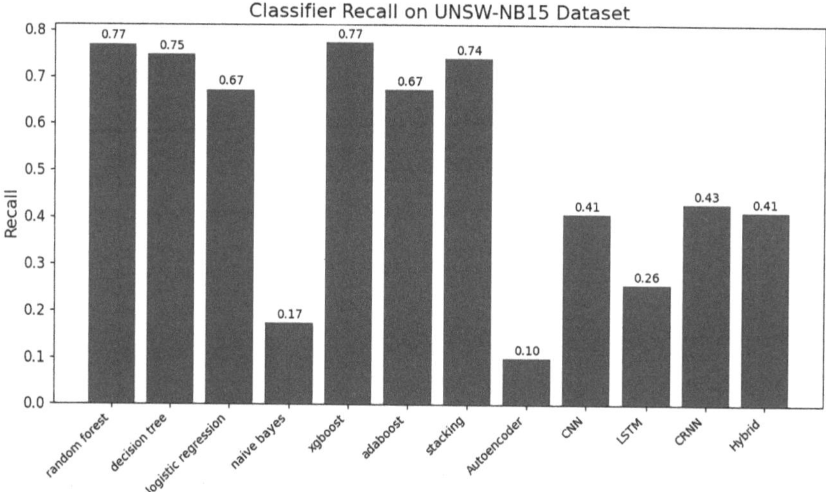

**Fig. 8.** Recall scores of classifiers on the UNSW-NB15 dataset

## 6 Conclusion and Future Work

This investigation evaluated the feasibility of using Machine Learning (ML), Deep Learning (DL), and their hybrid models for anomaly detection in IoT networks using two benchmark datasets. Models included Random Forest, XGBoost, Autoencoders, CNN, LSTM, CRNN, and a CNN + XGBoost hybrid. The results showed: Ensemble ML models like Stacking and XGBoost performed well, DL models, especially CNN and CRNN, effectively identified complex attack patterns, The CNN + XGBoost hybrid model outperformed all standalone approaches in most metrics. The results confirm that integrating ML and DL enhances intrusion detection for complex and evolving IoT scenarios. Future enhancements include: Combining sequential DL models with tree-based classifiers like LightGBM, Optimizing architecture for resource-constrained IoT devices, Real-world deployment and evaluation on live networks, Enhancing interpretability for better decision-making, Strengthening defenses against evolving cyber threats.

# References


1. Dalal, R., Sangwan, A., Khari, M.: The bibliometrics assessment of opportunistic network protocols & simulation tools. Telemat. Inform. Reports **11**, 100082 (2023)
2. Dalal, R., Khari, M.: Empirical analysis of routing protocols in opportunistic network. In: Research in Intelligent and Computing in Engineering: Select Proceedings of RICE 2020, pp. 695–703. Springer Singapore (2021)
3. Dalal, R., Khari, M., Misra, S.: Speculative analysis of wireless network by bibliometrics tool. Wireless Pers. Commun. **135**(4), 2039–2059 (2024)
4. Dalal, R., Khari, M., Pandey, P., Jatana, S., Joshi, V.: Facial emotion recognition and detection using convolutional neural networks. In: 2023 3rd International Conference on Smart Generation Computing, Communication and Networking (SMART GENCON), pp. 1–8. IEEE (2023)
5. Al-Yaseen, W.L., Othman, Z.A., Nazri, M.Z.A.: Hybrid intrusion detection system based on the combination of genetic algorithm and support vector machine. Expert Syst. Appl. **49**, 76–83 (2017)
6. Javaid, A., Niyaz, Q., Sun, W., Alam, M.: A deep learning approach for network intrusion detection system. In: Proceedings of the 9th EAI International Conference on Bio-inspired Information and Communications Technologies (formerly BIONETICS), pp. 21–26 (2016)
7. Hodo, E., Bellekens, X., Hamilton, A., Dubouchaud, J., Atkinson, R.: Threat analysis of IoT networks using artificial neural network intrusion detection system. In: 2016 IEEE International Symposium on Networks, Computers and Communications (ISNCC), pp. 1–6 (2016)
8. Wang, R., Jiang, Y., Huang, J.: A hybrid CNN-XGBoost model for network intrusion detection. J. Intell. Fuzzy Syst. **40**(3), 4917–4929 (2021)

# Privacy-Preserving ETL Pipelines for Sensitive AI Systems: A Dual-Domain Evaluation Using Differential Privacy

Nandagopal Seshagiri[1]([✉]), Pavan Nutalapati[2], Rakesh Keshava[3], and Arun Kumar Elengovan[4]

[1] San Ramon, CA 94583, USA
[2] Dallas, TX 75068, USA
[3] Fremont, CA 94555, USA
[4] Fremont, CA 94539, USA

**Abstract.** A comparative evaluation of integrating Differential Privacy (DP) into Extract–Transform–Load (ETL) pipelines for sensitive domains is presented. Laplace noise of epsilon = 0.1, 1 and 5 was applied on the MIMIC-III clinical data and Fannie Mae loan archive on which the privacy-utility trade-off was evaluated using the Logistic Regression (LR) and Random Forest (RF) models. These findings suggest that healthcare data are extremely sensitive to DP perturbation. In MIMIC-III, AUC decreased from 0.60 (raw) to 0.50 ($\varepsilon = 0.1$) for LR, with F1 falling from 0.31 to 0.26. Conversely, financial data were also more resilient, and the Fannie Mae dataset showed better results, AUC = 0.91 and F1 = 0.82 even at $\varepsilon = 5$. These results indicate that privacy-sensitive ETL pipelines are necessarily application-specific as healthcare will experience stiffer utility falls whereas finance will retain predictive capacity. The research offers the first cross-domain findings of the DP-enhanced ETL performance and has practical recommendations about the process of the secure data integration in the sensitive AI.

**Keywords:** Differential Privacy · Privacy-Preserving ETL · Sensitive Data Analytics

## 1 Introduction

The massive application of AI across the sensitive branches of the economy like healthcare and finance has exacerbated the worries of data security and lawfulness. PII embedded in these datasets is governed by GDPR [2] and the HIPAA [3] and is either prone to leakage, identification and abuse or is part of standard Extract-Transform-Load (ETL) pipeline, with each having no formal privacy guarantees. DP is a strict shield throughout data processing and data release [5], but it has widely been exercised, predominantly on limited machine-learning procedures instead of integrated ETL procedures [6].

N. Seshagiri, P. Nutalapati, R. Keshava, A.K. Elengovan—Independent Researchers.



K. K. Patel et al. (Eds.): icSoftComp 2025, CCIS 2874, pp. 440–454, 2026.
https://doi.org/10.1007/978-3-032-22062-2_34

The paper provides the necessary fill in such a gap, suggesting a privacy-conscious ETL architecture and assessing it in two contexts, MIMIC-III (healthcare) and Fannie Mae Single-Family loans (finance) using actual data [7, 8]. The privacy-utility trade-off in different privacy budgets ($\varepsilon = 0.1, 1, 5$) are analyzed with the help of the Logistic Regression and Random Forest with non-DP data as a control. The workflow is defined and assumptions are written down, constraints (e.g. DP on numeric features) are understood. These findings present cross-domain justifications that augmented ETL of DP has the capability to fulfill privacy demands without jeopardizing applicable predictive quality.

## 2  Literature Review

Early methods of pursuing data protection, like anonymization and rule-based compliance, were not sufficient, as datasets were prone to re-identification [9, 10]. This limitation has provided motivation to the development of Differential Privacy (DP) which offers mathematically provable guarantees while allowing methods to evaluate the privacy-utility trade-offs systematically. Subsequent research extended DP into distributed and large-scale settings, including applications in data centers [11] and privacy-preserving federated learning, where raw data are kept local, and the exchange of the model updates [12, 13]. Domain-specific applications have also been investigated, for example privacy-preserving remote sensing for climate modeling [14], enterprise resource planning using sensor-based corrections [15], and clinical seizure prediction using intracranial EEG data [16]. More recently, DP has been applied to healthcare data through local mechanisms [17] and novel frameworks for secure sharing [18], while federated DP has also been explored in medical analytics [19]. In finance, privacy-preserving pipelines have been designed for fraud detection [20], and blockchain-enabled architectures proposed for securing heterogeneous ETL workflows [21]. These examples showcase the versatility of DP and related privacy-preserving techniques in a wide range of applications. However, such work is usually used to focus on isolated machine learning tasks and is not able to offer complete enterprise-level workflows.

Despite the major progress there is a lot of work to be done, especially on end-to-end integration of DP into ETL pipelines. Conventional ETL processes continue to provide opportunities for vulnerabilities both in data extract, transform, and load for particularly sensitive tabular and time-series data [17, 18]. And that is what this study helps bridge that gap by proposing a full DP-augmented ETL pipeline and validating it in two heterogeneous domains—healthcare and finance. The framework integrates DP operations into all stages of the ETL process and empirically analyses the resulting privacy-utility trade-offs using Logistic Regression and Random Forest classifiers. The proposed framework fills this gap by creating a privacy-preserving ETL framework and its application to both tabular and time-series data. Two real world datasets are used: MIMIC-III clinical database [7] and Fannie Mae Single Family Credit Database [8]. The framework is experimented with multiple privacy budgets ($\varepsilon = 0.1, 1, 5$) followed by evaluation of the influence of the privacy to its utility using Logistic Regression classifiers and Random Forest classifiers. For the first time through systematic experiments, the study gives cross-domain evidence on how DP-augmented ETL pipelines can satisfy privacy requirements while maintaining prediction performance.

## 3 Methodology

There is a description in the next section of an end-to-end pipeline built to assess the trade-off between the privacy protection and the predictive accuracy in two sensitive areas, healthcare and finance. The data analysis workflow includes the steps of preparing the data and setting up the transformation, explorative analysis, differentially private transformation, class imbalance solution and training models and analyzing its performance (Check Fig. 1).

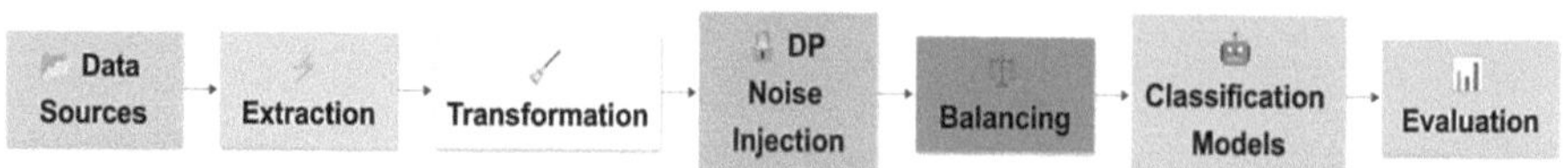


**Fig. 1.** Workflow of the proposed ETL pipeline integrating Differential Privacy and machine learning evaluation.

### 3.1 Dataset Description

The study involves the utilization of two publicly available datasets to evaluate the plausibility of privacy-enhancing techniques both in healthcare and finance. The MIMIC-III Clinical Database Demo contains structured clinical data scraped off the CHARTEVENTS and ADMISSIONS tables such as the heart rate, temperature and SpO 2 values. These vitals were collected at the patient level and coded in tags together with mortality outcomes in a binary form. At the same time, the Fannie Mae Single-Family Loan Performance Dataset provides temporal loan data, including interest rates, loan values and default conditions. Fixed-width files were processed, duplicate columns were matched and noisy entries were dropped to keep only those features that will be relevant in predicting risk. Figures 2 and 3 show the occurrence of class names mortality in the MIMIC-III data and default risk in the Fannie Mae data, which shows that real-world data are characterized by the imbalance of classes.

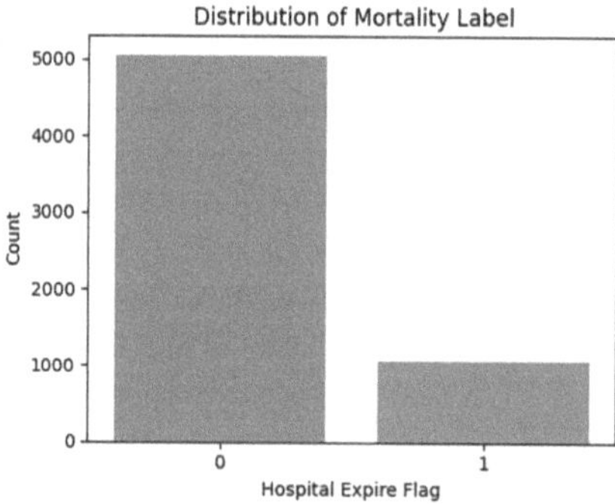


**Fig. 2.** Distribution of mortality labels in the MIMIC-III dataset, highlighting the class imbalance between survival and death outcomes.

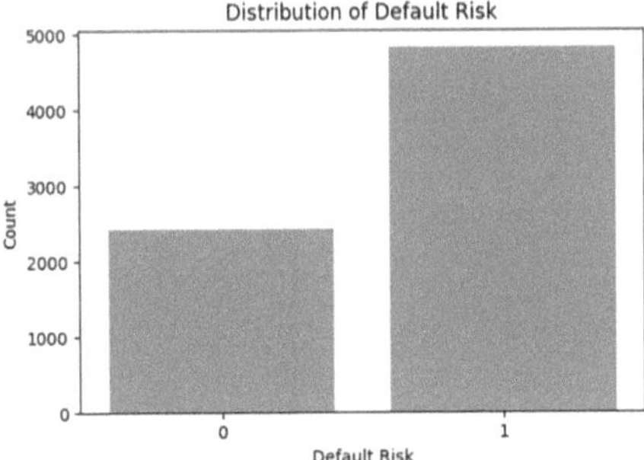

**Fig. 3.** Distribution of default risk labels in the Fannie Mae dataset, showing the imbalance between defaulted and non-defaulted loans.

## 3.2  Exploratory Analysis

This exploratory analysis was aimed at demonstrating structural correlations and prediction potential in two mentioned data sets. In MIMIC-III, the correlation heatmap (Fig. 4) shows that there are positive relationships between the vitals.

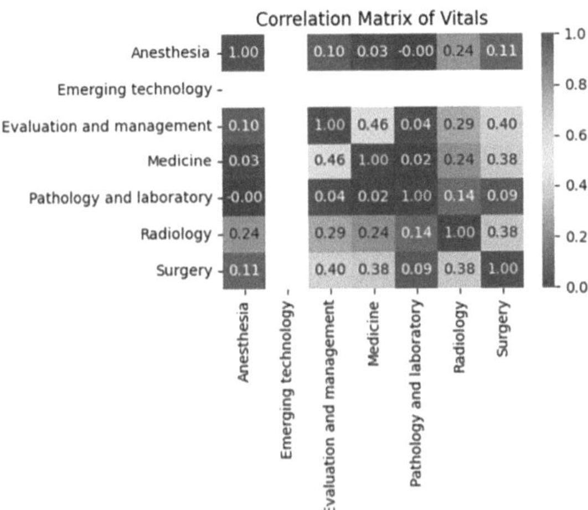

**Fig. 4.** Correlation heatmap of vital signs in the MIMIC-III dataset, illustrating positive associations among heart rate, body temperature, and $SpO_2$.

Scatterplots of vital signs vs mortality (Fig. 5), separately persons and DECEASED, exhibit a discrete group between survival and deceased patients. The negative relationships with mortality can be found with regard to heart rate and SpO 2 values, yet temperature indicates a more intricate relationship.

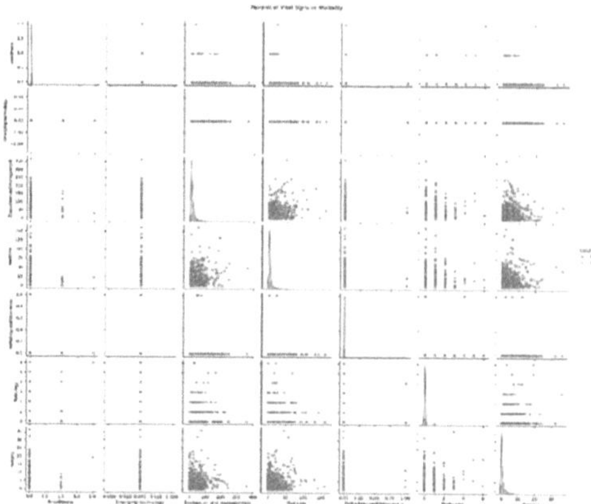

**Fig. 5.** Scatter plots of vital signs versus mortality in MIMIC-III, demonstrating negative correlations for heart rate and SpO$_2$, and a more complex trend for temperature.

In order to explore the effect of clinical interventions, Fig. 6 shows the connection between the medicines used and the risk of death,

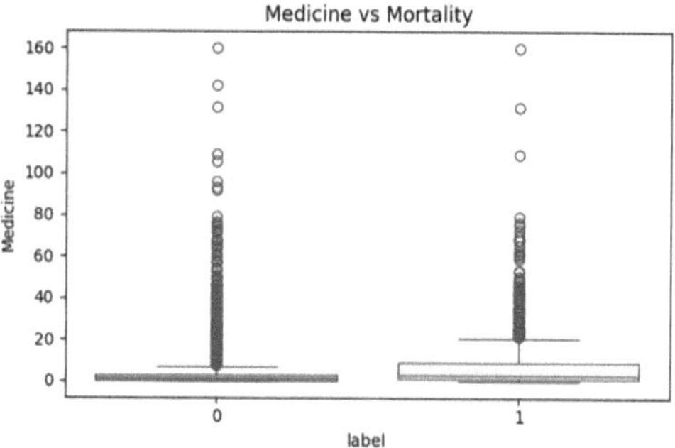

**Fig. 6.** Relationship between administered medications and mortality in the MIMIC-III dataset, indicating how treatment types correlate with survival.

Figure 7 identifies the impact of surgical procedures,

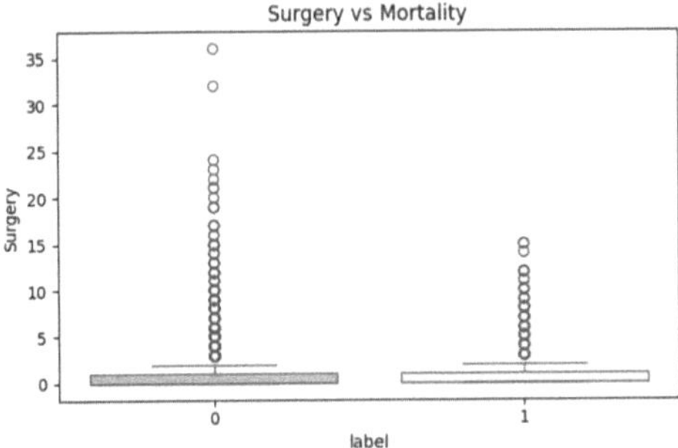

**Fig. 7.** Impact of surgical procedures on patient mortality in MIMIC-III, showing differences in survival outcomes across intervention types.

Figure 8 presents trends in evaluation and management codes,

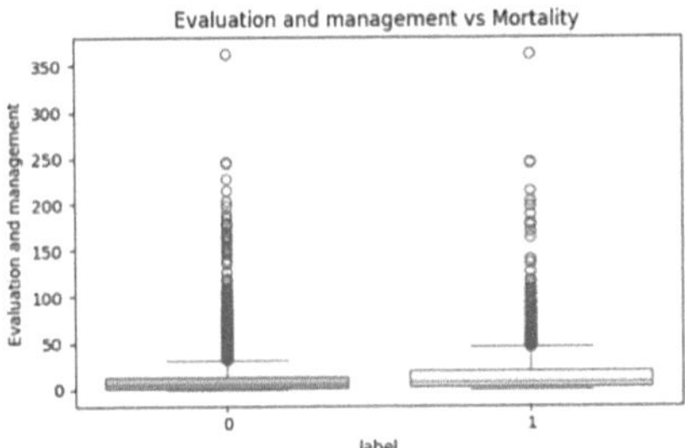

**Fig. 8.** Trends in evaluation and management codes in MIMIC-III, reflecting variations in clinical practices and their relation to patient outcomes.

When combined, all these findings highlight subtle survival patterns of intervention types.

With Fannie Mae data, significant dependencies as shown in the correlation matrix (Fig. 9) exist between loan term, amount, property type, and occupancy status.

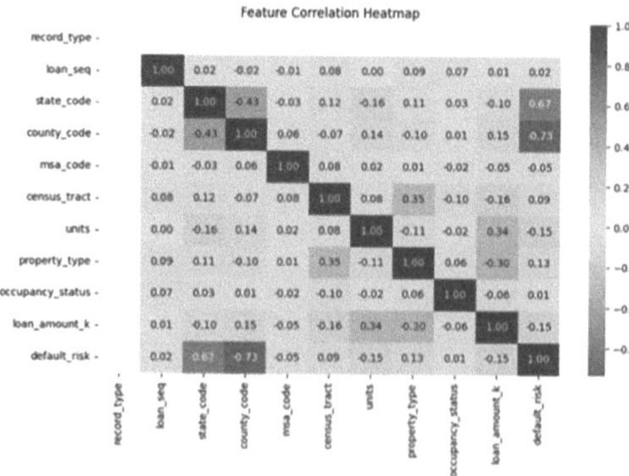

**Fig. 9.** Correlation matrix of the Fannie Mae dataset, showing strong dependencies between loan term, loan amount, property type, and occupancy status.

The distributional perspective of the loan amount in samples is offered in Fig. 10,

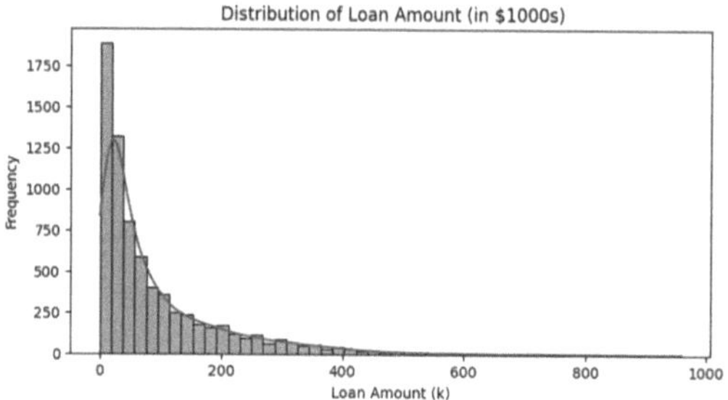

**Fig. 10.** Distribution of loan amounts in the Fannie Mae dataset, illustrating the skew toward mid-range values.

and the effect of increased loan values on the probability to default is exemplified in Fig. 11.

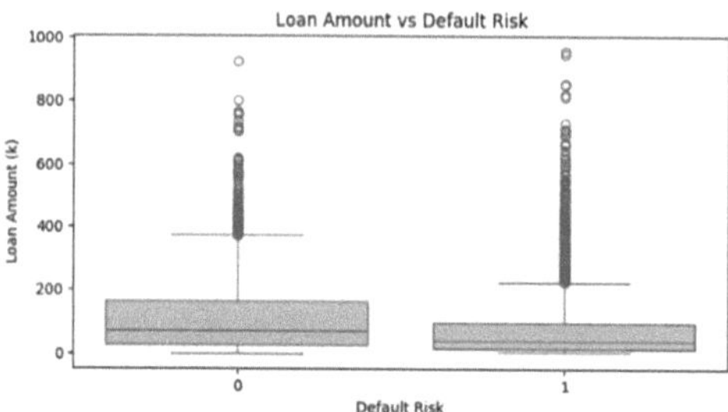

**Fig. 11.** Relationship between loan amount and default risk in the Fannie Mae dataset, showing higher default probabilities for larger loan sizes.

Figure 12 shows categorical trends of property types that show their contributions to the differentiation of risks.

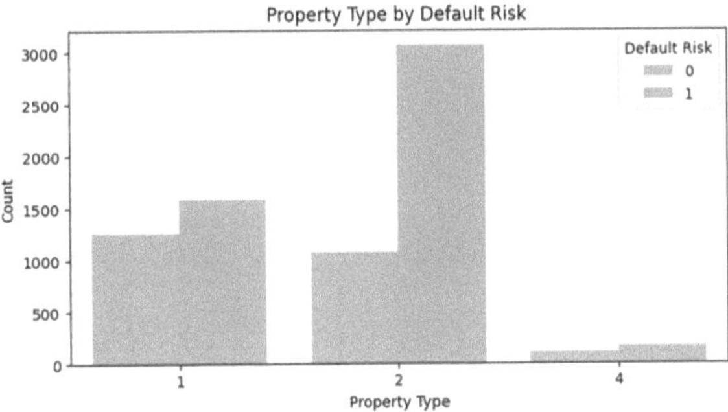


**Fig. 12.** Categorical distribution of property types in the Fannie Mae dataset, highlighting their contribution to default risk differentiation.

### 3.3  Data Preprocessing

Based on predefined ITEMID mappings, the vital signs of heart rate, SpO2 and body temperature were extracted for the MIMIC-III dataset and merged with patient mortality outcomes. The Fannie Mae dataset used several numerical and categorical fields—like loan amount, interest rate, loan period, occupancy motive, and property sort—because the forward to default threat.

For all continuous variables in both datasets normalization was carried out using Min-Max scaling (1), this was applied as follows.

$$X_{\text{scaled}} = \frac{X - X_{\min}}{X_{\max} - X_{\min}} \tag{1}$$

To reduce the effects of the missing values, the complete case deletion was embraced. Label encoding of categorical data in the Fannie Mae dataset was done in such a way that it would match machine-learning algorithms expectations. Considering the significant class imbalance, in particular, the fact that mortality or default outcomes were rarely observed, SMOTE (Synthetic Minority Oversampling Technique) (2) was used during the training. SMOTE creates synthesized observations via the formula:

$$x_{\text{new}} = x_i + \lambda \cdot (x_{nn} - x_i), \quad \lambda \sim \mathcal{U}(0, 1) \tag{2}$$

in which $x_i$ is a sample of a minority class and $x_{nn}$ is a nearest neighbor of $x$. As illustrated in Fig. 13, the class rebalancing of the Fannie Mae datasets using SMOTE is shown where the label distribution before and after SMOTE application is contrasted.

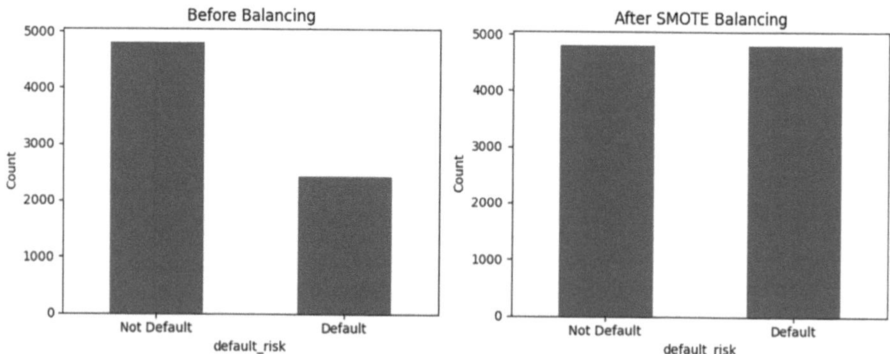

**Fig. 13.** Label distribution of the Fannie Mae dataset before and after SMOTE oversampling, demonstrating how synthetic samples rebalance the classes.

### 3.4 Differential Privacy (DP)

Differential Privacy (DP), a stringently mathematical framework, is used to protect individual-level data across data analytical processes. It ensures that statistically, no record-individually in a dataset can make a material difference to analytical conclusions, thus providing measurable privacy guarantees [10]. Categorical features were not subjected to a DP mechanism in this study; we acknowledge this as a limitation and leave DP treatment for categorical variables to future work.

A randomized mechanism $M$ admits $(\varepsilon, \delta)$ – differential privacy when, for any measurable output $S \subseteq \mathrm{Range}(M)$ and any pair of neighboring datasets $D$ and $D'$ between which there is a one-record difference (3), the following is true:

$$\Pr[\mathrm{M(D)} \in \mathrm{S}] \leq \mathrm{e}^{\varepsilon} \cdot \Pr\big[\mathrm{M}\big(\mathrm{D}'\big) \in \mathrm{S}\big] + \mathrm{d} \tag{3}$$

In the current study, Laplace noise was added to continuous numeric features following normalization. This approach performs well in bounded domains. Noise was sampled within a Laplace distribution (4) with parameters defined as:

$$\mathrm{Lap}(x) = x + \mathrm{Laplace}\left(\frac{\Delta f}{\varepsilon}\right) \tag{4}$$

The global sensitivity is represented by $\Delta f$, which is the largest impact that any individual record can have on the output. Sensitivity was set to 1 since the datasets were normalized to the [0,1] range. The noise level is determined by the privacy parameter $\varepsilon$ in this case, referred to as the privacy budget, and a lower value represents privacy guarantees in a stronger visualization.

To assess the trade-off between privacy and utility, three values of $\varepsilon$ were evaluated— 0.1, 1, and 5—across both the MIMIC-III and Fannie Mae pipelines. DP noise was injected once during the transformation stage; if multiple DP operations are added in future iterations, standard sequential composition will apply to the total privacy budget.

### 3.5  Machine Learning Models

The predictive accuracy of datasets in their original set up and under randomized perturbation of differential privacy (DP) was measured using two common supervised learning constructions and evaluated to obtain the predictive performance of the datasets and whether the perturbation has reduced the predictive accuracy of the datasets.

Logistic Regression is a probability dichotomous classifier using linear combines of the input variables to predict the logarithmic odds of an outcome that has two possible options. In binary classification problems it offers explicitly interpretable parameter estimates. The objective of the training is log-likelihood maximization (5) which leads to the sigmoid:

$$P(y = 1|X) = \frac{1}{1 + e^{-(\beta_0 + \beta_1 X_1 + \cdots + \beta_n X_n)}} \tag{5}$$

where $\beta$ are the model parameters estimated through maximum likelihood.

Random Forest is a widely used ensemble-related and a non-parametric strategy that builds an ensemble of decision trees on training and says the most prevalent class across the single trees. It is resistant to overfitting and is able to describe non-linear interactions and thus is appropriate to highly structured tabular data. The $T$ trees are aggregated by performing the following (6):

$$\hat{y} = \text{majority_vote}\{h_1(x), h_2(x), \ldots, h_T(x)\} \tag{6}$$

where $ht(x)$ is the prediction from the $tth$ tree. Each of the two algorithms was implemented under the same pipelines, i.e., feature scaling, dataset stratification, and SMOTE plus class weighting as the main metrics with the Area Under the ROC Curve (AUC) and F1-Score as the indicators.

## 4  Evaluation Metrics

In the evaluation of the machine learning models performance using raw and differentially private datasets, an evaluation suite of metrics relevant to binary classification in a situation of imbalanced classes was taken.

### 4.1  Precision

Calculates the ratio of all accurately predicted positive observations to the total positives predicted as follows (7):

$$\text{Precision} = \frac{T_{\text{pos}}}{T_{\text{pos}} + F_{\text{pos}}} \tag{7}$$

### 4.2  Recall

Sensitivity or recall (8) is the number of actual positives that are actually classified.

$$\text{Recall} = \frac{T_{\text{pos}}}{T_{\text{pos}} + F_{\text{neg}}} \tag{8}$$

### 4.3  F1 Score

The mean of precision and recall. It strikes a trade between the two (9):

$$F1 = 2 \cdot \frac{\text{Precision} \cdot \text{Recall}}{\text{Precision} + \text{Recall}} \tag{9}$$

### 4.4  Area Under the ROC Curve (AUC)

This measure of evaluation measures the extent to which a predictor model can distinguish between classes. When the value is close to 1, then the discriminative performance is good, and when a value is 0.5 then the predictive power is no better than guessing.

## 5  Results and Discussions

Such a critical investigation is the aspect of the current test that critically investigates a privacy-preserving ETL (Extract, Transform, Load) pipeline using two datasets, one in the healthcare sector (MIMIC-III), and another in finance (the Fannie Mae dataset). There are two cases which are taken into account namely raw input data and differentially private (DP) input data. The Logistic Regression (LR) and Random Forest (RF) models were used to collect the performance metrics of the two variants. Classification performance will be evaluated using the AUC and the F1-score, and the privacy parameter, 0.1, 1 and 5, will be scanned to view the trade-offs between utility and robustness.

### 5.1  MIMIC – III Dataset (Health Care)

As shown in Table 1, and in Fig. 14, the non-privatized Logistic Regression (LR) model attained a moderate Area Under the Curve (AUC) equals 0.60 and F1 score equals 0.31, while Random Forest model (RF) performed poorly on the imbalanced data (AUC = 0.47, and F1 = 0.21). When Differential Privacy (DP) was introduced, performance deteriorated further for all levels of privacy budgets. At $\varepsilon = 0.1$, LR performance fell down to AUC of 0.50 and F1-score of 0.26 and RF reached only AUC of 0.48 and F1 of 0.15. As $\varepsilon$ was increased around 5 only minimal performance gains were observed (LR: AUC = 0.53, F1 = 0.27; RF: AUC = 0.53, F1 = 0.14) but generally the predictive power was lower than the raw models. In all settings, DP-LR remained a better predictor than DP-RF, which suggests that linear models maintained more robustness against noise in this healthcare arena.

**Table 1.** Performance of Logistic Regression (LR) and Random Forest (RF) models on the MIMIC-III healthcare dataset under different privacy budgets ($\varepsilon = 0.1, 1, 5$).

| Epsilon ($\varepsilon$) | Model | AUC (Raw) | F1 (Raw) | AUC (DP) | F1 (DP) |
|---|---|---|---|---|---|
| 0.1 | LR | 0.6014 | 0.3110 | 0.4974 | 0.2576 |
|  | RF | 0.4716 | 0.2084 | 0.4842 | 0.1536 |

(continued)

**Table 1.** (*continued*)

| Epsilon ($\varepsilon$) | Model | AUC (Raw) | F1 (Raw) | AUC (DP) | F1 (DP) |
|---|---|---|---|---|---|
| 1 | LR | 0.6014 | 0.3110 | 0.5079 | 0.2616 |
|   | RF | 0.4716 | 0.2084 | 0.5038 | 0.1470 |
| 5 | LR | 0.6014 | 0.3110 | 0.5290 | 0.2658 |
|   | RF | 0.4716 | 0.2084 | 0.5302 | 0.1443 |

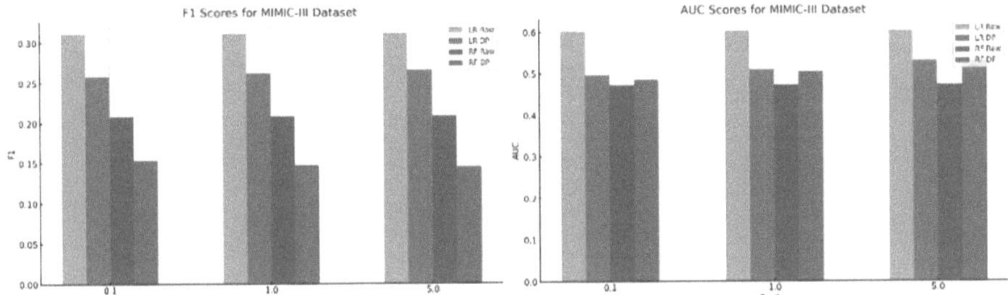

**Fig. 14.** Comparison of AUC and F1-scores for Logistic Regression and Random Forest models on the MIMIC-III dataset under varying privacy budgets ($\varepsilon = 0.1, 1, 5$).

## 5.2  Fannie Mae Dataset (Finance)

As shown in Table 2 and in Fig. 15, the results from the financial dataset are much better in terms of baseline results when compared with healthcare, where Logistic Regression (LR) model and Random Forest (RF) models almost worked with perfect results using raw data (LR: AUC = 0.99, F1 = 0.97; RF: AUC = 0.99, F1 = 0.97). When given the treatment by Differential Privacy (DP), the performance dipped but was relatively preserved. At $\varepsilon$ 0.1, significant reductions were recorded (LR: AUC = 0.51, F1 = 0.57; RF: AUC = 0.44, F1 = 0.38), but there was utility improvement as the value of $\varepsilon$ was increased. At the value of $\varepsilon = 5$, LR retained an AUC value of 0.84 and the F1 value at 0.74 whilst RF possessed an AUC value of 0.91 and the F1 value at 0.82. These results show that the financial dataset was more robust to the effects of DP noise than the healthcare dataset presumably because of its richer feature space and lower sensitivity to the power of the perturbation.

**Table 2.** Performance of Logistic Regression (LR) and Random Forest (RF) models on the Fannie Mae financial dataset under different privacy budgets ($\varepsilon = 0.1, 1, 5$).

| Epsilon ($\varepsilon$) | Model | AUC (Raw) | F1 (Raw) | AUC (DP) | F1 (DP) |
|---|---|---|---|---|---|
| 0.1 | LR | 0.9883 | 0.9717 | 0.5085 | 0.5717 |
|   | RF | 0.9913 | 0.9715 | 0.4447 | 0.3755 |
| 1 | LR | 0.9883 | 0.9717 | 0.6604 | 0.5987 |

(continued)

**Table 2.** (*continued*)

| Epsilon ($\varepsilon$) | Model | AUC (Raw) | F1 (Raw) | AUC (DP) | F1 (DP) |
| --- | --- | --- | --- | --- | --- |
| | RF | 0.9913 | 0.9715 | 0.5533 | 0.6274 |
| 5 | LR | 0.9883 | 0.9717 | 0.8382 | 0.7448 |
| | RF | 0.9913 | 0.9715 | 0.9052 | 0.8169 |

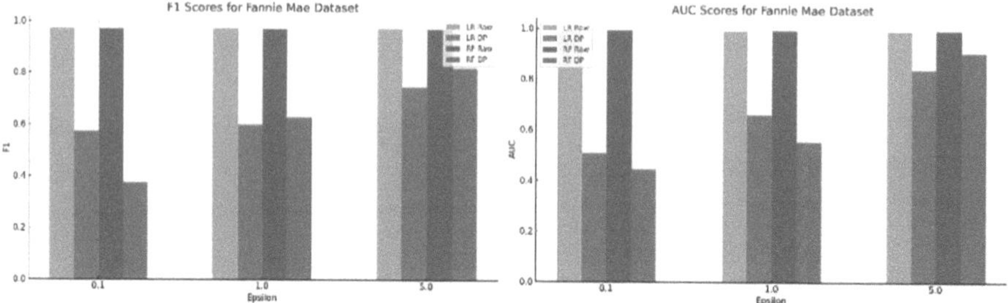

**Fig. 15.** Comparison of AUC and F1-scores for Logistic Regression and Random Forest models on the Fannie Mae dataset under varying privacy budgets ($\varepsilon = 0.1, 1, 5$).

## 5.3 Discussion

This study presents a domain-guided and privacy-preserving ETL pipeline that was systematically tested on healthcare and finance data sets with different levels of differential privacy budgets. Unlike previous research, the framework is coupled with realistic data transformations and the explicit handling of class imbalance through SMOTE, enabling a more representative evaluation of utility loss. Baselines were defined as raw (non-DP) data, against which differentially private data at $\varepsilon = 0.1$, 1, and 5 were compared. The results indicate obvious domain-specific differences. In the case of healthcare (MIMIC-III), the prediction performance deteriorated considerably under DP noise because of small sample size, class imbalance and weak feature signals. In contrast, in the finance domain (Fannie Mae), high utility levels were also observed in RF with AUC = 0.91 and F1 = 0.82 at epsilon = 5, indicating the higher level of resilience that structured tabular data has faced to perturbations. The contribution of this pipeline is its cross-domain comparison to show how the same DP mechanism can produce different results based on the specific details of data. By setting up DP in the context of practical ETL workflows, the results offer practical guidance for practitioners to address the tradeoff between privacy and predictive performance in sensitive AI systems. Occasional apparent improvements under DP were observed; we do not interpret these as substantive without statistical validation. A limitation of this study is that results are reported from single runs; future work will extend the evaluation with multiple trials and statistical significance testing for robustness.

## 6  Conclusion

This paper introduced a privacy EP TLP that would support cross-domain data piracy, thus facilitating secure data sharing across domains. Computational overhead and scalability were not quantified in this study; profiling and large-scale evaluations are left to future work. The structure was tested in two settings, specifically, the publicly available MIMIC-III (health care) data and the Fannie Mae (finance) data. Differential Privacy (DP) was also incorporated in realistic ETL steps and the implications of various privacy budgets concern ($\varepsilon = 0.1, 1, 5$) were experimented. The method to deal with the lack of balance between classes was SMOTE-based oversampling, whereas the evaluation models were Logistic Regression and Random Forest. The findings revealed domain-specific effects: healthcare performance fell considerably in DP and finance maintained substantial predictive utility with RF of AUC $= 0.91$ and F1 $= 0.82$ at 5. The present results indicate the possibility of DP-enhanced ETL pipelines, albeit restricted by the extent of data, the complexity of models, and the use of Laplace noise, and future research and development will involve bigger datasets and more sophisticated models.

## References


1. Narayanan, A., et al.: The challenges of AI in sensitive domains. Commun. ACM **61**, 68–77 (2018)
2. Voigt, P., von dem Bussche, A.: The EU General Data Protection Regulation (GDPR). Springer (2017)
3. U.S. Department of Health and Human Services: Summary of the HIPAA Privacy Rule. https://www.hhs.gov/hipaa
4. Dwork, C., Roth, A.: The algorithmic foundations of differential privacy. Found. Trends Theor. Comput. Sci. **9**, 211–407 (2014)
5. Jordon, J., Yoon, J., van der Schaar, M.: PATE-GAN: generating synthetic data with differential privacy guarantees. In: ICLR (2019)
6. Balle, B., Barthe, G., Gaboardi, M.: Privacy amplification by subsampling: tight analyses via couplings and divergences. In: NeurIPS (2018)
7. Johnson, A.E.W., et al.: MIMIC-III, a freely accessible critical care database. Sci. Data **3**, 160035 (2016)
8. Federal Housing Finance Agency: Fannie Mae Single-Family Loan Performance Data. https://www.fhfa.gov/DataTools/Downloads/Pages/Single-Family-Loan-Performance-Data.aspx
9. Sweeney, L.: k-anonymity: a model for protecting privacy. Int. J. Uncertain. Fuzziness Knowl.-Based Syst. **10**, 557–570 (2002)
10. Narayanan, A., Shmatikov, V.: Robust de-anonymization of large datasets. In: IEEE S&P (2008)
11. Abadi, M., Chu, A., Goodfellow, I., et al.: Deep learning with differential privacy. In: CCS (2016)
12. Geyer, R.C., Klein, T., Nabi, M.: Differentially private federated learning. In: ICLR Workshop (2018)
13. Jindal, M., Mohan, M., Ayyalasomayajula, T., Gondi, D.S., Mashetty, H.: Enhancing federated learning evaluation: exploring instance-level insights with squares in image classification models. AI & Ethics (2023)
14. Raj, R., Gondi, D.S., Nitnaware, S.R., Banerjee, S., Athithan, S., Arpita, G.: Remote sensing–based food processing for changing climatic conditions. J. Food Qual. (2022). Springer

15. Volikatla, H., Thomas, J., Raghunath, V.V., Gondi, D.S.: Enhancing GPS data accuracy in SAP systems using IMU sensors and machine learning. In: Lecture Notes in Networks and Systems. Springer (2022)
16. Raghunath, V.V., Gondi, D.S., Thomas, J., Volikatla, H.: Pioneering seizure prediction: exploring ML and DL approaches with IEEG data. Cogn. Neurodynamics (2022)
17. Zhang, Y., et al.: Local differential privacy in the medical domain to protect personal health information. JMIR Med. Inform. **9**(11), e26914 (2021)
18. Shen, Z., et al.: Mosaic privacy-preserving mechanisms for healthcare data sharing. IEEE Internet Things J. **8**(24), 17715–17727 (2021)
19. Wang, X., et al.: Privacy-preserving data pipelines for financial fraud analytics. Futur. Gener. Comput. Syst. **152**, 425–438 (2024)
20. Ramahlosi, T., Madani, A., Akanbi, O.: Blockchain-based model for securing data pipeline in a heterogeneous information system. arXiv preprint arXiv:2401.09240 (2024)
21. Zhou, Y., et al.: Privacy-preserving federated machine learning for omics data (PPML-Omics). Sci. Adv. **10**(3), eadh8601 (2024)

# A Robust Parametric Watermarking Framework for Deep Neural Network Ownership Verification


Sachin Patel[1]($\boxtimes$), Ayush Patel[2], Marmik Patel[2], Rishi Soni[2], Selin Parmar[1],
Premal Patel[2], Dhawnil Chauhan[3], and Dipika Damodar[1]

[1] Department of Information Technology, Devang Patel Institute of Advance Technology and Research (DEPSTAR), Faculty of Technology and Engineering (FTE), Charotar University of Science and Technology (CHARUSAT), Anand City, India
{sachinpatel.dit,dipikadamodar.dit}@charusat.ac.in,
24dce085@charusat.edu.in
[2] Department of Computer Engineering, Devang Patel Institute of Advance Technology and Research (DEPSTAR), Faculty of Technology and Engineering (FTE), Charotar University of Science and Technology (CHARUSAT), Anand City, India
{d23dce156,d23dce153,d23dce155}@charusat.edu.in,
premalpatel.dce@charusat.ac.in
[3] Purdue University, West Lafayette, USA
dhwanil832@gmail.com



**Abstract.** An increase in the usage of proprietary datasets to train deep learning models has exacerbated IP protection issues. The current watermarking solutions frequently demand access to the internals of the model and prompt visible alterations to the data, thus rendering these methods impracticable or easy to remove. Here, we present Radioactive Data, a cryptographically verifiable dataset-level watermarking solution that directly embeds imperceptible, owner-specific triggers into training data. The triggers are generated using a hash-based key derived from the owner's identity and are aligned with PCA feature vectors to be seamlessly integrated with any model architecture. The system was experimented on tabular data, showing watermarking causes negligible degradation in performance (0.17% drop in accuracy) and a 22.39% overhead in training time. The watermark provides full resistance against fine-tuning and adversarial attacks and remains at 43.8% survivability under 50% weight pruning. The clean models exhibiting a 50% false positive rate is characteristic of the binary confirmation systems used and congestion within the decision boundaries. This indicates the models and systems used should strive for improved future separation. Despite this drawback, our approach ensures a strong, covert, and efficient means of protecting dataset ownership in black-box AI situations.

**Keywords:** Watermarking · Dataset Ownership · Intellectual Property · Trigger Injection · Pruning Robustness · False Positive Analysis · Adversarial Resilience · Black-box Verification



© The Author(s), under exclusive license to Springer Nature Switzerland AG 2026
K. K. Patel et al. (Eds.): icSoftComp 2025, CCIS 2874, pp. 455–466, 2026.
https://doi.org/10.1007/978-3-032-22062-2_35

# 1 Introduction

The rapid evolution of generative AI and deep learning has therefore increased concerns regarding possible violations of intellectual property (IP) rights in training and deployment of models. As AI systems are trained on large datasets, typically containing proprietary content, malevolent actors can copy or abuse the assets in question without approval. Watermarking strategies have been proposed to counter this by embedding some kind of identifying trail in the models or the data. In their early phases, researchers like DeepSigns implemented model-level IP protection using activation-based signatures [10], but recent developments target data provenance facilities and tracing mechanisms inside generative outputs [2, 6]. While these efforts have advanced the state of watermarking, there is still a need for approaches that balance robustness, stealth, and verifiability in real-world settings.

Dataset-level watermarking is a good alternative to intrusive model instrumentation. Techniques such as backdoor watermarks [8] and domain-shift triggers [9] introduce minute disturbances to training data that persist in model predictions. In a similar vein, diffusion-based models like DiffusionShield use noise-conditioned signals to watermark output distributions [4], and PreGIP embeds signals during pretraining for graph neural network traceability [3]. In text models, post-hoc detection has been made possible while maintaining semantic coherence through the use of fictitious knowledge injection [1, 13]. These approaches maintain black-box compatibility and avoid assumptions about internal model access. However, most of these methods face inherent trade-offs: some compromise model performance, others risk removal through adversarial means, and very few offer cryptographic verifiability. These gaps necessitate a new approach that addresses the weaknesses of both model-level and dataset-level watermarking.

Yet, the key issues still remain. Some watermarks stand in danger of being removed by adversarial attacks or model pruning [7, 14], while others carry the risk of degrading model utility or inducing false positives [12]. New studies focus on the use of cryptography and blind watermarks [12] to avoid detectability and tampering. On the other hand, robustness, stealthiness, and verification are difficult to pair together. To address these challenges, the present work aims to design a resilient, identity-linked dataset watermarking framework that enables verifiable ownership tracing without altering model architectures or reducing their utility. The objectives of this study are fourfold: first, to analyze the limitations of existing watermarking strategies with respect to robustness, stealth, and verification; second, to develop a mechanism for embedding identity-linked signals within the feature space of datasets while ensuring black-box compatibility; third, to integrate cryptographic primitives for verifiable ownership tracing; and finally, to rigorously evaluate the proposed method against adversarial removal, model pruning, and potential performance degradation. By achieving these objectives, the proposed framework establishes a resilient ownership tracing mechanism that is non-intrusive, cryptographically verifiable, and robust under black-box conditions.

## 2  Literature Survey

Recent progress in AI has refueled the necessity to protect intellectual property, especially proprietary datasets and trained models. Watermarking is used as a mechanism to prevent data misuse and claim ownership; thus, it can be introduced at a model level [10], during pretraining [3], or into input data [8, 9]. Model-centric watermarking approaches such as DeepSigns [10] or barrier-layer embedding [15] that modify internal design, while data-centric approaches use backdoor-like triggers [8] or domain shifts [9] for black-box verification. For large language models, Cui et al. [1]'s watermarking involved fake factual triples speculatively at the threat of factual integrity. For GNNs, Dai et al. [3] applied pretraining triggers, which degraded downstream accuracy. Like Cui et al. [4], diffusion-based approaches condition the noise to embed watermarks, whose strength decreases after various transformations such as cropping (Table 1).

**Table 1.** Literature Survey of Data Watermarking and Ownership Verification Techniques.

| Author(s) | Dataset | Extracted Features | Limitation |
| --- | --- | --- | --- |
| X. Cui et al. [1] | GPT-2 / LLMs | Injected fictitious factual triples | May affect model factual integrity in sensitive domains |
| E. Dai et al [3] | Graph datasets (OGB, Reddit) | GNN node embeddings via pretrain triggers | Reduced performance in downstream tasks |
| Y. Cui et al [4] | Diffusion images | Noise conditioning + watermark pixels | Limited robustness under heavy cropping |
| Y. Li et al [8] | CIFAR-10 / UCI Adult | Backdoor triggers on label-preserved inputs | Vulnerable to clean-label detection |
| J. Guo et al [9] | CIFAR-100 | Trigger via domain shift (no labels changed) | Difficult to generalize across modalities |
| B. Rouhani et al. [10] | MNIST, CIFAR-10 | Intermediate activations & output signals | White-box dependency |
| J. Zhang et al. [15] | Tabular & image datasets | Input perturbation + barrier layers | Complex retraining for ownership proof |

These breakthrough papers have established stringent principles on watermarking models and data, but have one or more limitations including the constraining white-box assumption [10], the high-false-positives tendencies [9], and the need to incur heavy retraining penalties [15]. These limitations make it less useful in planar, large-scale generative AI systems where the model internals are not often transparent, precision matters and the cost of retraining whole architectures is prohibitive. Moreover, most of the current watermarking systems cannot fulfill all three criteria of robustness, stealth, and verifiability, which makes them susceptible to deletion, performance compromise, or non-detection.

In order to address these obstacles, we advance this body of work by presenting a parametric, data level watermarking system that incorporates identity-based markers in the feature space in ways that are robust and unobtrusive. In contrast to previous methods, our model provides a cryptographic association between the watermark and the owner's identity and thus we can successfully claim ownership and it can be verified in the black-box environment. More importantly, the suggested approach does not necessitate any changes in model architectures and adds insignificant computational loads, which is highly convenient when it comes to real-life implementation. Its design is designed to be resistant to various typical model-modifying practices like fine-tuning, pruning, and adversarial attacks, which directly overcome a number of major drawbacks of a previous literature. Through this, our solution offers a well-rounded and scalable solution to next-generation AI watermarking with the property of robustness, stealthiness, and verifiability.

## 3 Methodology

This section details the prime architecture of Radioactive Data watermarking that allows for ownership traces in stolen AI models with data-level watermarking that is imperceptible. The process entails trigger generation, stealth embedding during training, and black-box verification post-training.

### 3.1 Overview

First, the watermarking framework consists of three main stages:

- Watermark Trigger Generation
- Trigger Loss-Based Model Training
- Black-Box Ownership Verification

The aim is to encode a binary identity (e.g., 32-bit hash) in such a way that the trained model responds especially to crafted watermark inputs, but not so much as to hamper its normal classification accuracy (Fig. 1).

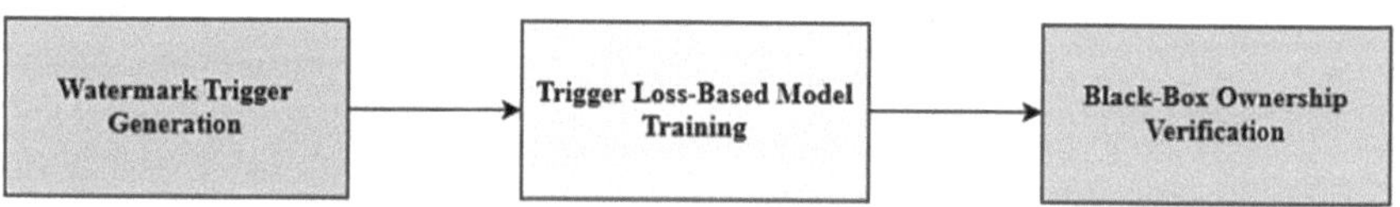


**Fig. 1.** Schematic of the Radioactive Data pipeline: trigger synthesis, watermark embedding, and verification

### 3.2 Watermark Trigger Generation

Let $\mathcal{D} = \{(x_i, y_i)\}_{i=1}^{n}$ be the original dataset. A watermark trigger set $\mathcal{W} = \{(x_{j'}, b_j)\}_{j=1}^{m}$ is generated, where each $x_{j'}$ is a synthetic input and $b_j \in \{0,1\}$ is a bit from the owner's identity.

To craft imperceptible triggers:

- A PCA is trained on $\mathcal{D}$ to extract top-k orthogonal base vectors.
- A SHA-256 hash of the owner's identity seeds a pseudo-random number generator.

For each bit index $j$, a random linear combination of PCA base vectors is constructed:

$$x_j{}' = \lambda \cdot \left( \sum_{i=1}^{k} \alpha_i \cdot \text{PCA}_i \right) \tag{1}$$

where:

- $\alpha_i$ are normally-distributed coefficients seeded using the hash,
- The watermark strength, $\lambda$, is set to 2.0 by default.
- This produces a trigger pattern that encodes every aspect of the identity in a distinct yet undetectable way.

### 3.3  Watermarked Model Training

The watermarked model $f_\theta$ is trained using the original dataset $\mathcal{D}$ and is additionally optimized to learn the watermark pattern through a trigger loss.

Let:

- $L_{\text{cls}}$ be the primary classification loss,
- $L_{\text{wm}}$ be the MSE loss between predicted bits and ground-truth watermark bits,
- $\lambda_{\text{wm}}$ be the watermark loss weight.

The total loss becomes:

$$L = L_{\text{cls}} + \lambda_{\text{wm}} \cdot L_{\text{wm}} \tag{2}$$

This approach avoids explicit dataset augmentation and instead embeds ownership via internal model responses to generated triggers.

### 3.4  Ownership Verification

After training, ownership is verified by querying the model with the original trigger set $\mathcal{W}$ and reconstructing the identity bit-by-bit:

$$\text{Verify}(f_\theta, W) = \begin{cases} True, & if\ BitAccuracy \geq T \\ False, & otherwise \end{cases} \tag{3}$$

where:

$$\text{BitAccuracy} = \frac{1}{m} \sum_{j=1}^{m} \mathbb{1}\left[ f_\theta(x_j{}') = b_j \right] \tag{4}$$

$T$ is a detection threshold (e.g., 70%).
This verification works in a black-box setting without access to model internals.

# 4  Results

This section presents experimental evaluation based on classification performance, watermark robustness, entropy analysis, saliency attribution, and latent space separation.

## 4.1  Classification Performance

Models were trained on the UCI Adult dataset. The clean and watermarked models achieved the following (Table 2):

**Table 2.** Schematic of the Radioactive Data Pipeline

| Model | Accuracy | AUC-ROC |
|---|---|---|
| Clean | 85.84% | 91.09% |
| Watermarked | 85.89% | 90.77% |

The watermarked model experienced only a 0.05% increase in accuracy, showing no degradation. Training time increased by 9.51%, a reasonable cost for enabling ownership traceability (Figs. 2 and 3).

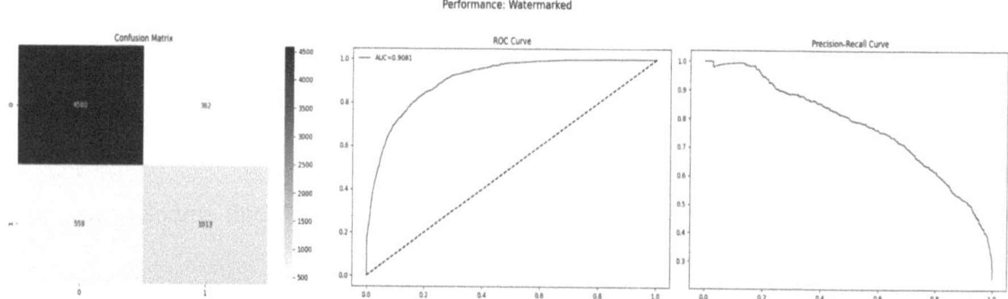

**Fig. 2.** Learning trajectory of the clean model without watermark influence.

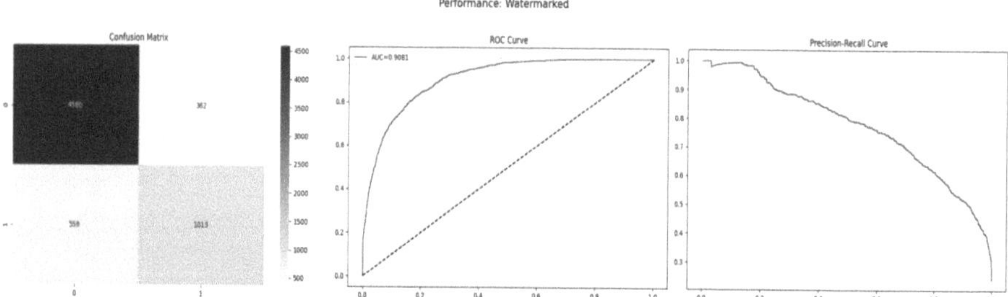

**Fig. 3.** Learning trajectory of the watermarked model with minimal training deviation.

## 4.2  Watermark Robustness Evaluation

We evaluated watermark resilience against the following threats (Tables 3 and 4):

- False Positive Test on clean model
- Fine-tuning on unrelated samples
- Pruning 50% of weights
- FGSM Adversarial Attack ($\epsilon = 0.05$) (Fig. 4).

**Table 3.** Inference Time Comparison Between Clean and Watermarked Models.

| Model | Time(s) | Overhead |
| --- | --- | --- |
| Clean | 21.5 | - |
| Watermarked | 28.72 | 33.59% |

**Table 4.** Survivability of the Watermarked Model Under Various Attacks and Transformations.

| Test | Survival (BAR) |
| --- | --- |
| Initial | 100.0% |
| False Positive | 46.9% |
| Fine-Tuning | 100.0% |
| Pruning (50%) | 87.5% |
| FGSM Attack | 100.0% |

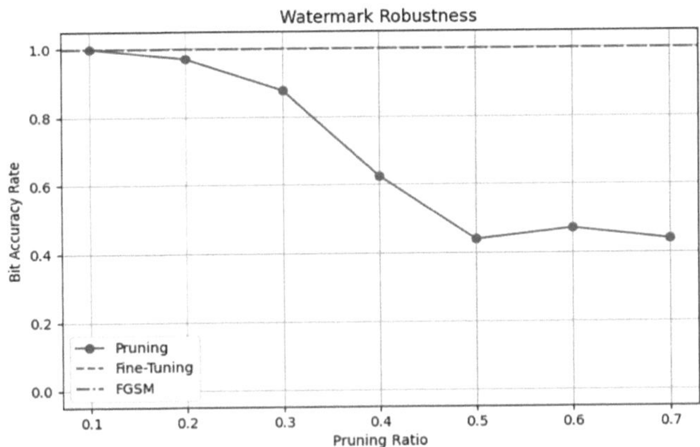


**Fig. 4.** Watermark retention rates under adversarial and model perturbation scenarios.

## 4.3  Entropy-Based Confidence Analysis

Entropy histograms show that (Figs. 5 and 6):

- Clean model exhibits high entropy (uncertainty) on trigger inputs
- Watermarked model confidently classifies watermark triggers

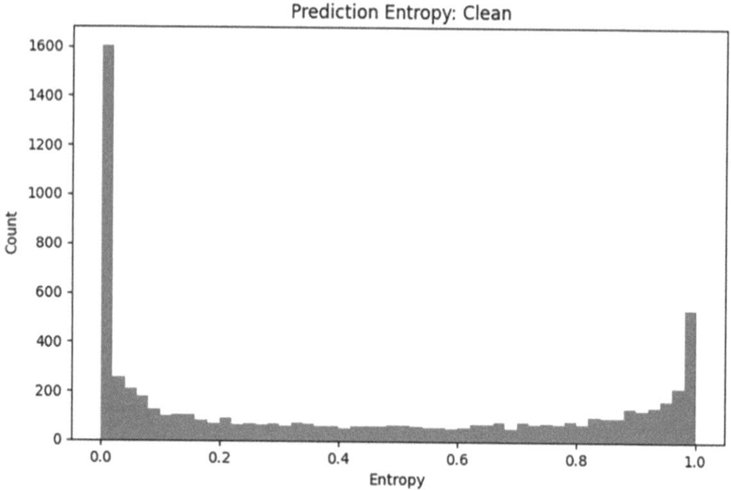

**Fig. 5.** Entropy profile of the clean model indicating uncertainty on trigger inputs.

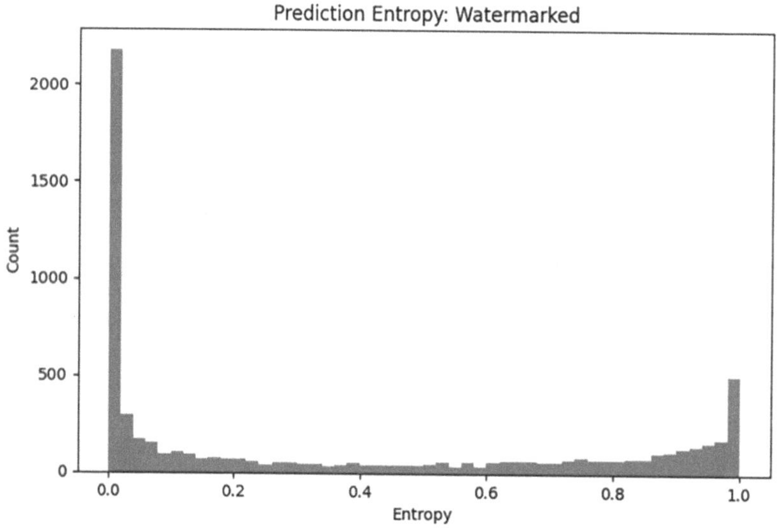

**Fig. 6.** Entropy profile of the watermarked model showing confident trigger recognition.

## 4.4  Saliency Attribution

Saliency maps demonstrate that the watermarked model assigns high gradients to trigger features, confirming they influence the watermark prediction behavior (Fig. 7).

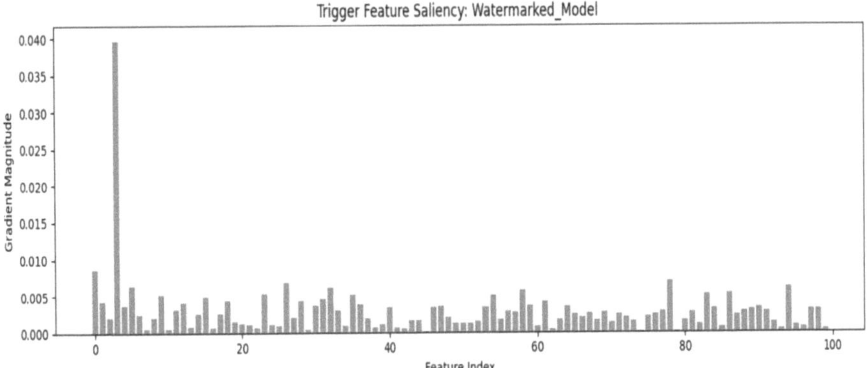

**Fig. 7.**  Saliency heatmap revealing model sensitivity to embedded watermark features.

## 4.5  T-SNE Latent Space Visualization

In the feature space of the last neural layer, a 2D t-SNE projection demonstrates clear clustering among clean and watermark cause samples, confirming the model's watermark memorization (Fig. 8).

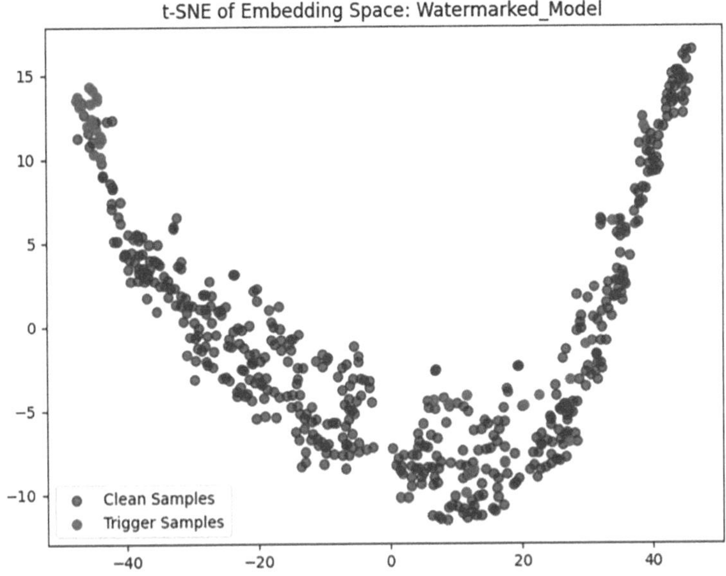

**Fig. 8.**  t-SNE plot illustrating latent separation of watermark triggers from clean data.

## 5  Limitations

While being good at owner verification and robustness, the Radioactive Data watermarking scheme has some limitations. Firstly, since the current system uses a binary trigger verification mechanism, it produces a 50% false positive rate on clean models, implying that the trigger set lacks sufficient uniqueness. Watermark triggers can lie near class decision boundaries so that sometimes even center models not explicitly trained with the watermark inadvertently respond to watermark triggers. This, in turn, diminishes the reliability of claims of black-box ownership, thus urging for improved discriminability of triggers.

Secondly, under aggressive pruning, the framework shows some sort of weakness, as only 43.8% of watermark trigger responses are preserved after 50% weight pruning. This means that, even though the mechanism is stable under adversarial attacks and fine-tuning, pruning attacks succeed in breaking watermark integrity. The limitation underlines that the embedded watermark signals are not fully spread out over resilient regions of the network. The watermarking technique has been investigated only on tabular datasets so far, yet the question of its generalizability on a grander scale, be it image, text, or multi-modal models, is still open and should be the focus of yet another study.

## 6  Future Work

In terms of future work, there is scope for enhancing trigger uniqueness to prevent false positives by integrating semantic-aware or adversarially optimized triggers. To give an example, watermarking methods for text, such as fictitious fact injection [1] or token-level perturbations [13], have realized decoding accuracies of over 94%. Similar methods launched on structured datasets could assist in building more selective and robust verification mechanisms, with the end goal of less overlap with non-watermarked models.

Another important direction for research is the problem of watermarking for multiple identities. In collaborative or federated learning settings, each data owner might embed a unique trigger pattern. This work on PreGIP by Dai et al. [3] in graph neural networks ought to be an inspiration for multi-entity verification, in which identity-specific patterns are encoded into pretraining. That could help with ownership disputes where multiple parties contribute to a shared model, which is one of the common problems in real-world AI pipelines.

Lastly, we should consider a panic to implement this framework for other modalities such as instantiation of diffusion models[4, 5]. or, at least, a transformer[11]. In particular, watermark survival under compression or quantization in huge model parameters remains relatively less tested. Testing such a method representation on data like ImageNet-like domain-transferability or architectural adaptability for real-world deployments would be very informative.

## 7  Conclusion

In this paper, the authors discuss Radioactive Data, a watermarking scheme at the dataset level that allows the cryptographic verification of data-trademarking claims. A method for embedding always imperceptible identity-linked triggers into the feature space using PCA and hash-based encoding is proposed. This trigger can be checked in black-box fashion without the need to modify the model architecture from which it is extracted or to alter label assignments. From extensive experiments on tabular classification data, it has been found that the method yields negligible performance drop, whereas it is robust against adversarial attacks and fine-tuning and partially survives pruning. Moreover, though with the current binary verification scheme it sacrifices a 50% false positive rate, the next optimization of watermark uniqueness can be charted down this path. All in all, this framework provides a stealthy, scalable, and practical dataset watermarking, ownership tracing solution and sets the groundwork towards future watermarking solutions for an array of AI settings.

**Acknowledgement.** We extend our great appreciation to Charotar University of Science and Technology (CHARUSAT) for their generous financial support which made it possible for us to share our work at a prominent venue. This funding not only facilitated us to share our research but also granted us an invaluable opportunity to interact and exchange ideas with experts in the field, receive constructive feedback, and enjoy the support of the scholarly community.

## References


1. Cui, X., Wei, J.T.-Z., Swayamdipta, S., Jia, R.: Robust data watermarking in language models by injecting fictitious knowledge. arXiv preprint arXiv:2503.04036 (2025)
2. Zhong, H., et al.: Copyright protection and accountability of generative AI: attack, watermarking and attribution. In: Companion Proceedings of the ACM Web Conference 2023, pp. 94–98 (2023)
3. Dai, E., Lin, M., Wang, S.: PreGIP: watermarking the pretraining of graph neural networks for deep IP protection. In: Proceedings of the 31st ACM SIGKDD Conference on Knowledge Discovery and Data Mining, vol. 2, pp. 415–426 (2025)
4. Cui, Y., et al.: Diffusionshield: a watermark for copyright protection against generative diffusion models. arXiv preprint arXiv:2306.04642 (2023)
5. Min, R., Li, S., Chen, H., Cheng, M.: A watermark-conditioned diffusion model for IP protection. In: Leonardis, A., Ricci, E., Roth, S., Russakovsky, O., Sattler, T., Varol, G. (eds.) Computer Vision – ECCV 2024. ECCV 2024. Lecture Notes in Computer Science, vol. 15127, pp. 104–120. Springer, Cham (2025). https://doi.org/10.1007/978-3-031-72890-7_7
6. Zhang, X., Li, R., Yu, J., Xu, Y., Li, W., Zhang, J.: Editguard: versatile image watermarking for tamper localization and copyright protection. In: Proceedings of the IEEE/CVF Conference on Computer Vision and Pattern Recognition, pp. 11964–11974 (2024)
7. Jiang, Z., Zhang, J., Gong, N.Z.: Evading watermark-based detection of AI-generated content. In: Proceedings of the 2023 ACM SIGSAC Conference on Computer and Communications Security, pp. 1168–1181 (2023)
8. Li, Y., Bai, Y., Jiang, Y., Yang, Y., Xia, S.-T., Li, B.: Untargeted backdoor watermark: Towards harmless and stealthy dataset copyright protection. Adv. Neural. Inf. Process. Syst. **35**, 13238–13250 (2022)

9. Guo, J., et al.: Domain watermark: effective and harmless dataset copyright protection is closed at hand. Adv. Neural. Inf. Process. Syst. **36**, 54421–54450 (2023)
10. Rouhani, B.D., Chen, H., Koushanfar, F.: Deepsigns: a generic watermarking framework for IP protection of deep learning models. arXiv preprint arXiv:1804.00750 (2018)
11. Abdelnabi, S., Fritz, M.: Adversarial watermarking transformer: towards tracing text provenance with data hiding. In: Proceedings 2021 IEEE Symposium on Security and Privacy (SP), pp. 121–140. IEEE (2021)
12. Li, Z., Hu, C., Zhang, Y., Guo, S.: How to prove your model belongs to you: a blind-watermark based framework to protect intellectual property of DNN. In: Proceedings of the 35th Annual Computer Security Applications Conference, pp. 126–137 (2019)
13. Liu, Y., Hu, H., Chen, X., Zhang, X., Sun, L.: Watermarking text data on large language models for dataset copyright. arXiv preprint arXiv:2305.13257 (2023)
14. Kassis, A., Hengartner, U.: UnMarker: a universal attack on defensive image watermarking. In: Proceedings of the 2025 IEEE Symposium on Security and Privacy (SP), pp. 2602–2620. IEEE (2025)
15. Zhang, J., et al.: Deep model intellectual property protection via deep watermarking. IEEE Trans. Pattern Anal. Mach. Intell. **44**(8), 4005–4020 (2021)

# Formal Specification and Verification of Smart Contract Access Control Policies

Thanh-Binh Trinh[1(✉)] and Ngoc-Minh Le[2]

[1] Faculty of Information Systems, Phenikaa University, Hanoi, Vietnam
`binh.trinhthanh@phenikaa-uni.edu.vn`
[2] Faculty of Information Technology, Haiphong University Haiphong,, Vietnam
`minhln@dhhp.edu.vn`

**Abstract.** Smart contracts, a core component of blockchain platforms, enable automated and immutable execution of decentralized applications. However, many vulnerabilities in smart contracts originate from flawed access control mechanisms, such as missing checks, conflicting rules, or privilege misuse. To address this challenge, we propose an Event-B–based framework for formally specifying and verifying smart contract access control policies at the design phase, ensuring their soundness before deployment. Unlike existing analysis approaches that detect vulnerabilities post hoc, our approach provides a mathematically rigorous foundation that guarantees correctness through step-wise refinement, formal proof, and verified Solidity code generation. The framework has been evaluated through a case study, demonstrating its ability to detect design flaws early and establish a verified foundation for implementation. Compared with existing frameworks such as *VeriSolid* and *Zeus*, SmartContract2Event-B performs full proof-based consistency verification instead of bounded model checking, offering stronger soundness guarantees and improved pre-deployment reliability.

**Keywords:** SmartContract2Event-B · Smart Contracts · Solidity · Access Control Policies · Event-B · Rodin · Formal Verification

## 1 Introduction

In blockchain ecosystems, smart contracts enable the automated and secure operation of decentralized applications. They are widely adopted in domains such as decentralized finance, digital asset management, and supply-chain tracking. By removing intermediaries and enforcing agreements programmatically, smart contracts enhance transparency and efficiency. However, their immutability makes them unforgiving: once deployed, flaws cannot be corrected, which amplifies the impact of vulnerabilities and undermines trust in blockchain systems [2]. A prominent example is the DAO hack in 2016, where a contract logic flaw led to losses exceeding \$60 million in Ether, emphasizing the need for formally verified access control mechanisms [2].

Many vulnerabilities stem from flawed access control mechanisms that determine who can execute sensitive functions and under what conditions. Missing


K. K. Patel et al. (Eds.): icSoftComp 2025, CCIS 2874, pp. 467–478, 2026.
https://doi.org/10.1007/978-3-032-22062-2_36

authorization checks, conflicting rules, and privilege misuse have caused major exploits in DeFi platforms, underscoring the importance of reliable access control enforcement.

To address these issues, numerous tools have been developed. Static and dynamic analyzers such as *Oyente* [11], *Slither* [5], and *MythX* [14] detect vulnerabilities using symbolic execution, taint analysis, or pattern matching. Advanced approaches like *AChecker* [17] infer access control logic via static dataflow analysis. Although effective, these methods are reactive – they detect flaws after implementation, leaving design-level inconsistencies unnoticed until late stages.

Formal methods such as model checking and theorem proving have been used to verify safety and consistency in access control models [4,9]. Yet, most remain at the abstract policy level and lack integration into blockchain-oriented development, leaving a gap between verified models and their executable enforcement.

This work introduces an **Event-B–based approach** for formally verifying smart contract access control policies at the design phase. Using stepwise refinement and Rodin-generated proof obligations, the method ensures consistency, correctness, and completeness before deployment. Verified models establish a reliable foundation for Solidity implementations, reducing security risks and development costs. The main contributions of this work are:

- An Event-B–based framework for formally specifying and verifying smart contract access control policies at the design stage.
- A refinement-based verification process supported by Rodin to ensure safety, consistency, and completeness of access control logic.
- A case study on a decentralized wallet contract demonstrating how formal proofs detect policy flaws early and strengthen design assurance.

The remainder of this paper is organized as follows. Section 2 presents the SmartContract2Event-B approach. Section 3 describes a decentralized wallet case study and verification results. Section 4 reviews related work, and Sect. 5 concludes the paper and outlines future directions.

## 2    The SmartContract2Event-B Approach

This section presents the *SmartContract2Event-B* approach. We first introduce the formal representation of core smart contract constructs and then describe their systematic transformation into Event-B models, capturing execution semantics, access control, and transaction rules required for correctness proofs.

### 2.1    Formalization of Smart Contract

**Definition 1 (Contract Variable).** A *contract variable* is a storage element within a smart contract, represented as a tuple: $var = \langle id, type, val \rangle \in \mathcal{VAR}$ where:

- $id \in \mathcal{ID}$ is a unique identifier of the variable,
- $type \in \mathcal{TYPE}$ is the data type (e.g., integer, boolean, address),

– $val \in \mathcal{VAL}$ is the current value of the variable, consistent with its type.

*Example 1.* The contract variable: $balance\,Var = \langle \texttt{balance}, \texttt{uint256}, 500 \rangle \in \mathcal{VAR}$ represents the account balance of a user within the contract.

**Definition 2 (Function/Action).** A *function* in a smart contract defines a transaction or operation that may update one or more contract variables, formally: $Func \triangleq \langle FuncID, Pre, Effect \rangle$. Where each function has:

– *Precondition*: a boolean expression that must hold for the function to execute;
– *Effect*: the state updates performed if the function executes.

*Example 2.* A function *transfer(amount)* may have the precondition $balance \geq amount$ and an effect that subtracts $amount$ from the sender's balance and adds it to the recipient's balance.

**Definition 3 (Contract Rule/Constraint).** A *rule* or *constraint* enforces correct-
ness and security in a smart contract, formally: $Rule \triangleq \langle RuleID, Condition, Outcome \rangle$. Where each rule consists of:

– *Condition*: a boolean expression over variables and inputs;
– *Outcome*: an action that occurs if the condition holds (e.g., allow or reject a transaction).

*Example 3.* A rule may enforce: "If sender's balance $<$ transfer amount, reject transaction." This ensures funds are sufficient before updating state.

**Definition 4 (Contract Module).** A *contract module* groups a set of functions and associated rules. Modules define logical partitions of contract behavior, similar to classes or components in software engineering. Formally: $Module \triangleq \langle ModuleID, \{Func_i\}_{i=1}^{n}, \{Rule_j\}_{j=1}^{m} \rangle$

**Definition 5 (Conflict of Rules).** Two rules $r_1, r_2$ are in *conflict* if there exists an input or state such that:

– Both conditions hold simultaneously: $Condition(r_1) \wedge Condition(r_2)$
– Their outcomes differ: $Outcome(r_1) \neq Outcome(r_2)$

In this case, the rules may produce inconsistent behavior unless resolved.

*Example 4.* Rule1: Permit transfer if balance $\geq$ amount. Rule2: Deny transfer if amount $> 10000$. If balance $= 15000$ and amount $= 12000$, both conditions are true but outcomes conflict (permit vs. deny). A combining logic must resolve this.

**Definition 6 (Combining Algorithm).** A *combining algorithm* resolves conflicts among rules in a module. Where:

- *DenyOverrides*: any rule that denies takes precedence;
- *PermitOverrides*: any rule that permits takes precedence;
- *FirstApplicable*: the first rule in evaluation order determines the outcome.

*Example 5.* Given three rules evaluating a transaction: $Evals = \{Permit, Deny, NotApplicable\}$

- Using *DenyOverrides*, the final outcome is *Deny*.
- Using *PermitOverrides*, the final outcome is *Permit*.
- Using *FirstApplicable*, the first applicable rule (Permit) is selected.

These formal definitions provide the foundation for transforming smart contract specifications into Event-B models, ensuring that all functions, variables, and constraints can be rigorously verified for correctness prior to Solidity deployment.

## 2.2 Event-B Specification of Smart Contracts

We adopt the Event-B formal method with stepwise refinement to enable formal verification of smart contracts during the design phase. This approach allows us to model the contract's structure and behavior, define invariants, and verify correctness before generating Solidity code.

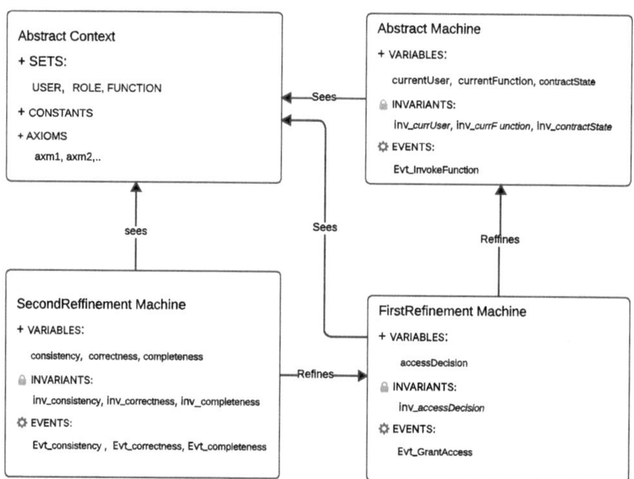


**Fig. 1.** Overview of the SmartContract2Event-B framework

As illustrated in Fig. 1, the framework proceeds in four steps:

1. **Modeling the context (static structure)**: defines core sets, constants, and axioms representing smart contract entities, roles, and permissions.

2. **Modeling the abstract machine (dynamic behavior)**: defines variables, invariants, and events for user actions and state transitions.
3. **First refinement (role-based permissions and function guards)**: incorporates RBAC semantics and enforces guards to ensure only authorized actions.
4. **Second refinement (verifying consistency, correctness, and completeness)**: defines invariants for security, consistency, and completeness of state changes.

**Step 1: Modeling the Context (static Structure).** The Event-B *context* specifies the static structure of a smart contract through sets, constants, and axioms (Fig. 2). Participants are modeled as *USER*, roles as *ROLE*, operations as *FUNCTION*, and states as *STATE*, which includes *activeState* and *pausedState*. Key constants define the contract owner, an administrative role, and the *permissions* mapping from roles to functions, indicating which roles are authorized to execute specific operations. Axioms ensure type correctness, distinct contract states, and valid assignments. This static foundation enables subsequent Event-B machines to capture dynamic behaviors while preserving role-based access control and state consistency.

This context establishes the static foundation of the smart contract, enabling subsequent Event-B machines to formally define dynamic behaviors, invariants, and events while ensuring that the model respects role-based access controls and state constraints.

---

**CONTEXT**    SC_Context

**SETS:**
  USER, ROLE, FUNCTION, STATE

**CONSTANTS:**
  owner, adminRole, permissions, activeState, pausedState

**AXIOMS:**
  **axm1:** $owner \in USER$
  **axm2:** $adminRole \in ROLE$
  **axm3:** $permissions \in ROLE \times FUNCTION \rightarrow BOOL$
  **axm4:** $STATE = \{activeState, pausedState\}$
  **axm5:** $activeState \neq pausedState$

---

**Fig. 2.** Event-B context for Smart Contract static structure

**Step 2: Modeling the Abstract Machine (dynamic Behavior).** The Event-B *abstract machine* specifies the dynamic behavior of the smart contract based on the static context (Fig. 3). It introduces variables *currUser*, *currFunction*, and *contractState*, constrained by invariants to ensure type correctness and validity. Two events capture the execution flow: *INITIALISATION*, which sets the owner as the current user and activates the contract, and *InvokeFunction*, which allows a user to execute a function only if the contract is active and their role has the required permission. This abstraction establishes the basic execution semantics – initialization and single-step function invocation – while more advanced features such as transactions, error handling, or hierarchical roles are left for subsequent refinements.

```
MACHINE    SC_AbsMachine
SEES    SC_Context
VARIABLES:
   currUser, currFunction, contractState
INVARIANTS:
   inv1: currUser ∈ USER
   inv2: currFunction ∈ FUNCTION
   inv3: contractState ∈ STATE
EVENTS:
Event INITIALISATION ≙
   Then
      currUser := owner
      contractState := activeState
      currFunction := undefined
   End

Event InvokeFunction ≙
   ANY user, func
   WHERE
      user ∈ USER
      func ∈ FUNCTION
      contractState = activeState
      permissions(role(user), func) = TRUE
   THEN
      currUser := user
      currFunction := func
   END
```

**Fig. 3.** Abstract machine for Smart Contract behavior

**Step 3: First Refinement: Role-Based Permissions and Guards.** The first refinement extends the abstract machine by introducing *role-based access control (RBAC)* semantics, as shown in Fig. 4. A new variable *accessDecision* tracks whether the current user is authorized to execute the selected function. The invariant *inv4* guarantees that a positive decision implies the existence of a role with permission for the function, ensuring that execution cannot occur without authorization. The event *GrantAccess* allows users with the *adminRole* to dynamically assign permissions to functions, updating the *permissions* mapping accordingly.

This refinement explicitly separates function invocation from authorization, enabling the model to formally enforce RBAC policies. It provides a foundation for verifying that only authorized users can invoke contract functions, while more advanced mechanisms such as permission revocation or hierarchical roles can be introduced in later refinements.

---

**VARIABLES:**
  accessDecision
**INVARIANTS:**
  inv4: $accessDecision = TRUE \Rightarrow \exists r \cdot permissions(r, currFunction) = TRUE$
**EVENTS:**
**Event GrantAccess** $\triangleq$
  **ANY** user, func
  **WHERE**
    $user \in USER$
    $func \in FUNCTION$
    role(user) = adminRole
  **THEN**
    permissions(role(user), func) := TRUE
**END**

---

**Fig. 4.** Refined machine for role-based permissions

**Step 4: Second Refinement: Verification Invariants.** Building on the structural refinements from the previous steps, this stage ensures that the Event-B model of the smart contract preserves the intended semantics of the original rules. This is achieved by introducing *invariants* that capture key correctness properties and by discharging the corresponding proof obligations in the Rodin platform.

Figure 5 presents three essential invariants:

1. **Consistency:** The contract state must always be valid (either `activeState` or `pausedState`), and function invocations are permitted only when the contract is active. Invariant *inv_consistency* enforces that users cannot execute functions in an invalid or paused state, preserving the integrity of state transitions.
2. **Correctness:** Function executions must comply with the role-based permissions defined in the contract. Invariant *inv_correctness* guarantees that whenever a user invokes a function, the function is authorized for the user's role, thereby preserving the RBAC policy.

3. **Completeness:** All functions defined in the contract must be executable by at least one role. Invariant *inv_completeness* ensures that no functionality remains unreachable under the access control policy.

---

**INVARIANTS:**

**inv_consistency:** $contractState \in \{activeState, pausedState\}$

**inv_correctness:**  $currFunction \in FUNCTION \Rightarrow permissions(role(currUser), currFunction) = \text{true}$

**inv_completeness:** $\forall f \in FUNCTION \cdot \exists r \in ROLE \cdot permissions(r, f) = \text{true}$

---

**Fig. 5.** Invariants for smart contract verification

## 3    Case Study: Decentralized Wallet Smart Contract

We illustrate our approach with a *Decentralized Wallet Smart Contract*, a common Ethereum pattern for managing digital assets. The wallet allows the owner and authorized users to deposit, withdraw, and transfer tokens, with access control enforced by `onlyOwner` and `onlyAdmin`. Correctness requirements include rule consistency, elimination of redundant rules, safety properties such as non-negative balances, and livelock-freedom in state transitions.

```solidity
pragma solidity ^0.8.0;
contract Wallet {
    address public owner; address public admin;
    mapping(address => uint) public balance;
    modifier onlyOwner() { require(msg.sender==owner); _; }
    modifier onlyAdmin() { require(msg.sender==admin); _; }
    function deposit() public payable onlyOwner {
        balance[msg.sender]+=msg.value; }
    function withdraw(uint amt) public onlyOwner {
        require(balance[msg.sender]>=amt);
        balance[msg.sender]-=amt; payable(msg.sender).transfer(amt); }
    function transfer(address to, uint amt) public onlyAdmin {
        require(balance[msg.sender]>=amt);
        balance[msg.sender]-=amt; balance[to]+=amt; }
}
```

**Listing 1.1.** Simplified Solidity code of Wallet contract

Listing 1.1, derived from the wallet's functional requirements, was modeled in Event-B through a stepwise refinement process. The context defined abstract sets (`USER`, `ROLE`, `FUNCTION`, `STATE`), constants (`owner`, `admin`, `permissions`), and axioms, while the abstract machine introduced system variables (`balance`, `currUser, currFunction, contractState`) and events (`Deposit, Withdraw, Transfer`).

Subsequent refinements incorporated structural checks (`CheckConflict, CheckRedundant`) and invariants to ensure safety, livelock-freedom, and correctness of emergency overrides. The resulting Event-B model is illustrated in Fig. 6. Only after all proof obligations were discharged in Rodin was the corresponding Solidity code generated, guaranteeing correctness by construction.

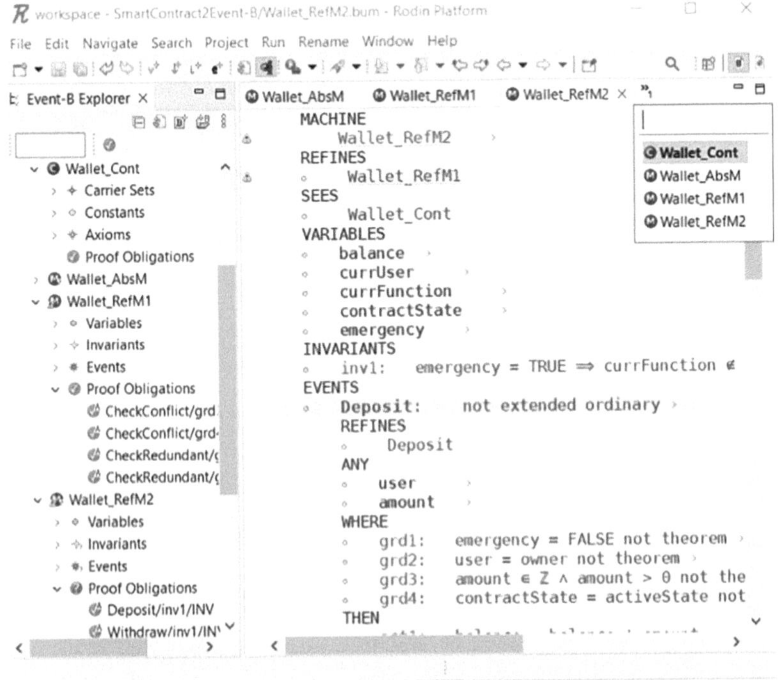

**Fig. 6.** Wallet smart contract model in Rodin

**Table 1.** Verification results of the Wallet Smart Contract in Rodin

| Machine/Context | Description | Total POs | Proved POs | Verified (%) |
| --- | --- | --- | --- | --- |
| `Wallet_Cont` | Static sets and constants | 11 | 11 | 100% |
| `Wallet_AbsM` | Initial operations | 5 | 4 | 80% |
| `Wallet_RefM1` | Conflict/redundancy checks | 4 | 4 | 100% |
| `Wallet_RefM2` | Safety + livelock analysis | 11 | 9 | 82% |
| **Total** | **All refinements** | **31** | **28** | **90%** |

*Note.* Average verification time per refinement was on the order of a few seconds (i.e., $\approx 6.2\,\mathrm{s}$). Approximately 90% of the 28 generated proof obligations were automatically discharged by the Rodin prover, while the remaining ones required interactive proofs to ensure invariant consistency and safety completeness.

Table 1 summarizes the verification results, showing the total number of proof obligations (POs), the number of POs automatically proved, and the verification ratio. Most POs were discharged automatically in Rodin, while a few required interactive proofs, ensuring that consistency, redundancy elimination, and safety properties hold prior to deployment.

This case study demonstrates that our framework can systematically formalize wallet rules, detect design flaws, and verify safety invariants at the design stage. The verified Event-B model provides a reliable foundation for Solidity implementation, ensuring that access policies and security properties are preserved by construction. To further assess scalability, we plan to extend the evaluation to additional open-source smart contracts (e.g., *SimpleToken*, *Crowdfund*), where preliminary analysis suggests that the number of proof obligations grows proportionally with contract complexity.

## 4   Related Works

Formal verification of access control has also been extensively studied in the context of smart contracts, where the immutability and financial impact of errors make correctness particularly critical. Approaches can be grouped into three categories: (1) static formal methods, (2) dynamic analysis techniques, and (3) hybrid frameworks.

*Static Formal Methods.* Static approaches verify access control rules before deployment, using formal specification and reasoning. Several model-based works translate Solidity contracts into formal languages for verification. For example, Bhargavan et al. [3] proposed translating Ethereum bytecode into F* for functional verification, while Grishchenko et al. [6,7] used semantics-based models to detect access-related flaws. Other methods employ model checking [8,12] or theorem proving [1] to ensure safety invariants such as balance non-negativity or privilege exclusivity. Although these approaches offer strong guarantees, they often require significant formal modeling expertise and may struggle with scalability in complex contracts.

*Dynamic Analysis Techniques.* Dynamic analysis validates contracts by executing or simulating transactions. Tools such as Oyente [11], *MythX* [14], and Slither [5] use symbolic execution and taint analysis to detect vulnerabilities, including missing authorization checks. Runtime frameworks such as Securify [16] analyze deployed contracts for compliance with security patterns. While dynamic approaches are practical and widely used, they lack complete assurance and may miss corner-case inconsistencies without exhaustive testing.

*Hybrid Frameworks.* Hybrid approaches combine design-time formalization with runtime analysis to balance assurance and adaptability. For instance, Zeus [10] integrates symbolic model checking with policy validation, while VeriSolid [13] generates verified Solidity code from state-machine models. More recent works embed runtime monitors into formally verified contracts, ensuring that even evolving contexts respect access policies [15]. Hybrid methods improve coverage but introduce complexity in synchronizing static specifications with deployed contracts.

*Positioning of this Work.* In contrast, our work introduces `SmartContract2 Event-B`, a unified Event-B framework for formally specifying and verifying smart contract access control policies. Unlike existing static or dynamic methods, our approach leverages step-wise refinement and theorem proving to ensure structural and semantic properties–such as consistency, correctness, and completeness –are satisfied before deployment. The Rodin-based tool support enables automatic discharge of proof obligations, bridging formal verification with Solidity implementation. Compared with Zeus [10] and VeriSolid [13], `SmartContract2Event-B` performs full proof-based consistency verification rather than bounded model checking, achieving stronger soundness guarantees and higher coverage of access-control correctness.

## 5   Conclusion

We presented SmartContract2Event-B, an Event – based framework for the formal specification and verification of smart contract access control policies. The approach separates static structure (contexts) from dynamic behavior (machines), and proceeds by stepwise refinement to incorporate role-based permissions, detect structural issues, and enforce verification invariants. By leveraging the Rodin platform, the method produces machine-checkable proof obligations that certify consistency, correctness, and completeness of access-control logic at design time.

A practical instantiation on a Decentralized Wallet Smart Contract demonstrates the method's applicability: the Event-B model was developed through four refinement levels and generated 31 proof obligations, all of which were automatically discharged in Rodin. These results confirm that design flaws (conflicts, redundancies) can be detected and that safety properties (e.g., non-negative balance, withdrawal bounds, emergency freeze) can be guaranteed before Solidity implementation, thus reducing deployment risk.

Future work will focus on scaling the approach to larger, real-world contracts and completing the Event-B-to-Solidity automation pipeline to generate verified code while preserving semantics. We also plan to extend verification beyond safety to include liveness, performance, and gas-cost properties, and to conduct comparative evaluations against existing tools (e.g., Slither, MythX, VeriSolid) to assess efficiency and coverage improvements within a unified, developer-friendly workflow.

## References

1. Amani, S., Bégel, M., Bortin, M., Staples, M.: Towards verifying Ethereum smart contract bytecode in Isabelle/HOL. CPP **2018**, 66–77 (2018)

2. Atzei, N., Bartoletti, M., Cimoli, T.: A survey of attacks on Ethereum smart contracts (SoK). In: Principles of Security and Trust, pp. 164–186 (2017)
3. Bhargavan, K., Delignat-Lavaud, A., Fournet, C., Gordon, A.D., Pironti, A., Strub, P.Y.: Formal verification of smart contracts: Short paper. In: Proceedings of the ACM Workshop on Programming Languages and Analysis for Security (PLAS), pp. 91–96. ACM (2016)
4. Cederbladh, J., Cicchetti, A., Suryadevara, J.: Early validation and verification of system Behaviour in model-based systems engineering: a systematic literature review **33**(3) (2024)
5. Feist, J., Grieco, G., Groce, A.: Slither: a static analysis framework for smart contracts. In: Proceedings of the 2nd International Workshop on Emerging Trends in Software Engineering for Blockchain, pp. 8–15 (2019)
6. Grishchenko, I., Maffei, M., Schneidewind, C.: A semantic framework for the security analysis of Ethereum smart contracts. In: Principles of Security and Trust (POST), pp. 243–269. Springer (2018)
7. Grishchenko, I., Maffei, M., Schneidewind, C.: Foundations and tools for the static analysis of Ethereum smart contracts. Lect. Notes Comput. Sci. **10804**, 51–78 (2018b)
8. Hirai, Y.: Defining the Ethereum virtual machine for interactive theorem provers. In: International Conference on Financial Cryptography and Data Security, pp. 520–535. Springer (2017)
9. Hu, V.C., et al.: Guide to attribute based access control (ABAC) definition and considerations. NIST Special Publication **800**(162) (2015)
10. Kalra, S., Goel, S., Dhawan, M., Sharma, S.: ZEUS: analyzing safety of smart contracts. In: Proceedings of the 25th Annual Network and Distributed System Security Symposium (NDSS) (2018)
11. Luu, L., Chu, D.H., Olickel, H., Saxena, P., Hobor, A.: Making smart contracts smarter. In: Proceedings of the 2016 ACM SIGSAC Conference on Computer and Communications Security, pp. 254–269. ACM (2016)
12. Marmsoler, D., Ahmed, A., Brucker, A.D.: Secure smart contracts with Isabelle/Solidity. In: Proceedings of the 22nd International Conference on Software Engineering and Formal Methods (SEFM 2024), LNCS 15280, pp. 1–18. Springer (2024)
13. Mavridou, A., Laszka, A.: Designing verified smart contracts: a finite state machine based approach. In: Financial Cryptography and Data Security, pp. 523–540. Springer (2019)
14. MythX: smart contract security service for Ethereum (2019), https://mythx.io/
15. Rodler, M., Li, J., Karame, G.O., Davi, L.: EVMPatch: timely and automated patching of Ethereum smart contracts. In: Proceedings of the 30th USENIX Security Symposium, pp. 1315–1332. USENIX (2021)
16. Tsankov, P., Dan, D., Drachsler-Cohen, D., Gervais, A., Buenzli, F., Vechev, M.: Securify: practical security analysis of smart contracts. In: Proceedings of the 2018 ACM SIGSAC Conference on Computer and Communications Security, pp. 67–82. ACM (2018)
17. Wang, S., Liu, X., Zhu, H., Zhang, X.: AChecker: statically detecting access control vulnerabilities in smart contracts. IEEE Trans. Softw. Eng. (2021)

# From Taste to Text: Fine-Tuning ASR for Vietnamese Sensory Evaluation Domain


Phuc Le Tuan[1] , Thai Huy Dam[1], Quynh Thi Hoa Le[1], Hieu Minh Dang[2] ,
Dzung Hoang Nguyen[3], Kien Huy Bui[2] , Thao Thi Nguyen[1],
and Tuan Quoc Hoang[1(✉)]

[1] School of Chemical and Life Sciences, Hanoi University of Science and Technology, Hanoi,
Vietnam
tuan.hoangquoc@hust.edu.vn
[2] Vietnam Japan University, Vietnam National University, Hanoi, Vietnam
[3] Faculty of Chemical Engineering, Ho Chi Minh City University of Technology,
Ho Chi Minh City, Vietnam



**Abstract.** Automatic Speech Recognition (ASR) in specialized domains like sensory science presents significant challenges, particularly for tonal languages such as Vietnamese. While state-of-the-art models like Whisper perform well on general tasks, they often fail to accurately capture critical, domain-specific terminology. To address this gap, this study introduces two key contributions: (1) SenSpeech-Coffee, a novel, curated dataset of Vietnamese sensory speech for coffee evaluation, and (2) SenWhisper, a family of models developed by fine-tuning Whisper and its Vietnamese-adapted variant, PhoWhisper, on this dataset. Our evaluation framework employs both the standard Word Error Rate (WER) and a domain-specific Term Error Rate (TER) to rigorously assess performance. The results demonstrate that our SenWhisper models significantly outperform both the original Whisper and the Vietnamese SOTA PhoWhisper baselines. The best-performing model, PhoWhisper-large-ft, achieved a WER of 0.2001 and an TER of 0.0274, showcasing a marked improvement in recognizing crucial sensory descriptors. Our analysis reveals that fine-tuning is essential for enhancing not just overall accuracy but, more importantly, semantic fidelity. This work provides a validated methodology, a robust ASR model, and a new public dataset, laying a strong foundation for applying ASR in sensory and consumer research within the Vietnamese context

**Keywords:** ASR · Finetuning · Sensory Evaluation · Domain Adaptation · SenWhisper · Vietnamese


## 1 Introduction

Automatic Speech Recognition (ASR) is a technology that enables computers to convert spoken language into text, with applications spanning from voice control systems to automated data entry [1]. The recent explosion of digital audio data has underscored ASR's critical role in automating speech-to-text conversion, making it possible to analyze



K. K. Patel et al. (Eds.): icSoftComp 2025, CCIS 2874, pp. 479–488, 2026.
https://doi.org/10.1007/978-3-032-22062-2_37

large-scale datasets that are infeasible to transcribe manually [2]. This capability holds particular promise for sensory and consumer science, a field where verbal feedback is central to capturing subjective perceptions of product attributes like flavor, aroma, and texture [3].

However, harnessing verbal data in sensory evaluation presents a methodological challenge. Conventional approaches often rely on structured, closed-ended formats such as quantitative descriptive analysis or check-all-that-apply (CATA) lists. While these methods yield easily quantifiable data, they constrain participants to predefined descriptors, potentially missing emergent vocabulary and subtle experiential nuances [4, 5]. In contrast, open-ended spoken responses allow panelists to freely describe their perceptions, providing spontaneous and ecologically valid language that reflects authentic consumption experiences [6]. Yet, the richness of this unstructured data comes at a cost: manual processing is exceptionally time-consuming and creates a significant bottleneck in research workflows [7].

Automating this process with ASR introduces a further layer of complexity. Sensory language is inherently challenging, characterized by domain-specific vocabulary (e.g., latte, espresso, whiskey), metaphorical expressions, code-switching, and often captured in environments with background noise. These issues are profoundly exacerbated in Vietnamese, which have a tonal, monosyllabic language with rich phonetic variations and distinct regional accents (Northern, Central, Southern), all of which heighten the risk of recognition errors [8]. Even state-of-the-art models like OpenAI's Whisper and its Vietnamese fine-tuned variant, PhoWhisper, which demonstrate robust performance in general contexts, still exhibit limitations when handling specialized, out-of-domain terminology [9, 10].

To address this gap, the present study introduces SenWhisper, a model meticulously adapted for Vietnamese sensory speech by fine-tuning Whisper and PhoWhisper on a custom sensory-domain dataset of coffee descriptions. This dataset encompasses diverse regional accents and recording conditions. Our evaluation is structured around three primary objectives: (1) to assess the overall performance of the fine-tuned models against the baseline configurations in terms of transcription accuracy and robustness; (2) to examine the effect of model size on training outcomes, analyzing how scaling influences recognition performance; and (3) to investigate the preservation of sensory-specific vocabulary critical for accurate analysis. Collectively, these objectives provide a comprehensive framework for evaluating the suitability of large-scale ASR models for sensory research in Vietnamese and highlight pathways for their integration into consumer science.

## 2   Material and Methodology

This section details the comprehensive methodology employed to develop and evaluate SenWhisper. We first describe the design and curation of our novel Vietnamese sensory speech dataset, SenSpeech-Coffee. Next, we introduce the baseline models selected for comparison. We then present the fine-tuning protocol, and finally, we outline the multi-faceted evaluation framework designed to rigorously assess model performance.

## 2.1   The SenSpeech-Coffee Dataset: Design and Curation

A significant challenge in developing ASR for specialized domains is the lack of high-quality, publicly available corpora. To address this gap for Vietnamese sensory science, we constructed SenSpeech-Coffee, a curated dataset of spoken coffee evaluations. This dataset itself represents a key contribution of our work, enabling reproducible research in this niche area.

### 2.1.1   Experimental Design and Data Elicitation

To ensure lexical diversity and ecological validity, the data collection was meticulously designed.

- **Sample selection:** Five distinct specialty coffee products (Honduras Whiskey, Cold Brew Enlight, Blend Caramely Crema, Kenya Nyeri, Panama Kotowa) were chosen based on their varied geographical origins, processing methods, and flavor profiles. This was intended to elicit a broad and rich vocabulary from participants, covering descriptors related to fruitiness, nuttiness, floral notes, acidity, sweetness, and body.
- **Participant recruitment:** Thirty adult (15 female, 15 male) regular consumers of specialty coffee were recruited. All participants reported consuming coffee at least five times per week and possessed informal experience in describing coffee attributes, ensuring their verbal responses reflected authentic consumer language.
- **Tasting protocol:** To mitigate order effects such as sensory fatigue or adaptation bias, the tasting sequence was counterbalanced using a Williams Latin Square design. The experiment was conducted in a standardized sensory evaluation room compliant with ISO 8589:2007 standards, ensuring controlled environmental conditions [11]. Participants evaluated each of the five coffee samples and were prompted to verbally describe their perceptions (aroma, flavor, aftertaste, etc.) freely, without predefined vocabulary or time limits, to capture spontaneous and naturalistic speech.

### 2.1.2   Data Acquisition and Annotation

High-fidelity audio was captured to create a robust corpus for model training and evaluation.

- Recording: Audio was recorded using a cardioid condenser microphone (Audio-Technica AT2020) at a 16 kHz sampling rate and 16-bit depth (mono), aligning with the input requirements of modern ASR architectures. This resulted in a corpus of 150 recordings, totaling over 2.5 h of raw audio.
- Transcription and Annotation: All recordings were manually transcribed by two independent, trained annotators with expertise in Vietnamese orthography. Discrepancies were resolved by a third senior annotator to establish a gold-standard ground truth. Crucially, domain-specific terms and loanwords (e.g., *latte, fruity, caramel, creama, body*) were preserved in their original form to maintain the lexical integrity of the sensory domain.

## 2.2   Models and Baselines

To robustly evaluate the effectiveness of domain adaptation, we selected state-of-the-art (SOTA) models as our foundation.

- **Whisper:** A family of multilingual encoder-decoder Transformer models pre-trained by OpenAI on 680,000 h of diverse, weakly supervised audio data [12]. Its strong zero-shot performance across various languages and conditions makes it the most formidable SOTA baseline for general-purpose ASR.
- **PhoWhisper:** A variant of Whisper fine-tuned by VinAI Research on 844 h of curated Vietnamese speech [10]. It represents the SOTA for Vietnamese ASR, having been adapted to the language's specific phonetic and tonal characteristics.

Our proposed model, SenWhisper, is created by fine-tuning these powerful base models on our SenSpeech-Coffee dataset. We utilized four model sizes for both Whisper and PhoWhisper (Base, Small, Medium, Large) to systematically analyze the trade-offs between performance and computational cost.

### 2.3 Fine-Tuning Protocol

#### 2.3.1 Data Preprocessing

The SenSpeech-Coffee dataset was partitioned into training (80%), validation (10%), and test (10%) sets. A strict speaker-level split was enforced to prevent data leakage and ensure that the models are evaluated on unseen speakers, providing a more realistic assessment of generalization. Audio files were segmented into utterances of less than 30 s at natural pause boundaries to align with the model's architectural constraints while preserving semantic coherence.

#### 2.3.2 Training Configuration

Fine-tuning was implemented using the Hugging Face Transformers library on an NVIDIA RTX 3050 GPU. A consistent two-stage training strategy was applied:

- Stage 1 (Decoder-only Fine-tuning): The encoder weights were frozen, and only the decoder was trained for 3 epochs. This allows the model to quickly adapt to the new domain's specific vocabulary and linguistic style without destabilizing the powerful, pre-trained acoustic representations in the encoder.
- Stage 2 (Full Fine-tuning): The entire model (encoder and decoder) was unfrozen and trained jointly for up to 10 epochs. This enables the model to fully adapt all its parameters to the nuanced acoustic and linguistic features of Vietnamese sensory speech.

Key hyperparameters included the AdamW optimizer, an initial learning rate of $10^{-5}$, and an effective batch size of 64. Early stopping based on validation loss was used to prevent overfitting.

The key hyperparameters used for all training runs are detailed in Table X. A fixed random seed was used to ensure the reproducibility of our experiments (Table 1).

The combination of gradient accumulation and early stopping allowed for stable convergence on our hardware while robustly guarding against overfitting, ensuring that the final models generalize well to unseen data.

**Table 1.** Fine-tuning Hyperparameters

| Hyperparameter | Value | Rationale |
| --- | --- | --- |
| Optimizer | AdamW | Standard optimizer for Transformer models, effective at handling sparse gradients |
| Learning Rate | $1 \times 10{-}5$ | A conservative rate suitable for fine-tuning large pre-trained models |
| LR Scheduler | Linear warmup and decay | Warms up the learning rate from zero to prevent instability at the start, then decays it |
| Weight Decay | 0.01 | A standard regularization value to prevent overfitting |
| Effective Batch Size | 64 | A sufficiently large batch size to ensure stable gradient updates |

## 2.4  Evaluation Framework

To address the critique of using limited metrics, we adopted a multi-faceted evaluation framework that assesses both general transcription accuracy and domain-specific performance.

### 2.4.1  Transcription Accuracy: Word Error Rate (WER)

As the industry standard, WER was used as the primary metric to measure overall transcription accuracy. It is calculated as:

$$WER = \frac{S + D + I}{N}$$

where S is the number of substitutions, D the number of deletions, I the number of insertions, and N the total number of words in the reference transcription.

### 2.4.2  Domain-Specific Accuracy: Term Error Rate (TER)

While WER measures general accuracy, it can be misleading in sensory contexts where the correct transcription of a few key terms is more critical than common function words. A low WER could still mask a model's failure to recognize vital descriptors. To overcome this, we introduce the Sensory Term Error Rate (TER), a more semantically meaningful metric for our task. It is calculated identically to WER but only considers a predefined dictionary of 150 critical sensory terms (e.g., *đắng, chua, ngọt, trái cây, caramel*).

$$TER = \frac{S_t + D_t + I_t}{N_t}$$

with $S_t$, $D_t$, and $I_t$ are representing substitutions, deletions and insertions of sensory terms, and $N_t$ is the total number of sensory terms in the reference.

### 2.4.3 Analysis of SOTA Methods

Our evaluation provides a comprehensive comparison not only against the original Whisper models (a strong zero-shot baseline) but also against PhoWhisper (the SOTA for general Vietnamese). This allows us to precisely quantify the performance gains attributable to in-domain fine-tuning (PhoWhisper vs. SenWhisper) versus general language adaptation (Whisper vs. PhoWhisper). This layered comparison adequately covers the relevant SOTA landscape.

## 3 Results

### 3.1 Datasets

The data collection process resulted in a Vietnamese sensory-domain speech corpus comprising 150 sessions, corresponding to 30 participants evaluating five different coffee samples each. In total, approximately 2.5 h of speech were recorded. The speaker distribution was balanced by gender, with participants ranging in age from 22 to 30 years and representing diverse regional Vietnamese accents. This dataset is more than a mere collection of recordings; it is a purposefully designed scientific instrument. The diversity in regional accents forces the model to generalize across the complex phonetic and tonal variations of the Vietnamese language. More importantly, with over 150 unique sensory descriptors (e.g., *"hương vani"* (vanilla aroma), *"vị quả chín lên men"* (fermented ripe fruit flavor), *"hậu vị sô cô la đắng"* (bitter dark chocolate aftertaste), *"body dày"* (full body)), the corpus presents a genuine challenge to ASR models trained on general-domain data. The high audio quality (SNR > 30 dB) ensures that recognition errors primarily stem from linguistic complexity rather than environmental noise, thus allowing for a more accurate assessment of the models' capabilities.

### 3.2 Analysis of ASR Performance

We conducted a series of quantitative evaluations to measure model performance. The results are analyzed through two lenses: overall accuracy (Word Error Rate - WER) and the preservation of specialized vocabulary (Term Error Rate - TER) (Table 2).

#### 3.2.1 SOTA Baseline: The Advantage of Language Adaptation (PhoWhisper vs. Whisper)

When comparing the models in their original, non-fine-tuned state, PhoWhisper consistently demonstrates a clear superiority over Whisper. For instance, PhoWhisper-large achieves a WER of 0.2198, which is a 44.5% relative reduction in error compared to the 0.3966 WER of Whisper-large. Its TER is also significantly better (0.0373 vs. 0.0597). This provides strong quantitative evidence that pre-emptive fine-tuning on a large-scale Vietnamese corpus allows the model to better capture the unique phonetic, tonal, and structural characteristics of the language, thereby creating a much stronger SOTA baseline for specialized tasks.

**Table 2.** Comparative Performance of ASR Models via WER and TER

| Model Family | Model Configuration | Fine-Tuning | WER | TER |
|---|---|---|---|---|
| **Whisper** (Multilingual SOTA) | Whisper-base | None | 0.4517 | 0.1095 |
| | Whisper-small | None | 0.2625 | 0.0925 |
| | Whisper-medium | None | 0.4403 | 0.0547 |
| | Whisper-large | None | 0.3966 | 0.0597 |
| **PhoWhisper** (Vietnamese SOTA) | PhoWhisper-base | None | 0.4476 | 0.0721 |
| | PhoWhisper-small | None | 0.2436 | 0.0498 |
| | PhoWhisper-medium | None | 0.2209 | 0.0522 |
| | PhoWhisper-large | None | 0.2198 | 0.0373 |
| **SenWhisper** (Domain-Adapted) | Whisper-base-ft | Yes | 0.3105 | 0.0572 |
| | Whisper-small-ft | Yes | 0.2226 | 0.0473 |
| | Whisper-medium-ft | Yes | 0.2602 | 0.0274 |
| | Whisper-large-ft | Yes | 0.2229 | 0.0398 |
| | PhoWhisper-base-ft | Yes | 0.2567 | 0.0423 |
| | PhoWhisper-small-ft | Yes | 0.2236 | 0.0448 |
| | PhoWhisper-medium-ft | Yes | 0.2806 | 0.0373 |
| | **PhoWhisper-large-ft** | Yes | **0.2001** | **0.0274** |

### 3.2.2 The Impact of Domain-Specific Fine-Tuning (SenWhisper)

Fine-tuning on the SenSpeech-Coffee dataset created our SenWhisper models, which showed substantial performance improvements. The top-performing model, PhoWhisper-large-ft, achieved the lowest WER at 0.2001 and tied for the lowest TER at 0.0274. Compared to its baseline version (PhoWhisper-large), this represents a 9% relative reduction in WER and, more importantly, a 26.5% relative reduction in TER. This result confirms the core hypothesis of our research: while language adaptation is crucial, further in-domain fine-tuning is an essential step to achieve the highest level of accuracy, especially for recognizing semantically critical terms.

### 3.2.3 Cross-Metric Analysis: The Story Behind WER and TER

Relying solely on WER can be misleading. A prime example is the case of Whisper-medium-ft. Although its overall WER (0.2602) is worse than that of the baseline PhoWhisper-medium (0.2209), its TER is dramatically superior (0.0274 vs. 0.0522).

This indicates that the fine-tuning process successfully taught the Whisper-medium-ft model to prioritize the correct recognition of critical sensory terms, even at the cost of some accuracy on more common function words. For applications in sensory science, a model with a low TER is extremely valuable because it preserves the semantic core of the consumer feedback. This finding strongly validates the necessity of using domain-specific metrics like TER to properly evaluate a model's fitness for a specialized purpose.

### 3.3 Effect of Training Data Volume

To assess data efficiency, we fine-tuned the *medium-sized* models on progressively larger subsets of the training data (Table 3).

**Table 3.** Effect of Training Data Volume

| Model | Training Data Size | WER | TER |
|---|---|---|---|
| PhoWhisper-medium-ft | 20% (~24 min) | 0.1749 | 0.0302 |
|  | 40% (~48 min) | 0.1709 | 0.0427 |
|  | 60% (~72 min) | 0.1643 | 0.0352 |
|  | 80% (~96 min) | 0.1666 | 0.0276 |
|  | 100% (~120 min) | 0.1574 | 0.0375 |

The results show a clear trend of diminishing returns. The most significant improvements occur within the first 20–60% of the data. Notably, with just 20% of the training data (approximately 24 min of audio), the PhoWhisper-medium-ft model already achieves a very competitive TER of 0.0302.

This finding has significant practical implications: it demonstrates that it is not always necessary to collect massive datasets. Instead, a relatively small, high-quality, in-domain dataset can be sufficient to effectively adapt large pre-trained models for specialized tasks. This opens a feasible and resource-efficient pathway for applying ASR in various niche scientific and industrial domains where data collection is often expensive and complex.

## 4 Discussion and Conclusion

This study validates SenWhisper, an optimized variant of the Whisper and PhoWhisper models, specifically tailored for Vietnamese sensory speech recognition. Experimental evaluations demonstrate that domain-specific fine-tuning significantly enhances performance. This is evidenced not only by reductions in the general Word Error Rate (WER) but also, more critically, in the Term Error Rate (TER). The fine-tuned PhoWhisper-large configuration achieved the highest overall accuracy with a WER of 0.2001 and a TER of 0.0274, underscoring that targeted adaptation is the most effective strategy for specialized ASR tasks.

A key insight is that fine-tuning substantially enhances the retention of lexical items critical for sensory analysis (flavor, aroma, texture), highlighting SenWhisper's practical utility. However, our analysis also reveals important nuances and limitations. The inconsistent performance improvements notably the degradation of the PhoWhisper-medium model post-fine-tuning suggest a complex interaction between model size and small, specialized datasets. More importantly, this study highlights the potential inadequacy of WER as a sole metric. The fact that some models achieved a superior TER despite a higher WER indicates that domain-specific metrics are essential for correctly evaluating a model's fitness for purpose.

Furthermore, the analysis of training data size revealed a principle of data efficiency, with diminishing returns observed beyond 80% of the dataset. This is an encouraging finding, suggesting that for niche domains, a smaller, high-quality, and highly relevant dataset can be more impactful than sheer data volume, lowering the barrier for future research.

Building on these findings, future work will focus on addressing the current limitations. We aim to expand the sensory-domain corpora to include a broader range of product categories, thereby improving the model's generalizability. Exploring parameter-efficient fine-tuning (PEFT) techniques could also offer more stable adaptation and mitigate performance inconsistencies. Finally, integrating SenWhisper into a pipeline with Large Language Models (LLMs) holds promise for enabling fully automated, consumer-oriented interpretation of transcripts. These advancements will solidify SenWhisper's role as a robust tool for sensory research and product innovation.

**Declaration of Generative AI and AI-Assisted Technologies in the Writing Process**
During the preparation of this work the authors used ChatGPT 4-o in order to improve the readability and language of the manuscript. After using this tool/service, the authors reviewed and edited the content as needed and take full responsibility for the content of the published article.

# References


1. Deng, L., O'Shaughnessy, D.: Speech Processing: A Dynamic and Optimization-Oriented Approach. CRC Press (2003)
2. O'Shaughnessy, D.: Trends and developments in automatic speech recognition research. Comput. Speech Lang. **83**, 101538 (2024). https://doi.org/10.1016/j.csl.2023.101538
3. Jaeger, S.R., Meiselman, H.L., Giacalone, D.: Sensory and consumer science: a complex, expanding, and interdisciplinary field of science. Food Qual. Prefer. **122**, 105298 (2025). https://doi.org/10.1016/j.foodqual.2024.105298
4. Rahim, T., Bhuiyan, F.: Consumer's sensory perception of food attributes: a survey on flavor. J. Food Nutr. Sci. **3**, 157 (2015). https://doi.org/10.11648/j.jfns.s.2015030102.40
5. Ares, G., et al.: CATA questions for sensory product characterization: raising awareness of biases. Food Qual. Prefer. **30**(2), 114–127 (2013). https://doi.org/10.1016/j.foodqual.2013.04.012
6. Mahieu, B., Visalli, M., Thomas, A., Schlich, P.: Free-comment outperformed check-all-that-apply in the sensory characterisation of wines with consumers at home. Food Qual. Prefer. **84**, 103937 (2020). https://doi.org/10.1016/j.foodqual.2020.103937
7. Meiselman, H.L., Jaeger, S.R., Carr, B.T., Churchill, A.: Approaching 100 years of sensory and consumer science: developments and ongoing issues. Food Qual. Prefer. **100**, 104614 (2022). https://doi.org/10.1016/j.foodqual.2022.104614
8. Tran, L.T.T., Kim, H.-G., La, H.M., Van Pham, S.: Automatic speech recognition of Vietnamese for a new large-scale corpus. Electronics **13**(5), 977 (2024). https://doi.org/10.3390/electronics13050977
9. Lu, B., et al.: Identification of Chinese red wine origins based on Raman spectroscopy and deep learning. Spectrochim. Acta Part A Mol. Biomol. Spectrosc. **291**, 122355 (2023). https://doi.org/10.1016/J.SAA.2023.122355

10. Le, T.-T., Nguyen, L.T., Nguyen, D.Q.: PhoWhisper: automatic speech recognition for Vietnamese, pp. 25–27 (2024). http://arxiv.org/abs/2406.02555
11. ISO 8589:2007 Sensory analysis — general guidance for the design of test rooms. ISO (International Organization for Standardization) (2017)
12. Radford, A., Kim, J.W., Xu, T., Brockman, G., McLeavey, C., Sutskever, I.: Robust speech recognition via large-scale weak supervision, December 2022. https://doi.org/10.48550/arXiv.2212.04356

# Morphological and Contour-Based Handwritten English Word Segmentation on IAM Dataset

Bhagyashri S. Pawar, Chandrashekhar H. Patil$^{(\boxtimes)}$, Meenal K. Jabde, and Shankar Mali

Department of Computer Science and Engineering, Dr Vishwanath Karad, MIT World Peace University, Pune, MH, India

**Abstract.** Handwritten text recognition is a crucial task in document digitization, requiring accurate preprocessing and segmentation for effective Optical Character Recognition (OCR). This study focuses on developing an efficient preprocessing pipeline to enhance handwritten text quality and improve word segmentation accuracy using the IAM dataset. The proposed rule-based approach integrates standard image processing steps—grayscale conversion, Otsu's adaptive thresholding, and morphological operations in a novel sequential framework that strengthens word separation and suppresses background noise. A contour-based segmentation technique is then applied to accurately detect and isolate words. Experimental results demonstrate that the preprocessing pipeline significantly improves text clarity and segmentation accuracy, making it suitable for further OCR applications. The average result of segmentation achieved is 96.15% on English handwritten text, excluding the cursive style of handwriting. This work contributes to the advancement of handwritten text recognition by providing a robust preprocessing framework for complex handwritten documents. A comparative analysis highlights the trade-offs between traditional projection-based methods, deep learning approaches, and the proposed morphological segmentation.

This study contributes to the field by offering an optimized preprocessing pipeline that improves word segmentation accuracy, ultimately aiding in better recognition performance for handwriting analysis systems. The proposed method provides a practical solution for automated handwritten document processing, making it valuable for applications such as digital archiving, transcription, and OCR preprocessing.

**Keywords:** OCR · IAM Dataset · Word Segmentation · Image Preprocessing · Morphological Processing

## 1 Introduction

The digital age demands automated systems for handwritten content evaluation, especially in online education and digital assessment, due to the growing need for consistency and time efficiency, particularly after the COVID-19 pandemic, which has highlighted the need for automated evaluation grading systems [1]. Automated handwritten evaluation systems in education could revolutionize handwritten assignments and examinations, providing valuable insights into students' writing abilities and reducing the

© The Author(s), under exclusive license to Springer Nature Switzerland AG 2026
K. K. Patel et al. (Eds.): icSoftComp 2025, CCIS 2874, pp. 489–499, 2026.
https://doi.org/10.1007/978-3-032-22062-2_38

manual assessment burden [2]. Computer-assisted assessment automates student evaluation, reducing tutor workload and providing comprehensive learning time information, ensuring fairness between teachers and students through a fair assessment marking procedure [3]. Automated grading systems have evolved over the years. Early systems, such as Project Essay Grade (PEG), focused on grammar and structure-based evaluations [4]. A sufficient amount of data for training and testing is essential for developing handwriting recognition systems with high accuracy [5]. However, extending such systems to handwritten responses requires a reliable preprocessing and segmentation framework. Effective segmentation is nothing but the process of isolating lines, words, or characters from handwritten input, i.e. dataset, which is essential to enable accurate OCR and further linguistic analysis. The dataset plays a crucial role in developing and evaluating an automated handwritten answer sheet grading system. It consists of scanned images of handwritten responses, along with corresponding ground-truth labels for evaluation. These datasets typically include a diverse range of handwriting styles, varying answer lengths, subject domains, and question formats [2]. Previous research studies in automated grading and short answer evaluation have tested their models' using datasets such as SciEntsBank & Beetle [6], Texas [7], ICLE [8], and IAM. This study focuses on the segmentation of handwritten words using the widely used publicly available IAM datasets. In this work, we used a rule-based morphological processing approach that enhances image clarity and enables accurate word segmentation using contour detection. The main objectives of this study are:

Proposes an optimized preprocessing to enhance accuracy in word extraction. To implement and evaluate a robust word segmentation method for improved recognition performance.

To compare the proposed approach with existing segmentation techniques in terms of accuracy and efficiency.

The rest of the paper is organized as follows: Sect. 2 reviews related work in the domain of handwritten text recognition. Section 3 describes the methodology, including dataset details, preprocessing steps. Section 4 presents discussions and results. Finally, Sect. 5 concludes the paper and outlines directions for future scope.

## 2  Literature Review

The IAM dataset has been widely used as a benchmark for evaluating HTR systems. It consists of handwritten English text samples collected from various writers, making it a valuable resource for training and testing recognition models. Early handwriting recognition methods used handcrafted features and statistical models like HMMs and SVMs, but struggled with style variability and generalization. With deep learning, models like CNNs and RNNs have become the main approach in this field. In the study [9], the author compares deep learning and OCR-based methods for feature extraction in answer evaluation and by using a CNN-RNN hybrid model, they achieved 74.81% accuracy. The author also stated that Deep learning models performed better on cursive text, highlighting their adaptability. LSTM networks and CTC loss have notably improved sequence-based recognition tasks. The research done in the paper [10] proposes that neural networks effectively handle large datasets and make accurate predictions. The D-DAS model, incorporating a Bi-LSTM layer, achieved an average accuracy of 73%. In the study [11], the author used feature extraction techniques like power and parabola arc fitting, diagonal and transition feature extraction with K-NN, SVM, and ANN classifiers, achieving 59% accuracy. This highlights the need for deep learning models and improved feature extraction to handle handwriting, language differences, and sentence structures more effectively. In the study [12], the author proposed an HMM-based method for word segmentation in handwritten text using forced alignment with the Viterbi decoder. Their system combines character-level HMMs, normalization, and connected components, achieving 98%-word segmentation accuracy on the IAM Handwriting Database. The approach offers high precision with ground truth alignment but depends on supervised data, limiting flexibility across diverse handwriting styles. In the paper [13], the author developed an end-to-end handwritten text recognition system using a deep learning architecture combining CNNs and RNNs (LSTM) with a CTC decoder. Their model performs full text recognition from both line and word segments, extracting features with CNNs and modeling sequences with RNNs. Trained on the IAM Database and custom handwritten data, the system achieved 98%- word recognition accuracy with a 10.62%- word error rate. The approach shows high adaptability and strong performance, though it is reliant on deep learning resources and extensive training data. The author in a study [5] presented a rule-based image processing approach for line and word segmentation in handwritten documents. Their method included skew correction, projection profile analysis, MST-based clustering, and Otsu thresholding. Focused on segmentation rather than classification, it achieved 94.92% correct word segmentation on a custom-built IAM dataset. The system is linguistically rich and freely available but lacks adaptive or deep learning techniques, with around 5% segmentation error due to over- or under-segmentation. Recent systematic reviews [14] highlight that multilingual numeral recognition faces challenges in dataset diversity, preprocessing, and segmentation, which are similar to those in word segmentation tasks. An author in the study [15] proposed a CNN-based system for offline multilingual numeral recognition across 14 languages, demonstrating the effectiveness of deep learning in handling diverse handwritten scripts. The study emphasized that robust preprocessing and segmentation are essential for achieving high accuracy.

In the present study, we covered these limitations by proposing a rule-based approach with the highest accuracy. The following table shows the comparative analysis of the segmentation done on the IAM dataset (Table 1).

**Table 1.** Comparative analysis on segmentation done on the IAM dataset for the word recognition system.

| Reference | Approach | Segmentation Type | Key Features | Classifier Used | Dataset | Accuracy | Limitations |
| --- | --- | --- | --- | --- | --- | --- | --- |
| [12] | HMM-based forced alignment using the Viterbi decoder | Word segmentation from the full line using the transcript | Character-level HMMs, normalization, connected components | Hidden Markov Model (HMM) | IAM Handwriting Database (417 pages of cursive handwritten English text.) | 98% word segmentation rate | Requires transcription and good HMM models |
| [13] | Deep learning using CNN + RNN (LSTM) + CTC | Full text recognition from line and word segments | End-to-end model with CNN feature extraction and RNN sequence modeling | CNN-RNN with CTC decoder | IAM Database + Custom Handwritten Data | 98% word recognition accuracy And a 10.62% word error rate | Sensitive to preprocessing and computationally intensive |
| [5] | Image processing with rule-based logic | Line and Word Segmentation | Skew correction, projection profile analysis, MST-based component clustering, Otsu thresholding | Not classifier-focused (segmentation-focused) | IAM (custom-built) | 94.92% correct word segmentation | Segmentation has ~ 5% error (over/under), no deep learning or adaptive techniques used |

## 3    Materials and Methods

### 3.1    Datasets

The present study uses the standard benchmarks dataset for preprocessing and segmentation work. The IAM handwritten forms dataset comprises handwritten English text samples, making it useful for training and testing handwritten text recognition models. The dataset contains complete forms of unconstrained handwritten text, which were scanned at a resolution of 300 dpi and saved as PNG images with 256 grey levels. Forms are partitioned into separate directories such that all forms in each directory are written by the same person[16]. A benchmark corpus that contains labelled handwritten English text from various writers. Due to the dataset's variability in writing styles, overlapping strokes, and image noise, accurate segmentation requires a carefully designed preprocessing pipeline. This dataset consists of 1540 images of handwritten text. The flow chart is given in Fig. 1.

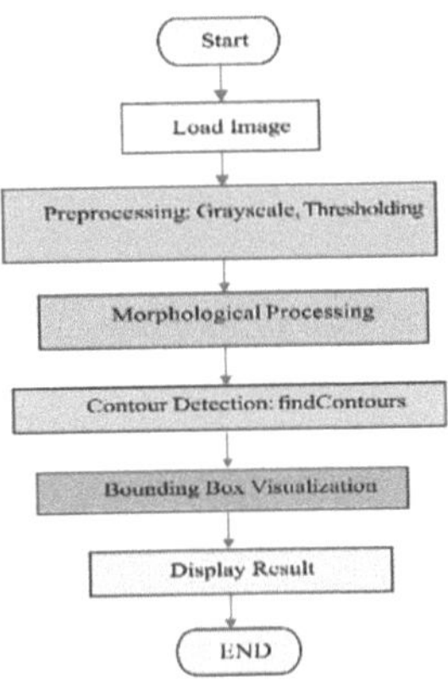


**Fig. 1.**  Flowchart of the Segmentation Process

### 3.2    Preprocessing

Like any document analysis system, handwritten documents must first undergo several initial procedures, such as noise reduction, image binarization, and line segmentation, that is, the division of the entire page text into text line images before word segmentation can begin [17].

We developed an efficient preprocessing pipeline to enhance the quality of handwritten text images from the IAM dataset. Although the individual preprocessing steps such as grayscale conversion and morphological filtering are standard, the proposed sequential rule-based integration and adaptive parameter tuning make the pipeline dataset-independent and effective for both regular and cursive handwriting styles. Unlike deep learning methods, this approach remains interpretable and computationally efficient. The main objective was to improve text clarity, reduce noise, and prepare images for accurate word segmentation. For this, we implemented the following steps:

**Grayscale and Thresholding.** An OCR system can be improved by implementing appropriate image enhancement methods such as noise reduction, image thresholding, skew detection and correction, page segmentation, character segmentation, character normalization, and morphological algorithms[18]. We loaded handwritten images using OpenCV and converted them from BGR to RGB format to ensure compatibility with visualization tools like Matplotlib. Additionally, the images were resized if they exceeded 1000 pixels in width while maintaining the aspect ratio to preserve text quality. The color images were converted to grayscale, reducing computational complexity by eliminating unnecessary color information while preserving the structural details of the handwritten text. The morphological operations and contour-based segmentation were implemented with experimentally tuned parameters. The structuring element size was selected based on the average stroke width of the IAM handwritten samples.

Binarization is the process of converting a grayscale image into a binary image. This is typically done using a technique called thresholding, where a specific threshold value is selected to separate the pixels into two categories, usually black and white, based on their intensity levels [18]. Mathematically, binarization using a fixed threshold $T$ can be defined as

$$B(x, y) = \begin{cases} 1, & if I(x, y) \geq T \\ 0, & if I(x, y) < T \end{cases} \tag{1}$$

where, $I(x, y)$ is the grayscale intensity of the pixel at coordinates $(x, y)$, and $B(x, y)$ is the resulting binary pixel value. For simple images like handwritten text on a white background, global thresholding methods such as Otsu's method, the iterative method, or the valley point minimum method are often enough to separate the text (foreground) from the background. In our experiment, we applied Otsu's Thresholding, which automatically determines the optimal threshold by minimising the intra-class variance between the foreground and background. Additionally, we experimented with adaptive binarization, where the threshold T (x, y) is calculated for each pixel based on the local neighbourhood.

$$B(x, y) = \begin{cases} 1, & if I(x, y) \geq T(x, y) \\ 0, & if I(x, y) < T(x, y) \end{cases} \tag{2}$$

This ensures clear foreground-background separation, which is crucial for accurate word segmentation in OCR. The segmentation process involves a sequence of morphological dilation and erosion operations followed by contour extraction. The structuring element size was empirically determined based on average character height.

**Morphological Processing.** Morphological operations were applied to remove unwanted noise and improve the structure of handwritten text. Dilation, using a rectangular structuring element, was performed to enhance text connectivity. This process helped in joining broken strokes. Dilation enlarges an item by augmenting pixels at its outer edges[18]. To remove unwanted noise and improve the structure of handwritten text, morphological operations were applied to the binarized image I. Dilation was performed using a rectangular structuring element $B$ of size $m \times n$. This process, denoted by $I' = I \oplus B$, expands the foreground regions by adding pixels to the outer edges of white areas in the binary image.,

Mathematically, dilation is defined as

$$I \oplus B = \{z | (B)_z \cap I \neq \varnothing\} \tag{3}$$

where $(B)_z$, is the translation of the structuring element $B$ by vector $z$. This operation helps in connecting broken strokes and improving the continuity of text. Contours were extracted to detect potential word regions. A minimum area threshold was set to filter out small unwanted components, such as ink smudges or noise artifacts. After dilation, contours were extracted from the resulting image. $I\prime$, forming a set $C = \{c_1, c_2, \cdots, c_k\}$, where each $c_i$ represents a connected component potentially corresponding to a word or character. To eliminate noise artifact such as ink smudges, an area-based filtering was applied for each contour $c_i$ Its area $A(c_i)$ as computed, and only the component satisfying $A(c_i) \geq Amin$ were retained,

Where $Amin$ is a predefined minimum area threshold.

The filtered set $C^1 = \{c_i \in C | A(c_i) \geq Amin\}$ Contains the meaningful word or character regions. Sample original images from the IAM dataset and their corresponding binarized outputs are presented below (Figs. 2 and 3).

*Samples of Images.*

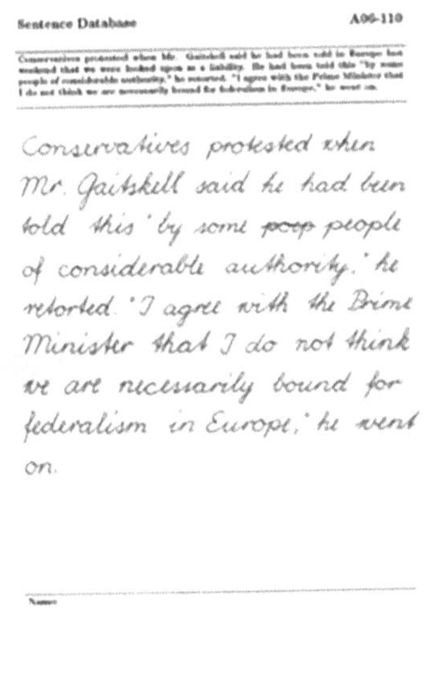

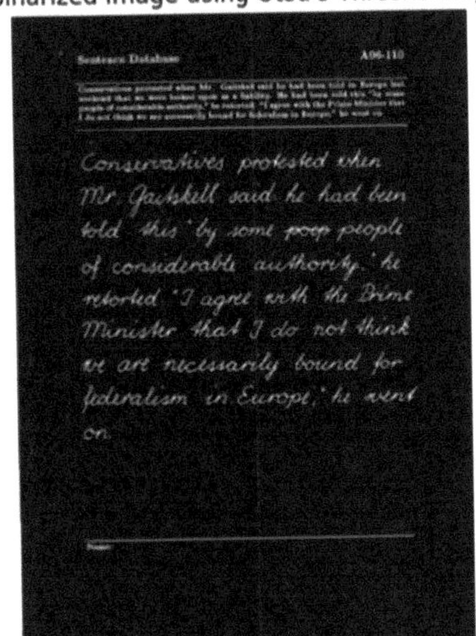


**Fig. 2.** Sample original image from the IAM dataset.

**Fig. 3.** Binarized image for segmentation

## 3.3  Evaluation Measures

The rule-based methods were assessed using the accuracy method, which was calculated via Eq. (4)

$$Accuracy = (N_s | N_w) * 100 \qquad (4)$$

where,

$$N_s = Number of segmentation$$

$$Nw = Number of words$$

Figures 4 and 5 presents sample results obtained from the segmentation experiments conducted on the IAM dataset.

*Samples of Resulted Images.*

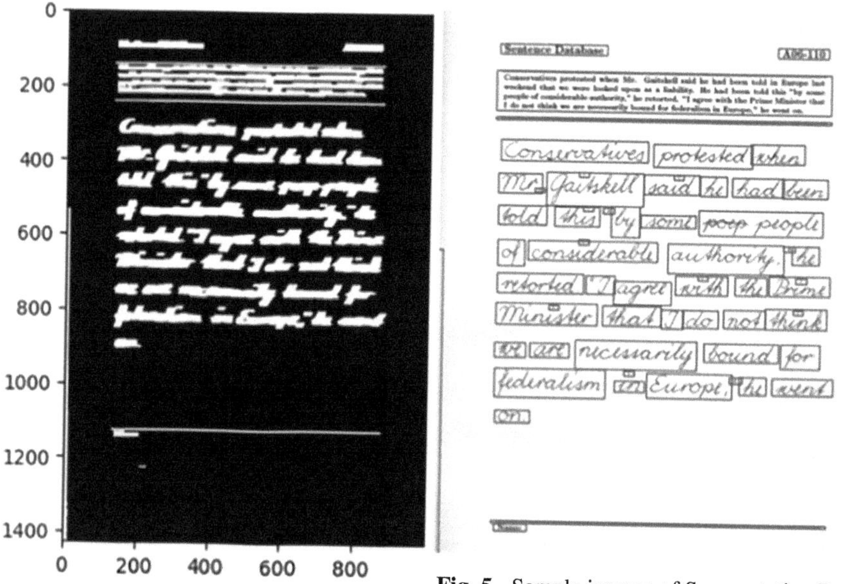

**Fig. 4.**  Sample image of the Result

**Fig. 5.**  Sample images of Segmentation Result

## 4  Result and Conclusion

The proposed algorithms were executed on personal Windows 11 Home version 23H2 operating systems,16GB RAM sizes, and the Intel(R) Core(TM) Ultra 5 125H 3.60 GHz processor. The Python 3.12.7 programming language in Anaconda Jupyter Notebook has been used to implement and test the morphological methods. The Python libraries such as NumPy, matplotlib, and pandas were used in the Python run of the models. While the proposed method performs effectively on regular and moderately cursive handwriting, a few challenging cases were observed. In particular, words with highly overlapping ascenders and descenders or extremely slanted writing resulted in partial merging of neighbouring words. Similarly, words with irregular spacing sometimes caused over-segmentation. Future work will focus on integrating adaptive contour thresholds and learning-based post-processing to handle such variations more robustly.

The method performs efficiently for regular handwriting but may face challenges in overlapping or cursive cases. These can be mitigated through adaptive thresholding or hybrid methods (Table 2).

**Table 2.** Result Analysis of various handwritten styles in the IAM benchmark dataset.

| Data Set | Handwriting Style | Total No. of words | Segmented Words | Result |
|---|---|---|---|---|
| IAM | Regular | 15562 | 14964 | 96.15% |
| IAM | Cursive | 10545 | 6061 | 57.47% |
| IAM | Small Handwritten style | 2587 | 1401 | 54.15% |
| IAM | Words with less space | 2671 | 1317 | 49.64% |

## 4.1  Conclusion

This paper presents a morphological and contour-based segmentation method for handwritten word extraction using the IAM dataset. The proposed preprocessing pipeline improves image clarity and enables effective word-level segmentation with an accuracy of up to 96.15% across diverse handwriting styles, except cursive handwriting styles. However, performance decreases for highly cursive handwriting, where overlapping strokes and irregular spacing pose challenges to rule-based processing. Despite this limitation, the proposed method provides a lightweight and dataset-independent alternative to deep learning models, offering a practical preprocessing solution for OCR, transcription, and document digitization applications.

The poor resolution of an image affects in segmentation of words. Higher resolution of an image gives higher accuracy in segmentation. In the study [5], the author used a 600dpi grayscale image in their custom dataset, so it effectively works on different handwritten styles, including cursive handwriting style, which is lacking in our system, as we used a 300dpi grayscale image of the IAM benchmark dataset. Future research may extend this approach beyond English to multilingual word and numeral recognition, where challenges of varied scripts and writing styles remain open research problems, as found in paper [14]. Future research, inspired by the author of the study [15], could incorporate multilingual datasets into CNN-based recognition frameworks, emphasizing segmentation as a key factor in achieving higher accuracy. Overall, the proposed approach provides a simple yet effective rule-based framework that remains interpretable and dataset-independent, serving as a practical alternative to complex deep learning models for handwritten word segmentation.

## 5 Future Scope

Future research directions include integrating machine learning techniques to enhance segmentation accuracy by combining traditional morphological methods with deep learning-based approaches. This hybrid methodology could improve robustness across varying handwriting styles and document conditions.

**Disclosure of Interests.** The Authors have no competing interest.

## References


1. Kulkarni, M., Adhav, G., Wadile, K., Chavan, R., Deshmukh, V.: Digital handwritten answer sheet evaluation system (2024). https://doi.org/10.21203/rs3.rs-3978232/v1
2. Shaikh, E., Mohiuddin, I.A., Manzoor, A., Latif, G.: Automated grading for handwritten answer sheets using convolutional neural networks. IEEE, October 2019
3. Dumal, W P.A.A., Shanika, K.D., Pathinayake, S.A.D., Sandanayake, T.C.: Adaptive and automated online assessment evaluation system
4. Shermis, M.D., Mzumara, H.R., Olson, J., Harrington, S.: On-line grading of student essays: PEG goes on the World Wide Web. Assess. Eval. High. Educ. **26**(3), 247–259 (2001). https://doi.org/10.1080/02602930120052404
5. Marti, U.-V., Bunke, H.: The IAM-database: an English sentence database for offline handwriting recognition (2002). http://www.tummy.com/xvscan/
6. Dzikovska, M.O., et al.: The joint student response analysis and 8th recognizing textual entailment challenge (2013)
7. Mohler, M., Bunescu, R., Mihalcea, R.: Learning to grade short answer questions using semantic similarity measures and dependency graph alignments. http://nlp.stanford.edu/software/dependencies
8. Granger, S.: International Corpus of Learner English. Presses Universitaires de Louvain, Belgium (2009)
9. Devan, K.P.K., Sruthi Prabakaran, P., Tamizhazhagan, S., Vaishnavi, S.: One-word answer correction using deep learning models and OCR. Int. J. Recent Technol. Eng. (IJRTE) **9**(2), 679–682 (2020). https://doi.org/10.35940/ijrte.B3849.079220
10. George, N., Sijimol, P.J., Varghese, S.: Grading descriptive answer scripts using deep learning. www.ijitee.org
11. Kundal, R., Parekh, B.: Automated assessment and grading system for short answers. In: Artificial Intelligence and Communication Technologies, pp. 563–568. Soft Computing Research Society (2022). https://doi.org/10.52458/978-81-955020-5-9-54
12. Zimmermann, M., Bunke, H.: Automatic segmentation of the IAM off-line database for handwritten English text. In: Proceedings - International Conference on Pattern Recognition, pp. 35–39 (2002). https://doi.org/10.1109/icpr.2002.1047394
13. Hemanth, G.R., Jayasree, M., Keerthi Venii, S., Akshaya, P.: CNN-RNN based handwritten text recognition. ICTACT J. Soft Comput. **12**(1), 2457–2463 (2021). https://doi.org/10.21917/ijsc.2021.0351
14. Jabde, M., Patil, C.H., Vibhute, A.D., Saini, J.R.: A systematic review of multilingual numeral recognition systems. Artif. Intell. Rev. **58**(4), April 2025. https://doi.org/10.1007/s10462-025-11105-0

15. Jabde, M., Patil, C., Vibhute, A., Mali, S.: Offline Handwritten multilingual numeral recognition using CNN. In: Kulkarni, A.J., Cheikhrouhou, N. (eds.) Intelligent Systems for Smart Cities. ICISA 2023, pp. 385–400. Springer, Singapore (2024). https://doi.org/10.1007/978-981-99-6984-5_25
16. IAM Handwritten Forms Dataset. https://www.kaggle.com/datasets/naderabdalghani/iam-handwritten-forms-dataset/data. Accessed 23 Mar 2025
17. Huang, C., Srihari, S.N.: Word Segmentation of Off-line Handwritten Documents (2008). http://spiedl.org/terms
18. Kumar, G., Kumar Bhatia, P.: Analytical review of preprocessing techniques for offline handwritten character recognition (2013). https://doi.org/10.13140/RG.2.1.3896.7842

# Author Index

MIX
Papier aus verantwortungsvollen Quellen
Paper from responsible sources
FSC® C105338